UFOs 1947 – 1987
THE 40 YEAR SEARCH FOR AN EXPLANATION

UFOs 1947-1987

THE 40- YEAR SEARCH FOR AN EXPLANATION

COMPILED AND EDITED BY **HILARY EVANS**
WITH **JOHN SPENCER**
FOR **THE BRITISH UFO RESEARCH ASSOCIATION**

FORTEAN TOMES   LONDON

First publication: 1987

FORTEAN TOMES
1 Shoebury Road, East Ham, London E6 2AQ

This book was edited on an IBM PC using Prefis *BookMachine* ® ;
photoset in 9 on 10 point Korinna by **D.R. Neaves** of Northampton;
and printed and bound by **Whitstable Litho Ltd** of Whitstable, Kent.

British Library Cataloguing in Publication Data

UFOs 1947 - 1987 : the 40 year search for an explanation.
1. Unidentified flying objects -- History
I. Evans, Hilary II. Spencer, John, *1954-* III. British UFO Research Association
001.9'42'09 TL789

ISBN 1-870021-02-9

4 EXPLAINING THE PHENOMENA

5 UFOs AND SOCIETY

6 UFOs AND SKEPTICISM

7 APPENDICES

PREFACE

UFO research is a worldwide activity, and this book reflects that fact. Its contributors are from Australia, Belgium, Britain, Canada, Denmark, France, Germany, Italy, Norway, Poland, Portugal, Spain, Sweden, the United States and Zimbabwe. We would have liked to include contributions from yet other countries but this was unfortunately not possible. Big as it is, this book could have been much bigger if space had not been limited: we are unhappily conscious that some aspects of our subject have received less attention than they deserve.

Deciding who to invite was a delicate and difficult matter. Obviously they had to be persons who are seriously involved, and who have demonstrated their ability to make a lasting contribution to our understanding of the subject. But we had to exclude many whose work has been chiefly as investigators, for though their practical work in the field is essential, it does not form part of the purpose of this book, which is essentially one of standing back and assessing the sum of our knowledge.

Other reasons prevented others from being included. Sometimes we had to choose between more than one person specialising in the same field. Some promised papers never made the final deadline. Some declined our invitation because they were too busy, or for other reasons or for none. A few simply didn't reply at all.

For these reasons, we would like to take the opportunity to pay tribute to those not represented here, but whose contribution to UFO research should not pass unacknowledged: Keith Basterfield; Ted Bloecher; Charles Bowen; Michel Carrouges; Jerome Clark; Gordon Creighton; Paul Devereux; Joaquim Fernandes; Michel Figuet; Salvador Freixedo; Irene Granchi; Loren Gross; Pierre Guerin; Richard Hall; Leif Havik; Allan Hendry; Milton Hourcade; Carl Jung; Philip Klass; Fernand Lagarde; Alvin Lawson; Coral and Jim Lorenzen; Bruce Maccabee; James MacDonald; Aime Michel; John Michell; Jim Moseley; Paul Norman; Michael Persinger; Thierry Pinvidic; Gosta Rehn; Sebastian Robiou-Lamarche; Scott Rogo; Harley Rutledge; Margaret Sachs; Frank Salisbury; Ivan Sanderson; Berthold Schwarz; Jacques Scornaux; Jean Sider; Leo Sprinkle; Ronald Story; Renato Vesco; Pierre Vieroudy; David Webb; Jennie Zeidman - and Kenneth Arnold himself. To those named in this very subjective list, and to scores of others not named, UFO research owes as much as it does to our contributors.

There is one other name, which recurs frequently in these pages, and which deserves special mention; it is, of course, that of the late J Allen Hynek. Many of us knew him personally, as a friend as well as a researcher; but even those who knew him only from his writings and public appearances knew that he embodied all that is best in UFO research - the persistence, but also the lack of dogmatism; the confident belief in the importance of his cause, but also the willingness to listen to the ideas of others. Almost single-handed he showed how UFO research, though it might not constitute a science in its own right, could and should be conducted on scientific principles. We were fortunate, and privileged, to have such a man among us at such a time.

Inevitably our international approach has involved problems. It seemed sensible for all contributions to be in English, but this has meant difficulties of translation. We apologise for shortcomings in this respect; most translations have been made by unpaid volunteers, often coping with unfamiliar terminology and novel concepts.

We have done our best to work to professional standards, but we ask you to bear in mind that this book was produced - like virtually everything else in UFO research - by unpaid amateurs working in their spare time. Inevitably, therefore, it falls short of the highest standards: referencing and cross-referencing, for example, are not as thorough as we would have wished. For such short-comings the editors, not the contributors, must take the responsibility. Nor did time permit the preparation of a comprehensive index and cumulative bibliography (which may be included in any further editions).

The views expressed are the authors': there has been no censorship, and only such direction as was needed to make a reasonably balanced book. For this reason you will find one text contradicting another, some personal opinions which you may find unacceptable, viewpoints you may consider wrong-headed, even perverse. Nevertheless, each of our contributors is a serious researcher, whose opinions were not arrived at lightly; all deserve a hearing. BUFORA takes no responsibility for what are presented as facts (though we have done a reasonable amount of checking): even less is it responsible for the ideas expressed.

Copyright in the book as a whole is BUFORA's: copyright in individual texts remains with the authors, who should be approached directly on all matters relating to their contributions: addresses are provided. If we ourselves have unwittingly infringed any copyrights, we hereby apologise.

Measurements are metric, except where an original text is quoted verbatim.

Dates are given in European style, for example 3.9.1939 = third of September 1939.

Finally, on behalf not only of BUFORA but of the worldwide ufological community, the editors thank the authors and translators who have worked so hard and so enthusiastically, for no material reward, to make this book possible. That busy men and women, many of them able to command fees as writers and lecturers, have been willing to give their time and trouble at no financial gain, is a magnificent tribute to the unselfish pursuit of truth which makes UFO research truly one of the greatest quests for knowledge in the history of scientific research.

H.E. **J.S.**

1
INTRODUCTION

1.1

UFOs 1947 - 1987

by Hilary Evans

What happened on 24 June 1947? A man saw something in the sky which didn't seem to be anything with which he was familiar. [See Section 2.3.2 Case 1]

Nothing unusual in that. So what made this particular incident special? Just this: in the past when such things happened, either the object was eventually identified as something familiar, or it was assumed it could have been so identified if sufficient data were available. But on this occasion it was suggested the witness had seen something with which neither he nor anyone else *could* be familiar: a new phenomenon, not simply unidentified, but *unidentifiable* in the light of our current knowledge.

Forty years later, we still don't know if that suggestion is sense or nonsense. We don't know what Kenneth Arnold saw; we don't know what is being seen by all those who, like him, have reported seeing UFOs.

If we don't have the answers, it's not for want of looking for them. For forty years a good many minds - and many good minds - have been occupied with that search. If we'd found no evidence, we would have given up looking. If we'd found conclusive evidence, we'd have no need to go on looking. As it is, we found some evidence that pointed one way, some that pointed another - so we go on looking!

Though the answers still elude us, we have none the less learnt a great deal in the process.

We have learnt, in particular, not to expect easy answers. The fact that our questions are still unanswered suggests that perhaps they are not the right questions. Maybe the question, 'Did Kenneth Arnold see a UFO?' is essentially meaningless.

Maybe it would be more meaningful to ask 'Why did it happen to Kenneth Arnold and not to someone else?' or 'Why in 1947 and not some other year?' or 'Why in the United States and not somewhere else?' or 'Why did this sighting, whatever it was, make such an impression both on him and on society?'

At the time of Arnold's sighting it would have seemed unnecessarily complicated - devious even - to ask such questions. All that had happened, surely, was that an experienced pilot had seen some flying objects he couldn't identify; which made them, by definition, unidentified flying objects. It was simply a question of finding out what those objects were.

Now, after forty years, we have learnt that nothing in this UFO business is simple. The same complicated, devious questions we might have asked about the Arnold sighting, we might ask about any and every case that has occurred during those forty years.

■ We have caught witnesses deliberately lying, so we must face the possibility that every witness, from Arnold on, though seemingly sincere, may be playing some game of deceit, perhaps for personal reasons, perhaps on behalf of some higher authority.

■ We have found witnesses unconsciously lying, perhaps because they are in some altered state of consciousness in which normal reality has temporarily been replaced by some alternative reality, or perhaps because they are being deliberately deceived by others, or perhaps because they are unconsciously deceiving themselves.

■ We have seen other alleged UFO witnesses acted upon by all kinds of intangible influences - their personal preoccupations, the beliefs and assumptions of their cultural milieu. Post-war boredom; cold war fears; space-age premonitions; the passing of old gods and a hunger for new gods - cultural factors like these may bias both the ability to perceive and/or the ability to interpret what is perceived.

More than that, we know that similar factors influence everyone who is touched by experiences such as Arnold's - the newspaper reporters who smell a good story; the researchers whose curiosity is aroused; the believers who see it as a confirmation of their hopes and fears; the skeptics who assail it as a monstrous rumour which must be checked at all costs.

These things and many more we have learnt, making UFO research the immensely complex field whose diversity is reflected in these pages. We have learnt that we can't hope to resolve the problem without calling on all kinds of expertise:

■ We need the astronomer to tell us if it is likely the UFOs could be of extraterrestrial origin.

■ We need the physicist to tell us how these machines could perform the way they are said to do, and the engineer to tell us how they could affect our vehicles and motors.

■ We need the meteorologist and the earth scientist to tell us about effects and forces in nature which could generate or be mistaken for such phenomena.

■ We need the psychologist to tell us what may be going on in the mind of the witness and the physiologist to tell us what may be going on in his body.

■ We need the sociologist to tell us how he may be influenced by those around him, the anthropologist to tell us about the underlying assumptions of his cultural background, and the mythologist to tell us about traditional beliefs which may be exerting their own subtle influence.

Yet at the same time we have learnt to suspect that there is more to the phenomenon than any one of these aspects in isolation. The challenge of the UFO can be met not only by taking into account what each of these disciplines can tell us, but also by taking a broader view and recognising the possibility that the UFO may involve something new, something outside the experience of any and all of these experts.

What is true of the Arnold case has been true of virtually every case which has been reported and studied throughout these forty years. Sightings, all provisionally labelled 'UFOs', have been of lights crossing the heavens at steady speed in straight-line trajectories - and they have been of lights dancing about the sky in awesome manoeuvres. They have been of shapeless forms which witnesses could describe with no more precision than as balls of fire or light - or they have been of structured objects with retractable landing gear and transparent domes. They have been of shape-changing objects, objects which separate and combine, objects which mimic terrestrial artifacts. And they have contained occupants of all shapes and sizes, some as human as you or I, some like gods, some like jellies, some like machines, and all indulging in a bewildering variety of seemingly senseless behaviour.

And all the time we have felt the nagging doubt: did the witness really see anything at all? And even if he did, did he see it on the same level of reality as he sees the everyday world around him?

Many researchers have been impatient of this kind of question. It's only natural to want simple answers, and most of us would no doubt prefer that the UFO should turn out to be simply this or simply that. But after forty years during which the phenomenon has been matched against every model that man could conceive - including many which he never conceived until the UFO came along and put the idea in his head - it is evident that no reductionist or simplistic approach will suffice. The believer's simple conviction that it is a nuts-and-bolts alien spacecraft, the conspiracy-monger's simple belief that it is a secret device of sinister terrestrial powers, the fundamentalist's simple warning that it is a new trick of the old Devil, the skeptic's simple insistence that it can be dismissed as illusion or misinterpretation - these, and many other all-or-nothing proposals, have proved simply inadequate.

So, on whatever level of reality the UFO exists, it certainly exists as a new and uniquely complex challenge.

NO LACK OF EVIDENCE

The past forty years have seen the accumulation of a vast quantity of data - sufficient, in any other sphere of human activity, to provide an adequate base from which to draw conclusions. Paradoxically, it is the nature of that evidence which is responsible for the doubts and uncertainties.

For one thing, almost every scrap of it is eyewitness testimony only, unsupported by any confirming evidence. When we are offered tangible evidence, it invariably falls short of being totally convincing; there is always ambiguity, room for doubt.

On the other hand, the sheer quantity of testimony is impressive. Hundreds of thousands of reports have been made, and even if only one in a thousand merits serious attention, that is still a very great number of anomalous events, reported by people whose word we would have no reason to doubt in other circumstances.

The situation is complicated by some additional factors:

- Many, perhaps most, investigators have acted on the supposition that there is a single 'UFO phenomenon': but it is far from certain that this is so. Maybe what is holding up research is the fact that the true UFO phenomenon is tangled up with various pseudo-UFOs - which, of course, are just as 'unidentified' as the true phenomenon!

- The testimony includes not only sightings of UFOs but also encounters with their occupants. Are these true UFO events, or are they behavioral pseudo-events in which the UFO stereotype is used as a framework for private fantasy?

- The base phenomenon - the things seen by people in the sky - has been overlaid by gratuitous interpretations derived from specific belief-systems. They have been damned as Satanic devices heralding the coming of Anti-Christ, or hailed as the carriers of Cosmic Guardians who will save mankind from the consequences of our foolish and evil nature. The fact that these hypotheses often reach the status of widespread cults testifies to the power of the UFO stereotype as a psychological trigger, and this must call in doubt *all* testimony. For who can be sure that such motivations are not operating in *every* case?

It is within this complexity of circumstances that UFO research has been conducted, and they have discouraged those whose professional abilities best qualify them to conduct that research. So, with rare exceptions, UFO research has been conducted not by trained scientists but by amateurs, lacking both finance and equipment; on the rare occasions of involvement by members of the scientific or military establishment, they have disdained co-operation with the investigators who, amateurs though they may be, have accumulated a considerable expertise as well as substantial data. It is not surprising that many researchers have wondered if this is deliberate policy by powers or authorities, terrestrial or even extraterrestrial.

HIGH STANDARDS, HIGH STRANGENESS

Despite these circumstances, adverse to the point of absurdity, UFO research has developed to standards which at their best measure up favorably with those of scientifically-conducted research in any other field. Since the praiseworthy but simplistic efforts of the first investigators, we have learnt both to ask more penetrating questions and to analyse more carefully the answers. Ironically, if superior procedures have succeeded in helping us to discard much that is extraneous and irrelevant, the core phenomenon, now that we see it more clearly, is more baffling than ever.

It seems that a UFO, if it is not a misinterpretation of something known but not recognised (whether a natural phenomenon or an unidentified artifact such as a secret military device), is most probably one of the following:

- A natural physical object
- An artifical physical object
- No object at all, but the psychosocial response to a stimulus which may be something perfectly simple, but perceived under circumstances where its true nature is not recognised.

That some UFOs are unknown natural physical objects is impressively suggested by cases such as Hessdalen [see Section 2.3.2 Case 13] which furnish abundant photographic and instrumentally-recorded evidence.

That some are artifical physical objects is not supported by any totally convincing direct evidence, but there is a wealth of circumstantial evidence drawn from cases such as the Bentwaters / Lakenheath radar-visual event [see Section 3.4.4] which seem overwhelmingly to support the claim that structured objects beyond any terrestrial capability are deploying intelligently in our atmosphere. The lack of any unambiguous photograph or trace - not to mention any direct access to a UFO - is discouraging but not conclusive; and the alternative - that every single such report is some kind of misidentification - is hardly more plausible.

That many sightings are no more than a psychosocial response is clearly evident from the many occasions where the stimulus for the report is shown to be a natural object such as Venus, enabling us to see how much the witness has added, and to speculate how and why.

In this stalemate situation, and until better evidence is forthcoming, many theorists have chosen to proceed, some cautiously, others not so cautiously, on an 'as if' basis - that is, 'as if' the witnesses are telling not only subjective but also objective truth.

Such efforts have not been altogether satisfactory because there is no consensus how far such 'as if' procedure should be carried. Should it, for instance, accept claims by witnesses to have been abducted on board alien spacecraft?

Another drawback of the 'as if' approach is that it encourages such controversial practices as the channelling of alleged messages from space beings which, perhaps more than any other feature of the subject, has discouraged serious interest.

Despite all these difficulties and discouragements, it is those who have studied the phenomenon most attentively who are most convinced that it warrants their study. If we continue the quest, it is for two main reasons:

First, because whatever the nature of the phenomenon, it offers unique potential for the scientist: if not for the physical scientist, then for the life scientist. Even such knowledge as has already been acquired contains valuable information both as to events in nature (for example, the study of ball-of-light phenomena associated with geophysical and atmospheric conditions) and to human behaviour (for example, the nature of witness-compliance in altered states, as demonstrated by the Lawson imaginary-abductee experiments).

Second, because thousands of people are having experiences which genuinely puzzle, and often frighten them, and someone should be able to tell them what is happening to them.

Though it is true we still don't know what Kenneth Arnold saw on June 24, 1947, or what so many thousands have seen since then, the pages which follow show how much we *have* learnt from the UFO phenomenon - about people, and what they see, and how they respond to what they see; about our world and what it contains; about things that are, and things that aren't, and things that may be.

2
THE PHENOMENA

2.1.1
UFOs BEFORE 1947

We may think of 'the Age of the Flying Saucer' as commencing with Arnold's sighting, but of course people have been failing to identify anomalous flying objects throughout history.

To some extent such incidents were catalogued, in a haphazard kind of way: thus in the *Histoires Admirables et Memorables de notre temps* of Simon Goulart, researchers Olivyer and Boëdec discovered sufficient references to anomalous phenomena to justify collecting them into a book which they subtitled 'the UFO wave of 1500 to 1600.' [**1**] A great many such anecdotes have been collected by authors like W. Raymond Drake [**2**] and our contributor Michel Bougard [**3**], and though a comprehensive, methodical and critical catalogue has yet to be prepared, Louis Winkler's *Catalog of UFO-like data before 1947*, prepared for FUFOR, is a valuable preliminary stage, containing several hundred intriguing reports. [**4**]

Though we may suspect that the great majority of these early cases were rare natural phenomena, that does not make them any the less UFOs. Sufficient evidence exists, in short, for us to be certain that UFOs have a prehistory no less baffling than what may be called their historical period.

Understandably, it is the immediate prehistory of the UFO which is the best documented. This period is dominated by the great airship waves which are currently the subject of substantial research in the United States [**5**], France [**6**] and in England by our contributor Nigel Watson and his collaborators. In the 1930s came the phantom airplane wave about which contributor John Keel has written [**7**] and then the ghost rocket wave of 1946 on which contributors Anders Liljegren and Clas Svahn are conducting ongoing research. While in some of these cases the evidence that the phenomenon was largely psychosocial is very persuasive, such an explanation is hardly adequate to explain each and every one of the anomalous incidents.

In addition there were many one-off sightings before 1947, though because many of them were not published until after Arnold had broken the ice, their evidential value is limited. But read the reports gathered by Loren Gross in his fascinating *Charles Fort, the Fortean Society & UFOs* [**8**], and you will surely end with the conviction that the Arnold sighting, though a landmark in the sense that it caused a heterogeneous assortment of happenings to become a public issue, was in itself no more than one further incident in an ongoing series.

REFERENCES

1 - **Olivier**, I L, & **Boëdec**, Jean-Francois: *Les Soleils de Simon Goulart; la vague OVNI de 1500 a 1600* (Runes d'Or, Marseille, 1981). ■ 2 - **Drake**, W Raymond: *Gods or spacemen?* (Amherst Press, 1964), and 6 others in the 'Gods and spacemen' series, 1968 - 1976. ■ 3 - **Bougard**, Michel: *Des Soucoupes Volantes aux OVNI* (SOBEPs, 1976); *La chronique des OVNI* (Delarge, Paris, 1977). ■ 4 - **Winkler**, Louis: *Catalog of UFO-like data before 1947* (Fund for UFO Research, 1984). ■ 5 - **Cohen**, Daniel: *The great airship mystery* (Dodd, Mead, NY, 1981). ■ 6 - **Sider**, Jean: in *Lumieres dans la nuit*, no 199, 1980; and elsewhere. ■ 7 - **Keel**, John A: in *Flying Saucer Review*, vol 16, nos 3 & 4. ■ 8 - **Gross**, Loren: *Charles Fort, the Fortean Society, & UFOs* (private, 1974).

2.1.2
UFOs THROUGHOUT HISTORY
by Michel Bougard

■ **MICHEL BOUGARD**. Born 1947. Attended l'Université Libre de Bruxelles where, in 1970, he obtained a Diplome de Licencié in the chemical sciences. Since then he has taught chemistry, and he is currently Professor of Chemistry at the Athénée Provincial de la Louvière. He is married, and the adoptive father of two Korean girls.

■ **UFO involvement**: Since 1972 Bougard has been President of SOBEPS (Société Belge d'Etude des Phénomènes Spatiaux) and for many years has edited its journal *Inforespace*, regarded by many as the most serious journal of ideas in the ufological world.

■ **Publications**: *Des soucoupes volantes aux OVNI* [From Flying Saucers to UFOs] (Delarge / SOBEPS 1974): *La chronique des OVNI* [The UFO chronicle] (Delarge 1977). The latter has been translated into several other languages, but unfortunately not yet into English.

■ **Address**: Rue des Bouveries, 18 / B6568 Merbes-le Chateau / Belgium. SOBEPS/Inforespace: Avenue Paul Janson, 74 / 1070 Bruxelles.

We are surrounded by mysteries, some of them illusory, others genuine. There are phenomena which are seemingly extraordinary but which soon resolve themselves with disconcerting banality. Others - and UFOs are one of them - have yet to receive a satisfactory explanation. Despite the concerted efforts of many valiant researchers, forty years of study have produced no more than crumbs of explanation or a partial interpretation. And in the meantime the scientific community remains silent, ignoring the subject.

Over and above the study of the phenomena per se, recent years have seen the growth of a new approach more concerned with the social and cultural context of the witnesses than with the stories they have to tell. In this perspective, the historical dimension of the subject becomes of particular importance.

Because the reports were unreliable and the sources difficult to check and often contradictory, researchers have too often neglected old sightings, in particular those previous to 1947. Yet, if it is indeed the case that the UFO phenomenon has recurred at different epochs of human history, such study may reveal an evolution in the reported characteristics, and enable a parallel to be traced with the social, economic and cultural context of the period under consideration.

For this reason, as complete as possible a census of the sightings of the past is essential: for a start, we must first study the annals of ufology.

I have had occasion to work in this field, and made my contribution by compiling a catalogue of bibliographical sources in which old cases were published. [1] From this it was obvious that in all periods anomalous aerial phenomena have been observed which did not at the time receive satisfactory explanation: in the literal sense of the phrase, UFOs.

Fabulous meteors, giant comets, unexpected auroras, capricious and untimely refractions, or real artificial objects of supposedly extraterrestrial origin? At this stage of our research, the question is premature. Instead, let us travel back in time and listen to these people as they voice their astonishment at the curious phenomena unfolding before them.

THE EARLIEST EPOCHS

If we admit the possibility that UFOs have traversed our skies at all epochs, it is logical to suppose that the first representations of them must originate with humanity's earliest days. Paleolithic cave and grotto paintings offer us an opportunity to verify whether, at these distant times, strange objects had already been observed.

The French ufologist Aimé Michel interested himself in this matter. [2] Patiently, he examined copies of graffiti from the walls of French and Spanish sites, looking for indications that UFOs were being depicted. However, to interpret these geometrical designs as representations of aerial objects is a hazardous proceeding. It is certainly disconcerting to find graphic shapes seeming to depict lenticular objects, even with a suggestion of movement; but experts see in them nothing more than a kind of signature by the paleolithic artist; magic signs associated with some initiatory rite; or even stereotyped representations of femal genitals.

Skipping lightly over several millennia, we come

to our first written records. The legendary texts of India, particularly the *Samarangana-Sartradhara,* a kind of treatise on architecture and town planning, mentions in Chapter 31 some very strange machines (*yantras*). Among these are the *'vimanas',* described as machines capable of flight, moving as directed by the pilot, and propelled by various systems which, though described at length, remain incomprehensible to 20th century man.

Other epics, such as the *Mahabaharata* and the *Ramayana,* refer to these *'vimana'* as military devices capable of carrying death to any part of the world. Though their vivid language is liable to lead us astray, we cannot but be struck by the modernity of certain passages, where we seem to be reading an account of a nuclear war.

FROM CLASSICAL TO MEDIEVAL TIMES

A leap in time carries us to classical Greece and Rome, where in Pliny the Elder's *De Natura Rerum* we find references to 'burning shields', 'flying torches', 'gleaming beams in the sky' and so forth. Simple though rare natural phenomena, or something else?

The so-called 'Dark Ages' certainly do not seem to have been enlightened by many luminous aerial phenomena, but in 1518 there was born Conrad Wolffhart, a curious person whose work is still little known; he was professor of grammar at Basel University and deacon of St Leonard's Church. In 1557, under the nom de plume of Lycosthenes, he published his *Prodigorium ac Ostentorum Chronicon,* where are described a vast range of unbelievable prodigies, similar to those later unearthed by Charles Fort; honey, wood, blood or flesh falling from the sky, monsters, unexplained disappearances &c. And of course, among this mass of mysteries, instances of UFOs.

Another chronicler, Gregory of Tours, in his *Historia Francorum* offers similar accounts, for example: "In the year 584 there appeared in the sky brilliant rays of light which seemed to cross and collide with one another... in 585, in the month of September certain people saw signs, that is to say rays or domes such as are customarily seen and which seemed to race across the sky."

It would be tiresome to recount in detail the cases reported by the various chroniclers of the Middle Ages. Often it's a question of 'aerial armies', of parades of luminous lights, of aerial combats between monstrous figures, or yet another passage of coloured lights in the sky. Were the times unusually favoured by astronomical or meteorological anomalies, were comets particularly noticeable, were meteors and auroras specially spectacular?

To illustrate this point, here is an extract from the *Historia Anglorum* of the English chronicler Matthew of Paris, which was not published until 1969; he is telling of a phenomenon which occurred on 24 July 1239, during the reign of Henry III. "At sunset, but before the stars were out and the sky was still clear, serene and brilliant, a great star like a torch appeared. It rose in the south and climbed the sky giving out a great light. When it was high in the sky, it turned towards the north, slowly, as if intending to take up position in the sky. But when it was about the middle of the sky, in our northern hemisphere, it left behind it smoke and sparks. It was shaped like a great head, the front part was sparkling and the back part gave out smoke and flashes."

Or take this account by Jacques Duclerc (or Duclarcq), duc de Bourgogne, Philippe III le Bon's advocate, entitled *Memoirs of a citizen of Arras*: "On All Saints' Day, the 1st of November 1461, appeared in the sky an object as bright as a bar of iron, as long and wide as a half-moon; it hung stationary for about a quarter hour, clearly visible, then suddenly the strange object spiralled, twisted and turned like a spring and rose into the heavens..." Does not that bring to mind present-day descriptions of the movements of unknown aerial objects?

THE RENAISSANCE

The skies of 16th century Europe were again the stage for exceptional aerial events. Most notably, the *Nurnberg Gazette* recounts how on 4 April 1561 a "very frightening vision" occurred at sunrise. Many men and women saw 'balls' coloured blue, black or blood-red, and 'circular discs' in great profusion, in the proximity of the sun; three or so in a line, sometimes four in a square, others on their own; among the balls a number of blood-red crosses'. Later were seen two huge cylinders, containing other cylinders small and large, spheres in threes and fours, all of which began to fight one against the others.

This combat appears to have lasted an hour, then all fell to earth as if burning and all was consumed in a great smoke. Among the spheres was noted a long shape "like a big black lance." These extraordinary signs were of course taken at the time as a divine warning. The phenomenon is strangely similar to that seen a little less than three centuries later, on 17 October 1952, when a cylindrical object was seen moving slowly above a cloud above Oloron (Pyrenées-Atlantiques): "A cottony cloud of strange shape was floating against the blue sky. Above it, a long narrow cylinder - whitish, non-luminous, and very distinctly defined. A sort of plume of white smoke was escaping from its upper end. At some distance in front of the cylinder, about thirty other objects were following the same trajectory. To the naked eye they appeared as featureless balls resembling puffs of smoke. But with the help of opera glasses, it was possible to make out a central red sphere, surrounded by a sort of yellowish ring inclined at an angle... These 'saucers' moved in pairs, following a broken path characterised in general by rapid and short zigzags. When two saucers drew away from one another, a whitish streak, like an electric arc, was produced between them." [2] Here we find again the 'cylinder' accompanied by balls, and the zigzag motion is a fair imitation of a fight.

Five years after the Nurnberg event, a similar sighting was reported by the *Gazette de Bâle*, published in the patois of the day by Samuel Coccius, "student in Sacred Writings and the Liberal Arts": "On 7 August 1566, at sunrise, were seen many large black spheres in the air which head at great speed towards the sun, then made a half-turn, colliding with one another as if fighting; many became red and fiery, ending by being consumed and vanishing."

Several other European cities, including Rotterdam, witnessed such aerial ballets in the course of the century.

The events which occurred over Paris on 12 September 1621 are also worth mentioning, for here we have more than one recorded testimony. The writer Pierre de l-Estoile, in his *Journal of Events during the reigns of Henri III and Henri IV*, reports: "Several little white clouds appeared which, as if in squadrons separated one from another, struck one against the other with enormous speed then disappeared, after which others appeared which as they approached sent out what seemed to be lances and arrows one against another, and after combating for a while, vanished and were not seen again..."

Jacques Thevenyn, a lawyer from the rue Saint-Martin who kept a journal of the strange things he saw, also witnessed this strange phenomenon: "The night of Sunday 12 September, though moonless was very clear, and swans could be seen flying. About 10 pm I saw from my door what looked like three long white paths in the sky, one smaller than the others, and moving. I supposed this to be due to the wind, but I don't know what it was. I then saw something like an open crown against which came many other objects which seemed to melt into it."

For the first time in our prehistory of the UFO phenomenon, we have the ideal situation, independent accounts of the same phenomenon from witnesses in different locations and who didn't know each other.

THE FIRST SCIENTIFIC REPORTS

The 17th and still more the 18th centuries bring us the first scientific reports from astronomers, notably Edmund Halley, who observed many curious aerial phenomena which he could not identify as known astronomical objects.

On 9 December 1731, immediately preceding an earthquake, a 'luminous cloud' was seen in the sky over Firenze, and observed until it disappeared below the horizon. More strangely, on 5 December 1737, at Sheffield, towards 5 pm, Thomas Short observed "the apparition of a dark red cloud, below which was a luminous body which emitted intense beams of light. It was not at all like the aurora borealis for the light beams moved slowly for a while, then stopped. Suddenly it became so hot that I could take off my shirt even though I was out of doors. This meteor was observed over Kilkenny, Ireland, where

The Basel sighting of 7August 1566. [Woodcut in Zentral-bibliothek, Zurich]

it seemed like a great ball of fire. It was reported that it shook the entire island and that the whole sky seemed to burst into flames."

Nor did it stop there; next day it was seen over Romania. In a manuscript account (*Manuscris Românesc 2343 folio 3-4*) we read that "on the afternoon of Saint Nicolas' Day there appeared in the west a great sign in the sky, blood-red and very large. It stayed in place for two hours, then separated in two parts which then rejoined, and the object disappeared towards the west" - an unexpected confirmation of Short's observation. It is certainly a curious 'meteor' which takes 24 hours to travel from England to Romania...

On 18 October 1783 Tiberius Cavallo made another interesting observation from the terrace of Windsor Castle: "To the NE of the terrace, in a clear sky and in warm weather, I suddenly saw appear an oblong cloud moving more or less parallel to the horizon. Under this cloud could be seen a luminous object which soon became spherical, brilliantly lit, which came to a halt. It was then about 9.45 pm. This strange sphere seemed at first to be pale blue in colour, but its luminosity increased and soon it set off again towards the east. Then the object changed direction and moved parallel to the horizon before diappearing towards the south-east. I watched it for half a minute, and the light it gave out was prodigious; it lit up everything on the ground. Before it vanished it changed its shape, became oblong, and at the same time as a sort of trail appeared, it seemed to separate into two small bodies. Scarecely two minutes later the sound of an explosion was heard."

Similar phenomena were reported from Deptford (Wiltshire), not far from Stonehenge, and at Hartlepool, Co Durham.

THE 19TH CENTURY

The 19th century was one of contrasts, in which spectacular progress was made in the course of a few decades. Of particular interest for us is the growing role of the press, which henceforward plays a significant part in the collection of UFO reports. Scientific journals began to relate events reported to them by their correspondents. Thus, the *Journal of Natural History & Philosophy & Chemistry* reports the sighting of by Sir John Staveley, 10 August 1809, at Hatton Garden, London: "I saw many meteors near the corner of a black cloud from which lights were emitted. It was as though patches of blinding light were dancing and passing across the cloud. One grew until it attained the brilliance and size of Venus, but I could see no body in the light. This moved with great rapidity, lost its brightness and disappeared. For nearly an hour these strange lights went in and out of the cloud at countless points. At the time when the meteors grew in size, they seemed to descend closer to the earth..." What a strange aerial ballet! What could that 'black cloud' have been, which moved and halted at will?

The term 'meteor' was certainly in fashion during this first half of the 19th century. Just as the citizens of the Middle Ages spoke of comets in and out of season, so our nearer ancestors interpreted the surprising phenomena they saw as so many astronomical curiosities. Yet, though sometimes they displayed the characteristics we today associate with meteors, more frequently there are references to properties which these debris of space do not possess. Certainly there exist meteors which traverse the sky majestically, but they are few and apparently small in size. If we invoke such an explanation for the foregoing accounts, we must add that there was nothing exceptional about them, for on average at least three such observations per year were reported throughout the 19th century.

Modern times bring modern explanations. At the end of the century, the myth of the balloon and airship began to replace that of the meteor. When a stray balloon escaped from English shores, it served to explain every curious sighting for a month to come.

In 1886 we find our first report of physiological effects caused by an unidentified luminous phenomenon. The *Scientific American* for 18 December published a letter from Walter Cowgill, US Consul at Maracaibo, Venezuela, who examined witnesses to an aerial phenomenon and noted loss of hair, burns, blisters and wounds over the whole body - effects which suggest intense radiation.

THE 1896-1897 SIGHTINGS

1896 - and even more 1897 - saw the first true wave of anomalous aerial observations. Over several months the NE states of America were the stage for singular events, thousands of witnesses reporting the flight over several towns of a mysterious 'unknown airship'. What strikes one, in the face of this wealth of testimony, is the consistency of description by people distant one from another, with only minimal possibility of contact. From this emerges a fairly precise image: an immense cigar-shaped object, with a structure - seemingly a control cabin - below it. This device was furnished with lights, frequently of different colours, and often with a system of wheels whose purpose is hard to understand. The occupants of these machines were just like ourselves and their conversations with those privileged to converse with them are dismayingly humdrum.

Many theories were proposed: individual and collective hallucination, the effects of alcohol, simple rumour. But all were discarded in favour of the hypothesis of an airship invented by an engineer - unnamed, though several candidates were suggested. Undeniably, we must acknowledge that all the accounts bring to mind an airship; but alas for the partisans of this hypothesis, no airship existed in 1897 capable of the feats recorded. No truly viable airship existed before the end of the century, when in 1901 Santos-Dumont succeeded in travelling 10 km in half an hour, rounding the Eiffel Tower to return to his point of departure. It is out of the question that such an airship could have been flying over Texas or the Great Lakes in 1897.

The 1896 wave was confined to the western states, between 6 and 30 November. That of 1897 comprised two separate waves, one in Texas which lasted from the end of March to the beginning of May, the other in the Great Lakes area, where the duration was shorter - from 13 to 26 April.

What are we to make of these events? Three things are clear: first, that in 1896-7 objects remarkably similar to airships were flying over the United States; second, that given the date it is impossible that one or more such airships could have been flying here or in any other country; third, that in view of the foregoing, these objects remain unexplained and were therefore UFOs in the true sense of the phrase.

What was their true origin? Could it be that the UFO phenomenon presents itself in a form susceptible of being understood by the witnesses of the day: airships for the end of the 19th century, 'flying saucers' for our own time? Or does it seek to deceive us by manifesting in changing, incoherent forms?

THE TWENTIETH CENTURY

1909 witnessed another wave of observations of an airship-like object, this time over Britain. Here again, an impression of consistency emerges from the witness reports, enabling us to draw an identikit picture of a dark cigar, furnished with one or more powerful lights; about 30 m long; highly manoeuvrable. Such a description obliges us to think in terms of an airship, and that was the preferred explanation at the time. The generally-held view was that German airships were carrying out reconnaissance flights over Britain with a view to subsequent invasion. The legend of 'aerial spies' was featured by the daily newspapers, along with other stories of the same sort, such as the discovery of a stockpile of German weapons in the heart of London. So intense became the fear of German spies that in the *Daily Mail* of 21 May 1909 Lord Northcliffe observed that "the Germans must think England has become a haven for mental degenerates."

What justifies the inclusion of these reports in a chronicle of UFOs is the fact that they present certain troubling aspects. In many respects they recall the events which had occurred a dozen years previously in America. Here too the performances described were beyond that of any device of the time, however feeble they may seem to us today, and it is virtually out of the question that they could have related to an actual airship. It is true that by 1909 aerial navigation was a practical proposition, but aviation was still in its infancy and its achievements still far short of what was recounted of the mysterious airships.

Study of these reports confronts us with a simple alternative: either they relate to a number of man-made machines with capabilities which were not duplicated until much later; or to devices whose technology was quite anachronistic for the time.

To believe that German airships could cross the Channel and fly over large areas of Britain for more than a month without causing an uproar in military circles is hard enough; it becomes harder still when we find that from mid-July to the first week of September 1909 - that is, a few short weeks after the reports of the 'unidentified airships' over England - astonished New Zealanders were reporting the movements of a device which they invariably described as a 'flying cigar'.

BETWEEN THE WARS

The between-the-wars period had its share of UFO sightings, but with no waves attributable to a collective psychosis. Now the cases are isolated, well related and open to investigation by present-day researchers: even if a witness's memory dates back over many years, it may be rich in significant details which interest today's ufologist.

For example, there is the testimony of traveller Nicholas Roerich, who in his 1929 book *Altai Himalaya* describes his sighting on 5 August 1926 [1927, according to Dr Leon Davidson]. While travelling in the Kokonor region of Mongolia, members of his expedition were watching an eagle flying high above: "Several of us began to watch this unusual bird. At the same moment another of our caraveneers remarked: 'There is something far above the bird,' and we all saw something big and shiny reflecting the sun, like a huge oval moving at great speed...we even had time to take our field glasses, and saw quite distinctly an oval form with a shiny surface, one side of which was brilliant from the sun."

Moving on to the period of World War Two, we find the most notable event, ufologically speaking, was the widespread appearances of small discs and spheres of unknown origin which were at the time nicknamed 'foo-fighters'. Their first official appearance was on 14 October 1943, during a bomber raid on the German industrial complex at Schweinfurt, Mission 115:

"As the bombers of the 384th Group swung into the final bomb run, the fighter attacks fell off. This point is vital, and pilots were queried extensively, as were other crew members, as to the position at that time of the German fighter planes. Every man interrogated was firm in his statement that 'at the time there were no enemy aircraft above'."

At this moment the pilots and top turret gunners, as well as several crewmen in the plexiglass noses of the bombers, reported a cluster of discs in the path of the 384's formation and closing with the bombers. The startled exclamations focused attention on the phenomenon, and the crews talked back and forth, discussing and confirming the astonishing sight before them.

The discs in the cluster were agreed upon as being silver coloured, about one inch thick and three inches in diameter. They were easily seen, gliding down slowly in a very uniform cluster.

And then the 'impossible' happened. B-17 Number 026 closed rapidly with a cluster of discs; the pilot attempted to evade an imminent collision, but was unsuccessful in his manoeuver. He reported at the intelligence debriefing that his "right wing went directly through a cluster with absolutely no effect on engines or plane surface."

The intelligence officers pressed their questioning, and the pilot stated further that one of the discs was heard to strike the tail assembly, but that neither he nor any member of the crew heard or witnessed an explosion. He further explained that about twenty feet from the discs the pilots sighted a mass of black debris of varying sizes in clusters of three by four feet. The SECRET report added: "Also observed two other A/C flying through silver discs with no apparent damage. Observed discs and debris two other times but could not determine where it came from.

No further information on this baffling incident has been uncovered, with the exception that such discs were observed by pilots and crew members on missions prior to, and after, Mission 115 of October 14, 1943." [**3**]

The 'foo-fighter' wave picked up again towards the end of 1944, when at 2200 h on 23 November 1944, Lieut Schluter, pilot in 415 Fighter Group of the USAF at Dijon, took off for a routine mission over the Vosges mountains. The sky was clear and the American radar had detected no enemy presence in the area. About 30km from Strasbourg Lieut Ringwald, Information Officer, saw towards the west a linear formation of 8 to 10 red fireballs moving at great speed. Four days later, Lieuts Giblin and Cleary, on a mission south of Mannheim, saw over Speyer an enormous luminous orange sphere moving at about 400 km/h, scarcely 500 m above their aircraft. As with the previous incident, the radar operators had nothing to report - so far as they were concerned, there was nothing else in the sky at the time.

In December 1944, USAF Major Leet, in a B-17 bomber, observed an amber disc which seemed to follow the manoeuvres of his aircraft over Klagenfurt (Austria). On 22 December two other pilots of 415 Fighter Group were flying over Hagenau at an altitude of 3000 m when at 1800 h the pilot reported: "Two very bright lights have left the ground and are headed towards us. Right now they are following us." For two minutes the two orange spheres stayed in the aircraft's wake, then suddenly they abandoned the aircraft and vanished. Two nights later the same pilots had another similar encounter. In January 1945 other pilots from the same squadron were followed in the same fashion by three of these balls, red and white this time. The *New York Times* of 2 January 1945 reported several other cases of foo-fighters seen over France over a period of several months.

Throughout August 1946, 'ghost rockets' were seen over Scandinavia, as described in another section of this book. We should note, however, that other countries besides Scandinavia were visited by 'mysterious rockets' during the summer of 1946; they were seen in Switzerland, Belgium, and at Waterford in Ireland.

During the night of 1 September 1946, several military units stationed in Greece reported mysterious rockets in the sky. According to a communique passed on to AFP by the authorities of the British Embassy there, the objects were at altitudes ranging from 500m to 10 km. Altogether, thirteen reports were received for that night; the objects had been seen in all parts of the country, but particularly Macedonia and Salonika, over the principal cities.

11 September brought a report from Srinagar, India, and during the week of 14-21 September the rockets were reported over Portugal. An AFP dispatch of 21 September reports a number of unexplained aerial phenomena in the Portuguese sky during this period: on 14 September at Alemtejo on the 16th, over Porto and the Duoro; also two 'green globes' to the north of Lisbon on the 18th. Towards the end of September, the rockets seemed to migrate to Belgium; on the 27th they were seen over Ostend, and on the 28 and 29 near Verviers.

As the year 1946 closed, on 30 December, Ella Young was in the company of a girlfriend near Morrow Bay (CA), when she saw heading towards them a curious object: "The sun had just set and it must have been 17.35pm. Suddenly, a dark object appeared in the sky, and as it came closer to us its shape became more distinct. You'd say it was a black stick with wings. It stayed motionless for a few moments, then it went off towards the horizon and disappeared behind a cloud. Immediately after, a bright flash of light lit up the sky over the ocean."

And then it was 1947, with its striking wave of unknown discs which flew over the United States from the end of June to mid-July, and that most famous date of all, Kenneth Arnold's celebrated sighting of 24 June 1947.

But from then on, UFOs entered a new era...

REFERENCES

1 - **Bougard,** Michel *La chronique des OVNI*, J-P Delarge, 1977. ■ 2 - **Michel**, Aimé, *Lueurs sur les Soucoupes Volantes*, Mame, 1954. ■ 3 - **Caidin,** Martin, *Black Thursday*, Dutton, 1960.

2.1.3

BEFORE THE FLYING SAUCERS CAME

by Nigel Watson

■ **NIGEL WATSON**: After studying psychology part-time for five years with the Open University, is currently on a full-time degree course in Film & Literature at Warwick University.
■ **UFO involvement**: His particular interests have been: the role and impact of science fiction ideas on the UFO subject; historical sightings of UFO-like phenomena; and the psychological aspects of close encounter and contactee experiences.
■ **Publications**: Many articles on the above subjects have appeared in *BUFORA Bulletin, Fortean Times* and *Magonia*; he is a regular contributor to the latter. With David Clarke and Granville Oldroyd (who also contribute to this present publication) he is currently compiling a detailed catalogue of the British 1912-1913 phantom airship scare, and articles on other historical facets from the same collaboration are forthcoming.
■ **Address**: Westfield Cottage / 7 Crowle Bank Road / Althorpe / South Humberside DN17 3HZ / England.

Throughout history the heavens have been the domain of gods, devils, angels, serpents, dragons, wandering spirits, signs and warnings, and miraculous wonders that we can barely understand. The skies above us are the great realm of the unknown and the unexplained. As long as our feet remained on the ground, only our imaginations could roam these regions. This separation between man and heaven was shattered on 21 November 1783 when the Marquis d'Arlandes and Pilâtre de Rozier made the world's first balloon flight. The first flight in Britain occurred on 15 September 1784. When the balloon landed in a field nearby farmworkers ran away calling the vessel the Devil's horse. [**1**] Once infringed, would this aerial territory ever again be left entirely undisturbed?

One result of manned flight was that if anything strange was seen in the sky it tended to be interpreted as a balloon. What might be called the first balloon scares occurred towards the end of the 19th century. One began on 10 December 1881, when the balloon *Saladin* was accidentally released from Bridport, England, with Member of Parliament Walter Powell on board. The extensive inquiries made to locate this craft caused several observers to report what they thought were sightings of the *Saladin*. On 11 December from Dartmouth Harbour two lights were seen 7 to 20 metres above the water moving rapidly at 8.00 pm. In Hartlepool, on the morning of 13 December a huge balloon was seen going northwards. The next day a balloon was seen near Manney Hill on the island of Alderney at 7.00 am. The following morning a light was seen over Montrose Ness, Scotland, by the crew of the steamer *Countess*. On the 16th, three custom-house guards saw a balloon over Monte de Fuerte, Spain, and the next day it was seen near Bilbao. [**2,3**] Although it seems likely that Powell and his balloon fell into the Channel not long after taking off, sightings of him came from a wide geographical area over a relatively long period of time. What the observers called a balloon was their own gloss on sightings of odd lights in the sky seen during night-time.

The expectations of observers no doubt coloured their perceptions during 1896 and 1897 in Canada. In both years people were on the look out for a balloon captained by Salomon A. Andrée, who intended to fly over the North Pole in a balloon. What was assumed to be his air vessel was seen passing over Winnipeg on 1 July 1896. Two days later a boy at Hazleton saw a black balloon at 7.35 pm. On Blackwater lake some Indians saw the lights of a balloon at about the same time. Yet the fact is that Andrée never even took to the air that year!

On 10 June 1897, two fishermen in Northern British Columbia saw a light attached to a pear-shaped body flying towards the south. By the end of July and during August many Canadians allegedly saw Andrée's balloon. Thousands in Vancouver on the night of 13 August viewed it. The next day the balloon was seen in the interior of Siberia. When the remains of Andrée's expedition were found it was discovered that his flight, launched on 11 July 1897, came down to earth on 14 July 1897. He never went anywhere near Siberia or Canada. [**4, 5, 6**]

With the development of petrol engines and

aluminium production in the 1880s, it was possible to construct viable airships that could be powered and steered. So anything strange in the sky could now be interpreted as being an airship. The earliest 'phantom airship' scare, only recently re-discovered by Thomas Bullard, erupted in Russian Poland during March 1892. At the time there was a great deal of border tension between Russia and Germany. So when hovering lights were seen almost daily over Sosnowice, Dombrova and Stremeszice, the Germans were accused of sending steerable balloons on spying missions. On at least two occasions the craft was shot at when it was seen near military establishments. This, like all the phantom airship scares that followed, featured observations of a powerful searchlight beam streaming down from the airship, usually during the hours of darkness. Yet, at that time searchlight equipment was extremely heavy and difficult to fit to any aircraft.

We must also bear in mind that night flying was in itself a very hazardous enterprise even without the additional danger of spying on enemy territory. The flimsy aircraft of the pre-World War One period found it difficult enough to maintain a flight-path over friendly land in full daylight without crashing or straying off course.

The newspapers of that period spoke of phantom airships for the same reason people today speak of UFOs. They were not observations of real aircraft, either because all such craft were accounted for, or because they displayed an ability to navigate the sky that surpassed currently known human technology.

The largest and most puzzling phantom airship scare began in the closing months of 1896 in California. For example, on the night of 17 November between 6 and 7 o'clock hundreds of people saw an 'electric arc lamp' pass over Sacramento. Some witnesses said they heard voices coming from the aircraft that carried the light. Music was also heard and a voice from it said: "Well, we ought to get to San Francisco by tomorrow noon." A few witnesses saw a balloon shape, and one said it had a wheel that spun round. [**7**]

As the sightings spread eastwards the reports became more fanciful. Secret inventors allowed themselves to be discovered but none of them seem to have been capable of creating the great many reports that filled the American newspapers.

One farmer said that near the end of March 1897, the anchor of an airship caught him by the seat of his trousers while he was on his cow lot near Sioux City, Iowa. Robert Hibbard travelled some distance before he was able to grab a sapling and rip himself to the ground. Another story, repeated in many UFO books, was equally unusual. This concerned the arrival of an airship containing six strange beings over Alexander Hamilton's farm near Vernon, Kansas. One night in mid-April he watched it winch up a three-year-old heifer and fly away. On the 17 April an airship crashed at Aurora, Texas. The wreckage consisted of strange metals, and papers filled with odd writing were found on the body of the dead pilot, who did not look as if he was from this planet. Such stories have been taken more seriously than they deserve. Many similar accounts were published and were obviously meant as humorous hoaxes. The intriguing thing is that so many people reported having inside knowledge of the mystery, which they obtained by meeting the occupants of the airship(s) who sought directions, provisions, or time to repair their craft. A few people even claimed they rode in the airship. One man who lived on Troy Hill, Allegheny, PA, was taken by two men on the night of 11 April on an aerial ride to Mount Washington. Here they left him, but he did not remember much of the flight because he had been drinking. [**8**]

The sheer quantity of newspaper reports indicates that the citizens of America were excited by the idea of a wonderful new flying machine and suggests that this 'scare' was a form of wish fulfilment.

For the next few years there were no more airship scares anywhere near the dimensions of the American 1896-97 events. On 12 December 1903 the Wright brothers at Kitty Hawk, North Carolina, made the first powered and controlled aeroplane flight. At the same time Count Zeppelin continued to develop the airship in Germany. Every year steady progress in aeronautics was made. What troubled many people, particularly in Europe, was that aircraft could have a dramatic impact in any future war. Such machines could spy on enemy forces and bomb them with little risk to themselves. Even worse, it brought the civilian population into the front-line. No longer could battles be fought at a distance; now everybody from peasant to king was vulnerable to attack.

When a strange light was frequently seen over Cherbourg, France, in April 1905, it was suspected that a British torpedo boat was experimenting with signal lights suspended from a captive balloon. [**9**] Later, in June and July 1908, when an object with lights and wings was seen in Denmark, it was thought British warships exercising in the North Sea had launched it. [**10**]

After being suspected of being the creator of airship scares, Britain became the victim of a widespread panic between March and May 1909. Virtually all the observations of searchlights from the sky occurred at night. Sometimes the whirr of the airship's machinery was heard, and a glimpse of an object behind the light or lights was noted. In May, a Mr Lethbridge encountered two men on the top of Caerphilly Mountain who jumped into the carriage of an airship and flew away. Another grounded airship was encountered on Ham Common, but both reports are of suspect validity. The press, and the public, believed the lights came from a German airship on an espionage mission. [**11**] The same idea was held by New Zealanders in July and August of 1909 who were plagued by numerous lights in the sky. Some boat-shaped objects were seen in daylight and one or two descriptions of occupants were provided, but the amount of hoaxers and just plain misperceptions of stars, planets, etc., made it difficult to conclude if there was anything genuinely strange about them. Other than the theory that these airships were launched from a German ship, there was speculation that a secret inventor was experimenting, and a couple of writers to the press claimed the vessel was from Mars. In August, for a couple of weeks, lights were sighted in the sky in Australia. [**12**]

In September and December 1909 an elliptical object with wings was seen in Sweden. On 2 December at Göteborg a fast-moving lighted balloon was seen heading out to sea. Before it departed from sight it fired a rocket at Redburgs Park. [**13**]

The fear of infringements by enemy aircraft experienced in most parts of the world was replaced by optimism in the USA. On the night of 8 September 1909, Wallace Elmer Tillinghast claimed he flew from Worcester, Massachusetts, to within a mile of the Statue of Liberty and safely returned back to his secret base near Worcester. When this was made public in mid-December, sightings of aerial activities soared. From the 19th to Christmas Eve thousands of people in Worcester, Boston, and most surrounding parts, saw Tillinghast flying in his new invention. Some saw the body and wings of the craft, the majority merely saw a moving light in the sky. As usual, jokers capitalised on the craze by sending up toy balloons with lights attached. Venus was possibly responsible for lots of sightings. As well as Massachusetts, unusual lights were seen in Maine, Connecticut, Rhode Island and Vermont. Tillinghast tried to get money to build an aircraft factory, and he even promised to exhibit, in a more conventional fashion, his machine. But his machines and dreams never materialised into anything substantial. In January 1910 sightings were made in Tennessee, Alabama and Arkansas, but they did not help solve this mystery. [**14**]

The pranks of people like Tillinghast in the USA served only to make people look ridiculous or drain them of any cash they might invest in such high-flying schemes. In Europe, international tensions were close to their breaking point. A strange buzzing sound and a dark object seen over Sheerness and nearby Eastchurch Naval Flying School, England, on the night of 14 October 1912 caused a major panic that could have resulted in a world war. The event obtained wide-scale publicity on 27 November when the First Lord of the Admiralty, Winston Churchill, made a statement about it in the House of Commons. His objective seems to have been to make the public more aware of the growing danger of Germany's aerial superiority and thereby obtain more funds and backing for his naval fliers. His tactic worked well, too well in fact! By the middle of January 1913 lights in the sky were seen in South Wales nearly every night. In February sightings became more concentrated in Yorkshire and the east coast. Thousands saw the light of the airship and of course the Germans were blamed. The press took a great interest in these stories and the public concern hastened the introduction of the *Aerial Navigation Act, March 1, 1913* which prohibited unauthorised aircraft from flying over certain areas of Britain. More sightings were made in the Orkneys and Scotland at the end of February until mid-March but they received little national publicity. The effect of this scare was to alert the government to public worries, and as a result, legislation and practical measures that might be initiated to protect Britain from air warfare were at least discussed and decided upon. [**15**]

In the rest of Europe there were similar fears about foreign aircraft. The Russians accused the Austrians of sending two aircraft over Kamenetz-Prodosk, Russia, at the end of 1912. In turn, Russian aircraft were blamed for using searchlights on military sites in Jaroslaw, Austria. One Russian aircraft crashed killing its pilot in that incident which took place on 18 January 1913. Twelve days later a Russian aircraft with a searchlight was shot at by soldiers in Jassy, Roumania. Next, two Austrian pilots were accused of roping a mayor of a town near Plock, Russian Poland, to their aeroplane and flying him a good distance before releasing him. These types of incident continued into February.

The more familiar fear of German airships emerged in Belgium and Holland during February 1913. During the same period people in the eastern regions of France claimed German airships were spying at night, and cars equipped with searchlights were sent out to search for them. And in Germany itself, phantom airships began being seen. On 4 March an airship was seen at Tarnowitz, Prussia, that was suspected to have come from Russia. On the Caputh side of Lake Schwielow, a burning airship was seen to crash into the forest, but no wreckage was found after extensive searching. [**16**]

Prior to and just after the declaration of war with Germany, a phantom aircraft was seen in many parts of South Africa. In Durban natives feared falling bombs, and at Pretoria on 31 August 1914 an aircraft was shot at. Most of these sightings consisted of lights in the sky, but it was feared that aircraft were being flown from German South-West Africa. [**17**]

The outbreak of the First World War created many airship and aeroplane scares. Due to censorship, many of the reports were not made public, but in the past few years many reports that were filed with the authorities and taken seriously by them have been discovered in government record offices. Certainly in Britain many such cases occurred and consisted of observations that the witnesses believed were of enemy aircraft. [**18**]

In Canada hostile aerial phantoms were frequently seen from September 1914 to February 1916. Airships and aeroplanes were observed mainly in the area of Niagara Falls. During September 1914 an airship with red lights dropped a rocket near the Welland canal. In the following months guards at military installations saw the lights of aircraft. Two men were seen to get out of an aircraft near Noyan Junction, Quebec, at 7.00 pm in July 1915. They returned to the vehicle and then flew off towards Montreal. At Chateaugay an aircraft was seen to land and collect a German officer who had been living in the neighbourhood. Over the winter of 1915 and 1916 lights were again seen near the Welland canal. On 5 February 1916 at 5.00 am two aircraft flew near the Victoria railway bridge and later in the day a suspicious character who was spotted in the vicinity was shot at. The major fear was that German aircraft were responsible for the flights and that air raids might occur. [**19**]

Other sinister events occurred in conjunction with mystery aircraft in New Jersey and Pennsylvania during January and February 1916. Three du Pont gunpowder plants suffered explosions, then at the end of January a white light was seen hovering over one of these plants, and a low-flying aircraft was observed over another du Pont plant. A phantom sniper shot at a home in Glassboro, NJ, on 2 February. A huge aircraft was seen circling over a chemical factory at Tionesta, PA, by many skaters. After this spate of sightings, mystery fires and explosions ignited in Philadelphia and several du Pont plants until the end of the month. [**20**]

After the first World War, there do not seem to have been any scares or panics associated with aircraft until the 1930s. Perhaps newspaper research might rediscover some in the future; or was it that people just wanted to forget anything associated with warfare? However, during the 1930s the phantoms made up for lost time. On 26 December 1933 a mystery aircraft circled New York city, and on 1 February 1934 another mystery flier circled over London.

The majority of the sightings, however, occurred in Scandinavia. The aeroplane was often described as grey-coloured, the engines were heard, and it carried a powerful searchlight. Sometimes it was seen to land. It was suspected that smugglers or Russian or German military forces were at work. Between 1929 and 1934 the German Luftwaffe made secret training flights from Russia that could have 'strayed' into Sweden. Also, secret flight testing was made from the island of Rügen by the Germans. Yet the extensive searches and investigations made by Sweden and Norway seem to indicate that they could not easily solve the mystery. After many sightings in 1934, there

The German airship scare: current fears reflected in the popular press. [*The Queen,* **1913**]

was a lull until the winter of 1936 and 1937, when it was again seen over Scandinavia. In February 1937 there was a sighting in Vienna, Austria, and in July the British Air Ministry made inquiries into the activities of a mystery night flier in Britain. [21]

The next panic, not directly associated with airships or aeroplanes, did show the public's ability to believe in life on other planets in certain circumstances. This was triggered by the now famous *War of the Worlds* radio broadcast on the night of 30 October 1938. This Orson Welles production induced thousands of people to escape the heat rays of the invading Martians. [22]

Suggestions had been made during the American 1896-97 airship scare, and during some of the other scares, that the sightings were caused by ships from outer space, but such ideas had generally been tongue-in-cheek and never seriously considered. [23]

In the Second World War things called foo-fighters were seen in the sky. Pilots on bombing missions to Germany often saw silver spheres or discs, that were somtimes translucent, follow them. These small aerial mysteries either flew in formations or on their own. They were seen over Japan, Northern Europe and the Mediterranean. The best theory was that they were some new type of psychological weapon and/or a means of confusing radar systems built secretly by the Germans. However, German pilots saw them too and were equally mystified. No satisfactory explanation has ever been postulated to account for these reports. [24]

In February 1942 Los Angeles suffered an extraordinary war scare. Rumours of Japanese submarines off the coast circulated and sightings of unidentified aircraft caused anti-aircraft guns to fire thousands of rounds into the air. It seems they were shooting at phantoms. The panic was used as the foundation for Steven Spielberg's comedy film *1941* (released to public disinterest in 1979).

Before the term 'flying saucer' and speculation about visitors from outer space took root, a major panic spread across Sweden from May to October 1946. Cigar-shaped objects that had a predilection for crashing into bodies of water were seen frequently. They were nicknamed 'ghost bombs' or 'ghost rockets'. In Sweden a special committee was formed to investigate the matter, and the British and American forces took an interest in the situation, since it was thought that the Russians might have been testing captured German weapons. Despite all the sightings and investigations, no answer was found. To add to the mystery, odd fireballs were also seen over France, Denmark, Finland, Greece, Northern Africa, Portugal, Spain and Italy during September 1946. [25]

Ufologists have eagerly latched onto these reports to prove that flying saucers are not just a post-war fad created by fear of Communism and the atomic bomb. They have maintained that the intruders in our skies merely adapt themselves to the shapes and features we expect to see. Thus, in the 1890s and 1900s they dressed themselves up as airships; in the 1930s as aeroplanes; and in the 1940s as secret weapons; and in 1947 onwards as advanced types of spacecraft. This idea seems to impute an undue amount of sophistication and effort to the aliens for no clear reason. Also, ufologists have interpreted religious visions, such as those experienced at Fatima, Portugal, in 1915 to 1917 in the context of the new UFO frame of reference. [26] The handy thing about such a procedure is that it fuses the secular world of science and rationality with the magical and mystical world of religion. As a consequence God becomes a technological hero who can be 'proved' to be operating in our world all the time. This is a powerful impulse for both UFO investigators and witnesses. Vessels that are 'seen' in the sky have been invested with great symbolic and mythological power throughout history. Heaven has always been conceived as above us, so that anything flying in the skies can be regarded as a link between us and salvation and/or death. [27]

The perception and reporting of things in the sky is also conditioned by other more mundane frames of reference. On a social level, newspaper coverage of technological developments, and science fiction stories about their consequences, plus anxieties about international and internal national problems, provide a climate for UFO witnesses. This general background of knowledge can then be focused by more specific information, such as the alerts to look out for Andrée's and Powell's balloons. In the pre-World War One period, to report a sighting was almost a part of a citizen's patriotic duty, and newspapers that advocated greater defence spending promoted the stories fully. The eagerness of America for a flying machine helped perpetuate the 1896-97 scare. It could be argued that such scares are maintained by a whole series of promoters: the witnesses, newspaper reporters and editors, politicians, manufacturers, inventors, war-mongers, and fiction writers, all of whom might wittingly or unwittingly help keep the interest in the sightings alive, just as ufologists try to do in our present day.

Since it seems that sightings of odd things in the sky are a periodic occurrence, and were so even in the pre-1947 years, why do they erupt into massive scares at certain specific times and places? One explanation is that they bring half-imagined fears into the open and as a consequence provide a vehicle for debate and action. At other times, or concurrently, scares about muggers, Hell's Angels, bombers, stranglers, pollution, atomic power, spies, inflation, unemployment, etc., can manifest themselves in the public consciousness and lead to decisions that are based on as much or as little evidence as the airship scares.

What this discussion boils down to is this: "Are witnesses now and in the past really seeing something out there which we cannot explain or are they all deluded fools or liars?" An easy way out is to say that meteors, fireballs, planets, stars, comets, birds, kites, toy balloons, reflections from clouds, mirages, and unusual optical and meteorological phenomena, etc., can all be relied upon to provide strange visions in the sky at any time, particularly if they are seen in extraordinary circumstances and/or when the witnesses have been subject to physical or mental stress or strain. In addition, certain types of psychological condition can induce a person to report a variety of hallucinatory and visionary experiences as real. But even allowing for the unreliability of human testimony, we are still left to ponder on a body of reports that could indicate things flying about out there which we have been unable to understand. If this is true, and despite the onslaught of sceptics like myself most ufologists think it is, then we have to determine what they are. As this book shows, the question has brought forth a multitude of theories and conjectures and much debate, but THE ANSWER seems as remote now as a phantom airship in the night sky.

REFERENCES

1 - **Rolt,** L.T.C., *The Aeronauts,* Alan Sutton, Gloucester, 1985, p71. ■ 2 - **Bullard,** Thomas E., *The Airship File,* priv.pub., Indiana, USA, pp8-11. ■ 3 - **Fort,** Charles H., *The Complete Books of Charles Fort,* Dover Publications, New York, 1974, pp461-462. ■ 4 - **Bullard,** op.cit., pp14-15 and pp245-249. ■ 5 - **Cottrell,** Leonard, *Up in a Balloon,* World's Work Ltd., Tadworth, Surrey, 1974, pp162-190. ■ 6 - **Rolt,** op.cit., pp152-158. **Clarke,** David, 'A Balloon in the North' in *UFO Brigantia,* No 21, pp5-9 and 10. ■ 7 - *Sacramento Evening Bee,* 18 November 1896. **Bullard,** op.cit.15-6. ■ 8 - *Pittsburg Dispatch,* 12 April 1897. **Bullard,** op.cit.p199. ■ 9 - **Gross,** Loren E., *Charles Fort, The Fortean Society, and Unidentified Flying Objects,* priv.pub. Fremont, California, 1976, p25. **Bullard,** op.cit., pp251-252. **Fort,** op.cit., pp496-499. ■ 10 - **Wegner,** Willy, 'The Danish "Airship" of 1908' in *MUFOB* new series No 9, pp11-13. ■ 11 - **Anon,** 'What did PC Kettle See?' in *FSR* Vol 6 No 4, pp11-12. **Anon,** 'The First Contact of the Century?' in *FSR* Vol 6 No 2, pp19-20. **Clarke,** David, 'The Airship Syndrome' in *Quest,* Sept./Oct. 1985, pp17-22. **Grove,** Carl, 'The Airship Wave of 1909' in *FSR,* Vol 16 No 6, pp9-11 and Vol 17 No 1 pp17-19. **Hind,** John, 'The 1909 Mystery Airships in the Irish Papers' in *Irish UFO News* No 6 pp4-11 and *Pursuit* Vol 13 No 3 pp105-108. **Screeton,** Paul, 'A Newspaper Looks at the Airship' in *MUFOB* new series No 11 pp17-18. **Watson,** Nigel, 'Airships and Invaders' in *Magonia,* No 3 pp3-8. **Watson,** Nigel, 'Phantom Airships over Britain in 1909' in *Common Ground* No 3 pp18-23. **Watson,** Nigel, 'The British Scareship Invasion' in *The Alien World,* Orbis, London, 1984, pp54-576. ■ 12 - **Brunt,** Tony, 'The New Zealand UFO Wave of 1909' in *Xenolog'* No 100 and 101. **Chalker,** Bill, 'Australian 1909 and 1910 Sightings', unpublished manuscript. **Hinfelaar,** Mrs., 'The New Zealand "Flap" of 1909' in *FSR* Vol 10 No 6 pp32-iii. **Norman,** Paul, 'Items from the Australian Flap; 1909-1910' in *FSR* Vol 22 No 6 p15. ■ 13 - **Bullard,** John A., *UFOs: Operation Trojan Horse,* Abacus, London, 1973, p110. ■ 14 - **Bullard,** op.cit., pp267-291 and 384. **Gross,** op.cit., p29 and pp42-44. **Keel,** op.cit., pp110-121. ■ 15 - **Clark,** Jerome, and **Farish,** Lucius, 'The Phantom Airships of 1913' in *UFO Report,* Vol 7 No 6 pp36-38. **Clarke,** David, 'UFOs over Yorkshire in 1913' in *Quest* Vol 4 No 1 pp11-17. **Watson,** Nigel, 'Who sent the Scareships?' in *The Alien World,* Orbis, London, 1984, pp58-60. **Watson,** Nigel and **Oldroyd,** Granville, 'The British Phantom Airship Mystery', to be published in *FlyPast.* **Watson,** Nigel, 'The Fear that Flies by Night is over Yorkshire' in *UFO Brigantia* No 21 pp23-27. ■ 16 - **Bullard,** op.cit., pp293-296, 298, 300, 304-306. ■ 17 - **Bullard,** op.cit., 306-314. **Creighton,** Gordon, 'Saucers and South Africa' in *FSR* Vol 8 No 4 pp18-21. **Keel,** op.cit., p121. ■ 18 - **Clarke,** David and **Oldroyd,** Granville, *Spooklights,* priv.pub., 1986, pp7-10 and 28. ■ 19 - **Whalen,** Dwight, 'What were those Strange Airborne Noises?' in *The Standard* 13 November 1982. And *Fate* September 1983. **Lorenzen,** Coral and Jim, *Flying Saucer Occupants,* Signet, New York, 1967, pp19-25. **Bullard,** Thomas E., *The Airship File: Supplement I,* priv.pub., Indiana, USA, pp36-41. ■ 20 - **Shoemaker,** Michael T., 'UFO Saboteurs' in *Fate,* December 1985, pp59-64. ■ 21 - **Keel,** John A., 'Mystery Aeroplanes of the 1930s' in *FSR* Vol 16 No 3 pp10-13; Vol 16 No 4 pp9-14; Vol 17 No 4 pp17-19; Vol 17 No 5 pp20-22 and 28. **Liljegren,** Anders, 'The Ghost Fliers of the 1930s' in *AFU Newsletter* No 24 pp6-8. **Liljegren,** Anders, 'Mysterious Airships and Aeroplanes' in *AFU Newsletter* No 24 pp5-6. **Winterbotham,** F.W., *The Nazi Connection,* Weidenfeld & Nicolson, London, 1978, pp108-109 and 136. ■ 22 - **Cantril,** Hadley, *The Invasion from Mars.* Harper Torchbooks, New York, 1966, orig.pub.1940. ■ 23 - **Farish,** Lucius, 'The ET Concept in History' in *FSR* Vol 19 No 4 pp14-15 and 26. ■ 24 - **Creighton,** Gordon, 'Foo Fighters' in *FSR* Vol 8 No 2 pp11-15. **Gross,** op.cit., pp52-62. **Harbinson,** W.A., *Genesis,* Corgi, London, 1980. **Heering,** Jan, 'UFO Physics - Part 2' in *FSR* Vol 24 No 5 pp22- 23. ■ 25 - **Gross,** Loren E., *The Mystery of the Ghost Rockets,* priv.pub., Fremont, California, 1982 (second edition). **Liljegren,** Anders, ghost rocket research notes in *AFU Newsletter* No 25 pp13-14; No 27 p8; and No 28 pp2-5. **Liljegren,** Anders, and **Svahn,** Clas, 'The Kolmjarv Ghost Rocket Crash Revisited' in *AFU Newsletter* No 27 pp1-5. **Overbye,** Bjorn, 'Ghost Bombs over Sweden' in *FSR* Vol 15 No 2 pp17-18 and Vol 15 No 3 pp18-19. ■ 26 - **Alexandra,** M., 'UFO seen by Sixty Thousand' in *FSR* Vol 4 No 1 pp10-11. **Fernandes,** Joaquim, 'The "Apparitions of the Virgin" at Fatima considered in relation to the UFO Phenomenon' in *FSR* Vol 28 No 6 pp9-14. **Keel,** op.cit., pp255-264. **McClure,** Kevin, *The Evidence for Visions of the Virgin Mary,* The Aquarian Press, Wellingborough, 1983, pp71-86. **Ribera,** Antonio, 'What happened at Fatima?' in *FSR* Vol 10 No 2 pp12-14. **Rogerson,** Peter, 'The Sun Maiden' in *MUFOB* Vol 4 No 2 pp22-26. **Rogerson,** Peter, 'Children of Another God' in *Magonia* No 20 pp11-14. ■ 27 - **Rogerson,** Peter, 'The Phantom Ship and the UFO' in *MUFOB* new series No 1 pp4-10.

FURTHER READING

Other than the works cited in the references, useful information is contained in the William Corliss *Sourcebooks* and in Peter Rogerson's *Intcat* published in *MUFOB* Vol 5 No 4 to Vol 6 No 1 and *MUFOB* new series No 1. Due to the current interest in historical UFO cases, most journals carry data on the subject. Also the *BOLIDE* project and the Comite Ile-de-France des Groupements Ufologiques take a serious view of these phenomena, and the latter has published an extensive listing in their *Annuaire Du C.I.G.U.* No 2, June 1985. Useful books are: **Carter,** Paul A., *The Creation of Tomorrow: Fifty Years of Magazine Science Fiction,* Columbia University Press, New York, 1977. **Clark,** Jerome, and **Coleman,** Loren, *The Unidentified,* Warner, New York, 1975. **Cohen,** Daniel, *The Great Airship Mystery,* Dodd, Mead & Co., New York, 1981. **Gross,** Loren E., *The UFO Wave of 1896,* priv.pub., Fremont, California, 1974. **Meheust,** Bertrand, *Science Fiction et les Soucoupes Volantes,* Mercure de France, 1978. **Meheust,** Bertrand, *Soucoupes Volantes et Folklore,* Mercure de France, 1985.

2.1.4

THE GHOST ROCKETS

by Anders Liljegren and Clas Svahn

■ **ANDERS LILJEGREN**: Born 1950. Professionally, a systems analyst and computer programmer.

■ **UFO involvement**: His interest in unidentified aerial phenomena dates back to the mid-1960s, when he started to read UFO literature. He is one of the founders of AFU (Archives for UFO Research), a private foundation established to ensure that collections and archives of Swedish UFO literature are preserved. He is also editor of the *AFU Newsletter*.

His personal speciality is historical UFO research. Since 1977 he has been searching Swedish official archives for information relevant to his 'life project' of compiling a history of Swedish UFO investigations. He is particularly interested by Sweden's early waves of 'ghost fliers' and 'ghost rockets': such phenomena have been investigated by Swedish military organisations since 1933.

■ **Publications**: include a great many contributions to UFO journals, both in Sweden and internationally.

■ **Address**: PO Box 11027, S-60011 Norrkoping, Sweden. Phone (home) 46-11-14-46-50.

■ **CLAS SVAHN**. Born 1958. By profession a journalist with *Norrbottens-Kuriren*, a newspaper in northern Sweden. He specialises in astronomy and space technology, in addition to his specific interest in the UFO phenomenon.

■ **UFO involvement**: He has investigated and studied cases of alleged UFOs since 1974, when he founded and headed a small group of enthusiasts in southern Sweden. During the past five years he has focused on sightings in the extreme north of Sweden. He is a board member of AFU (Archives for UFO Research).

■ **Publications** include: a monthly UFO column and book reviews for *Norbottens-Kuriren* as well as regular contributions to Swedish UFO journals. In 1954 he was responsible for the most extensive study of UFOs ever published in a single issue of a Swedish newspaper, when *Norrbottens-Kuriren* carried no less than seven pages on the subject!

■ **Address:** Norrbottens-Kuriren / S-951 81 Lulea / Sweden. Phone 0920-105 00.

The European continent had been devastated to ruins as it saw the dawn of the first peace-time year after World War II. Rumours of new, even more frightening, weapons and wars circulated in the news columns. The American nuclear bomb and German progress in missile technology cast their shadows. Doomsday prophets of those days combined the two new weapon technologies as they saw nuclear rockets crossing the skies, heading for an unthinkable destruction. Today we know this catastrophe could happen any hour, any day - and it would be much worse than anyone could imagine more than 40 years ago.

To people living in 1946, the concept of guided missiles and rockets travelling the skies was just a few years old. German progress with V-1 remotely-guided planes and V-2 supersonic rockets came too late to win the war for the Nazis, but still they were major engineering achievements. The two post-war powers-to-be raced to secure German rocket technology, hidden in south German caves. [1]

Sweden, still a rural society, had escaped from the war without major destruction. If anything, the Swedes were not subject to "war nerves". If some obscure psychological or sociological phenomen of *that* sort played a part in what happened over Sweden in the summer of 1946, it is very strange that this phenomenon did not centre on the European continent, Britain, or the Balkans.

Five German V-1s and at least one V-2 rocket had fallen on Swedish soil during 1943 and 1944. On the sunny afternoon of June 13 1944 a farmer near Bäckebo in south Sweden was ploughing his field when he and his horses were thrown to the ground by a heavy explosion. The first V-2 had fallen on non-German soil. Swedish Air Force technicians collected 10,000 parts of the exploded rocket and managed, in a few weeks, to solve the mystery of its construction and motive power. 2.5 tons of metallic scrap was soon transferred to Britain, where Allied scientists confirmed the Swedish finds. [**1**] and [**2**].

THE FIRST SIGHTINGS

Swedish knowledge of rocket technology was thus not non-existent when - two years later - rocket-shaped objects started to appear over the Swedish countryside. Official Swedish statistics counted 997 'ghost rocket' reports for 1946, but this is an underestimate of the true number of sightings.

Mysterious phenomena were first spotted in southern and mid-Sweden in the latter part of May 1946. Night-time observers described them as luminous phenomena or as dark, rocket-shaped objects with intermittent bursts of fire from the tail, quite similar to the war-time V-1s. Day-time sighters saw slow-moving zeppelin- or cigar-shaped metallic objects.

The Swedish Defence Staff, on June 12, secretly ordered reports to be collected by all military and civilian defence units (police, home defence and customs). [**3**] A Swedish astronomer, consulted by the Staff on the first set of reports, remarked that "especially the adjective 'cigar-shaped' is something new". [**4**]

Until July 9, just about 30 reports had reached the Defence Staff. On that day the flood-gates opened wide.

THE JULY 9 BOLIDE

The afternoon of Tuesday, July 9, was sunny. A great part of the Swedish population spent their well-earned vacation on beaches, or drinking afternoon coffee outside their summer cottages. Farmers were in their fields. Suddenly a bright meteor-type phenomenon flashed in the sky at about 14.35. People in the south of Sweden saw the phenomenon in the NE, people in the northern parts generally saw it in the East or SE, as it dived in a steep angle towards the ground. People were blinded by the light, which was described as teardrop-shaped and shining silvery. The sighting area had a radius of about 500 kilometres - quite unusual for a bolide or day-time meteor.

Newspaper offices and the Defence headquarters were flooded with reports. On July 10 the commander-in-chief made a general call for reports through the Swedish news agency TT. Some 250 sightings, for July 9 alone, were carefully logged by the Staff. Hundreds of citizens wrote letters to the Staff or phoned in their reports. The reports were numbered, typewritten on summary sheets and pinpointed on analysis maps with course and direction where the phenomenon was seen.

One fortunate observer, Erik Reutersward, had the extreme luck to capture the July 9 phenomenon with his camera. This is the one and only, much circulated, photograph of a 'ghost rocket'. Despite rumours in the British *Daily Telegraph* [**7**] that the photograph supported the newspaper's theory of "a new method of propulsion", the photo was so poor that it offered nothing of interest to the Swedish Defence Staff analysts. The July 9 light was probably a rare example of a day-time meteor, with some question marks left for the reported slag remains and the wide sighting area.

THE SPACE PROJECTILE COMMITTEE

On July 10, the commander-in-chief set up a special investigation committee. The general suspicion was that Soviet rocket weapons were involved. The committee included the same people who had worked on the V-1 and V-2 finds two years before. It existed for more than five months and involved the work of about 40 people. About half of these were specialists whose knowledge was called for only once or twice. The other half were, more or less, permanent members of the committee, taking part in many, or all, of the 12 or 13 recorded meetings. [**5**]

Chairman was Colonel *Bengt Jacobsson*, head of the Air Administration's Materials department. From the Air Administration also came *Henry Kjellson*, the chief man behind the V-2 analysis, and *Eric Malmberg*, who had written the V-2 report. Malmberg became secretary and chief field investigator for the committee.

From the Defence Staff's Air Defence department came its head, Major *Nils Ahlgren* and his assistant Captain *Gerdt Stangenberg*. The chemical department of the Research Institute of National Defence (FOA 1) was mainly represented by its head, professor *Gustaf Ljunggren*. The physics department of FOA (FOA 3) was represented by its head *Martin Fehrm*, an expert in radio and radar technology. Another permanent member was *Olof Kempe*, a signals intelligence expert with FRA, the Defence Radio Institute. The committee also included specialists on radar, radio and reconnaissance from the Air Force and the Navy. Investigation records were ordered SECRET and this classification remained until May 1983.

The committee's main objective was to secure evidence for the nature of the sightings. The leading theory was that the sightings involved German-Russian technology of V-weapon type. The luminous phenomenon on July 9 was connected to about a dozen finds, in mid-Sweden, of mysterious substances. To the disappointment of the FOA chemists, there was nothing metallic in these remains, as had been the case two years before. Instead, the remains rather uniformly consisted of coal-or slag-like lumps with parts of vegetation embedded into them. Professor Gustaf Ljunggren, on September 21, summarised his department's analysis of twenty-seven finds: "...they do not come from any kind of space projectile, nor from any meteorite. It has been possible to find other solutions in every case".

All finds had been tested for radioactivity. The results proved that nuclear energy was not the motive power behind the phenomenon. [**6**]

THE KÖLMJÄRV CRASH

The public at large was now invited to send in their reports, however, and the result was a continuous stream of reports. Observers described objects and phenomena much more controversial than the July 9 flash. The general description, in the better reports, was of cigar-, rocket-, airplane-or bird-shaped objects travelling at airplane speeds or slightly more. Some

Erik Reutersward's 1946 photo, the only one known of a 'ghost rocket', may only show a daylight meteor.

reports involved close-up sightings and a few were even linked to EM effects. The wave of such "substantial" reports continued throughout July and August, with some cases also during the remaining months of 1946. The Defence Staff logged 225 cases of spool-shaped objects, but we are somewhat more conservative in our estimate, knowing the weaknesses of human vision. (We have, on the other hand, uncovered quite a few interesting cases that were unknown to the Defence Staff in 1946.)

On July 19 a two-meter-long ashen-gray rocket plunged into the long and shallow Lake Kölmjärv, in the extreme north of Sweden. The Kölmjärv crash happened at noon on a sunny day and was witnessed by several people on the shores, including farmer Knut Lindbäck. Two similar objects had crashed into Norway's Lake Mjösa some 24 hours before.

The Kölmjärv crash seemingly presented the Defence Staff with more tangible evidence and a troop of engineers, headed by Lieutenant Karl-Gosta Bartoll, was immediately dispatched to the small lake. They were later aided by specialists from FOA in Stockholm and from the Boliden mining company. During three weeks the lake was carefully mapped from a wooden raft. Almost every square meter of the lake was searched with electrical probes and an ore-finding apparatus hired from Boliden. Nothing was ever found, except mundane objects. [**8**]

The Kölmjärv incident became a double mystery: How could a V-type plane, or rocket, travel 1,500 km from a north-German base (or 700 km from a west-Russian or Estonian base) to a perfect touchdown in a narrow north-Swedish lake, when 370 km had been the maximum range of V-weapons just 16 months before? Why was no scrap of the machine found in the lake? Had it self-destructed to very small pieces? Nearby witnesses heard a heavy detonation as it went down.

INTELLIGENCE INTEREST

The appearance of these 'ghost rockets', or 'ghost bombs', started off a chain of reconnaissance and intelligence actions. On July 17, south-Swedish radar stations were put on alert. Ground stations of the FRA radio institute began to monitor for signals like the ones that had guided the V-1s at the end of the war. On July 22 the news agency TT distributed a demand from the Defence Staff to all newspapers not to publish the names of sighting places and other intimate details that would be a lead to "the power making the experiments". [**9**]

The US Secretary of the Navy, James Forrestal, suddenly appeared in Stockholm, July 16, on his worldwide tour home from the Bikini nuclear test. Apparently he made a hasty change in his flight plan. Forrestal was a member of the Central Intelligence Group, formed by Truman on January 22 1946. [**10**] He met the Swedish Secretary of War, Allan Vought. Immediately, Vought asked the committee for details and two committee members visited him, July 23, for a briefing of their work.

In late July and early August, members of the committee interviewed German refugees on the issue of V-weapon development in the Soviet zone of East Germany. The committee was now holding weekly sessions. At the 22 July meeting, Air Director Henry Kjellson speculated on a development of the American 'Ram Jet' projectile.

By early August a B-3 (Junkers Ju 86) bomber was equipped with FRA radios and a recording apparatus. The bomber flew over the Baltic towards the Soviet Union and the north-German coast. Some mysterious signals (similar to the V-1 remote control signals) were monitored, but the radio recordings seldom co-ordinated with visual sightings on Swedish territory. Aerial reconnaissance was attempted on Peenemunde, but Soviet fighters prohibited any close inspection of the former German rocket test area.

SAMPLE OF SIGHTINGS

The sightings continued with several interesting new cases each day for the committee to study. A selection of good reports with significant details emphasised:

At 1320 hours on July 24, engineer Tennlund from Älvenäs saw a small, cigar-shaped object with a pair of small wings. The object came *from the direction of Norway* at great speed and with no sound. It had a south-easterly course and Tennlund thought it crashed into Lake Vänern.

At 1512 hours on July 30, a military serviceman of the KA1 base at Oscar-Fredricsborg (east of Stockholm), William Jorgensen, reported a flying object with short wings and no sound at a distance of about 2,000 meters. *Speed was greater than a jet aircraft* (the Vampire jet was introduced in the Swedish Air Force in June).

About two hours *before* Jorgensen's sighting, "two dark crosses" were spotted by a man at Filipstad. One hour and 42 minutes *after* Jorgensen's, a silvery torpedo with short wings was observed by a customs officer on the Norwegian border. This object came from the south but *changed direction* with a sharp turn and continued towards east with a whining sound. Sightings often displayed this pattern: One report from one part of Sweden, then a lapse of one or two hours, then another report from quite another part of the country. This frustrated the military, used to being able to follow aerial objects on continuous routes.

August 5 saw another similar series of sightings: At 1400 hours (the very minute that Colonel Jacobsson opened one of the committee's meetings) a motorist and his father saw a dark, spool-shaped object pass *below the telephone wires* in front of their car. At 1826 hrs a similar object, but this time luminous, was reported by a motorist near Landskrona in south Sweden.

Nine minutes later, another military serviceman of the KA1 regiment saw a cigar-shaped object through a measuring instrument with a x28 but could only be run a few hours each day, due to lack of experienced personnel. At least four radar 'sightings' occurred in July, and another seven between August 19 and 22. At the present time it is difficult to judge the value of these reports and we are seeking someone with the technical capacity to do that. Several radar returns probably concerned flights of birds. One radar registration (at the F1 wing at Västerås on August 20), however, involved a simultaneous visual outdoor sighting of a vague luminous phenomenon.

The transportable units were activated several times. In August they were positioned in the Stockholm archipelago. During the Air Force training, in September, they were posted in southern Sweden. At both times there were no results (as far as is apparent from the documents we've studied). In November a radar at Ottenby on öland registered a large object landing on the island. Analysts concluded this had been a flock of birds. The report was of great interest to the then Chief of the Air Staff, not in his official capacity, but in his role as the chairman of a bird-watching society! [**12**]

DOOLITTLE AND SARNOFF

On August 20, former US General David Sarnoff, employed as vice president of the RCA company, arrived at Stockholm's Bromma airport. Later that day, another former US General, James Doolittle, also arrived, in the company of ex-RAF Colonel Douglas Bader. Both of them were officially representatives of the Shell Company. On August 21, the three joined for lunch with the top brass of the Swedish Air Force.

Reportedly Sarnoff visited President Truman in the White House on his return from Europe. [**13**] Doolittle was probably quite well informed on UFO-type sightings, since he had commanded the 8th Air Force during the assaults on Germany and Japan, when reports of 'foo fighters' were frequent. Doolittle was later often employed by American intelligence in the 1950s and 60s [**10,**] so it is quite probable that he was "an intelligence man" in 1946 as well.

Allied intelligence interest in the ghost rockets is further substantiated by several archival documents: British Air intelligence produced a detailed five-page folio report [**14,**] which was distributed to at least 150 British and American military units. "Tremendous pressure" was exerted "on the (US) Air Force Intelligence to conduct research and collect information in an effort to identify these sightings", according to an FBI document. [**15**] A US Air Force list mentions no less than 44 different documents on the ghost rockets in their intelligence archives. [**16**] Also, the American air attachê in Stockholm produced a list of questions, which was duly answered by the committee.

FINAL SWEDISH REPORT

On December 23 1946, the Swedish commander-in-chief received the final report from the committee. The report summarised:

"Despite the extensive effort which has been carried out with all available means, there is no actual proof that a test of rocket projectiles has taken place over Sweden. The committee has therefore been are forced to decide that the investigation has been unsuccessful and that it is useless to continue the activity in its present form and with the present limited resources. Even if the main part of the reports can be referred to as celestial phenomena the committee cannot dismiss certain facts as being purely public imagination. From knowledge of German activity on the Baltic coast during the war and developments later on, one cannot deny the implications of the reports which have been received through various sources."

In our continuing work on follow-ups to the official documents we have discovered quite a few leads to a possible TOP SECRET document, or file, on the ghost rockets. It appears that several intelligence reports, case investigations and interviews are lacking in the now-opened files.

THE GHOST FLIERS

Thus ended Sweden's *second* attempt at identifying a larger number of sightings of unidentified flying objects.

Sightings of luminous phenomena, and airplane-shaped objects had, in fact, started as early as in December 1933 (we know unsubstantiated rumours of even earlier waves). The great 1930s wave opened in the border area between Norway and Sweden, close to the 66th parallel. the 'ghost flier' sightings soon spread to the whole of northern Sweden and to other parts of northern Norway and Finland. [**17**]

Mysterious light phenomena (behaving as airplanes) interacted with close-up observations of airplanes that sometimes behaved strangely: flying about aimlessly at low level in the night or during snow storms. As usual, the Russians were suspected, but more recently a Swedish historian has claimed that the sightings originated from secret German pre-war flight training missions in northern Scandinavia. [**18**]

The 'ghost fliers' sightings were carefully recorded by local policemen and by military investigators. The resulting files, accumulated in the years 1933-1937, are still kept at the Stockholm War Archives. [**18**]

The more than 1,000 reports of ghost fliers in the 1930s, the 1,600 reports of ghost rockets in 1946, and more than 2,000 reports of 'light-and sound-phenomena' accumulated by the Swedish Defence Staff and the FOA research institute since 1947, form a great body of official data for study. A main part of the 1930s and 1946 data was recorded by local policemen and contains much that would be of interest, not only to ufologists, but to sociologists or folklorists.

magnification. The Air Administration's field investigator Eric Malmberg made a detailed report of this case. A J-9 Seversky-Republic EP-1 fighter was flown under similar circumstances to acquire comparison data, but with no resolution of the case.

A military pilot, flying a B-18 bomber in broad daylight on August 14, saw yet another of the mysterious 'rockets' pass right in front of his airplane. He was questioned by Staff people in Stockholm and by Eric Malmberg. This pilot later became one of the foremost Swedish test pilots and head of the Air Force's experimental centre. He is considered as probably the most trustworthy witness of the 1946 wave.

A preliminary computer study (September 1986) of 165 of the best ghost rockets reports indicate that about 66% of good-quality reports had an initial flight direction that correlates well with the theory of Russian projectiles (a northerly or westerly direction), while the remaining 34% of the 'rockets' were flying towards the east or south, at least at the initial phase of the observation. [**11**]

THE AUGUST 11 PHENOMENON

It was almost dark, at about a quarter to nine in the evening of August 11, as another strange display hit south- and mid-Sweden. Luminous objects crossed the sky, generally with a northerly direction. Descriptions varied widely. One astronomer, consultant to the Defence Staff, saw the phenomenon from his summer cottage on the island of Gotland. He thought it was a bright meteor on the western horizon. A more vivid description came from an FOA engineer, who said he saw a spool-shaped object without wings, in the Stockholm archipelago.

So far we have logged almost 400 sightings concerning this "fireworks display". As with the July 9 phenomenon, there are certain reasons not to draw definite conclusions. For instance, the August 11 phenomenon resulted in several heaps of slag on the ground, like those produced by the July 9 "daytime meteor".

RADAR SIGHTINGS

In 1944, the Swedish Air Force had purchased 30 sets of AMES 6 Mk III radars from Britain. One stationary type was allocated to each of the Air Force wings and another was transportable, on truck, to any place where it was needed.

The wing radars had been activated in mid-July

The Swedish War Archives 'ghost rocket' file contains hundreds of reports. [AFU]

So far we refrain from making very definite claims or stating any final theories on the nature of these phenomena. Premature conclusions have saturated the UFO field in the past 40 years and have proven, in the past, to be one of the obstacles for a well-organised research effort. We hope, however, that the knowledge we now accumulate on these early waves will one day contribute towards a better understanding of the UFO phenomena as a whole.

Input to our 'Project 1946' is welcome. Write us at: **Archives for UFO Research** (AFU), PO Box 11027, S-600 11 Norrköping, Sweden.

NOTES AND REFERENCES

1 - The V-1/V-2 war and post-war era is documented in several works, such as: **von Braun,** Wernher & **Ordway,** Frederick I: *History of rocketry & space travel.* Thomas Y. Crowell, New York, 1975. **Ley,** Willy: *Rockets, missiles and men in space.* The Viking Press, New York, 1968. **Dornberger,** Walter: *Der Schuss ins Weltall.* Bechtle Verlag, Esslingen, BRD, 1952. **Klee,** Ernst & **Merk,** Otto: *The birth of the missile. The secrets of Peenemunde.* George G. Harrap, London, 1965. **Garlinski,** Josef: *Hitler's last weapons. The underground war against the V1 and V2.* Julian Friedmann, London, 1978. **Stoiko,** Michael: *Soviet rocketry: past, present and future.* Holt, Rinehart and Winston, New York, 1970. ■ 2 - Air Staff. *History of the emergency service* (WWII), volumes 53, 54 and 55. (War Archives, Stockholm). ■ 3 - Defence Staff, Air Defence department: HQ order nr. 7:49. (War Archives). ■ 4 - Letter from prof. Bertil Lindblad of the Stockholm observatory to the Defence Staff. July 6, 1946. (War Archives). ■ 5 - Space projectile committee: proceedings. Written records of 12 meetings. About 40 pages. (War Archives). The proceedings of the first meeting (July 10) is not available. ■ 6 Preliminary report, August 9 and Preliminary report nr. 2, September 21, from FOA to the committee. 49 pages in all. (War Archives). ■ 7 - *Daily Telegraph,* September 6 1946. ■ 8 - Reports by K-G Bartoll, FOA personnel and Eric Malmberg. Sketches and photos, numerous newspaper articles. 1984 interviews by Clas Svahn. English summary: **Svahn,** Clas & **Liljegren,** Anders, The Kölmjärv ghost rocket crash revisited, in *AFU Newsletter,* Norrkoping, Sweden, January-December 1984, issue nr. 27. ■ 9 - A July 22 newswire from the Defence Staff's press department, signed by the head of the news agency TT and co-signed by the chairman of the Swedish union of journalists. (War Archives). ■ 10 - **Wise,** David & **Ross,** Thomas B: *The invisible government.* Random House, New York, 1964. ■ 11 - Based on data from the SCANCAT computer file of 1946 reports, now comprising more than 1,700 incidents. ■ 12 - Interview with Eric Malmberg, principal investigator of the committee, May 13 1986. ■ 13 - Telegram, September 16 1946 from the White House to General Sarnoff. Credit: William L. Moore, Burbank, Cal., USA. ■ 14 - A.1.2 (g): *Paper 271/46: Investigations of missile activity over Scandinavia,* 9th September 1946. Credit: Don Berliner, Alexandria, Virginia, USA. ■ 15 - FBI: Office memorandum from E.G. Fitch to D.M. Ladd, August 19 1947. Credit: Fund for UFO research, Maryland, USA. ■ 16 - Letter from Lt.Col. Douglas W. Eisemann, USAD HQ to 'Project Sign', February 1948. Credit: William L. Moore. ■ 17 - **Liljegren,** Anders, 'The ghost fliers of the 1930s' - a status report (May 1982), in *AFU Newsletter,* Norrköping, Sweden, May-August 1982, issue nr. 24. ■ 18 - Correspondence with Sven **Wäström,** Uppsala, who is writing a thesis on the Swedish military's signal reconnaissance in the years 1914-1948. ■ 19 - The file of ghost flier data at the War Archives was discovered in 1977. AFU holds copies of the most interesting report investigations, but a general mapping of the many reports still remains to be done. We hope to cover this area when our 'Project 1946' has been reasonably finished, a few years ahead.

2.2.1

UFOs IN 1947

Psychologists know that the 'instant conversion' claimed by some naive religious groups rarely if ever occurs: rather, there is liable to be a long incubating period in which, without realising it, the individual is being subconsciously processed. Then some event, perhaps trivial in itself, triggers the transition from subconscious to conscious awareness - and the individual 'sees the light.' [1]

In 1947, something of the sort seems to have happened on a social scale with regard to UFOs. As the preceding papers have demonstrated, there was nothing new about the phenomenon; what was new was that now it became a public rather than a private matter.

For this reason, it has been suggested by some critics that the flying saucer phenomenon was no more than a 'media event.' But this is inverted thinking. The media mirror public preoccupations - our hopes and our fears. To a limited degree they can manipulate our ideas and attitudes - but only if we are subconsciously willing to be manipulated. [2]

The primary role of the media, during the years following the Arnold sighting, was to reinforce the new public awareness of the UFO as a phenomenon in its own right. Much the same process occurred in the Middle Ages in regard to witches; and more recently David Hufford had the same experience when he conducted research into the remarkable phenomenon of the 'bedroom invader'. He found that no sooner had he ascribed a label to a certain kind of experience than he received letters like this:

"I just heard you on the radio...I would like to tell you that I have been experiencing this for many years... I never before heard of a name for it & no one that I have described it to has ever known what I was talking about." [3]

This kind of response encouraged him to question the traditional 'cultural source hypothesis' for the Bedroom Invader - that is (to put it crudely) the view that people experience what they expect to experience. Instead, he found that the evidence pointed strongly in favour of the 'experiential source hypothesis' - that reports derive directly from personal experience.

We must consider seriously that what Hufford found to be true of the Bedroom Invader may be equally true of the UFO. Ted Bloecher's study of 1947 UFO reports [4] shows how, once Arnold's experience had become public property, a host of witnesses came forward with their stories, many of which ante-dated the Arnold sighting.

To this day we still do not know for sure what Arnold saw; what we *do* know is that a great many alleged UFO sightings have been very different from his experience. Yet, if the reports which began to flood into the media as a direct result of his experience had been (to continue with Hufford's terminology) culturally based, we would expect them to have more or less resembled Arnold's sighting.

Instead, as we all know, UFOs were, from the start, reported in all shapes and sizes, and this diversity is a telling argument in favour of their being reflections of specific experience rather than cultural contagion. And of course it works the other way about: the fact that Arnold's sighting was a daylight sighting of a group of distant objects in continuous movement encourages us to think that whatever saw, it was not a psychosocial artifact created by interaction between his subconscious mind and the cultural milieu...

REFERENCES

1 - **James**, William, *The varieties of religious experience* (1902) **Sante de Sanctis** *Religious conversion* (1927). ■ 2 - Studies of media involvement in the early manifestations of the UFO include **Strentz**, Herbert J., *A survey of press coverage of UFOs* (1970 reprinted Arcturus, 1982). ■ 3 - **Hufford**, David J, *The terror that comes in the night* (University of Pennsylvania, 1982) ■ 4 - **Bloecher**, Ted, *Report on the UFO wave of 1947* (private, 1967)

2.2.2

THE MAURY ISLAND CAPER

by John A. Keel

■ **JOHN A KEEL**: Born 1930. A professional writer since age 16, he has been a contributor to numerous journals, science editor for Funk & Wagnall's encyclopedia, a regular columnist on mysteries in *Saga* and sometime editor of the Society for the Investigation of the Unexplained's journal *Pursuit*. His autobiographical *Jadoo: mysteries of the Orient* was published when he was 27.

■ **UFO involvement**: If Keel is often regarded as the *enfant terrible* of ufology, this is due to his willingness to voice ideas that the rest of us hardly dare formulate. His *Operation Trojan Horse* is widely regarded as one of the most notable sources of advanced thinking in the field, while other writings have emphasised the need to explore links between UFOs and fringe phenomena such as 'mothman' and 'men in black'. He states: 'I abandoned the ETH in 1967 when my field investigations disclosed an astonishing overlap between psychic phenomena and UFOs... a large part of the UFO lore is subjective and many alleged UFO events are actually the products of a complex hallucinatory process, particularly in the contactee and CE III-type reports. The same process stimulated religious beliefs, fairy lore, and occult systems of belief in other centuries. A very small percentage of sightings and events indicate that other strange, but natural, phenomena are often included, or absorbed, into the UFO data. While we cannot satisfactorily explain all UFO events in terms of present-day knowledge and technology, I feel that the ultimate solution will involve a complicated system of new physics related to theories of the space-time continuum. It is possible, even highly probable, that a subtle cosmological system of control has been in effect since the dawn of mankind and that UFOs are a part of that system.'

■ **Publications**: include *Operation Trojan Horse* (Putnam 1970); *Strange creatures from time & space* (Fawcett 1970); *Our haunted planet* (Fawcett 1971); *The Mothman prophecies* (Saturday Review / Dutton 1975); *The eighth tower* (Saturday Review / Dutton 1976).

■ **Address**: PO Box 20024 / New York / NY 10025 / USA.

At 10 pm on the evening of October 4 1968, two cars were splashing through a misty rain on the River Road outside of Tacoma, Washington, when suddenly one of them darted ahead of the other and a flame spurted from its rear window. The windshield on the second car exploded and the driver felt a sharp blow on his face. His car went out of control as blood gushed into his eyes, blinding him. The other vehicle sped into the darkness.

"I could not see from my right eye and I knew that this could be from either the shock of being hit or from having lost the eye," he recalled later. "I had been wounded in combat and I recognised that same numb shock feeling that a wound by a high-speed bullet brings."

Fortunately, the bullet had fragmented as it penetrated the windshield and pieces of it had only broken his cheekbone. It was not a serious wound. He managed to bring the car under control and drove himself to a hospital. For Jon Gold, star of a telephone talk show on radio station KAYE, this was just another harrowing episode in a lifetime of adventure.

A few weeks later, while driving slowly and carefully in his brand new Oldsmobile, purchased to replace the car damaged in the shooting incident, Gold was stopped by the local police and arrested for "reckless driving". After his bail bondsman had arranged his release from the Tacoma jail, a newspaperman informed him that he was being summoned to New Orleans, Louisiana, by District Attorney James Garrison, who was then conducting an enquiry into the assassination of President John F. Kennedy... It seems that a person resembling Gold had appeared in some photographs taken in Dealey Plaza, Dallas, Texas, on the day that Kennedy was shot. New Orleans is thousands of miles from Tacoma but Jon Gold made the trip and testified before the Grand Jury. Even before he left Tacoma, however, the local newscasters were broadcasting that he had been indicted for the murder of President Kennedy! Obviously he had made enemies among his colleagues in the radio business, as well as on the police force. Eventually those enemies succeeded in driving him off the air, but he continued to raise hell by publishing books and pamphlets attacking the local political structure in Seattle-Tacoma (those cities were very corrupt at that time) until he died a natural death in 1975.

Who was this man? Here's how one of his associates described him: "Fast talking, abrasive, highly opinionated, aggressive... With experience in many fields, a varied and colorful background, a keen intelligence and a well-honed wit, he was an excellent raconteur and could cross swords with any opponent... Then there is the man Fred L. Crisman. Quiet, soft spoken, diffident by nature, he is totally different from his alter ego - Jon Gold, but it is as Jon Gold that he will be remembered in Tacoma".

Jon Gold and Fred L. Crisman were the same man, although their personalities were radically different. Both have become legendary in their own way. Back in 1947, flying saucer researchers turned him into a mystery man who had engineered a UFO "hoax" and then vanished forever. Actually, he was born and raised in Tacoma and spent most of his life in that area. He was a fighter pilot in World War II, and was recalled for another thirty months of service in the Air Force during the Korean War in the early 1950s. After that, he became a school teacher and was employed in various school systems in the states of Washington and Oregon before returning to Tacoma and becoming a muck-raking broadcaster. British author Harold T. Wilkins tried to write to Crisman in 1951, in care of the US Coast Guard in Tacoma. Not surprisingly, the letter was eventually returned stamped "Address Unknown". Mr. Wilkins viewed this as a very sinister governmental conspiracy to render Crisman incommunicado and magnified the incident to unseemly proportions in his book *Flying Saucers on the Attack*. Crisman was in Korea in 1951, and, in any case, no one in the Coast Guard could have known how to contact him because he had no connection with that service. A newspaper report had once erroneously identified him as the head of a Coast Guard harbor patrol.

"In 1946-47, as a recently released fighter pilot," he claimed, "I had been appointed a Special Investigator and assigned to a now defunct department of the state government, the State Department of Veterans' Affairs. My job - take a look at the variety of rackets, con jobs and outright cheating of newly discharged veterans from our Washington-located camps of the armed forces."

Aside from being a "Special Investigator" for the state of Washington, Crisman had his fingers in many other pies. He was a part-owner of an old boat operated by one Harold Dahl. Dahl used the boat to haul lumber and supplies around Tacoma harbor, sharing the profits with Crisman. On June 23 1947, Dahl was on the boat with his teenage son, the boy's dog and another man (who has never been publicly identified). Crisman was not aboard. As they sailed near a peninsula known as Maury Island, an almost totally uninhabited body of land at that time, two or more aircraft appeared overhead. Suddenly they began to discharge vast quantities of radioactive slag. Many of these pieces fell on the boat, injuring the boy's arm and killing his dog! Dahl had a camera and snapped several pictures. The slag continued to fall into the water and on the shores of Maury island. Dahl raced the boat back to Tacoma, where he rushed the boy to the local hospital. (A Chicago editor, Raymond Palmer, later obtained copies of the hospital records.)

That, essentially, is the famous Maury Island event.

The next day, a private pilot was flying over Mt. Rainier in the state of Washington when he saw some strange objects weaving through the mountain range. He later called them "Flying Saucers" and the modern UFO era began.

Meanwhile, Harold Dahl was in big trouble. That morning a black automobile drove up in front of his house and a man in a black suit came to his door and invited him to breakfast. While they drank their coffee, the stranger soberly recounted everything that had happened to Dahl the day before and then grimly warned him to keep quiet, suggesting that if he talked about the incident there could be dire consequences for him, his family, and the world generally.

Dahl took the man seriously and was very unnerved by the visit. When Fred Crisman came to call, Dahl was in a very agitated state. They developed the film in Dahl's camera and found the negatives ruined, covered with white specks resulting from exposure to radiation. The boat itself had been damaged by the pieces of heavy slag. Crisman took another boat to Maury island and viewed the heaps of slag there. Then Kenneth Arnold's "Flying Saucer" report hit the newspapers and for two weeks hundreds of sightings were published. Crisman, not Dahl, finally told a local reporter about the Maury Island incident and it was Crisman who turned the aircraft seen by Dahl into circular "donut-shaped" objects spewing slag. Crisman had been in touch with Ray Palmer, editor of *Amazing Stories*, for two years so he drew up his version of the Maury Island story and sent it to Chicago. Palmer immediately contacted Arnold, sent him $200 for expenses, and asked him to visit Tacoma to interview Dahl and Crisman.

Dahl was a very reluctant witness, feeling that he was forced to confirm Crisman's story. Kenneth Arnold's detailed account of the whole Maury Island affair later appeared in the first issue of *Fate* magazine, published by Palmer, and eventually became a book, *The Coming of the Saucers*. An astute observer and a meticulous reporter, Arnold left us a classic record of his experiences in Tacoma. He called in two friends from the US Air Force who were then the only official UFO invstigators. They were very interested in the case until Crisman slipped up and said something that gave him away. The two officers, Brown and Davidson, got into their plane and flew into oblivion. An engine caught fire and they crashed.

Meanwhile, Dahl's young son vanished!

Maury Island was now turning into a real mystery.

Crisman and Dahl panicked. Fearing they would be blamed for the death of the two Air Force officers, they rushed to the local Air Force base and recanted. *There was never a real Air Force investigation into any of this*. Crisman and Dahl were genuinely terrified by the chain of events (many other things happened to the men, such as the loss of important business deals, etc.) They wanted out. The Air Force and the FBI were disinterested. Brown and Davidson had crashed in their A-25 because an engine had caught fire and the bottle of CO2 fire extinguisher connected to it was empty.

After Arnold's article appeared in *FATE* magazine, the Air Force published a single paragraph in an obscure service journal, denouncing the Maury Island affair as a hoax.

The truth is frustratingly simple. In 1947, the Atomic Energy Commission's (AEC) huge metallurgical plant at Hanford, Washington, was processing plutonium and creating vast quantities of radioactive waste. Getting rid of this material was already a major problem and one method was to load it into cargo planes and dump it unceremoniously into various large bodies of water... such as Puget Sound and Tacoma harbor. Dahl happened to be an unwitting witness to one of these dumping operations. When newspaperman Paul Lance visited Maury Island a few weeks later, he found a high chain fence had been erected around the slag piles and there was a sign: "PROPERTY OF U.S. GOVERNMENT. KEEP OUT."

Apparently a group of cargo planes was heading north-west from Hanford to a dumping ground in the Pacific when one of the aircraft developed serious trouble. It unceremoniously dumped its ugly cargo into Tacoma harbor and onto Maury Island, then returned to Hanford. Dahl and his crew were seen from the air and photographed. It was easy for AEC security officers to check with the hospital later and track Dahl down. *The Man-in-Black who visited Dahl was actually an agent for the AEC intent on covering up what was even then an illegal dumping of dangerous atomic waste.*

Unbeknownst to Arnold, Crisman, Dahl and most of the citizens of Tacoma, another dramatic situation was taking place at Hanford and the Tacoma-Seattle area in 1947. In those days, the CIA barely existed as a small group of men left over from World War II and hanging around a small office in Washington, DC. However, the AEC had a large, efficient force of well-trained security agents. They had managed to keep the atomic bomb secret during the war. Now they were caught up in a desperate anti-espionage effort. They were aware that someone in and around the three secret atomic cities (Oak Ridge, Tenn., Hanford, Wash., and Savannah River Project, Georgia) was leaking vital secrets to the Soviet Union. Everyone was under suspicion. Hotel rooms in Tacoma and Seattle were wired. Telephones were widely tapped. Strangers to the areas around all three "secret cities" were kept under surveillance. This accounted for Arnold's strange experiences when he arrived in Tacoma. Confidential conversations in his hotel room were immediately passed on to the press by mysterious telephone informants, etc. Why? Because the AEC knew it had committed a No-No and security officials saw the Crisman story of a "flying donut" as a perfect cover for a botched operation. Misdirection and disinformation became the rule of the day. But reporter Paul Lance may have sensed the larger truth as he chased down every lead.

In 1949, the Soviet Union set off its first atomic bomb. Shortly afterwards, 65 atomic scientists, most of them Jews who had fled Nazi Europe, were arrested and tried as spies. Three of them were eventually executed.

Kenneth Arnold had managed to send Ray Palmer some samples of the original Maury Island slag and Palmer had them analysed. He was baffled by the laboratory analysis because he knew nothing about metallurgy and he certainly didn't know anything about the Top Secret process for creating plutonium. It was not until the 1960s that information about that process was publicly revealed. Part of it included piping deadly fluorine gas through tubes of pure nickel. The slag-like material that accumulated in these tubes was high in calcium and matched Palmer's sample. But Ray Palmer died in 1977, without ever knowing that the mysterious slag from Maury Island was not from outer space but was merely garbage from the miles of metal tubing in the world's largest factory building in Hanford. Garbage so important to the national security in 1947 that the AEC agents harassed many harmless, well-meaning citizens and helped foster the growing flying saucer myths.

He never admitted it, but it is possible that Crisman was also engaged by the AEC and had been advised to turn the Dahl story of a crippled aircraft into the "flying donut" story. Brown and Davidson lost all interest in the Maury Island caper, according to Arnold, after Crisman had idly bragged about some vague association with Hanford and the AEC. When they departed, Crisman presented them with a cardboard carton containing pieces of slag. They dumped it in the back of their Army sedan and when they reached the airport they told their driver to dispose of it. The slag was never placed aboard their aircraft. A heavy box of personnel files was loaded onto the plane, however, and this inspired ufological rumors for years that the box of slag had somehow contributed to the crash.

After Jim Garrison summoned Crisman to New Orleans for his ill-fated Kennedy assassination trial (Garrison accused one Clay Shaw of engineering the shooting and he was subsequently acquitted), a new breed of researcher zero-ed in on Crisman. They were the amateur sleuths devoted to investigating the assassinations of the 1960s. They were much better equipped than the UFO buffs of the 1950s who had devoured Arnold's Maury Island report and made Crisman's life so miserable that he had to hide behind unlisted phones and various aliases. Most of the assassination buffs were college professors, lawyers and journalists whose intellects, training and methodology were vastly superior to the unsophisticated, uncritical UFO believers. Only a handful overlapped into both fields, such as Paris Flammonde, a struggling author who had published two "Gee Whiz" books about flying saucers and who had also spent time in New Orleans with Garrison. These assorted researchers, buffs and outright crackpots, gleefully circulated documents of dubious worth about the "mysterious" Fred Crisman. One widely distributed dossier was purportedly a summary of Crisman's CIA file and it linked him with everything from Teapot Dome to Watergate. It is quite possible that Crisman himself wrote it and put it into circulation, if only to cover the humiliating fact that he had spent most of the 1950s and early 1960s teaching in public schools. But after returning to Tacoma in 1966, it took him only two years to antagonise enough people so that someone hired a hit man.

After the deaths of Brown and Davidson, Crisman spread a runmour that he was moving to Alaska. Dahl simply packed up and moved to a new address. His son was eventually located in a small town in Colorado, suffering from total amnesia!

Today Fred Crisman is only dimly remembered by the ufological hardcore as the perpetrator of what Captain Edward Ruppelt of the US Air Force once termed "the dirtiest hoax" in flying saucer history. Yet it was the most discussed UFO case of the 1940s and served to launch the key components of the saucer mythology... the fiendish governmental conspiracy to hide "the truth" from the public, the sinister Men-in-Black who have obligingly reappeared in countless UFO cases since, mysterious telephone harassment, mail interference and all the more paranoid aspects that form the basis for modern ufology. Historian Dr. David Jacobs spent years tediously researching the UFO subject for his revisionist book *The UFO Controversy in America*, devoting only a single paragraph to Maury Island... and in that paragraph he managed to get all the salient facts wrong. He also slighted Ray Palmer, who was actually the father of modern ufology and kept the subject alive through his magazines and books during the long periods of public disinterest. It is even probable that if Palmer had not existed, the whole flying saucer business would never have taken form and gripped the public imagination as it did in the 1940s and again in the 1960s. Maury island was the beginning. And the ultimate irony was that it had nothing to do with flying saucers. It merely coincided with the national UFO craze that summer. Three men died that year - Brown, Davidson and Paul Lance - and one was left badly frightened and discouraged (Kenneth Arnold). Massive and somewhat mysterious efforts were made by someone to discredit Ray Palmer. Even his office was broken into and someone stole the slag he had on display there. Others, as Palmer was to recall later, were driven into bankruptcy or worse, and the whole subject of UFOs was to become fodder in the US for a brigade of paranoiacs who were perpetually seeking causes, preferably hopeless ones, and worrying about the slag that was falling from the sky.

2.3.1

UFOs AS GLOBAL PHENOMENON

by Hilary Evans

'A purely statistical study of a phenomenon as elusive as the UFO has no value in itself'

Jacques Vallée [**19**]

'How many UFOs have been seen?' - a natural question to ask; an impossible question to answer. Impossible by definition, because the unknown cannot be measured.

Nevertheless, in this 40-year anniversary publication, it is appropriate at least to note such attempts at quantitive assessment of the UFO phenomenon as have been made. Most of those who have participated in such attempts would echo Vallée's warning; but though statistics may lie through their teeth, they tell us something, if only about people's beliefs.

It must be clearly understood, however, that **what follows cannot be regarded as a serious quantitative assessment of the UFO phenomenon.** Every estimate summarised here is as full of holes as a gruyère cheese, arrived at by methods which outrage common sense, to say nothing of the laws of mathematics. At best, the data are straws held up to indicate in which direction, and how strongly, the wind is blowing.

SIGHTINGS REPORTED TO OFFICIAL AGENCIES

Sightings reported to official agencies are in some respects the most solid basis for calculation, though by their very nature they are pre-selected and therefore atypical. In particular, virtually all such surveys are based on United States experience; it would clearly be dangerous to make the assumption that what is true of America is true of the rest of the world, if only because of the sociological factors involved.

■ **Ruppelt** was one of the first to make an attempt at quantification, on the basis of the cases that came to his department. 'We investigated dozens of UFO reports, and read and analyzed thousands more', he tells us [**16, p7**], and adds that 'several thousand' reports were received between 1947 and 1956 [**16, p10**]. Of these 15-20% were classed as 'unknown'. Assuming that 'several' means at least 3000, that gives us at least 450 unknowns.

We can extrapolate this figure in both time and space. If we assume (while recognising that it may be reckless to do so) that the number of UFOs manifesting in our atmosphere is more or less constant, we get a round 2000 unknowns over 40 years.

But that's for the United States alone. As it happens, both the population and the land area of the United States are roughly 1/16 of the whole world: so, making the further reckless assumption that UFOs share their visits evenly across the globe from Papua to Pascagoula, we arrive - even using Ruppelt's most conservative figure - at **32,000 unknowns.**

■ **Project Blue Book** received 2199 reports during its first five years from 1947 and 1952, [**6,p.32**] and eventually 'nearly 13,000' according to Steiger [**18,p.4**] or '13,134' according to Hynek [**9,p.254**] for the 22 years from 1947 to 1969. Why there should be this discrepancy I don't know; but if we settle for a compromise 13,000, we get a 40-year figure of 23,600 and a worldwide figure of 380,000. Applying Ruppelt's lower factor of 15% leaves us with 57,000 true unknowns; even if we decide, on the grounds that Blue Book's figures were not as closely screened as Ruppelt's, to be yet more conservative and reduce the factor to 10%, we are still left with **38,000 unknowns.** Given our rough-and-ready protocol, this is encouragingly close to our previous figure.

■ **Jacques Vallée**, while warning us against statistics, was none the less unable to resist the temptation to apply his professional skills to the UFO numbers game. [**19**] As we should expect, his interpretations are perceptive and thought-provoking; but like all interpretations, they are only as good as the data they are based on. He uses a working base of 8260 sightings sent to the US Air Force by military or civilian observers between 1942 and 1965, of which all but a few originate from the United States. Extrapolating as before, these give us a global figure of **210,000 reports.** However, it is evident that this is a very mixed bunch of data indeed - in more than 100 we do not have precise date and location, for instance - so that caution is called for, and as with Blue Book, a reduction by 90% seems called for, leaving us with some **21,000 probable unknowns.**

OPINION POLLS

Opinion Polls offer a different kind of starting point. Gallup Polls to find out what the American public thinks about UFOs were conducted in 1947, 1950, 1966, 1973 and 1978. The 1966 poll revealed that 5 million Americans over the age of 18 thought they had seen a UFO. This figure was used by **Otto Binder** [2] in one of the bravest attempts to get at some absolute figures.

> 'Even if 80% were optical illusions or conventional objects mistaken for saucers, that still leaves 1,000,000 more-or-less genuine sightings in 20 years, or 50,000 annually. In America alone. Since the US has about one-tenth of the world's population, and since UFOs visit every part of the earth without exception, the worldwide figure then becomes 500,000 saucers each year for 20 years. That comes to 1370 per day, or 57 each hour.
>
> Thus, in the average, a UFO is sighted *once every minute* somewhere on earth. In America alone, the figure would be 6 per hour, still an amazing quantity.
>
> But let us be ultra-conservative and eliminate 99.9% of all sightings. That leaves some 50,000 'hardcore' sightings around the world in 20 years.'

Extrapolating from that to cover the full 40 years, we get a figure of **100,000 probable unknowns** - considerably more than figures based only on those sightings which were reported to official agencies; which is just what we should expect.

At the same time, Binder's estimate that the US has 'about one-tenth' of the world population, when the true figure is closer to 1/16th, shows that his figures are to be taken only very cautiously.

By 1973, however, the opinion poll figures has risen sharply; now 11% of Americans - 15 million - claimed to have seen a UFO, three times the 1967 figure. If Binder had updated his book, he might have been tempted to multiply his findings by a factor of three. Even if, again, we use his ultra-conservative caution and eliminate 99.9% of the 300 million overall total, we are left with an impressive worldwide figure of **300,000 hardcore sightings** for the 40-year period.

How safe is it to extrapolate from the United States to other countries? Claude Mauge [**12**] finds that French opinion polls are more or less consistent with their American equivalent. A poll by SOFRES/Bonne soiree in 1981, for instance, found that of those who responded, 7% reckoned they had seen a UFO, roughly midway between the 1967 and 1973 American figures. However, by this time Americans too were not quite so sure about what they had seen; the percentage had dropped back to 9%, or some 13 million persons.

Working from these figures, Mauge arrived at between 10 and 100 million cases since 1947 (like us, he found it hard to know how selective to be) which works out at between 800 and 8000 cases a day. This, he found, falls within the limits of a previous independent assessment by Belgian researcher **Jacques Scornaux** [**17**] who had arrived at a figure of 1000 cases a day.

Needless to say, two such hard-headed researchers as Scornaux and Mauge did not accept such figures at face value. Scornaux comments: 'Every researcher knows very well that in the majority of cases, the word 'UFO' is simply a label stuck onto a banal description where the phenomenon responsible is easily identified. The only cases which deserve to be taken into account are those which remain unexplained even after they have been investigated...in which case, we come down to a figure which is of the order of 100,000.' That is to say, **100,000 true unknowns** - the same figure as we reached using Binder's calculations.

It is not only opinion polls among the general public which can lead to vast numbers. Veteran French researcher **Aimé Michel** in 1976 [**13**] took as his starting point the results obtained by American astronomer Peter Sturrock, who in 1974 questioned members of the American Institute of Aeronautics & Astronautics. Extrapolating from Sturrock's figures, he found himself with a figure of 2,312,000 sightings for the US alone, of which one in ten, he thought, would be 'high strangeness' cases - equivalent to the 'true unknown' of our calculations. Michel then extrapolated again, not for the world as a whole but - for reasons which no doubt seemed good to him - to 'the other advanced nations', multiplying by a factor of ten, giving him a total of some **2.5 million true unknowns**, most of which he supposed would be close encounters or physical trace cases.

Needless to say, both Mauge and Scornaux regard such a figure as somewhat extravagant. Scornaux considered that Sturrock's small and selective sample was insufficiently representative to warrant such extrapolation. Yet even reducing the total by Binder's ultra-conservative 99.9% would leave us with an impressive 23,000 true unknowns for the 'advanced nations', which (working from his very rough figures as to what constitutes 'an advanced nation') extrapolates as **37,000 true unknowns** globally - surprisingly close to the Blue Book figure.

INVESTIGATORS' FILES

The research files kept by investigators should, in principle, represent the most reliable of all starting points, based as they are on the compiler's experience. Veteran French investigator **Claude Poher**, preferring to start from what he knew, used his own files as a basis [**15**]. They gave him a figure of 5000 cases, over a six-year period, in France alone. Projecting these figures in time and space, we would reach a figure of two million cases. It is not clear from Poher's account precisely what was the status of these cases, but they would hardly have been in a serious investigator's files if they had not themselves been serious reports meriting serious attention.

We may assume, then, that they are not such raw data as that of the Gallup polls, which Binder thought it prudent to reduce by a factor of 99.9%. On the other hand, it is also probable that not all of them had been subjected to thorough investigation.

But even if we discount them by the same 90% factor that we used for Blue Book, we are left with **200,000 true unknowns**.

CATALOGUES

Case catalogues of a sort have no doubt existed since ufology began, but when figures of this order are involved, it needed the making-available of high-tech data processing to transform mere collections of cases into meaningful research resources.

David Saunders' UFOCAT was the first major attempt. Poher in 1976 reported it as housing some 80,000 entries relating to 37,000 distinct events, and when Thierry Pinvidic met Saunders in 1979 the figure had risen to 84,000 [**12**], drawn from 138 different countries.

Admirable as this pioneering effort was, it is now generally recognised that UFOCAT's data are so raw as to be valueless except as a first-stage source of reference; it is to be hoped that the new generation of catalogues will be of greater practical use. Dr Willy Smith with UNICAT, Mike Wootten with the BUFORA archives, Michel Figuet with France's FRANCAT, and no doubt others in their respective countries, are currently purging their files and eliminating rubbish. When this has been achieved, they may provide us with a more reliable statistical basis that any we have at present.

SELECTIVE CATALOGUES

There are many selective, partial or specialist lists which help to fill out the overall picture. Examples are:

■ Regional studies, such as the **Gindilis** survey of 256 sightings in the Soviet Union [**7**]

■ Specialist studies, such as BUFORA's catalogue of 420+ vehicle interference cases [**4**]; **Ballester Olmos**' survey of 200 landing cases in Spain [**1**]; and **Figuet**'s similar survey of 600+ such cases in France [**5**]; **Moravec**'s survey of 88 Psi-UFO cases in Australia [**14**], &c.

All of these are valuable, and often the figures are significant. Any attempt to extrapolate from them would, however, be even more hazardous than doing so from the more general catalogues.

THE TIP OF THE ICEBERG

There is one further factor we have not yet taken into account which adds an extra dimension of uncertainty to figures which are already sufficiently conjectural: what proportion of sightings ever get to be reported?

Several attempts have been made to establish this. **Hynek** [**9**] askd an audience how many of them had seen UFOs; 18% raised their hands, but only one had reported their sighting. Unfortunately he omits to tell us how big his audience was: a speaker of such repute may be supposed to attract a statistically significant audience, but we still don't know what proportion that one reporter represents.

On the basis of his experience, he concluded that there might be '100 sightings in a night some place around the world.' [**10, p254**] This would extrapolate out at 1.5 million sightings over the 40-year period, but it is not clear whether he is speaking of raw sightings or true unknowns.

Sturrock's survey [**13**] showed that of 18 respondents who had seen UFOs, only two had reported them; this suggests we should multiply our figures by a factor of 9.

The **Condon Report** [**3**] concluded that 13% of those who had sightings reported their experiences, suggesting we should multiply by 8.

Ron Westrum [**12**] thought that 22% reported their sightings, so we should multiply by 5.

Even if we take the most conservative of these guidelines, it would seem as though we might reasonably multiply by five any totals based on reported sightings; which brings them pretty close to the figures achieved by working from the opinion polls.

The French group GABRIEL joined in the numbers-game with a delightful - if wildly speculative - series of calculations based on the assumption that UFOs are ET in origin:

■ 1 - If UFOs visit the earth uniformly - clearly a totally unwarrantable assumption! - only 1 in 16 would even be capable of being seen by humans, because the rest will be over the sea or uninhabited regions.

■ 2 - The time of day, coinciding with sleep or work, would reduce the figure to 1 in 64.

■ 3 - At least half the UFOs will be dark silent shapes moving at night and so literally invisible, so the figure becomes 1 in 128.

■ 4 - The fact that for two-thirds of the world no effective reporting agencies exist means that the figure is reduced to 1 in 384.

■ 5 - Additionally we could estimate that only 1 sighting in 10 is reported, and of those only 1 in 10 is published.

■ 6 - Consequently, **we learn of only one UFO in 38,400** that visits our planet, and a realistic assessment of the UFO as global phenomenon would multiply any figures based on reported sightings by this factor. [**8, p12-14**]

All this has been little more than game-playing, as every serious ufologist recognises. Nevertheless, the game has a meaning: there is some kind of reality underlying it. These are not random figures, plucked out of the air and juggled for fun; they are derived, as best we can, from what people do and say. And though many of the judgments involved are subjective, they represent a fervent wish to reach an objective basis for judgment.

If we tabulate the computations noted above, something approaching consistency emerges, even if it is objected that it is a spurious consistency resulting from arbitrary figure-juggling. None the less, if only as a matter of interest, here are the numbers of **true unknowns** we obtain from the various attempts at quantification:

Ruppelt	160,000
Blue Book	190,000
Vallée	105,000
Binder	100,000
Gallup 1973	300,000
Scornaux	100,000
Michel	185,000
Poher	200,000

Even if we make every allowance for the arbitrariness of these figures; even if we adopt in every case the most conservative estimate; even if we accept the possibility that UFOs are selective, and are *not* evenly distributed in time and space; even if we admit the possibility of cultural and psychosocial factors which would skew our figures out of all recognition - even if we take every conceivable factor into account, it remains a fact that the UFO phenomenon is a global phenomenon of unique and awe-inspiring scale.

REFERENCES

■ 1 - **Ballester Olmos**, VJ, *OVNIs, el fenomeno aterrizaje*, Plaza y Janes, 1978 (catalogue section translated as *A catalogue of 200 type-1 UFO events in Spain & Portugal*, CUFOS, 1976). ■ 2 - **Binder**, Otto, *What we really know about Flying Saucers*, Fawcett, 1967. ■ 3 - **Condon**, Edward U, (dir) *The scientific study of UFOs,*, University of Colorado, 1969. ■ 4 - **Falla**, Geoffrey, *Vehicle interference project*, BUFORA, 1979. ■ 5 - **Figuet**, Michel, & **Ruchon**, J-L, *OVNI, le premier dossier complet des rencontres rapprochees en France*, Lefeuvre, 1979. ■ 6 - **Fowler**, Raymond, *UFOs, interplanetary visitors*, Exposition, 1974. ■ 7 - **Gindilis** et al, *Observations of anomaloous atmospheric phenomena in the USSR*, trans CUFOS, 1979. ■ 8 - **Giraud**, J (ed) *Les soucoupes volantes, le grand refus*, GABRIEL groupe, 1979. ■ 9 - **Hynek**, J Allen, *The Hynek UFO report*, Dell, 1977. ■ 10 - **Hynek**, J Allen, & **Vallée**, J, *The edge of reality*, Regnery, 1975. ■ 11 - **Jacobs**, David, in **Story** (ed) *The encyclopedia of UFOs*, Doubleday, 1980. ■ 12 - **Maugé**, Claude, 'OVNI-OVI', in *Inforespace* no 63, Brussels. ■ 13 - **Michel**, Aime, 'Sur la nature reelle de l'observation rapprochee', in *Lumieres dans la nuit* no 151, 1976. ■ 14 - **Moravec**, Mark, *Psiufo phenomena*, ACUFOS, 1981. ■ 15 - **Poher**, Claude, 'Deux questions essentielles', in **Bourret**, J-C (ed) *Le nouveau defi des OVNI*, France-Empire, 1976. ■ 16 - **Ruppelt**, E J, *The report on UFOs*, Doubleday, 1955. ■ 17 - **Scornaux**, Jacques, 'Et si Michel Monnerie n'avait pas tout a fait tort?' in *Inforespace* no 49, Brussels. ■ 18 - **Steiger**, Brad, *Project Blue Book*, Ballantine, 1976. ■ 19 - **Vallée**, J, in *Flying Saucer Review* vol 14 no 3, 1968.

2.3.2

UFO CASEBOOK

by Kim Hansen

■ **KIM MOLLER HANSEN**. Born 1957; occupation, school teacher & school librarian.

■ **UFO involvement**: Has been a Council Member of SUFOI since 1980; he is currently director of the research departments and editor of its journal *UFO-Nyt* and also of *UFO-vision*, a yearbook of UFO literature. 'I am especially interested in UFO-phenomena seen from a psychological and folklore point of view. I believe that there still are among the unresolved cases many which could be explained if we had more data. Probable explanations, in my opinion, are psychological mechanisms and experiments with secret weapons, nor can we rule out the possibility that some sightings involve rare natural phenomena for which there is currently no explanation. I regard visits from other planets

as very unlikely.

'Ufology is not a department of science. But though it is researched by amateurs, we should none the less follow scientific procedures and use legitimate scientific methods if we wish to extend our knowledge of the phenomenon. At the same time, science could also benefit in the long run by examining the UFO phenomenon more closely.'

■ **Publications** for SUFOI: *UFO'er over New Zealand* (1980); *Focus pa UFO'er* (slides, textbook & tape, 1982, 4-6); *Bortfort; Travis Walton sagen* (1983); *Rex Heflin sagen* (1983); *UFO-Sloring* (UFO cover-up; re RAAF released information, 1985); *Piloter ser UFOer* (re the Valentich & other Australian cases, 1985); *Spogelsesraketterne; UFO'er over Norden i 1946* (re 'ghost rockets, 1986). For other publishers: *UFO* (Gyldendal, 1987).

■ **Address**: Eilekiersvej 14 / Benlose / DK-4100 Ringsted / Denmark.

INTRODUCTION

What makes a UFO-observation into a classic case?

There can be several reasons. It may be a case which has been told and retold again and again, sometimes so often that it has become an anecdote. Sometimes it becomes a model case by which other cases are evaluated. Sometimes it is regarded as solid and used as proof when battling with skeptics. But always it provides a common point of reference when discussing the evidence for or against the existence of UFO phenomena.

I do not believe that any of the classic cases can be regarded as 100% authentic. In every case alternative explanations can be found, doubts can be raised about the correctness of the information, &c. Despite this, I find the UFO-classics both interesting and valuable for the understanding of the history of the phenomenon and the problems of UFO research, as well as for highlighting the differences of opinion among those who work with or are interested in the phenomena.

Since 1981 I have been writing about classic cases in the Danish journal *UFO-Nyt*. Only a few can be discussed in this book. Photographic cases such as McMinnville 1950 and Trindade 1958 are omitted because they are treated elsewhere in these pages, and so are those which have been explained with virtually 100% certainty, such as Mantell 1948 and President Carter 1969. [*The Bentwaters / Lakenheath case, also one of those selected by Hansen, is also omitted since it is discussed in detail in the chapter on radar cases - Ed.*]

Those selected are partly the result of editorial choice, but also because they meet the prerequisites mentioned earlier. This does not imply that they prove the existence of the UFO phenomennon, because no case can do that. Alternative explanations are taken into account wherever possible, and even experienced ufologists may encounter details not generally known, and be inspired to look at these old cases with fresh eyes.

1: MOUNT RAINIER, 24 JUNE 1947

Businessman Kenneth Arnold has been called "the man who started it all". His sighting of nine silvery shining objects near Mount Rainier on 24 June 1947 marks the beginning of the modern UFO-era, as its 40th anniversary is the occasion for this book.

His story has been told so many times that it has become something of a cliche in the literature. So we do well to start with his own account, as given in his 1952 book *The coming of the saucers*.

ARNOLD'S OWN ACCOUNT

"It was Tuesday, June 24 1947. I had just finished installing some fire fighting apparatus at Chehalis, Washington. The job finished, I began a chat with Herb Critzer, chief pilot for Central Air Service. We talked about the possible location of a lost Marine transport which had gone down in the mountains. I decided to look for it. It meant a $5,000 reward and

I hoped that via my proposed route to Yakima, Washington, I might be lucky enough to find it. I decided to spend enough time in the air in the vicinity of Mount Rainier to make a good attempt at locating the wreckage.

I was flying a specially designed mountain airplane, and having had considerable experience in this type of flying, I felt qualified to undertake the dangerous search. I took off from the Chehalis, Washington airport at approximately two o'clock in the afternoon with the intention in mind of delaying my trip to Yakima for at least an hour, which I would spend on top, in and around the high plateau of Mount Rainier. I flew directly toward this plateau, which has an elevation varying from nine to over ten thousand feet.

It was during this search and while making a turn of 180 degrees over Mineral, Washington, at approximately 9200 feet altitude, that a tremendously bright flash lit up the surfaces of my aircraft. I was startled. I thought I was very close to collision with some other aircraft whose approach I had not noted. I spent the next twenty to thirty seconds urgently searching the sky all around - to the sides, above and below me - in an attempt to determine where the flash of light had come from. The only actual plane I saw was a DC-4 far to my left and rear, apparently on its San Francisco to Seattle run. My momentary explanation to myself was that some lieutenant in a P-51 had given me a buzz job across my nose and that it was the sun reflecting from the surface of his wings as he passed that had caused the flash.

Before I had time to collect my thoughts or to find any close aircraft, the flash happened again. This time I caught the direction from which it had come. I observed, far to my left and to the north, a formation of very bright objects coming from the vicinity of Mount Baker, flying very close to the mountain tops and traveling at tremendous speed.

At first I couldn't make out their shapes as they were still at a distance of over a hundred miles. I could see the formation was going to pass directly in front of me, as it was flying at approximately 170 degrees. I watched as these objects rapidly neared the snow border of Mount Rainier, all the time thinking to myself that I was observing a whole formation of jets. In group count, such as I have used in counting cattle and game from the air, they numbered nine. They were flying diagonally in an echelon formation with a larger gap in their echelon between the first four and the last five.

What startled me most at this point was the fact that I could not find any tails on them. I felt sure that, being jets, they had tails, but figured they must be camouflaged in some way so that my eyesight could not perceive them. I knew the Air Force was very artful in the knowledge and use of camouflage. I observed the objects' outlines plainly as they flipped and flashed along against the snow and also against the sky. Since this formation of craft was at almost right angles to me and was traveling from north to south, I was in an excellent position to clock their speed. I determined to make an attempt to do so.

It was a beautiful sunny afternoon and the giant bulks of both Mount Rainier and Mount Adams made perfect markers. Now, clocking speeds by only your sweep second hand cannot be entirely accurate because several seconds could be lost in breaking your gaze to observe your clock. I recall that when the first craft of this formation jetted to the southward from the snow-based cleft of Mount Rainier my second hand was approaching the top of my hour dial and the time was within a few seconds to one minute of three.

I was fascinated by this formation of aircraft. They didn't fly like any aircraft I had ever seen before. In the first place, their echelon formation was backward from that practiced by our Air Force. The elevation of the first craft was greater than that of the last. They flew in a definite formation, but erratically. As I described them at the time, their flight was like speed boats on rough water or similar to the tail of a Chinese kite that I once saw blowing in the wind. Or maybe it would be best to describe their flight characteristics as very similar to a formation of geese, in a rather diagonal chain-like line, as if they were linked together. As I put it to newsmen in Pendleton, Oregon, they flew like a saucer would if you skipped it across the water.

Another characteristic of these craft that made a tremendous impression on me was how they fluttered and sailed, tipping their wings alternately and emitting those very bright blue-white flashes from their surfaces. At the time I did not get the impression that these flashes were emitted by them, but rather that it was the sun's reflection from the extremely highly polished surface of their wings.

Even though they held a constant direction they swerved in and out of the high mountain peaks which are found on the hogsback of the Cascade mountains between Mount Rainier and Mount Adams. I determined my distance from their pathway to be in the vicinity of twenty-three miles because I knew where I was and they revealed their true position by disappearing from my sight momentarily behind a jagged peak that juts out from the base of Mount Rainier proper. Considering that I was flying all this time in the direction of their formation, this determination can be only approximate, but it is not too far off.

Between Mount Rainier and Mount Adams there is a very high plateau with quite definite north and south edges. Part of this chain-like formation traveled above this plateau towards Mount Adams, while part of the formation actually dipped below the near edge. As the first unit of these craft cleared the southernmost edge of this background, the last of the formation was just entering the northern edge. I later flew over this plateau in my plane and came to a close approximation that this whole formation of craft, whatever they were, formed a chain in the neighborhood of five miles long.

As the last of this group of objects sped past and seemed to gather altitude at a point beyond the southernmost crest of Mount Adams, I glanced at the sweep second hand of my instrument clock. As closely as I could determine, this strange formation of aircraft had covered the distance between Mount Rainier to the north and Mount Adams to the south in one minute and forty-two seconds.

I can say honestly that I was amazed, thinking all the time: what will these aeronautical engineers dream up next? Although readily explaining it all in this way in my mind, I definitely did have an eerie feeling about the whole experience. I tried to focus my mind on a continued search for the downed C-46 which had crashed some months earlier with thirty-two Marines aboard, but somehow the $5,000 didn't seem important. I wanted to get on to Yakima and tell some of the boys what I had seen.

Around airports pilots are continually arguing about how fast our Army and Navy jets and missiles really can go. Most pilots conceded that the fastest aircraft that had been invented at that time could go in the vicinity of seven hundred miles per hour. Up to this point I hadn't done any paper figuring on the distance and time, but I felt sure this formation of strange craft was traveling in excess of a thousand miles an hour.

It was about four o'clock in the afternoon when I landed at Yakima and went straight to Al Baxter, general manager of Central Aircraft. I met him in his outer office and rather breathlessly asked to see him in private. He dropped whatever it was he was doing and in his private office I related the story of my observation and drew him pictures of what I had seen. I recall that he looked at me in a rather puzzled way, but seemed quite positive that I hadn't gone crazy and wasn't seeing things. He called in several of his flight pilots and helicopter instructors to listen to my story.

The high point of my enthusiasm got its top knocked off when one of the helicopter pilots said, "Ah, it's just a flight of those guided missiles from Moses Lake."

I proceeded to gather my scattered wits together, got back in my airplane, and took off for Pendleton, Oregon. I remembered that I had forgotten to mention the fact that one of these craft looked different from the rest, was darker and of a slightly different shape, and that I hadn't told the Yakima boys that I had clocked the speed of this formation within fairly accurate limits. While flying to Pendleton I took my map from its snap holder on the extreme edge of my instrument panel, grabbed a ruler, and began figuring mathematically miles per hour. Figuring and flying my airplane at the same time was a little confusing, and I thought my figures were wrong and that I had better wait until I landed at Pendleton to do some serious calculating.

When I landed at the large airfield at Pendleton there was quite a group of people to greet me. When I got out of my plane no one said anything. They just stood around and looked at me. I don't recall just how the subject came up in those first few minutes after I had landed, but before very long it seemled everybody around the airfield was listening to the story of my experience. I mentioned the speed I had calculated but assured everybody that I was positive that my mathematics were lousy.

I don't know how many fellows sat down and started figuring it out. When it kept coming out in excess of seventeen hundred miles an hour I thought, "Holy smoke, we're taking the measurement of distance far too high up on both Mount Rainier and Mount Adams." So we took a measurement of the very base, as closely as it could be determined, and which I knew from the map was far below the snow line. The distance was 39.8 miles. Even covering this distance, which was so far on the conservative side that I knew it was incorrect, we still had a speed of over thirteen hundred and fifty miles per hour. To me, that evening, that was that. They were guided missiles, robotly controlled. I knew that speeds of this velocity the human body simply could not stand, particularly considering the flipping, erratic movements of these strange craft.

After talking to the editor of the East Oregonian newspaper, I was fairly convinced that it was some new government invention along the line of guided missiles. I could almost tell what this editor thought when the story went scudding over the news wires - that the government had taken this way to announce a new principle of flight.

I could have gone to sleep that night if the reporters, newsmen, and press agencies of every conceivable description had left me alone. I didn't share the general excitement. I can't begin to estimate the number of people, letters, telegrams, and phone calls I tried to answer. After three days of this hubbub I came to the conclusion that I was the only sane one in the bunch. From then on, if I was to go by the number of reports that came in of other sightings and of which I kept close track, I thought it wouldn't be long before there would be one of these things in every garage. In order to stop what I thought was a lot of foolishness and since I couldn't get any work done, I went out to the airport, cranked up my airplane, and flew home to Boise.

It wasn't long after I arrived home when Dave Johnson called on me. Dave Johnson is aviation editor of *The Idaho Statesman* newspaper, and a man of respected ability and intelligence in matters related to military and civilian aviation. When I caught the look in his eye and the tone of his words, flying saucers suddenly took on a different and a serious significance. The doubt he displayed of the authenticity of my story told me, and I am sure he was in a position to know, that it was not a new miltary guided missile and that if what I had seen was true it did not belong to the good old U.S.A. It was then I really began to wonder."

PROJECT SIGN INCIDENT #17

Arnold sent in a detailed report to the U.S. Air Force, which was the basis of their investigation. In certain respects it differed from his 1952 account.

In his comments on the Arnold report, Hynek, then UFO consultant to the Air Force, wrote: "There appears to be no astronomical explanation for this classic incident, which is the prototype of many of the later flying saucer stories. It is impossible to explain this incident away as sheer nonsense, if any credence at all is given to Mr Arnold's integrity."

However, as he points out in his report, there are many inconsistencies in Arnold's account as given to the Air Force:

- Arnold says his attention was first drawn to the objects by a bright flash. But at a distance of 30-40 km a direct reflection would be very small and unlikely to catch the attention of an observer.
- According to Arnold's calculation the objects were 13-15 m in length: their thickness was some 20 times smaller. Taking into account his estimate of their distance, this would mean that their thickness would correspond to an angle of 80 seconds of arc, which is definitely below the limit of resolution of the human eye which is about 3 minutes, and in practice must be considerably greater for any detail at all to be perceived.
- If his estimate of distance is correct, the size of the objects must have been at least 35 m thick and 600 m long for any details to be perceived.
- If his estimate of size is correct, the distance of the objects must have been closer to 2 km than to 30.

In short, if Arnold's estimate of distance is correct, his estimate of size must be wrong, and vice versa. Hynek therefore concluded that Arnold's figures were exaggerated. Estimating from Arnold's drawings, he decided that a size about 6 x 130 m, at a distance of about 10 km, was more reasonable. At this distance the objects would have travelled 18 km (rather than 75) in 102 seconds, giving a speed of 650 km/h rather than Arnold's estimated 2750 km/h. Consequently, Hynek concluded, "it appears probable

The first issue of Ray Palmer's *Fate*, Spring 1948, featured Arnold's sighting, wildly distorted.

that whatever objects were observed were travelling at subsonic speeds and may, therefore, have been some sort of known aircraft." (Note that the so-called 'sound barrier' was first broken through in October of that year by Chuck Yeager.)

In his report, Arnold himself accepted the airplane hypothesis: "*I am convinced in my own mind that they were some type of airplanes, even though they didn't conform with the many aspects of the conventional type of planes that I know.*"

Later, when he had told and re-told his experience several times, he changed his mind. Later, moreover, he said the objects were 160 km away when he first saw them, whereas to the Air Force he had given a figure of 35-40 km: if this revised figure is accepted, the objects would have to be measured in kilometres!

MIRAGES AND RAINDROPS

The UFO-skeptic, astronomer Donald H Menzel, also sought to explain the sighting. Given Arnold's flying experience, he thought it unlikely that he would misidentify a formation of aircraft. On the other hand he might have been tricked by raindrops on his window catching the light from the distant sky and giving the illusion of aircraft in formation when his eyes were directed towards the distant mountains.

Menzel himself had experienced such a phenomenon in a DC.9 over Amsterdam. He seemed to see three aircraft in formation approaching his plane, and their appearance immediately reminded him of Arnold's description. They turned out to be raindrops driving across the window.

Alternatively, he suggested, Arnold might have seen mirages round the mountain tops. Such phenomena often occur on clear sunny days at certain temperatures. Commenting on these suggestions Arnold wrote in his report to Project Sign: "This I know to be absolutely false, as I observed these objects not only through the glass of my airplane but turned my airplane sideways where I could open my window and observe them with a completely unobstructed view - without sun glasses."

Menzel also sought to detract from Arnold's credibility by pointing out that when he decided to write an account of his experience, he did so with the assistance from sci-fi publisher Ray Palmer, editor of *Fate* magazine, a man not known for his strict adherence to fact...

UFO WAVE

Press coverage of the incident triggered a veritable wave of observations during the following months, more than 850 sightings being reported in June-July alone, the wave reaching its crest between 25 June - 16 July.

However, Arnold's sighting was far from being the first. In April a meteorologist tracking a balloon instead found himself observing a saucer-shaped object: on 5 May a silvery object was said to have dropped from the sky and disintegrated over Washington state: on 18-19 May a silvery object was observed in Virginia and later over the Colorado desert: a chain of flying objects was seen from Weiser, Idaho, on 12 June, and two days later a pilot named Rankin saw a triangular formation composed of 10 'saucers.' All these sightings preceded that of Arnold which, by chance, happened to be the one to set the ball rolling.

During the succeeding years Arnold was more and more involved in the UFO matter. On the one hand he was a frequent participant in UFO-congresses, on the other he did much investigation of sighting reports. Right up to his death on 16 January 1984 he was very active.

In 1981 during an interview with ufologist Greg Long he commented on the reaction to his sighting. From the start he had to contend with skepticism which often turned to outright spite: "These nameless, faceless people ridiculed me. I was considered an Orson Welles, a fraud... I loved my country. I was very naive about the whole thing. I was the unfortunate goat who first reported them... Governments are more afraid than anything else of Joan of Arcs, religious saints or 'phenomena' that cause their self-destruction." He thought this deep-rooted fear of UFOs was felt in many countries.

He learned this lesson shortly after his sighting when he was visited by Capts. Brown and Davidson from the military intelligence service A-2. After discussing his sighting, the officers went through his mail, picking out letters from religious groups and organisations who had written asking Arnold to give an account of his experience. Davidson told Arnold the government was aware of the effect of the enthusiasm of some religious sects, and that they didn't want anything like that occurring here.

Arnold spent $30,000 of his own money on private investigations of UFOs and related phenomena. This led him to the conclusion that UFOs really exist, but he found few except a handful of believers who wanted to hear what he had to say.

He was astonished to find how his sighting was received - ridiculed by some, criticised by others, exploited by yet others. He soon learned, too, how the attitude of the Air Force, so friendly and eager to learn at first, suddenly changed, perhaps because they sensed that it presented a threat to the government.

ALTERNATIVE THEORIES

On one occasion Arnold sent President Eisenhower a telegram warning him that America was being visited by 'other worlds'. The November 1962 issue of *Flying Saucers* quoted him as saying: "After some 14 years of extensive research, it is my conclusion that the so-called unidentified flying objects that have been seen in our atmosphere are not space ships from another planet at all, but are groups and masses of living organisms that are as much a part of our atmosphere and space as the life we find in the depths of our oceans. The only major difference in the space and atmospheric organisms are that they have a natural ability to change their densities at will."

Five years later Arnold repeated this theory in a special edition of the magazine *Look*: "The impression I have held after observing these strange objects a second time was that they were something alive rather than machines - a living organism of some type that apparently has the ability to change its density, similar to fish that are found in our oceans, without losing their apparent identity."

Since uttering these words, all sorts of theories had been published by different people, and in 1981 he was more cautious: "It's a complicated sort of thing." Even though "after 30 years, if there's proof of UFOs, the government has it," he thought that the world would never accept the reality of their existence since "we are so engrossed in economic or selfish pursuits."

MANY SIGHTINGS

Arnold had many, less-known sightings in the course of his 68-year life, some of which he described briefly at *Fate*'s International UFO Congress at Chicago in 1971. In 1952 he had his eighth sighting, near Susanville CA, of two 'craft', one of which was transparent: "They looked like something alive. I've had the feeling with these things that they are aware of me, but they made no effort to come close."

On 9 July 1966, at 2 pm, he took a 16-mm movie of a glowing 'cylinder' over Idaho Falls, Ohio. The object looked like an atmospheric balloon, but flew at a speed of 70-120 km/h into a NNW wind.

Despite the evidence for the existence of UFOs he believed he had collected, he was in no hurry to publish; he told Greg Long that he had lived on 'hunches' his whole life, and "the time simply isn't right."

In a sense, it never had been. In part he saw his own involvement in the UFO controversy in terms of his responsibility to fellow professional pilots. He disliked people impugning their integrity, and for this reason he spoke out. But his public involvement left him with frustration and hurt. "When it happens to you, you're completely helpless."

REFERENCES

■ 1 - **Arnold**, Kenneth, & **Palmer**, Ray *The coming of the saucers*, Amherst, 1952 ■ 2 - *The TRUE report on Flying Saucers*, no 1, 1967 ■ 3 - *LOOK* special, 'Flying Saucers'. 1967 ■ 4 - **Pedersen**, F & **Kjems**, I O, *UFO-orientering*, Kobenhavn, 1969 ■ 5 - **Jacobs**, David M, *The UFO controversy in America*, 1976 ■ 6 - **Steiger**, Brad (ed) *Project Blue Book*, (1976) ■ 7 - **Menzel**, Donald H, & **Taves**, Ernest H, *The UFO enigma*, 1977 ■ 8 - **Hynek**, J Allen, *The Hynek UFO report*, 1978 ■ 9 - **Knight**, David C, *UFOs, a pictorial history*, 1979 ■ 10 - **Sachs**, Margaret, *The UFO encyclopedia*, 1980 ■ 11 - **Wegner**, Willy, *UFOer - Top secret?*, Kobenhavn, 1980 ■ 12 - **Story**, Ronald D, *UFOs and the limits of science*, 1981 ■ 13 - *MUFON UFO Journal* no 165, 1981; no 191, 1984 ■ 14 - *APRO Bulletin* vol 32, no 3 ■ 15 - *UFORAN*, no 3, 1984.

2: KELLY-HOPKINSVILLE - 21 AUG. 1955

Kelly is a little collection of houses 11 km north of the town of Hopkinsville, Kentucky. Here, on the night of 21-22 August 1955, a farm was the scene of an incident which - if it indeed occurred - matches any of our recent horror movies. In this real-life event, eleven down-to-earth country folk claimed to have been besieged by "little people" with big luminous eyes and claw-like hands.

The case is referred to by Hynek, but he was not personally involved in the investigation. A few months after the incident, he was engaged in setting up satellite tracking stations round the world and had little time to spare for UFO research. However, it happened that one of the engineers employed in the work was a certain Andrew (Bud) Ledwith.

Ledwith had been a technician at the radio station WHOP in Hopkinsville. The morning following the incident, he began his own thorough inquiry into what seemed a patently absurd case. As a result, Hynek received the complete story, including signed statements from all the adult witnesses, their original sketches of the humanoids, and the drawings Ledwith himself made based on the sketches.

Arriving at the radio station on the morning of 22 August, Ledwith was greeted with the words "Have you seen the little green men yet?" He asked for and got a vague account of the night"s happenings. "Remembering a magazine article about the way police reconstruct facial features from witness descriptions, I decided to try to clarify the situation. I had once studied art and thought I might be able to get sketches. With me went Mike Lackey, son of the owner of station WHOP; he could watch and listen and make sure that I was not leading or guiding the people."

Those gathered at the Sutton farm the previous night included:

- Mrs Glennie Lankford, 50, widow after the death of her second husband Oscar Lankford;
- Elmer ('Lucky') Sutton, 25, Glennie's son by her first husband Tillman;
- Vera Sutton, 29, Lucky's wife;
- John Charley Sutton (J.C.), 21, Lucky's younger brother;
- Alene Sutton, 27, J.C.'s wife;
- Lonnie Lankford, 12; Charlton, 10; and Mary, 7 - Glennie's three children by her second marriage;
- Billy Ray Taylor, 21, a close friend of 'Lucky'
- June Taylor, 21, Billy's wife; she was too frightened to look at the little beings and so was not a witness;

O.P. Baker, 30 or 35, brother of Alene.

Seven of the eight adults - all except Alene - had seen the frightening beings; Ledwith interviewed them in three groups during the course of 22 August. Glennie, Vera and Alene were interviewed in the morning (for 3 hours!). Billy Ray, who had been hunting with a neighbour since 8 am, was interviewed in the afternoon. The other men - Lucky, J.C. and O.P. Baker, who despite the dramatic occurrences of the previous night had been into Evansville, Indiana, to buy tools for the farm - were all interviewed in the evening about 8.30 pm, immediately after their return and before they had the opportunity to discuss the events with the others.

VISITORS IN THE DARK

About 7 pm on 21 August Billy Ray Taylor, a family friend, went out to the farm well to get some water. While he was taking a cool refreshing drink he saw to his great surprise a huge shining object "real bright, with an exhaust all the colors of the rainbow" come down in a dried-up river-bed close to the farm. He immediately went in to tell the others that a UFO had landed, but nobody believed him and he was laughed at. No one could be bothered to go out to the supposed landing site, since they reckoned he had seen a shooting star.

Less than an hour later the occupants were alarmed by the furious barking of the dog in the yard. Lucky, as head of the family, went with Taylor to the kitchen door to see if anyone was there. A little "shining" man with enormous eyes, his arms stretched in the air over his head "as if someone had told him he was about to be robbed", was slowly approaching the house.

Those who live in these country districts in such financial and social circumstances as the Suttons are accustomed to "shoot first and ask questions afterwards" - and this was exactly what Lucky and Taylor did. Armed respectively with a shotgun and a .22 rifle, both fired when the little man was about 7 m from the house. The sound was "exactly as if you had shot into a pail." The visitor somersaulted backwards and scurried away into the darkness.

One incident in particular shows the little beings' apparent ability to "hover". While all were indoors, a scraping or knocking sound was heard from the kitchen roof. The men ran out into the yard and saw a creature moving on the roof. They fired and the creature fell. It then "floated" 12 m down to a fence in the backyard, where it seemed to settle. But the respite was short. Lucky and Billy Ray fired together; the creature fell and disappeared into the high weeds on all four limbs.

THE APPEARANCE OF THE VISITORS

The ghostlike figures were a little over 1 m tall, and looked as if they were illuminated from the inside. Their heads were round or egg-shaped, and completely bald. Their eyes, yellow and big as saucers, were placed half-way round the side of the face; they were apparently very light-sensitive, for the house lights rather than the rifle bullets seemed to be the chief deterrent to their forcing an entry into the house. The mouth was just a crack stretching from ear to ear, and the ears were huge and elephant-like.

According to the women, the body was slim with a shapeless, straight figure and with no visible neck. The arms were long, ending in claw-like hands. The legs were thin without visible knees. Both head and body were the same silvery shining colour. The light emitted from the body grew more intense every time they were fired at or called on, as though noise influenced the light emission.

The creatures uttered no sound when they walked or fell. The undergrowth crackled when they walked through it, but there was no sound of footsteps. When they approached the house they did so slowly and with arms stretched forward over the head. When hit by a bullet or the light from a torch, they dropped their arms and made off on four limbs.

The stretched arms and claw-like hands had at first sight a hostile appearance, but this could have been a peaceful gesture to show they were unarmed. Their behaviour was not aggressive at any time. They did not attempt to force their way into the house, but only stood staring until they were frightened off. Several times when the light in front of and behind the house was turned off, they approached from all sides.

HEAD-LONG ESCAPE

Nothing dismayed these Kentucky farm folk more than the ineffectiveness of their guns, and soon the whole family was gathered inside the house behind locked doors. From time to time their visitors could be seen at the windows. After about three hours they decided they had had enough of this one-sided siege, and made a rapid decision to pack into two cars and head for Hopkinsville and the police. It was then 11 pm. Since it takes a lot to pack 11 people into two cars late in the evening and rush 10 miles to the police station to ask for help, this is an impressive indication of the fear which had taken hold of the family.

The Hopkinsville Chief of Police, Russell Greenwell, deputy George Batts, Sgt Malcolm Pritchett, three other officers from the Kentucky State Police, and a photographer from the local newspaper *Kentucky New Era*, followed the family back to the farm to investigate and if necessary take up the fight with the unknowns.

Three or four km out of Hopkinsville on the Kelly Road, at the Shady Oaks restaurant, they saw and heard two meteors passing overhead in the direction of the Sutton Farm "with a noise like artillery fire."

The police examined the area with flashlights, and made a great stir. They found no trace of the little men or the UFO, but found the bullet-holes, and

Chief of Police Greenwell later stated that "something frightened these people, something beyond their comprehension." He emphasised that "these are not the kind of people who normally run to the police for help. When they sense danger they reach for their guns."

Since it was dark and quiet, and they could find nothing, the police returned to Hopkinsville about 2 pm, planning to return in daylight to continue the investigation.

BUT WAS THE NIGHTMARE OVER?

About 2.30 pm, when all had gone to bed, Glennie, lying in bed facing the window, noticed something shining at the window. A little figure, holding his claw-like hands against the window, stood absolutely motionless, staring into the bedroom with wide shining eyes. Throughout the evening Glennie had been the most calm and reasonable of them all, and had tried to cool down the others and discourage them from shooting, since the creatures were not doing them any harm.

Now she called softly to the other members of the family. Lucky immediately came running with his rifle at the ready, and though his mother said "For God's sake, don't!", Lucky replied "Mama, I'm goin' to shoot that little man," and fired at the voyeur, who disappeared into the darkness.

The last time the uninvited guests were seen that night was about half an hour before sunrise, at 5.15 am on the morning of Monday 22 August.

NO 'PROTECTING RATIONALISATION'

When news of the incident spread beyond the family, it was distorted in every possible way and for a long time the family was pestered by sight-seeing hordes. The critics directed the spotlight onto the personality of the witnesses, who were accused of being affected by religious hysteria (they were fundamentalists, and

Elmer Sutton and Billy Ray Taylor at the door of the farmhouse. [*Kentucky New Era* / **CUFOS**]

had attended a church service the evening before the events).

Despite the unfavorable publicity and the personal harassment, Isabel Davis of Civilian Saucer Intelligence was able to make a thorough investigation a year later, in June 1956; her findings in the main confirm those of Ledwith. The Sutton family remained convinced that they had been involved in a real experience. In her report Davis writes: "The Suttons stuck to their story. Stubbornly, angrily, they insisted that they were telling the truth. Neither adults nor children ever so much as hinted at the possibility of an exaggeration or a mistake - neither in public nor to relatives: there was no trace of a retraction."

In her comprehensive report she mentions the lack of the concept of 'protecting rationalisation' used by UFO-observers who, though personally convinced, wish to retain the respect of their friends, and so say something like "of course it must have been a plane...I may have been wrong" - with self-conscious laugh or giggle. Davis writes: "Never have the Suttons been tempted to retract their story and thereby retrieve the respect of the community... Their refusal to concede an inch to skepticism may not prove anything about the truth of their story, but it does tell us something about them."

WHERE DID THEY COME FROM FROM?

We have only one witness for the UFO itself, while ten testify to the humanoids; this is an encounter case rather than a UFO sighting. Is there any correlation between the beings and the supposed UFO? Impossible to say for sure, but Davis offers some supporting testimony.

Early on Sunday evening a neighbour, some 400 m north of the Sutton farm, had seen lights moving around on the fields behind the farm; he thought the Suttons' pigs had got out and were being rounded up. "I thought maybe I ought to go and help them. But I'm glad I didn't go out there - I might have been shot."

The witness is sure he saw the lights between 7.30 and 8 pm - between the time of the alleged landing and that of the first appearance of the creatures.

CIRCUS MONKEYS, ROBOTS, FOLKLORE BEINGS, OR...?

Hynek, though not directly involved, wondered if a travelling circus might have been in the area, from which monkeys could have escaped. However, the monkey hypothesis must be rejected if the witness testimony is accepted: with so much shooting going on, including apparent direct hits from experienced hunters at close range, it would be most improbable for not one dead monkey to be found, or at least traces of blood. Nor do monkeys "float" from trees. Moreover, though as it happens the King Circus did indeed pass through Hopkinsville that day, there is no evidence that they possessed any monkeys, let alone that any escaped - a fact which would surely have emerged at the time.

Another suggestion was that the beings had brought photographic equipment with them, since they approached the house from the darkest side and were disturbed when the outdoor light was put on.

Were these country folk besieged by invulnerable robots? Or are the little shining men American examples of ufonauts which, according to Aage Skjelborg, who has a master's degree in folklore, are the "result of chimeras, wishful thinking and hallucinatory experience, but also created by intense, human elements from a confused conflict-filled world of experience"? Or is the confrontation at Kelly a tragically unsuccessful attempt at a meeting between two worlds?

Project Blue Book never examined the case officially, but Major J E Albert looked at it informally. The records are sketchy, and little or no investigation was conducted. Still, as Hynek notes, "the case is carried in Blue Book files as "Unidentified". That much it certainly is."

REFERENCES

1 - **Pedersen,** F & **Kjems,** I O, *UFO-Orientering*, SUFOI, 1969 ■ 2- **Hynek,** J Allen, *The UFO experience*, Regnery, 1972; *The Hynek UFO Report*, Dell, 1977 ■ 3- **Skjelborg,** Aage, *Pa sporet af UFOnauten*, Berlingske, Kobenhavn, 1979 ■ 4- **Lob,** J & **Gigi** R, *Ceux venus d'Ailleurs*, Dargaud, 1973 ■ 5- **Bowen,** Charles (ed) *The humanoids*, Flying Saucer Review, 1974 ■ 6-**Steiger,** Brad, (ed) *Project Blue Book*, Ballantine, 1976 ■ 7- **Story,** Ronald D (ed) *The encyclopedia of UFOs*, NEL, 1980 ■ 8- **Davis,** Isabel, & Bloecher, Ted, *Close encounter at Kelly and others of 1955*, CUFOS, 1978.

3: ANTONIO VILLAS BOAS - 14-15 OCT., 1957

In the Brazilian state of Minas Gerais, something unbelievable is said to have occurred in October 1957. Antonio Villas Boas, a 23-year-old farmer from Sao Francisco de Salles, near the state border with Sao Paulo, was forced to have sexual intercourse with a "space-woman" - a close encounter of the most intimate kind.

Nine days earlier, Antonio and his brother Joao had seen through their bedroom window a blinding beam of light; they could see that it came from the sky, but could not see what was its source, even when it seemed to approach their window.

On 14 October, at about 10 pm, Antonio was out with his brother, plowing with the tractor. (The family had labourers to work during the day, and he himself worked at night, sleeping during the day.) He suddenly saw in the northern part of the field a dim red ball of light, the size of a cartwheel, hovering at a height of approximately 100 m. The light was too glaring for him to look directly at it. He called his brother to help him find out what it was, but when his brother refused to accompany him he had to go alone.

When he approached the stationary light, it moved suddenly at high speed to the far end of the field. In this way Antonio chased the ball of light from one end of the field to the other. After twenty such attempts he gave up; he stopped and returned to his brother. The light remained a little longer, intermittently emitting rays in all directions.

AN 'EXPERIMENTAL ANIMAL' MUST BE CAUGHT!

The following night, 15 October, Antonio was out plowing again, alone this time, when at 1 am he saw a great red "star" which approached, becoming larger and larger. In a very short time it had grown into a very bright, egg-shaped object hovering about 100 m overhead, illuminating him so brightly that the tractor's own headlights could not be seen.

While he considered means of making a getaway with his tractor, the object landed about 10-15 m in front of him, on three metallic legs. A rotating dome on top of the object changed colour from red to green when the speed of the object decreased. Three spurs projected from the front and were illuminated by a red phosphorescent or fluorescent light from the object.

Antonio jumped from the tractor and started to run away, but his arm was caught by a small figure dressed in strange clothes. He pushed it to the ground, but at the same time he was attacked by three men, who took him by the arms and lifted him off the ground and dragged him towards their machine. He was lifted onto a flexible ladder and forced inside.

He found himself in a small square room with polished metal walls, brightly lit; when the door was closed it was invisible. He was led through several rooms to one larger than the others, where "for endless moments", while held by his captors, he was inspected by the creatures, who seemed to be debating what to do with him. His five abductors all wore tightly-fitting grey suits of soft, thick, unevenly striped grey material, and helmets which hid everything but their small, blue-ish eyes. From the helmets three tubes ran down into their clothes at back and sides.

An impression of the Villas Boas encounter. [Henrik Pedersen / *UFO-Nyt*]

The beings began forcibly to undress him. He resisted, "cursing them with loud yells, at which they stopped and stared at me as if trying to make me understand that they were being polite." One of the men began to spread a clear, thick liquid over his skin.

Next he was taken by two of the men into another, smaller room, where a strange device was used to take a blood sample, giving him a scar that he was able later to show his investigators.

Then he was left alone, and had time to study the room, which was empty except for a kind of couch on which, tired, he now sat. He then noticed an odd smell which made him feel sick; the source seemed to be a row of small pipes in the wall, from which tufts of grey smoke spread and dissolved in the air. He ended by vomiting in a corner of the room.

SEDUCTION

After a little over half an hour, a naked woman suddenly came into the room. She had blond hair, fair skin, big blue slanting eyes, small lips, a little nose and small ears; her most unusual facial features were the high, broad cheekbones which gave her a face wider than normal but with a pointed chin. "Her body was much more beautiful than any I have ever seen before. It was slim, and her breasts stood up high and well separated. Her waistline was thin, her belly flat, her hips well developed, and her thighs were large... She was much shorter than I am, her head only reaching my shoulder." Her arms were freckled. He believes the strange smoke allowed her to breathe in the room without wearing a helmet.

"The woman came toward me in silence, looking at me all the while as if she wanted something from me, and suddenly she hugged me and began to rub her head against my face from side to side. At the same time I also felt her body glued to mine and it also was moving... I began to get excited... This sounds quite incredible, considering the circumstances." (He speculated that the liquid that had been spread on him may have been some kind of stimulant.) He responded to her caresses with enthusiam: "We ended up on the couch, where we lay together for the first time. It was a normal act and she reacted as any other woman would. Then we had some petting, followed by another act, but by now she had begun to deny herself to me, to end the matter... I too became frigid, seeing that that was all they wanted, a good stallion to improve their own stock. I was angry, but decided not to attach any importance to the fact, for anyhow I had spent a few agreeable moments with the woman." He added that "some of the growls that came from her at certain times nearly spoiled everything, as they gave me the disagreeable impression of lying with an animal." One thing he noticed was that she never kissed him, though once she bit him softly on the chin.

A man appeared at the door and called to the woman. Before she left she pointed first at her belly, then at the sky; "I interpreted the signs as meaning to say that she intended to return and take me with her to wherever it was that she lived. That is why I still feel afraid; if they came back to fetch me, I'd be lost."

Antonio was given his clothes back and was shown round the craft. After he had made a fruitless attempt to get hold of one of the instruments as a proof of his experience, he was carried out of the craft and left back in the field. The craft began to ascend, the light became more intense and the landing gear was retracted. When it had reached an altitude of about 30 m the craft hovered momentarily, the light became more intense and changed to red, the object rotated at a terrific speed and disappeared at an incredible speed like a bullet.

Antonio noted that he had spent 4 hrs 15 min aboard the craft. During the following weeks he was tormented by some strange wounds on his hands, forearms and legs. These became violet while they healed, and left a scar.

A FIGMENT OF EROTIC FANCY?

In the following month, Antonio wrote a letter to the journalist Joao Martins, who had advertised for UFO-witnesses in the magazine *O Cruzeiro*. The following February he was questioned by the well-known UFO investigator Dr Olavo Fontes of Rio de Janeiro. Both researchers interviewed and interrogated Antonio, but were impressed by the man and could not fault his story.

Fontes conducted a medical examination which revealed the cheek scar and some skin-burning which might have been caused by radioactive radiation. Fontes was inclined to put great confidence in Antonio's account because he seemed honest and was in full mental command of his experience. At the same time he pointed out that the account was so rich in fantastic detail that Antonio must either have a remarkably good visual memory or be an accomplished liar.

Danish folklorist Aage Skjelborg has anlysed the Villas Boas from a regional/social point of view, in the light of what we know about the inhabitants of the area. In his view, Antonio's experience should be considered in the context of his family situation on the collective farm. As a bachelor he lived together with his married brothers and sisters-in-law and his parents. Night-working could induce conditions of sleeplessness, in which males frequently experience pleasant and often erotic fancies, often as realistic visual impressions.

Skjelborg suggests that Antonio's "spacewoman" resembled an attractive sub-species of the *guarani* woman - European/Indian, with fair hair, blue eyes and a light freckled skin, considered very desirable in that region. In his opinion, therefore, the "spacewoman" was a figment of Antonio's imagination, but an important part of the sexual reality of a young man. But for Antonio himself, it was a real experience.

SUBSEQUENT EVENTS

In 1980 CUFOS received from Brazilian researcher Irene Granchi the tape of a 1978 Brazilian TV show (in Portuguese with translation) in which Antonio Villas Boas made his first public appearance in 21 years. He is now Dr Villas Boas, a respected lawyer in a little town not far from Brasilia. He is happily married, with four children.

He explained that he was breaking his long silence because he felt injured over the way his experience and the UFO subject in general had been treated by the press; his adventure had even been presented in a French comic strip! His re-telling of his account contained no contradictions, but he added one detail to the original account. The woman used a container to collect a sperm sample after their second intercourse. He assumes this was preserved.

After the programme, Granchi asked Marlena, Antonio's wife, how she felt about the possibility that her husband had more offspring than their own terrestrial four. She said she didn't mind the idea at all: in fact, she would be rather proud of it.

As Allen Hendry commented, "One thing is certain: if Antonio Villas Boas *had* been the victim of serious radiation exposure in 1957, it doesn't seem to have affected the last 23 years of his life."

REFERENCES

■ 1 - **Bowen,** Charles (ed) *The humanoids*, Flying Saucer Review, 1966 ■ 2- **Fontes,** Olavo, & **Martins,** Joao, *Report on the Villas-Boas incident*, in **Lorenzen,** Coral & Jim, *Flying Saucer occupants*, Signet, 1967 ■ 3- *Probe* update, September 1980 ■ 4- **Sachs,** Margaret, *The UFO encyclopedia*, 1980 ■ 5- **Skjelborg,** Aage, *Pa sporet af UFO-nauten*, Berlingske, Kobenhavn, 1979 ■ 6- **Story,** Ronald D (ed) *The encyclopedia of UFOs*, 1980.

4: PAPUA, NEW GUINEA - 26-27 JUNE 1959

"A large UFO was sighted... we watched figures appear on top - four of them - there is no doubt that they were human. On the larger one, two of the figures seemed to be doing something near the centre of the deck - they were occasionally bending over and raising their arm as though adjusting or 'setting up' something. One figure seemed to be standing, looking down at us. I stretched my arm above my head and waved. To our surprise, the figure did the same."

Though it sounds like a scene from the movie *Close Encounters,* this is actually a quotation from a report by a clergyman in Papua.

Papua forms the southeast coast of the world's second largest island, New Guinea, and since 1975 has been a republic under the name Papua-New Guinea. In 1959, when the sightings took place, Papua was administered by Australia.

At that time it was seemingly the centre of intense UFO activity. Seventy-nine sightings were reported, 61 of them in 1959, and mostly in June-July. Three reports stand out, because of the large number of witnesses and especially because in two of them "human beings" were observed in connection with the UFOs.

THE INVESTIGATING MISSIONARY

The Rev. Norman Cruttwell, head of the mission at Menapi, Papua, collected these 79 reports into a dossier which was published as a special edition of the respected *Flying Saucer Review*. He interviewed many of the witnesses, several of whom were known to him personally. Further reports were sent to him by other missionaries in Papua; one of them was the Rev. William Bruce Gill, head of the mission at Boianai. The account of the sensational events at Boianai is taken from Cruttwell's *FSR* article.

THE FIRST EVENING

After dinner on 26 June, at 6.45 pm, Gill went out in front of the main building looking for Venus, which was conspicuous at the time. "I saw Venus, but I also saw this sparkling object, which to me was peculiar because it sparkled, and because it was very, very bright, and it was above Venus and so that caused me to watch it for a while, then I saw it descend towards us.

He called two of the mission staff, teacher Stephen Gill Moi and Eric Langford, and shortly after the rest of the men were summoned. Gill estimated the object's angular diameter as about 13 cm at arm's length. Stephen Gill Moi said that if he stretched out his closed hand, it would cover about half the object.

In their signed statement the witnesses agreed that the object was circular with a wide base and a narrower upper 'deck'. It had something resembling legs beneath it. At intervals a shaft of blue light was switched on and off at a 45-degree angle up into the sky, and on top of the object four human-like beings appeared. Some witnesses thought they could see four portholes or windows on the side of the object. Gill saw "what appeared to be panels in the side", but did not interpret them as portholes.

"As we watched it, men came out from this object and appeared on the top of it, on what seemed to be a deck on top of the huge disc. There were four men in all, occasionally two, then one, then three, then four; we noted the various times the men appeared... Another peculiar thing was this shaft of blue light, which emanated from what appeared to be the centre of the deck. The men appeared to be illuminated not only by this light reflected on them, but also by a sort of glow which completely surrounded them as well as the craft. The glow did not touch them, but there appeared to be a little space between their outline and the light..."

During the sighting Gill noted his observations in a notebook: the following are excerpts:

"6.45 P.M. - Patches of low clouds. Sighted bright white light from front door.
6.50 - Clear over Dagura and Menape. Call Stephen and Eric Langford.
6.52 - Stephen arrives. Confirms not a star. Five hundred feet? Orange?
6.55 - Sent Eric to call the people. One object on top moves - man? Now three men, moving, glowing, doing something on deck. Gone.
7.00 - Men one and two again.
7.04 - Gone again.
7.10 - Cloud ceiling covered sky; ceiling 2000 feet [and thus, not stars or planets]. Men three, four, two [appeared in that order]. Thin electric blue spotlight. Men gone. Spotlight still there.
7.12 - Men one and two appear again. Blue light.
7.20 - UFO goes through clouds.
8.28 - Clear sky here, heavy cloud over Dagura. UFO seen by me overhead. Called station people.
8.50 - Clouds forming again. Big one stationary and larger - the original? Others coming and going through the clouds. As they descend through clouds, light reflected like a large halo on the cloud - no more than 2,000 feet, probably less (height of clouds is judged by height of nearby mountain).
9.46 - Overhead UFO reappears; is hovering.
10.50 - No sign of UFO.
11.04 - Heavy rain. "

The objects, especially the smaller ones, flew in a very irregular manner - sometimes fast, then slow, changing course, coming closer then moving away, sometimes swinging backwards and forwards like a pendulum. A single object flew away and looked as if it was going to land at the village of Wadobuna. The people on the mission ran down to the beach, but the object shot upwards and flew towards the mountains, where it disppeared as it changed colour to red.

The big object was dim yellow (maybe light orange) except when it was moving, where it became much brighter. Before it disappeared at 9.30 pm, it made a light waving movement and suddenly rushed away at tremendous speed, changing colour from yellow to red and then to blue-green: it disappeared silently over the bay towards Giwa.

THE SECOND EVENING

The following evening a large object was seen by Annie Laurie Borewa, a nurse at the hospital. She called Gill, who got in touch with Ananias Parata and others at the mission. This is his account:

"... We stood in the open to watch. Although the sun had set (behind the mountains), it was quite light for the following fifteen minutes. We watched figures appear on top - four of them - there was no doubt that they were human. This is possibly the same object that I took to be the 'mother ship' last night. Two smaller UFOs were seen at the same time, stationary, one over the hills, west, and one overhead.

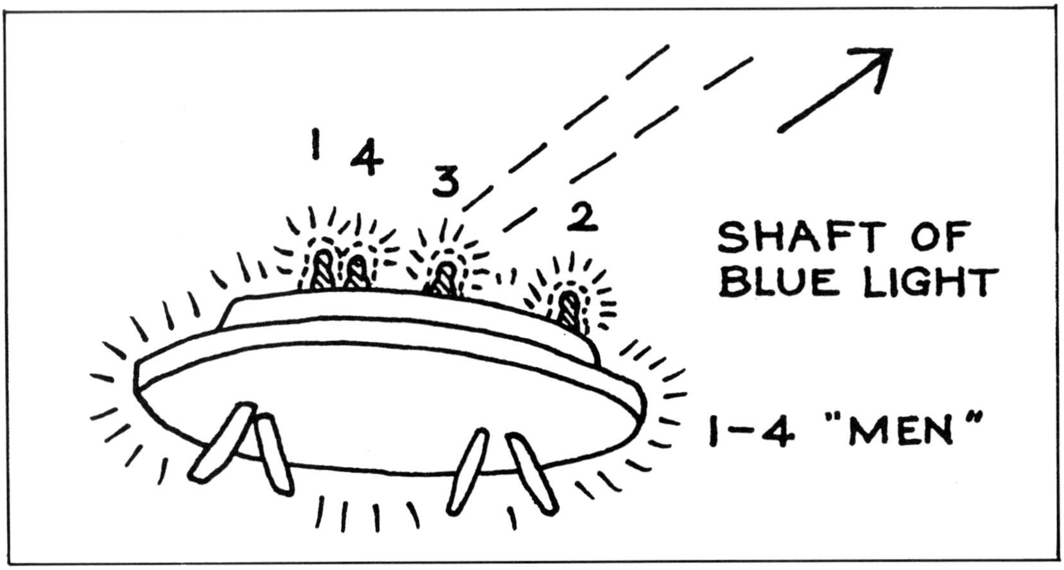

Gill's own sketch.

On the large one, two of the figures seemed to be doing something in the center of the deck - they were occasionaly bending over and raising their arms as though adjusting or setting up something. One figure seemed to be standing, looking down on us (a group of about a dozen)."

Now comes the climax. Father Gill stretched his arm above his head and waved. To his surprise, the figure waved back. One of his companions waved both arms over his head and then the two outside figures did the same. There was more waving and now all four of the beings seemed to wave back!

"There seemed to be no doubt that our movements were answered. All the mission boys made audible gasps.

As dark was beginning to close in, I sent Eric for a torch and directed a series of long dashes towards the UFO. After a minute or two of this, the UFO apparently acknowledged by making several waving motions back and forth (in a sideways direction, like a pendulum). The waving by us was repeated and this was followed by more passes with the torch and then the UFO began to become slowly bigger, apparently coming in our direction. It ceased after perhaps half a minute and came on no further. After a further two or three minutes, the figures apparently lost interest in us for they disappeared below deck."

At 6.25 two figures resumed their activity, and the blue spotlight came on for a few seconds twice in succession. At 6.30 Gill went in to dinner! According to his notes, he came out from dinner at 7 pm, and the UFO was still visible, though now it appeared somewhat smaller. Then everyone went into the church for Evensong. When they came out visibility was poor, the sky covered with clouds, and no UFOs were to be seen.

At 10.40 Gill noted: "A terrific explosion just outside the mission house. Nothing seen." According to Cruttwell's account, the explosion woke everyone on the station and made Gill jump out of bed, giving him a tremendous shock. Whether this "penetrating, ear-splitting" explosion had anything to do with the UFO is only conjectural.

Gill and his 37 witnesses at Boianai were not the only ones to see peculiar things in the sky that evening. Additional observations at Giwa, Baniara and Sideia confirm that something unusual was going on over Papua.

On Sunday 28 June the phenomenon returned. The objects did not come so low, and no ufonauts were seen - but now the number of objects had multiplied. At 6.45 Gill could see one hovering right above his head: at 9 pm there were three UFOs, in an almost straight line, all high above. The sky was clear.

Two hours later they could see *eight* UFOs! One of them was quite low, but apart from slight drifting movements, no activities were seen.

At 11.20 a piercing, high metallic crack sounded from the roof of the mission station, as if it had been hit by a piece of metal; but nothing came rolling down its sloping surface. Four UFOs were seen circling round the station, all very high. The next day Gill checked the roof but found no mark that could relate to the sound.

SHORTSIGHTEDNESS AND NARROW-MINDEDNESS

The most outspoken critic of the case was astronomer Donald Menzel; his comments demonstrate that if many so-called UFO investigators can be justifiably blamed for overlooking crucial data and allowing their pet theory to colour their reports, the same is no less true of the skeptics. Menzel's writings purport to explain many well-known cases, and they can certainly not be accused of dullness; his suggested explanation for the Papua case is no exception. He writes the entire case off as an observation of Venus, founded on the hypothesis that Gill was not wearing his spectacles at the time:

"... We are first to assume that Father Gill and Stephen Gill Moi (teacher) both suffer from appreciable myopia and that they were not wearing spectacles during the sighting. They probably had appreciable stigmatism as well, so that the image of Venus was large and definitely elongated. Something of this sort is necessary to account for the difference in appearance of the UFO as reported by the two individuals. Father Gill had the long axis of the vehicle horizontal; Stephen had it more nearly vertical. The human eye executes erratic motions, which make an object such as a star or planet appear to be vibrating when, in fact, the object is standing still. Atmospheric effects account for the rapid changes in color.

But what about the reported men waving? Could this have been an illusion? With a myopic eye, the excursions of the eyelid over the pupil perform a sort of optical knife edge. Out-of-focus nature of the eyelashes and out-of-focus images of the eyelashes and a defraction resulting from squinting as a near-sighted person tries to improve his vision. The waving to the occupants and the reported waving back might not have been as universally observed as Father Gill thought. He reported gasps of either joy or surprise, perhaps both. Could these gasps have been of incredulity because of the inability to see what Father Gill was reporting? After all, in a Mission of this sort, the natives must have been conditioned to miracles and the like..."

Menzel unfortunately fails to note the following facts:

- The UFO was sometimes seen *beneath* the clouds.
- Gill specifically noted Venus *in addition* to the UFO.
- Gill *was* wearing the right spectacles.

AN ANTHROPOLOGICAL VIEW

Anthropologists have pointed out that the Papua observations could be connected with the 'Cargo Cult' phenomenon, a millenarist movement which has appeared sporadically in several parts of the Pacific. However, in his book *The trumpet shall sound*, Peter Worsley says that though comparable myths relating to a second coming of the Messiah have occurred in a few places in northern Papua, the true Cargo Cult, involving flying machines, has not been noted in Papua except from small remote places in the northwest corner, on the border of the former German territory.

Thus the Cargo Cult is completely unknown in the areas where Cruttwell collected his many reports, and it is highly improbable that the observers in Papua were influenced by the cult's belief in supernatural flying machines. In any case, the UFOs are totally different in appearance from any existing stereotype.

NOT SECRET CRAFT

Many commentators have expressed surprise that Gill went in for dinner during the exciting observation of 27 June. During a visit to the United States in 1977 he was questioned on this point by Hynek and Hendry: he answered:

"We were a bit fed up that they wouldn't come down, after all the waving. The waving was not an unusual thing to happen; it's the same sort of procedure that would go on, including signalling with the flashlight, if a vessel arrived. There was no difference. It got so large and close that we were trying to beckon it to land on the playing field. We expected the four occupants, probably dressed in army or navy uniforms, to come in. It all seemed so perfectly ordinary and natural; there was nothing spooky or 'flying saucerish' about it.

This is the difficult thing to get across to people... 'Here was a flying saucer; therefore, it must have been a traumatic experience.' It was nothing of the kind."

He also told Hynek that at the time he had supposed the objects to be new American aircraft.

The Department of Air, Commonwealth of Australia, know of no such craft, as appears in a letter addressed to a colleague:

" Canberra Act
28 january 1970

Dear Sir,
I refer to your letter dated 12 November 1969 concerning an unusual aerial sighting at Boainai, in Papua, New Guinea. The RAAF could come to no definite conclusion on the report, and enquiries with the United Kingdom and the United States could add no clues or answers. As a result these sightings have been classified as aerial phenomenon, but most probably they were reflections on a cloud of a major light source of unknown origin.
Yours faithfully"

What did Father Gill and so many other witnesses actually see? There seem to be only two possibilities: either they saw Venus and stars, distorted in size and shape by extraordinary atmospheric conditions, and imagined the rest of the detail; or they did indeed see UFOs as they described them.

REFERENCES

■ **1**- *Flying Saucer Review*, special issue no 4, 1971 ■ **2**- **Hynek,** J Allen, *The Hynek UFO report*, 1977; *UFO-Dokumenteret*, SUFOI, 1974 ■ **3** - *International UFO Reporter*, nos 11-12. 1977 ■ **4** - **Klass,** Philip J, *UFOs explained*, 1974 ■ **5** - **Knight,** David C, *UFOs, a pictorial history*, 1979 ■ **6** - **Menzel,** Donald ■ **7** - **Pedersen,** F, & Kjems, O, *UFO-Orientering*, SUFOI, 1969 ■ **8**- **Sagan,** Carl & **Page,** Thornton (eds) *UFOs, a scientific debate*, Cornell, 1972 ■ **9** - **Story,** Ronald D (ed) *The encyclopedia of UFOs*, 1980.

5: SOCORRO - 24 APRIL 1964

At 5.45 pm on 24 April 1964, police officer Lonnie Zamora observed an egg-shaped craft outside the town of Socorro, New Mexico. By the side of the craft two little beings in white suits were standing. It was a close encounter of the third kind which, even after thorough investigation, the U.S. Air Force has been unable to explain.

The tale of the Landing at Socorro has been told and retold time and time again, and with each retelling it becomes more and more sensational - even in the writings of respected researchers. Lonnie Zamora himself has embellished his own story since his first interviews in 1964 - but who wouldn't, when assailed by countless amateur enthusiasts bombarding him with leading questions about spaceships, radio black-outs, beep-beep sounds, "fizzing" rock at the landing site and much more of the same kind?

Zamora was interviewed only a few hours after the incident by FBI agent J Arthur Byrnes Jr, who chanced to be visting Socorro that day on other business. Together, Zamora and Byrnes drew up a detailed report which Zamora signed at 1 am on 25 April. Byrnes is a very experienced interviewer, and since the report was written while Zamora still had a vivid recollection of the incident, this first deposition is of the greatest interest.

ZAMORA'S UFO-REPORT

Policeman Lonnie Zamora, 30 years-old, tells:

"About 5:45 P.M., April 24, 1964, while in Socorro Two police car, I started to chase a car due south from west side of the courthouse. Car was apparently speeding and was about three blocks in front. At point on Old Rodeo Street, near George Murillo residence, the chased car was going ahead towards the rodeo grounds. Car chased was a new black Chevrolet...

At this time I heard a roar and saw a flame in the sky to the southwest some distance away - possibly one-half mile or a mile. Came to mind that a dynamite shack in that area had blown up, decided to leave chased car go. Flame was bluish and sort of orange, too. Could not tell size of flame. Sort of motionless flame. Slowly descending. Was still driving car and could not pay too much attention to the flame. It was a narrow type of flame. It was like a "streamed down" - a funnel type - narrower at the top than at bottom. Flame possibly three degrees or so in width - not wide.

Flame was about twice as wide at bottom than top, and about four times as high as top was wide. Did not notice any object at top, did not notice if top of flame was level. Sun was to west and did not help glasses. Could not see bottom of flame because it was behind the hill.

No smoke noted. Noted some "commotion" at bottom - dust? Possibly from windy day - wind was blowing hard. Clear, sunny sky otherwise - just a few clouds scattered over area.

Noise was a roar, not a blast. Not like a jet. Changed from high frequency to low frequency and then stopped. Roar lasted possibly ten seconds, I was going towards it at the time on a rough gravel road. Saw flames same color as best I recall. Sound distinctly from high to low until disappeared. Windows both were down. No other spectators noted - no traffic except the car in front. Car in front might have heard it but possibly did not see it because car in front was too close to hill in front to see flame.

After the roar and flame, did not note anything while going up the somewhat steep, rough hill - had to back up and try again, two more times. Got up about halfway first time, wheels started skidding (roar still going on), had to back down and try again before made the hill. Hill about sixty feet long, fairly steep and with loose gravel and rock. While beginning third time, noise and flame not noted.

After got to top, traveled slowly on the gravel road westwardly. Noted nothing for a while - for possibly ten or fifteen seconds. Went slow, looking around for the shack - did not recall exactly where the dynamite shack was.

Suddenly noted a shiny type object to south about one hundred fifty to two hundred yards. It was off the road. My green sunglasses over prescription. At first glance, stopped. It looked at first like a car turned upside down. Thought some kids might have turned it over. Saw two people in white coveralls very close to object. One of these persons seemed to turn and look straight at my car and seemed startled - seemed to quickly jump somewhat.

At this time I began moving my car towards them quickly with the idea to help. Had stopped only about a couple of seconds. Objects were like aluminium - was whitish against the mesa background, not chrome. Seemed like oval in shape and I, at first glance, took it to be an overturned white car. Car appeared turned up like standing on radiator or trunk, at this first glance.

The only time I saw these two persons was when I had stopped for possibly two seconds or so, to glance at the object. I don't recall noting any particular shape or possibly any hats or headgear. Those persons appeared normal in shape - but possibly they were small adults or large kids. Then paid attention to road while driving. Radioed to sheriff's office, "Socorro Two to Socorro. Possible 10-40 [accident]. I'll be 10-6 [busy]." Out of car, checking the car down in the arroyo.

Stopped car, was still talking on radio, started to get out; mike fell down, reached back to pick up mike then replaced mike in slot and got out of car. Hardly turned around from car when heard roar (was not exactly a blast), very loud roar - at that close, it was real loud. Not like a jet - know what jets sound like. Started low frequency quickly, then rose in frequency (towards higher tone) and in loudness - loud to very loud. At same time as roar, saw flame. Flame was under the object. Object was starting to go straight up - slowly up. Object slowly rose straight up. Flame was light blue, and at bottom was sort of orange-colored. From this angle, saw what might be the side of object (not end as first noted). Difficult to describe flame. Thought, from roar, it might blow up. Flame might have come from underside of object, at middle, possibly a four feet area - very rough guess. Cannot describe flames further except blue and orange. No smoke except dust in immediate area.

Object was oval in shape. It was smooth - no windows or doors. As roar started, it was still on or near the ground. Noted red lettering of some type. Insignia about two and a half feet wide, guess. Was in middle of object like drawing. Object still like aluminium - white.

Can't tell how long saw object second time (the "close" time). [Zamora was at this time seventy-five to one hundred feet from the object itself.] Possibly seconds - just guess - from time got out of car, glanced at object, jumped over edge of hill, then got back to car and radioed as object disappeared.

As my mike fell as I got out of the car, at scene area, I heard about two or three loud thumps, like someone hammering or shutting a door hard. These thumps were possibly a second or less apart. This was just before the roar. The persons were not seen when I got up to the scene area.

As soon as saw flames and heard roar, turned away, ran from object but did turn head towards object. Bumped leg on car, back fender area. Car facing southwest.

After fell by car and glasses fell off, kept running towards north with car between me and the object (for protection in case object exploded). Glanced back a couple of times. Noticed that subject arose to about level of car, about twenty to twenty-five feet (guess). (Car was appreciably above object which was in a gully.) Took, I guess, about six seconds from when object started to rise and I glanced back. I guess I ran about halfway to where I ducked down, just over edge of hill. I guess I had run about twenty-five feet when I glanced back and saw the object about level with the car and it appeared directly over the place where it rose from.

I was still running and I ducked just over the hill - I stopped because I did not hear the roar. I was scared of the roar, I had planned to continue running down the hill. I turned around towards the ground, covering my face with my arms. Being that there was no roar, I looked up, and I saw the object going away from me in a southwest direction. When the roar stopped, heard nothing. It appeared to go at the same height and in a straight line, possibly ten to fifteen feet from the ground, and it cleared the dynamite shack by about three feet. The shack was about eight feet high. Object was traveling very fast. It seemed to rise up and take off immediately cross-country. I ran back to my car and as I ran back, I kept an eye on the object. I picked up my glasses (I left the sunglasses on the ground), got into the car, and radioed to Ned Lopez, the radio operator to "look out of the window to see if you can see an object." He asked, "What is it?" I answered, "It looks like a balloon." I don't know if he saw it. If Ned looked out of his window which faces north, he couldn't have seen it. I did not tell him at the moment which window to look out.

As I was calling Ned, I could still see the object. The object seemed to lift up slowly and to get small in the distance very fast. It seemed to just clear Box Canyon or Six Mile Canyon Mountain. It disappeared as it went over the mountains. It had no flame whatsoever as it was traveling over the ground and made no smoke or noise.

Just before Sergeant Chavez got to the scene, I got my pencil and drew a picture of the insignia..."

THE INVESTIGATION

Deputy James Lucky, who heard the conversation between Zamora and Chavez on the radio, went at once to join the two policemen at the site. Shortly after, Byrnes also arrived: he was at Chavez' office working on another case, and when he heard Zamora calling the station he too came along, out of pure curiosity.

Later Byrnes called Capt Richard Holder, in charge of the tracking station at the Army's White Sand missile base, located to the south of Socorro.

LANDING MARKS AND FOOTPRINTS

At the observation site, four impressions were clearly seen in the soft sand, and in several places between the imprints the brush was burned.

The imprints had an irregular shape and may best be described as flat-bottomed V-shaped grooves, between 30-60 cm long and 2-5 cm deep. Little stones were placed round them as a protection and next morning they were photographed by Chavez. The prints were arranged in such a way that they made an asymmetrical diamond pattern; this agreed with Zamora's account, and they were consequently referred to as "landing marks".

Close to one of the landing marks were five other marks, thinner, more irregular and less well defined. Since they too seemed to correlate with Zamora's testimony, they were referred to as "footprints".

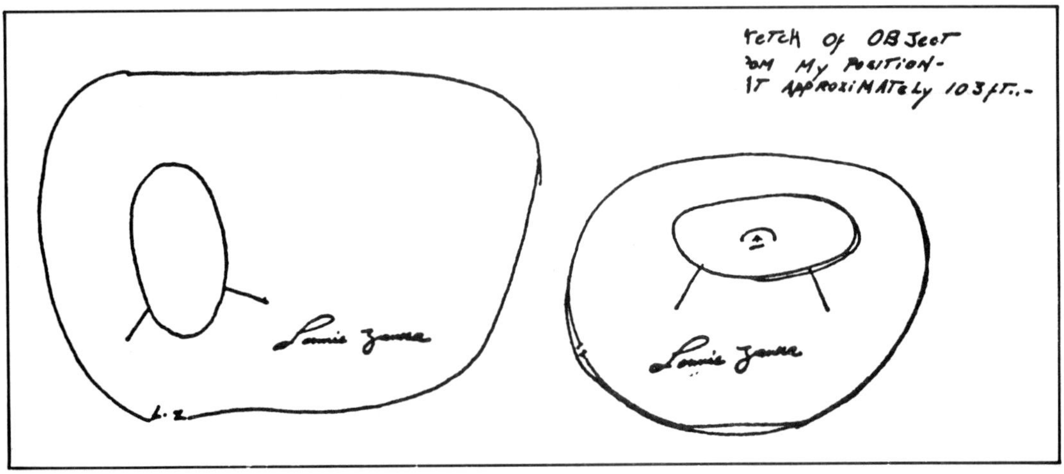

Zamora's sketches from 250 and 30 metres respectively.

TOP SECRET WEAPON?

On 28 April - that is, four days after the incident - Dr Hynek, then associated with the Air Force's Project Blue Book, came to investigate. Since the technical aspects of measurement and photography of the traces had been taken care of, he concentrated on the human aspects of the case; on this and later occasions he probed the character and mutual relations of those involved as thoroughly as he was able.

Hynek's efforts to fault Zamora's testimony by looking for mutual contradictions were fruitless. Zamora seemed to be a reliable and much-liked man with "both feet on the ground", and Hynek considered it most unlikely that Zamora would participate in a hoax. In his report to the Air Force he wrote:

"Any common object would certainly have been recognised. It would seem virtually incredible that an ordinary object, such as a balloon, helicopter, private small airplane &c could have remained unidentified (by Zamora) and, further, could have caused Zamora to become as frightened as he did."

His conclusion was that "Zamora saw a tangible, physical object... It appears essential that we discover what the physical object actually was", and recommended that "the object which produced this, if it was a new device under test or in manoeuvres, be brought to the same location and movies be taken of it departing in the manner described by Zamora."

The Air Force followed Hynek's advice in part, and even contacted every aircraft plant in the country to learn if they had developed any such craft on their own initiative without informing the authorities. Their search was fruitless, nor has any craft subsequently come to light which matches Zamora's description.

CIA INVOLVEMENT?

The CIA is often suspected of standing behind the scenes and pulling the wires of many events in recent history; the landing at Socorro was no exception. One ingenious American demonstrated that by a little manipulation of the lines of the red insignia observed on the object by Zamora, the letters 'CIA' are revealed! "Cut a heel and clip a toe, and the shoe will fit!"

OTHER WITNESSES

When Capt Holder returned to the police station together with the officers, Ned Lopez reported that he had received three telephone calls from persons who had seen a bluish flame in the area. Unfortunately he had not noted the names and addresses of the informants.

During one of his later visits, Hynek interviewed a Mr Grinder, who managed a gas station on Highway 85. Grinder reported that on the day of the sighting a motorist who had stopped at the gas station observed that planes flew awfully low in the area. Grinder replied that there were a lot of helicopters about, to which the motorist answered, "It was a funny-looking helicopter, if that's what it was." He had seen the object just south of the town; it was obviously in trouble and was landing. He said there must have been trouble because he had seen a police car (Zamora's) going out across the sandy terrain to where it was landing. Hynek tried to get the Air Force to seek the unknown witness through the intelligence services, but they showed absolutely no interest.

OBJECTIONS

Philip Klass, known to all readers of the UFO literature as a skeptic who has made persistent attempts to explain away classic sightings, offers two possible explanations for the Socorro incident, operating separately or together. The first explains it as a natural phenomenon, the second as a publicity stunt for the town of Socorro.

According to Klass, what Zamora saw was not a physical object but a plasma (an accumulation of ionised air) which either disengaged itself from the clouds over Socorro or was a corona discharge from the 115,000-volt power line running less than 2 km west of the site. This hypothesis supposes that the plasma travelled that distance (there was a strong wind blowing) and neatly positioned itself in the little ravine where Zamora saw it. The two landing legs were a couple of long branches from a nearby bush, and the "persons" were energy discharge from the plasma which Zamora, on account of the distance, identified as people. The 'landing traces" and burned brush were likewise caused by energy discharged by the plasma against the sandy soil.

Klass points out that a married couple, Mr and Mrs Felix Phillips, living some 300 m from the site, were at home at the time, and heard neither the roar nor the loud shrieking although all the windows in the house were open at the time. Klass therefore suggests that Zamora heard nothing, either when he saw the blue flame in the sky or when he watched the object take off and disappear; the ear-splitting noise which scared Zamora out of his wits was simply a product of his imagination.

It must be said that the plasma explanation is even more fanciful than Zamora's own account...

PUBLICITY TRICK?

In 1964 Socorro was a town of approx 7000 inhabitants. It is traversed by Highways 60 and 85. Income from travellers is slight - but if a spaceship from another planet should choose to land in the not too trackless terrain between the two highways, the site could become an attraction for the tourists who at present drive through the town without putting anything in its money-box...

Klass surmises that Zamora and his fellow officer, together with Mayor Bursom, invented the story; Zamora made the marks with a spade, and set the brush afire. The Mayor has an evident interest in boosting tourism: moreover, he is one of the town's bank managers, and owns part of the land where the UFO landed.

But would Zamora really have been willing to risk his good reputation and his career in a hoax whose chief beneficiary would be the Mayor? How long could such a secret be maintained? And how could such an explanation have eluded the official investigations?

UNIDENTIFIED

Major Hector Quintanilla, then head of Project Blue Book, said "We had soil samples tested at the Air Material Lab. The burned bushes were analysed for propellant residue. We measured the distance between the pod marks. There were even footprints left on the sand. My first reaction was that it was a lunar test module from NASA or the Air Force - that seemed the only logical explanation.

"This was probably the best documented case in the Air Force files and I've checked it out everywhere. All the way up to the top, even the White House Command Post... and nothing, nothing. I wish I could put my finger on it... although I'm not convinced that it was anything extraterrestrial."

The official report on the Zamora sighting concludes: "Initially believed to be observation of Lunar module type configuration. Effort to date cannot place vehicle at site. Case carried as UNIDENTIFIED pending additional data."

Finally, Hynek writes in *The Hynek UFO Report*: "Maybe there is a simple, natural explanation for the Socorro incident, but having made a complete study of the event I don't think so. It is my opinion that a real physical event occurred on the outskirts of Socorro that afternoon of April 24, 1964."

REFERENCE

■ 1 - *Project Blue Book*, file no 8766 ■ 2- **Hynek,** J Allen, *The UFO experience*, 1972: *The Hynek UFO report*, 1977 ■ 3 - **Emenegger,** Robert, *UFOs past, present & future*, 1974 ■ 4 - **Bowen,** Charles (ed) *The humanoids*, 1969 ■ 5 - **Klass,** Philip J, *UFOs identified*, 1968; *UFOs explained*, 1974 ■ 6 - **Knight,** David C, *UFOs, a pictoral history*, 1979.

6: VALENSOLE - 1 JULY 1965

On the morning of 1 July 1965, in his lavender field near Valensole in southern France, farmer Maurice Masse saw an egg-shaped object with six thin legs and a door. Two little beings standing beside the object were so alarmed that they immediately 'paralysed' him with a weapon-like device before hastily departing.

Masse was 41 years old, married with two children. He had left his house about 5 am and walked to the field, some 2 km northwest of Valensole, where he cultivated lavender which he then distilled for use in the perfume industry.

Before starting work he paused to smoke a cigarette in the shade of a small heap of stones, when he was puzzled by a strange sound, or rather whistling. He thought it must be a military helicopter, for he was used to them landing on his fields during their exercises. He would always chat with their pilots, particularly if they shared his interest in hunting. When he heard the strange sound, his first thought was, Well, he might have found some other place to land than in my lavender.

He walked round the mound and saw a 'machine' about 90 m away, which was not like a helicopter or any other aircraft known to him. It was shaped like a rugby football, with a cupola on top, and was about the size of a Dauphine car. It stood on six thin 'legs', and had a central support resembling a thick pipe.

Beside the object Masse saw two figures, who looked like boys about 8 years old, who were evidently examining the lavender plants. During the preceding weeks he and his father had frequently found their plants damaged, as though somebody had been breaking off the new shoots; thinking he had caught the vandals, he started walking cautiously towards them, skirting round an intervening vineyard, hoping to take them by surprise. However, in a later statement Masse said: 'From the moment I started out from the heap of stones, I knew that it wasn't with men that I had to deal.'

According to the statement he made later, offering to swear to it on oath to commandant Olivia, chief of police at Valensole, the two beings were dressed in grey-green one-piece suits like boiler suits. Their bald, bare heads were pumpkin-shaped, three times the regular human size, with high fleshy cheeks, big oblique eyes, a lipless mouth and a very pronounced chin. Their skin was white.

On the left side of their belts was a little cylinder or box, and another a little larger on the other side.

Masse was about 7 m away when the two beings noticed him and were at once alarmed. One of them took a little cylinder from his belt and aimed a beam at Masse, who was immediately rooted to the spot, unable to move. For a minute they looked at him while seemingly making comments on him with gurgling guttural sounds. Their look was in no way hostile. Masse didn't feel he was standing facing two monsters, and was not afraid even though he could not move. In his opinon their intentions were undoubtedly peaceful.

After about a minute the two beings returned with surprising agility to their craft, which they entered by a sliding door. After that the object again emitted a loud whistling, hovered a few metres over the ground while the six legs began rotating, and disappeared at incredible speed in a westerly direction at an angle of 45 degrees. After only 20 m flight the object disappeared into the blue air. 'One moment I could see it clearly, the next it was gone.'

He thought he would feel normal again as soon as the object and the beings had disappeared, but it took a quarter of an hour for the 'paralysis' to wear off. On the site where the object had been standing he found some impressions consisting of a great flat imprint just over 1 metre in diameter. In the centre of these prints, where the centre support had been, was a cylindrical hole about 30 cm deep and about 15 cm in diameter. From here four flat grooves radiated to make an x-shape. Each groove was 2 m long and 25 cm deep. Two of the six legs seemed to have left no imprint.

After release from his invisible chains, Masse gave up all thought of working that day and returned to Valensole, where he told his story to his friend M Moisson, proprietor of the Café des Sports. Moisson could see that Masse was shaken and did not doubt his story. Masse added that he had not told everything but would tell no more since probably no one would believe him. Moisson advised Masse to go to the police, but Masse, who had never had any trouble with the police and didn't want any, now said that actually it was all just a joke. But Moisson hurried to the field, saw the traces, and on his own initiative informed the police. Soon the press had got wind of the affair - and the avalanche started to roll.

PHYSICAL TRACES

In the evening Masse returned to the site together with his 18-year-old daughter. They inspected the traces and noted that the soil around the central imprint was as though petrified, hard as cement, whereas elsewhere the soil crumbled in the hand. Yet, according to Masse, immediately after the disappearance of the object the soil had been of a near-

Maurice Masse at his lavender field.

liquid consistency, though it hadn't rained for a long time.

The Valensole incident was very thoroughly investigated by the French UFO-organisation GEPA (Groupement d'Etudes des Phénomènes Aériens et Objets Spatiaux Insolites) in collaboration with Aimé Michel and two unnamed scientists who visited Valensole on several occasions, interviewing the witness, photographing the site and gathering information.

A chemical analysis of soil samples arranged by GEPA revealed nothing abnormal except an unusually high calcium content. However, shortly after the event, the lavender plants on the site began to die. The imprints also disappeared quickly beneath the trampling feet of the hordes of sightseers!

Finally Masse decided to fill up the deep central hole with earth, level the other imprints and plant new lavender bushes to discourage curious sightseers, but also to erase the memory of his alarming experience. The new plants died after a short time, whereas self-sown wheat from a nearby field established itself perfectly. Dr 'Jacques Lamaitre' (pseudonym of a well-known French physicist and consultant to GEPA) found the site still easily recognisable in March 1969, because wheat and grass were growing there instead of lavender.

Only a few weeks later a similar event occurred - but on another continent. On 19 July an unidentified object landed on the beach of Ciudad Colonio, Uruguay, near Buenos Aires, Argentina. Several witnesses saw the object take off and disappear, leaving impressions in the sand similar to those at Valensole.

In May 1967 French police investigated a pattern of imprints in a clover field near the village of Marliens. Though no object was seen in connection with the prints, they were regarded as UFO-related since no known object or phenomenon could have caused them. The Marliens impressions resembled those of Valensole. There were 6 grooves, covered with a kind of grey-violet dust, which analysis by the scientific faculty at Dijon revealed to be quartz crystals used in the smelting process. Chemical engineer F R de Brem put samples from both Marliens and Valensole through drying and humidity processes and showed that samples from the impression zone absorbed humidity 60% less rapidly than control samples from elsewhere in the field.

According to Masse, the object disappeared westwards towards the town of Manosque. When Michel visited Valensole five weeks after the incident, he learned that lavender plants along a 100 m long, 2-3 m wide strip in the direction of Manosque were damaged. On every plant one or more twigs were dried up as though they had been exposed to strong heat - something that only an expert would recognise. The gendarmes who arrived immediately after the incident had noticed nothing.

PHYSICAL AFTER-EFFECTS

For the first three days after the incident Masse had felt very well, but on the fourth day he suddenly collapsed, feeling a great need for sleep. Had his wife and father, in their concern, not wakened him, he would have slept the whole day and night. He would no longer talk, and continued sleepy. Michel noted that his hands were trembling. Before the incident he had slept 4-5 hours, now he slept 12-15.

During Michel's visit Masse was nervous and intense, and on two occasions distinctly distressed. Once when Michel moved his compass to and fro close to Masse's wristwatch, seeing the needle move, he cried, 'Then what about me? Haven't I too been touched by anything? By a ray?'

The second occasion was when, after obtaining Masse's own description, Michel showed him a picture of a model of the object seen by Zamora at Socorro, a year previously. Masse's reaction was fantastic: at first he thought someone had photographed 'his' craft, then, relieved, he said, 'You see then that I wasn't dreaming, and that I'm not mad.'

Michel visited Masse again, in the company of Charles Bowen, editor of *Flying Saucer Review*. They found Masse calm and relaxed. The following exchange took place:

Michel: I have always had the impression that you did not tell me everything.

Masse: That is true. I did not tell all. But I have already said too much. It would have been better if I had kept it all to myself.

Michel explained that what Masse had to tell would surely mean a lot to many people; **Masse** replied: Yes, it's very important, but I can't explain anything. All I could do would be to say things that would not be understood. You have to have undergone it to understand it.

Michel: How do you know that? Just try.

Masse: Monsieur, what I have not told you, I have not told anybody, not even my wife, and nobody will make me tell it. Do not insist on it, and let us say no more about it.

HELICOPTER WITH LITTLE PILOTS?

According to the newspaper *Le Dauphine Liberte*, the military authorities declared that a large-scale military exercise, code-name 'Provence 65', had been taking place in the Valensole area, and the object seen by Masse was probably a military helicopter - possibly of the Alouette 2 or 3 type. However, the imprints measured by the police are not consistent with the military hypothesis.

Danish folklorist Age Skjelborg offers an explanation which even he admits is somewhat far-fetched, but is nevertheless thought-provoking when taken in relation to other accounts of ufonauts.

In 1954 there was a massive wave of ufonaut reports throughout France and northern Italy. The

Valensole account was similar in several respects to the North Italian reports, where the ufonauts used 'paralysing nozzles', spoke with a 'gurgling guttural sound' and had a grey or greenish colour of the skin or dressed in a tight-fitting 'boiler suit'. Skjelborg suggests that Masse may have unconsciously received the inspiration for his account from such stories told by seasonal workers from Italy. According to him, Masse's experience was not physical but purely visual, a kind of waking dream such as may occur as the result of stress, when floating images and dreams are seen before falling into true sleep.

The 'waking dream' hypothesis explains, among other things, the sudden and inexplicable disappearance of the object, and the resemblance of the beings he described to those seen by tired motorists on empty highways - beings with big heads and rumbling voices.

What causes this waking dream? Masse, like other farmers on the Valensole plateau, may have felt his livelihood threatened by a government which had a plan (never put into action) to restructure cultivation patterns in the area through canal construction and the introduction of new technology. Skjelborg suggests that this latent fear, combined with the attack on his plants, may have triggered the experience.

As for the incident with the 'paralysing' gun, this may be a repressed memory of a war incident dating from Masse's experience in the resistance movement.

Ingenious as it is, Skjelborg's hypothesis fails to take into account the physical traces.

ASTRONOMERS SAW A UFO

Unexpected confirmation may be given by other incidents occurring in the neighbourhood of Valensole. About 3 months later, at 3 am in the night of 17-18 September, three astronomers at the Saint Michel Observatory, some 25 km from Masse's field, saw a huge, egg-shaped orange-red light. They saw it over a period of 10-15 minutes from the main dome, placed high, south of the observatory. The light came either directly from an unoccupied house near the landing site, or very close to it. Aime Michel confirmed that from the landing site one can see sunlight reflecting on the observatory dome.

Perhaps we today would know a lot more about the Valensole incident if on 1 July an astronomer at the Saint Michel observatory had been standing with binoculars in his hands looking over the Valensole plateau.

REFERENCES

1 - *UFO-NYT* 1967/1 and 4, 1968/1 and 3 ■ **2** - *Phenomenes Spatiaux*, Sept 1966, Sept 1967 ■ **3** - *Flying Saucer Review*, vol 11 nos 5 & 6; vol 12 nos 2 & 3; vol 14 no 1; vol 15 nos 1 & 4 **4 Rehn,** K Gosta, *Nya fakta om de flygande tefaten: UFO* (Zindermans, 1969) ■ **5** - **Vallee,** Jacques, *Passport to Magonia*, (Regnery, 1969) ■ **6** - **Lob,** J, & **Gigi,** R, *OVNI, dimension autre*, (Dargaud, 1975) ■ **7** - **Skjelborg,** Age, *Pa sporet af UFOnauten*, (Berlingske, 1979).

7: EXETER, 3 SEPTEMBER 1965

In 1966 journalist John G Fuller investigated some strange reports from Exeter, New Hampshire. His articles and the subsequent book *Incident at Exeter*, which sold more than 500,000 copies, focused worldwide attention on events which even today are believed by many to defy explanation. The events became even more mysterious thanks to later tellings in which they were narrated with all kinds of inaccuracy and embellishment.

The most dramatic sighting in the Exeter wave of Fall 1965 occurred on 3 September. The witnesses were Norman Muscarello, 18, and police patrolmen Eugen Bertrand, 30, and David Hunt, 28. Muscarello's statement to Project Blue Book was as follows:

"I, Norman J. Muscarello, was hitchhiking on Rt. 150, three miles south of Exeter, New Hampshire, at 0200 hours on the 3rd of September. A group of five bright red lights appeared over a house about a hundred feet from where I was standing. The lights were in a line at about a sixty-degree angle. They were so bright, they lighted up the area. The lights then moved out over a large field and acted at times like a floating leaf. They would go down behind the trees, behind a house and then reappear. They always moved in the same sixty-degree angle. Only one light would be on at a time. They were pulsating: one, two, three, four, five, four, three, two, one. They were so bright I could not distinguish a form to the object. I watched these lights for about fifteen minutes and they finally disappeared behind some trees and seemed to go into a field. At one time while I was watching them, they seemed to come so close I jumped into a ditch to keep from being hit. After the lights went into a field, I caught a ride to the Exeter Police Station and reported what I had seen."

This was confirmed and added to by police patrolman Bertrand:

"I, Eugene F. Bertrand, Jr., was cruising on the morning of the 3rd of September at 0100 on Rt. 108 bypass near Exeter, New Hampshire. I noticed an automobile parked on the side of the road and stopped to investigate. I found a woman in the car who stated that she was too upset to drive. She stated that a light had been following her car and had stopped over her car. I stayed with her about fifteen minutes but was unable to see anything. I departed and reported back to Exeter Police Station where I found Norman Muscarello. He related his story of seeing some bright red lights in the field. After talking with him a while, I decided to take him back to where he stated that he had seen the lights. When we had gone about fifty feet, a group of five bright red lights came from behind a group of trees near us. They were extremely bright and flashed on one at a time. The lights started to move around over the field. At one time, they came so close I fell to the ground and started to draw my gun. The lights were so bright, I was unable to make out any form. There was no sound or vibration but the farm animals were upset in the area and were making a lot of noise. When the lights started coming near us again, Mr. Muscarello and I ran to the car. I radioed Patrolman David Hunt who arrived in a few minutes. He also observed the lights which were still over the field but not as close as before. The lights moved out across the field at an estimated altitude of one hundred feet, and finally disappeared in the distance at the same altitude. The lights were always in line at about a sixty-degree angle. When the object moved, the lower lights were always forward of the others."

Hunt received a call from Bertrand at 02.55 am, and drove to the site, where he too saw the lights; his description of them and their movements is in complete accord with the testimony of the others.

According to an observation report dated 15.9.1965 from Pease Air Force Base, which investigated the incident, the weather that night was clear with unlimited visibility. At Pease AFB a light westerly wind was recorded. Their report concluded:

"...at this time I have been unable to arrive at a probable cause of this sighting. The three observers seem to be stable, reliable persons, especially the two patrolmen. I viewed the area of the sighting and found nothing in the area that could be the probable cause. Pease AFB had five B-47 aircraft flying in the area during this period but I do not believe that they had any connection with this sighting."

Shortly after the Exeter lights had disappeared out of sight, the police duty officer that night, Reginald 'Scratch' Toland, received a phone call from a telephone operator in Exeter; she had just received a call from a hysterical man in a phone cabin who claimed that a flying saucer was flying right towards him. Suddenly the connection with the anonymous caller was interrupted; attempts to trace him were unsuccessful.

THE EXETER UFO PURSUED BY A JET-FIGHTER!

The well-known journalist John Fuller learnt of the case from NICAP and wrote an article on it for *The Saturday Review*. On the strength of this article, the publishing house of Putnams signed him up to write a book-length account.

Fuller stayed in Exeter for over a month and interviewed more than 60 persons who had seen inexplicable things in the sky - often near high-voltage power lines - during a period of several weeks in Fall 1965. He learnt that Muscarello had been so impressed by his experience that for three weeks after the sighting he and his mother would sit on a hillside watching and waiting: on one such evening they saw a UFO again. Other people drove out in the evening and parked near power lines hoping to see the celebrated UFO. Fuller took part in one of these excursions, and claims he too saw a high-flying orange-red disc followed by a jet-fighter!

Some other reports are worth mentioning:

- Mrs Jalbert and her four teenage sons claimed they repeatedly observed a glittering silvery object hovering over power lines near their home. On it were lights flashing in many colours, so bright that it was possible to read a book by them. They also reported that when an object appeared, a plane would now and then appear and 'pursue' it.
- Two young people at Hampton Beach told how they had seen an object appear from the sea; it followed their car at a very low altitude despite their attempts to shake it off.
- A Mrs Blodgett told of a 'bright and blinding' ball of light she had seen at a distance of only 30 m. It hovered over the treetops rotating at a very high speed.

OFFICIAL STATEMENTS

On 27.10.1967 the Pentagon issued a press release which was published in many newspapers.

"The Pentagon believes that, after intensive investigation, it has come up with a natural explanation of the UFO sightings in Exeter, New Hampshire, on September 3.

A spokesman said the several reports stemmed from 'multiple objects in the area,' by which they mean a high-altitude Strategic Air Command exercise out of Westover Mass., was going on at the time in the area.

A second important factor was what is called a 'weather inversion' wherein a layer of cold air is trapped between warm layers.

The Pentagon spokesman said this natural phenomena causes stars and planets to dance and twinkle.

The spokesman said 'We believe what the people saw that night was stars and planets in unusual formations'."

This inaccurate version, purporting to give an official and conclusive explanation, was received in astonishment and skepticism, and not only by the people of Exeter. An even greater surprise came about a month later, when police officers Bertrand

and Hunt received an undated letter from Major Hector Quintanilla, then head of Project Blue Book:

"GENTLEMEN,
The sighting of various unidentified objects by you and Mr. Norman Muscarello was investigated by officials from Pease Air Force Base, New Hampshire, and their report has been forwarded to our office at Wright-Patterson Air Force Base. This sighting at Exeter, New Hampshire, on the night of 2 September has been given considerable publicity through various news releases and in magazine articles similar to that from the 'Saturday Review' of 2 October, 1965. A portion of this article is attached for your information. This information was released by the National Investigations Committee on Aerial Phenomena, a private organization which has no connection with the government. As a result of these articles, the Air Force has received inquiry as to the cause of this report.

Our investigation and evaluation of the sighting indicates a possible association with an 8th Air Force Operation, 'Big Blast'. In addition to aircraft from this operation, there were five B-47 type aircraft flying in the area during this period. Before a final evaluation of your sighting can be made, it is essential for us to know if either of you witnessed any aircraft in the area during this time period either independently or in connection with the objects observed. Since there were many aircraft in the area, at that time, and there were no reports of unidentified objects from personnel engaged in this air operation, we might then assume that the objects observed between midnight and 2 A.M. might be associated with this military air operation. If, however, these aircraft were noted by either of you, then this would tend to eliminate this air operation as a plausible explanation for the objects observed.

Sincerely
HECTOR QUINTANILLA, JR., Major, USAF
Chief, Project Blue Book
1 atch.
Article 'Saturday Review'."

Not only did this letter lack a date and a postmark, but it contained glaring errors: both the date and the

Muscarello with polices officers Hunt, Bertrand and (seated) Toland. [*Manchester Union Leader*]

time of the observation are wrong! However, the most remarkable item is Quintanilla's indication that he did not consider the case closed, though a month earlier the Pentagon had published the 'final conclusion'.

These were among the points mentioned by Bertrand and Hunt in their reply to Quintanilla. They added that Bertrand had spent four years in the Air Force, servicing different types of aircraft, and was familiar with them and their flight characteristics. They said that immediately after the object had disappeared they had seen something like a B-47 at high altitude, and that this had in no way resembled the UFO.

Bertrand and Hunt received no answer to this letter, and it was not until Fuller, in the course of his research, wrote to Air Force HQ in the Pentagon, and published his article 'Outer space ghost story' in *Look*, that the Air Force reacted. On 9.2.1966 Lieut Col John P Spaulding wrote to Bertrand and Hunt: 'Based on additional information you submitted to our UFO investigation office at Wright-Patterson Air Force Base, Ohio, we have been unable to identify the object you observed on September 3, 1965.'

A CRITICAL VIEW OF THE EXETER UFO

The great number of observations reported by Fuller in *Incident at Exeter* are impressive at first sight, but closer reading reveals their unsatisfactory nature. Fuller's primary interest was in the feelings and reactions of the witnesses: many of the accounts lack such elementary data as date and time. Direction is precisely indicated in only a very few cases.

UFO-skeptic Robert Sheaffer made a closer examination of those cases in which direction *is* indicated, and found that in every one the object appeared from the direction of the sea and followed the time schedule for the planet Jupiter! This emerges very clearly when the sightings are plotted into a graph alongside the appearance of Jupiter. Other sightings, Sheaffer claimed, would fit the positions of Venus and Saturn.

Sheaffer is of course aware that planets are not able to execute the manoeuvres which the Exeter UFO is reported as performing, but as Jenny Randles clearly demonstrated in her classic exposition 'Close Encounter with the Moon', witnesses are quite capable of ascribing - in all sincerity - complex manoeuvres to objects which on investigation are unambiguously shown to have been natural phenomena. Atmospheric anomalies coupled with the human imagination are responsible.

Other skeptics have also sought to de-mystify the Exeter case. Menzel, for one, considered that mass hysteria played a conclusive role in creating the wave.

The fact that many of the shining objects were seen in the vicinity of high-voltage lines suggested to Philip Klass an example of the plasma thesis he had presented in his *UFOs identified*. He proposed that the objects were corona discharges luminescent ionised air containing electrical particles - which are known to manifest along high-voltage lines under appropriate weather conditions. According to Klass, the weather conditions at the time were perfect for such a phenomenon, just as the colour of the UFOs matched that most frequently reported for ball lightning.

The sightings at Exeter are in many ways similar to the phenomena at Hessdalen in Norway [see case 13 below], and perhaps are not as mysterious as seem to be suggested by the more dramatic accounts, starting with those narrated by Fuller in his journalistic report. But whether or not there is a natural explanation for the sightings, the three principal witnesses remain to this day convinced they saw something inexplicable.

In 1980 a group of journalism students from Exeter High School re-opened the case. They located Muscarello, the police patrolmen and others who had been involved. Not only did they collect information relating to the sightings, but they noted the reaction and attitude of the witnesses to what happened more than 20 years ago. Officer Hunt told the students: 'It's just a thing that happened and we reported it the way it happened at the time, which you know is about all you can do, I guess.'

REFERENCES

1 - **Fuller,** John G, *Incident at Exeter,* 1967 ■ 2 - *LOOK* Flying Saucer Special, 1967 ■ 3 - *The TRUE report on Flying Saucers,* no 1, 1967 ■ 4 - **Klass,** Philip J, *UFOs identified,* 1968 ■ 5 - **Jacobs,** David M, *The UFO controversy in America,* 1975 ■ 6 - **Hynek,** J Allen, *The Hynek UFO Report,* 1978 ■ 7 - **Sachs,** Margaret, *The UFO Encyclopedia,* 1980 ■ 8 - **Sheaffer,** Robert, *The UFO verdict,* 1981 ■ 9 - *International UFO Reporter,* Vol 8 no 5, Sept/Oct 1983.

8: THE MAARUP SIGHTINGS OF 13 AUGUST 1970 and 14 AUGUST 1973

The 1970 sighting by police officer Evald Hansen Maarup near Hadersley, Denmark, during which he was able to take three photographs of the object, was widely reported in the Danish press and in the journals of foreign UFO organisations. His second sighting, almost precisely three years later, is less known but is of interest in view of its almost exact duplication of the earlier incident.

THE 1970 SIGHTING

At 10.50 pm on Thursday 13 August Maarup was driving home in his police car, and had just turned east off the main road onto a secondary road. 'I had been driving about 10 km when suddenly the car was surrounded by a bright bluish-white light, and at the same time the car engine stopped. The lights of the car also went out, even the dashboard lights. I drove to the side of the road and stopped. The bright neon-like light outside was so dazzling that I could see nothing. With my arm shielding my eyes - to protect them against the light - I succeeded in groping my way to the radio. When I got the microphone and tried to call the station, it appeared that the radio was just as dead as any of the other electrical parts of the car.

The temperature inside the car was increasing and it became pleasantly hot. How hot I cannot tell, but it could be compared to the heat you feel when you drive against the sun on a summer day. After a while the light was rising. It was a conical light with a diameter at the bottom of about 4-5 metres. When I was bending forward and looking up I could see that the light cone ended at the bottom of the big grey thing. Not a sound was heard.

After a few seconds the light was 'drawn' into the thing. It is difficult to explain how: the light was not extinguished, but the bottom of the light was rising so that it became dark beneath the cone. It took about 5 minutes for the light to be drawn up. I stepped out of the car and saw how the last remnant of the light cone disappeared into the bottom of the thing in a hole with a diameter of almost a metre.

When the light had disappeared into the thing, this started moving. In a few seconds it vanished vertically into the air. It accelerated swiftly - still without sound. When the object moved away, all lights in the car's system returned. It started quite normally, and I was able to get in touch with the station. I reported to them what I had experienced.

Before I stepped out of the car I had taken three pictures with the fastened camera of the patrol car. Now I took three more photographs of the highway, which was lit up by my headlights.' (The automatic-focus FUJAXA camera has automatic wind-on and can take about one picture per second; it was loaded with Neopan SS film.)

Having talked to the station I once more stepped out of the car to see if there was any residue or evidence left by the thing in the area around the car, but I found nothing. While I was collecting myself a little, I laid my hand on the front mudguard and could feel that it was still hot.

If I should describe the thing, I can only say that it was circular and about 10 m in diameter seen from my position below it. It had a luminous hole in the bottom from which the cone of light erupted. This hole was about 1 metre wide, consequently about 1/10 of the total diameter. The object had two extensions or domes on the underside, about 1.5 m in

An impression of Maarup's experience. [Henrik Pedersen / *UFO-Nyt*]

diameter. When I saw the thing through the windshield I will estimate it was about 20 m from me.'

When he reported back by radio to the police station, some wag replied, 'Should we come with a red hospital-admission note?' - the kind used when committing someone to mental hospital. This was the only occasion when Maarup was not taken seriously. When journalists questioned his colleagues on the force, all without exception said they believed his story.

When Maarup arrived home, his wife thought he looked pale, so he told her of his experience though he had no intention of making it public. Next day, when his film had been developed and he saw that he had captured an image, he took it to Skrydstrup Air Force base.

One of his colleagues - the one who had made the joke about the red note - informed the press, otherwise the story might not have got out. By the following evening he was being questioned both by the military and by journalists not only from Denmark but the world over, even from Ghana!

INVESTIGATIONS

As soon as Maarup's film was received at Skrydstrup AFB on the Friday evening, analysis began, and on Saturday a statement to the press said that the preliminary study indicated a spot of light in the first three pictures, while three more showed the road with the crash fence illuminated by headlights. There was no doubt they were consistent with Maarup's account.

On Sunday it was announced that the photographs had been passed to Defence Command at Vedbaek, who were questioning radar operators and pilots who might have been on duty on the Thursday evening. That evening, Maarup heard the television news report that, according to Major Hellden of Flyvertaktisk Kommando (= Air Tactical Command), what Maarup had seen was *the landing light of a T-33 jet trainer.*

On this Maarup commented that 10 minutes after the sighting he had indeed seen an aircraft, and he could not have mistaken one for the other: the plane's light was nothing like what he had photographed. And indeed Major Hellden was himself displeased that the TV news had taken his explanation so literally. 'I merely told them about the theoretical possibilities, nothing concrete. It is conceivable that the police officer might have seen the exhaust of a jet aircraft or an aeroplane's anti-collision light, which might look more intense in a layer of clouds.'

The following day Major Brons-Hansen, press officer of the Air Force, stated: 'The Air Force does not recognise the existence of unidentified flying objects. But on the other hand it cannot be denied that over the years we have received a number of observation reports in which we were not able to say what was seen. We have the greatest confidence in the police officer. He is a trained observer, and we do not seek in any way to dismiss this kind of observation. We look for an explanation, and already we can say for sure that no Air Force aircraft was responsible.'

Six pilots on the day of the sighting had flown over the location in T-33 trainers. None had seen or done anything unusual, though one recalled seeing a comet or shooting star, but could not specify the time and place. The landing lights can be switched on only when the aircraft were flying with their undercarriage down, so, normally, only when landing; on that Thursday evening landing approaches were being made from quite a different direction, so if there was an aircraft in Maarup's vicinity with its landing light accidentally switched on, it must have been after take-off rather than landing. This would mean it would be very noisy, whereas Maarup had heard no sound.

Having rejected the aircraft hypothesis, the Air Force considered alternative natural explanations. A series of coincidences was proposed, involving a light reflected in a window and distorted by the hazy atmospheric conditions, or a static electricity phenomenon.

The newspapers were full of accounts from other people who claimed to have seen something remarkable on the night of 13 August. Many had seen a very bright comet or shooting star at the same time as Maarup's sighting - some accounts suggested it was 3 to 6 times as bright as such phenomena normally are, with a long tail. The Air Force's last suggestion was that this was the basis of Maarup's observation.

The Air Force investigation was finally closed on 6 November, in inconclusive fashion. Though it accepted that the light which Maarup photographed did not originate from his car, and though it could not explain what it was, it was confident it had nothing to do with UFOs! Rather, a series of independent natural events had accidentally coincided. Questioned by SUFOI in 1972, the Air Force suggested that the power failure had been caused by a periodic or temporary technical failure, such as a slack cable terminal; though, because no such suggestion was made at the time, the car was not investigated for such damage.

The Air Force did not specify what it meant by a series of independent events accidentally coinciding, but by studying their reports and press releases, one can reconstruct the following scenario:

Police Officer Maarup comes driving in his new patrol car. Suddenly the car is flooded by glaring light coming from an unusually bright comet; or alternatively from a T-33 jet trainer from Skrydstrup AFB. These normally fly at 2000 m minimum altitude, so either the landing or anti-collision light is extremely powerful, or the pilot has come down to a very low altitude in silence. Simultaneously the accumulator terminal cable in Maarup's car falls off, and power disappears. The jet plane hovers silently over the car for nearly two minutes with the full blaze of its light, then vanishes, at which point Maarup perhaps see another shooting star or something of the sort. The cable then jumps back into place and he is able to drive home.

The contradictions and illogicalities of the Air Force investigation as reported by the press gave many people the idea that they were trying to mislead the public or to ridicule Maarup. The cover-up myth was fuelled when a newspaper reported that about a month after the sighting, a young woman told a UFO meeting that her husband, an Air Force radar operator, had been on duty the night of the sighting, and that a UFO had been tracked that night over a very long period.

Nothing more is known of this claim; but SUFOI's investigation leads to the conclusion that the Air Force was telling all it knew and honestly seeking an explanation. Their final report shows that they failed to do so: yet though the object photographed by Maarup remains unidentified, the Air Force will not describe it as an unidentified flying object - doubtless because, for them, UFO is synonymous with alien spaceship!

So far as SUFOI is concerned, however, the Maarup case remains unsolved.

THE SECOND SIGHTING

'One thing my sighting taught me; to keep my mouth shut. No way would I want to go through that 'brainwashing' again. Can you imagine what it's like, telling the same story over and over again, answering questions from journalists and military investigators who then change your story to suit their book. In addition I've had letters from most parts of the world, with religious fanatics wanting me to send them an account of my story...'

But in 1974 Maarup did admit to a second inexplicable experience, and once again he was able to secure a series of photographs. Here is his account:

'On Tuesday 14 August 1973, at about 10.50 pm, I was driving in a patrol car. About 6 km north of Haderley I turned east along a secondary road, and soon afterwards became aware of an intense light over the field north of the road I was driving on. The light appeared from the air, lighting up a herd of cattle, and a couple of horses were rushing about bewildered in the beam. The light moved swiftly to the road where I was bringing my car to a stop: just as I stopped, my car was caught in the light and the car lights went out. The beam approached slanting from the north, after which the object tilted about 45 degrees and stayed in front of the car in this slanting position; then it returned to the horizontal, then tilted 45 degrees to the opposite side.

While the object was within range I took four photos with my automatic camera; unfortunately they show only a spot of light, but you can see how the object approaches from the left of the car, then rises to the right. When the object tilted, the outline and the lower surface of a huge object about 15 m in diameter, with three large domes protruding from the bottom, could be seen.

After the object had moved in front of the car and again tilted to the opposite side, the light beam swept over the field south of the road, but soon after it began to retract. As the object tilted I saw a low domed superstructure with windows all the way around. The windows were rectangular with rounded corners, as in a passenger plane. All of the windows were lit up, as if by daylight. The object was steel-grey in colour, but of a velvet-like texture.

After the object had retracted the beam, it climbed towards the east, appearing as a huge disc. It gave a whistling sound like a strong gust of wind in trees as it disappeared at enormous speed. The entire sighting had lasted about 5 minutes.

Apart from that, I can only refer to my previous experience, 3 years and 1 day earlier. To me the most important question still is, *Why?* I have no doubt of what I've seen, but why at almost exactly the same time? Why on no other day in the year, why in almost exactly the same place?'

REFERENCES

1 - *UFO-NYT* nr 5, 1970; no 6, 1974 ■ 2 - SUFOI Archives ■ 3 - *Flying Saucer Review Case Histories* no 1 ■ 4 - *APRO Bulletin* Jan-Feb 1971 ■ 5 - *Phenomenes Spatiaux* no 26.

9: IMJÄRVI, 7 JANUARY 1970

'I was standing completely still. Suddenly I felt as if somebody had seized my waist from behind and pulled me backwards. I think I took a step backwards, and in the same second I caught sight of the creature. It was standing in the middle of the light beam with a black box in its hands. Out of a round opening in the box there came a yellow light, which was pulsating...'

The time was 4.45 pm on Wednesday 7 January 1970, the place was Imjärvi, 15 km NW of Heinola in southern Finland. Woodman Aarno Heinonen, 36, and farmer Esko Viljo, 38, both active competition skiers, were out skiing. They came down from a little hill to a glade where they usually take a pause. It was sunset, and a few stars were visible in the unclouded sky. It was very cold (-17 Celsius) and windless.

They had been standing in the glade for about 5 minutes when they heard a buzzing sound, and caught sight of a very strong light moving through the sky. It approached from the north, made a wide sweep, and came at them from the south, descending as it came. The faint buzzing sound became louder. The light halted, and then they could see that a luminous red-grey mist was swirling round it. Puffs of smoke were thrown up from the top of the cloud.

The two men stood quite still staring into the air, saying nothing. The cloud was soon down as low as 15 m, and they could see what was inside it: a round object, flat at the bottom, metallic in appearance and about 3 m in diameter.

Heinonen's account, as reported by GICOFF (the Göteberg UFO information centre) runs: 'The round craft hovered awhile completely motionless above us while the buzzing sound could still be heard, quite low. Then the huge disc began to descend along with the red-grey fog which became more thin and transparent. It stopped at a height of 3-4 m, so near I could have touched it if I had reached with my ski-stick.

'The craft was completely round. When it came down obliquely towards us we saw it had a dome on the upper side. Along the lower edge was a kind of raised part on which were three spheres or domes spaced equidistantly. From the centre of the bottom projected a tube, approximately 25 cm in diameter, from which suddenly there came an intense beam of light.

'I don't think we said anything to each other at all. We were completely amazed. We saw the light move a couple of times before stopping and intensely illuminating a patch of snow about a metre in diameter, with round it a dark edge, almost coal-black and 1 cm wide.

'I was standing completely still. Suddenly I felt as if somebody had seized my waist from behind and pulled me backwards. I think I took a step backwards, and in the same second I caught sight of the creature. It was standing in the middle of the light beam with a black box in its hands. Out of a round opening in the box there came a yellow light, pulsating. The creature was about 90 cm tall, with very thin arms and legs. Its face was pale like wax. I didn't notice the eyes, but the nose was very strange. It was a hook rather than a nose. The ears were very small and narrowed towards the head. The creature wore some kind of overall in a light green material. On its feet were boots of a darker green colour, which stretched above the knees. There were also white gauntlets going up to the elbows, and the fingers were bent like claws around the black box.'

Viljo: 'The creature stood in the middle of the bright light and was luminous like phosphorus, but its face was very pale. Its shoulders were very thin and slanting, with thin arms like a child's. I did not think of the clothes, only noticing that they were greenish in colour. On its head was a conical helmet shining like metal. The creature was less than 1 m tall.'

Suddenly it turned and directed the opening of the box towards Heinonen: 'The pulsating light was very bright, almost blinding. It was very silent in the forest. Suddenly a red-grey mist came flowing down from the object and large sparks started to fly from the illuminated circle of snow. The sparks were like tapers, about 10 cm long, red, green and violet. They floated out in long curves, rather slowly; many of them hit me, but though I expected them to burn me, I did not feel anything.'

Viljo: 'The sparks were shining in several colours. It was very beautiful. At the same time the red mist became thicker and hid the creature. Suddenly it was so dense that I could not see Aarno even though I knew he was standing only a few metres away from me.'

Heinonen: 'I could only just see Esko. The mist was very thick and I could no longer see the creature.'

Viljo: 'I saw the being for perhaps 15-20 seconds, no longer. Suddenly the beam melted, flew up like a flickering flame, and was sucked into the gap in the craft. After that it was as if the fog curtain was torn to pieces. The air above us was empty! I don't think you can say we were afraid. We were laughing and talking about this light. But at the same time we felt a little uneasy.'

They stayed there for perhaps three minutes. Gradually Heinonen became aware of a numbness in his right side. When he stepped forward on his skis, his right leg wouldn't support him and he fell in the snow. 'My right leg had been nearest the light. The whole leg was stiff and aching. My foot was as if anaesthetised.'

Viljo: 'It was growing dark. I asked Aarno if we should be on our way. I thought he was joking when he sat down in the snow. But then I saw he couldn't get up though he tried over and over again.'

SYMPTOMS

Viljo had to half-carry, half-drag his friend to his home, some 3 km distant. 'When they got home,' said Heinonen's mother, 'it was dark outside. They knocked on the door, which they don't usually do. When I opened the door Aarno was outside leaning against Esko. I helped them in. Neither seemed frightened, but I could see Esko's face was red and swollen. We got Aarno over to a sofa.'

Heinonen: 'I felt ill. My back was aching and all my joints were painful. My head ached and after a while I had to vomit. When I went to pee the urine was nearly black, it was like pouring black coffee onto the snow. This continued for a couple of months.'

Viljo: 'I hurried to the nearest neighbour, who lived some 600 m away; he has a telephone. The first two doctors I called couldn't come, but Dr Kajanoja said he would meet us at Heinola clinic in an hour's time. The neighbour drove us there.'

To the doctor, Heinonen complained about his aching joints and his headache. The doctor prescribed sleeping pills, and next day sedatives, telling him the symptoms would be gone in 10 days. But they continued, and Heinonen was unable to work. In May he reported he was still ill, with pains in head and neck; the least effort tired him. The numbness in his right leg had gone, but he still had trouble with his balance. His memory was so bad that if he left home he had to say where he was going so that he could be picked up if he didn't return. A visit to the site of the incident made him feel worse. Several people who had visited the site, said Viljo, had felt sick for some days afterwards; he wondered if the place was infected in some way. He too suffered after-effects, including headaches and eye troubles.

Dr Pauli Kajanoja reports: 'I think the men have

An impression of the Imjärvi incident. [*UFO-Nyt*]

suffered a great shock. Viljo was very red in the face and seemed a little swollen. Both seemed absent-minded. They talked quickly and incoherently. I could not find anything clinically wrong with Heinonen. He did not feel well, but that could have been his stomach reacting to the shock. The symptoms he described are like those after being exposed to radioactivity. Unfortunately I had no instrument to measure that. As to the black urine, it seems inexplicable. Possibly it could have been blood in it, but this cannot go on for several months. If blood samples had been taken they might have revealed changes in his blood.

'Both men seemed sincere, and I don't think they had made the thing up. I'm sure they were in a state of shock when they came to me; something must have frightened them.'

A strange thing happened in June 1970 when the two witnesses revisited the site together with a Swedish journalist, a photographer and an interpreter; the hands of the three strangers suddenly became red, and Heinonen had to leave the site with a powerful headache.

CONFIRMATIONS

On the same day and at the same time as the skiers had their experience, two other people saw a bright light in the sky. A farmer's wife, Elna Siitari, in Paistjárvi, about 15 km from Imjärvi, was on her way to the cow-house when she saw a strange light in the direction of Imjärvi. In Paaso, 10 km north of Imjärvi, the son of a household had gone out for firewood when he observed a light phenomenon; it was then 4.45 pm.

STATEMENTS FROM EXPERTS

Matti Tuuri, professor in electro-physics at Helsinki University, was very interested in the incident: 'We can't exclude the possibility that the injuries could have been caused by electrical radiation. But both state that the light was blinding and white, so it can't have been ultraviolet radiation, which is always bluish. Besides, it does not penetrate clothing. If the radiation penetrated Heinonen's clothing, it must have been a short-wave radiation such as X-rays; an overdose of these would cause symptoms such as those he reported...

'There is much in electro-physics which has yet to be explored. One has only to mention ball lightning; we know it exists, but the physical laws defining its existence have yet to be established. According to the known laws of physics, ball lightning should blow up immediately - but it doesn't! The incident at Heinola seems likely to be an abnormal electrical phenomenon.'

The Institute for High Voltage Research at Uppsala University told GICOFF they did not think the phenomenon was related to any kind of atmospheric electricity.

Soil, vegetation and snow samples from the site were sent to Chalmers Institute of Technology for radiation tests, but revealed no more than normal background radiation.

SINCE 1970

To complicate a situation which already defies explanation, we have to consider Heinonen's claim that between the time of the incident and August 1972 he had no less than 23 further UFO sightings. As if that were not enough, he has become a contactee: on two occasions he met an 'extremely beautiful' spacewoman, after a loud female voice had directed him to a secluded rendezvous.

At the first encounter he also saw a man, standing about 60 m behind the woman. She was wearing a yellow trouser suit which rustled when she moved; she was 1.5 m tall, with shoulder-length hair and blue eyes - a description recalling Adamski's Venusian. She didn't walk like a human but 'floated' or 'hovered'. Though she looked about 20 she told him she was 180, as Menger's Venusian did. In her hand she held a silvery ball with three aerials pointing at Heinonen.

Fortunately she spoke Finnish, and began her conversation with "Hyvää päivää" (= How do you do?); she told him she came from a green and pleasant land. Three different species of humanoids had visited Imjärvi, she said, some smaller than her, some of her height (140 cm) and some about 2 m high. [Researchers looking for UFO/folklore connections will be reminded of Goldilocks' three bears? - Ed.] She said that the January incident had lasted 3 minutes, not just a few seconds as the two witnesses thought.

At their second meeting Heinonen again asked where she came from. She told him to hurry home and he would see the beautiful craft she had come in. And indeed when he got home he saw an object some 5-7 m in diameter in the sky.

On each occasion Heinonen spoke with the spacewoman for five minutes, but can recall surprisingly little of what was said. On another occasion both he and Viljo saw a being in Viljo's home: a being a little more than 1.5 m, wearing a grey suit with white stripes, suddenly stepped out of the wall and remained standing in the middle of the floor; the two men gaped at it for 30 seconds, after which it vanished.

Swedish ufologist Liljegren has drawn attention to the failure of Heinonen and Viljo to offer anything by way of concrete evidence. On one occasion Heinonen received a green pen from the space beings, but he lent it to a researcher and never saw it again: he was given a stone but made to throw it away; when he tried to photograph the spacewoman both she *and* his camera disappeared! Viljo too tried to take a photograph of a mysterious light, but the camera was knocked out of his hand and the film was burned to ashes. All in all, Liljegren concludes, their accounts are more likes sagas and myths than a logical contact attempt by an intergalactic civilisation.

Without question, these later accounts undermine the credibility of the witnesses and throw a dubious light on their original story. As in the Dewilde case in France, the Hill case in the United States, and many more, what seems at first to be an interesting and serious incident is made to seem doubtful by subsequent events.

Is it that the *real* UFO experience causes the witnesses to subsequently have *imaginary* experiences? Or was the first, like those that followed, the symptom of some psychic state, triggered by some unknown cause to bring about a UFO 'sighting'? (In this connection it is perhaps significant that, according to Anders Liljegren, this was not Heinonen's first UFO sighting; he had had one six years previously!)

Or is there yet a third explanation?

A CURIOUS POSTSCRIPT

In February 1969 a 16-year-old boy, Matti Kontulainen, had a strange experience only 100 m or so from the slope where Heinonen and Viljo had their encounter:

'It was a cloudy winter evening about 11 pm. I was skiing home through the forest after visiting a friend. It was dark but suddenly the forest was lit up by an intense light which rushed just above the treetops at so low an altitude that I threw myself down in the snow. It was like a huge welding flame, and it disappeared in no time. I have never seen such an intense light; it was like staring at the sun! It was coming from the south and heading north. I heard no sound, so I'm sure it wasn't an airplane.'

Matti Haapaniemi, 46, is a farmer in Imjarvi and a member of Heinola rural district council; his farm is only 1 km distant from Heinonen's home. He says: 'Many people in this neighbourhood have laughed at this story. But I don't think it's anything to joke about. I've known both Aarno and Esko since they were little boys. Both are quiet, rational fellows, and moreover they are abstainers. I'm sure their story is true!'

REFERENCES

1 - *UFO-NYT* no 5, 1970 ■ 2 - *Flying Saucer Review* vol 16 nos 3, 4 & 5; vol 26 nos 3 & 5 ■ 3 - *GICOFF Information* no 4, 1978 ■ 4 - Personal correspondence Ilkka Serra/Kim Moller Hansen, September 1985.

10: DELPHOS, 2 NOVEMBER 1971

'*Close encounters of the Second Kind bear a special importance, for when it is reported that a UFO left tangible evidence of its presence, here is clearly the area in which to begin digging for 'scientific paydirt'... It is in this category of UFO-reports that we find the real challenge to scientific inquiry.*'

J. Allen Hynek.

On 27 May 1973 *The National Enquirer* announced that a panel of UFO experts had decided that the Delphos case was 'a major scientific mystery - the most baffling case the panel encountered in a full year of investigation... The panel carefully investigated the possibility of a hoax, but are completely satisfied that the sighting was real.'

From more than 1000 entries, the panel had voted all but unanimously to award the $5000 prize for the UFO story 'that supplied the most scientifically valuable evidence' to farmer Durel Johnson, 54, who lived just outside the small Kansas town of Delphos. Since then the case has been a favourite for ufologists to produce when skeptics demand physical evidence for the existence of UFOs.

The incident occurred on 2 November 1971. Johnson and his wife had already gone into the house for supper; Ronnie, their 16-year-old son, was supposed to join them when he had finished feeding the sheep. When he didn't arrive his mother called him, but receiving no answer the parents got on with their meal without waiting for him.

At 7 pm they had just finished when Ronnie came running in to tell how, after hearing a rumbling sound, he had seen a bright mushroom-shaped object hovering about 60 cm above the ground, about 25 m away from him in a group of trees behind the farm. About 3 m in diameter, it glowed with intensely bright light, every colour of the rainbow, 'like the light of a welder's arc.' From its bottom a shaft of white light shone towards the ground. He was blinded and completely paralyzed by the object; after about five minutes it suddenly rose, headed towards the hog shed, 15 m away, and disappeared southwards towards Delphos. After about 15 minutes he could see and move again, and rushed indoors to tell his parents.

THE GLOWING IMPRESSION

At first his parents wouldn't believe him, but when eventually they went out with him, Durel Johnson states that they were in time to see the UFO moving southward among the trees near the road, only a few hundred metres away - close enough for Erma Johnson to describe it as looking 'like a giant washtub.'

They hurried to the site where Ronnie had seen it hovering; as they approached they saw a circle, a little under 3 m in diameter, which 'glowed in the dark. The soil was glowing a bright grey-white. Portions of the nearby trees glowed also.'

In such a situation most people would have kept their distance in case of dangerous radiation. But the Johnsons not only approached the glowing ring but stooped to touch the white powdery substance on the ground, which seemed not to be warm. Later Mrs Johnson declared she had a feeling of numbness in her fingertips and so rubbed them against her legs to get rid of the stuff, with the result that her legs became numb too. Mr Johnson said that his fingers, too, were briefly numbed, whereas Mrs Johnson's numbness persisted for nearly two weeks, so as to prevent her taking the pulse of patients in the rest home where she worked; oddly, though, she didn't consult a doctor about it.

Ronnie said that after the sighting his eyes were bloodshot for several days, and later he got a headache.

After studying the shining ring Mrs Johnson, despite her numb fingers, went into the house to fetch the family's polaroid, so as to take pictures of the ring. Meanwhile Mr Johnson and his son drove into Delphos, not to consult a doctor but to invite Willard Critchfield, editor of the local *Delphos Republican*, to come and see the 'landing site.' However, saying the paper was being prepared for press, Critchfield could not spare even the 20 minutes for the visit.

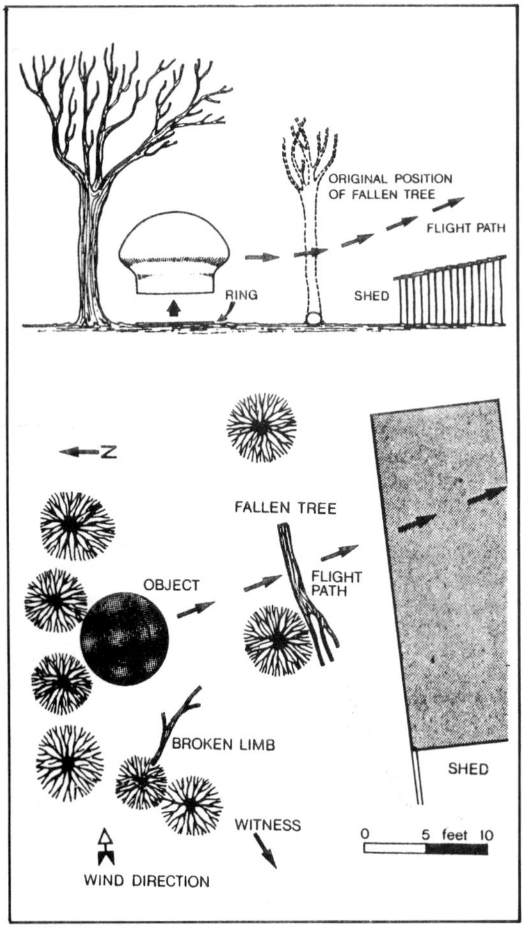

A diagram of the Delphos site.

Next morning Durel Johnson again went into Delphos, hoping to meet the editor; instead he met one of the paper's reporters, Mrs Lester Smith, who already knew them as respectable and trustworthy farming folk. She accepted his invitation, and went out there immediately with her husband and son-in-law. She took pictures of the ring, collected soil samples and some branches apparently broken off by the departing UFO, and noticed that the ground inside and outside the ring was muddy from the recent rain, but the ring itself was dry and very light in colour compared with the nearby soil.

The site was surrounded with trees on three sides, so the object must have arrived from the south and passed over the hog shed. Mrs Smith noticed a dead tree exactly in the probable flight path; it was overturned and lying in an east-west direction. If it had been overturned by the UFO when it arrived from the south, or disappeared towards the south, as Ronnie described, it should have been lying in a north-south direction. In addition it showed no marks suggesting such a collision.

A VISIT FROM THE POLICE - AND A MECCA FOR UFOLOGISTS

Mrs Smith advised Johnson to report the incident to the police, which he refused to do. So she contacted them herself, and that afternoon sheriff Ralph Enlow and two colleagues visited the site and took pictures and samples. The white substance was found down to a depth of at least 20 cm; it was found nowhere else but in the ring - not on the surrounding trees or the shelter roof.

Enlow's photos show clearly that the ground had *not* been exposed to pressure of any kind or heat radiation; some small twigs lying in the ring show no sign of either pressure or heat.

The first UFO researcher to visit the farm was Ted Phillips, an associate of CUFOS whose speciality was physical traces. He interviewed the family on 4 December, a month after the incident, and took away soil samples; he paid several subsequent visits. A local lawyer interested in UFOs, Clancy D Tull, also made a very thorough examination and contributed important information. Other prominent ufologists to visit the Johnson farm included Dr James Harder, Stanton Friedman and Philip Klass; soon the farm had become such a mecca for ufologists that the Johnsons had to erect a fence so that the big attraction - the horshoe-shaped ring - should not be totally destroyed.

MYSTERIOUS REPERCUSSIONS

The ultimate tribute came in May 1973 when the Johnson family received *The National Enquirer*'s $5000 cheque. The attendant publicity did not seem to bother the family; quite the contrary - they enjoyed the fame which was theirs until they were over-shadowed by two other sensational cases, the Pascagoula abduction and the Coyne helicopter encounter. It looked as though the Delphos incident would be forgotten.

Fortunately, a new development occurred: the UFO returned! In a long interview in the *Salina Journal* for 13 October 1974, Durel Johnson reported that on the evening of 27 April Ronnie had come running into the house crying 'I told you it was coming back again!'

The Johnsons hurried out: 'It was the same one or one just like it. It circled the same spot where it was before, then circled the house and took off east.'

Though the incident occurred in full daylight, no one else saw the UFO. But Johnson could tell of other mysterious consequences: he alleged that Ronnie had acquired psychic abilities. Only a few days after the sighting, Ronnie had begged his sister not to drive to Salina. However, she had driven - and had been involved in a motor accident. Now, he had foreseen the return of the UFO.

Johnson also reported that since the visit of the UFO two-thirds of their prize-winning pigs had become sterile, while it had had the opposite effect on the sheep. They had been ready to lamb when the UFO appeared; less than 6 months later they bore another batch of young, without being served, but these young died soon after.

What is more, the wrist-watches of both Mr Johnson and his son had gone out of order two days after the incident; a watchmaker in Salina couldn't find what was wrong with them.

THE WOLF GIRL STRIKES AGAIN

The most sensational repercussion, however, was Ronnie's encounter with the 'wolf girl' - a being 1 metre tall, with wild blonde hair, wearing a torn red dress of cloth, who had been seen by others in the Delphos area.

Ronnie said that when it ran, it got down on all fours and ran away faster than anything human can run.'

In the light of these reports, the sheriff conducted further investigations, but when he suggested to the witnesses that they take a polygraph (lie-detector) test, they refused. Since when there have been no more 'wolf girl' reports from the Delphos area.

The Delphos ring outlined by unmelted snow, 4 December 1971.

CREDIBILITY CRUMBLES

With so many investigators and journalists visiting the farm there was ample opportunity to test the family's testimony: as time went by, their credibility steadily crumbled.

Johnson told Klass in 1973 that the local post office was opening and censoring his mail, closing the envelopes afterwards with tape. But when Klass asked to see one of the envelopes, Durel was unable to find one and said his wife must have thrown them away.

When the Johnsons showed Klass the photos taken on the night of the sighting, it was clear that the trees were lit by the setting sun, which meant that the photographs could not have been taken at the time claimed. As for the picture showing the luminous rings, it was clearly invalidated by the fact that a flash had been used.

The Johnsons claimed the ring and the surrounding trees glowed for five days; but none of the many visitors saw this, nor did the soil samples display this effect. There had been a full moon on the night of the sighting and the nights immediately after; perhaps this made the Johnsons think the ring and trees were emitting light?

FAIRY RING

Champions of the case like to point out that no less than 18 laboratories examined the samples from the horseshoe-shaped impression but could reach no final conclusion as to its nature. However, this suggests a slip of the memory, for a French biologist identified the white material as a vegetal substance of the family *Actinomycetacae* and the genus *Nocardia*. Furthermore, he stated that this organism is often found in conjunction with the fungus *Bacidiomycepes,* which often fluoresces and forms circular fungus rings.

The *National Enquirer* pointed out that 'independent laboratory tests have shown that it [the soil] mysteriously resists water...retards plant growth...has a calcium content up to 10 times higher than the earth around it...contains a "white fibrous substance" that is not in nearby soil.' What is even more extraordinary, as Ronald Story points out, is that so many experts should have failed to notice that these are the classic symptoms of the fairy ring fungus.

Many fungi form 'fairy rings' which result from the fact that the growth of the fungus releases nitrogen which stimulates the growth of other plants. Thus in a lawn, grass so stimulated will be lusher and darker than elsewhere.

SUPERSTITION, ELF MAIDS AND UFOs

Despite the strong indication that the Delphos ring is a fairy ring, many ufologists are reluctant to accept that nothing mysterious happened at Delphos that night in 1971. Vallée, for example, considers it a curious coincidence that a UFO chose to hover over a fairy ring!

In bygone days it was believed that fairy rings showed where elf maids danced, or where lightning had struck, or where animals had grazed in a circle and manured the soil... UFOs are simply the latest in a line of ingenious explanations!

REFERENCES

1 - **Hynek,** J Allen, *The UFO experience,* 1972 ■ 2 - **Klass,** Philip J, *UFOs explained,* 1974; *UFOs, the public deceived,* 1983 ■ 3 - **Nilsson,** Sven, *Svampe i naturen,* bind 1, 1977 ■ 4 - **Hendry,** Allan, *The UFO handbook,* 1979 ■ 5 - **Story,** Ronald D, *The encyclopedia of UFOs,* 1980; *UFOs and the limits of science,* 1981 ■ 6 - **Sheaffer,** Robert. *The UFO verdict,* 1981 ■ 7 - **Oberg,** James, *UFOs & outer space mysteries,* 1982.

11: CAPT. COYNE, OHIO - 18 OCT. 1973

On 18 October 1973, four Army Reserve men - Captain Laurence Coyne, 36, 1st Lieut Arrigo Jezzi, 26, Sgts John Healey, 35, and Robert Yanacsek, 23 - were returning in a Bell UH-1H helicopter to their base at Cleveland Hopkins AFB from Columbus, Ohio, a 150 km trip. The night was starry, with visibility 60 km, temperature about 6 degrees Celsius. Jezzi was piloting the helicopter at about 165 km/h at 800 m altitude. They were flying over a mainly agricultural terrain, with some hills of 330 to 400 m. They had left about 10.30 pm.

About halfway through their journey, some 16 kms S of Mansfield, Healey, sitting in the left rear seat behind Jezzi, saw a single red light to their left (west); it was headed south and seemed brighter than the usual port navigation light of an aircraft, but since it wasn't relevant to their flight he didn't mention it.

Three or four minutes later, at 11.02 pm, Yanacsek, sitting behind Coyne on the right, saw a steady red light on the eastern horizon. It seemed to be pacing them. After watching it for perhaps a minute he told Coyne, who told him to keep an eye on it. Thirty seconds later he remarked that it seemed to be closing on them. Coyne and Yanacsek watched it from their seats while Healey stood up and bent forward in the aisle to see it; Jezzi's view was obstructed.

The light continued to approach. Coyne took over control and started a descent of approx 165 m/min, and contacted Mansfield Flight Control to ask about other traffic in the area. He knew a group of F-100 fighters was stationed at Mansfield; but such aircraft were not supposed to fly so fast at so low an altitude as this light. But after an opening acknowledgement 'This is Mansfield Tower, go ahead Army 1-5-triple-4', no further replies were obtained, though the radio seemed to be functioning.

The red light became steadily brighter and seemed to be on a collision course at approx 1100 km/h; Coyne responded by increasing his descent speed to 610 m/min. His final altimeter reading was approx 520 m above sea level.

A collision seemed inevitable, but the light stopped and hovered over and in front of the helicopter!

Later, Coyne, Healey and Yanacsek reported that a cigar-shaped metallic grey object filled the entire front windshield. In the 'nose' of the object a red light could be seen, at the tail a white light, and from the bottom emanated a green pyramid-shaped beam, which suddenly swept up over the nose of the helicopter and front window to the tinted upper window panels, flooding the cockpit with green light. No sound or air turbulence was noted.

After hovering for a few seconds the object accelerated and moved off towards the west; only the white 'tail light' was visible. Coyne and Healey followed the object with their eyes and saw it make a 45-degree change of course towards the NW. Jezzi noticed no course change, and Yanacsek's view was obstructed.

While the object was still visible, Jezzi and Coyne read the instruments showing they were at an altitude of 1150 m, with a rate of climb of 330 m/min - and the collective control column was in the full-down position. Coyne carefully raised it; the helicopter climbed approximately a further 100 m before responding normally, and the crew noticed a slight bump.

As the object retired, the intensity of the 'tail light' increased together with its speed. It disappeared towards the NW horizon after passing over Mansfield Airport. Coyne manoeuvred the helicopter down to their previous flying altitude of 820 m, and they had no trouble making radio contact with Akron-Canton. The flight continued to Cleveland without further incident.

Next day Coyne asked P J Vollmer, in charge of flight control at Hopkins Field, how and where he should report the incident. Vollmer later told Hynek: 'I'll never, all the rest of my life, forget that man coming in here. I have known Coyne for some time, not personally, not even socially, but I personally have an extremely high regard for his integrity and his capability. In a case of this kind, I don't know anybody that I would believe any more. I trust his judgment without a question of a doubt. I don't know what happened, but I *do* know - I could tell from the tremor of his voice, which wasn't much - that he was shook. He felt the feeling, inside of himself - this is what I gathered - that it had to come out of him. This knowledge and information. He needed advice on reporting it somewhere, but he didn't know where to go.'

Vollmer, however, could not suggest any official authority, so nothing happened until three days later when Coyne described the incident to a cousin who was a journalist on the *Cleveland Plain Dealer*. The authorities were still apparently not interested, but to ensure that the case was officially on record, Coyne a month later filled in an 'Operational Hazard' form, used when a military person has been exposed to danger while using an aircraft of any kind.

INVESTIGATION

A thorough investigation spread over one-and-a-half years was made by Dr Hynek and his CUFOS colleague Jennie Zeidman, who had previously been his assistant when he was a consultant for Project Blue Book. They secured taped interviews with everyone involved. However, the earliest taped interview was made by a friend of Sgt Healey's in the Cleveland Police Department, only 18 hours after the event. Apart from minor discrepancies, all accounts tally perfectly.

Zeidman found they were agreed that the object was about 20 m long, and at its closest was 30 m above and 150 m distant. However, this doesn't fit with the witness statement that it filled the entire front windshield; to do that, the object would have had to be only 21 m away and be no less than 30 m long.

The speed of the object varied during the sighting from 0 to 1200 km/h, and it was able to accelerate/decelerate very quickly, and at least one sharp turn was observed.

Their estimates of the duration of the sighting varied because not all the witnesses were able to see the object all the time; the average seems to have been 5 minutes, with a margin of half a minute.

POSSIBLE EXPLANATIONS

Two possibilities that Zeidman had to consider were an *advanced aircraft* or a *meteor*.

The following data argue against the aircraft hypothesis:

- The object was able to decelerate from high speed to hovering in a few seconds.
- It was flying much faster than is permitted at this low altitude.
- It created no turbulence and seemed silent.
- No wings, undercarriage, or stabilisers were seen despite its demonstrated ability to alter/maintain altitude and direction, and change speed.
- The light configuration didn't match that on any known aircraft, no matter which way it is looked at. Also, the lights were steady.
- The closest likely aircraft were the F-100s at Mansfield, but the last one of these came down at 10.47 pm, more than a quarter-hour before the encounter.

The following data argue against the meteor hypothesis:

- The red, white and green lights were positioned at specific points on the object.

- No tail, after-glow or such were seen.
- The flight characteristics of the object - eg change of direction, hovering, varying speed - were not consistent with meteor behaviour.
- The object was seen for approx 5 minutes, whereas the longest-observed meteors in the best weather conditions are visible for only 30-40 seconds.

'SUCKED' BY A UFO?

The terrain SE of Mansfield is at its highest 400 m above sea level. Coyne reported that when the red light approached and collision seemed unavoidable, his final altitude reading was 520 m, with a descent speed of 610 m/min. Zeidman's investigation established that the incident occurred over Charles Mill Reservoir, altitude 330 m, surrounded by trees of 10-15 m. Thus Coyne's actual height above the trees was some 210-225 m. At a descent speed of 610 m/min, the helicopter would crash into the trees in some 20 seconds; this reduces the time the men would have had to give the object their attention. Coyne said: 'The reason I didn't crash into the ground was because I could *see* the ground. I had night vision. We were down to 160 m, maybe. But I've flown a helicopter low-level many times - 60 m, even 15 m. The big thing of course is wires, obstructions.'

It is not known exactly what altitude the helicopter was at when it stopped diving and started to climb, but the change can't have been sudden for none of the crew noticed any G-forces caused by a sudden change of course. The helicopter was thoroughly examined afterwards and no damage caused by such strains was found.

Coyne says that the collective was in the full-down position when he discovered they were actually climbing, not diving. He remembers his left arm was stretched to hold it. Zeidman wondered if, staring up at the object, he might have been in a half-lying position and have unconsciously pulled the column up; Yanacsek replied that, on the contrary, Coyne was bent forward in a kind of defensive position. Coyne himself remembers stiffening and flinching in anticipation of a collision; he was looking forwards, not up.

Klass suggests that the unexpected climb was caused by Coyne or Yanacsek instinctively bringing the helicopter out of the dive when a crash was imminent; an experienced pilot, he thinks, would react automatically in such a situation.

RADIO BLACK-OUT

Radio communication failed after a few seconds when the unknown light approached. Coyne, and later Jezzi, repeatedly but vainly tried different frequencies. They could hear the channel tone every time they changed frequency. The radio was working, but no transmission was taking place and so Flight Control could not hear them. How unusual was this, and was there necessarily any connection with the object?

Jezzi: 'It happened from time to time. Our maintenance, our avionics, were not that good. You'd have poor transmission and then all of a sudden it

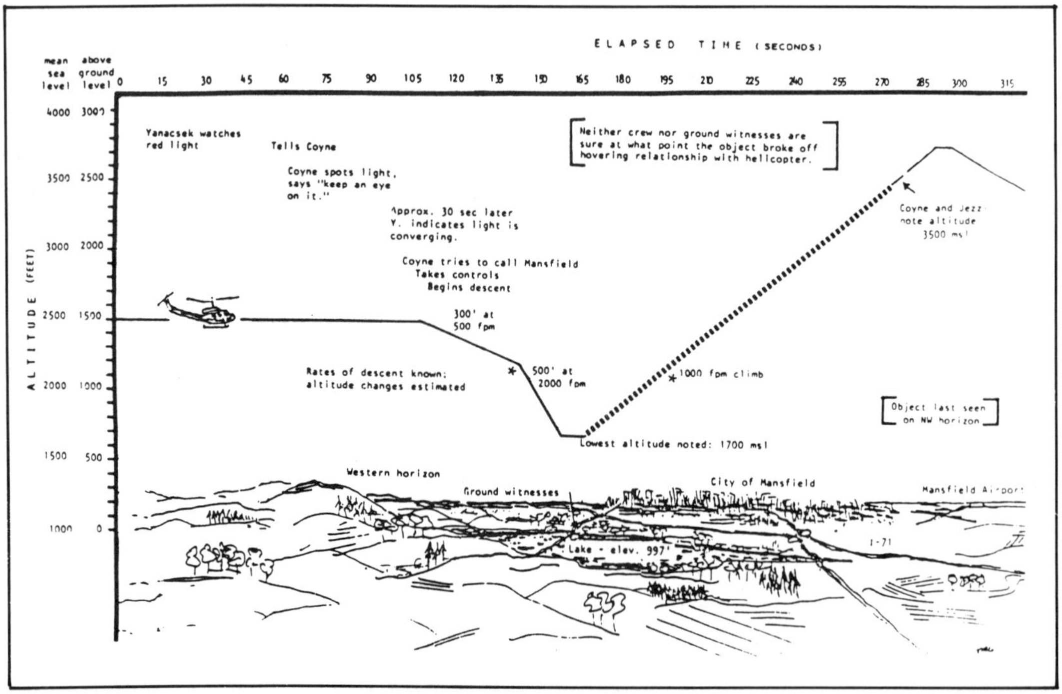

The sequence of events, as prepared for the CUFOS report.

came in, or it was garbled. So I don't know if it was part of the incident or not.'

Next day Coyne asked Mansfield Flight Control to play the previous night's tape. He learned that Flight Control had heard them, but couldn't find the opening communication, which occurred normally, on their tapes.

Klass asked Coyne, next time he was in the neighbourhood of the occurrence, to try to make radio contact with Flight Control at Mansfield, Cleveland, Columbus and Akron-Canton. Coyne did so, and told Klass he hadn't been able to contact the three latter because he was out of their range at that low altitude; but he was able to contact Mansfield.

Klass suggested several reasons why Mansfield might not have answered Coyne on 18 October. There might have been a defect in the mike's on/off switch; Flight Control might have been busy guiding other aircraft; the fuselage of the helicopter might have shielded the aerial in the direction of Mansfield; fast frequency changes in the helicopter might have meant that the radio didn't have time to stabilise on the selected channel. So the communication breakdown can't necessarily be seen as a mysterious incident related to the unknown object.

THE ROTATING COMPASS

A new and previously unrevealed detail turned up in the course of investigation. During the most hectic seconds of the sighting when the helicopter was diving and after the beam from the object had flooded the cockpit with green light, the magnetic compass had begun slowly rotating at approx 4 rpm. Previously it had always worked satisfactorily, but after the incident it was totally kaput and had to be replaced.

WITNESSES WANTED, WITNESSES FOUND

The possibility must be considered that the four men were deceived by a combination of three abnormal factors: the appearance of a huge meteor, whose glowing tail lit up their cockpit and gave the illusion of a hovering object; the seemingly mysterious behaviour of their craft due to instinctive reactions on the crew's part; and the coincidental breakdown of radio communication due to natural causes.

But such an explanation becomes even more improbable when we find that their accounts are supported by five other witnesses.

On 19 August 1976 the Mansfield *News Journal* published an article on the Coyne case and asked possible witnesses to contact a local UFO group, CCAP (Civil Commission on Aerial Phenomena). The article paid off.

Five persons, Mrs C and four teenage children, had seen the bright, steady red light from their car; five minutes later, near Charles Mill Reservoir, they stopped and witnessed the encounter between the two craft. Their account tallies in detail with that of the helicopter crew:

- The date was 18 October, the time a few minutes past 11 pm
- The incident ocurred east of Mansfield, east of I-71 and east of Mansfield NDB (non-directional beacon)
- The helicopter approached from the SW
- There was a steady red light at the front of the object
- There was a short, intense green beam, but apart from this the red light was the dominant one
- The object wasn't quite symmetrical
- The object was over the helicopter
- The helicopter did not change course; its final course was NE
- The final course of the object was NW
- The course of the object was as described by the helicopter crew

Following on Zeidman's investigations, the conclusion by CUFOS was that the object seen by Coyne and his crew, and by the witnesses on the ground, remains unidentified. The men were awarded the *National Enquirer*'s $5000 prize for 'the most scientifically valuable report of 1973.'

REFERENCES

1 - **Zeidman,** Jennie, *Helicopter-UFO encounter over Ohio*, CUFOS, 1979 ■ 2 - **Story,** Ronald D, *The encyclopedia of UFOs*, 1980; *UFOs and the limits of science*, 1981 ■ 3 - **Klass,** Philip J, *UFOs explained*, 1974; *UFOs, The public deceived*, 1985 ■ 4 - *UFO-NYT* 1979-2.

12: TEHRAN, 19 SEPTEMBER 1976

Two sophisticated F-4 Phantom fighters of the Imperial Iranian Air Force rendered impotent while pursuing UFOs north of Tehran... radio communication, instruments and weapon system all put out of action... a UFO seeming to fire a missile at one of our aircraft... are the UFOs hostile and aggressive after all?

That seemed to be the case, according to the dramatic events of September 1976. Immediately after the incident, the IIAF asked their military advisors from the USAF-MAAG (Military Assistance Advisory Group) to investigate. The official record prepared by Lieut Col Mooy is as follows:

'1. At about 12:30 AM 19 September 1976 the IIAF Command Post received a telephone call from the ADOC [Air Defense Operations Center] representative at Mehrabad [civil-military airport near Tehran]. He said that Mehrabad had received four telephone calls from citizens living in the Shemiran area saying that they had seen strange objects in the sky. One lady described them as a kind of bird, while another lady said, "Please tell this helicopter with a light on to get away from my house because I'm scared." (There were no helicopters airborne at that time.) The citizens were told it was probably stars.

2. The Command Post called Brigadier General Yousefi, assistant deputy commander of operations. After Yousefi talked to Mehrabad tower and determined Babolsar and Shahrokhi radars did not have the object [that is, no unidentified target on these air-defense radars], he decided to look for himself. He noticed an object in the sky similar to a star but bigger and brighter. [Note: the planet Jupiter was especially bright at the time.] He decided to scramble and [sic] F-4 from Shahrokhi to investigate. [Shahrokhi was an IIAF air base located approximately 130 miles southwest of Tehran.]

3. The F-4 took off at 01:30 AM and proceeded to a point about 40 NM [nautical miles] north of Tehran. Due to its brilliance the object was easily visible from 70 miles away. As the F-4 approached a range of 25 NM he lost all instrumentation and communications (UHF and Intercom). He broke off the intercept and headed back to Shahrokhi. When the F-4 turned away from the object and apparently was no longer a threat to it the aircraft regained all instrumentation and communications.

4. A second F-4 was launched at 01:40 AM. The backseater [radar operator] acquired a lock-on at 27 NM, 12 o'clock high position [directly ahead and above] with the Vc (rate of closure) at 150 MPH. As the range decreased to 25 NM the object moved away at a speed that was visible on the radar scope and stayed at 25 NM.

5. The size of the radar return [echo-blip] was comparable to that of a [Boeing] 707 tanker [aircraft]. The visual size of the object was difficult to discern because of its intense brilliance. The light that it gave off was that of flashing strobe lights arranged in a rectangular pattern and alternating blue, green, red and orange in color. The sequence of lights was so fast that all colors could be seen at once.

6. The object and the pursuing F-4 continued a course to the south of Tehran, when another brightly lighted object, estimated to be 1/2 to 1/3 the apparent size of the moon, came out of the original object. This second object headed straight toward the F-4 at a very fast rate. The pilot attempted to fire an AIM-9 [infrared-guided] missile at the object but at that instant his weapons-control panel went off and he lost all communications (UHF and interphone). At this point the pilot initiated a turn and negative-G dive to get away. As he turned the object fell in trail at what appeared the [sic] be about 3-4 NM. As he continued in his turn away from the primary object the second object went to the inside of his turn, then returned to the primary object for a perfect rejoin [that is, returned and merged with the primary object.]

7. Shortly after the second object joined up with the primary object another object appeared to come out of the other side of the primary object going straight down, at a great rate of speed. The F-4 crew had regained communications and the weapons-control panel and watched the object approaching the ground anticipating a large explosion. This object appeared to come to rest gently on the earth and cast a very bright light over an area of about 2-3 kilometers.

8. The crew descended from their altitude of 26M [26,000 ft.] to 15M and continued to observe and mark the object's position. They had some difficulty in adjusting their night visibility for landing so after orbiting Mehrabad a few times they went out for a straight-in landing. There was a lot of interference on the UHF [ultra-high-frequency air-ground radio] and each time they passed through a Mag. [magnetic] bearing of 150 degrees from Mehrabad they lost their communications (UHF and Interphone) and the INS [inertial navigation system] fluctuated from 30-degree to 50-degrees. The one civil airliner that was approaching Mehrabad during this same time experienced communications failure in the same vicinity (Kilo Zulu) but did not report seeing anything.

9. While the F-4 was on a long final approach the crew noticed another cylinder shaped object (about the size of a T-bird [jet-trainer aircraft] at 10 NM) with bright steady lights on each end and a flasher in the middle. When queried, the tower stated there was no other known traffic in the area. During the time that the object passed over the F-4 the tower did not have a visual on it [that is, saw nothing], but picked it up after the pilot told them to look between the mountains and the refinery.

10. During daylight the F-4 crew was taken out to the area in a helicopter where the object apparently had landed. Nothing was noticed at the spot where they thought the object landed (a dry lake bed), but as they circled off to the west of the area they picked up a very noticeable beeper signal. At the point where the [beeper] return was the loudest was a small house with a garden. They landed and asked the people within if they had noticed anything strange last night. They [sic] people talked about a loud noise and a very bright light-like lightning.

11. The aircraft and the area where the object is believed to have landed are being checked for possible radiation. More information will be forwarded when it becomes available.'

If the details of this event are as reported, the implication is that an advanced jet-fighter, widely used by the USAF and US Navy, was incapacitated by an unknown object. If so, it is reasonable to suppose that a massive investigation was immediately launched, and the late Shah asked to keep the case secret.

Yet neither of these things happened. Far from being put under security wraps, the case was boosted by the Iranian papers, even with 'official' statements. Mooy's report was sent to the CIA, the State Department and the Pentagon, but classified not 'Top Secret' but 'Confidential' - the lowest level of secrecy. The USAF treated the affair so casually that a copy of the report leaked out to NICAP, which was able to publish it in its *UFO Investigator* for November 1976. When Mooy - now Colonel - returned to the US, Klass questioned him about the case in October 1977, and was told that since the initial interrogation of the pilots the USAF in Iran had carried out no further examination of the case; nor, to the best of his knowledge, had the IIAF conducted any thorough examination of the second Phantom to seek the cause for the alleged electric/electronic malfunction.

Does this lack of interest, on the face of it so extraordinary, indicate that the case was recognised as being somewhat less mysterious than Mooy's report suggests?

REVEALING TAPE RECORDINGS

Since May the Tehran newspapers had been publishing tales of innumerable UFO sightings in the Bushehr area on the south coast; in one case a man claimed he had been abducted from a forest and taken to Esfahan. The Tehran air chase brought new headlines: but the press was able to contribute new and interesting information on the event.

The Persian-language newspaper *Ettela'at* had had a chance to listen to tape recordings of the communication between Mehrabad Flight Control and Lieut Jafari, pilot of the first Phantom. From the taped exchange it seems that Jafari found himself unable to get close to the object, even at maximum speed. Mehrabad instructed him to return if he could not get closer, but shortly after he reported:

'Something is coming at me from behind. It is 24 km away... now 16 km away... now 8 km... It is level now, I think it is going to crash into me. It has just passed by, missing me narrowly...' The newspaper said that 'the disturbed voice of the pilot...then asked to be guided back to base. It was at this time that a second plane was ordered to take off.'

In contradiction to Mooy's report, there is no mention in the recording of anything that suggests electrical malfunction. This discrepancy could be due to the fact that Mooy's investigation was directed to the experience of the other crew, and that the two crews had not had time to compare notes before the interrogation.

It is also interesting that when Jafari was hunting the huge object *ahead* of him, he should have been approached from *behind*. This raises the possibility that there was no connection between the object he was pursuing and the one that was pursuing *him*.

The tape recording containing the radio communication with the second Phantom was also published. The English-language *Tehran Journal* told its readers that 'the pilot reported having seen the UFO and told the control tower that it had reduced its speed. The pilot said his plane was working well and he was preparing to fire missiles at the UFO. After a moment's silence he said he had seen a bright round object, with a circumference of about 4.5 m, leave the UFO. A few seconds later the bright object rejoined the mother craft and it flew away at many times the speed of sound.'

Here again there is no mention of electrical malfunction; but if any such had taken place it would have put the radio communication system out of action and we would have no recording. Also not mentioned was any registering of the object on the aircraft radar (the radar at Mehrabad was out of action at the time).

EXPERT STATEMENTS

The Phantom is equipped with a Westinghouse APQ-120 radar. Two Westinghouse technicians were at the Shahrokhi base at the time of the incident, and their firsthand knowledge is very illuminating. [Since they requested anonymity they are here named 'Smith' and 'Jones'.]

Smith stated that the second Phantom was put in 'quarantine' behind an outlying bank of sandbags (for use in the event of surprise attack). This confirms that only this second aircraft had after-effects following the encounter. American personnel were not permitted to approach the plane; however, it was back in operation less than a week later.

Among the American experts at the Shahrokhi base was a technician from McDonnell Douglas, who was curious about the case. Comparing notes with Smith and Jones he found that this particular Phantom had continually been plagued with defects in its electronic system, which IIAF's technicians had never been able to set right satisfactorily.

Jones asked the Iranian technicians if they had examined the Phantom after the incident. They had, but the only thing they had found was that one of the radios was 'filled with static electricity', which is not unusual for airborne radios.

Both Smith and Jones were eager to test the plane's radar, following the incident; but their first chance to do so was a month later when the plane had its routine inspection. Smith was then called on to make adjustments to the radar, which had obviously not been working satisfactorily.

Smith and Jones also revealed that the Iranian pilots at Shahrokhi were not trained in night flying; nor were the radar operators highly skilled, for they were junior pilots whose chief interest was to become senior fighter pilots as quickly as possible. This makes it more likely that the crew in the two planes misidentified a known object. The huge UFO could have been Jupiter, which was extremely bright at the time, and the smaller objects and 'missiles' could have been meteors or fireballs.

Indeed, two meteor swarms, Aquarides and southern Piscides, were at their maximum on 19 September. That such a mistake can occur even to trained pilots is demonstrated by what happened at St Louis on 5 June 1969, when the pilots of a large airliner and a fighter both thought they were about to clash with a swarm of UFOs, which were photographed by a press photographer and observed from the ground. The fireball which was thought to be on a collision course with the aircraft was actually 200 km away!

If experienced pilots can make such mistakes, we need not be surprised if pilots unused to night flying do likewise. Moreover, the crew of the second Phantom seem to have lost their heads: according to Mooy's report, the target on the airborne radar was 46 km distant, yet they were prepared to launch at it an AIM-9 missile, which is a close-combat weapon with a range of only a few km.

But what about the strange 'beep' signal heard aboard the helicopter when the pilots next day inspected the drained lake to find the impact site of the object the crew saw crash?

Col Mooy offered a possible explanation. Several aircraft, including the C-141 transport, are equipped with an emergency radio transmitter which, after the plane is crashed, is able to transmit signals which may be received by a rescue plane. Mooy said there had been a lot of trouble with these instruments, which are supposed to detach from the aircraft only in the event of a crash but which were frequently dislodged by powerful air turbulence - often encountered in the mountains near Tehran.

OPEN FOR SPECULATION

The facts of the Tehran case are not easily established, but the data which have been accumulated, if they do not explain it for certain, do suggest prosaic ways of accounting for the events of that night.

If so, it is understandable that the IIAF would not wish for a large-scale investigation involving the Americans. The Air Force was the Shah's pride and joy; he had invested billions in a super modern air force, and was planning to replace his F-4s with the more advanced F-14. It would have been a little embarrassing if the IIAF revealed to the Americans that they had considerable trouble keeping even the older F-4s in good operational order, and that the training of their crews was so inadequate that an F-4 pilot could try to shoot down the planet Jupiter with a short-range missile. Under the circumstances, it was easiest to endorse the news stories about UFOs; for even the USAF has had to admit that it cannot explain all the UFO reports it receives.

THE UFO EVENT OF THE YEAR?

The Tehran case was chosen by the *National Enquirer*'s panel as the 1977 case possessing the greatest scientific value, publishing at the same time a dramatic and incorrect account of the event.

If the incidents reported in the Mooy memorandum really took place, there is justification for Gen Abdullah Azerbarzin's verdict, three months after the event: 'It was unidentified. Definitely it was. Because we had six witnesses.' As Bruce Maccabee has pointed out, those witnesses are agreed that 'the strange object was considerably more mobile than Jupiter.'

If, on the other hand, we accept the possibility of a series of natural phenomena occurring to insufficiently skilled persons who would be liable to misinterpret them, especially at a time when UFOs were very much 'in the air' - in the newspaper headlines if not in reality - then the events can be accounted for more mundanely.

It seems to be a stalemate situation. However, there is one comfort. In January 1977 Ardeshir Zahedi, then Iran's ambassador to the United States, accepted the *National Enquirer*'s $5000 cheque, and because the IIAF pilots, like all military and state employees, are not permitted to receive the money, it went to the Iranian Red Cross... which just goes to show that there's nothing so bad that good can't come of it!

REFERENCES

1 - US official memorandum IR 6 846 0139 76 ■ 2 - *Phenomenes Spatiaux*, March 1977 ■ 3 - *National Enquirer*, 31.1.1978 ■ 4 - **Story**, Ronald D, *The Encyclopedia of UFOs*, 1980 ■ 5 - **Sachs**, Margaret, *The UFO Encyclopedia*, 1980 ■ 6 - **Klass**, Philip J, *UFOs, the public deceived*, 1983 ■ 7 - **Maccabee**, Bruce, 'UFOs - still unexplained', in *Fate*, March 1984.

13: HESSDALEN, 1981-1985

It must be every ufologist's dream to be able to study the UFO phenomenon over a prolonged period of time in a fixed location, just as other scientists in other fields are able to conduct research in controlled conditions. Since the autumn of 1981, researchers in Norway have had this opportunity.

In November of that year the people of the 12 km-long valley of Hessdalen (southwest of Trondheim, 30 km northwest of Røros) began to report the occurrence of strange light phenomena. Lights would come sweeping between the mountains and stop abruptly, make rapid ascents or accelerate horizontally. Hundreds of witnesses were involved, and many of them described the objects as egg-shaped, with rather old-fashioned window-like features, and soundless. They were seen more frequently around 7.30 pm and between 10.30-11 pm, but also at other times of day.

On 26 March 1982, Norway's leading UFO research organisation, *UFO-Norge*, conducted a survey among the 130 locals who came to a meeting held at Ålen:

- 17 witnesses reported seeing a yellow spherical light
- 12 reported possible cigar-shaped objects
- 8 reported possible egg-shaped objects
- 6 reported oblong objects with 2 yellow and 1 red light
- 1 reported a daylight sighting.

No one had experienced physical or psychical effects. One had noticed that animals were influenced, and three noted interference with radio or TV. Altogether 30 people had had sightings since December 1981. In February 1982 NRK, the Norwegian Broadcasting System, came to the area hoping to document the phenomenon; they recorded some 50 m of the light phenomena, but at such distances the quality was poor.

SOME OF THE ACCOUNTS

On several occasions during the December-January period, Ruth Mary Moe, Age Moe and John Aspass, from the Aspass Farm, saw a bright shining object, oval or egg-shaped with a well-defined outline; frequently they saw it hovering over the top of Finnsahogda, a hill some 3 km away. Once they saw the object low over a mountain pasture, but when they reached the site there were no traces in the snow; there was no sound from the object.

Sightings fluctuated with the weather: nothing was seen when the weather was grey and clouds hanging low. Only when the sky was dark and clear. Never more than one object was seen at a time. Characteristically it would appear slowly from the southwest, hover over Finnsahogda, descend vertically behind the mountain, after which it would rise again and return towards the southwest. Sometimes it would rise and descend several times.

About 7 pm on 20 December 1981 several independent witnesses, including journalists Nils Kare Nesvold and Per Holden, at Vongraven saw a shining spherical object the apparent size of a large star; the light was steady and intense, with no corona or surround. The weather was clear and dark. The

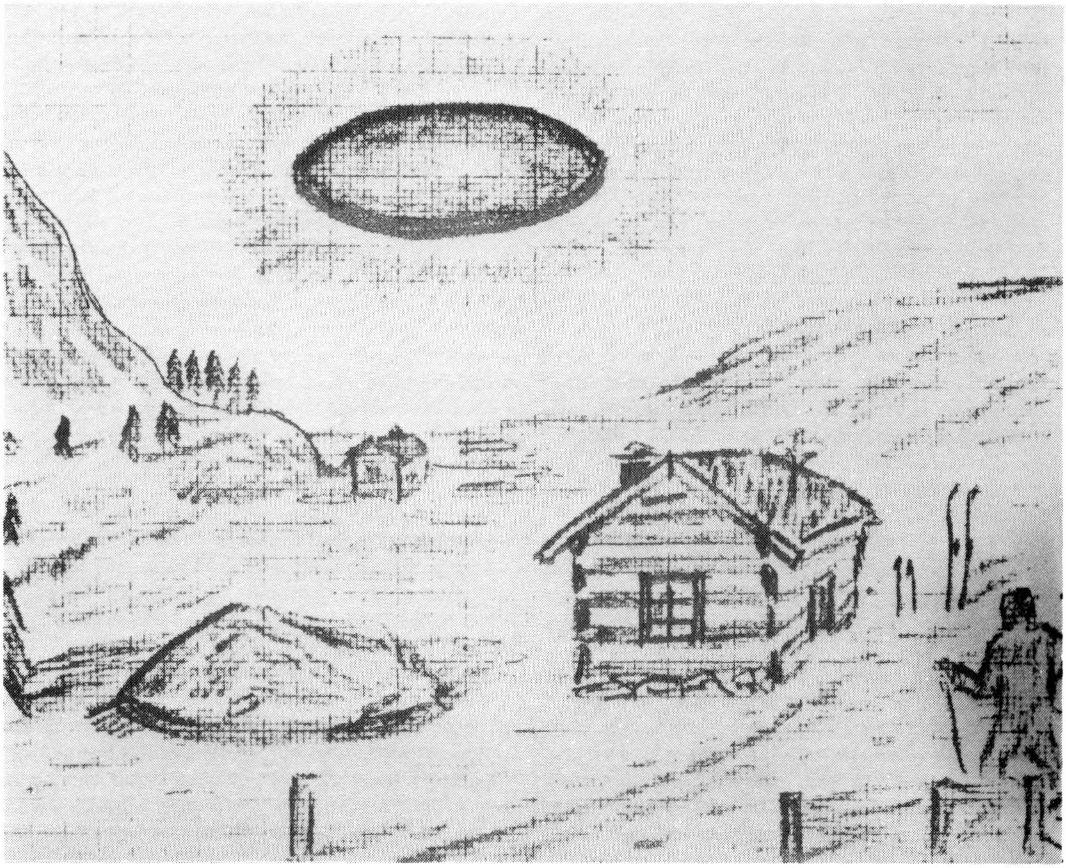

Hessdalen: what the witnesses describe [sketched by Leif Havik from witness accounts] ...

object was flying above a mountain about 3 km distant, at an altitude between 1000-2000 m above the mountain. Its speed was irregular, and it changed both course and altitude. Suddenly it disappeared as though an electric light had been switched off.

NORWEGIAN DEFENCE GOES UFO-HUNTING

At the end of March 1982 two officers from Vaernes AFB, Capt Nyland and Lieut Reymert, came to Hessdalen to study the phenomenon at close quarters. So far as we know, this was the first time Norwegian Defence had ever sent its men to hunt UFOs.

They camped for a short time in a tent in Hessdalen: 'We didn't see any UFOs. On the other hand, we saw 30 shooting stars and satellites and 6 or 7 planes. And not least, we saw a lot of UFO-hunters in the area... The people of Hessdalen have been seeing luminous objects since 1944, but many years passed before they dared to talk about the sightings. But the accounts are credible, and we in the Defence must take them seriously. There are more things between Heaven and Earth than can be explained at first sight.'

The officer responsible for the investigation was Maj Gen Schibbye, head of Air Command in southern Norway, who stated: 'We have received credible reports about objects which people have not been able to explain. This is something we have to take seriously. There are natural explanations for what people see in the sky at night, but sometimes it can be difficult to indicate the correct cause. The phenomena in Hessdalen may be atmospheric reflections, ball lightning or other meteorological phenomena.'

SCIENTIFIC STUDIES

With sightings being reported by the hundred, investigators flocked to the area, and journalist Arne Wisth wrote a book on the subject. But the first organised investigations were carried out at the end of 1983/spring 1984.

On 3 June 1983 'Project Hessdalen' was formed in co-operation between UFO-Norge, UFO-Sverige, Foreningen for psykobiofysik ('society for psychobiophysics') and Finnish ufologists. The project was directed by Leif Havik, Odd-Gunnar Røed, Håkan Ekstrand, Jan Fjellander and Erling Strand.

They were able to borrow technical equipment from universities, including an Atlas 2000 radar, a seismograph, a fluxgate magnetometer, a spectrum analyser, infra-red viewers, geiger counters, and different kinds of camera. It was decided that from 21 January to 26 February 1984 - the time of year which, according to the records, was most favourable for sightings - these instruments would be set up in hope to catch the phenomenon.

The results were published in *Project Hessdalen 1984; final technical report part One*, edited by engineer Erling Strand. In contrast to previous sighting reports from Hessdalen, which involved subjective interpretations of flickering lights coloured by the preconceptions of witnesses and investigators, this report presents, soberly and without jumping to conclusions, the data obtained by the instruments, noting not only the achievements but also sources of error which should be guarded again in future investigations.

RESULTS OF PROJECT HESSDALEN

During the period of the project, 188 reports of lights (not necessarily 'objects') were noted. Each report was assigned two indices: one indicating the quality or reliability of the report (G1 to G9), the other its 'strangeness', implying that attempts to explain it in conventional terms had failed (F1 to F10). Only two reports were rated high on both axes (F10/G9); two others had high strangeness (F10) but were less reliable (G7).

The most inexplicable sighting was made by Leif Havik at 6.12 pm on 20 February, standing in the snow outside the headquarters caravan on Aspaskjolen: a red light flew round his feet and disappeared into the air. Witnessed also by Age Moe, there seems no conceivable source for this light.

The overall conclusion of Project Hessdalen is positive, in that it demonstrates that the phenomenon *is* capable of being registered on measuring instruments; but negative in that it indicates that more data is required before any conclusions can be drawn. The following year the Project was mounted again, and was visited by Dr Hynek on 26 January 1985: 'It seems we have something important in Hessdalen, nowhere else in the world has the UFO phenomenon been known to stay put for so long a time.' Unfortunately, unfavorable weather diminished the chances of obtaining good results during this second year of the project.

EXPLANATIONS

As may be expected, many hypotheses have been proposed to account for the Hessdalen phenomena.

Scientist Thomas McClimans at the Harbour Laboratory in Trondheim, in an interview in *Adresseavisen* on 16 March 1982, said: 'I won't claim with 100% assurance that I have the solution to the Hessdalen UFO sightings, but I think the explanation is this: Cold air is forced down into the valley, where it meets a layer of warmer air. Where the two strata meet, a mirror surface is created which may reflect light from the sun, moon or other sources. This is a well-known meteorological phenomenon.'

Several sightings have been shown to coincide with known flight traffic in the area. Witnesses tell of soundless, wingless silvery objects, concerning which flight captain Kjell Bjerkan comments: 'Aircraft have already begun their landing approach to Vaernes when they are over Tolga, in the Hessdal area. You can easily imagine the effect when their landing lights are seen from the hill at the moment they are switched on... I can well believe that you might not hear a plane over Hessdalen if the wind is blowing in the wrong direction or whistling through the forest trees; besides, the aircraft engines are running idle when we make our approach.' He does not rule out the possibility that hoaxers are pulling the legs of the Hessdalen inhabitants by remote-control helicopters equipped with lights!

One of the more far-out explanations comes from Asbjorn Hallan in a letter to *Arbeiderbladet*: 'The UFO hysteria which is afflicting the people of Røros and Hessdalen is unique in our day. However, it is a known fact that people who live in such remote areas are more prone to superstition than those who live in other parts of the country. Even when remnants of meteorological balloons are found in Hessdalen, the dogged superstition of the residents is unshaken. It is possible that in such Godforsaken places as Hessdalen, in-breeding had taken place over the centuries. In-breeding is associated with physical defects, as science has conclusively proved. Among the defects are hallucinations. So the conclusion that the people of Hessdalen are suffering from hallucinations due to in-breeding must be regarded as the explanation unless the contrary can be proved.'

METEOROLOGICAL STATION

During the period 1 April to 1 May 1984, NIVFO (the Norwegian Institute of Scientific Research and Enlightenment) set up a meteorological station in Hessdalen for the purpose of testing two possible explanations for the phenomena: plasma phenomena, and the inversion phenomena proposed by McClimans. For this it was necessary to collect information about weather conditions in the valley, and since there was no weather station in the area, NIVFO had to set up one of their own.

Jan Krogh, NIVFO's representative for the area, was able to borrow equipment from the Norwegian Meteorological Institute, including radio balloons, which were launched on 20 occasions, to altitudes as high as 1300 m. Krogh's report concludes: 'We now have clear indications that plasma phenomena may have been seen, and are currently seen, in Hessdalen. The same is true of inversion phenomena. In addition, many other lights were observed which help to give an explanation, eg lights

... and what the camera recorded at 19:50 on 25 September 1982. In the original coulour photo the outline of hills can be seen behind the bright yellow light, enabling its distance and other parameters to be estimated. [Arne Thomassen / *UFO Norge*]

from stars, planets, meteors, satellites and planes. Most of the sightings are not of large objects but of relatively small point-like lights. In this context the autokinetic effect may play an important role.

'When these have been excluded, we are still left with a residue. Most of these are relatively large lights, and often moving in waves. In the daytime they often look like metallic balls or discs surrounded by a glow or halo. When such lights are seen they often look as though a metallic object has been placed in the light. Such a description is quite fitting with light from plasma. It is the glowing ionised gas which looks like a metallic fuselage. Such balls of plasma can arise time after time and in the same way as a wind might appear regularly in the valley. The wind in the valley exists and the electrical gradient exists. Our measurements show that the wind in the valley, whatever the weather conditions, comes from 160-200 degrees, and its force is steady for long periods at a time. The ideal conditions for producing the plasma phenomenon are constant wind with a constant direction and speed.

'Another type of phenomenon is the inversion phenomenon... Light moving rapidly across the sky, often in different directions and of different sizes, may be inversion lights. To create these, what is needed is a cold wind above a warm one. Measurements, as well as talks with the inhabitants, confirm this theory. We found different winds at different altitudes. In addition the air in the valley will often be colder coming in from the south.'

The NIVFO Report concludes that 'none of the descriptions of light phenomena seen in Hessdalen fall outside known explainable phenomena or objects.'

DEFECTIVE HIGH-VOLTAGE POWER LINE CREATES UFOs

One of the weaknesses of the NIVFO thesis has hitherto been the absence of a mechanism to trigger off the plasma effect. NIVFO now believe they have found this trigger. A person with good connections to Televerket (the Norwegian Telegraph Service) has reported that crossing Hessdalen is an old high-voltage line which should long ago have been replaced. He has measured radio and TV noise close to this line exactly in the area where the UFO phenomena are seen simultaneously when witnesses have reported flicker on their TV screens. Writing to NIVFO, he says, among other things:

'What has to be remembered is that noise from high voltage lines occurs frequently in dry weather, more rarely when it is humid. The high voltage network in Ålen is old and defective. So far as we know, there is a voltage of 22kV on the line; it is not usual for 'glimming' to occur on so low a voltage, but this can happen if the lines are covered by salt and the like. People from the power station claim that this can happen too with substandard insulators, such as are known to be sometimes fitted: electric arcing may occur between china and metal.

'Whether the Hessdalen phenomena have anything to do with the high-voltage network I can't say. But I can say in summary:

- Interference has been recorded simultaneously with 'the light'; is this coincidence or correlation?
- The light phenomenon is seen only in clear or dry weather.
- The inhabitants have noticed more disturbance on TV when the light is seen.
- On the other hand, 22kV is a relatively low voltage for air ionisation surrounding the insulators. An electric arc will have some trouble switching itself off.'

DECREASING ACTIVITY AND LASER EFFECTS

The Project Hessdalen team do not share the NIVFO's satisfaction that the problem of the Hessdalen sightings are solved, for many reasons including:

- It seems at the moment that the Hessdalen phenomenon is not as active as before. If there is a natural explanation for the phenomenon, it should continue so long as conditions in the valley remain unchanged. Nor can the fall-off in sightings be attributed to a declining interest among the people of Hessdalen, for thanks to the unique circumstances of Hessdalen, we can say that it is not simply reports of the phenomenon, but the phenomenon itself, which is displaying the decline.
- Though UFO-Norge accepts that *most* of the Hessdalen sightings have a natural explanation, no explanation yet produced, by NIVFO or anyone else, can account for *all* of the findings. In particular, the remarkable fact that when a laser beam was directed towards a periodically-flashing 'UFO', immediately the flash period was doubled, only to resume its previous flashing pattern when the laser was switched off. When the laser was again directed at it, the flashing doubled again. This occurred a total of eight out of nine times in a way which, to quote Hynek, is 'straining coincidence and suggests intelligent behavior' (*IUR* Mar-Apr 1985).
- Finally, if we accept a purely local solution, such as the defective power line, we have to explain the similarities with data obtained elsewhere, notably by Rutledge in Missouri, as reported in *Project Identification*.

REFERENCES

1 - *UFO-NYT* 1982/6; 1983/1 & 2; 1984/2, 7, 4; 1985/4-5; 1986/5-6. ■ 2 - **Krogh**, Jan S., *Hessdalsrapporten*, NIVFO, 1984 (summary in English, *The Hessdalen Report*) ■ 3 - **Strand**, Erling, *Project Hessdalen 1984, final technical report; part one*, UFO-Norge, 1984.

2.3.3

UFOs AND THE AFRICAN TRIBAL SYSTEM

by Cynthia Hind

■ **CYNTHIA HIND**: Born in South Arica; educated in Cape Town; she has lived in Africa for most of her life. She emigrated with her husband Norman (d. 1986) to Zimbabwe, where she now lives. She has been a writer all her life, on travel, history and African commentary as well as fiction.

■ **UFO involvement**: In the course of her writing she became increasingly involved in researching stories about UFOs, leading eventually to her becoming MUFON co-ordinator for Africa. 'Co-operation with officialdom here is often difficult or non-existent, and although I have a large net of interested people who assist me from all over Africa, none are able to give the time and money that dedicated Ufology deserves. Therefore I continue to work alone.' She travels widely on behalf of her interest, and is a popular speaker at conferences throughout the world.

■ **Publications**: include articles in a great many UFO and anomaly journals: her book *UFOs, African Encounters* (Gemini, Zimbabwe 1982) is the only English-language study of UFOs in Africa; it has been translated into Portuguese.

■ **Address**: PO Box 768 / Harare / Zimbabwe. Phone Harare 701515.

If there was ever need to know that the UFO phenomenon was worth a worldwide scientific study, African case histories are a major incentive in favour of this, for there is no alternative explanation for the CE IIIs these unsophisticated people have. They are not aware of UFOs, nor can they relate to them, so psychologists would have a problem in proving an hallucinatory effect.

In my book *UFOs - African Encounters*, I discussed many UFO cases which occured mainly in South Africa, for the simple reason that it was the more sophisticated people who would report UFO events, whereas the majority of the tribes-people had no idea what they were seeing and certainly did not communicate the events to persons outside their locale or village. It is only recently that I have been able to move around more easily and safely and have come across cases where black Africans have been involved in a possible UFO contact.

What was interesting to me was that none of the people interviewed treated their experiences as anything other than something which was associated with the spirits of their ancestors.

The people of Africa are from many backgrounds and many tribes and it would be impossible to examine them from every tribal viewpoint.

What I have done is to take the spiritual beliefs of the Mashona/Ndebele people in Zimbabwe (where I live) for they are close enough, in general terms, to what most of the African people believe.

All the tribes whom I have dealt with accept the concept of a Universal God. This does not preclude lesser gods. Politics, health and economics are all tied up with their spiritual belief. In other words, the Creator and their religion is part of the whole of life, not merely a portion of it.

With the Mashona themselves, there are three main spirits:

■ the *Chitukwane* is the unfortunate ghost of a person immediately resurrected after death. The reason for this quick resurrection is that an *nganga* (a tribal doctor) has trapped the escaping spirit. The ghost then falls into the manipulative hands of the sorceror who can do untold damage to his enemies. Thus the *chitukwane* is an evil spirit.

■ the *Mudzima* is the normal spirit which passes from a person at the time of death. The spirit allegedly comes out through the mouth and makes for its home; that is, the place of its earthly domicile. The head of the corpse must always face in the direction of his/her home, wherever the death may occur. The *mudzima* then comes home and settles comfortably there.

■ the *shave* is a lost spirit who has not found its way home. The *shave* will seek out a suitable medium to notify its descendants that they have not done their duty by him. The spirit is angry and belligerent and will often appear to frighten and chastise the offender.

The spirits of one's ancestors therefore feature in the lives of the people to a large extent and ancestor-worship has remained resistant to change. Most of the ceremonies pertaining to the ancestors, although serious in content, are lively affairs with much beer-drinking and partying. This means that the concept of spirits and ghosts are not necessarily awesome or frightening. The ancestors are accepted as supernatural bodies and it is only when there is a threat of evil, of unknown events, or portents of disaster, that fear is experienced.

In one of the *Nada Journals*, I picked up a story told by District Commissioner C.B. Archer about some interesting cases he had come across. He tells the story of Maganga who lived in his district. Coming home one night on his own, Maganga saw an extremely bright light on the path in front of him. No matter which way he turned, the light was before him and drawing nearer. Suddenly, the light went out and he felt invisible hands clutching at his throat, handling him roughly. When his unseen attacker finally let him go, he fell to the ground and only after some time was he able to summon enough strength to crawl back to his *kraal* (village).

He lay there partially paralysed and found he had lost his speech. Later, his relatives were able to bring a special *nganga* to him who gave him herbal medicine whereupon he vomited green froth and soon returned to normal.

Archer, who saw Maganga before the visit of the *nganga*, had given him up for dead and could not believe it when he saw he had recovered completely.

One could evaluate the situation by saying that Maganga might have been subject to fits, but that would not account for the next story, also by C.B. Archer. In this case a man and his dog were chased by a light on a remote path. The dog was as badly affected as his master (hardly a question of *folie au deux*) and both man and animal nearly succumbed before being restored to health by the local *nganga*.

There are many cases I have come across recently which could be attributed to a UFO, although the witnesses themselves produced a tribal hypothesis. The best and most detailed witness report-case was that which occurred at La Rochelle on the evening of August 15th, 1981.

La Rochelle is a large estate 9 km outside Mutare in Zimbabwe, a town close to the Mocambican border.

La Rochelle was originally owned by Sir Stephen and Lady Virginia Courtauld and they gave their home to the nation when they left the country. It is situated in the beautiful Imbeza Valley and is now part of the Nyabara Forest Training School, and its gardens and buildings have been a tourist attraction for some years.

As one approaches the estate, wide sweeping lawns slope up to the homestead and buildings at the back which is comprised of an observation tower, the main living quarters and, behind the main house, a futuristic type of building which is known as the 'Fantasy' and was used by Lady Courtauld as a retreat and orchid house.

On the right-hand side facing the buildings is a long narrow building which is the tea-room and, behind this, the quarters for the workers.

The place is kept in meticulous condition by the Forestry Commission, who employ about 30 workers and 3 Game Park Wardens to supervise and run the place.

I heard of the sighting through one of the Wardens, Andrew Connolley, and in November 1982 I went to visit the Estate. One of the first people I met was Clifford Muchena, the main witness. Clifford is 1.65 mts tall, slightly built and pleasant-faced. He is not highly educated but he can read and speaks a reasonable English.

He said, "It was around half-past six when I saw a ball of light near the tea-room from my house nearby. Then everyone saw it! It was very big and it rolled towards the tea-room. Some people only saw it when it reached the observation tower, rolling around inside the room, and they thought the tower was on fire as there were flames coming out of the window. All the grounds were brightly lit.

"They were frightened - very frightened. I ran to ring the emergency bell which is at the side of the house and some more men came running out.

"Then the ball of fire went in front of the building and past me into the Fantasy building. I stopped ringing the bell and ran to the Fantasy building to see what was happening. I could see that it was all alight and filled with flames. Then I saw three men standing there. It might have been four but I think it was three. I was very afraid and I wondered what kind of a fire this was.

"At first I thought one of the men was Mr. Connolley and he had come because of the fire. So I called to him by name. The men were tall, more than 1.8 mts and when I called Mr. Connolley's name they turned around, *very* slowly; not just their heads, but their whole bodies. They were wearing shiny overalls, the colour of this," - he produced a silver twenty-coin from his pocket - "I couldn't see their faces because there was so much light shining from them that I had to put my hands up to protect my eyes. I couldn't see if they were wearing anything on their heads. I didn't look very closely because of the light; it just blinded me.

"And then, when I put my hands up to cover my eyes, I fell down. All the time I was very frightened."

I couldn't understand why Clifford had fallen down. He couldn't have been pushed as he indicated to me where he was standing and where the men were and they were about three meters away.

"There was a power coming from them and too much light shining in my eyes, so I fell down."

I established, with further questions, that his legs had given way. I asked Clifford if he had trouble with his eyes subsequently but he told me 'no'.

Who did he think the men were?

"I thought at first it was Mr. Connolley and some friends of his but then I could see that they had such strange clothes on so I knew it wasn't Mr. Connolley.

Then I thought, it could not have been friends of his either as there was no car in the car park. They must have come by car, but where was the car?"

He went on, "The shape of their clothes was like overalls, and all one colour. I didn't see anything more because they turned to me as I called out and it was such a shock to my eyes."

I asked Clifford if he had ever read anything about outer space; about the possibility of people and craft coming from space. He was obviously puzzled. "I don't know. Do you mean astronauts? I read about astronauts in a book."

Had he seen pictures of the astronauts in this book he read? Did these men look like them?

"I don't know," Clifford replied. "There were no pictures in the book I read. Just the story." He hesitated. "Some of the twenty or more people who saw this 'thing', they think it was ghosts. We think it was the spirits of our ancestors."

I put it to Clifford that his ancestors, with all due respect, would surely have worn clothes made of hide and not silver overalls. Was it not true that they wore fur and beads and necklaces of lion or crocodile teeth?

"Yes," he said, a little hesitantly, "but you know, times change."

While I had been talking to Clifford, one of the gardeners had fetched another witness, Eunice Kachiti, who was a domestic worker at the Forestry Commission house in the grounds. In fact, I learned later that Eunice was also in charge of the Homecrafts Workshop for handicraft, crocheting and knitting.

Eunice said, "It was a Saturday and I was at my house when I saw some fire at that tree"... she indicated a Cassia tree (in the centre of the lawn), now bare of foliage... "There were two men that I could see standing there; two strange men. They had torches in their hands. The light that was shining was like the light from a torch, but very, very bright.

"They had on what seemed like blue jeans but I couldn't see the top half of their bodies as the torch was only shining on their legs. I thought they were standing and looking at the ball of fire in front of them."

I asked Eunice to describe the torches, or what she could see of them. She told me they appeared to be longer than a normal torch, with an elongated end from which the light emanated.

"The ball of light started to move towards the tea-room. The colour of the ball changed from yellow to bright red and, as it moved, it became bigger and bigger until it was 1.5 metres wide.

"It started from the Cassia tree over there, then it stood at the tea-room for about two to three minutes and then it came back to the tree. All the time, the men were still there; they never moved. At the time I thought the men were just ordinary visitors watching the fire. Then the ball went back to the tea-room again and later to the wall of the observation tower. It walked up the wall of the tower and into the room at the top."

Based only on the memory of the people involved, there were no visitors to La Rochelle that afternoon. The entrance fee is fifty cents and it is receipted in a book with weekly, not a daily, total. However, it was not a day for visitors. The weather was poor, overcast and drizzling most of the time and none of the workers could recall any tourists calling that day.

I asked Eunice if it seemed to her that the men had anything to do with the ball of fire, or were they just observing it?

"I don't know," she said, "I think they were just looking at it because it jumped in the air and began bouncing higher and higher. Then it bounced to the tower and crept up the wall and I saw it walking around the tower inside. It looked like the tower was on fire. When I looked back to where the men were, they had gone. Then the fire went away."

Soon after Clifford had rung the emergency bell, Eunice told me that one of the Game Park Wardens, Mr. Gardener, arrived on the scene. She said, "I asked Mr. Gardener what it was and even he did not know. The people here say it was ghosts because they have seen ghosts before."

The next person I spoke to was Naison Sampindi, who was formerly head gardener to the Courtaulds and is now garden-foreman.

He said, "It was after six o'clock and I was coming from the Apostolic Church where I had been. I saw the fire coming up to the tower and burning through the top window. The light was so bright that it lit up the whole house and all the garden. I saw the fire going down the tower wall and then walking to where the emergency bell was. I went to my house and then I heard the bell ringing. I wondered who was ringing the bell as it was too dark to see. It was Clifford, calling the Wardens to come because of the strange fire. Then Clifford came to my house and told me that he had been ringing the bell because he saw this big fire at the Fantasy and the people standing there..."

Who did he think they were? I asked Naison.

He laughed, "They were ghosts - we have many ancestral spirits."

Gardener could find no evidence of the fire. There was no smell, no smoke, no sign of physical burning. The carpet in the tower was quite untouched, not even a sign of singeing.

He tried to calm the excited crowd, as most of the women had run off into the bush with their children, too frightened to wait and see what it was all about.

When I spoke to Gardener he dismissed it all. "They usually have a Saturday night booze-up," he said. "They were probably all drunk."

I gathered that Clifford was one 'of the boys' but being drunk could not account for what Naison and Eunice saw. Neither of them were drinkers and

Gardener agreed with me on this point. Also, if they have a beer-drink every Saturday night, why did the strange fire not occur on any other Saturday?

On the Monday (following the 15th August), when Connolley came on duty, he was told about the incident and checked the grounds thoroughly with some of the witnesses. He said, "I looked inside the observation tower for any sign of a fire. There was nothing. Nor were there any footprints, burn marks or smells."

However, he did tell me that there was some methane gas down in the valley. The Fantasy and homestead stands high up and looks down into a steep valley at the bottom of which is a small dam filled with rotting vegetation, an ideal situation for methane gas to form.

I subsequently spoke to Professor Geoffrey Bond of the University of Zimbabwe (he has since died) and asked about methane gas and its general behaviour. Methane is a colourless, odourless gas (CH_4). Professor Bond informed me that it was produced from swampy ground where there was rotting vegetation. The methane collects into a large ball below the vegetation and then bursts forth, burns readily in contact with air, and explodes. When burning it forms into carbon dioxide and water vapour which, of course, has no smell.

Thomas Kachiti, Eunice's husband, recalled that on August 7th 1981 they were coming over the rise behind La Rochelle when they also saw a light in the tower which vanished after a few seconds. One of the senior staff thought that the place was haunted by the ghosts of the Courtaulds coming back to their home (as with the *mudzima*).

I thought perhaps ball lightning might have been involved (always an easy explanation) but the sky was heavily overcast, and no sign of lightning or thunder.

Another hypothesis was put forward by a friend of mine, Bill Magness. He thought that perhaps some visitors had arrived and entered without paying (the entry gate is closed at 5 pm, but I had a good look round and thought that the grounds could easily be entered illegally) and were having a free viewing with a torch. That would account for the 'blue jeans' that Eunice described, and the torches they were carrying.

On Tuesday March 29 1983, I again drove down to La Rochelle to test Bill's theory and take some more photographs of the area. With the assistance of Andrew Connolley (who had been most co-operative all the time), a friend, Helene Hildick, Clifford, Naison and myself met at La Rochelle at 6.30 pm. It was soon dark. Connolley had brought with him a very powerful torch used by the Forestry Commission, and we started the experiment.

Helene walked with the torch in her hand across the grounds and there was no doubt that it bounced. But, said Clifford, it wasn't the right colour, nor was it bright enough. Also the ball of light they had seen had been far larger, and growing all the time. Naison agreed with him.

When we reached the tower, Clifford again said the light of the torch 'climbing the walls' was not nearly bright enough. When we shone the torch-light on the observation tower windows both men immediately pointed out that this was not the way it had been at all. When the ball had entered the top of the tower, flames appeared to burst out of the windows, whereas when we shone our torch on the glass, the inside was quite black and did not appear to be on fire. Naison pointed out that when the ball of fire had entered the tower, the light from it had been bright enough to light up the entire grounds of La Rochelle.

We shone the light directly into Clifford's face. He admitted that it was bright but, again, nothing like the light and power he had experienced on the 15th August. Also, he said, after he had fallen to the ground, the men had disappeared. Could they have run away? Helene ran across the grass, the concrete and finally down the gravel driveway. Each time, light as she was, we could hear her footsteps. Clifford had heard nothing.

I am not suggesting a solution, one way or another, but there are several facts to bear in mind:

- None of the witnesses had ever heard of UFOs or spacemen. Clifford had read about astronauts, but not seen a picture of one and never, in any case, connected them with what he saw that night.
- Clifford could not describe the silvery metallic look of the clothes the beings wore. There is no word for silver in Shona. He had to produce a coin to demonstrate the colour to me.
- The immediate reaction to the 'ball of fire' was that it was a spirit of some sort and not a friendly ghost because of its behaviour.
- There was never any doubt in any of their minds that these were anything other than ghosts... ancestral spirits.
- Eunice's second thoughts about the men was that they must have been friendly spirits, probably the Courtaulds.
- Although Clifford at first assumed the figures were those of Connolley and friends, he soon dismissed this and thought they were perhaps the spirits of his ancestors, but not necessarily 'friendly' ones.

If these rural people were hallucinating, then surely the figures would have been dressed in hides, furs and tribal regalia. Clifford would hardly imagine 'silvery clothing' - a colour he had difficulty in describing. And if the men used a torch, as Eunice claims, she would surely relate to a type of torch with which she was familar.

I have no doubt that a lot of UFO cases are natural phenomena, or miscalculations, or even hysterical misinterpretations. But one could hardly apply these explanations to the La Rochelle case; or some others with which I have come in contact.

So again, if ever there was reason for good scientific investigation, surely some of the African case-histories would suggest such a study.

2.3.4

UFOs IN LATIN AMERICA

by Willy Smith

■ **WILLY SMITH**: Received his MS and PhD from the University of Michigan. After working for a year at the Atomic Energy Commission Facility in Puerto Rico, he devoted the rest of his professional career to education, teaching physics at the University of Michigan and at Lycoming College in the USA, and at the University of Valencia in Spain.

■ **UFO involvement**: His interest in UFOs began in the 1950s, and was strongly revived after a sabbatical leave in 1973, when he met leading researchers in Spain and France. In 1980 he finally decided to devote himself full time to the study of the UFO phenomenon. At the end of 1983 he initiated, together with Dr Hynek, the **UNICAT Project**, initially conceived as a data-base of high-quality UFO cases. Following the death of Dr Hynek, he has assumed full responsibility for UNICAT, which has now expanded into a full-fledged research activity with more than 60 collaborators and associates all over the world.

Through his international contacts, and his work with UNICAT, he has acquired a wide and intimate knowledge of present-day ufology in the US and abroad, travelling and lecturing in many countries, notably Latin America. He is a MUFON State Section Director.

■ **Publications**: include many papers published in journals in the USA and Europe, on UNICAT and many other aspects of UFO research.

■ **Address**: 1200 Murcott Court / Longwood / FL 32779 / USA.

INTRODUCTION

A prevalent misconception in the United States is that Latin America, extending south from the Mexican border to Tierra del Fuego, has a single and unique cultural identity; moreover, that those cultural traits are those of our immediate neighbour, Mexico.

Nothing could be further from reality. The assumed cultural identity was perhaps true at the beginning of the 19th century, during and following the wars of independence; but as time went by and different factors came into play, such as the immigration of diversified ethnic groups, various governments and frequent revolutions, marked changes appeared and developed. What we find today are the results dictated by this evolution, but we cannot say that each country has developed an individual and typical culture. In spite of very strong and prevalent nationalist feelings, which have in fact handicapped economic advancement, what we have are regions often composed of several countries, in each one of which the milieu is very similar, both economically and culturally. At the same time, each of those regions presents marked differences from the others, which tend to increase with geographic separation. For instance, what the traveller finds in Argentina is quite distinct from what he would find in Ecuador or in Central America.

All of the above is relevant in order to comprehend and interpret the ufological information originating in Latin America, as the interest and depth of involvement of the ufologist are strongly coloured by the cultural environment in which he develops his activities, very often in complete isolation.

I will not presume to be an expert in Latin American ufology as a whole, because I am not. But in connection with the UNICAT Project, I have become quite familiar with ufologists and the ufology of some areas, enough to be able to offer a comparison between the UFO reports that reach me from South America and those from other parts of the world.

I hasten to add that my knowledge is a direct function of the connections I have been able to cultivate in a particular country, and those connections, in turn, depend on the active presence of the UFO phenomenon and the interest and follow-up it has developed. In some countries, like Colombia and Venezuela, I have been unable to locate a reliable correspondent, but of course this doesn't mean that such persons or groups do not exist.

The three regions I will discuss are:

■ the **Southern Cone,** roughly encompassing the geographical zone below the Tropic of Capricorn. This includes mainly three countries: Argentina, Chile and Uruguay.

■ **Brazil,** a rather large territory with a great deal of UFO activity.

■ the central area of South America, but restricted to the two countries I have visited personally: **Ecuador and Paraguay.**

With the exception of only Brazil, Spanish is spoken in all Latin American countries. True, there are differences in usage and enunciations, ranging from a well-preserved Spanish heritage in countries like Ecuador and Peru, to a totally impoverished language in places like Cuba. But the differences do not constitute a barrier, and with the advent of television the uniformity of the language within the regions has improved.

South American ufologists, as a group, are not much different from those encountered in other parts of the world. A great majority consider ufology a hobby and devote to the topic their scant free time and their limited personal resources. They come from all social layers, and the quality of their research depends heavily on their educational background. Unfortunately, the majority have no scientific training whatsoever, but they do the best they can. Moreover, many are very conscious of their basic limitations and quite willing to learn ways to improve the quality of their output. In fact, some of them have become quite competent, and their investigation reports are equal to if not better than those I receive from correspondents in the United States.

In a very broad context, ufologists in Latin America can be divided into two groups: those who have a genuine interest in the phenomenon, pursuing it to satisfy their intellectual curiosity; and those who live from the phenomenon, that is, those whose interest is more financial than otherwise. Such individuals exist also in other countries, like Spain, and they are usually newspapermen doubling as writers of popular books.

For lack of a better name, I will call them 'leeches' of ufology, with no derogatory intention in mind, because like the *Hirudo medicinalis*, they fulfil a beneficial role within the framework of ufology. Although I do not sympathise with their mercenary position, I understand their crustiness is a matter of necessity.

Because of their profession, they are good investigators and capable of doing satisfactory fieldwork. The problem appears when they have to report what they have investigated, as in their eyes it is more newsworthy to talk about a "type-3 extraterrestrial craft" (like J.J. Benitez) than to admit that all the evidence points out it was only a helicopter, or to talk about a mysterious UFO flying over Buenos Aires than to simply identify the object with a high-altitude French probe.

Perhaps the reader is wondering why I am devoting so much space to these journalists, but there are two reasons for that. First of all, whatever they investigate is published, sooner or later, either as a book or in a magazine, sometimes with the blessings of ufologists of repute (like Jacques Vallée, in the case of Fabio Zerpa) who should know better. This is what the general public reads, in fact, probably what it wants to read, but is nonetheless a disservice to ufology, particularly in the eyes of the scientific establishment, which sees in this a confirmation of its faulty assessment of the UFO phenomenon. So, *caveat emptor* when you buy their prolific production.

The second reason is equally important. As I already indicated, they are good field investigators, and their private files contain many excellent cases which will never see print as they are not sensational enough. But from the viewpoint of serious ufology, those files contain valuable information, and the analyst should attempt his best to gain access to them.

THE SOUTHERN CONE

The predominant immigration to these countries was Italian and Spanish, which had an important effect on the culture, orienting it towards the European mentality. This closeness with Europe is quite typical of this part of South America.

A consequence of some significance is that English and particularly French are common second languages, and thus ufologists have access to journals like *Lumieres dans la Nuit* and *Phenomenes Spatiaux*. In fact, they not only read those publications, but many Argentinian ufologists have systematically found an outlet for their work in those magazines, and to a lesser extent in *Flying Saucer Review*.

The importance of this interchange is that the ufologist of the Southern Cone does not live in a vacuum, and is well acquainted with developments in other corners of the world. This is an astonishing difference from the typical American ufologist, whose knowledge extends more often than not only to those manifestations of the UFO phenomenon published in English, the only language he can read. Although he is aware of the universality of the phenomenon, his ignorance of foreign cases is abysmal; and as I have noticed in my lectures throughout the United States, he feels embarrassed by Argentinian cases he never heard of. Of course, it is not his fault, but rather the fault of supposedly international publications that in practice pay little attention to foreign cases. By contrast, the typical Southern Cone ufologist is better informed about cases outside his national boundaries, as I noticed when lecturing in Buenos Aires and Montevideo.

Organised ufology is strong in Argentina, where we find FAECE, a federation of numerous small groups. When I first became acquainted with FAECE during my trip with Dr. Hynek to a meeting in Rosario de Santa Fe in 1982, we were amazed at the low level of the papers presented, mostly on esoteric topics unrelated to ufology. The poor quality of the papers was matched only by the lack of information and/or knowledge of those presenting the talks. I cannot resist citing the example of a very nice gentleman who sincerely believed that quarks had real colors and flavors, and who had elaborated a complex theory based on those premises. Or the psychologist who honestly believed that he could send the minds of his patients on trips -- not through hypnosis, but by some vague concoction that he called "the fourth state" -- to spacecraft circling the Earth, so successfully in fact that he had been able to do a statistical study of these innumerable galactic civilisations.

But all this is ancient history. Under the able leadership of Roberto Rovere and Eduardo Ficarotti,

FAECE has turned over a new leaf, and the papers now presented in their annual meetings are of higher quality, and much more oriented toward the scientiic approach.

The problem with FAECE, as I see it, is that it devotes the efforts of its members, as well as its limited financial resources, to organizing the meetings, and the actual research is left to individuals. But perhaps this is the wise thing to do, because the FAECE congresses provide a forum for researchers, and also keep alive interest in the subject for the general public.

■ ARGENTINA

One of the earlier investigators of the UFO phenomenon in Argentina was Omar R. Pagani, an officer in the Navy who collected information in his official capacity. Although he is no longer active, his name appears in the list of references of many published papers, and that, by itself, is a warrant of credibility. For instance, as a captain of the Argentinian Navy he investigated the lengthy and complex Trancas sighting, which in my opinion is one of the best cases from that country.

Another Argentinian investigator is Dr. Oscar A. Galindez, whose name has appeared many times in the pages of *FSR* [**1**] as well as in other journals. His latest work has centered on the discussion of sightings of entities in the absence of an actual UFO (type CO). [**2, 3**] However, the Villa Carlos Paz events have been reinvestigated and strong criticism has been raised about his unquestioning acceptance of this case.

The name of Prof. Oscar A. Uriondo is also well known as a researcher who has specialized in the preparation of catalogs of UFO sightings in Argentina. In addition, his work has appeared in European publications [**4**] and he is the author of several books.

His initial catalog was compiled in 1972, but was updated in 1976, and I have used it extensively while selecting Argentinian cases for inclusion in UNICAT. Having thus become quite familiar with this work, I have two criticisms to make about it:

(i) Although in his introduction Uriondo recognizes the shortcomings of the Vallée classification, such as enclosing under the name "landings" a conceptually much larger variety of events that could be better described by using Dr. Hynek's system, he persists in using the obsolete Vallée terminology. As a result, the catalog is divided into four parts and is not a single chronological arrangement, which makes its use rather cumbersome; it is practically impossible to remember all the subdivisions of the modified classification to determine where to look, specially when one is not certain about the type of the case at hand.

(ii) The catalog is based almost exclusively on information collected from newspapers and popular magazines, although a few of the 200 entries are taken from more reliable sources.

Oscar Uriondo is quite aware of the limitations of his catalog and indicates that he has tried (in the 1976 version) to reduce the noise/signal to a minimum. I don't believe he handled this screening successfully, as many of the included cases lack even the basic bits of information and have only anecdotal value.

In spite of its heterogeneous contents, the catalog is a good reference work provided one is fully aware of its deficiencies and limitations. A new and more up-to-date listing of raw Argentinian cases is now being prepared by Carlos A. Demaria, an amateur astronomer.

Both Dr. Galindez and Prof. Oscar Uriondo don't seem to be active any longer on the Argentinian scene.

No review of the earlier UFO writers in Argentina would be complete without the mention of Pedro Romaniuk, whose name became known in Europe stemming from the publication of at least one of his books in German. While all previously named researchers can be considered serious, Romaniuk is precisely the opposite. His published work not only is tainted by his personal ideas on unrelated topics, but also presents information that on many occasions is distorted and even fraudulent. In short, he is not a reliable source.

The next name to mention is that of Lic. Guillermo C. Roncoroni, whose more significant work has been done in the last 10 or 12 years. In 1976 he founded *UFO PRESS*, a well edited magazine that by the early 80s had become the most important UFO magazine published in Spanish. Although it took many articles from other UFO publications, mainly the IUR, it also included reports on well investigated Argentinian cases, and *UFO PRESS* is an important reference for many cases that have not been published elsewhere. Unfortunately, as seems to be the fate of most UFO publications, at the writing of these lines (Sept. 1986) *UFO PRESS* has ceased to be a purely ufological publication, having moved to the newsstands. Under new management, its future seems dubious. The new editor is Alejandro Agostinelli, who is essentially a field investigator, and who has done some good work in the past.

But the most valuable contribution of Lic. Roncoroni is undoubtedly ARGENCAT, a computer catalog of Argentinian cases in which each entry contains quite a bit of information. I have used this catalog extensively in my work with UNICAT, and the only criticism that I have is that, as in many other catalogs (for instance UFOCAT), the entries are sequential, thus requiring codification as well as the use of a code book to read the output, column by column. The last version of ARGENCAT that has been received by the UNICAT Project is dated May 1985 and contains 290 entries. Significantly, the quality of the cases is listed in a special field, and although personally I don't agree totally with Roncoroni's grading system, to have a co-efficient of evaluation is a definite plus.

Regrettably, and due to the presures of his work, Lic. Roncoroni has also deserted the field of active ufology.

Another serious investigator is Roberto E. Banchs. By profession an architect, he has a passionate interest in the UFO phenomenon, and has been an active researcher for many years. As he is also a student of the philosophy and methodology of science, his work has not been limited to the discussion of cases, and he has produced illuminating articles reflecting his other interests as applied to ufology. He has published several books, of which perhaps the most important is *Los Ovnis y sus Ocupantes* [**5**] and he continues to be active in the field. [**6**]

His work should be considered careful and reliable, and he has made a significant contribution by unmasking some cases that, although given remarkable media coverage, are nothing more than frauds. Perhaps the most outstanding of those is the Llanca case (731028, near Bahia Blanca, Buenos Aires).

Another reliable Argentinian ufologist who has done significant work is Oscar Alemanno. Among other contributions, he has analyzed in depth the best cases with entities reported in Argentina. Unfortunately, his work is practically unknown outside his country.

A ufologist whose work has perhaps not been properly recognized is Alberto A. Diaz. Among his contributions is a compilation of massive sightings in the Southern Cone, ie events reported simultaneously by observers located in very large geographical areas. Although practically all of those cases have been identified (in some instances with the help of James Oberg) as produced by satellites and associate phenomena, his work is still valuable. incident reported in Uruguay.

Lic. Milton Hourcade has written a book in Spanish [**8**] and several papers which unfortunately are unknown outside his country as none of his work has been published in leading journals like *FSR* and *LDLN*. This is regrettable as many significant cases remain in limbo and out of reach for world ufology.

The Armed Forces in Uruguay have taken a serious and non-secretive stand regarding the UFO phenomenon, and in 1979 the Uruguayan Air Force created CRIDOVNI, a special commission responsible for the investigation and study of all UFO reports generated in the country. Membership in CRIDOVNI is not restricted by any means to military personnel, but includes representatives of many interested groups, as well as individual ufologists. When I visited Uruguay in 1982 with Dr. Hynek, CRIDOVNI received us extremely well and promised future cooperation, which did not materialize as no cases have occurred since.

CIOVI was invited to sit on this commission, but to maintain its independence of action, it was decided that its participation would be through individuals, like Hermann Jegerlehner and James Carren, rather than as a group.

I have waited purposely to the end of this section before naming Capt. Daniel A. Perisse. A career officer of the Argentinian Navy, he has recently retired and now devotes a great deal of his time to the study of the UFO phenomenon. His interest is not casual but dates from many years back, when he was the officer in charge during two incidents that are well known in the UFO literature: the sightings of June-July 1965 at Deception Island in Antarctica; and the chase of an unknown submarine in Gulf St. George in Argentinian territorial waters. This firsthand exposure to the UFO phenomenon has made him quite enthusiastic about the topic, and he is doing a rather novel piece of research in which he attempts to correlate the reported size of the UFOs with the dimensions of the associated humanoids. He is using the necessary information as provided by the UNICAT data base. In my opinion, he is one of the most promising researchers alive today in Argentina, and his influence and association with FAECE have given new life to this organization.

■ URUGUAY

Uruguay is smaller than its neighbors, Argentina and Brazil, both in territory and in population, thus offering a quite different ufological picture. Of all the civilian groups that existed briefly in the past, only one has resisted the erosion of time and the decline of interest in the topic, and that is CIOVI. This organization was founded in 1958 by Lic. Milton Hourcade, whose dedicated collaborators -- too numerous to list -- have been continuously active to the present day. CIOVI not only investigates the reports of UFO sightings within the country, but also sponsors lectures, TV and radio programs and other activities aimed at keeping alive interest in UFOs and divulging the subject to the general public.

The main characteristic of CIOVI is its serious scientific orientation, and it has intermingled with the scientific and academic establishment, organizing meetings and conferences, and more recently, advising official agencies on subjects related to the UFO phenomenon. Its most important contribution was collaborating in the revision of astronomy textbooks used at the high school level to incorporate a factual and unbiased presentation of the UFO problem.

Over the years the group has studied in depth ALL the sightings reported and has significantly contributed to unmasking cases that had been publicized as genuine on a global level, such as the 1968 Lopez photographs. [**7**]

The thoroughness and dedication of CIOVI is better evidenced by the fact that since 1940 a little over 300 UFO sightings have been reported in Uruguay. All of them have been investigatd in depth by CIOVI, with only a few surviving the persistent scrutiny. Of those, six have been accepted in the

UNICAT data base; in particular, the Isla de Lobos case (721028) is a textbook model of how a serious investigation should be done, and perhaps the best

■ CHILE

According to the last numbers released by UFOCAT before folding (1978), the number of sightings originating in Chile was about 500. If the statistics developed by the UNICAT project are valid for this country, the number of "good" reports should be between 5 and 15, but as of this writing (Sept. 1986), there is only one case from Chile in the data base, mostly because the country has not yet been fully studied. The basic reason for this is the lack of success in finding serious and reliable correspondents, which I hope to correct in the near future.

The information for this section has been obtained thanks to the kindness of Antonio Humeeus, a Chilean-born freelance journalist now living in New York. [**9**]

According to Humeeus, Chile never developed UFO groups capable of conducting suitable investigations of sightings, and only individuals have pursued ufology. The general public is interested in the phenomenon, but a large majority have tended to follow a mystical or religious interpretation of "extraterrestrials" very much like the "contactees" in the United States.

There are a few contactee groups operating in Chile, among which two deserve a warning mention: i) the RAMA groups, founded by a Peruvian contactee named Sixto Paz Wells following the "teachings" of another famous contactee, the Italian Eugenio Siragusa; and ii) a spiritual community in the valley of the Elqui, headed by a Mother Cecilia which follows the tradition of the "White Brotherhood" and claims to have contact with the "galactic fleet." These contactee groups are perhaps not too large in numbers, but they are certainly loud and vocal.

One of the more influential ufologists is Patricio Varela, a professional broadcaster who has had a late night radio program devoted to UFOs for the last 20 years. He is more a popularizer than a field researcher, but over the years he has compiled extensive files and interviewed numerous witnesses and UFO experts. He has a wide following and could be a key figure for any UFO-related project to be developed in his country.

The second name listed by Humeeus is that of Fernando Noel, a professional astronomer who works at the Cerro Calan Observatory of the University of Chile. He is a member of Dr. Sturrock's Society for Scientific Exploration, and his interest in the subject is slanted more toward the academic. Like many others, he had a change of attitude with respect to UFOs when he witnessed a UFO formation that could not be explained.

The name of Hugo Correa should be mentioned next. He is a well-known science fiction writer and newspaper columnist, and a former head of UFO Chile, a now-defunct small research group. Through his work with one of the daughters of President Pinochet in a foundation called Fundacion Chile, he maintains good connections with the government. At present, he writes a weekly column in the newspaper *La Tercera*.

The only organized civilian group existing in Chile is CIO, having a small membership (25-50 members) and headed by Hugo Pacheco. This group is somewhat discredited due to its religious overtones, which resulted in a split with the scientifically-oriented members, Luis Riquelme and Aquiles Castillo. These two investigators are the core of the ORION group, which is the closest thing to a scientifically-oriented UFO investigating organization.

As in many other countries, the Armed Forces have their own secret history regarding their involvement and interest in the UFO phenomenon, which in a way has been forced upon them by the unwilling participation of military personnel in notorious sightings. For this country, the most famous incidents are perhaps the case of Caporal Armando Valdez (770425, Arica), and the scrambling of F-5E fighters from Cerro Morena AFB in Antofagasta in 1978 and 1979.

The rumor is that the Armed Forces have information on many more cases, but again, as in many other countries including the USA and Great Britain, the military is not talking.

BRAZIL

Brazil, an enormous country both in extent and in natural resources, offers a completely different ufological picture. Indeed, many cases have been reported, mainly from the areas along the Atlantic Ocean where the population density is higher and the important cities are located. The problem is not an absence of the UFO phenomenon, but the low credibility of the reports.

Not only do these reports contain, in many instances, intrinsic shortcomings that deny their validity, but almost invariably they are tainted with the more or less esoteric beliefs of the writer, which can range very widely from spiritualism to witchcraft.

The UNICAT Project has received many so-called investigation reports from Brazil, but very few have met the basic requirements to be added to the data base. By comparison with reports received from other parts of the world, I have encountered three distinctive characteristics.

■ **a)** The writer himself, even if he is a professional, exaggerates the events that he is investigating, sometimes to the extreme of presenting speculations as fact, in direct and obvious contradiction with the pertinent information on which the case is based.

■ **b)** There is a high incidence of sexual episodes, either implicit or explicit, to the point that it seems that most reports from the last two decades present this particularity. During my last trip to Brazil,

I questioned my correspondents there, as well as some of the alleged witnesses, about this; the reply was, "We Brazilians are very sexy." That may be true, but no more so than in other Latin countries, where sex in UFO reports is practically unknown. Perhaps the Villas Boas case (571016), which of course is well known not only by ufologists but by the general public, might have some bearing on the situation, but the impression I got is that the witnesses are more interested in bragging about their sexual prowess than in discussing the stranger fact of their UFO encounter. This consideration alone makes me very skeptical about the great majority of modern Brazilian cases.

■ **c)** This third element may not be clear to those who are not familiar with UNICAT and its procedures for analyzing a case prior to accepting it for the data base. As we have processed more and more cases, we have noted that some rules seem to obtain. For instance, when NC (NC = number of UNICAT parameters found to pertain to a case) is small and the number of witnesses is more than 2, further investigation has shown in many instances that it was a misinterpretation by the witnesses. Or when in a case with a single witness, apparently supported, of course, by other physical evidence, NC is abnormally high (say, more than 30), almost invariably the case turns out to be a fraud.

Now, the analysis of contemporary Brazilian cases shows very often a large NC, sometimes 50% more than found in a similar case in other countries. Granted, this rule has no basis except that experience points to it as true, but at any rate it places a red flag on many of the investigation reports originating in Brazil.

It is difficult to put a finger on why Brazilian reports are lacking and leave the analyst with an unsatisfactory feeling. It is not the language, because reports translated into English and reports that I read directly in Portuguese have the same effect. Neither is it the style of the report nor the education of the author, as one of those fraudulent reports was sent to me by a professional psychologist. Whatever it is, the inescapable conclusion is that ufology in Brazil is not on a par with that in other parts of the world

Perhaps one could divide the history of the UFO phenomenon for this country into two periods: the classic, extending perhaps to the late 60s or early 70s, in which reports of UFO activity seem to insinuate a systematic exploratory effort; and the modern period, extending to the early 80s and typified by a predominance of CE3 and abduction reports, usually investigated poorly and documented worse. Few significant cases, if any, were reported during this period; but in May 1986 the pattern changed when UFOs apparently played for several hours with a frustrated Brazilian Air Force in the Sao Paulo area.

During the classic period, the name of Dr. Olavo Fontes (1924-1968) is outstanding. He was not only a very educated man, a physician with a distinguished career, but his position in society gave him connections with what he called "confidential sources" in the Armed Services. He was thus privy to information inaccessible to other investigators. I know this very well, as I have had an opportunity to examine in detail at least part of his private files. In fact, many of his investigation reports were never published, and the UNICAT Project has rescued several good cases from oblivion. As he was a scientist, his reports are written in the language of science, factual and without padding speculation. It is my considered opinion that Dr. Fontes was the best investigator of all time in Brazil. Among many other cases, he personally investigated some that time has made classic, such as the already-mentioned Villas Boas case, the Trindade Island photographs, and the Ubatuba incident, which is still under investigation.

The name of Dr. Walter K. Buhler has been a household word in Brazil since 1957, and he is still active in UFO research. His work has appeared many times in the pages of UFO journals like FSR. [**10, 11**]

He has recently co-authored a book [**12**] in which I have found the most concise description of the Villas Boas incident. Unfortunately, the quality of the content is very varied, with numerous incidents, involving mediums and psychics, most of them without merit. In addition, more than half of the pages are devoted to unjustified speculations, UFO politics and a definite attack on Dr. J. Allen Hynek. It follows that information now coming from Dr. Buhler must be taken with a grain of salt.

Another well-known ufologist is Irene Granchi, who for years has been the CUFOS representative in Brazil. She is very active in the field, as evidenced by her work appearing continuously in Brazilian newspapers and popular magazines such as *Planeta* and *Ufologia Nacional e Internacional*, and also in many UFO journals like IUR [**13**] and FSR. [**14**] It must be said, sadly, that Mrs. Granchi's enthusiasm sometimes causes her to rush out reports without having verified their correctness, and some cases in which she has been involved have been shown to be false. As a result, her credibility has suffered during the last few years.

Among the younger ufologists, the best known is A.J. Gevaerd, who has sent us, from time to time, lengthy reports about incidents in Brazil. His reports, like others, follow the pattern detailed above, and the analyst is left with many unresolved questions. He is also the editor of a rather new ufological publication, *Ufologia Nacional e Internacional*, a magazine that in editorial policies and content could compare to the *National Enquirer*. In recent times he has been associating with Wendelle Stevens, and although this makes him popular in Brazil, it detracts from his credibility with serious ufologists elsewhere.

A review of Brazilian ufology is not complete unless the binomial Marco A. Petit-Wanda Campos is mentioned. This young couple is obsessed with Billy Meier's photographs, which they consider genuine and the final proof of the extraterrestrial origin of UFOs. Their views have been given wide publicity in *Ufologia Nacional e Internacional*, while in the same magazine Irene Granchi states correctly that the Meier photos are the biggest hoax ever perpetrated. All of this may seem trivial to the reader of these pages, but it is not in Brazil, where Petit has a very wide and noisy following, and where the issue has divided the Brazilian ufologists into two groups at odds: those who analyze the UFO phenomenon scientifically, and the others, like Petit and Campos, for whom rationality has ceased to exist. I experienced their fanaticism and rudeness firsthand when they disrupted a lecture I had been invited to present in Rio de Janeiro, simply because I stated that in my opinion the Meier photographs were phonies.

PARAGUAY AND ECUADOR

Paraguay is a sleepy little country in the center of South America in which no organized ufological groups exist. But interest in the subject is present, and my lectures in Asuncion were well attended, even by high-placed government officers.

Although not investigated, UFO cases exist, particularly in the remote rural areas inhabited predominantly by Indians. They have seen things which they recognize as unusual, but the language barrier makes extracting the pertinent information from them rather difficult. Most of the Indians speak only Guarani, a musical language totally inappropriate for communicating this particular type of information. It is very frustrating to realize that there have been sightings, but that the investigation of them is practically impossible. Another interesting thing of which I became aware during my trip (December 1984) is that the problem of cattle mutilation is not unknown to breeders in that country, although they place the blame on jaguars which are abundant in the area. They were, however, quite unable to explain how jaguars could have transversely cut off the tongues of the dead animals.

The UNICAT representative in Paraguay is Carlos R. Jacks, a businessman from Asuncion, who has been trying to organize a research group for several years -- without much success, I must add.

My visit to Ecuador (April 1986) was very short, but I was invited to present UFO lectures at the two main universities in Quito. The talks were well attended, and I used the opportunity to try to locate any organized civilian group, or even individual ufologists. Although the audiences were really interested in the topic, no one was able to provide me with a usable lead, except for saying that at some time in the distant past the military had been interested in the subject. No one seemed to recall any UFO incident, past or present, so apparently the inescapable conclusion is that the UFO phenomenon is practically unknown in Ecuador. This does not mean that it doesn't occur, particularly -- as in Paraguay -- in the remote areas inhabited mainly by Indians. I am not talking here of savages, since the Indians in Ecuador, while maintaining separate cultures, have intense commerce with the rest of the population and even have retail outlets for their products abroad.

REFERENCES

1 - **Galindez,** Oscar A.: 'Trancas, after Seven Years'; *FSR* Vol 17, No.4, 1971, p.14 ■ 2 - **Galindez,** Oscar A.: 'The Anthropomorphic Phenomena at Santa Isabel': *FSR* Vol.21, No.2, 3, 4 and 5, 1975. ■ 3 - **Galindez,** Oscar A.: 'The Antropomorphic Entity at Villa Carlos Paz': *FSR* Vol.26, No.5, 1981, p.8. ■ 4 - **Uriondo,** Oscar A.: 'Preliminary Catalog of Type I Cases in Argentina': *FSR Case Histories* No.12. 1972. ■ 5 - **Banchs,** Roberto E.: *Los OVNIS y sus Ocupantes*, Ediciones Tres Tiempos, 1980. ■ 6 - **Banchs,** R.E. and Heiden, R.W.: in *The Journal for UFO Studies*, Vol.II, 1980, p.58. ■ 7 - **FSR** *Case Histories*, Supplement No.8, Dec.1971, p.4. ■ 8 - **Hourcade,** Milton W.: *Fenomeno OVNI, Desafio a la Ciencia*, Ediciones de la Plaza, Montevideo, 1978. ■ 9 - **Humeeus,** J.Antonio: 'A Chilean Overview': in *MUFON UFO JR*. No.218, June 1986, p.5. ■ 10 - **Buhler,** Walter K.: 'Extraterrestrial Dwarves attack Farm Worker': in *FSR* Vol.28, No.1, 1982, p.5. ■ 11 - **Buhler,** Walter K.: 'Ufonauts study a Brazilian Farm': in *FSR* Vol.28, No.2, 1982, p.12. ■ 12 - **Buhler,** W.K. and Pereira, G.: *Livro Branco dos Discos Voadores*: Petropolis, 1985. ■ 13 - **Granchi,** Irene: 'The Paciencia, Rio de Janeiro Case', in *IUR* Vol.2, No.11, Nov.1977. ■ 14 - **Granchi,** Irene: 'An encounter with "Rat-Faces" in Brazil', in *FSR* Vol.29, No.1, 1983, p.6.

A SAMPLER OF OUTSTANDING CASES

This survey of Ufology in South America would not be complete without including a few significant case histories. The most important and perhaps the best studied incident in Argentina is the Trancas case, but since it has been discussed satisfactorily in the literature (see, for instance, Ref.1 above) it would be redundant to add it here. The Trinidade photos have also been widely discussed, but the case has been included because new details have been disclosed by a careful study of the personal files of Dr. Olavo Fontes.

The Isla de Lobos sighting in Uruguay and the Yacanto, Argentina photo are hardly known outside their respective countries. However, both are unique cases that remain unexplained and should be presented to the non-Spanish-speaking public.

The fourth case, finally, describes a very recent radar-visual episode, in which the Brazilian Air Force was teased by unknowns for about three hours. This incident is not only intrinsically interesting, but poses a more fundamental question when one considers how fast the official sources of information dried up following an initially open disclosure policy. The same after-effect occurred following the Trinidade incident.

THE YACANTO PHOTOGRAPH

UFOTYPE: **CE1**
DATE: **July 3, 1960.**
TIME: **4.30pm.**
DURATION: **40 sec.**
WITNESSES: **1**
PLACE: **Yacanto, Cordoba, Argentina.**

This sighting is one of the best-recorded in Argentina, but it is practically unknown to English-speaking ufologists as it has been published in Spanish magazines only. Perhaps for that very reason it has escaped the attention of the professional debunkers, but a more likely cause is that it is an extraordinary case for which their usual hand-waving techniques simply would not work.

It is a single-witness case, but this witness is a high-ranking officer of the Argentinian Air Force (AAF), who by a fluke was able to obtain a remarkable photograph as supporting evidence of his encounter.

Even in Argentina, and perhaps due to the association of the witness with the AAF, the case was not given much publicity until 1977, when it finally was reported in *UFO Press*. [**15**]

The witness in this sighting is Hugo F. Niotti, then a captain of the AAF assigned to the Air Force School for Sub-officers located in the city of Cordoba. Contrary to what many would expect, his involvement in the case did not affect his military career, and seventeen years later, when finally interviewed by Roncoroni, he had risen to the high rank of vice-commodore, occupying a responsible position with the AAF.

THE INCIDENT

On July 3 1960, the then Captain Niotti was driving from Yacanto toward Cordoba. The weather was inclement, typical of what one would expect for that area in the middle of winter. It was drizzling off and on, and the cloud deck was very low, perhaps 100-150 m. The road was rather slippery, and Capt. Niotti was concentrating hard on his driving.

At approximately 4.30 PM, he was in the area of Villa General Belgrano, about 70 km from the city of Cordoba. He had finished negotiating a wide S-curve, when he suddenly noticed a rather close and unusual object hovering near the ground to the right of the road.

Startled, he stopped the car, grabbed his camera, fortunately next to him on the seat, moved a few steps away, and proceeded to take a photo of the object, which was moving slowly. While he was engaged in winding the film to take a second shot,

the object started to accelerate and disappeared into the clouds, which, as stated, were very low.

The whole incident had lasted about 40 seconds and had developed in the most absolute silence. This eerie silence, coupled with the bad weather and the abruptness of the incident, gave Capt. Niotti a sense of unreality, which puzzled and confused him. In this mood, he jumped back into his car and continued his trip to Cordoba, where he proceeded to have the film processed.

Here is Capt. Niotti's description of what he had seen. The object was conical in shape, with a height of 7-8 meters and a base diameter of 3-4 meters, with its axis almost parallel to the ground and its base facing the witness. It was at a distance of 80 to 100 meters from his location and moving very slowly toward the south, perhaps at 10 KPH, always parallel to the ground. It was rotating, also very slowly. It then accelerated very rapidly, attaining a speed of perhaps 200 KPH in 3 or 4 seconds, and disappeared into the low cloud bank. This sudden acceleration without any sound was inexplicable to the witness in view of his proximity.

The color of the object was a uniform dark gray. The surface was perfectly smooth without joints or rivets and had a definite metallic aspect.

THE PHOTOGRAPH

As an officer of the AAF, Niotti was naturally reluctant to divulge his experience and initially told only a few fellow officers, who persuaded him to send the negatives and copies to the *Revista Nacional de Aeronautica* (RNA); the editors of this official magazine transmitted the photos to the *Servicio de Informaciones de Aeronautica* (SIA), a technical service available to the Air Force.

The SIA gave a good bill of health to the photo, and the sighting was reported by the RNA in its issue of November 1960. It is remarkable that never before or after have the Armed Forces made public the results of a UFO investigation.

In the years to follow, many examinations of this photo have been done except, perhaps, by the so-called debunkers, and no negative opinions have been voiced.

There are two interesting details in the photo which must be emphasized. When Capt. Niotti saw the object, his perception was of a uniform color; thus, he was surprised -- after developing the film -- that in the photographic image the base of the cone is a dull black, without any gradation of color in spite of being oriented toward the sun, which was hidden by the clouds. The rest of the cone appears much lighter, to the point that it is sometimes difficult to obtain copies showing it clearly, due to the high contrast between the base and the sky background. The edges of the base, in the original negative, appear sharp and well defined, even more defined than other elements appearing in the photograph. It seems as if the base of the cone were a total sink of radiation, reflecting no light.

The copy of the photo presented in this report is from a second-generation negative, and its quality does not compare with the prints made from the original negative.

The other anomalous detail in the photo is the presence of a horse whose head is turned around, its attention apparently drawn by the object. As anyone familiar with a rural environment knows, horses kept in pastures near roads become totally indifferent to traffic and will not interrupt their grazing for the presence of a car. Nevertheless, the horse seems to be looking directly at the object, placed halfway between him and the road.

The existence of the horse is fortunate, as it has allowed some estimates of sizes and distances. The Argentinian investigators have performed some photogrammetry using the original negative, and report that the horse is about 80 meters from the road, which places the object at no more than 50 meters from Capt. Niotti. No wonder he was surprised by the absolute silence!

On the basis of these estimates, the dimensions of the cone were 7 m in height and 6 m in diameter, and it was 17 meters above the ground, in good agreement with the numbers indicated by Capt. Niotti.

But the most interesting detail, which I have reserved for the end, is that Capt. Niotti was extremely surprised when he inspected the copies of the photo and saw the horse, as he had not noticed its presence during the incident. This is a clear indication of his concentration while taking the photo, and his disorientation after the sudden departure of the object when he just jumped back into his car and continued his trip.

COMMENTS

A case with a single witness usually is not even considered for incorporation into UNICAT, but in this instance we have two circumstances that allow an exception to the rule.

First, we have a competent witness, trained by his profession to observe details, who did not lose his presence of mind when confronted with the unknown. On the contrary, he reacted promptly, snatching his camera and jumping out of his car to obtain a unique graphic document.

And second, the photograph by itself lends enough credibility to the case to make it deserve serious consideration. Not only has the photo repeatedly been shown to be genuine, but it is inconceivable that an Air Force officer would compromise his career with a fabrication that would bring him nothing but problems and discredit. For those who know Vice-commodore Niotti, this option is unthinkable.

From the UNICAT viewpoint, the case also offers some interesting characteristics which confirm its value. Among the many parameters searched for when studying a case, there are two that are considered as particularly significant because of their high statistical incidence. Both of them apply to this sighting:

DR: driving a vehicle

LR: lonely road or place.

The first of these parameters appears in the UNICAT data base with a frequency of 33.8%, while LR shows a frequency of 37.9%, both of them being included within the ten most frequent parameters.

A third parameter that is not so frequent, but that seems to occur in significant cases, is also found for this incident. It is the RC parameter, ie "rounding a curve." It indicates that the witness suddenly notices the phenomenon when coming out of a curve in the road.

In short then, the Yacanto photo is unique and outstanding among the Argentinian cases, one of the best reported from that country.

REFERENCE

15 - **Roncoroni,** G.: 'Foto de *OVNI* Avalada por la Fuerza Aerea Argentina', in *UFO Press* No.3, April 1977.

THE BEST URUGUAYAN CASE

UFO TYPE: **CE3**
DATE: **October 28, 1972.**
TIME: **10.15 pm.**
DURATION: **1 minute.**
WITNESSES: **1**
PLACE: **Isla de Lobos, Uruguay.**
35 deg. 1' S; 54 deg. 53' W.

Isla de Lobos is a small island a few miles off the Uruguayan coast, just where the River Plate meets the Atlantic Ocean. Its name means literally "island of the fur seals", as these animals roam freely, and it is a lonely place where the only outstanding feature is the lighthouse.

The maintenance of this lighthouse is the responsibility of the Navy, and for that purpose a small garrison of 4 or 5 men is kept on the island. Their main task is to attend to the electric generators, as the actual operation of the beam is automatic. It is a routine and non-stressing job, and the tours of duty are 15 days in and 15 days out.

THE INCIDENT

On the night of October 28 1972, there were five men at the house which serves as headquarters for the Navy personnel: the witness, Corporal Juan Fuentes Figueroa; two enlisted men, Jose Gomez and Hector Gimenez; a telegraph operator, Jose Lima; and the sub-officer in charge, Francisco Cascudo. After dinner, the men sat around the table for a while, talking and playing cards, until at 10.10 pm it was time for Cpl. Fuentes to inspect the generators, which are located at the base of the lighthouse proper.

The lighthouse is a 66-meter-high tower sitting at the center of a large building which contains the electric generators, the telegraph office and other dependencies. The top of this building is a flat terrace, which is about 6 meters above the adjacent terrain **(Fig.1)**. The house where the garrison lives is at a distance of 45 meters from the lighthouse.

As soon as Cpl. Fuentes started to walk towards the lighthouse, he noticed on top of the terrace some lights that shouldn't be there. In fact, he thought first of a car, a complete impossibility, and his reaction was to return to the house and procure a pistol that he had in his room. To do this, he didn't have to pass through the kitchen where the other men were, so he didn't speak to them. As will be discussed later, this behavior is typical of the personality of the witness.

Carrying the pistol, he went outside again and started walking decisively but not fast toward the lighthouse, meanwhile removing the safety from the gun and cocking it. As he advanced, he noted that the object had several lights: some white, some yellowish, and a third color that he describes as violet, as in the "rainbow". Those lights were sufficient to allow him a good view, and he saw that a figure was next to the object and that a second was in the process of descending. A third and taller figure started to descend almost at once, but at that moment, the initial two figures noticed Fuentes progressing toward them. They had what appeared to Fuentes as a moment of communication, and all three of them faced him.

By that time, Fuentes was at about 27 meters from the object, which, we will recall, was on top of a 6-meter terrace. Hence, the object was above him, and he started to raise his extended arm to shoot. He was never to complete his motion, as the entities prevented him from doing so. Fuentes, a man of limited education, tried in vain to explain to the investigators how this was accomplished. It was not telepathy, and he felt some physical effects, like a "vibration" and his hair standing on end; but more than anything else it was like a premonition, in his words like: "Don't shoot because it is useless". At any rate, he felt paralyzed and confused, and was unable to shoot.

The action continued rather fast: the entities reentered their craft, the tallest one first. Although Fuentes did not see steps or a handrail, he could see quite well the motion of the figures against the lights of the object, outlined by the light coming out through the open door. He is certain that there were steps, as while the entities were climbing up with their backs toward the witness, their motions were like those of a person pulling himself up with handrails.

The door closed sideways, and the craft started to move straight up, emitting a humming sound until it reached about 45 meters, as judged by the adjacent lighthouse tower. It then tilted, belched a blinding fireball from the bottom, and disappeared in silence

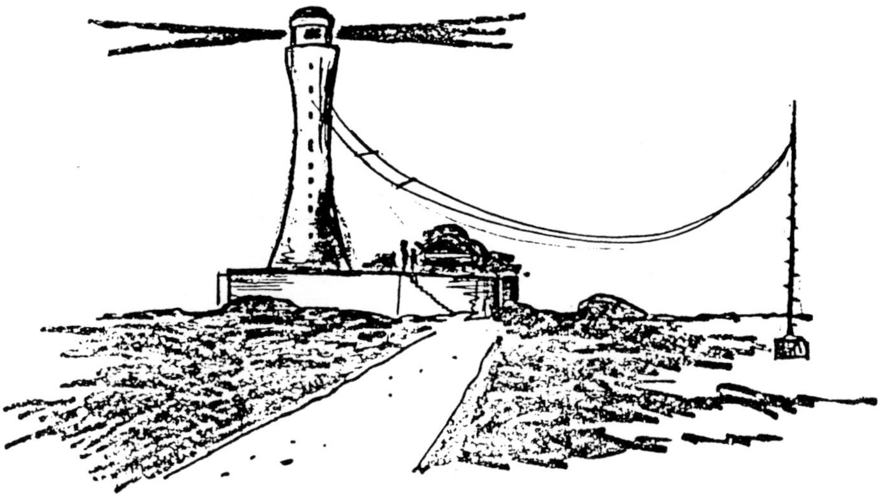

FIGURE 1.

at a tremendous speed toward the south-east.

The witness returned to the house, where the other men noticed him white as a paper and still with gun in hand. When he said that he had seen a flying saucer, he was not believed, except perhaps by Sub-Officer Cascudo.

Corporal Fuentes was rather upset that his equals and his immediate superiors were dubious of his story, and was planning when he returned to Montevideo to go to one of the leading newspapers and make his experience public. However, before this was accomplished, he was ordered to report to a higher ranking officer, who carefully listened to what Fuentes had to say. He then disappeared into an office in which two members of the personnel of the American Embassy had been waiting.

According to Fuentes, they were officers of the "*Spatial Affairs Service*", (sic) and their presence in the Command Offices was not unusual. Fuentes was left waiting in the corridor, and after a while someone came out and offered him some drawings for inspection and asked him to select the one closest to what he had seen. He did so and was dismissed. He never talked directly to the Americans, but from the conversation overheard through the door, he concluded that they were surprised at the short distance of Fuentes' observation. And I am amazed at the continuous interest shown by American Embassies in collecting information about a phenomenon that we have been told many times does not exist...

CRAFT AND ENTITIES

While the whole incident lasted about one minute, Cpl. Fuentes had the object in direct view for no more than about 15 seconds. It was well illuminated by its own lights, and it was fortuitous that the external lights usually illuminating the exterior of the installations were not on at the time, as the generators that feed those lights were not in operation that night. If the floodlights had been on, they would have prevented a clear view by the witness, even blinding him at the location of the observation. As things turned out, he observed the entities in the background light of their own craft, and even if this prevented him from seeing facial details, for example, their outline and motions were quite evident.

When Cpl. Fuentes started to walk toward the lighthouse, the first entity was already on the terrace, while the second was alighting from the craft. These two entities were about 1.50 m (5 ft), while the third one, the last to descend, was 1.75-1.80 m (6 ft). Thus, their heights were within the normal human limits **(Fig.2)**. Their silhouettes were dark, as if they were wearing heavy black rubber suits. The witness attributed their slow and deliberate motions to the weight of their suits, and thinks that his presence surprised the strangers at the beginning of an operation never to be completed. Their descent from the craft was done backwards, as if using a ladder

FIGURE 2.

not seen by the witness. Likewise, when they climbed back into the object, their motions were those of a person pulling himself up using handrails.

The most distinctive feature of the entities, clearly noticeable in the profile view that they offered to the witness, was the elongated shape of the back of their heads. It is not clear if this corresponds to the heads themselves, or if it was the result of some type of hood or garment.

The craft itself had the shape of an inverted bowl, with a diameter of between 4 and 5 meters. It had a dome on top and a rectangular aperture or door, used by the entities to descend **(Fig.3)**. It also had legs, which the witness saw clearly during the first stage of the departure, as the craft was slowly gaining altitude. Those legs did not fold like the landing gear of a plane, but retracted telescopically.

The surface of the craft was undoubtedly metallic, with a somewhat reddish color that Fuentes compared to mahogany. The most distinctive feature of the object was the antenna that topped it, shaped like a corkscrew and rotating.

The lights have already been described, and it only is necessary to add that they seemed to Fuentes like "*little squares*", moving and flashing like "*an advertising sign*".

Of course, what Fuentes actually saw is the superposition of Figs. 2 and 3, as shown in **Fig.4**.

FIGURE 3.

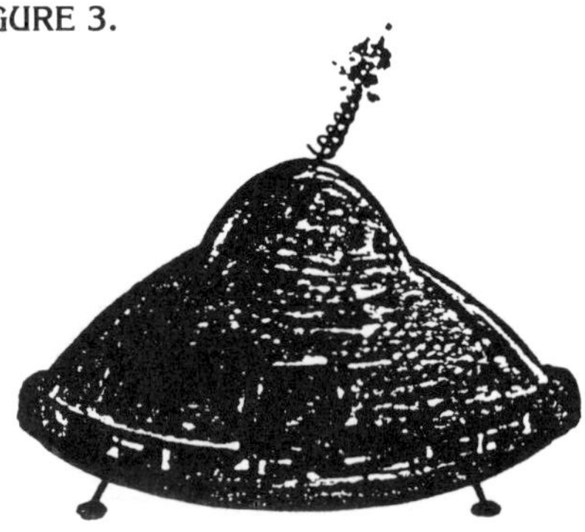

THE WITNESS

This is a single-witness sighting, and yet it has become the best case coming from Uruguay due to the in-depth investigation done by the members of CIOVI. This paper is based on the information contained in their report on this case. [**16**]

The first stage of the investigation consisted of two lengthy interviews with the witness in his own home. The two interviews were recorded, and the transcripts do not reveal any discrepancies in the narrative.

This was followed by an *in situ* reconstruction of the events, with the participation of the witness. Sub-officer Cascudo, present on the island that night, verified that the initial version by Cpl. Fuentes was similar to the subsequent descriptions relayed later to the investigating team. Sub-officer Cascudo, as well as other superiors of Corporal Fuentes, described him as a "*simple and honest man, incapable of inventing a story of this nature.*"

But indeed the most fascinating part of the CIOVI investigation was to request the assistance of a professional and to submit the witness to a battery of psychological tests that extended over a total of 9 hours, and that included, among others, Raven, Bender, Rorschach and PMK.

The results of those various tests dwell on positive and negative aspects of the personality of the witness, but when analysed in the light of the narrative presented by Corporal Fuentes, they complement each other and tend to lend credibility to the story.

In what follows, the key elements of the psychological evaluation will be indicated with quotation marks, interspaced with comments on how they relate to the particular facets of the case.

FIGURE 4.

First of all, the witness is described as "*sincere, uncomplicated and simple*." He expresses what for him is the truth, and he does that in a straightforward manner, with no cultural burden distorting what he has to say.

The witness "*has no tendency to fabrication or fantasy*", which if existing would damage his credibility. Moreover, he has "*less than average intellectual capacity*", to which the psychologist adds that he "*lacks an average imagination*" and "*has a remarkably poor knowledge of what is going on in the social environment*". All of these are plusses from the viewpoint of the credibility of the witness, and negate the possibility of him having created the whole story. And in fact, the investigators were able to determine that the ufological knowledge of the witness was practically non-existent.

From the emotional viewpoint, the witness is typified as "*insecure, prompt to react anxiously and even aggressively*" to an unexpected situation. That is exactly what the witness did when confronted with the impossible presence of a car on the terrace: his first reaction was to arm himself, although he could not explain later to the investigators what he intended to do with the gun. But he was following his training, and thus bolstered his confidence.

Another result of the psychological tests is that the witness has "*a balanced psychic personality*", and it is "*unlikely that he would confabulate by himself, unless an external event would upset him*". To summarize, his poor intellectual capacity and lack of imagination did not allow him to reason what was best to do when confronted with the unexpected, and instead of firing his gun or alerting his companions, he failed to do either, remaining paralyzed and confused. When he returned to the house, the other men noticed his trembling voice and his pale color, so there is no question that an external stimulus affected him deeply.

The conclusion, then, is that the psychology and personality of the witness are such that his reactions and behavior under the circumstances are totally compatible. Therefore, the probability that the witness is telling the truth is very great.

Of course, there is always an uncertainty about what percentage of the description of the witness corresponds to the physical reality of the object and the entities, but we can assert that in fact some event took place that night. If this is combined with the fact that Isla de Lobos is a remote place, moreover, a restricted area with difficult access, controlled by the Uruguayan Navy, and where no conventional explanations are viable, the inescapable conclusion is that this case is, using Dr. Maccabee's coined word, a TRUFO.

REFERENCE

16 - Hourcade, Milton, et al.; *Informe Final en el Caso de la Isla de Lobos del 28 de Octubre de 1972*; C.I.O.V.I., March 1975.

TRINIDADE ISLAND

UFO TYPE: **CE1**
DATE: **January 16, 1958.**
TIME: **12.20 pm.**
DURATION: **1-2 minutes.**
WITNESSES: **48**
PLACE: **Trinidade Island, Brazil.**
20 deg. 30' S.; 29 deg. 20' W.

It is curious how some cases occurring many years ago have apparently been immune to the attack of the self-appointed debunkers, remaining to this day "unexplained." But it is more curious when those sightings are hardly ever mentioned in the modern literature, in spite of their potential probatory value for the reality of the UFO phenomenon. The photographs taken on Trinidade Island by Almiro Barauna are one such case, and it is appropriate to mention it here as an example of Brazilian sightings.

THE SCENARIO

Trinidade Island is in the Atlantic Ocean, about 1200 km (750 miles) from the east coast of Brazil, the country to which it belongs. It is a small rocky place, used as an anti-submarine base by the USA during World War II, and abandoned afterward. In October 1957, during the International Geophysical Year, the Brazilian Navy reopened the installations, establishing a meteorological station and an oceanographic post. During January 1958, the vessel *Almirante Saldanha* of the Hydrographic and Navigation Service of the Brazilian Navy had arrived at the island on a routine trip, and on the morning of January 16 was anchored close to shore, making ready to sail back to Rio de Janeiro.

THE CAST

Besides the normal crew of the *Almirante Saldanha*, under the command of Jose Saldanha da Gama, there was on board a group of submarine divers who had been invited by the navy to take underwater photographs around the island. This civilian group was headed by Amilar Vieira Filho, a lawyer and bank executive, and included among others a retired captain of the Brazilian Air Force, Jose Teobaldo Viegas, as well as Almiro Barauna, a professional photographer. All in all, 48 eyewitnesses were on the deck during the incident, including the ship's dentist, Lt. Homero Ribeiro. Also on board, but not on the deck, was Capt. Carlos Alberto Bacellar, who had been responsible for revamping the installations on the island and had commanded the oeanographic station since October 1957, and who was now returning to Rio.

A few words concerning Barauna are mandatory, as the circumstances made him the leading character of the play. Barauna was 42 years old at the time, and had had some previous involvement with UFOs when in 1953 he disputed the authenticity of the photos taken by Ed Keffel in a place known as Barra da Tijuca [**18 p41**], publishing an article in a popular magazine to demonstrate how the photos could have been obtained. It is unfortunate that Dr. Menzel, a somewhat unsuccessful debunker, as well as others, used this article to cast dispersions on Barauna, presenting him as a professional hoaxer.

THE PLAY

On January 16 1958, preparations to cast anchor were under way, and Barauna was on the deck with his Rolleiflex Model E camera, with a f2.8 lens. [**17 p167**] As he intended to photograph the boat used for shore transfers during its final trip and while it was taken on board, he had set his camera at f8 and a speed of 1/125. The sea was not calm and this had upset Barauna, who had forgotten to take his seasickness pills.

At 12.20 pm, a disturbance occurred when everyone on the deck became excited by the fast approach of a bright object moving toward the island. Mr. Vieira Filho and Mr. Viegas, as well as Lt. Ribeiro, shouted to Barauna, gesticulating and pointing to the area of the overcast sky where the object was. After about 30 seconds, Barauna proceeded to take six photographs in a time interval of 14 seconds, as determined by later tests. The photos have been so widely published in the literature [**17, 18, 19**] that it would be superfluous to reproduce them here. The first two photographs were taken while the object was approaching the island. It then disappeared behind the central mountain (Desejado Peak) only to reappear a few seconds later moving in the opposite direction, apparently closer and bigger (photo 3). It then moved at high speed toward the ocean, but due to the confusion prevailing on the deck, Barauna missed the object in his next two frames. He managed, however, to obtain a fourth photo when the object was already far out at sea, and apparently it had stopped momentarily in mid-air. After about 10 seconds, it moved away and disappeared in the distance.

Following the incident, Comm. Bacellar as well as other officers insisted that the film be developed at once, in spite of the poor facilities existing on board and the lack of photographic paper to make prints. A bathroom was transformed into a darkroom and the film was developed. The negatives were examined by Bacellar and others. Frames 4 and 5 did not show the object, only the sea and the rocky coast.

An interesting detail revealed by Dr. Olavo Fontes [**20**] is that to make certain that no substitution would be possible, Comm. Bacellar forced Barauna to enter the darkroom in his swimming trunks. Comm. Bacellar had good reasons for this, as he knew that previous sightings had occurred on the island.

THE PROPS

The photos were taken on a bright overcast day and as the settings of the camera were not quite correct, they are slightly over-exposed. It was, however, a wise decision by Barauna not to attempt to modify the settings, since if he had done so he probably would have lost his opportunity.

Acording to Capt. Viegas, the object was like a flattened sphere encircled at the equator by a large ring or platform. In the words of Barauna:

"It made no noise, although with the shouting of the people on the deck and the noise of the sea I cannot be certain. It had a metallic look, of an ash color, and had like a condensation of a green vapor around the perimeter, particularly on the advancing edge. Its motion was undulating, like the flight of a bat."

As determined by the photographs, the object was tilted slightly, with the upper part oriented in the direction of the motion. It appears quite sharply in photos 2 and 3, corresponding to the closest approach and minimum speed, while the contours appear slightly blurred in photos 1 and 4, corresponding to the maximum distance. In view of the separation between object and camera, a shutter speed of 1/125 sec is enough to freeze an object moving at speeds of several hundred miles per hour, and the Brazilian Navy estimated the speed to be 600-700 mph. [**17 p168**] The object shown in the four photos resembles the planet Saturn, and it is not luminous.

The photos were proclaimed authentic by John T. Hopf, APRO photographic analyst, as well as by the Cruzeiro do Sul Aerophoto-grammetric Service, to which they were referred by the Brazilian Navy.

The Cruzeiro do Sul made very large copies of the photographs, which were examined by the Ministry of the Navy and the American Embassy. According to Dr. Fontes [**20**] who had confidential sources in the Brazilian Navy, enlargements show details not clear in the released copies, like two semi-spherical protuberances, or cupolas, in the bottom part, from which things similar to antennas seem to stick out.

THE CRITICS

The incident and the photos caused a furore in Brazil and were given wide press coverage. An inquiry to the Ministry of the Navy by a member of Parliament (Sergio Magalhaes) prompted an investigation. The resulting dossier was never made public in its totality but some details became known to the press, which also discovered additional information. The incident was not isolated, but at least seven other sightings had occurred during the end of 1957 and in early 1958, one of them in broad daylight on March 7 1958. [**20**] Some of the earlier events were witnessed and confirmed by Comm. Bacellar. A fifth photograph, taken with a box camera by a sergeant of the garrison prior to January 16, was part of the dossier. Although never officiallly released, it was shown to Barauna when interrogated at the Ministry of the Navy, and is also mentioned by Dr. Fontes. [**20**] The Barauna photographs were released to the press by the then President of Brazil, Mr. Juscelino Kubitschek, in person.

The US Naval Attache in Rio (M. Sunderland, Capt. USN) filed a report [21] on the incident on March 11 1958, characterized by its inaccuracies and the obvious bias of the writer, epitomized by the closing paragraph aimed at pleasing his superior officers:

"...a flying saucer sighting would be unlikely at the very barren island of Trinidade, as everyone knows Martians are extremely comfort loving creatures..."

Yet this report transcribes the official position of the Brazilian government, referring to a carefully worded communique issued by the Ministry of the Navy, which denies any attempt to suppress the release of the photos that *were taken by Mr. Almiro Barauna* in the presence of Navy officers on board the *Almirante Saldanha,* and remarks that the Navy could not venture an opinion on the nature of the *object that was observed over Trinidade Island.* The emphasis has been added to indicate that for the Brazilaian Navy two things were beyond question: i) that an unidentified object had been detected over Trinidade Island; and ii) that the Barauna photos were indeed taken at that location and showed that object, whatever its nature.

REFERENCES

17 - **Lorenzen,** Coral E.; *The Great Flying Saucer Hoax.* Signet Books edition, 1966, pp.164-74. ■ 18 - **Story,** Ronald; *The Encyclopedia of UFOs,* Doubleday, 1980, pp.366-69. ■ 19 - **Bougard,** Michel; in *Stendek* No.26, December 1976, p.14. Translated from original in French. ■ 20 - **Fontes,** Dr. Olavo; Memorandum in private research papers, UNICAT files. ■ 21 - **Sunderland,** M., Capt. *US Navy. Information Report 39-58,* dated 11 March 1958. Office of Naval Intelligence.

THE BRAZILIAN INCIDENT

UFO TYPE: **RV**
DATE: **May 19, 1986.**
TIME: **9 pm.**
DURATION: **approx. 3 hrs.**
WITNESSES: **numerous.**
PLACE: **States of Sao Paulo & Rio, Brazil.**

After maintaining a low profile for a period of several years, UFOs have regained the world headlines following an incident in Brazilian air space during the night of May 19 1986.

In spite of the large amount of clippings received from UNICAT correspondents in Brazil and Argentina, as well as reprints of news items that appeared in American newspapers, I find it difficult to organize the information into a coherent narrative. The different Brazilian news-papers and the statements of government officials provide somewhat contradictory versions of the events, but it is clear that something out of the ordinary occurred, enough to shake the complacency of the authorities.

SEQUENCE OF EVENTS

The night of May 19 1986, a Monday, was clear with good visibility, devoid of heavy clouds that could affect radar.

An executive plane, a Brazilian-made two-engine Xingu owned by EMBRAER (Empresa Brasilena de Aeronautica), was en route from Brasilia to Sao Jose dos Campos (near Sao Paulo). While starting its descent, it was alerted by the Sao Paulo radar control that an unknown object was in the area. The presence of this unknown was confirmed shortly by the radar at Brasilia. [22]

In the pilot seat of the Xingu was a well known man: Colonel Osires Silva, former president of EMBRAER, who had just been appointed head of PETROBRAS, the Brazilian state-owned oil company. According to the official version, Col. Silva was the first to visually spot the unidentified object as a "dancing point in the sky". [23] The time was 21.10. [29]

Next to Osires Silva was a civilian pilot for EMBRAER: Commander Alcir Pereira da Silva, age 37, with more than 6000 hours of flying time. In his statement to the press [22] Comm. Pereira da Silva indicated that when the Xingu had descended to 2000 ft., the pilots perceived a strong light and turned the plane in its direction. The light is described as "brighter than a star, emitting a constant red-orange light" and also as being on for 10-15 seconds, then off, only to reappear at a different location. [22] Whatever the cause was, the pilots were very soon discouraged and abandoned the chase after about 30 minutes.

By that time, the Brazilian Defense Center (CINDACTA = Centro Integrado de Defesa Aerea e Controle de Trafego Aereo) which apparently controls all air traffic, was on full alert, as the radar screens in the vicinity of Sao Jose dos Campos and nearby Sao Paulo were saturated and all air traffic had been disrupted. [23]

Only minutes after the appearance of the unknown objects on the radar screens, jets were scrambled from two Air Force bases (see map): Santa Cruz, in the State of Sao Paulo, and Anapolis, near Brasilia. Although the number of jet fighters scrambled, as well as the number of UFOs that were detected, varies depending on the spokesman, the indisputable fact is that planes were dispatched, attempted to approach the lights, and failed.

The UFOs had initially appeared over a mountainous region between the states of Rio de Janeiro and Minas Geraes, known as the Sierra de la Manchiqueira. [23] The incident terminated near midnight as suddenly as it had started, with the UFO disappearing simultaneously from radar and from visual observation after moving toward the ocean beyond the Brazilian coast. The duration of the sighting was close to three hours.

THE PILOTS' TALES

The Brazilian Air Force allowed the pilots to have a press conference in which they freely expressed their versions of the events of May 19. According to our correspondent in Rio, Mrs. Irene Granchi, the 7 pilots and 3 radar controllers that participated in the incidents appeared on television. [**25**]

We summarize their statements from the information received from Mrs Granchi, as well as from the version published by the prestigious newspaper *O Globo*. [**24**]

All of the seven pilots were military, except the already named Comm. Alcir Pereira da Silva.

Three F-5E jets were scrambled from the Santa Cruz AFB near Sao Paulo, two of them at 22.23 and the third at 22.55. In addition, three Mirage III jet fighters were scrambled from the Anapolis AFB at 22.50 [**29,**] but only one had an effective contact. The time of the actual contacts has been established as between 22.55 and 23.20. [**29**]

The pilot of one of the F-5Es was Lt. Kleber Caldas Marinho, age 25. Following the instructions of the radar controller, he vectored his plane to a target 35 miles distant, but was unable to close in. The radar control in Brasilia informed him at this point that the target was approaching him rapidly. However, the pilot didn't see anything, and in his own words, "One gets scared of what one sees, and I saw nothing." But later in the chase, he finally obtained a visual contact. As verified by both the ground radar and the on-board radar, the target was at a distance of 35 miles, but when the pilot tried to narrow the gap it was "like attempting to reach a point at infinity," in spite of his 1000 km/hr (625 mph) speed. As his fuel was getting low, he returned to the Santa Cruz Air Force Base. [**24**] He describes the target as a reddish light, very intense, which changed colors when the chase was aborted, first to white, then to green and to red again. [**24**]

The pilot of the second F-5E, Capt. Marcio Jordao, age 29, was luckier, as he was able to reduce the distance to the target to 12 miles. He described the UFO as a very strong light of continuous intensity, which changed colors continuously from white to green. Capt. Jordao broke off contact when the object moved over the sea beyond the 200-mile limit from Santa Cruz. [**24**]

Of the three Mirages scrambled from the Anapolis base, only one was able to establish actual contact. It was piloted by Capt. Armindo Souza Viriato de Freitas, age 30, whose statements we transcribe:

"I was warned by ground control that there were several targets ahead of me, at a distance of 20 miles and ranging in number from 10 to 13. I was also advised that the targets were approaching my plane, and finally that they were following me at a distance of 2 miles (sic). I had to lower my plane, as the lights had descended, but from then on they climbed vertically. This was my only visual contact, but I could see them in my radar at a distance of 12 miles". [**25, 29**]

The radar controller at the Anapolis AFB was Lt. Hugo Nunes Freitas (notice the similarity of names) and he advised Capt. Viriato that he had several targets behind his plane, six to one side and seven to the other.

Acording to *O Globo* [**24**] Capt. Viriato added that the targets made 80 degree turns (possibly 180 degrees was meant) and that he could not manage to have a visual contact right ahead of his plane. "No plane I know can make turns like that at 1000 km/hr," he concluded.

One of the traffic controllers, Lt. Valdecir Fernando Coehlo, stated: "In my 14 years of experience as a radar operator, I never saw anything like this." ... Familiar, isn't it?

At the close of the press conference, and immediately following the pilots' reports, the Air Ministry declared that no further reports are to be expected on the incidents until the special commission appointed to investigate the events has reached a conclusion.

AIR MINISTER

Some unusual and out of character developments must be pointed out. The Air Minister, Brigadier Octavio Julio Moreira Lima, after informing the President of Brazil, Jose Sarney, of the incident, proceeded to inform the press that the radar screen of CINDACTA in Sao Paulo had been saturated, that jets had been scrambled, and that visual-radar contacts had been established with "balls of light of multiple colors."

This is the first time that a high-ranking officer of the air force of any nation has come forward and admitted the presence of unidentified objects, and moreover, that intercept attempts had failed. [**23, 26**]

In addition, the Air Minister carried on his press conference in a semi-humorous tone, indicating that he "always wanted to see a UFO as a child," but adding "that radar is not subject to optical illusions. The radar echoes are due to solid objects or to massive clouds, which were not present that night."

Strangely enough, the Air Minister Brig. Moreira Lima, did not seem concerned about this unchecked penetration of Brazilian air space, but was rather proud of the prompt response of the Air Force to an alert. [**28**]

According to *CLARIN* [**23,**] the decision to release the news to the public was made personally by President Sarney; another first.

CONCLUSIONS

Although their number is uncertain, numerous UFOs were observed visually and detected by both ground and airborne radars. The episode lasted for near three hours, but the only concrete information is that they were balls of light of different and changing colors, which the jet fighters could not really approach. As in many other cases, the initiation and termination of the incident were sudden and unexpected.

Weather was good, a clear night without clouds, so that radar echoes remain unexplained. The number of echoes was very large, enough to saturate the radar screens and, according to the Air Minister, corresponded to solid targets.

Nowhere in the original Brazilian newspaper clippings have I found a direct quote about the ping-pong balls mentioned in the American press. *CLARIN* of Buenos Aires [**23**] states that the UFOs were described alternatively as stars, football balls, or ping-pong balls.

As for the speeds of the UFOs, only two specific quotes were made by the Brazilian press. The first refers to the statements made by Colonel Osires Silva, an aeronautical engineer by training, while commenting on his attempt to approach the lights. He indicated that the maximum speed of his plane was 400 km/hr (250 mph), while the lights were apparently moving at a speed of 1500 km/hr (937 mph). [**27**]

The second concrete mention of speeds was made by Major Ney Cerqueira, head of CINDACTA, who actively participated in the tracking operations. According to Maj. Cerqueira, "due to technical limitations in the radar equipment" the speeds could not be determined with precision. "The speeds detected varied in an interval of 5 to 10 minutes from 150 knots/hr [sic] to 800 knots/hr [sic]". [**26**] In miles per hour, this corresponds to a range of 173 to 921 mph, and matches well with the information that jets with speeds of 1000 km/hr (625 mph) were unable to close on the lights.

The sighting started, according to the Air Ministry, at 20.50 and ended about midnight, having thus a total duration of 3 hours. [**29**] Finally, the number of UFOs has been quoted by the media as between 13 and 21. The Air Minister placed the number at 20. [**28**]

Since most of the information on which this report is based was obtained from newspaper clippings, usually a very unreliable source, it is necessary to emphasize that in this particular instance the media did a very faithful reporting job. Most of the details were released at the press conference during which the pilots related their experiences and were directly questioned by reporters. The information written in the different papers is consistent and accurate. In addition, the Air Ministry released further information as a chronology of the events. [**29**] All together, then, we are satisfied that the incident occurred as narrated.

REFERENCES

22 - *Jornal do Brasil*, May 23 1986. ■ **23** - *Clarin*, Buenos Aires, May 23 1986. ■ **24** - *O Globo*, May 24 1986. ■ **25** - Irene **Granchi** (UNICAT Project correspondent in Rio de Janeiro), private communication. ■ **26** - *Jornal do Brasil*, May 22 1986. ■ **27** - *O Dia*, May 23 1986. ■ **28** - *O Dia*, May 22 1986. ■ **29** - *Fohla de S.Paulo*, May 24 1986.

2.3.5

UFOs IN THE SOVIET UNION

by Enrique Vicente

■ **ENRIQUE de VICENTE MARTIN:** Born Madrid, 1950. Graduate in Information Sciences, Universidad Complutense de Madrid. He has also studied history at the Ecole des Hautes Etudes, Sorbonne, Paris, and computer programming (IBM, Madrid). He works as an advertising technician and specialist journalist on science and para-science subjects.

■ **UFO involvement:** His interest in UFOs and other anomalous phenomena and heterodox ideas dates from 1963. Since 1968 he has been very active throughout Spain and in Latin America, lecturing and broadcasting widely, writing numerous articles, organising conferences and seminars (including in 1978 the only seminar on UFO phenomena ever held in the Universidad Autonoma de Madrid).

Mundo Desconocido

He is an active investigator, having interviewed hundreds of UFO witnesses (including seventy Spanish pilots). He is also a member (often a founder) of many associations and research groups. He serves on the managing boards of many organisations devoted to parapsychology and interplanetary, studies as well as ufology.

■ **Publications:** Besides being a prolific contributor to anomaly journals, he has been editor of *Contactos Extraterrestres* (the only popular journal devoted to UFOs in Spain and Mexico), *Supermente, Revista de Parapsicologia, Psi-Comunicacion* and others. He is an associate editor of the new *Caudernos de Ufologia.*

■ **Address:** Porto Sta Maria de la Cabeza, 64, 16#D / 28045 Madrid / Spain. Phone: 474 95 23.

FROM "NOTHING IS HAPPENING" TO "EVERYTHING IS UNDER CONTROL"

'Neopozhannie Letaiushkie Objekts' (UFOs), formerly known as 'Letaiushkie Tarelki' (Flying Saucers), are no less a matter of concern to Soviet citizens and their governmental, military and scientific authorities than they are to their Western colleagues - perhaps more so. In the Soviet Union - as is appropriate to a technocracy - it is the scientists who participate in the research, while the official spokesmen carry out their sacred function of preserving the established order and reassuring the alarmed minds of the comrade-citizens. First, it must be shown that UFOs are being studied, so that later it can be explained that they are no more than natural phenomena unknown to us. For nothing exists that cannot be squared with the orthodox co-ordinates of dialectical materialism.

UFOs IN CZARIST RUSSIA

Back in 1953, Moscow Radio would make such assertions as: 'Flying saucers are a fantasy invented by Western militarists to frighten their taxpayers into accepting higher defence budgets.' But those days are over. Soon the Russian media became totally silent on the subject, leading the CIA to suspect that this silence was itself a Soviet psychological warfare device.

Such statements as that just quoted, or the one made in 1957 by Karpenko, Secretary for Interplanetary Communications, to the effect that 'flying saucers have no connection whatever with factual reality, as such things have never been seen by us', were direct lies, intended to hush the anxiety of a population concerned by the increasing number of sightings. For the fact is that Russians have been seeing UFOs since early times.

The first known to us occurred on 15 August 1663, when a great fireball, some 45 metres in diameter, descended on the village of Rozoboro projecting two blazing beams from its front. It vanished abruptly, only to reappear an hour later over a nearby lake, where it stayed for an hour and a half, inflicting severe burns on two fishermen.

During World War Two there were several reports of strange objects over Soviet territory, such as the disc seen in September 1943 near Pushkino by Spanish volunteer-fighters of the 'Division Azul', who supposed they were watching a battle between the German and Russian air forces until the object vanished at great speed.

According to Zigel, the modern Russian period begins in May 1946 with some nocturnal observations by pilots, farmers and citizens: three years later, in July 1949, there was a wave of sightings over northwest Russia.

We can get an idea of the extent of the Soviet cases from some of the sightings reported from Moscow and its outskirts, which for obvious reasons are better known to the rest of the world than events in other parts of the country. In spring 1949 a UFO was reported leaving the characteristic evanescent filaments known as 'angel hair'. On 27 November 1954, and again on 14 February 1955, strange celestial cigars were seen which, after remaining stationary for a considerable time, disappeared at great speed. Close to Moscow a huge saucer-shaped object was seen landing on 19 March 1958: it vanished after a spiral ascent. On 2 August 1959 the radar system of the civil airport recorded three saucer-shaped objects at a height of some 800 m, which were pursued by military planes. In the same month there were rumours that in a Georgia village a UFO had exploded, leaving the remains of a dead monster whose chemical composition was silica-based...

STRANGE CORPSES, A KIDNAPPED PARACHUTIST, AND OTHER RUMOURS

Such tales seem appropriate to a country where science fiction writers flourish, and where the possibility of ET intelligence has greater scientific as well as popular support than in the West. UFO-related rumours are more prevalent there; perhaps because until the 1960s the mass media provided so little reliable information. Various accounts circulated from mouth to mouth, undergoing a progressive deformation which left them utterly unrecognisable. Despite the passage of time, it is still impossible to tell which of these stories can be assigned to objective reality, which to popular imagination, and which to official disinformation. For example:

■ Polish newspapers reported how, on 21 May 1959, dockworkers at Gdynia saw a bright object fall into the harbour basin. Divers retrieved a piece of rustless metal, but nothing was ever released concerning the analyses allegedly carried out subsequently by the Polish Navy and the local Polytechnic. But several days later some guards were said to have found a strange figure crawling exhausted along the beach, wearing 'a sort of uniform' seemingly made of very resistant metal. At the University Hospital he was isolated and closely studied: he was found to have very different organs and blood system from ours, and an abnormal number of fingers and toes. He survived for several days, until a bracelet round his arm was removed. His remains were taken to the Soviet Union for further examination...

■ In 1962 Italian journalist Alberto Fenoglio relayed the story of a Russian female parachutist who jumped at an altitude of 9000 m near Santov - and vanished for two days. When she reappeared, she reported having been kidnapped by a flying saucer in the course of her descent. She had been very well treated by its three occupants, who showed her our planet from a great height, and entrusted her with a case containing a message for the authorities, which she handed to the police on her return.

■ Author Degaunzi reported further amazing stories published by the Soviet press during 1976: luminous tentacles taking samples of our plants; egg-shaped objects which seemed to be alive; a manned UFO apparently in difficulties over a lagoon near Tachkent, followed by the discovery of a small grey-skinned man with no ears, and of a long mark on the floor of the lagoon; even an insect 1.5 metres in length with a human-like brain, which just before expiring seemed to express itself in a melodic way.

'We believe,' Hobana and Weverbergh explain, 'that the rumours, which come from people who do not in general seem to be afflicted with UFO-mania and often are not even familiar with the term "flying saucer", arise because, while UFOs are real phenomena, any attempt to explain them in normal, logical terms fails completely.'

...BUT ALSO TESTIMONY FROM PILOTS, SCIENTISTS AND THE MILITARY.

By contrast with the sensational rumours, there is clear evidence of many sightings by Soviet scientists, pilots, armed forces and radar installations. Examples:

■ In February 1955 'coloured strips' were observed in the sky by Gomely Shlobin Meteorological Centre.

■ In 1956, while the famous pilot, Commanding Officer of the polar routes, Valentin Akkusatov, was exploring a strategical region near Greenland, a huge inverted saucer-shaped object flew parallel to them for an hour, avoiding all attempts to evade or approach it. Later a second, similar object joined the first; finally both vanished at unbelievable speed.

■ In spring 1959 panic was provoked when 'saucers' visited the Sverdlovsk rocket base over a 24-hour period. They were detected by radar, and at times could be seen hovering stationary over the launch platforms.

■ On 16 August 1960 eight members of a geophysical expedition in Kazakhstan, led by Dr Nikolai Sotchevanov, professor of Geology and Minerology at Leningrad University, saw a bright lens-shaped object whose apparent diameter was greater than the moon, and whose extremities were not as radiant as its centre.

■ In August 1961 a pilot flying over Kiev was accosted by a UFO which seemed to be playing games with him, flying round his plane in ever closer spirals, then moving away. The pilot followed the object, which seemed to stop, but as he came near it rapidly moved off. After some 12 minutes of aerial antics it disappeared at a speed of 10,000 km/h.

■ On 26 July 1965 astronomers Robert and Esmeralda Vitolniek and Yan Melderis, at the Ogre Observatory in Latvia, saw a star-like triangular object. Through the telescope they could see a combination of three smaller green balls which spun round a central sphere some 100 metres in diameter, then went away; they estimated the objects could have been at an altitude of 100 km.

■ During 1966 an intense wave was registered in the USSR, Poland, Czechoslovakia, as well as in other parts of the world. In April, Air Force Major Baidukov obtained visual and radar sighting over the Odessa region of a UFO which descended from an altitude of 50 to 18 km: this was confirmed by ground radar. On 17 June V G Krylov and a team of geophysicists at Blista (northern Caucasus) saw a small reddish disc which descended from 48 to 17 km in 45 minutes. In October V I Duginov, director of the Hydromagnetic School at Kherson, with 45 other witnesses, observed a saucer-shaped object with an apparent diameter three times that of the sun.

■ During 1967 *Soviet Weekly* reported some 200 UFO sightings in southern Russia. On 18 August astronomer Anatoli Sazanov, and 11 colleagues of the astrophysical station near Kislovodsk in the Caucasus, watched the movements of a yellowish crescent-shaped, asymmetrical object at least 150 metres long, moving at 18,000 km/h; it emitted a puff of what looked like steam, and was accompanied by a luminous point. Similar phenomena were seen by some of his colleagues, and other inhabitants of the area, on 18 July, 4 September and 18 October: the sightings were confirmed by the staff of Kazan Observatory.

One could carry on endlessly with such reports.

1965 : A COMPULSORY CHANGE OF DIRECTION

Meanwhile, what was happening at an official level?

The Soviet Air Force compiles records from sightings only when these are made by pilots; so the figure of 15,000 UFOs on file, which someone gave Jacques Vallee, seems rather astonishing. But explanations must be left to the scientists, who seem as confused as their counterparts in the United States.

On 8 January 1961, *Komsomolskaia Pravda*, official organ of the CPSU, published a weird photograph of a UFO. About the same period, reports were received from Uzbekistan and Tangakistan of UFOs flying very low over inhabited areas, frightening the population and animals: they even left circular traces where they landed on thick ice and melted it. To make matters worse, rumours circulated about beings who appeared in an isolated village and telepathetically compelled the staff of a co-operative store to hand them sweet food...

Next day, *Pravda* declared 'Soviet citizens who claim to have seen these saucers are idiots or incorrigible liars'; pointing out that Russian reports duplicated those from America, it accused the witnesses of being traitors who listened to *Voice of America* broadcasts.

The end of the cold war meant an exchange of information between scientists on both sides of the Iron Curtain, and Soviet authorities learnt that UFOs were as big a problem in the West as for them; according to Frank Edwards, they proceeded to pursue the same cover-up policy as did the authorities in North America.

1965 saw an important change in official policy. The Kazakstan region was flooded with reports and rumours which were so distorted as to reach alarming proportions. A government force was sent to the zone to provide 'explanations' which would mitigate the effects of the sightings, which were interpreted as a supernatural premonition of imminent catastrophe and were leading to a widespread religious revival.

At the beginning of 1965 the Russian government sent several scientists to South America, source of many UFO reports, to study the phenomenon. One was Dr Mitrofan Zverev, who on 10 February was reported in *Kazakstan Pravda* as telling the Chileans 'Something which we do not understand is going around the earth.' Why was this published in that local paper? It suggests that the authorities, impotent in the face of the sightings, could only insist that Soviet scientists were studying the phenomenon, and there was no need for people to be afraid.

Nevertheless, it is rather surprising that later that same year Moscow Radio reverted to defining UFOs as 'an invention of the American Minister of Defense, McNamara, in order to spread alarm in the world.'

THE SHORT-LIVED STOLIAROV COMMITTEE

During the 1966 International Congress of Mathematicians at Moscow, Jacques Vallée gave a lecture about UFOs and even published articles in the press. This encouraged Felix Zigel - professor of the Aeronautical Institute, one of the monitors of the Russian cosmonauts, and the best-known Soviet ufologist - and some other scientists who were interested in the subject, to express their views publicly.

In April 1967 an article by Zigel in *Smena*, a widely circulating youth magazine edited by the eminent scientist B P Konstantinov, reflecting his point of view, was favorably accepted by the great majority of the public who were eager for news on the subject.

On 18 October 1967, before more than 400 people, a meeting took place in Moscow of a UFO survey team created by the All-Union Committee on Astronautics. It was headed by Air Force Maj.Gen. Porfiry Stoliarov, vice-presidents were Zigel and writer Aleksandr Kazantsev, one of the first to sustain the 'ancient astronaut' theory, together with a cosmonaut, 18 scientists, and 200 qualified observers. A month later they appeared on television. Zigel showed photographs and sketches of UFOs: Stoliarov explained that he and his colleagues considered UFOs 'a serious subject meriting thorough study', denouncing pseudo-scientific interpretations of unexplained phenomena. He invited witnesses to send in accounts of their experiences, and received hundreds of detailed reports in response.

This TV presentation made an enormous impact throughout the world, and media in the West inaccurately reported the creation of an 'official' UFO organisation backed by the Soviet government. Hynek declared that Zigel would not have been allowed to claim the attention of the public if UFOs were not being officially researched.

The UAS (Academy of Sciences) quickly corrected this mistake: Dr Arcimovich explained that the committee was no more than a free association of Russian scientists, and deplored the public manifestation as unscientific.

If the 'Committee' obtained the official approval necessary for any association, this was probably because in the highest political circles there were people convinced of the seriousness of the subject. Nevertheless, certain sectors of the UAS kept up their furious attacks. On 29 February 1968, *Pravda* published a tough article, signed by Mustjel, Chairman of the Academy's Astronautics Committee, Martinov, Chairman of the Astronomic-Geophysical Society, and Ljeschkovtzev, Secretary to the National Committee of Physicists, in which they defined the official Soviet attitude, explaining that the 'flying saucer myth' had been clarified years before. It was a fraud, a misunderstanding of natural or artificial phenomena, and the reports had no scientific value since the observers were not astronomers, meteorologists or military personnel.

Following this publication, the Soviet press was extremely careful not to publish anything contradicting the opinion of these high authorities, and began a campaign of ridicule. The Committee was soon obliged to cease its activities.

THE SILENT DECADE

During the decade which followed, UFO research in the USSR was virtually an underground activity. But

Dr Felix Y. Zigel.

the sightings themselves continued, and with them, the activity of a few ufologists who, though their private activities were not actually prohibited, none the less had to proceed with caution.

An extreme case was that of Zigel, who from 1968 abandoned all public activity and gave no more interviews. Despite this, both by his fellow citizens and outside the USSR he was regarded as the leading Soviet ufologist, while establishment scientists considered him 'a dangerous dreamer'.

When, in the late 1960s, American journalists Ostrander and Schroeder visited the USSR to compile their 1970 report on *Psychic discoveries behind the Iron Curtain,* Zigel was was the one scientist they were unable to interview. Eight years later, Gris and Dick, financed by the *National Enquirer*, were more successful, eventually interviewing him in the home of his friend Kazantsev, and reported his views in their 1978 book *The new Soviet psychic discoveries*.

Although Zigel cannot speak for Soviet ufology as a whole, it is interesting to observe the development of his thought. He had become interested in UFOs in the late 1950s, and by 1967 had written *UFO sightings in the USSR*, containing some 200 selected UFO cases; unfortunately this book was not published, though it circulated in manuscript form, as did many other works by himself and other Soviet ufologists.

In his 1967 book, Zigel considers various UFO hypotheses and dismisses fraud, hallucination, optical illusion, atmospheric phenomena and terrestrial spacecraft as explanations for the totality of recorded sightings; the most probable hypothesis he considered to be unmanned research probes of extra-terrestrial origin. Reports of landings and encounters with occupants he considered to be fictional or hallucinatory.

It is because we do not possess sufficient high-quality experimental material that we tend to deny the existence of UFOs or explain it in conventional terms. Though they present 'a sort of reality which has not yet been explored', UFO sightings are capable of scientific explanation if analysed objectively. He recommends:

■ 1. Use of astronomical and other observatories, radar, artificial satellites &c in a systematic surveillance of the skies to obtain scientific data of real value.
■ 2. Exhaustive study of interesting and well-documented reports.
■ 3. Theoretical study of such empirical material as we possess.
■ 4. Laboratory replication of processes observed in connection with UFOs.
■ 5. Two parallel organisations for UFO study should be created. First, a *public* one to compile data, organise countrywide sky-watches, and encourage scientific discussion; and second, an *official* co-ordinating centre to compile and process the information, and conduct a certain amount of secret research.

Seven years later, interviewed by Gris and Dick, Zigel's views were substantially unchanged. The lack of contact with the UFO-intelligences he attributed to the fact that 'they were waiting for our civilisation to advance to a safer level.' He explained many anomalies associated with UFOs as resulting from the use of other dimensions for the long space journeys. He still denied that landings or encounters with occupants have occurred in the USSR.

THE 'FORBIDDEN LECTURE'

In early summer 1977, a rumour was circulating in Moscow that Zigel had been relieved of his post. He was nowhere to be found. It was said his sacking was due to the clandestine circulation of a lecture given to a close circle of scientists, and attributed to him despite his vigorous denials. The old quarrel was re-opened. *Konsomolskaia Pravda* declared 'All who interest themselves in UFOs are subversive; influenced by Western mass media they display suspicious - even religious - tendencies.' One journalist added 'All the Americans I know consider the extra-terrestrial explanation a stupid rumour.'

The alleged manuscript purports to be a status report on UFOs, and tells in general terms the story of the UFO phenomenon, with some blatant errors and gratuitous comment; it asserts that the Soviet Academy of Sciences is collaborating in mutual agreement with the USA. It adds that 3000 cases have been reported in the USSR, that in January 1976 two landings took place in the region of Vologonsk, and that UFOs induce paralysis in witnesses and bring machines to a dead stop if they are close enough. Cigar-shaped mother-ships and others of crescent shape have been detected, reaching sizes of 500 and even 1500 metres.

UFO occupants are classified in three main groups according to height, and yeti-like entities are also seen, supposed to be some kind of intelligent extra-terrestrial animal used by the ufonauts for certain purposes. It states that the physicist Kirichenko and other Soviet experts have analysed substances found on landing sites, concluding that they cannot be identified with any terrestrial substance.

Finally, the official refusal to publish UFO reports is explained as fear that they would create uncertainty and confusion, which some people would exploit for their own ends; furthermore, mankind is not yet ready for knowledge of this kind.

THE PETROZAVODSK 'JELLYFISH'

Meanwhile, Soviet ufology began to experience a slight change. In 1976 a UFO wave took place in Moscow, Leningrad and Kiev, as well as from more isolated districts. Many reports came from pilots and military observers. Though the official position was still to deny the existence of UFOs, the press began to publish some of the cases.

This continued in 1977 with a great spring wave in Georgia, the sighting of a UFO with occupants by a military pilot, and the landing on 19 August of something like a focus of violet light which, before disappearing in a fluorescent cloud, was seen by three scientists camping near Serpukov, who were awakened by loud voices speaking an unknown tongue: a circular hole some 5 metres in diameter was left as a souvenir of their presence.

Excitement reached new heights at dawn on 20 September 1977 when a spectacular aerial display occurred over Petrozavodsk (Karelia), while a scientific installation to study the aurora borealis recorded various anomalies. Dr Mikhail Dimitriev, one of the many scientists who studied the phenomena, compared it to a gigantic jellyfish. Its changes of shape made many people panicky, some fearing an American nuclear attack, others becoming mentally confused or hysterical. Other simultaneous sightings encouraged ufologists to presume that several different UFOs were involved. Meanwhile, in the United States, 'sympathetic skeptic' James Oberg, an expert on the Soviet space programme, explained the jellyfish as the booster contrails associated with the launch of the Kosmos 955 spy satellite, launched from the secret Plesetsk rocket establishment, an explanation which was readily accepted by Hynek and other American ufologists.

The Moscow press, meanwhile, described it as a natural phenomenon of unknown etiology. Subsequently, it was explained by Dr Dimitriev as a 'chemoluminescence zone' enhanced by nitrous oxide pollution from a Petrozavodsk factory, and by Dr Migulin as 'physical changes in the upper atmosphere' provoked by a wave of solar electrons and other factors.

KOSMIC VISITORS IN MOSCOW

On 14 June 1980 and 15 May 1981 some spectacular luminous phenomena were recorded at dawn in Moscow and other Soviet cities, which provoked further alarm among the population. As with the Petrozavodsk incident, Henry Gris published a sensational report in *The National Enquirer* and elsewhere, counting on the open collaboration of Zigel, who had assured them that the Petrozavodsk phenomenon was 'a true UFO'.

Skeptical ufologist Marcelo Copetti said that 'UFOs seen at Moscow are probably new inventions of Soviet manufacture, under test', adding 'Zigel and his colleagues know much more than they reveal.' Again, American and Finnish experts ascertained

The Petrosavodsk sighting as depicted by the *National Enquirer*.

that these sightings were provoked by the launch of Kosmos 1188 and Meteor 2-7 from Plesetsk.

This explains why the Soviet authorities granted Gris facilities to concoct his spectacular UFO stories: it was he who in 1979 alleged that the Russian ambassador's interpreter in Washington was giving telepathic orders to President Carter's subconscious mind!

Nikita A Schnee, on behalf of a leading private UFO group, declared that some Leningrad ufologists had checked on landing reports and humanoid sightings published by Zigel, and not a single one was true. He accused Zigel of encouraging the Communist Party and the KGB to harass his group.

UFOs OVER STRATEGIC INSTALLATIONS... OR A MILITARY INTELLIGENCE GAME?

Devious official policy could account for several otherwise inexplicable incidents, such as the 1978 publication of an article by the young astrophysicist Juri Poslepov, in which he states that on 7 June 1976, just before the launch at Plesetsk of a Kosmos communications satellite, technicians photographed a chain of luminous cylinders flying over the launch platform. They remained there for 20 minutes, but fighters sent to intercept them could do nothing because their controls were mysteriously de-activated, as also were the ground radar installations which had previously been able to detect and follow the UFOs.

Repeated reports came from Plesetsk of strange green or red balls which were unharmed by shots from jet fighters. Poslepov adds that in November 1977, just before the launch of a satellite containing orbital bombs at Turyatam, several egg-shaped luminous balls danced over the launch area for more than a quarter of an hour, finally combining and leaving. During this time, electrical equipment failed to function and three jet fighters were unable to take off. The records and photographs were being kept secret in order not to frighten the population.

Such stories might lead one to ask whether the UFOs are interested in satellites and ground military plants: but if so, why would the Soviet authorities permit the publication of stories which reveal their inability to deal with the UFOs?

On the other hand, it makes sense to see them as a cloak for military operations, allowing the public - just as the Americans have surely been doing - to believe that extra-terrestrial spaceships are responsible. To achieve this, there is nothing more effective than rumours and foreign journalists, who have greater credibility than the local press.

RUMOURS WHICH WENT BACK TO MOSCOW

It is interesting to see how the pulp stories in *The National Enquirer* and such like - generally ignored by serious ufologists - had their repercussion in the rumours which circulate in Moscow. Some examples:

■ On 14 July 1983 a metallic capsule of characteristics unknown to the scientists and military personnel who examined it, was found near Sosnovska (Kirghizstan) just after the sky had turned red and various explosions had been heard. Inside was a strange hairless baby with violet skin and webbed fingers and toes. It was taken to the Institute of Medical Research of Frunze, and died three months later of infection.

■ In 1979, the ufologist Bozhich - backed by other colleagues - asserted that a crippled spaceship of unknown origin had been orbiting earth since 1955. According to Oberg, this discovery - refuted by satellite tracking experts - originated in a 1969 article by the American Dr John P Bagby, who rejects the spaceship hypothesis. Yet let us not forget that in 1975 the USSR Academy of Sciences published a document proposing 'systematic continuous observation of the skies' with 'special attention to the possibility of discovery of probes sent out by extra-terrestrial civilisations which may even be in orbit around earth.'

■ According to Zigel, at 5 pm on 16 June 1976, Nikolai Affounskin of Podolsky (Koursk) was wrapped in a strange mist which caused him to faint. When he recovered, he found that at least an hour had elapsed, his watch had stopped and he was 90 km from where he had been. He was taken to the police station of Rogotzy where his story was checked. On that very day, witnesses saw strange sights in the sky, particularly in the woods where the man had disappeared... In May 1979, a woman of Iegorievsk (southeast Moscow) claimed to have undergone a similar experience, being teleported a distance of 200 km in 30 minutes.

THE QUICK-CHANGE ACT OF FELIX ZIGEL

Meanwhile, in an interview given to Gris, Zigel spoke of the suspicious 1980 incident in Moscow as the biggest alien apparition on earth: which shows an almost incredible change in his attitude to the problem, throwing all caution to the winds. He made assertions which seem clearly inspired by the statements of his Western colleagues, and expressed views which would sound ridiculous to any Western ufologist.

Zigel appears convinced that UFOs have a special reason to be more interested in the USSR than in any other country, explaining 'they will not land in the USSR before requesting and receiving our permission.' He does not reject the possibility that some ET beings are already living among us, to study our civilisation, and expects them to establish direct relations with us in the near future.

Beside the four categories of ufonauts already mentioned, he thinks we are being visited by robots or androids who are able to appear or disappear as if 'deliberately constructed to confound all our notions of space, time and dimension.' He declares that he knows of four cases of true abduction, but will provide no details.

Subsequently, some events of this kind have been published. Among them is the story of a veterinary surgeon, V G Palzev, who encountered a saucer near Borisoglebsk and thinks he was conducted inside by three beings with heads like ostrich eggs and exceptionally long fingers. Waking 1½ hours later, his new briefcase seemed worn out as a result of having been taken aboard the device, according to revelations made during hypnotic regression.

It has been suggested that Zigel became a pawn of the Soviet government in return for access to secret documents. But his behaviour can be more simply explained: perhaps it was enough for him to be recognised as the leading ufologist, after so many years of enforced silence, to give way to megalomaniac impulses as he disseminates throughout the world the information filtered to him by official sources. However, this can only be speculation.

ANOMALOUS ATMOSPHERIC PHENOMENA AND THE NEW SOVIET UFOLOGY

In the absence of any valid answer to the UFO enigma, the authorities have decided to ignore it or use it for their own aims, while officially maintaining that they are either man-made artifacts or atmospheric phenomena.

During the last decade it seems to have been this latter interpretation which has prevailed, and when Menzel's work was published in the USSR in 1963, it was favourably received among the scientific authorities who found it gave them the weapons they needed to counter the popular enthusiasm for UFOs. Since then, there have been continual references to ionised particles, dust bags suspended in the air, atmospheric plasma gatherings, gaseous chemiluminescent formations, solar phenomena, ball lightning, and so on.

During the past decade, the highest government levels seem to have laid aside their negative attitude, and given encouragement to research into what are officially known as 'anomalous atmospheric phenomena', and interest in them has grown in scientific circles.

In 1979, the Institute of Space Research published a statistical analysis of 256 AAP sightings, of which 76% occurred in 1967. Though the study contributes nothing new, it was enthusiastically accepted in the West in the absence of any other indications of Soviet research. Oberg suggests that most of the 1967 cases can be explained as the effects of undisclosed space launches.

In the meantime Soviet ufology has continued to develop in an interesting way. Nikita Schnee, in an article published in *FRS*, has described the situation in the late 1970s. As a result of lectures given by physicist Dr Vladimir G Azhazha (who he presents as the true leader of unofficial Soviet ufology), an 'Initiative Group' was started in 1978 by Schnee and Azhazha, hoping to stimulate official investigation.

In July 1979, the group was changed to the Section BPVTS (Search for Extra-terrestrial Civilisations in the neighbourhood of Earth by electronic means) of the A S Popov Scientific and Technical Society for Radio, Electronics and Communications (NTORES); its vice-president was Lev Gindilis, and its members included Vice-Admiral Krylov, cosmonaut Khrunov and other notable scientists and specialists, with collaborators throughout the USSR. Four months later, the NTORES authorities obliged them to change their name again, this time to Section for the Investigation of AAP. Eventually, continued sabotage from Party members, apparently incited by Zigel, put an end to its activities.

Schnee blames Zigel for acting as though he considers UFOs his private bailiwick, allowing nobody to share his vast information.

A PROMISING FUTURE

In 1981 a new department devoted to the study of AAP was created within the radio-astronomy section of the UAS, whose secretary, Gindilis, recognised that more than 20% of the cases studied could not be explained, and invited scientists throughout the world to 'co-operate in their efforts to study thoroughly the nature of these phenomena.'

A year later many scientists took part at Kiev in the first public conference on the study of AAP: others were to follow.

Within the UAP's Institute for the Study of Terrestrial Magnetism, Ionosphere and the Diffusion of Radio Waves, another AAP study group has been formed.

Finally, in July 1984 a **Social Commission on Abnormal Phenomena** was founded, generally regarded as the first official Soviet organisation devoted to UFO research. It is headed by the well-known UAS member V Troitskij, and the cosmonaut General Pavel Popovich, and its members include several reputable scientists including Anatoly Loganov, a vice-president of the UAS and a rector of Moscow University.

Popovich explains that there have been hundreds of UFO reports in the USSR and that most of them can be explained, but some defy all rational explanation, and as a consequence Soviet scientists take the subject seriously. A list of recent sightings has been released.

All this seems to show that, while in the rest of the world UFO activity seems to have declined during the last decade, along with public intertest and even that of many former ufologists, in the USSR the reverse is true. Besides the ufologists whose names have reached us during the last 20 years - Zigel, Azhazha, Kasantzev, Bozhich, Zolotov, Fomin, Zaiutsev, Girov, Lina and others - the phenomenon has attracted other enthusiasts of the unknown, such as unofficial para-psychologists Naumov and Barbara Ivanovna, and new scholars such as Valerii Sanarov and Eduard Ermilov.

It is interesting to observe that, though their views differ as much as those of their Western colleagues, they seem basically agreed that UFOs are extra-terrestrial, possibly ultra-dimensional.

From a merely political analysis, the new Soviet UFO policy can be seen as another aspect of de-Stalinisation and the ongoing propaganda battle against the United States, manipulating public enthusiasm to suit the government's purposes. However, the ufologist community throughout the world must welcome this more open policy, enabling science the opportunity to interest itself in the subject despite totalitarian pressure.

Despite political games, despite cover-ups, it seems likely that before long the brave new Soviet ufologists will have some surprises for us. Perhaps not everything will be 'under control' in the USSR. Time will tell.

REFERENCES

■ **Note:** This alphabetical list does not include articles and manuscript in Russian, but not translated into other languages. ■ **Arteaga**. F. -- 'Estudio estadistico: los OVNIs siguen preocupando a los sovieticos', in *Contactos extraterrestres*, Mexico, 107, Feb 4, 1981. ■ **Creighton**. G. -- 'A Russian "jellyfish"', in *FSR* 23(4), 1977. -- 'Russia: naughty Henry Gris says it again! "Soviet space-centre knocked out by UFOs"', in *FSR* 28(6), 1983. -- 'Dr Felix Zigel and the development of ufology in Russia', in *FSR* 27(3,4,5), 1981-1982. -- 'The Russians again', in *FSR* 30(4), 1985. ■ **Danyans**. E. -- *OVNIs: enigmas del espacio*, Plaza & Janes, Barcelona, 1980. ■ **Degaudenzi**. J.L. -- 'Des extreterrestres dans la presse russe', in A.A. **Roudene**, *Les extreterrestres*, Retz, Paris, 1977. -- 'Deux OVNIs bombardent un cosmodrome sovietique', in *Nostra* (Feb 7, 1983), Paris. ■ **Drouin**. J. -- 'OVNI et teleportation en Union Sovietique', in *Nostra* 475 (May 14, 1981), Paris. ■ **Ermilov** E.A. -- 'Study of Anomalous Atmospheris Phenomena (AAP) in the USSR', in *UPIAR Research in Progress*, Torino, 2 (2/3), 1984. ■ **Edwards**. F. -- *Flying saucers - serious business*, Lyle Stuart, NY, 1966. ■ **Favero**. G. -- 'Gli UFO in URSS', in *UFO*, Torino, 2, Dec 1986. ■ **Fenoglio**. A. -- 'Amazing news from Russia: can this be true?', in *FSR* 8(6), Nov-Dec 1962 (originally published in *Oltre il Cielo*, Rome, 105, June 1962). ■ **Gerin**. D. -- 'Les OVNI en URSS', in *OVNI approche*, 19, Toulon, 1978. ■ **Gindilis**. L.M., **Menkov**. D.A., and **Petrovskaya**. I.G. -- *Observations of Anomalous Atmospheric Phenomena in the USSR: a statistical analysis*, Institute of Space Research, Moscow, 1979 (in Russian); CUFOS, Evanston, 1980; GEPAN, Toulousse, 1980. ■ **Gris**. H., and **Dick**. W. -- *The new soviet psychic discoveries*, Prentice-Hall, NJ, 1978. -- 'First UFO to inflict damage on a city', in *National Enquirer*, Lantana, April 18, 1978. -- 'Crippled UFO orbiting Earth', in *National Enquirer*, Lantana, July 17, 1979. -- 'Un bebe de otro planeta... ', in *Lecturas* 1663, Barcelona, March 2, 1984. ■ **Hobana**. I., and **Weverbergh**. J. -- *UFOs from behind the Iron Curtain*, Souvenir Press, 1974. ■ **Keyhoe**. D.E. -- *Aliens from space*, Doubleday, NY, 1973. ■ **Kobyizev**. K. -- 'Visitors from Outer Space', in *The ESP papers*, edited by S. **Ostrander** and L. **Schroeder**, Bantam, NY, 1976. ■ **Krassa**. P. -- 'URSS: prohibido hablar de OVNIs', in *Mundo Desconocido*, Barcelona, 18, Dec 1977. ■ **Lina**. J. -- 'El "OVNI-Medusa" de Petrozavodsk', in *Contactos extraterrestres / Fenomeno OVNI*, Madrid, 1(2), 1979. -- 'Aterrizaje con tripulantes en Estonia', in *Contactos extraterrestres / Fenomeno OVNI*, Madrid, 1(6), 1980. ■ **Migulin**. V. -- 'Les phenomenes aerospatiaux non identifies a l'etude', in *La Recherche*, Paris, 102, July-Aug 1979. -- and **Platov**. U., 'Riddles of the Planet Earth', in *The MUFON Journal*, Seguin, 139, Sept 1979. ■ **Moore**. W.L. -- 'Red skies: a history of UFOs in Russia', in *UFO Report*, June 1980. ■ **Mustjel**. E., **Martinov**. D., and **Ljeschkovtzey**. -- '"Flying saucers" again?', in *Pravda*, Feb 29, 1968, (trans. into Spanish, MS; cedit: V.J. Ballester Olmos.) ■ **Nosdrina**. Y. -- 'El silencio de la Academia', in *Mundo Desconocido*, Barcelona, 72, June 1982.

■ **Oberg**. J. -- 'Flight of the jellyfish UFO', in *True Flying Saucers & UFOs Quarterly*, 10, Summer 1978. -- 'Phantom moonlet', in *Omni*, March 1980. -- 'The Russian connection', in *Omni*, July 1980. -- 'UFOs and Soviet space activities', in *Second Look / Frontiers of Science*, July-Aug 1982. -- *UFOs and Outer Space mysteries*, Donning, Norfolk, 1982. -- 'The great Soviet UFO cover-up', in *The MUFON Journal*, 176 &177, Oct &Nov 1982. -- 'UFO Update', in *Omni*, Nov 1982. ■ **Ostrander**. S., and **Schroeder**. L. -- *Psychic discoveries behind the Iron Curtain*, Prentice-Hall, NJ, 1970. -- 'OVNIs o identificacion sin careo', in *Sputnik* (Spanish ed.), Moscow, June 1981. ■ **Pinotti**. R. -- *UFO: la congiura del silenzio*, Armenia, Milano, 1974. ■ **Randles**. J. -- 'UFOs: an open secret', in *P.* **Brooksmith**, *The age of the UFO*, Orbis, London, 1984. ■ **Risoli**. R. -- 'NLO? Niet!', in *Contactos extraterrestres / Fenomeno OVNI*, Madrid, 1(20, 1979. ■ **Sanarov**. V.I. -- 'NLO and NLOnauts in the light of folklore', in *Sovetskaya Etnografiya*, Moscow, 2, March-April 1979 (trans. into English by Raymond Drake, MS). -- 'Observaciones en Rusia en el ano 1977', in *Stendek*, Barcelona, 35, March 1979. -- 'UFO probe in the Kremlin', in *APRO Bulletin*, Tucson, 28(4), Oct 1979. -- 'On the nature and origin of Flying Saucers and Little Green Men', in *Current Anthropology*, 22(2), April 1981. ■ **Schnee**. N.A. -- 'Soviet contact case near Pyrogovskoe Lake', in *FSR*, 26(6), 1980. -- 'Ufology in the USSR', in *FSR*, 27(1), June 1981. ■ **Schneider**. A. -- *Besucher aus dem all*, Hermann Bauer, Freiburg, 1973. ■ **Settler**. H. -- 'Nueva oleada OVNI en la URSS, el caso del portafolios que se des gasto misteriosamente', in *Contactos extraterrestres, Mexico, 113, April 4, 1981.* -- 'Soviets launch new UFO probe', in *APRO Bulletin*, 32(8), 1984. ■ **Teerikorpi**. P. -- 'Soviet "UFOs" identified as satellite launchings', in *FSR*, 27(6), 1982. -- 'UFO wave over Russia', in *FSR*, 24(3), 1978. -- 'Un russe et un polonai seraient entres en contact avec des extraterrestres', in *Nostra*, Paris, 432, July 17, 1980. ■ **Vicente**. E. -- '33 anos de OVNIs en Rusia', in *Contactos extraterrestres / Fenomeno OVNI*, Madrid, 1(2), 1979. ■ **Virtanen**. H. -- 'Soviet contact case near Pyrogovskoe Lake: the missing pages', in *FSR*, 28(3), 1983. ■ **White**. J. -- 'UFO research in Russia', in *APRO Bulletin*, Tucson, May-June 1976 (reprised in R. **Story**, *Encyclopedia of UFOs*). ■ **Zigel**. F.U. -- 'UFO ground effect cases in Russia', in *UFOlogy*, Fall 1976. -- 'OVNIs tras la Cortina de Acero', in *Contactos extraterrestres, Mexico,* 11 & 12 (April 27 & May 11, 1977). -- 'Los OVNIs ante la ciencia', in *Contactos extraterrestres, Mexico,* 27, (Dec 7, 1977). -- '1982: le bilan ufologique sovietique', in *Nostra*, 553, Jan 13, 1983. .

2.3.6

UFOs IN POLAND

by Bronislaw Rzepecki

■ **BRONISLAW RZEPECKI**: Born 1956; manager of a chemical shop in Krakow. Married with a son and daughter. Outside ufology his interests include Indian culture, paleo-astronautics and other fields of anomaly research.

■ **UFO involvement**: Has been actively interested in the UFO problem since 1972. In 1980 he established the UFO section of the Krakow Science Fiction Fan Club; in 1983 this developed into the Krakow Club of UFO Research and Popularisation, in 1984 the Krakovian UFO Research Society, in 1985 the UFO Research Group. He has also helped to found more than ten UFO societies in other Polish towns, and in 1983 helped organise the first Polish UFO Congress at Krakow.

■ **Publications**: From 1981-1984 he edited Poland's first UFO-bulletin, *'Peripheral Visions'* which ran for 18 issues. In 1986, with Krzysztof Piechota, he produced *'Catalogue of UFO observations in Poland 1947-1985'* and *'Bibliography of Polish UFO Publications 1945-1985'* which lists all UFO articles appearing in the Polish press.

■ **Address**: ul.Jozefa 22 / 14 / 31-056 Krakow / Poland.

The first attempt to interest the people of Poland in the UFO phenomenon occurred in 1958 when articles by Andrzej Trepka appeared in the magazines *Wieczor Wybrzeza* and *Skrzydlata Polska*. Providing serious information about UFOs and presented selected cases, they laid a foundation for the future development of the Polish ufological movement. Three years later the first Polish-language UFO book was published, Janusz Thor's *Latajace talerze* ('Flying Saucers').

In the early 1970s several leading Polish journalists began to write popular articles about UFOs, accounts of their occurrence, hypotheses as to their origin, propulsion methods &c., mainly based on Western scientific material. Several of these writers became well known: Lucjan Znicz, Andrzej Donmirski, Arnold Mostowicz, Zbigniew Blania. At the same time UFO enthusiasts formed groups in various Polish cities, though their activities were limited and mainly consisted of the private exchange of information.

ORGANISING UFO STUDIES IN POLAND

In 1976 the weekly *Fakty* began to publish a series of UFO articles by Znicz entitled 'Visitors from Space' which attracted a large correspndence. This suggested the idea of establishing a broad-based UFO society. 'Klub Kontaktow Kosmicznych' ('Space Contacts Club') was created on 8 July 1978, an informal organisation made up of interested persons throughout the country. From the creation of this organisation (which still exists) we may date the beginning of serious ufology in Poland.

A similar organisation, 'UFO Sonda' was formed in Wroclaw in December 1978, but was short-lived. Finally, in June 1981, there was registered in Warsaw the first legally-authorised UFO organisation, the Varsovian UFO Research Society 'UFO-Video', established by the man who is to this day its Chairman, Janusz Marczak M.S.

The first Polish-Language UFO bulletin was *Wizje Peryferyjne* ('Peripheral Visions') first published in November 1981 by an organisation which, commencing in January 1980 as the Ufological Section of the Cracow Science Fiction Fan Club, became independent just three years later as the 'Cracovian Club of UFO Research & Information'. The founder of the section and subsequent Chairman of the Club was the author of this article.

These organisations, together with Para-UFO, the Space Club of Lodz, formed in 1983, agreed to co-operate on such matters as reporting procedures, and combined to stage the First Polish UFO Congress at Cracow, on 23-25 September 1983; subsequent congresses were held in 1984 and 1985.

Over the years, in Poland as everywhere else, several UFO groups have come and gone. Today there are some nine serious organisations currently active including:

- Varsovian UFO Research Society 'UFO-Video'
- Pomeranian UFO Research Organisation 'Internol'
- Co-ordination centre of 'Space Contacts Club'
- Co-ordination centre of 'UFO Research Group'
- Wrocklawian Club of UFO Research & Information

■ UFO sections or groups in specific cities

Parallel with these, again like everywhere else, Poland has its so-called ufologists, working privately or in groups, who have no connection with serious ufology, but give interviews to the mass-media, and publish the results of their so-called 'research'. They do much harm because the media, failing to distinguish between them and serious ufologists, suppose that the entire movement shares their ridiculous ideas.

UFO SIGHTINGS IN POLAND

Fragmentary accounts show that unexplained aerial phenomena have been observed in Poland since the 16th and 17th centuries, but insufficient data is available about these early reports. It is not until the 20th century that we possess reliable data. Here is a selection:

■ 29.6.1908 - ZALESIE

Four witnesses observe the flight of a bright yellow object.

■ SUMMER 1922 - WARSAW

Many witnesses observe a silvery object - two hemispheres, divided by a rotating ring. The object 'shoots' a beam of light, then rises with a loud noise.

■ 31.7.1953 - WOLIN ISLAND (Baltic)

At 7pm, five Poles and two Germans see a disc-shaped object land in a field by a railroad track. It is about 22m in diameter and has numerous holes in its circumference. After a few minutes the object begins to move, and flies off at great speed.

■ 22.12.1958 - MUSZYNA

About 3pm, Dr (of medicine) Kowalczewski is the first Pole to photograph a UFO - a dark, disc-shaped object.

■ 3.1959 - KOLOBRZEG

Soldiers observe a strange triangular object emerge from the sea near the coast; its sides are about 4 m long. It flies into the air and starts to whirl in circles above the wavy surface of the water, then rapidly accelerates and vanishes.

On 21 January 1959, if local rumour can be believed, a UFO accident occurred in the harbour of Gdynia, after which a little humanoid being in a spacesuit was found, whose face was partially burned. He was taken to hospital, but died there. Though Shuttlewood mentions the incident in *Flying Saucerers*, he supplies no reference, and we in Poland have no documentary evidence for this event. [Editorial note: The same incident, though dated 21.2.1959, is narrated in some detail in Degaudenzi, *Les OVNI en Union Sovietique*, but again without precise references.]

TWO RECENT CASES

None of these cases, like many others not referred to here, was competently investigated, and are presented only for their historical interest. More worthwhile are two events selected from the period of the Polish 'ufo-flap' of 1978-1981:

■ 22.5.1979 - PÍASTÓW, near WARSAW

Waldemar R. left home to visit a café in the town park He reached the park about 10pm. There was complete silence round him suddenly he saw some bright lights about 5 m ahead of him. At once he stopped in surprise, and saw that two bright yellow beams were shining onto the concrete path. They came from the underside of a dark object, floating a few decimetres above the ground. Beneath the dark silhouette of the object, a little farther back, he could see a third beam of light, projecting to a distance of about 15 cm. In the glow of the yellow light, the object resembled an ice-hockey disc; it occupied nearly all the 3m width of the path.

Without knowing why, the witness approached the object, halting about 3 m from it. Suddenly, on the curved surface of the object green geometrical figures began to appear - triangles, squares, trapezoids, circles, in turn manifesting then extinguishing. In other places on the sides lights were glowing constantly.

At one moment a red light appeared on the upper surface, illuminating an H-shaped symbol which occupied nearly the whole of the upper surface. At one end of this symbol appeared a red light, blinking with a frequency of about 1 hz (once every second) as did the changing geometrical shapes on the side.

Suddenly the whole object shone with a white-blue light, and a scarcely-visible aura appeared round its shape. The witness felt heat and burning on his face. Instinctively he turned away and ran off home without looking behind him. In the morning he awoke with the feeling that something heavy was pressing on his head. After about two weeks burns appeared on his face, little sore abscesses containing jelly-like hardened blood drops. There were no other traces of the incident.

■ 8.1979 - CZLUCHOW

A case which could be classified as a CEIII on the Hynek scale occurred one beautiful evening when an inhabitant of Czluchow was rowing on the lake and suddenly saw a 'dark oblong object' moving on the surface. It slightly resembled a fishing boat, but moved much faster, making no sound and causing no waves. After a few seconds it vanished behind a peninsula.

A second witness saw the same object from the land , at almost the same moment as it disappeared from the first observer's view. Then he too lost sight of it behind a clump of reeds. He called his dogs and went with them to the spot where he thought the 'boat' would land, according to its apparent course. He had walked for no more than twenty paces when he noticed, about 20 m away, two beings in dark clothing going towards the forest. The dogs, sensing strangers, ran towards them. The beings turned to face the dogs: the dogs stopped, barked, then turned back. The stangers also turned again and began to move away.

During the few seconds of the observation the witness noted that the strangers were about 1.5 m tall, dressed in a hermetically-closed outfit somewhat like a diving suit. Level with their eyes were some plates resembling spectacles. Their hips were unnaturally wide, and each had something like a hump on his neck between the back of the head and the shoulders. Between their knees and the ground their legs were invisible. Their movement was not typical of two-legged beings; they glided over the ground as if on some perfectly smooth surface, though the ground below them was rough and uneven. Their hands were supported on their hips by their elbows, and half-bent to their sides.

The witness shouted to them to stop, but they started to move faster then vanished. He looked around for them, and then saw in the direction of the forest a bright shining object floating over the tree tops, about 100 m distant. About 30 m from the ground the object stopped. It looked like a smooth rectangular wall with its corners rounded; it glowed with a bright blue-green light on its sides, changing smoothly to a bright white in the centre. Then the object flew away.

No traces were found at the site where the object presumably 'parked', nor were any left by the entities. The behaviour of the dogs is remarkable: coming close to the humanoids, suddenly at about 2-3 m they ran off in great alarm; for half a year following the incident both dogs were paralysed in their forepaws, requiring treatment.

Other cases in the files of Polish UFO organisations span the spectrum of UFO observations from anomalous lights to close encounters involving telepathic communication with aliens, from BOL phenomena to apparent EM effects on turbogenerators. [Details of these cases will be supplied to representatives of serious organisations in exchange for reciprocal information-sharing.]

They demonstrate that UFO sightings in our country are similar to those reported elsewhere in Europe, the United States or Latin America. Moreover, the same is true of other countries of Eastern Europe, too, where both the UFO phenomenon and its investigation present the same features of interest as in other parts of the world.

2.4

UFO OCCUPANTS

by Peter Hough

■ **PETER A. HOUGH.** Has always been interested in phenomena which current science cannot explain. He was also mystified by the establishment view, that despite thousands of eye witness reports and other peripheral evidence, such phenomena could not in fact exist. At the other extreme, writers and TV planners often treated the subject merely as entertainment, with a cavalier disregard for factual accuracy.

He has studied psychology and sociology at an elementary level, and recently turned professional writer.

■ **UFO involvement**: In 1975 he decided to seek the truth for himself, and joined the Manchester UFO Research Association as investigator. In this capacity he has personally interviewed hundreds of witnesses to the UFO experience, as well as other strange phenomena. In 1983 he was elected Chairman.

Although he acknowledges that a degree of 'fence sitting' is required to remain open and objective, he believes that many phenomena such as alien contacts, poltergeists and 'spirit messages' have a common origin.

■ **Publications**: Features on the paranormal, and UFOs in particular, have appeared in such journals as *Beyond Science, Fate, Fortean Times, Magonia*, and *The Unknown*. He has also lectured widely, and taken part in many radio programmes including a BBC documnetary.

■ **Address**: 6 Silsden Avenue / Lowton / Warrington WA3 1EN / England.

'Bless them all, bless them all - the long and the short and the tall...'

Not least of the complex facets which compose the UFO experience are the so-called 'UFO occupants' - entities encountered in association with the anomalous UFOs themselves. Common sense tells us that they should be the key to answering the fundamental questions relating to UFOs perceived as nuts-and-bolts craft: Where do they come from? Who or what manufactures these machines? What is their purpose here? And what do they want from us? Logically, if we could only question the occupants, the entire enigma would be resolved.

Unfortunately, as hardened ufologists are aware, common sense and logic play but a small part in accounts of UFO events. Perhaps this is because the phenomenon is so completely alien as to be almost totally beyond our comprehension. Imagine a family of mice living beneath the stage of a theatre. Though they would occasionally be aware of the actors, they would have no conception at all of what a play is, let alone the story line of *The Tempest* being enacted above them, still less any inkling of the culture and complexities of human society presented in the drama. Even if a member of the mouse family made a few guesses to explain the sighting of these strange two-legged monsters, in all probability he would be completely wrong.

Mice and humans do not converse with one another, however, whereas many reports indicate that some UFO occupants understand our languages quite well. Thousands of people world wide, from all walks of life, races and religious doctrines claim to have questioned them face to face. Why, then, are we not fully knowledgeable concerning the UFO phenomenon?

THE DISINFORMATION FACTOR

UFO occupants seem to have an amazing capacity for issuing disinformation. The tall, slim, blond-haired humanoid that George Adamski claimed to meet in the California desert in 1952 informed Adamski he was from Venus, and that other planets in our solar system were also inhabited by space-journeying peoples. [1]

When a saucer-shaped craft abducted an entire family along a lonely country road in Oxfordshire, England, in 1978, they were first examined then given a conducted tour of the 'spaceship'. One of the occupants, named Uxiaulia, claimed the crew were but a tiny fraction of ten million refugees fleeing the planet Janos (a name which suggests Janus, the Roman god of gateways and passageways), destroyed by debris from a disintegrating moon. The 'Janos People', now in orbital expectation in various parts of the solar system, were waiting for the opportune moment to make themselves known to Earth's super-powers; they then hoped to settle in peace with us on our planet. Of course, before that day arrived, we would have to dismantle our nuclear toys. [2] (Adamski's aliens, and indeed very many UFO-occupants, are similarly concerned with the dangers of nuclear power.)

During the spring of 1964, a Mrs Lainchbury was disturbed during the night by an orange glow in her bedroom. Through the window she saw a bright-sphere pass quite close outside before *silently* exploding into a million pieces. Shortly afterwards she heard voices in her garden speaking an unknown language. When Arthur Tomlinson and I interviewed her in 1976, she claimed that two months after the sighting an entity appeared in her bedroom. About 1.5 metres (5 feet) tall, it was humanoid, but completely covered in grey circular rings. The entity informed her it was from the 'ship' she had witnessed exploding, and that it was now stranded on Earth, awaiting rescue. On a second occasion, *three* figures materialised in the room. She asked them where they came from, and several letters formed in the air spelling the word: PLUTO.

Old Mrs Lainchbury had no idea where Pluto could be, until she discovered in a book it is the ninth planet of the solar system. She had no conception at all that Pluto was also the Roman god of the underworld.

MUTUAL IGNORANCE

For some reason, the ten million Janosians were totally ignorant of the existence of Adamski's Venusians and Martians, still less were they aware of Mrs Lainchbury's aliens from Pluto. Each percipient seems to be visited by a different set of aliens, varying in physical appearance and originating from different planets. If we take these stories at face value, the universe is teeming with space-travelling civilisations, visiting Earth like bees around a honey-pot, yet all absolutely ignorant of the others.

Clearly, somebody - or something - is telling lies. Is subjective hallucination the explanation? Psychologists Leo Sprinkle and June Parnell studied more than 200 contactees, and determined that none was mentally ill. [**3**] Seasoned investigators know well that the majority of witnesses are confused, frightened - and above all, *sincere*. None the less, the fact remains that there is no evidence that UFO occupants are extraterrestrial aliens: they just like giving the impression that that is what they are.

A CULTURAL PHENOMENON

An impressive case has been made suggesting that alien occupants are a current manifestation of a phenomenon which adapts its external appearance to suit the technological and sociological expectations of the time.

Back in the 18th century Emanuel Swedenborg, Swedish scientist and visionary, claimed to be in regular contact with spirit entities. He learned quite soon that the spirits "tell lies". UFO occupants seem to have more in common with Swedenborg's spirit visitors than with the extraterrestrial aliens they are fond of portraying. Their lies are legion.

In his classic *Passport to Magonia* [**4**] Vallée uses the Eagle River, Wisconsin case of 18 April 1961 to make a historical comparison. Joe Simonton, a 60-year-old chicken farmer, discovered a saucer-shaped craft hovering outside his home. He went towards it and saw three "men" inside, "resembling Italians". They were 1.5 metres (5 feet) tall, with dark hair and skin, wearing blue knitted outfits, incorporating turtle-neck tops and knitted helmets. [**5**]

Time and again, witnesses demon-strate a remarkable anaesthesia of emotional reaction: natural fear is subdued while curiosity is heightened. Instead of fleeing, Joe went right up to the entities. One was cooking on "a flameless grill of some sort", and when Joe expressed interest in the food he was given three small flat cakes. In return, at their request, he gave them a jug of water.

Two of the cakes were tested in the Food & Drug Laboratory of the US Dept. of Health, Education & Welfare, at the request of the USAF; they were found to contain terrestrial ingredients, but surprisingly lacked salt. Vallée juxtaposes this incident with other, non-UFO cases from older periods. During encounters with 'the Gentry', small cakes were often exchanged for water; the Little People could not abide salt, as neither could Joe Simonton's visitors.

American researcher Evans Wentz published in 1911 a thesis based on stories of fairies which he had collected. [**6**] He was told the following by what we would term today a 'contactee': "They are able to appear in different forms. One once appeared to me and seemed only four feet high, and stoutly built. He said, 'I am bigger than I appear to you now. We can make the old young, the big small, the small big'."

What Wentz' informant seems to be saying is that the Gentry could assume any manner of appearance, size or proportion. And that is exactly what our UFO occupants seem able to do.

DEFYING CLASSIFICATION

Many researchers, in their efforts to make the ET hypothesis more tenable, have attempted to squeeze occupant descriptions into a mere handful of categories. One of the most recent is Walter Andrus, MUFON director, who after studying "thousands of cases" announced that there were four main types of alien visiting the Earth:

- the small humanoid
- the experimental animal
- the human-like entity
- the robot.

He then goes on to give precise physical descriptions for each category. [**7**]

While MUFON must be congratulated for carrying out this work, I fear they have evaluated their data while wearing blinkers. Within each of these categories there are hundreds of small differences between the reported entities. Consider some reports in which the occupants, though broadly similar to others, are none the less unique:

On the night of 16 November 1963, two courting couples received a severe fright near Sandling

Park, Saltwood, Kent, England. [4] They observed an oval-shaped 'star' descend then hover near some trees, about 8 metres away. Suddenly something emerged from the direction of the golden object. A human-sized entity shambled towards them. The witnesses described a black figure, headless, with webbed feet and wings like a bat: they fled in panic.

This bizarre monstrosity reminds us of the 'Mothman' reports from West Virginia in 1961, 1966 and 1967. [8] But 'mothman' was really a catch-all name for a variety of large humanoid creatures with bat-like wings. They were described variously as brown or grey in colour, some headless, others with glowing red eyes; most were as tall as a man, but one in Utah was "about as big as a Piper Cub aeroplane". [9] In Da Nang, Vietnam, in 1969, several US Marines saw a black naked woman with large bat-like wings who flew over them glowing with a green luminescence. [10] In Cornwall, England, during the mid-to-late 1970s, people were reporting something which came to be labelled 'Owlman': they described it as "like a big owl with pointed ears, as big as a man" with glowing slanting red eyes, a very large mouth, silvery grey feathers and clawed feet. There have been thousands of such monster reports, many of them sighted in conjunction with "strange lights" or "glowing objects".

One theory suggests that these monsters are purpose-built nightmares released by the UFO occupants to scare away intruders while they repair their craft or carry out tasks associated with their mission. However, it is no less likely, human nature being what it is, that monster reports would *attract* unwelcome visitors to the remote locations where these incidents tend to occur.

MINDLESS MONSTERS?

UFO occupants often give the impression of mindlessness; but even though they have the potential for causing serious physical harm and even death, they do not except in rare cases give witnesses more than a bad fright. Jerome Clark investigated the experience of William Bosak, a dairy farmer from Frederic, Wisconsin. Bosak was driving through patchy fog at 10.30 pm one night in December 1974. Ahead of him, resting on the road, he saw a disc-shaped UFO whose front, like curved glass, enabled him to see inside.

There he saw a humanoid creature "just as scared as I was". Its eyes were normal except that they protruded, and its body was covered with dark tan fur which left the face and chin bare. On the head this fur appeared to be brushed or combed back. Bosak was most impressed by the ears which resembled calf's ears, sticking out horizontally about 7.5 cm from the head. He described the mouth and nose as "flat". [11]

Unlike Adamski's aliens who had normal human features, most human-like occupants have at least one physical abnormality. An example is the entity encountered by middle-aged couple Joyce Bowles and Ted Pratt while driving near Winchester, England, in November 1976. [12] After noticing an orange glow in the sky, they lost control of their car which swerved onto a wide grass verge along a narrow country lane. Ahead of them, hovering just off the ground, was an orange cigar-shaped object, 5 metres (15 feet) in size. Through a window three heads were peering.

As the terrified couple clutched at each other, they saw a "man" pass through the side of the cigar and walk towards their car. He was about 1.8 m (6 feet) tall, slimly built, wearing a one-piece foil-like suit, with a zip which went up to his chin. He had long blond hair combed back from his forehead, but wore a dark beard; his complexion was pale.

Upon reaching their Mini Clubman he placed one hand on the roof and peered inside, enabling them to see that his nose was long and pointed, but his eyes were pink - *entirely* pink, without irises or pupils. . It would seem they were also luminescent, for when Mrs Bowles turned her head away, an after-image remained on her retina, similar to the effect of staring at a naked electric lamp.

This makes an interesting comparison with the glowing red eyes reported in some of the 'Mothman' reports; moreover, glowing eyes - usually red - abound in the annals of historical folklore, attributed to black dogs and other supernatural entities. There seems no biological reason why eyes should glow, although it does make the entities more "scary".

THE FOETUS-LIKE ENTITIES

The celebrated 1961 case of Betty and Barney Hill featured an occupant type similar to that reported elsewhere with slight variations. Under hypnosis, the couple revealed that after their UFO sighting, their car was ambushed and they were taken on board a UFO and examined. They described the aliens as about 1.5 metres (5 feet) tall (though perhaps significantly the "leader" and the "doctor" were taller than the rest of the crew) and wearing shiny black uniforms. They were hairless, with wrap-round almond-shaped eyes with cat-like pupils. Betty described the head shape as "mongoloid" - a round face and prominent forehead; the skin was bluish-grey.

Their uniform possessed neither buttons nor zippers (the absence of such details suggests a sketchy cartoon in which fine detail is simply omitted); the design emphasised their abnormal physique, which was characterised by deeper chest cavities and larger chests than would be found in a human. [13]

Betty Andreasson gave a similar description of the entities who visited her on 25 January 1967, at her home in South Ashburnham, Mass. During a power cut, Betty and her family noticed a glowing light through one of the windows. When the house lights suddenly came back on, everyone in the room except Betty became paralysed. Shortly afterwards four entities entered the house, passing through the closed front door. 1 to 1.2 metres (3.5-4 feet) tall, they had pear-shaped heads with broad foreheads and narrow chins. Their noses were merely two small holes, their mouths thin horizontal slits. Though paralysed, both Betty's father and her eldest daughter confirmed that they too had observed the entities. [**14**]

Occupants of this type, sometimes reported with thin emaciated arms and legs, are very reminiscent of the human foetus.

ROBOT-LIKE ENTITIES

In his press release Andrus mentions robot-type entities, and there have indeed been a number of reports of humanoid occupants who look and seem to be machines of some sort. But ETH proponents fail to see the implausibility that space-travelling races would construct humanoid-shaped robots: there is no necessity for it, which is why our own Lunar and Mars robots are not in the least human in appearance. The kind of robot occupants witnessed during UFO scenarios come straight out of *Buck Rogers* and *Dr Who*.

On 2 January 1978 four young men from Kirkby, near Liverpool, England, decided to have a night out in the nearby town of Rainford. To get there, they had to drive across Simonswood Moss - several square miles of flat boggy landscape relieved by clumps of stunted trees and short scraggy bushes.

Just after 11 pm the group left Rainford for home. Soon the sodium brightness of the streets was left behind for the blackness of the Moss. They were chatting, when the driver realised he had taken a wrong turning onto a narrow dirt track bordered by a ditch. While they considered what to do, a figure appeared in the glare of the headlights, some 8 metres ahead.

About 2 metres (7 feet) tall, the being was either wearing a white fluorescent one-piece suit, or its body was made from a bright metallic substance, with boots to match. The head was devoid of facial characteristics, or visor of any kind. Its arms were

The Winchester encounter. [**Jennifer Cook** / *BUFORA Journal*]

disproportionately short, ending in claws. On the chest was positioned a box with two flashing red lights.

The figure took a few steps towards the car, then abruptly stopped, apparently as surprised to see the men as they were to see it. No wonder the driver panicked, slammed the vehicle into reverse and headed for a nearby farm. The police searched the area in vain, but confirmed that the four witnesses were genuinely distressed. While waiting at the farm for the police to arrive, the driver had suffered an asthma attack.

Although there was a report of a UFO seen in the area, it could not be conclusively tied down to the same date. So was this robot-like entity a UFO occupant? Well, it *looked* "space age", and it had to come from *somewhere* - if not from a UFO, then from wherever UFOs come from. [**15**]

But robot-like entities do not have to be larger than life. In the early evening of 23 October 1965, Jerry Townsend, employee of a local radio station, was driving towards Long Prairie, Minnesota, when suddenly his engine, lights and radio went dead. Ahead, on the road, was a "space ship" culled straight from the pulp era of science fiction. It was rocket-shaped, 10 to 12 metres high, and rested on three fins. Townsend left his car and saw three 15 cm (6 in) "beer can" shaped beings coming towards him from beneath the rocket. They walked comically in an absurd "side to side" gait, on two small fins. When they halted, a third, stabiliser, fin came down at the rear. Eventually they returned to the rocket and it took off. This final phase was witnessed by two hunters some distance away. [**5**]

Jerry Townsend's "beer can" robots lead us to another occupant type - what Keel has called the "mini-people": entities just a few centimetres high. How many such encounters have occurred is uncertain, for this kind of experience, more than any other, is liable to be suppressed by the percipient: would *you* admit to relatives and friends, never mind a stranger, that you have seen tiny people at the bottom of your garden?

A fascinating incident of this type was reported from Lumut, Malaysia in 1980. Ahmad Jamaludin, editor of the *Malaysian UFO Bulletin*, stated that several manifestations had occurred at a school in the village. Most of the witnesses were pupils, though two teaching staff were also involved: they attempted to hush the whole matter up.

One morning at 10.30 am, two 12-year-old girls went outside the school building to deposit some rubbish. Imagine their surprise on seeing, just a metre or two away, two strange miniature figures in the grass. Though humanoid, they were monkey-like, and just five cm tall! The girls fled in terror and babbled out their story to a teacher. Convinced something had really happened, the teacher obtained a full description. Both entities wore safari-style suits complete with hats and boots. One was dressed all in white, the other in black, Both carried packs and long rods which the girls assumed to be weapons. Oddly (but not unusually) neither figure appeared to be actually standing on the ground.

Just two hours earlier, another girl had visited the toilet and claimed she encountered a large hairy monkey-like creature. When this rapidly shrunk to just a few inches high, the girl fainted.

Both incidents impressed the staff sufficiently for them to organise a search of the grounds at noon. During the search, three figures were seen, all dressed in white and carrying packs. What happened next is not quite clear, but the mini-people were lost behind a large rock. Some of the witnesses claimed they boarded a small UFO which then took off. Three days later, a small object was seen flying over the area.

WHO OR WHAT ARE THEY?

UFO occupants come in all shapes and sizes, from a few centimetres to over two metres tall: mini-people to hairy dwarfs, hairless aliens to giant hominids. They can look (almost) human, comically absurd or like the manifestation of a nightmare. Some leave footprints, others - ghost-like - float a few centimetres above the ground. They have the capacity to look like flesh and blood, yet they can pass through walls and doors. Some act like benevolent saints out to save the world, while others portray satanic miscreants bent on spreading terror among their human victims. When it comes to telling lies, they could give lessons to earthly politicians.

Hobbies include abducting and examining humans and other animals; collecting soil and vegetation samples; and repairing craft forever breaking down in places where people might just "happen" to come along.

In short, UFO occupants are all things to all men. Who or what are they *really*? Genuine alien entities from other planets? Inter-dimensional denizens? Time travellers? Refugees from Atlantis, operating from remote areas on or in the Earth? Or is there some entirely different answer?

Wherever they originate, the occupants display various eccentricities either in dress, physical malformation, behaviour or speech content. They act less like 'aliens' than as if they are fledgling temporary beings hastily assembled and scripted to act out a brief scenario.

"The examples of apparent absurdity are very numerous", Aime Michel has written, "and we find almost always one or two absurd details in every well-reported case. Some cases are veritable festivities of absurdity." [**5**]

In his *Visions, apparitions, alien visitors* [**17**] Hilary Evans discusses the whole menagerie of entity reports and ponders on the machinery required to produce them. One possibility is manufacture from ectoplasm, the substance said to exude from a spirit medium's body when in trance. Described as alive and sensitive to touch and to bright lights, ectoplasm has long been held by spiritualists to be the means whereby the spirits make themselves visible in our dimension.

So the idea is not new, but never before has it been applied so widely, and in particular to our 'extraterrestrial' visitors. Ectoplasm has been photographed, and described as a gelatinous vapour, which may relate to reports of UFOs surrounded by a strange mist or appearing from unusual clouds. Some have resembled balls of vaporous light to begin with, then subsequently assumed the appearance of solid flying machines. In some instances, a substance similar to ectoplasm - 'angel hair' - has been found at the location of a UFO event.

Even if this should be a clue as to what UFOs and their occupants are composed of, it tells us nothing about their true origins. Less still does it help us to understand why this bizarre interaction with the human race has been occurring for so many hundreds of years.

REFERENCES

1 - **Leslie,** Desmond and **Adamski,** George, *Flying Saucers have landed*, 1953. ■ 2 - **Johnson,** Frank, *The Janos people*, 1980. ■ 3- **Sprinkle,** Leo, *Personality characteristics of UFO witnesses*, 1986. ■ 4 - **Vallée,** Jacques, *Passport to Magonia*, 1969. ■ 5- **Bowen,** Charles (editor) *The humanoids*, 1969. ■ 6- **Evans Wentz,** W.Y., *The fairy faith in Celtic countries*, 1911. ■ 7 *Irish Independent*, Dublin, 1986. ■ 8 - **Keel,** John A, *The Mothman prophecies*, 1975. ■ 9 Bord, Janet and Colin, *Alien animals*, 1980. ■ 10 *Flying Saucer Review Case Histories*, No 10, 1972. ■ 11 *Flying Saucer Review*, Vol 21 No 1, 1975. ■ 12 *Flying Saucer Review*, Vol 22 No 5, 1976. ■ ■ 13 - **Fuller,** John G, *The interrupted journey*, 1966. ■ 14 - **Fowler,** Raymond, *The Andreasson affair*, 1979. ■ 15 - **Hough,** Peter, 'The humanoid contingent', in *The unknown*, September 1986. ■ 16 *Malaysian UFO Bulletin*, October 1981. ■ 17 - **Evans,** Hilary, *Visions, apparitions, alien visitors*, 1984.

2.5

ABDUCTIONS AND CONTACTEES

by Hilary Evans and John Spencer

HISTORY AND SUMMARY

Historically we may be unable to identify the first contactee or abduction cases. In the Bible, Ezekiel certainly seems, in one interpretation of events, to have been taken aloft in a 'flying saucer', though his experience seems to be more that of a contactee than an abductee. The 'Bibles' of other religions, like the folklore of cultures throughout the world, contain similar tales. Even before this kind of written history, cave paintings are held by some to recall sightings of 'flying saucers', and perhaps if they do then they also recount stories we would today classify as abductions or contacts. It is important to recognise that today's contact and abduction accounts are part of an ongoing tradition as old as the records of humanity. However, this is far from being a reason to dismiss the stories currently being told. If a tradition is sustained for so long, it is because it is important to those who sustain it. Today's contactee and abduction stories are unquestionably important. What *is* open to question is whether they are important, or even relevant, to UFO research. This speculation will not be examined at this point; the understanding of abductions as part of folklore and religion is examined in the last part of this article.

From the point of view of abductions and contacts reported as part of the UFO phenomenon we find, not surprisingly, that they seem to begin in the 1940s, when 'saucers' made their apparent entrance.

THE STEREOTYPE

The crucial feature of the reports is that **every case is unique**. This in itself is reason for suspecting that the 'external' event may have an 'internal' meaning specific to the individual witness.

At the same time, the reports share many common features. Patterns exist, and this leads to perhaps the key question we have to ask: **Is it what the experiences have in common, or what makes each one distinct, which is the key to understanding them?**

In the stereotype contact experience, an individual - who frequently has a pattern of curious incidents in his/her life story hitherto - is contacted by extraterrestrial beings, who tell him that they have chosen him to pass on a message (generally a warning) to humankind, or to perform a mission in preparation for profound developments in terrestrial/extraterrestrial affairs. Frequently he is taken aboard their spacecraft, and sometimes is taken to visit their home planet and given other wonderful insights.

In the stereotype abduction experience, the individual seems (but this is open to question) to be taken by surprise by an encounter with extraterrestrial beings; the witness is taken aboard the spacecraft and subjected, more or less involuntarily, to some kind of physical examination, which may include subcutaneous and even surgical probing, sample-taking, and even sexual operations leading in some cases to pregnancy.

Here are some examples taken from many hundreds of such reports:

■ 1946

George Adamski's first contact (of many). Adamski's meetings were generally with very human, tall, long-haired, beautiful creatures. Generally the meetings took place in the Californian deserts. Adamski reported being taken on rides to Venus, where the aliens reportedly came from. He was apparently also taken to Mars and the Moon. The tone of the contacts was one of a benevolent interest in mankind, the aliens for the most part issuing words of warning to mankind.

Many other contactees followed in Adamski's footsteps and told similar stories. By far the greater number of these claims occurred in the United States, but other cultures too produced examples - Siragusa in Italy, Monnet and Vorilhon ('Rael') in France, Julio F in Spain, Yosip Ibrahim in Peru, and so on.

■ 1953

Sarah Shaw and Jane Whiteley (aliases) at Tujunga Canyon. The event started with lights seen through the windows and included a classical abduction facet - lost time. The two were taken aboard a UFO, and subjected to medical examination. Aliens were generally said to be shadowy slender creatures, but no clear descriptions are given. Note, however, that the recall of these events was not made until many years after the given time of the abduction.

■ 1954

San Carlos, Venezuela. Three men were driving in a car, one left the car for a short time and claimed he was attacked by a small hairy creature that ran into a UFO that then took off. No contact or abduction reported. However, none appears to have been tested for.

■ 1957
Antonio Villas Boas. This case is covered in great detail in another section of the book. Generally, however, the events were as follows: The subject observed a light in the sky while farming at night. UFO then approached and the tractor would not start. Subject ran off but was chased and caught by occupants of the UFO. He was subjected to a form of medical examination and was then 'introduced to' and had sexual intercourse with a female alien entity. She is described as being under 5 feet tall and somewhat oriental in appearance. The subject tried to remove physical evidence but was prevented from doing so.

■ 1961
Betty and Barney Hill. This case is also examined in great detail in another section of the book and also later in this article. The facts are generally very well known, suffice to say here that it was a 'classical' abduction involving a UFO sighting, lost time, and medical examinations. Facts revealed by hypnotic regression some time after the event.

Joe Simonton; Wisconsin. A chicken farmer saw a UFO land in his backyard. Three men, approximately five feet tall, came out, wearing blue uniforms and balaclava helmets. They exchanged some pancakes for a pitcher of water. The pancakes were tested and revealed to be made of terrestrial material but contained no salt. There was no reported abduction, though again none was tested for.

■ 1967
Betty Andreasson, Massachusetts. Subject saw a light outside the window of her home. Then she saw creatures outside the window. They entered the house (through the wall). Subject was hypnotically regressed in 1977 (ten years after the events). She reported that she was taken aboard the craft and underwent a medical examination.

Patrolman Schirmer, Ashland, Nebraska. Subject reported a UFO landing. Hypnotic regression later revealed some of the classical facets of abductions: missing time, taken aboard UFO and interrogated, though no report of a medical examination. Occupants described as four-and-a-half to five feet high, muscular but wiry, large chests, head thin and long and had eyes like a cat's. They wore tight-fitting silver-grey suits and boots.

■ 1969
Belo Horizonte, Brazil. Jose da Silva, a member of the armed forces was night camping, and then fishing the next day. Two entities abducted him. They were described as having a stocky build, 4 feet high, human proportions, long beards and long hair. They wore what seemed to be some sort of breathing apparatus. Subject was abducted with violence, rather than the passive 'mental control' often described. Missing time reported. Subject was taken for a ride in the UFO. No apparent medical examination made. Object of the abduction seemed to be that subject should 'spy' for them. Subject refused. One alarming aspect of the case was the report of dead human specimens on board.

■ 1970
Shearer, Wisconsin. Very similar to the above two cases. There appears to have been an abduction but no real medical examination, just an interrogation. Entities were approximately 4½ to 5 feet high, good physical build and appeared to resemble the old Egyptian gods.

■ 1973
Pascagoula. Two fishing companions saw a UFO near them. Three figures floated through the air towards them from a door in the UFO. They were basically human-like, but nose and ears were conical. They had crab-like claws. Abductees were 'floated' into the UFO and given medical examinations.

■ 1974
Carl Higdon, a hunter in Medicine Bow National Forest. While hunting deer, he encountered being on foot which he described as being approximately 180 pounds, over six feet, face blended into his throat with no chin or jaw. Oriental cast to the skin. No eyebrows or lips, but large teeth, ears and eyes very small. Coarse gold hair standing on end and two antenna sticking out of his forehead. Apparently spoke in idiomatic local dialect. 'Floated' towards Higdon. UFO of a distinctly different type to the norm; more like a cube of small size into which subject was 'transferred'. No real medical examination given, though subject thought he had been rejected after screening as he had had a vasectomy. Subject was taken for a trip to their planet.

Aveley, Home Counties, UK. Driving home late at night, the family saw a UFO. Their car drove into a mist and went dead. Family then went on their way. Hypnotically regressed, and revealed a time loss, and abduction. Medical examination given on board the UFO.

■ 1975
Travis Walton. One of seven in a wood-cutting gang. Saw UFO. Subject ran to it, and was knocked out by blue light. His companions ran off, thereby losing the first real possibility of an external confirmation of an abduction. Subject was missing for five days. He had no memory of medical examinations but seems to have been taken on a trip by the UFO. Aliens noted as five feet tall, but no clear descriptions given.

'P & W', Maine. Two subjects driving together saw a

UFO. They then found themselves a mile away. Hypnotic regression revealed they had been abducted and that they had undergone a medical examination. Creatures fairly classical but with the unique feature of mushroom-shaped heads.

■ circa 1978

'Kathie Davis' and members of her family and friends participated in a complex 'multiple abduction' saga comprising a series of inter-related incidents, including many pregnancies, foetus-removal, mother-child confrontations and much more. [7]

■ 1979

Virginia. Turner, driving a truck, saw a UFO, the occupant got in the vehicle and was shot at. The whole truck was lifted aboard the UFO. Turner was subjected to a medical examination. He saw the entities but could offer no real description.

■ 1980

PC Alan Godfrey, West Yorkshire. At the end of a night patrol, subject thought he had seen a bus. Realised it was a UFO. Tried to report incident but neither car radio or personal radio would function. Object suddenly disappeared. Regressive hypnosis revealed abduction and medical examination.

■ 1984

Whitley Strieber had a more or less stereotyped experience, partially shared by his wife and son, of which, as a professional writer, he was able to provide an exceptionally detailed and articulate account. [12]

This is not the only such instance; in 1982 a well-known Spanish writer, Eduardo Pons Prades, published an account of his contact experience. Like Strieber, he wrote his account immediately afterwards and published it with a major publisher within a few months of the events.

Having now noted some major incidents above, we can use these to analyse the contactee/abduction scenarios generally. There are a number of points. Firstly, contact with the entities followed the beginning of 'saucer-fever' in the 1940s. First meetings were benevolent, and subjects were chosen to deliver messages. Later, contacts were subjected to less pleasant mental and physical violence. They were not given messages but were used as subjects for experimental work. In the case of Tujunga Canyon, this appears to be an earlier abduction rather than contact, but it is important to note that the events were not recalled until many years later. In the 'human' world, these events have a parallel; for the early days of flying saucer sightings coincided with great concern over the development of the atomic bomb - a concern which dwindled for decades until recently. Witness the Campaign for Nuclear Disarmament, which was a very strong force in the 1950s, much less so in the next two decades, and is only now regaining ground. Our early aliens appear to have shared our fears and gave grim warnings to contacts. Later aliens appear to have rid themselves of the fear and are very much in control of the situation; later theories included that the entire planet is a laboratory experiment and that the human race is a biological experiment periodically being checked on. There are a great many other such parallels, and later we shall consider their implications. First, however, we must consider another very important aspect; the way in which the information is revealed.

ALTERED STATES OF CONSCIOUSNESS (ASC) AND REGRESSION HYPNOSIS

Common to a great number of abduction accounts are indications which suggest that the witness may have been in an altered state of consciousness at the time.

ASCs vary greatly; from states such as sleep in which the individual appears to lose virtually all contact with the external world, to states such as fear or excitement in which he appears to be in full conscious control of his thoughts and actions. Between these extremes are various forms of ecstasy, rapture and trance, either voluntarily induced by meditation, drugs, spiritual or spritualist exercises etc, or involuntarily brought about by external events, atmospheric and other physical circumstances, personal physiological factors such as alteration in body chemistry; and many more.

Though each of these states has its specific characteristics, there are others which all or most of them have in common. One is enhanced suggestibility; this can take many forms, such as hallucination, seeing something that isn't physically there, or illusion, mistaking what is seen for something other. ASCs are also characterised by greater or lesser degrees of amnesia; thus a spirit medium doesn't consciously recall what she says in her trance, a hypnotic subject doesn't know what he did while hypnotised, and so on.

This amnesia can, however, often be removed by returning the subject to an altered state; he is then often able to retrieve his concealed memories. The great hypnosis researchers of the 19th century, such as Pierre Janet, made extensive use of this technique to reveal the subconscious processes at work, but the more discerning came to realise that the technique had serious limitations which had to be allowed for.

Unfortunately, these lessons were not taken to heart by everyone who used hypnosis as a way of obtaining access to hidden memory. This proved to be notably the case when researchers used regression hypnosis in order to obtain information about the subject's previous existences (as evidence for reincarnation) or about encounters with extraterrestrials on which some kind of amnesia was allegedly imposed by the abducting aliens.

Let us now confine ourselves to this one aspect of this area of Ufology.

REGRESSIVE HYPNOSIS

Hypnosis has been known and misunderstood since the latter half of the 18th century, and only in more recent years has much of the mysticism been removed. Even then, regression hypnosis is still less understood, and because of its frequent uses in the field of the so-called 'occult' it is an area still shrouded in mysticism. The two main uses to which this has been put, in this context, are in the study of reincarnation and in UFO-abduction cases.

In each field of research there is a well-documented case where the subject of regression hypnosis can be studied. In the case of the search for past lives, the classic case is that of Bridey Murphy [**14**], and in the case of UFO abduction investigations, as previously stated, it is that of Betty and Barney Hill.

Let us consider the basic premise on which it is believed that regression hypnosis is a worthwhile tool in UFO research. Firstly, the abduction is undergone by a person. That person has a memory. For some reason (the two most popular being either traumatic amnesia or a direct instruction from the alien entities), the person is unable to recall from his memory details of the contact. Regression hypnosis then takes that person back to the time of the contact in his mind and the person relives the experience, able to describe in detail what is happening around him as if he were there at that time.

But that may not be the case, and when you combine a method of research (regression hypnosis) which we do not yet fully understand, with a subject matter (UFOs/Reincarnation) that is still open to so many areas of speculation, the results must be open to much doubt. To quote from the introduction to "The Interrupted Journey" by Benjamin Simon, MD (who hypnotised Betty/Barney Hill):

"Hypnosis is the pathway to the Truth as it is felt and understood by the patient. The Truth is what he believes to be the truth, and this may or may not be consonant with the ultimate non-personal truth." [**3**] The author of the book, J G Fuller, points out that it is common in hypnosis for the subject to give the answer that will most please the hypnotist.

In order to study the use of regressive hypnosis, we must first study the case of Betty and Barney Hill. In summary, the case is this: In September 1961, driving home in New Hampshire, USA, they observed a UFO moving on an erratic course, which Barney at first believed to be an aeroplane. At a later point it was seen as a much larger structure, in front of the car, quite close, and Barney, taking some binoculars from the car, got out and moved closer to the object in order to look closely at it. He observed occupants looking at him through the object's windows, believed himself about to be captured, and ran back to the car. They drove off and began feeling drowsy, while at the same time being conscious of a "beeping" noise. As their drowsiness lifted and they could still hear the noise, they became aware that they were now some 35 miles from the first contact point.

They reached home somewhat shaken by their experience, and during the next few days Betty consulted UFO books in order to better understand what they had seen. This led to her making contact with NICAP and a visit from investigators; in the course of their questioning, it emerged that the Hills' journey had taken some two hours longer than would be expected, and other curious details emerged which made them wonder whether there may have been more to their experience than they could remember.

This was echoed in dreams which Betty began to have, in which the couple had a *second* experience with the UFO, this time involving an actual encounter with its occupants. For some reason, the Hills had taken a road other than the one they meant to be on; their car was stopped, they were seized and taken aboard a spaceship and there subjected, separately, to medical examination, after which they were taken back to their car. Though somewhat alarming, the experience was not too unpleasant, and at the end Betty was on surprisingly friendly terms with the leader of the ET crew.

However, when Barney's health began to deteriorate during the course of the next year or so, they speculated that this might be connected with their strange experience; their doctor accepted the suggestion, and arranged a series of hypnosis sessions with a reputable psychologist. In the course of these sessions both Barney and Betty narrated experiences which replicated Betty's dreams.

In order to study the reliability of the reporting of this case, we must first concentrate on the measuring and recording instruments themselves, ie Betty and Barney Hill. Before we do this, I would like to summarise my final conclusions first, as they form the framework of this chapter.

I believe that Betty and Barney Hill saw a UFO during their journey and I have no concrete thoughts on what that UFO might, in reality, have been, although it is worth noting at this point that Barney at first believed it to be an aeroplane, and J G Fuller described Barney as "an avid plane watcher" [**3**], and later on in the recalling of the incident both Betty and Barney Hill many times, both consciously and under hypnosis, referred to the UFO as the moon, although admittedly in a confused and agitated state. From the UFO researcher's point of view, the identification of this object is important, but from the point of view of a study of regressive hypnosis it need not be. What is clear is that they saw something, and that they believed that they saw something. What is also clear is that in the period after the incident they were both upset and agitated by it. I [JS] believe that Betty Hill subsequently had vivid nightmares based on the incident, in which she believed she had been taken aboard the flying saucer with her husband and subjected to a medical examination, and indeed it is admitted by all parties that she did have these nightmares, although those who believe the incident to have been a UFO reality consider that the nightmares were inspired by the incident. Betty discussed these nightmares with her husband, and there is a serious conflict of evidence surrounding this point in that it was believed that Betty had not remembered the experience in detail and had certainly not communicated it to her husband at least until during the regressive hypnosis treatment which commenced in 1964. John G Fuller says:

"The question of how Betty's dreams were absorbed by Barney would have to be carefully examined." [**3**]

However, it has been shown that in September 1962, following the incident but before the regressive hypnosis, they were invited to a UFO study group in Massachusetts, where they described in some detail the experience and the dreams resulting from the sighting, although they were unaware that this discussion had been tape-recorded. Clearly then, there is no difficulty in understanding how Barney became aware of Betty's dream, he had only to listen to her talking. In fact, other sections of Fuller's *Interrupted Journey* make it clear that they had discussed the dreams before the time of the regressive hypnosis therapy, with Barney playing the part of the sceptic.

If we conclude that the sighting of a UFO was the only incident involved, that it inspired fearful nightmares, that Betty and Barney Hill discussed these nightmares perhaps in a context of space exploration and UFOs generally, and that under regressive hypnosis a "hotchpotch" of memory, fantasy, anxieties, and dreams came out, then we have to study the two areas: firstly, why a seemingly uneventful sighting should inspire such a fearful fantasy, and secondly why the regressive hypnosis could not sort signal from substance.

Let us look, then, at Betty and Barney Hill. They are described as a pleasant, well-adjusted couple of average intelligence. However, a more searching

The Hill case: the first phase. [From Hilary Evans, ***UFOs: the greatest mystery*****]**

enquiry into their personal lives, while not exactly refuting this, does show clear areas of potential stress:

■ Their marriage was a mixed marriage, Barney being a negro and Betty a caucasion, and such a marriage is subject to stress even in this present day, and it is inconceivable that there would not be stresses in the late 'fifties/early 'sixties in Puritan New England, particularly when one considers that Martin Luther King was at his most vehement in his fight for civil rights. This was also a cause dear to the hearts of Betty and Barney Hill: "They stomped the State of New Hampshire speaking for the cause of Civil Rights." [**3**]

■ Secondly, Barney is said to have two sons from a former marriage, which indicates either a previous divorce or the death of his former wife, either of which would be a source of past or present potential stress.

■ Betty described Barney as "a worrier at times", his job "a daily 120-mile round trip" had, Barney felt, "been instrumental in causing his ulcer to kick up, a condition for which he was under medical treatment." In fact, at the time of the incident Barney "was waiting for the result of recent x-rays of his ulcer that his doctor had taken." [**3**]

■ On the subject of their intelligence: "Barney, with an IQ of nearly 140... found the frustration of the routine work..." [**3**] We recognise today that an intelligent mind, trapped in routine work, unstimulated, is like a vacuum waiting to be filled, and that far from high intelligence being unlikely to produce fantasies, the reverse is true in that it takes a strong mind to damage itself.

With this in mind, part of armed forces training in Germany is to place soldiers in forests alone throughout the night in order that they can understand the fantasies that lack of stimulation can produce. I have personally [JS] interviewed one such soldier, a reasonably level-headed and intelligent person, who found this experience quite frightening, and resulted in his both seeing and hearing things, both of which his own investigations showed to be non-existent. The Army has recognised for some time that the less intelligent soldiers they put in this position show no anxieties whatsoever, which they believe to be due to their having too little imagination to create fantasies with which to concern themselves.

■ Betty had previously undergone an operation which prevented her having children, and this is clearly a potential source of stress, and a comparison is worth making between this case and the case of Betty Andreasson, in which she describes a similar abduction and medical examination and an exactly similar technique being used to study her womb, and it is revealed in the medical reports that Betty Andreasson had previously undergone a hysterectomy. Betty Hill's dream also revealed that a sample of semen had been removed from Barney, her husband, and it is possible that such fantasies could be generated by, if not the desire for children, then the loss of ability to reproduce them. Of course, the comparison between the two cases is irrelevant if it were demonstrated that Betty Andreasson had read the reports of the Hill case.

A BIZARRE FANTASY?

Summarising our contactees, we have intelligent minds, perhaps unstretched by their circumstances, and certainly stretched by fears and anxieties.

If we accept the above, then why such a bizarre and elaborate fantasy when, after all, many hundreds of thousands of people face the same stresses and the same fears, which surface perhaps through dreams and sometimes through actions of a more literally down-to-earth nature. Why should their subconscious concoct the fantasy that it did, and if we accept that in Betty's case her acceptance of the fantasy as a reality is merely a result of the strength of the fantasy, then why should Barney be convinced of its reality merely by being told of the dreams by Betty? For this we have to mentally place ourselves in New Hampshire, USA, in 1961 to 1964, because at that time and in that place there would be many stimulations which could help generate a fantasy of this nature and one event which produced an emotion so intense that the subject of space exploration would have been foremost in everybody's mind.

With regard to general stimulus, the previous decade, following Kenneth Arnold's 1947 sighting and use of the words "flying saucer", had produced many UFO abduction stories in the form of films, many of which have become classics to this day. The following are the most famous: *The Day the Earth stood still* - 1951, *Earth versus The Flying Saucers* - 1956, *I married a monster from Outer Space* - 1958, *Invaders from Mars* - 1953, *Invasion of the Body Snatchers* - 1956, *Invasion of the Saucer Men* - 1957, *Man from Planet X* - 1951, *Target Earth* - 1954, *This Island Earth* - 1955, *War of the Worlds* - 1953. The general theme of these films is of UFOs coming to the earth, usually to conquer it and usually involving the capture and sometimes abduction of human beings. It must be borne in mind that in the 'fifties and 'sixties, and particularly in America, the cinema was not the same cultural medium that it is today. Whereas today we visit the cinema to see a particular film, in that period of time it was customary to go to the cinema on, say, a Saturday night, usually without even knowing what was on, and sit through the evening's programmes. As such, it was a social gathering and its importance was the meeting of other people, not primarily the seeing of films. We have no details of whether Barney and Betty Hill partook of this social gathering, but it is inconceivable that they would not have been in contact with people who did;

would not have been aware of the type of films that were being shown at some level in their consciousness. In addition to this, television was in the middle of showing its new series *The Twilight Zone*, and it is clear that they were aware of this series of programmes because part of the conversation revealed between Betty and Barney at the time of the contact is as follows:

Betty: "...and I laughed and asked him if he had watched *Twilight Zone* recently on TV."
Doctor: "Why did you mention *Twilight Zone*?"
Betty: "Because the idea was fantastic."
Betty does go on to say that she never sees *The Twilight Zone*, but the point is, she was clearly aware of it. [**3**]

The one extraordinary statement from Barney with regard to the potential background to the fantasy is that: "...but I have not talked about flying saucers since 1957, when we were talking about Sputnik." [**3**] And this was 1961. The implication would seem to be that there was no reason to generate this fantasy, that space exploration was not on his mind and had not been for four years, and he is therefore an impartial observer. We must regard this as a desire to be believed, as this surely cannot be true. Four months and two weeks to the day prior to the abduction, Alan Shepherd became the first American in space (on 5th May 1961). His tiny 15-minute space lob was unspectacular by today's standards, but at that time he was certainly regarded as the greatest living American, and his flight was seen as a rebuttal of Soviet dominance of space. The subsequent ticker-tape parade, media adulation and mass hysteria regarding him and his flight reveal much of the emotions of America generally towards him, his flight and the subject of space exploration. What is important is that Alan Shepherd came from Derry, New Hampshire, virtually on top of Betty and Barney Hill's doorstep, and by no stretch of the imagination would the local newspapers, television and radio media leading up to, during and subsequent to that flight, have allowed Betty and Barney Hill not to have discussed space exploration some way or the other, and if they discussed flying saucers in relation to Sputnik, then surely the subject was raised again here.

Perhaps we have now shown that the stimulus was right for a fantasy of this nature, but then we move on to our second area of difficulty and investigation, ie why the regressive hypnosis was unable to sort signal from substance, and the answer lies, as it inevitably must, in the minds of Betty and Barney Hill. Firstly, they were not strangers to the subject. "In 1957 Betty's sister and family had described seeing clearly a UFO in New Hampshire. Betty believed the story, Barney was more sceptical". [**3**] Secondly, having the dream some ten days after the incident inspired Betty to look into the subject closely, and she contacted Major D Keyhoe of NICAP and she followed up this contact by reading much UFO material. Of the dreams themselves, they continued for five successive nights, and never in her memory had she recalled dreams of such detail and intensity. They dominated her waking life during that week and continued to plague her afterwards. They assumed the proportion of nightmares. And they had discussed these dreams: "the reality or non-reality of the dreams was, of course, foremost in Betty's mind. For nearly two years now, the answer to this question had been gnawing away at her. For Barney, as he had already told Betty, he was hoping that once and for all she would accept the fact that her experience in regard to an abduction was no more than an intense series of dreams." [**3**]

Of the craft itself, Barney says "The physical structure of the craft itself fitted in with my conscious attitude of what a craft like this would look like." On later being questioned by Dr Allen Hynek, who asked: "How do you know what flying saucers look like?", Barney replied: "I was looking in a magazine, I think it was Post magazine." [**3**]

So we have a plethora of input to Betty and Barney Hill; an initial sighting, subsequent dreams, the transmission of those dreams to her husband, subsequent reading of UFO material (which could possibly have included abduction cases such as Antonio Villas Boas in 1957), Barney's subsequent reading of what a flying saucer might look like, and all this on top of the more subliminal suggestions that we have already mentioned relating to films and television of that time and the birth of the US manned space programme.

What we seem to have, then, is a fantasy constructed by intelligent minds from a simple stimulus overlaid by many of the attitudes of the time, but we would then have to look deeper at the fantasy itself, firstly to see why Betty and Barney Hill should generate it in their circumstances, and why it should be such a cause of later anxiety. As well as fantasy at the level of space exploration, which we have gone into above, we must consider fantasy at a level personal to Betty and Barney Hill. It seems that the greatest fears revealed by the regression hypnosis surround the medical examination on board the UFO. We have already said that Betty had undergone an operation (which had prevented her having children) and we know that Barney at that time is waiting for the results of x-rays on his ulcer. Under hypnosis Barney recalled, when being dragged to the spacecraft, "I don't want to be operated on" although *no such suggestion has yet been made during the incident.* If Betty's anxieties surround her inability to have children and in having described the dreams to Barney, would not his anxieties latch onto his fears that he would at some time have to undergo an operation for his ulcer?

Of the fantasy itself, it has a clear dream-like quality: "The doctor believed that the abduction to have taken place to be too improbable, much material was similar to dream material. Betty's recall under hypnosis paralleled her dream almost exactly." [**3**]

There are many dream-like qualities relating to the incident: "Floating or gliding on the part of both the reported humanoids and the subject... the inability of the subjects to strike out... temporary amnesia... ability to communicate by thought transference and inarticulate sounds..." ; and in the case of this particular abduction, Barney is obsessed with seeing piercing eyes which seem to dominate him although they do not seem attached to a body, which is a common enough characteristic of dream-like material. Also, there is a great inconsistency in the material itself, a point which is raised by John G Fuller himself, which is easily explained if you consider the quality of dreams. In conversation with the Ufonauts, they use what appears to be idiomatic English, for example, "You'll be on your way home in no time", and yet some of the questions asked include "What are vegetables?", "What is old?", "What is yellow?", which shows a remarkable lack of knowledge of the language inconsistent with the use of an idiom such as "in no time", meaningless at face value but meaningful at a deeper level of understanding of language.

The doctor himself notes [**3**]: "There seem to be indications that a great deal of the experience was absorbed by Barney Hill from Betty, in spite of his insistence that this was his own. And there are definite indications that her dreams had been suggested as a reality by her supervisor." The doctor later concludes "From the available evidence from all sources and present knowledge of mental functioning, he could accept the probability that the Hills had had an experience with an unusual aerial phenomenon, a sighting that stimulated an intense emotional experience in both of them. He felt that the abduction was improbable." And points out "Psychological amnesia exists for the purpose of repressing or wiping out intolerable emotional experiences. Is this amnesia in a sense wiping out real experience, or an amnesia relating to the wiping out of an intensely painful fantasy?"

The regressive hypnosis could clearly be searching in Betty's and Barney's minds for memory and coming up with this complex combination of memory and fantasy, unable to distinguish between the two. To be fair to Dr Simon, he takes great pains not to stimulate memory by too much directions, but by the very nature of the exercise, in order to concentrate Betty's and Barney's minds on the incident, he has to make references to airplanes, aerial phenomena, and these can take the form of suggestions. Much of the criticism of Morey Bernstein's regression of Ruth Simmons in his search for Bridey Murphy stems from the opening phrases of his hypnosis, which are: "Go still further back until, oddly enough, you find yourself in some other scene, in some other place, in some other time, and when I talk to you again you will tell me about it." [**14**] If we assume that there was no previous time for Ruth Simmons prior to her birth, the doctor's questions could act as an instruction to create one from fantasy, particularly given that the subject is keen to please the hypnotist by giving the answer he requires. It has been indicated that several of Ruth Simmons' pre-birth memories can easily be related to her young life as Ruth Simmons and the stories that were read to her when she was at that most impressionable of ages. Such a problem is not so clearly seen in the regression of Betty and Barney Hill, but a reading of the transcripts of the tapes shows that there are subtle similarities to this reinforcement of dreams, particularly given the possibility that they are desirous of pleasing the hynotist. On this, it is worth bearing in mind that both Betty and Barney Hill took very greatly to Dr Simon and missed him greatly when the sessions were completed.

Part of the problem relates to memory itself. The assumption that memory is fixed and unchanging at a given point in time is clearly incorrect. If regressive hypnosis is able to take a person back to a previous time, whether or not they are able to remember that time consciously, there is clear evidence that the remembrance does not take place as it would at that time but is affected by incidents subsequent to the event, prior to the regression. In the Bridey Murphy case, Ruth Simmons, when regressed to the life of Bridey Murphy, speaks in an Irish tongue, using many Irish phrases of which we are told she is normally unaware, and this is recorded as the strength of the case, but at the same time, she uses many Americanisms when she is ostensibly Bridey Murphy (such as calling sweets "candy"), and if you accept that the regression is really taking her to a previous life, then you have to accept that memory of that previous life is being coloured by later events. In the case of the regression of Barney and Betty Hill, therefore, any memory of September 1961 will be coloured by events subsequent to 1961 in some way or the other, and we have shown that these subsequent memories could include the reading of the NICAP material, the dreams themselves, and subsequent discussions about the dreams and the experience with Betty's family, her husband, and others.

Lastly, we must consider the question of why there are so many cases so similar to this one and so many similarities between other types of cases, which is often given as a strength of the reality of the incidents in UFO literature. This question is really a question for UFO researchers, but we can make the point here that the reading of one case can clearly influence the fantasies which become another case, each time being somewhat distorted by the particular anxieties of the contactee. In the case of Antonio Villas Boas, his own contact fantasy, if fantasy it was, included being forced to have intercourse with a reasonably attractive, if somewhat alien woman. If it was a fantasy, it does not take an enormous leap of intellect to analyse this person's causes of potential anxiety. In an analysis of the case in this book, the author points out that this subject was the only unattached male on the farm.

Regression hypnosis seems to be an unreliable tool for UFO research in the light of our discussion above. Basically, that the contactee may have hidden fears and anxieties of which the UFO researcher is unaware, that the subject of regression hypnosis is not fully understood even by those who practise it, and that there is no scientific control to the experiment, ie a framework within which to study the outcome of the experiment. We have never been able to categorically prove in any regression hypnosis case that the revelations under regressive hypnosis are true, other than in the sense of personal truth to the individual relating them. We refer here, of course, to areas involving trauma and psychological amnesia and not to the more pedestrian tests of regression hypnosis, such as remembering the names of everyone present at your fifth birthday party, etc, which does not constitute a controlled experiment because of the lack of trauma; the trauma being the important ingredient in UFO abduction cases. In this respect, the contactee is an uncalibrated instrument and the regression hypnosis a distorted hand-glass with which to read the instrument, and together they may ultimately prove totally unreliable.

There is, finally, an amusing note from Leslie Lecron's book *Experimental Hypnosis,* published in 1952, appropriate to this study. He was discussing whether or not a person could be instructed to do something under hypnosis which was not basically in his own character. Leslie Lecron said: "There is about as much danger for one to become involved in hypnotically-inspired anti-social actions as there is to being struck by a flying saucer." **[15]**

Perhaps he should talk to Betty and Barney Hill.

ASSESSING THE ABDUCTION EXPERIENCE

Abduction reports are the most dramatic manifestation of the UFO phenomenon. If they are valid - if abductions are really taking place as reported - we need look no further for an explanation of the UFOs and their visits to our planet. They would be clearly seen to be part of a larger scenario of extraterrestrial contact. What is more, they would be, quite simply, the most important event in the history of mankind. The central question then is: are abductions taking place as reported? There can be no doubt that *something* is taking place. That the abductees are having an experience of some sort is something we need not question; but we may question their interpretation of their experience. In one sense or another, abduction reports are real; what is in doubt is whether that reality is the everyday reality of the physical world, or the private reality of the witness's mind.

Like many other anomalous phenomena, abduction reports have a compelling plausibility. Reading an account such as Budd Hopkins' *Intruders* **[7]**, we find a bewildering assortment of elements which, at first sight, seem like the pieces of a jigsaw puzzle to be capable of being put together in only one way. It is only when we stand back from the event and view the picture as a whole, that we start to wonder whether there may be an alternative picture.

The first step in taking a wider perspective is to consider abduction reports in the context of the UFO phenomenon as a whole.

Abduction cases are by definition related to the UFO phenomenon, for it is in UFOs that the abductors travel to our planet, and onto the UFOs that most abductees are abducted. Every abduction case, therefore, involves a UFO, whether or not one is actually reported.

This fact alone immediately raises doubts. For if physical human beings are being abducted onto UFOs, those UFOs must themselves be physical and the act of abduction must be a physical act. Unless we are prepared to premise some temporary metamorphosis of the material substance of the abductee's physical body, it follows that the UFOs are in principle capable of being detected, either by human senses or by instruments. Yet despite the hundreds if not thousands of such reported events, not one single abduction-related UFO has ever been independently detected; and no abductee has ever been seen in the act of being taken on board or returning from a UFO. All this, despite the fact that there are thousands of reports of detection of 'other' UFOs.

Nor have the abductees themselves been more successful in obtaining material proof of their experience. Some have attempted to procure mementoes and souvenirs, but in every instance they have been prevented.

But even if no substantial proof of the physical existence of the abductees' UFO is forthcoming, would we not do well to adopt the abduction scenario as a working hypothesis? For, after all, it offers a coherent, logical explanation of the UFOs and their purpose; which is more than anyone else has been able to come up with.

When we have been seeking a solution to the UFO problem for so long, it is tempting to adopt one which at last seems to make sense. The danger is that, in our relief, we will accept the solution without examining it too closely.

One major objection is the curious recentness of the abduction phenomenon. Although many researchers have endeavoured to establish an ancient lineage for the UFO phenomenon, and even proposed earlier reports of abductions, the evidence is scanty and ambiguous. For all practical purposes, the UFO phenomenon, as we know it, commenced in the 1940s; during the 1950s it was made more complex by the appearance of the contactees, and they in their turn gave way to the abductees. This progression contains a certain logic. If there were UFOs, then it was likely they would contain occupants who had some kind of purpose; contact with the occupants was made, and their purposes were revealed. Usually it took the form of Cosmic Guardians, concerned for the well-being of our planet, selecting some allegedly exceptionally gifted member of the human race such as George Adamski, George King or Orfeo Angelucci, and entrusting him with a mission to save the world.

Though some contactees attracted a considerable following - some, indeed, still retain one - in general their claims have been discounted. Now, however, they have been replaced by the abductees, who certainly have a more plausible story to tell. We are not asked to believe that abductees like Barney and Betty Hill [**3**] or Kathie Davis [**7**] were chosen because they were **remarkable** people, only because they were **suitable** - for physical examination or genetic experimentation.

This certainly makes their stories easier to believe. It makes sense of a sort to suppose that the visiting ETs had reached a point in their study of Earth-people where they found it necessary to conduct physical examinations and breeding experiments with specimen humans. In support of this interpretation, some very ingenious scenarios have been offered, in many of which our human race is regarded as being at the level of livestock on a farm, or rats in a laboratory, placed on this planet by some more advanced species and periodically inspected to keep a track of our progress; the best-known formulation of this is Charles Fort's 'We are property'.

IMAGINARY ABDUCTEES

Those who entertain such entertaining speculations are working from the premises that abductions do in fact take place and are pretty much as described. There are others, though, for whom such a premise is less easy to accept than its contrary, that abductions do **not** occur but are a fantasy of some kind.

Support for this view has come from the work of Alvin Lawson and his colleagues in the 'imaginary abductee' experiment. [**8**] This came about as a consequence of a UFO investigation, the Brian Scott case, in which investigator John DeHerrera was puzzled by the ambiguous indications of a witness who refused to admit that any abduction had occurred, yet under hypnosis fabricated an **imaginary** abduction of extraordinary verisimilitude.

The experiment consisted of hypnotising volunteer subjects - who have no particular interest in the UFO phenomenon - then suggesting to them that they are involved in a UFO-abduction situation. They are led through its successive phases by means of guided questions, so there is no claim that the subjects fabricate the overall story. But the questions are mere bare bones; what the experiment showed was that the subjects will deck those bones with an elaborate, detailed and dramatic story - yet one which is, of course, entirely fiction.

Moreover, the fictitious stories fabricated by the 'imaginary abductees' are strikingly similar, not only in outline but in specific detail, to the stories told by the 'true' abductees.

There have been critical comments on Lawson's experiments, and because neither he nor anyone else has replicated or developed them, we should not draw more than preliminary conclusions from them. But the central finding is unequivocal and cannot reasonably be accounted for by either coincidence or cryptomnesia; while the experiments do not prove that the 'true' abductees are fabricating their accounts, **they do suggest that anyone who subconsciously wishes to do so can find within himself the necessary resources to fabricate a detailed and coherent abduction story.**

The Lawson experiments did indicate one major area of difference between the 'imaginary' and the 'true' abductees: the emotional effect, and sometimes the physiological effect, on the witness. The volunteers were not in a strongly emotive state, they had no psychological after-effects such as amnesia, dreams, nightmares or psychic experiences; 'true' abductees are liable to have all these things, including physiological effects.

This is often interpreted by critics of the experiment as a demonstration of the reality of the 'true' experiences. But it demonstrates nothing of the kind. True, it demonstrates that the 'true' abductees are in a truly emotional state; but **it is just as likely that the abduction experience occurs as a result of the emotional state as that the emotional state is the consequence of an abduction experience.**

Nobody will question that the abduction witness has a genuinely emotional experience; no one who sees the videotapes of Yorkshire policeman Alan Godfrey's recall of his alleged abduction experience [**9**] under hypnosis could be in any doubt of that. But while it shows that he had something to be emotional about, we must not jump to the conclusion that the abduction experience was the *cause*; it may have been part of the cure. The abduction experience may be a means whereby the individual externalises an internal psychological problem.

BIZARRE SIMILARITIES

An American psychologist who has made a special study of abductees, Dr Aphrodite Clamar, says: "The question persists: is the UFO experience genuine, or are those who claim to have been abducted the victims of hysteria or their own delusions? After spending more than fifty hours with a dozen subjects under hypnosis, I still cannot answer that question... I am persuaded that all of the subjects do believe that something strange and unknown did occur... It is the curious similarity of their experiences that gives pause." [**7,4**]

The fact that one witness after another, who could not be aware of one another's experiences, comes up with similar stories containing similar bizarre details, is probably the most impressive feature of the abduction experience. It is this which seems to have convinced American investigator Budd Hopkins that abductions are physical and literal fact: "For me, the conclusion is inescapable: They [the ETs] are already here... Though I do not *want* to believe this, and feel decidedly unnerved by it, I believe it is true; extra-terrestrials have been observing us in our innocence for many years." **[7]**

Apart from the similarity of the stories, he believes we have more tangible evidence. For instance, he finds that a great many of his subjects have inconspicuous scars, usually on their legs, and that these are often associated with some rather mysterious incident in childhood. The implication is that they relate to some kind of surveillance, and may indicate the implant of a monitoring device, or be the result of a blood test or some such.

Hopkins has more than once been able to successfully predict that a witness will find a scar on his body that he didn't know he had, and this certainly points to the reality of the phenomenon. But difficulties remain. If ETs are putting implants in substantial numbers of children, surely by now *some* doctors *somewhere*, examining a child, would have come across one? Again, our earthly surgeons can make incisions which leave virtually no scar; surely we could expect these advanced beings to have found a way of carrying out their tests without leaving tell-tale traces?

What alternative explanations are on offer?

- Coincidence: have you ever examined your body to check whether you, too, have a scar you have forgotten or never even noticed you had?
- Stigmata, subconsciously created by the witness himself to back up his story.

Admittedly, these suggestions are only speculative, but they are enough to show that it is too soon to stop looking for alternative explanations.

FOR AND AGAINST THE ABDUCTION EXPERIENCE

Abduction experiences confront us with a paradox, and with very little that might help us to resolve that paradox. They offer very little objective evidence, and that little ambiguous; they offer us only a **story**, told in all good faith, no doubt, but none the less subjective and unsubstantiated. And as every psychologist and every school-teacher knows, and as Lawson has shown to be no less true in this specific context, everyone can tell a story.

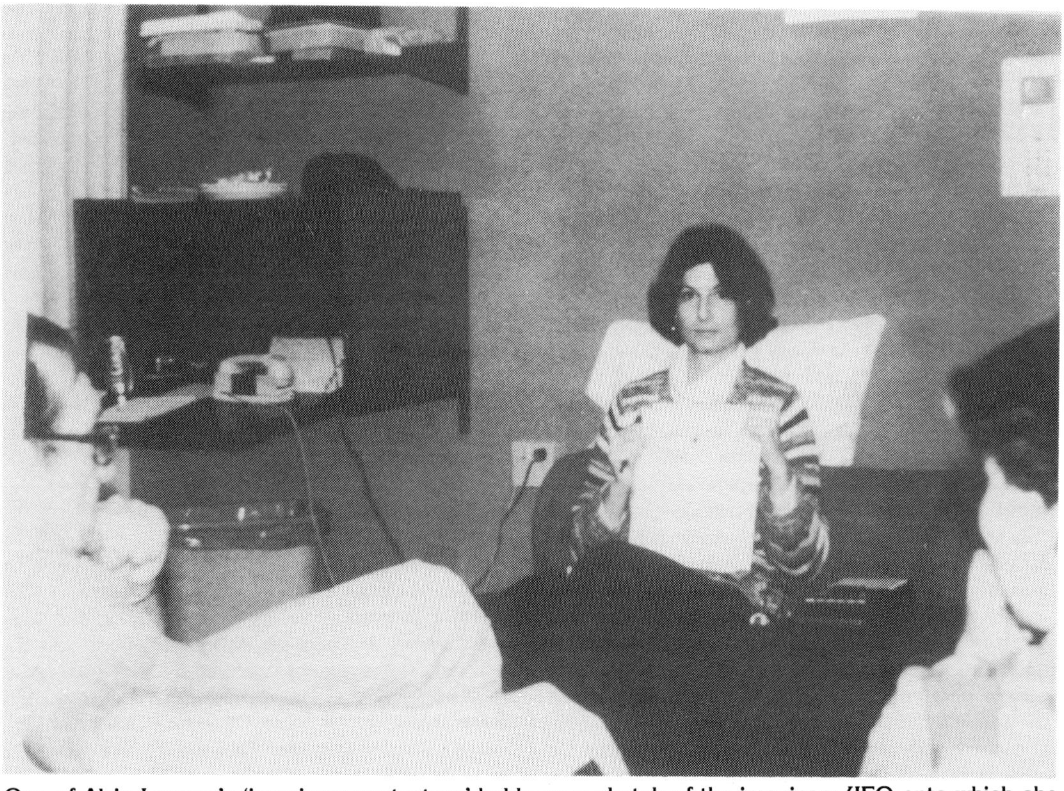

One of Alvin Lawson's 'imaginary contactees' holds up a sketch of the imaginary UFO onto which she wasn't abducted. [Courtesy of Alvin Lawson]

Nevertheless, those who, like Hopkins, feel that the weight of the evidence is **in favour** of real experience have persuasive grounds for their belief:

■ The abduction scenario, in its most elaborate form - for example, in the Kathie Davis [**7**] or Whitley Strieber [**12**] cases - contains an internal plausibility which gives us the best explanation yet for the UFO phenomenon.

■ Abduction experiences are spontaneously reported by witnesses who are not ostensibly seeking material advantage.

■ They involve a genuine emotional response. Lie-detector tests confirm that the stress is real enough.

■ In multiple abductions, the accounts tally close enough to persuade us that the witnesses participated in the same experience.

■ Recurrent features, reported by witnesses who would not be aware of others' testimony, suggest that the same external process is happening to many people.

■ Independent tests [**4**] have shown that abduction witnesses have no obvious pathological background or discernible predisposition to paranormal experience.

■ Abductees often report a change in life-style and outlook. The Gansbergs, who carried out follow-up investigation of several American abduction witnesses, reported that in almost every case the witness felt his life had benefited [**5**]; the same was true of the Aveley case in England. [**11**] Such real benefits suggest a real event.

This is a formidable challenge; however, the **objections** are hardly less forceful:

■ The stories of ET/UFO visits are improbable in themselves - it defies reasons (??reason) that so many spacecraft should successfully avoid detection while visiting our planet, particularly since no ET crews seem to be the same, implying a vast number of points of origin.

■ The behaviour of the abductors towards the witness is in many respects illogical, despite an overall plausibility. Clearly, we must allow for the possibility that ET logic may be different from ours. But how, for example, can we reconcile such contradictions as their frequently stated intention that the witnesses will not recall their experiences, with their apparent ignorance of recall under hypnosis? Or their detailed telepathic monitoring of witnesses with their ignorance of such basic facts as that a witness destined for genetic experiments has undergone a vasectomy? Note also the point made earlier that their grasp of language is very inconsistent.

■ There is a total lack of hard evidence. When witnesses try to retain souvenirs, they are always prevented. There are no convincing photographs of spaceships, not to mention the entities.

■ No abduction has ever been independently witnessed. The closest we come to it is in the 1975 Travis Walton case, in which six companions of a forestry worker signed an affidavit to say they saw the witness walk towards a spaceship; none saw him actually go aboard the craft where he claimed he spent the ensuing week. That sounds sufficiently impressive; but the manner of investigation has been criticised and the findings remain ambiguous. [**11**]

■ Though psychological tests suggest that abduction witnesses are normal people who are telling the truth as they know it, they also indicate that they suffer from 'a mild paranoia - hypersensitivity, wariness &c.' [**4**] Hardly enough to build a case on, admittedly, but a reminder that we rarely have psychological data on witnesses *before* their experience. We do often have anecdotal testimony, however, and this often points to some kind of predisposition. Both Betty Hill [**3**] and Charles Hickson [**6**] have testified to anomalous experiences previous to their abduction.

■ Not only do we know little about witnesses' psychological state, we are often not well informed about the outward circumstances of their lives, though these could well have a bearing on their attitudes and behaviour. John Rimmer [**10**] noted that out of eleven abduction witnesses whose personal circumstances are shown, eight were widowed, divorced or having sexual or marital difficulties at the time. He suggests that this would make them particularly vulnerable to suggestion.

■ American sociologist Ron Westrum has noted a 'contagion effect' whereby a rash of abduction reports occurs immediately after the publicising of a story like that of Barney and Betty Hill. [**4**] This is a complex sociological phenomenon which can be interpreted in different ways; but one of the possibilities is that the abduction experience has become as much part of American folklore as the phantom hitchhiker. That virtually every abduction encounter occurs in the Americas may simply relate to the social acceptability of being an abductee, but there could be a deeper explanation.

Setting these two sets of factors side by side, it is evident that neither adds up to a clear case for and against the reality of the abduction experience. Nor is it likely to until more solid evidence is offered us.

But if we put the abduction experience into a wider perspective still, we become aware of certain considerations which may help us to reach at any rate a provisional verdict:

■ 1. The existence of a folklore tradition of kidnapping by fairies and other other-worldly entities [**2,13**] shows that the **idea** of abduction is widespread and deeply rooted. While this is not an objection to the abductions claims per se, it reminds us that it is a mistake to think of the abduction experience as a novel phenomenon born of the Space Age. It has served as the basis for fantasy experiences in the past (unless, that is, you accept the tradition of fairy kidnapping as fact) and it may be doing so again.

■ 2. UFO abductions are not the only kinds of experience in which an apparent internal plausibility is balanced by an external implausibility. Other examples include 'possession', believed by fundamentalist Christians to involve molestation by the Devil, but interpreted otherwise by psychologists; 'poltergeist' experiences, once thought to be the work of 'noisy spirits' but currently attributed by parapsychologists to unconsciously manifesting psychokinetic powers; and witchcraft, once believed to be the devil's work, but today regarded as induced hysteria.

It is notable that the traditional explanations for all these phenomena gained their force from a specific belief system. We must consider the possibility that the same thing may be happening with the abduction experience. If so, what may be happening is this:

At any given time there are a number of individuals who are, as it were, shopping around for a suitable framework into which to project a private psychological hang-up. Such a framework would not only have to meet their personal need but also conform to current socially acceptable beliefs. In former days diabolical 'possession', witchcraft, lycanthropy and the like offered a suitable framework; later came communication with spirits of the dead; today the 'authorised myth' is one of extra-terrestrial visitation, derived from science fiction, space age thinking and a millenarist 'Cosmic Guardian' alternative to traditional religious belief. [**1**]

Since the myth is shared by the community, not only do the abductees find it easy to 'believe themselves into' the story, but others find it easy to believe them.

■ 3. Finally, though, there is only one simple consideration which may outweigh all others. Here we have accounts which, if they really occured as we are asked to believe, are the most extraordinary and most significant events which have taken place throughout the history of mankind. Yet how do we learn about them? By purchasing commercial books published by commercial publishers and sold in High Street bookstores! There is an incongruity between the events on the one hand, and how we hear of those events on the other hand, which must induce doubt, if not outright disbelief, that these experiences occur anywhere outside the imaginations of those who, for whatever reason, have them, and of those who, with whatever motive, report them.

REFERENCES

■ **1** - **Evans**, Hilary, *Visions, apparitions, alien visitors*, Aquarian, 1984; *Gods, spirits, Cosmic Guardians*, Aquarian, 1987. ■ **2** - **Evans-Wentz**, W.Y., *The fairy faith in celtic countries*, Frowde, 1911. ■ **3** - **Fuller**, John G., *The interrupted journey*, Dial, 1966. ■ **4** - **Fund for UFO Research**, *Final report on the psychological testing of UFO 'abductees'*, 1985. ■ **5** - **Gansberg**, Judith M & Alan L., *Direct encounters*, Walker, 1980. ■ **6** - **Hickson**, C., and **Mendez**, W., *UFO contact at Pascagoula*, UFO Photo Archives, 1983. ■ **7** - **Hopkins**, Budd, *Missing time*. Marek, 1981; *Intruders*, Random House, 1987. ■ **8** - **Lawson**, Alvin H., The hypnosis of imaginary UFO 'abductees' in *Journal of UFO studies*, CUFOS, ca 1983. ■ **9** - **Randles**, Jenny, *The Pennine UFO mystery*, Granada, 1983. ■ **10** - **Rimmer**, John, *The evidence for alien abductions*, Aquarian, 1984. ■ **11** - **Story**, Ronald D., *The encyclopedia of UFOs*, Doubleday, 1980. ■ **12** - **Strieber**, Whitley, *Communion*, Beech Tree Books, 1987. ■ **13** - **Vallee**, Jacques, *Passport to Magonia*, Regnery, 1969. ■ **14** - **Bernstein**, Morey, *The Search for Bridey Murphy*, Doubleday, 1956. ■ **15** - **LeCron**, Leslie, *Experimental Hypnosis*, McMillan, 1952.

2.6.1

THE CHASE FOR PROOF IN A SQUIRREL'S CAGE

by Leonard Stringfield

■ **LEONARD H. STRINGFIELD.** Born 1920. Professionally, was for 31 years an executive with Dubois Chemicals, retiring in 1981. During World War Two he served in 5th Air Force Intelligence and Counter-Intelligence in the Pacific arena, where a personal sighting of three UFOs, first directed his interest to the subject.

■ **UFO involvement**: Probably the most widely experienced UFO researcher still active. He has at various times been associated with NICAP, CUFOS and MUFON in a consultative or administrative capacity. Between 1953 and 1957 he worked with Air Defense Command, screening and reporting UFO activity; during this period he was director of CRIFO (Civilian Research, Interplanetary Flying Objects) and edited its journal *Orbit*, besides being president of the Cincinnati UFO Society. In 1967-9 he was assigned as Early Warning co-ordinator for the Colorado Project under Dr Condon.

As *Orbit* and his other publications testify, he has always pursued a strictly case-based approach to the UFO phenomenon, and the controversial crash/retrieval question especially has occupied his attention since 1978. His researches in this field, though frustratingly inconclusive, have persuaded his colleagues that whatever the basis of the reports he has collected, they represent a facet of the UFO phenomenon which cannot be dismissed as mere myth.

■ **Publications** include: *Inside Saucer Post 3-0 Blue* (CRIFO 1957); *Situation Red; the UFO siege* (Doubleday 1977); and four reports on his crash/retrieval researches: *Retrievals of the Third Kind* (MUFON Proceedings 1978), *The UFO crash/retrieval syndrome: status report II* (MUFON 1980), *UFO crash retrievals: amassing the evidence; status report III* (Cincinnati 1982), *The fatal encounter at Ft. Dix - McGuire: a case study* (MUFON Proceedings 1985). Some of these publications are available from the author.

■ **Address**: 4412 Grove Avenue / Cincinnati / OH 45227 / USA. Phone (513) 271 4248.

My subject, of course, is UFO Crash / Retrievals, a controversy that just won't go away despite many who wish it would. New, provocative evidence always surfaces to keep it astir, some of it suggesting a massive cover-up.

What, then, is behind this stubborn syndrome, stalking research, that defies scientific rationale, turns off the media, boggles and divides ufologists and frustrates those who probe for these hidden facts -- and proof? Some clues may be evident in the story of my research, probing for that proof.

For many years the only manifestation of the syndrome was a knee-jerk reaction to a cobwebbed skeleton in the proverbial closet rattling with stories of UFO crashes in the deserts of Southwest USA. They were so unbelievable that it was unfashionable for discussion among the lords of research fascinated by reports of daylight discs and green fireballs or in debates over the pros and cons of the extraterrestrial hypothesis or an exotic close encounter.

This phase of wonderment and of irresolution, or stagnation, went on through a score or more years. But, in 1977, the year Doubleday published my book, *Situation Red, the UFO Siege*, in which I had related several tantalising references to captive alien bodies, our skeleton began to form flesh and sinew to its bones. New sources emerged to tell me, firsthand, about their experiences of involvement in secret military retrieval operations or of having seen the alien craft or cadavers, some on a need-to-know basis. The floodgates had opened.

Pushed to the forefront with this sobering input, I accepted an offer by Walter Andrus, Director of MUFON, to present a paper at their 9th annual symposium in Dayton, Ohio, in July 1978. News of my presentation sparked an instant response from researchers, some who favored paranormal answers, voicing defensive disbelief; others, who knew me for my "conservative" views, wondered what I had uncovered as new evidence. The suspense, I feared at that time, was spreading out of control, beyond the facts on hand. UPI picked up the story which, in turn, triggered ABC radio and at least 100 affiliates, coast-to-coast, to call me day and night for interviews and talk shows. These, of course, brought the public into the hubbub and with it a deluge of mail and phone calls. Some were new sources with tales to tell, but most were the kind whose uncle, or cousin, or friend who, years ago while in the military, had seen the hardware or the critters. Only a few were traceable.

Among my early contacts, one stood out. There was little doubt in my mind, as time went by, that he was what he professed to be -- an agent in the CIA. Through "church affiliation" and probably for other reasons unknown to me, he had a close and trusted relationship with researcher Robert Barry of Yoe, Pennsylvania, who served as our intermediary. Known only as "Mr. Q" he was to remain invisible to me; his presence known only by a recognizable voice, terse, commanding and knowledgeable. I heard it many times as Barry replayed his tapes with information on worldwide UFO events and some useful advisories relative to UFO crashes. In fact, said Barry, he was a member of a retrieval team in a New Mexico crash, 1962, where he personally helped in the recovery of the dead humanoid occupants. (See Case A-6, Status Report II)

Surprisingly, Mr. Q's tips on past UFO crashes, which I had shared with no one, including Barry, often proved accurate. Also of note, on the eve of my departure to Dayton, he not only predicted a flare-up of trouble by agitators during my presentation, but strongly advised that if I had inside information concerning a UFO problem linked to West Germany and, vaguely, a reference to a UFO crash in Mexico, that I should avoid their use. He didn't say why. His final advisement, I recall, was that foreign agents would be present, and to reveal nothing of technical value about the craft that could breach US security.

Actually, I had nothing on a West German problem, only general knowledge about a Mexican crash in the early '50s and no deep-throat secrets about the craft's properties or, at that time, US attempts to duplicate a saucer at a secret base. No one was sure what I had to show-and-tell in my paper's final version, not even the CIA. But I found it wise to heed my friend's advice on sensitive matters. Sometimes he would say, "With that information you had better stay out of dark alleys" or, "It's safer to eat fast food." Indeed, the skeleton I had rattled began to grow horns!

In anticipation of the revelations in my paper, entitled *Retrievals of the Third Kind: A case Study of Alleged UFOs and Occupants in Military Custody*, I recall one attempt to set the mood for the expected large audience at the Convention Center: a member of the sponsoring group, The Ohio UFO Investigators League (OUFOIL), paraded around the halls wearing a green "little man" costume. Others, however, were less amused. One of my contemporaries in research since 1954, a close friend, went into a rage when he learned of my subject, saying it was nonsense and would hurt research and me; and it almost did.

Apart from the watchful eyes of "sentinels" obviously following me everywhere, even on elevators at the Stauffer Inn where I stayed, I found encouragement from many long-time associates, including Major Donald Keyhoe and Richard Hall, both authors and also speakers. Dr. Hynek, who was scheduled to arrive in the late afternoon from St. Louis to deliver his paper, came early to be on hand for my morning "bombshell". Also on hand were cameras representing all the networks in a "press room" where I was to be interviewed following my talk. When my moment of glory, or infamy, was over, having read 63 typewritten pages of anecdotal case histories, I was unprepared for the rush act of plainclothes Dayton police (perhaps the sentinels I had watched earlier) from below stage, who whisked me away to a rear elevator and took me, completely puzzled, to my room at the Inn.

It was explained that the sponsoring group's PR man had been approached twice, once the night before by phone and again, face-to-face, in the foyer just minutes before I spoke, with threats-to-kill if I pursued my talk. Said the PR man, "I was too stunned to react right away and he got away into the crowd."

After a harried news conference where I was hounded to reveal names and show proof, I was steered back to my room. There I tried in vain to order a sandwich and hoped to join my wife, Dell, and son-in-law, who had driven up from Cincinnati that day, but they were lost in the confusion. I was transferred to another room for my safety, and a personal bodyguard was assigned to stay with me at all times until my departure the next day. The culprit, whether a part of a local gag or a well-planned scare tactic by "the company" or a wound-up weirdo, was never identified.

Media coverage? Well, none of the network TV stations carried the story, nor did it fare any better on any of the three Cincinnati stations even though I had made dozens of appearances on previous occasions as special guest for far less significant matters. Also giving it a cold shoulder were the Cincinnati newspapers, ignoring OUFOIL, the Cincinnati-based sponsor; MUFON, with its large Ohio membership and popular speakers such as Dr. Hynek and CUFOS (Center for UFO Studies), and Major Keyhoe, former head of NICAP.

Was the story of UFO crashes and the little gray humanoids at Wright-Patterson too incredible, or too awkward and embarrassing an issue, for the media to throw coldly at a potentially critical public so ill-prepared, or cushioned, for its colossal impact? Certainly, there was reason for guilt, for they had done nothing over the years to dig into the facts.

Such was the beginning of my adventures into the realm of UFO crashes and retrievals. But I was not to easily forget the Dayton episode, as there was an assortment of strange incidents to happen at home, the kind of which I had never before experienced since I got into research back in 1950.

Notably, and in close order, were threatening phone calls at night by a low, monotone voice saying that my death was imminent; a skull with crossed bones drawn in red ink on notepad paper received in the mail; the daytime appearance of a short-bearded, neatly-clad stranger lingering in a nearby wooded property to the rear of my home, who, when challenged, pretended to be studying a leaf of a maple tree and then scampering away, and, the damnedness of them all, four muddy shoe-prints, sole and heel, appearing as though someone -- or something -- had tried to *walk up* the redwood siding of my house. Below, the gravel was disturbed. Was there a message in these and other bizarre happenings as I continued my probes?

Response from researchers after Dayton was an emotional mix. Kindled were the hopes of those who espoused the ETH, but many another with different views sometimes went to scurrilous ends to blast at my everlasting weakness, the anonymity of my sources. A few opportunists tried tricky ways to get me to loosen up with my sources' names and addresses. But I didn't loosen.

In June 1980 I released *The UFO Crash/Retrieval Syndrome, Status Report II*, which was a continuum of witness reports from new sources, including a letter I had received from a medical informant describing the alien anatomy. Published by MUFON, it got good reviews in friendly quarters and was widely read among researchers. Walt Andrus commented that he could tell when I had appeared on a radio talk show by the increased number of orders coming into his office.

Dr. Hynek called me one evening, first extending his compliments for my new paper as a "job well done", but lamenting the fact that my credibility was suffering by not releasing names of my sources. He wondered if there might be a *discretionary* way that it could be handled to the satisfaction of the sources and myself. A few weeks later he called again, this time offering his version of a "discretionary" plan, a package deal that would basically provide credence to the anonymous witnesses, especially when I faced the media or on talk shows.

According to the plan, Dr. Hynek would be privileged to see the names and their pertinent data, but the key to its success would rest on the third party, a renowned astronaut. Unfortunately, the plan came to nothing. I'll never know, of course, if there was an ulterior reason for the Hynek proposal or for the astronaut to bow out. I do know that they were close friends and had the opportunity to discuss the subject before I had agreed to the plan. Whatever the case, it was a spark of hope that flickered out.

In reflection of his straightforward yet witty way, Dr. Hynek admitted that he was forever bothered in later years, during lectures or talk shows, when he was questioned about the "little men on ice" at Wright-Patterson. But, apart from this understandable aversion, he did take a keen interest in my work, so often ignored by others of his scientific status.

After the release of my second paper, the odds working *against* me making progress in my endeavors leaped up dramatically. Signs of interference were clear. Fading away were many firsthand sources - unreachable by phone or mailing address - and no less explainable was the sudden dearth of new ones, the kind usually following a phone tip, unfortunately, with a name mentioned by the unwitting intermediary.

Even more disconcerting, during this short negative time frame, was the loss of two key contacts, the CIA advisor Mr. Q, and a medical doctor eminent in the field of hematology, who claimed he had performed an autopsy on an alien body at an Eastern hospital in the early 1950s. Mr. Q simply stated, through his friend, that a new stiffening policy forbade him from discussing the UFO issues any longer. The doctor's fade-out "explanation" bore a ringing similarity.

And there were many more odorous happenings. One was the bizarre episode of photographs supposedly lifted from CIA files and stealthily provided for me to present as a block-buster breakthrough at the MUFON Symposium in Houston, Texas in June 1980. The photos, taken at various angles, showed a cadaver, not human, under glass with vapor emanating from a beaker near the head. At the bottom and on either side of the body were rows of downdrafts.

One photo in the set, however, was not in conformity. It showed the same gear inside the rectangular glass case, but the body appeared to be maimed or dismembered with its limbs askew in an unlikely position. Although the mangled body features were blurry, the overall photo was morbid; it was the kind of pose a photographer would not rig up to win a blue ribbon - or even a convincing hoax.

And there was another photo in the lot that didn't make sense either. Showing a body in the normal face-up position, it was obviously retouched. Why? But my source, to be known as Mack, didn't know why, and when pressed for more facts about the procurement of his photos, he would not budge. Instead he preferred to envision my success in Houston and went on to promise even better photos in color of alien bodies for a future big showdown. Not quite sure what he meant by "showdown", I recall feeling uneasy in our motel meeting place and wondered why I went all the way to Erie, Pennsylvania to bargain with a stranger and his friend, and my intermediary who had made all the arrangements.

Nor was I sure of Mack's story about his arrest and jail sentence on trumped-up charges when caught with the hot photos and other secret documents during a lecture. (See US Government Memorandum dated July 22 1978, page 40, in my *Status Report III*).

If the photos were bogus, I mused, and Mack was a part of a phoney set-up, why would the orchestrators throw in two obviously oddball photos? The one showing a mangled body could be easily viewed as bona fide; the other, retouched, gave cause for suspicion. In May 1980, however, my speculation about the cadaver photos took a more serious turn.

Like being hit by a sledgehammer, a fellow researcher, who was aware of the photos, came into my office with a copy of the July issue of *UFO Sightings* (Vol.1, No.1), a new pulp magazine published by Myron and Irving Fass. Featured was an article by David McCarthy titled 'The Question for Teleportation' that included a full-page picture of a humanoid body lying face-up in a glass case with downdraft units and a beaker emitting vapors. The caption read, "A prototype of cryogenic freeze chamber. The 'person' inside is actually a mannequin encased in special protective mylar foil." Except for the body's position in the case and some extra accoutrements outside, the photo was strikingly similar to Mack's print.

Disturbed, I called our intermediary in New Hampshire and requested that he reach Mack for an explanation. Of course, his reaction was astonishment and he called the story a phoney, adding "Even the chamber in which the body is encased is slightly different than in my pictures." In a later letter, May 20 1980, Mack re-emphasized that his source was reliable and that he had had his photos since 1978.

I also tried to reach either one of the Fass Brothers at their publishing office in Fort Lee, New Jersey, but the operator said there was no phone listed. I was back on Square One. At this stage there were too many paradoxes and I felt like the weary squirrel on its treadmill. But I was determined to get answers. On the way to Houston by van with researchers Dick Hall and Tom Deuley, I was still trying to decide whether or not to show the photos, and I said more than once, "I'll be damned if I do and damned if I don't."

With permission from Walt Andrus, I announced possession of the photos at the beginning of the day's agenda of speakers. Having agreed beforehand to call my intermediary at a special number once I had made my announcement, I told him that, following my brief message, I chose not to show the photos to the audience and the media. I had made a wise decision.

Then the unexpected happened. Shortly after returning from Houston, an associate in MUFON reported he had dug into his magazine files and found a copy of the magazine *Ancient Astronauts*, December 1977 issue, featuring on its cover the picture of a *retouched* humanoid under glass -- the same photo supplied to me by Mack. Headlined *Secret Chamber Beneath the Empire State Building*, the story raved over the discovery of an alien body underground in cryogenic suspension.

The story was a fabrication, of course, but it was a blow to Mack's credibility. Crucial was the year 1977, the year the magazine (known in serious research for its low-grade contents) was released. This meant that the Fass Brothers, the publishers, had the prints (or similar ones) for nearly a year before Mack, who said he got his in 1978. And the question remains: from whom did the Fass Brothers get their prints when, according to Mack, his were exclusive and from all places, the CIA files?

While the game plan for Mack's part in the photo hocus-pocus is unclear to this day, it was clear then that the prints (or similar ones) on file in the Fass office were used again in *UFO Sightings* and released coincidental to my announcement in Houston.

I am left to wonder, if not a coincidence, was it a move with a deeper purpose, one which leaves me to question not only the new magazine's timing for release, but its editorial and marketing aims -- and its real ownership? Who then, if not the Fass Brothers, controlled the magazine's contents? Who made sure that the "secret" humanoid photos got into print and the magazine circulated just in time to let the world know that my photos matched theirs and would sooner or later be declared a fraud?

During this period of doubt and confusion, I called Jim Moseley, editor of *Saucer Smear* in Fort Lee, New Jersey, near the Fass operations, to see what he could learn about the questionable photos. In September he managed to finally get through to a former staff member who said, "They're phonies; the bodies were models, staged for entertainment purposes." Again I wondered about his reference to "entertainment" and what part Mack may have had in that end of it.

If, beyond any stretch of the imagination, my source, Mack, is innocent of what seems to be a case against him for leading me into a trap, and if everything he told me is true, then he already knows the feeling to be on the short end of a conspiracy.

On the premise that Mack's story is true in every respect, then his photos also should be genuine. This would explain the slight differences of those in his possession from the one used in *UFO Sightings*. It would also give more reason to believe that the one print showing the contorted and maimed humanoid was not the kind posed for "entertainment" purposes.

In a letter dated November 27 1980, he wrote in part, "...I am in full realization of the position you are in...but had no idea that the overtones were so serious. I know you are being pushed to reveal proofs and facts and that discrediting has begun and that's serious, but finally it seems that you have struck a nerve in the spinal cord of the jokers who know what is happening. I will try to answer all of your questions in your last two letters and mail out to you the final picture soon."

That was the last I ever heard from him.

But the evidence is stacked against Mack. If his stories describing his problems with the Intelligence agencies and the FBI were false, and our meeting in Erie a part of his masquerade, then what was his game? Was he and his intermediary both secret agents bent on making me a "goat" in Houston? Or was Mack really in trouble, as he claimed to be, with the FBI on grounds of seditious UFO activities, resulting in a jail sentence? If so, was his devious dealings with me a bargain he struck with the agency to get me discredited and himself a pardon? I can keep guessing and may never hit on the right answer.

Later, after Houston, still wondering about the authenticity of the photos, I took time to have them checked with several "insiders". To my surprise, I got conflicting responses. One, a physicist, who showed a set to a person he said was "very high up" in nuclear research, was told, "They're old but authentic." Said my contact, the hematologist, "Some features look similar to the one I autopsied, but the photos look like fakes." Another medical doctor, impressed by the photos I showed him privately in Houston, purchased a set requested, he said, by a top NASA official "with access to the president." In this deal I was promised a comment, which never came. Finally, Mr. Q of the CIA said that all photos circulating among researchers showing dead or live aliens were bogus and advised that I get out of the controversy.

What was the truth behind this bizarre episode? As I commented at the time, "There is no simple cut-and-dry answer unless the UFO problem is seriously greater than ever imagined and must be hidden at all costs."

Public interest in UFOs into the mid-1980s had perceptibly declined on the American scene, in ratio to fewer sighting reports, and these got only scant attention in the media. New faces in research gradually replaced the old, and once again there was a recycling of the fundamental arguments by pop-up experts either attempting to shoot down the ever-popular extraterrestrial hypothesis with scientific gibberish, or re-offering a variety of exotic themes or another new religion. To old-timers it was boring rehash. But at least it kept research alive.

In this climate my probes continued in low profile. But the soaring interest in crash/retrievals, with my pioneering work in that sector still in the forefront, meant that my writings provided targets to critics - some of them prominent writers and field-workers whom I had previously held in respect. Unbelievably, among them a few still insisted that crash/retrievals had no validity in serious research, but all, for reasons unclear, chose to snipe at me for publishing shallow, insubstantial, and of course anonymous witness reports in my papers with nary a sign of proof.

Despite their investigative track records, the snipers had either misread my papers or had disregarded my repeated statement that the purpose of my papers was to share *scarce* information -- the good and the bad -- with researchers to evaluate and judge for themselves. They also ignored the fact that I had not endorsed any one case in my reports as a bearer of proof. Philip Klass, arch foe of UFOs, told a researcher on the West Coast, "Stringfield would buy the Brooklyn Bridge", an innuendo which illustrates not only the wide differences between two opposite points of view, but the utter frustration that grips researchers whose pet theories are thwarted and so turn to a war of words.

In June 1982 I published *UFO Crash/Retrievals: Amassing the Evidence. Status Report III*, which gave my contemporaries a further chance to complain about the anonymity of my sources. But in the same paper I published the name of a distinguished scientist, Dr. Robert Sarbacher, who later was to give UFO believers a boost and perhaps an opening for the long-awaited breakthrough. A fellow researcher into C/R work, William Steinman of La Mirada, California, lost no time in pursuit of the high-level scientist and called me, relating his successes.

Listed in *Who's Who in America*, Dr. Sarbacher, who, on last word, heads the Washington Institute of Technology, admitted to Steinman and others later in 1950, when serving as a science consultant in the US Defense Department's Joint Research and Development Board, that he had received a visit from the Canadian engineer Wilbert B. Smith informing him about the alleged crash-retrieved USOs in US government custody. He also revealed to Smith that Dr. Vannevar Bush, top US physicist and at that time head of the JRDB in which he served, and mathematician John von Neumann were told at a secret meeting at Wright-Patterson that the vehicles "appeared to be spaceships from another solar system."

Credit for the Sarbacher disclosures, which confirmed Smith's 1950 memorandum (see *Status Report III*) belongs to Canadian Arthur Bray, author of *The UFO Connection* (published in Canada, 1979). It began in 1980, when Bray sent me a letter commenting on my disclosure of some Frank Scully correspondence, and with it enclosed a copy of Smith's 1950 memorandum. In my opinion, both his letter and the memo were of singificance, and while working on *Status Report III* I obtained permission to publish his letter, with the name of Sarbacher in it.

The Sarbacher disclosures got positive reaction in ufological circles. Jerry Clark wrote glowingly in the August 1985 issue of *OMNI* and quoted Bill Moore's appraisal: "It's the first time that someone with reputation has come forward to state publicly that the Pentagon has a recovered UFO..."

By 1986, research had nearly forgotten the noise over my firsthand claimants as witnesses to the alien craft and the morgue of corpses. The new focal point was documentation, whether cleared through the Freedom of Information Act or the kind of "official" memoranda that surfaces clandestinely purporting to be authentic. Anything of this documentary nature, revealing a hidden or tell-tale fact, would be the *piece de resistance*, and maybe the grand prize -- the proof! Credit must go to those stalwarts in this paper-chase, like Bill Steinman, Lee Graham, Dr. Bruce Maccabee, Robert Todd, and to the Citizens Against UFO Secrecy (CAUS) leadership, Larry Fawcett and Barry Greenwood; and the brave work of Larry Bryant, who, despite his employment at the Pentagon, has taken vigorous legal actions in the federal courts against the "cover up" in government agencies.

But government documents, I believe, from whatever source, still may not be the final and unequivocal *proof* that would be acceptable to the negative establishment. The pusillanimous press would surely find a way for skepticism and even outright dismissal. Among the hottest documents being chased down is *Majestic 12* (MJ12), referred to in various surfacing memoranda as the inner sanctum of scientists, who, since the early days under General George Marshall, has been in charge of the US government UFO research operations.

Project Aquarius is another conundrum. It is referred to in a copy of a telex communication dated November 17 1980 from "AFOSI, Bolling AFB, DC" to "AFOSI Dist 17, Kirkland AFB, NM." Downgraded from Secret, and surfacing in the usual surreptitious manner, the subject covered by the telex concerns the analysis of UFO film and negatives. Also mentioned is MJ12.

A new light, however, casting shadows of doubt on *Project Aquarius* and its UFO connection, came through FOIA inquiries made by Dale Goudie of CUFON (Computer UFO Network) in his correspondence with the National Security Agency. In a letter, March 3 1986, the NSA states in part, "Please be advised that Project Aquarius does not deal with unidentified aerial objects." Then in a letter, April 15 1986, responding to Goudie's follow-up, the NSA said in part, "...The document located in response to your request as stated in your 7 March letter has been reviewed by the FOIA and has been found to be currently and properly classified in accordance with Executive Order 12356... and remains classified TOP SECRET... The document is classified because its disclosure could reasonably be expected to cause exceptionally grave damage to the national security..."

And then there is the disquieting mystery surrounding an alleged secret Air Force document called *Project Grudge/Bluebook Report 13.* When accused of publishing the document and destroying it before distribution, the Air Force denied its existence, and further claimed, through a spokesman, that the Grudge series of reports, reaching the number of 14, skipped 13 because that number was considered unlucky. Unlucky? In military parlance?

The crash / retrieval stereotype. [Henrik Pedersen / ***UFO-Nyt*****]**

Nonsense. Whatever the real reason for the missing number 13, information alleging to support its existence emerged when an informant, having relocated in Tucson, Arizona from England, met the well-known researcher Wendelle Stevens and gave him the story of his experience with the "actual" *Grudge 13* document.

In 1981, the time had come, as I understand the circumstances, for the informant to avenge himself for past injustices in connection with the Grudge report. Tapes, recording the main contents of the text from memory, were given to Stevens for safekeeping, and from these a memorandum containing an outline version was sent to a few researchers. Among them were Linda Howe, writer and producer of the TV documentary *A Strange Harvest*, and Tom Adams, editor of *Stigmata*, long recognized for his investigations into animal mutilations. Both managed to get additional details from the source by phone interviews.

It all began when the source, a former Captain in the Green Berets in Vietnam and later assigned to Intelligence duties as analyst at an RAF post in Chicksands, England, claimed that he chanced upon reading a copy of *Grudge 13* under circumstances he never fully understood.

According to the former officer's story, the report, sealed in a diplomatic pouch, had been placed as routine business into his desk basket without explanation or a clue as to its source. Stunned by its content, he read the 624-page report over and over for several days, wrote up his usual analysis and routinely put it into the "outgoing" basket for pick-up. He thought no more about it until besieged by unthinkable troubles a short time later.

Basically, the impact of the report's disclosures was enough, as the saying goes, to scare the feathers off a cigar store's wooden Indian -- or even shake up the MJ12. Luridly described are incidents of animal and *human* mutilations, of violent encounters and abductions, and a concern for UFO weaponry and surveillance of military installations, and of their crashes and retrievals.

And not to be overlooked were the dead aliens which had been retrieved from their crashed vehicles. According to Stevens' tapes, the source recalled several photos, in color, included in the report; one showing the full prostrate, face-up body, another, on a metal autopsy table in an early stage of vivisection, the rest, close-ups of internal organs.

Once again, the external anatomical feature of the small humanoid, with over-sized head and with grayish skin, were essentially the same as those described by my medical and CIA sources and most other firsthand witnesses.

Like other cases dealing in sensitive matters, there are many pros and cons and empty spaces in the source's story. It was made known, however, before his sudden disappearance, that he and his Commanding Officer, a Colonel, at his post in England, got into deep trouble over Grudge 13 and both were terminated from service with "unsatisfactory performance of duty" marked on their records.

To add to our lexicon, we have a range of code names wallowing in the woodwork, each supposedly hiding a US military UFO secret of some sort. Among these are *Sigma*, dealing with communications with aliens, and *Redlight* for covert test flights of captured UFO (or replicas of UFOs) at Nellis AFB, and *Dreamland*, *Snowbird*, *Have Blue* and *Moondust* -- ad infinitum. For certain, all have been checked into by researchers through the FOIA at a high cost of time, money and patience. But getting the sought-after information has proved to be difficult when censors, in their replies, refuse to release documents or just delete out parts of a page, or all of it, for national security reasons.

Some day a document with all the satisfying requisites may be uncovered, but until then I will continue with my low-profile probes, hoping for that elusive firsthand witness who can produce good evidence with good back-up and who may opt to allow names to be used. This, I believe, is the bedrock of UFO crash/retrieval research.

Looking back into my own squirrel's cage, I now must take a positive note of several of my cases involving firsthand witnesses which I believe have withstood the test of time. These informants, all having served in the military, came across to me as normal people; educated, stable at their work or professions and, yes, patriotic. And I must stress that the circumstances of time and place set for their disclosures gave no cause to suspect a masked sinister motive, or, to put it more plainly, to lie for glory or financial gain, or fib just for the fun of it. Moreover, what each source said, independent from the others, clashed with information I already had without him knowing it.

Out of the 24 firsthand witness cases written up in my series of Status Reports, or on file, I believe that five stand out above the rest which are described briefly as follows:

■ Case A 7, from Status Report II:

Hardly enough can be said in praise for my medical source cited so often in my Status Reports and in this paper. Introduced to me through a close research friend who knew the "right" people, the doctor, a noted hematologist, who had allegedly performed an autopsy on an alien body, agreed in due course to share with me, under strict conditions, bits and pieces of its descriptive features.

While the doctor's "authoritative" information was helpful in opening doors to new sources, and as a stimulus for me in my drive for higher standards in my work, it was never explained to me the reason for his cooperative gesture.

It was at the high point of my C/R work in July 1979, after a year of "negotiations", that I received from the doctor a surprisingly informative statement in the mail, detailing in layman's language the head-to-toe anatomy of the alien and, returning with it, my drawing of a hypothetical being submitted earlier for his critical review, with corrective comments.

Thanks to the doctor's colleague, a biochemist whom I got to know well, and also in a position to view the alien tissue under microscope, a dialogue was limitedly maintained. But, as stated before, hard times took over in late 1980 when most of my sources dried up. As though orchestrated, I was told at that time, through the colleague, that no more information about the alien could be released.

I have had reasons to believe that my medical sources, from the beginning, were given the "nod" to provide general or limited information about the alien for a reason -- maybe as a test to determine public reaction, and how research might digest it.

The source and colleague both held key staff positions at a major Eastern hospital during the interlude of cooperation. The risks were too great to play games of charade. Trust was a factor in all our dealings then, and still is.

■ Case A 1, from Status Report II:

My source, a pilot in the Air National guard, claimed he witnessed "by accident", while on duty, three humanoid corpses flown to Wright-Patterson AFB from a UFO crash site in Arizona in 1953. He gave me this confidential information following my talk before the Cincinnati Chapter of World Wings, a pilots' organization, at Lunken Airport in 1977 just after my book *Situation Red, The UFO Siege* was published. Discreetly, he took me to the large map room, pointed to an isolated spot and said, "There's approximately where the saucer crashed."

According to the pilot, the bodies, four feet tall and atypical of other described specimens, were carted individually in small hastily-constructed wooden boxes. While the lids were temporarily opened by the overseeing officer, possibly to check the condition of his cargo, the pilot also got a glimpse of a plastic liner separating the body from a bed of dry ice, probably to prevent epidermis damage.

They were not human or simian, he stressed, which he had observed from a distance of 12 feet under strong hangar lights. Later that night, while billeted in the same barracks with officers of the flight crew who transported the secret cargo, he got confirmation of the UFO crash and other details of the retrieval operation.

In August 1978 I requested an affidavit, on tape, describing his experience. He declined because of his oath of secrecy. I then asked for a statement for possible posthumous use, to which he responded that he would have to check with his Security Officer. The answer: "You have seen nothing, heard nothing and as sure as shit you can sign nothing." That was the final word from my source. He and family suddenly became inaccessible, leaving no forwarding address or new phone number.

■ Case A 2, from Status Report II:

This encounter with cadavers at Wright-Patterson involved an Air Police sergeant who, in 1973, was called out for special duty at night. Blindfolded, he was driven to an area on the base and escorted down a flight of steps and led to a location where, free of his blindfold, he was given specific instructions to stand guard. It was a busy area for a while, with medics bustling in and out of the room he guarded. It was during this phase that he had a good glimpse of three small bodies on a table. They were not human.

The credibility for this case is not that the anatomy described by the sergeant is analogous to others, but the manner in which I got his admission as a witness to the event. For many months I had to be content with a secondhand source, the sergeant's wife. Her response to my numerous attempts to talk with her husband got only adamant refusals. My break came months later. The wife had become ill and was unable to help. However, I had managed beforehand to obtain her husband's place of work, his on-duty hours, and even his coffe-break periods. It was on a break when I reached him. Explaining my research objectives and assuring him anonymity, his only response was silence.

But he suddenly came alive when I shifted my subject to relate details of the creatures' anatomy, which, I emphasized, had come from a medical doctor who had performed an autopsy on an alien body. This was the clincher and, after a brief pause, I asked if what he had seen was similar to my description. He answered "yes". After another pause, he mentioned some additional details about the head which, except for a "short fuzz" he observed on the crown, were identical to the doctor's.

After another and longer pause, I thanked him and, saying no more, we hung up. I could have pressed for more information at the time, or tried again at a later date, but I didn't. I don't think he would have given me the chance, and feeling his uneasiness, I was satisfied with this simple admission of being on scene at an historic event.

■ Case A 3, from Status Report II:

Thanks to my son-in-law, Jeffrey Sparks, who, in 1978, was an Assistant Professor at St. Leo's College, Dade City, Florida, I gained a knowledgeable informant and another witness of the humanoids at Wright-Patterson AFB.

Jeff talked openly about my research on campus, which brought forth a number of UFO reports by students, but one fortuitous day, while visiting the finance office, he got into a discussion about the work of my daughter, a registered nurse at a hospital near campus, which in turn, as Jeff explained, led to my work in UFOs. Eyes opened when he told of my acquaintance with the doctor who performed the autopsy, and when he went on to describe its features he got a prompt response.

"He's right", spoke up a member of the office staff. Later, when work resumed, he called Jeff aside to elaborate on his computer work in Army Intelligence and having the privilege in 1966 to see nine alien bodies stored underground at Wright-Patterson.

In a matter of days I was in touch with Jeff's source. It was obvious that he had a keen awareness of the military posture relative to UFOs; their crashes, when and where; the method of recovery using a specially trained task force of Blue Berets, and much more. But he was also wise enough not to say much on some sensitive issues I brought up for the usual security reasons.

One significant point he made was Norad's use of a sophisticated electronic system able to detect a malfunctioning UFO and follow its trajectory flight to the point of crash. In this case, he said, the special Blue Berets took over for the recovery.

Once again, my source described the bodies as small with big heads, just like others who had the opportunity to see them. And, just like so many others, my source soon vanished into oblivion. No more contact, no new phone number, no forwarding address.

■ Case A 3, from Status Report III:

Complete coverage in *The Fatal Encounter at Ft. Dix-McGuire: A Case Study*, in *Status Report IV*, published in *MUFON Proceedings, 1985*. This case, above all others, remains in my *active* file, but while lacking in proof, it has amassed so much qualitative evidence that the hunt is on for new back-up sources.

Remarkably, my lone source, a former sergeant in the Air Security Police, who "disappeared" for three years after his initial contact, and resurfaced to impart additional substantive information, is still reachable by mail at an overseas address.

According to my source, referred to as Jeffrey Morse, he stood guard at a gate of the McGuire AFB in New Jersey, January 18 1978; dispatched there after an alien intruder had been shot and wounded by an MP at Ft. Dix, the adjacent army base. Said Morse, the creature somehow crossed the fence into McGuire and fell dead on an abandoned airstrip -- not far from an atomic storage area. That fatal night, UFOs were in the area, he said, and were confirmed by radar. Both bases went on the alert.

To review the complete story, including the events that followed in the life of Morse, is beyond the scope of this paper. However, it serves the reader to know the basic details of the incident, described in Morse's initial letter to me in 1980:

DEPARTMENT OF THE AIR FORCE
TH SECURITY POLICE SQUADRON (PACAF)
APO SAN FRANCISCO 96239

Subject: Response for Request of Information
in Relation to UFO Contact and Other Related Information

To: Len Stringfield

1. In January of 1978, I was station at McGuire AFB, N.J.. One evening , during the time frame of 0300hrs. and 0500hrs., there were a number of UFO sightins in the area over the air field and Ft. DIX Army camp. I am a security policeman and was on routine patrol at the time. N.J. State Police, and Ft. Dix MP's were runnig code in the direction of Brownsville,N.J.. A state trooper then entered Gate # 5, at the rear of the base, requesting assistance and permission to enter. I was dispatched and the trooper wanted access to the runway area which led to the very back of the air field and connected with a heavily wooded area which is part of the Dix training area. He informed me that a Ft. Dix MP was pursueing a low flying object which then hovered over his car. He described it as oval shaped, with no details, and glowing with a blueish green color. His radio transmission was cut off. At that time in front of his police car, appeared a thing, about 4ft. tall, greyish, brown, fat head, long arms, and slender body. The MP panicked and fired five rounds from his .45 Cal into the thing, and one round into the object above. The object then fled straight up and joined with eleven others high in the sky. This we all saw but didn't know the details at the time. Anyway, The thing ran into the woods towards our fenceline and they wanted to look for it. By this time several patrols were involved.

2. We found the body of the thing near the runway. It had apparently climbed the fence and died while running. It was all of a sudden hush-hush and no one was allowed near the area. We roped off the area and AF OSI came and took over. That was the last I saw of it. There was a bad stench coming from it too. Like ammonia smelling but it wasn't constent in the air. That day, a team from Wright-Patterson AFB came in a C141 and went to the area. They crated it in a wooden box, sprayed something over it, and then put it into a bigger metal container. They loaded it in the plane and took off. That was it, nothing more said, no report made and we were all told not to have anything to say about it or we would be court martialed.

3. I will be getting out of the air force in about two months. Do Not disclose my name as I could get into trouble. I am interested in pursuing this and other matters if you need help. Forgive me for not signing this but I can't take any chances. Please reply to the above address and my parents will forward it to me or I will be home already. Don't send it here because they monitor all mail closely and I again don't want to take any chances.

It all began, said Morse, when he was stationed on Okinawa, following his transfer there after the incident. There, by chance, he heard a replay of my interview, discussing UFO crashes, on a Los Angeles radio station carried by Armed Forces Far Eastern Radio Network in July 1980. Lucky for my research...

But unlucky for Morse. Once out of the service, he became the victim of surveillance, which he later said included seizure of some of his mail. On my end, I finally gave up writing to him.

Three years later in December 1983, after renewed attempts to reach him, Morse, feeling safe, decided to call me. This was to begin an exchange of correspondence and phone calls providing new details about the incident and his subsequent interrogation at Wright-Patterson by Air Force Intelligence.

Also, during this "safe" period I received from Morse a so-called "back office" copy of the official form *Incident/Complaint Report*, which was channeled to the usual higher echelons on the base and elsewhere. In the blocked section, designating *Evidence*, was this terse statement: "One body of unknown origin released to the care of OSI District Commander and special recovery team from Wright-Patterson AFB."

During 1984, Morse experienced renewed surveillance, and to his disappointment was turned down on a sought-after government law enforcement job, and the reason for it, he was told by a Justice Department official, "your disclosures to Stringfield". Refusing to compromise himself in a later offer to review more favorably his work status if he would deny his story, he instead departed for work overseas. Before his departure, fortunately, I had managed to arrange for Richard Hall, my research confidante for many years, to meet with him for an evaluation of the Fort Dix-McGuire episode and, more importantly, of Morse himself. Hall, following two meetings with Morse, said summarily, in part: "...Personally, he was well-groomed, friendly, relaxed and articulate. He spoke confidently and without hesitation in answer to questions, and did not come across as someone who had concocted a tall tale and might contradict himself or get caught in a trap if he weren't careful. He showed no mannerisms that would betray any obvious psychoses or 'hang up'... overall, I detected nothing in his manner, or story, to cause skepticism. To the contrary, he seemed very credible to me... Pending further investigation, I would tend to give him very high marks..."

Since my release of *Status Report IV*, I have had the names of the officers involved at McGuire AFB, and in the interrogation at Wright-Patterson, checked and authenticated at the National Personnel Records Center in St. Louis, Missouri. That was a plus if there were any doubts.

And one last note of hope. A MUFON researcher in New Jersey, while discussing the Ft. Dix-McGuire affair at work, found a former serviceman, a Master Sergeant, who, stationed at Ft. Dix in January 1978, remembered a UFO incident there.

According to the researcher, the former sergeant tried to investigate the incident on his own time and ran into a stone wall. All records, tapes, everything, he said, were destroyed and nobody was willing to talk about it. But what he didn't know was that most of the personnel involved had been quickly transferred, as a security measure, to separate bases overseas.

Having gotten the researcher's name and phone number from Tom Benson, MUFON State Director for New Jersey, I called him in February 1986 with a plea of urgency to follow up with his source for more specific details, and offered some key questions especially addressed to the kind of story, or rumor, he heard to prompt his investigation and if he was aware of a base alert at Fort Dix. If we got the *right* answers, I said, the case could be a major breakthrough. The researcher, however, said that he no longer worked with his source, who lived about 25 miles away, and made the point: "He seemed unusually nervous when we talked about the incident the first time." But the researcher, who spent long hours in the insurance business, assured me that he would see his friend and ask my questions.

A month later, in March, with no response, I called again. His answer: the source had an unlisted phone and he was unable to make an appointment but he had his address and would make the trip unannounced. No, a letter wouldn't do, he said, and added, remembering his source's nervousness before, "He probably would be too scared to answer it."

In June, with no word from my intermediary, I called again and was told that he planned to make the trip the following week -- maybe with Benson, who had been urging him to go. On July 16, I tried a letter to break another deadlock of silence. As I write this copy in late September, so far no reply. Here is an example of the treadmill in motion and I, like the proverbial squirrel, going nowhere.

But there is a reward for enduring patience. I may yet hear from the researcher, or Tom Benson, who has been helpful in the search for back-up material. *The case is not closed.* But now I have a new challenge to chase after.

In a letter dated August 22, 1986, from a California researcher, Michael Johnstone, a new source has emerged, an ex-marine who said he once stood guard in a building where a saucer-like craft was concealed. While the information related by the ex-marine dwells on the craft's extraordinary exterior refinements, it leaves many of the touchy questions unanswered, and understandably, in deference to his secrecy oath. We on the outside, therefore, must be content for the moment with Johnstone's bold preliminary probes and for his able assessment of the source in his letter which, in part, follows:

A client in my recording studio picked up your

Status Report II *and thumbed through it. He told me that his life-long friend had stood guard around a UFO years ago while in the marines. In fact, he had a photo of the craft which my client had seen several times over the years. To my dismay, the photo along with other possessions was lost in a flood three years ago in Pennsylvania.*

I then asked my client to try and arrange a meeting. After several days, and prodding calls from me, I finally met the man...He is in his 40s, looks like a young Gerald Ford: married with four children and three grandchildren. He's a kind of free spirit, an avid gardener, works odd jobs, plays chess, makes homemade wine. He's not really a UFO buff, but accepts them as part of life...He never heard of Hynek or yourself or the Condon Report...He saw Hangar 18 and says the gist of it is true but the rest is fabrication. A sergeant in the marines from 1960 to 1966, he taught weapons at Quantico. For two weeks in December 1963 he was one of the guards in charge of security for a large metal building in an undisclosed military base. The building housed a craft of a type unknown to him. It was a discus shaped vehicle with ovoid cross section totally symetrical, approximately 40 feet across and 13 feet thick at the center. It was silver in color with polished aluminum appearance. It was totally seamless except for hatch-like seams on the lower part of the craft which were so well-fitted that "you couldn't get a razor blade in the crack." What appeared to be windows circled the edge of the craft which had the appearance of smoked glass with approximately one foot of space between the windows. He said, "you couldn't see in them even when you got up close." The craft had no landing gear, no fins, no exhaust ports.

The marine witnessed over a two week period a technical crew working on the craft trying to gain entry. He witnessed attempted drilling and cutting with torches on areas of the craft indicated in a sketch that he drew. He said, "metal got hot under the torch but when it cooled you could wipe off the soot and the surface remained clean and undamaged." The same effect was observed when they tried to drill or burn into the lower right-hand part of the window above and to the left of the hatch. He also claims to have witnessed an attempt to cut into the craft with a high-powered laser device...This was ineffective as well, as the laser deflected off the curved side of the craft up into the rafters of the building doing some damage.

One day my source came on duty to find the craft off its blocks and sitting on a flat-bed trailer with men putting a tarp over it. Later that day it was driven away. He was told: "You saw nothing."

As far as bodies are concerned my source saw none. But he knows of several others C/Rs, secondhand, including one where three bodies were pulled from a craft...The bodies were 39 inches tall and had no thumbs. He said, "We've got quite a few craft and bodies now."

Upon discharge from the marines, he was made to sign a security oath that threatened 10 years in jail and $10,000 fine if he talked. Other things we talked about was the morality of going public with this whole story. He doesn't think the world would freak out. He feels just the opposite. He said, "there's a certain amount of people who, if the thing was on display down the street, would rather stay home and watch football."

Parts of the marine's story certainly jibe with other things I've read in your monographs and elsewhere. Like I've said, he's totally uninformed of your writings which I withheld knowledge of while he told his tale...Hopefully he can shed some light on some of the other cases or point out the one he was involved in without incriminating himself...He seems to know more about other C/Rs that he is currently willing to say...

A good and promising report, I told Johnstone on receipt of his letter and, as always when dealing with ex-servicemen on sensitive C/R matters, I gave him my assurance that his source's name would be kept in confidence. Also, I expressed the hope that I could work with his source eventually on a first-hand exchange basis to learn more about the recovered bodies. But, realistically, having second thoughts on the chances of getting more information on sensitive issues, Johnstone cautioned, "We must remember he didn't come to us and he doesn't have to prove anything."

The case is on "hold" for now. Like so many other anecdotes in the past, its keeps me *squirreling on the treadmill.* Finding the proof to convince the world about UFO crash/retrievals may never come in my lifetime. But I believe that much of what I have said in my papers may come close to the truth if and when the time comes to tell it by official proclamation.

2.6.2
SAUCERFUL OF SECRETS
by Andy Roberts

■ **ANDY ROBERTS** was born in 1956 and lists his occupation as househusband, on behalf of his wife and 4-year-old child.
■ **UFO involvement**: Has been interested in strange phenomena since the age of ten. Stimulated by Keel's *Jadoo* and Vallee's *Passport to Magonia*, he took up active UFO investigation in 1982, and is currently a member of the West Yorkshire UFO Research Group, ASSAP and BUFORA. His special interests include modern folklore and urban legends; mystery felines; and within the UFO field, foo fighters (on which he welcomes contributions and reference material) with the intention of preparing a definitive source work.

■ **Publications**: Editor of *UFO Brigantia*, the WYUFORG journal; a regular contributor to *Folklore Frontiers*; author of *Cat flaps*, a survey of North British mystery felines.

■ **Address**: 84 Elland Road / Brighouse / West Yorks HD6 2QR / England. Phone (0484) 721993.

Crashed saucer or retrieval stories are now 'officially' folklore. Jan Harold Brunvand in *The Choking Doberman* [**1**], a book on modern folk-tales, refers to the crashed saucer/retrieval motif and puts it in the category of a suppressed government truth story, going on to give an outline of just such a tale. It might be just a folk-tale to Brunvand, but there are thousands of UFO buffs all over the world who believe that various governments have in their possession crashed saucers. As a result of this, belief stories and rumour abound in an attempt to substantiate the burgeoning myth. Official documents, affidavits and death-bed confessions all exist from people who claim to have had direct and not-so-direct experience of them, and researchers who have delved too deeply even claim to have had their lives threatened. In looking at crashed saucer/retrieval tales from a modern folklore perspective it is possible to see how a folk-tale has sprung up, developed and is now being accepted as truth.

The basic story-line around which all the variants are based is as follows. An unknown aerial craft is either seen to crash or is found crashed and immobilised, invariably in a remote spot deep in the country. If civilians are involved they are quickly hushed up by officialdom and the object, most often a disc, is taken away by the military to a top secret airbase where it is kept in a high-security area. No more is then heard of the disc other than the rumours which emanate and spread in the wake of its alleged capture. Indeed, its very 'existence' is totally reliant on these rumours alone as no physical or photographic evidence is ever forthcoming. All retrieval tales have most of this basic story in their make-up. Additions and spin-offs to the basic story are common and include, amongst other things, the retrieval of alien bodies (usually dead, but in a few cases alive but who die shortly afterwards), Presidential, Senatorial and other authority figure involvement and acknowledgement and more arcane phenomena such as the mysterious Men in Black.

However we look at the retrieval stories, there are two main aspects to be considered and they are inextricably linked. Firstly, is it true? Do we *really* have crashed saucers here on earth; and secondly, how and why are the tales and rumours, leading to the eventual creation of the crashed saucer myth, created and spread?

Since the explosion of the idea of extraterrestrial UFOs in the years following 1947, the ultimate proof of aliens visiting earth would be actual, tangible, physical contact between mankind and extraterrestrials (ETs). The people who believe in ETs would dearly love this to happen, as would the media, and both parties eagerly spread any rumours which allege this to have happened. The existence of extraterrestrials is far from proven though, but belief in ETs has not lessened, and a growing assumption, one which brings the possibility of alien contact just (but not quite) within our grasp, is that many governments or their agencies have retrieved crashed alien craft and bodies. Once retrieved, the governments take any necessary steps to 'cover-up' the fact, denying all knowledge of the event.

This rumour is widely and enthusiastically accepted by the people who thrive on mystery and cover-ups and is readily and uncritically assimilated into much of the UFO literature. From there it easily permeates into the media and public consciousness. It then falls on the UFO organisations to prove to the rest of humanity that we have been duped in this way and are being prevented from learning the 'truth' about crashed saucers. Many UFO organisations and researchers thrive on rumour and secrecy, and from this base a body of folklore has been created which is in turn fed by the media, the UFO literature itself, the military and back to the UFO organisations and so on. Objective facts are scarce and usually non-verifiable. I mention the military here as being active in the creation of at least part of this myth as there is a good deal of evidence and reason to suggest that the military and its agencies may have a vested interest in keeping belief in retrievals going. More of this later.

The history of retrievals is riddled with hoax and mis-information, making it very difficult to discern where truth begins and ends. The subject is a vast and complex one and the best way to approach it here is to briefly look at a few of the main cases on which all other retrieval tales could well be based, and the possible reasons for their existence in the first place.

The first report of a crashed object comes from the USA Airship wave of 1897, when one such airship was reported to have crashed in the small Texas town of Aurora. The airship allegedly crashed after exploding, scattering wreckage over a wide area. The pilot was recovered and although badly burned, it was discernible that he 'was not of this world.' The airship itself was said to have been made from an unknown metal resembling aluminium and some reports stated that 'unknown hieroglyphics' had been found on some papers.

The pilot in the Aurora crash was buried in the local cemetery and the tale later passed into international UFO folklore as a 'true' occurrence. Later, however, diligent investigation by various critical UFO researchers revealed that no crash actually ever took place and that the whole story had been a fabrication, either by bored wireless telegraph operators or by a Dallas reporter hoping to attract tourists to the town. The story thus created could well have been the genesis for all future crashed saucer tales. The basics of crashed object/dead pilot or crew/unknown metal like aluminium/strange hieroglyphics, have remained constant in retrieval tales since. [**2**]

By the time of the first post-1947 crash the objects allegedly retrieved had gone from airships to discs. Two retrieval tales stand out as being the true forerunner of the crashed saucer myth of the last thirty years: one a hoax, and one which may well have side-tracked many a researcher.

THE RETRIEVAL AT AZTEC NEW MEXICO

The Aztec crash was popularised by newspaper columnist Frank Scully in his book *Behind the Flying Saucers* in which he stated that a 30-metre-diameter crashed saucer had been found on a plateau in the above state, with sixteen dead aliens inside. At last, this seemed real proof that ETs existed. Alas, the Aztec case suffered the same fate as the Aurora crash.

Researcher William Moore, who has looked into retrieval stories in some depth, unearthed the fact that Scully had received all his information on the Aztec case from two gentlemen, Silas M Newton and Leo GeBauer. Both were convicted confidence tricksters who had spent years creating complicated scenarios to help part people from their money. According to Moore's book on the subject, Newton and GeBauer had carefully prepared Scully over several years with tales of crashed saucers and dead aliens, but without ever producing any solid evidence. A significant development in this story, however, and one which has implications for the veracity of all other retrieval tales, is Newton and Scully's involvement with the biggest rumour-mill in the world, Hollywood.

In 1948/9 an actor by the name of Mike Conrad decided to make a film based on the idea that UFOs were operating out of Alaska, and in order to create prior interest in the film, began circulating rumours in Hollywood that his film would contain close-up footage of 'real' UFOs. As an added lure Conrad had also hired a man who posed for the media as an FBI agent who acknowledged that the FBI had possession of the film, which was safely locked away. This story, spread via the media, prompted Scully to announce to the public, via his newspaper column, the story he had been told by Newton and GeBauer, with the additional detail that the aliens had come from the planet Venus. Conrad later admitted his story was a publicity stunt, but it was too late. By then, Newton, who had no knowledge at the time that Conrad's tale was a hoax, was telling the Aztec tale, well blended with elements from the Conrad hoax, to anyone who would listen, in and around Hollywood. Furthermore, according to Moore's book, the tales differed vastly in content according to who he was telling them to. Hundreds of people must have heard variants of the tale from Newton in late 1949, a tale which must have been subsequently spread and altered and will doubtless have formed the basis of, or addition to, many a retrieval tale since. One of the tales circulating at that time involving a crashed saucer found its way to the FBI, who sent a memo based on it to J. Edgar Hoover. This memo has been seen by many as proof that retrievals of alien craft by the government have actually taken place. In fact, the story can be traced back to Silas M. Newton and his money-making schemes. [**3**]

The Aztec case, coming from the days of 'saucer fever' in the USA and obviously a hoax, has spread rumour variations throughout the UFO community ever since. The second case is one in which the military involvement with these tales becomes apparent.

THE ROSWELL INCIDENT

Investigation proper into the Roswell case did not begin until 1978, but since then over ninety individuals have been located who claim to have some first-hand knowledge of the case. Briefly, in July 1947 during a storm over Roswell, New Mexico, an explosion was heard, a bright object was seen in the sky and later a large amount of debris was found in the area by a local farmer. The wreckage was immediately recovered by the USAAF, who flew it to Wright Patterson airbase, the farmer who had discovered the object being held incommunicado by the USAAF for a week whilst the area was cleared of debris. A statement issued to the press said that a weather balloon had been recovered (although one Major Marcel was quoted as saying though, that '*it was nothing made on this earth*') and arguments have raged ever since as to whether the retrieval was a UFO or something else.

From various interviews with witnesses to the debris, the description of the wreckage seemed to be very similar to that allegedly found at the Aurora crash site, a thin aluminium-like substance and some small rods covered with hieroglyphic-type characters. Wire was also found, as was 'electrical' equipment.

The evidence that *something* did crash at Roswell and was retrieved by the USAAF is overwhelming. It happened, but it may well not have been a 'UFO', at least not in the extraterrestrial sense, which was retrieved. It is here that that the military involvement in the folklore of retrievals comes in. **[3,4]**

The desert area around Roswell and many such areas in the south and west of the USA are used by various agencies of the US military to test new and unconventional military and space craft. Supporters of the ETH will immediately say that this is why so many UFOs are seen in these areas: they are keeping an eye on the military activity. Many of the well-witnessed and documented retrieval cases also come from areas near these secret testing grounds, as do many so-called extraterrestrial landings and contacts, such as the Socorro case. Perhaps 'they' are keeping watch over us. But a more prosaic source of these stories and reason for at least part of the body of retrieval tales must be considered.

There is a strong case for some of the retrieval stories having some factual basis, but that what is actually being retrieved is some kind of secret test craft. This would account for the almost immediate high military involvement in the cases and the initial attributions to mundane causes such as weather balloons. The US military is well aware of the high public interest and media involvement in the UFO phenomenon, whatever its origin, and it would be a simple and very convenient job to later, if it was thought necessary, manipulate both witnesses and the media into thinking that an alien craft *had* crashed and had been retrieved.

MANIPULATION AND MIS-INFORMATION

This type of manipulation is not new, and military forces all over the world have used the prevailing beliefs of indigenous people for their own ends, albeit on a lesser scale, notably in the Congo and Vietnam. If this is occurring it serves two purposes; the government get what they want, which is secrecy, and furthermore an already existing myth is spread and fed which will serve to cover up further crashes and experiments of this kind. After all, who is going to believe the rantings of the UFO magazines?

Conspiracy theories involving governments and other secret agencies have been with us for thousands of years and retrievals merely provide us with a new one. In latter years this mis-information, feeding on an existing myth, has been used to good effect in the Rendlesham Forest case, in which it was alleged that something very strange had been flying around and landing at a USAAF base in Norfolk. When it became apparent to the USAAF that UFO researchers were not going to give up easily on the case, the USAAF themselves put out (mis) information suggesting that a UFO had landed and even that aliens had been conferred with. This effectively debunked the case in the eyes of the British public and the media. In reality it was almost certain to have been a military (possible space re-entry or 'stealth') test, perhaps not even 'one of ours'. Whatever it was is to some degree less important than the means used to disguise it. Even though this is apparent to the critical observer, the Rendlesham case has created and fanned many rumours both in Britain and abroad, notably about the knowledge possessed by the military in the UK about UFOs. You know the sort of thing, secret houses in the country where UFOs are being studied and US bases which secretly track UFOs. Just to confuse matters further, UFO authority Jenny Randles was told by a former British Government official that a crashed saucer was being kept in a South Wales military base. **[4]** These are relatively recent happenings and no doubt retrieval rumours will soon start spreading in the UK. A more recent (1986) occurrence in the USA, in which a 'stealth' bomber crashed in a National park, perhaps adds some weight to the above theory. These craft are ostensibly secret, and when this one crashed the entire area was sealed off and will apparently remain so for years to come. With it taking place in a public area the truth came out relatively easily. Had it crashed in a remote desert or mountain area the story behind it may have turned into yet another ET retrieval story. **[5,6]**

Whilst the Aztec and Roswell retrieval cases are the two best known and documented, many other retrieval accounts exist, quite a few of which are certainly variants on these two. UFOs have, according to veteran researcher Leonard Stringfield, been retrieved from many other countries as well as the USA. However, Stringfield, who reputedly holds vast amounts of data dealing with retrievals, is reluctant to name names and exact locations for many of these cases and so the rumours continue. [**7**] The possibility that *genuine* (alien craft) retrievals have taken place has given rise to spin-off tales connected with them. For instance, it has been suggested that alien bodies are stored in military establishments all over the world, sometimes on ice, somtimes pickled. Affidavits have been signed to this effect and senator Barry Goldwater was refused admittance to part of a base in which these aliens were allegedly kept. One of Stringfield's alien tales tells of a Presbyterian minister who as a child was taken on a tour of a museum in Chicago by his father. They got lost and by mistake wandered into a room in which small humanoid bodies were seen in a glass case. They were instantly seized by officials, and only released when the boy's father had signed some papers. If we are to believe Stringfield's unsubstantiated accounts there are at least thirty alien bodies being held in a freezer at Wright Patterson airbase. [**8**]

To support some of these retrieval tales, photographs have been occasionally circulated, and even though they have all been proved to be hoaxes these still keep popping up in UFO and 'mystery' books as proof that crashed saucers do exist. In Berlitz and Moore's book *The Roswell Incident*, there appears a photo of an alien supposedly retrieved from a saucer in Germany in the early 1950s. It was easily discovered, by the West German group CENAP, to have been an April Fool's joke by a German newspaper. [**4,9**]

The possibility that genuine alien craft have been retrieved and studied is as unrealistic as it is exciting. Had it happened and on the scale alleged, thousands of scientists, from every discipline ranging from anthropology to zoology, would have been needed over the years to study the craft and its occupants. The chances of involvement on this scale with no actual physical or irrefutable photographic leaks are nil. Add to this the fact that discoveries made would be manifesting themselves obviously via science generally, and the case for the existence of retrieved alien craft, looked at objectively, just does not hold water. Of course, adherents to the idea of retrievals will refute this and claim that the military are using the technology gleaned from crashed saucers in craft such as 'stealth' and via SDI (Star Wars) etc.

Essentially, then, the retrieval tales are modern folklore blended with conspiracy theory, with some basis in truth, well mixed with elements from mainstream UFO lore, which itself - by the very fact that we have only witness narratives to go on - is no more than folklore. The stories will continue and grow, and unless and until a genuine crashed saucer is produced by the authorities, the myth will never be resolved, only strengthened.

The most recent report I have seen of a retrieval story comes from the German newspaper *Bild* of 14 July 1983, which reported that the Russians had found a baby (presumably alien) in a crashed saucer, and had kept it alive for seven weeks before it eventually died of an earth virus. Rumour of captured aliens, dead or alive, and photographs keep the retrieval myth going by the addition of more and more spurious evidence.

If we take the crashed saucer/retrieval accounts as a modern folk-tale, there should, as with most folk-tales, be parallels elsewhere both in the past and at the present time. Similarities can be found with other discovery/secrecy/conspiracy tales. For example, the stories involving people who know there are underground shelters in the UK which house old steam locomotives. Or the stories in which people have stumbled on blocked-up tunnels in the underground train system, finding whole carriages full of corpses in Victorian clothes. This obsession with locating things underground, incidentally, is repeated elsewhere in the UFO lore, UFOs allegedly having bases underground everywhere from the Yorkshire Dales to the Arctic. Searching for folklore parallels elsewhere, an alleged crashed saucer incident from Mexico in 1964 has the saucer crashing on a mountain top. The local tribe refused official access to the saucer as it was a gift from God, a frequent folklore theme whether the gift is from God, the fairies or whoever. Had it been a true story surely the relevant government would not have considered divine worship a hindrance to retrieving the saucer for its own uses. Fairy lore, too, is full of references to artefacts and bodies being retrieved from the land of faerie, even down to the finding of cloth and metal with tremendous strength qualities. On a contemporary note, the tale told by Stringfield's informant above has its parallels in a story related by Peter Rogerson in the contemporary folklore magazine *Folklore Frontiers*. This told of a friend who, when visiting his son in hospital, found himself by accident in a strange ward full of babies with massive and impossible deformities. He was ushered out by a nurse who told him he should not have been there and the room should have been locked. [**10**]

REFERENCES

1 - *The choking Doberman & other 'New' Legends*, J. **Brunvand** (Norton 1984) ■ **2** - 'Once Upon a Time in the West', H.M. **Simmons** in *Magonia* (August 1985) ■ **3** - *Crashed UFOs: Evidence in the Search for Proof*, W. **Moore** (Moore pubs. '85) ■ **4** - *The Roswell Incident*, C. **Berlitz** & W. **Moore** (Granada 1980) ■ **5** - *Skycrash*, B. **Butler**, D. **Street**, J. **Randles** (Grafton 1985) ■ **6** - *Lies, Damned Lies*, Henry **Porter** (Coronet 1984) ■ **7** - 'UFO Crash/Retrieval Syndrome', L. **Stringfield** in *FSR* (Vol.28/2 1982) ■ **8** - *Situation Red*, L. **Stringfield** (Sphere 1977) ■ **9** - 'Mr X', Klaus Webner in *UFO Update* (No 9) ■ **10** - Letter in *Folklore Frontiers* (No.4 January 1987)

GENERAL REFERENCES

International UFO Reporter July/Aug 1985. ■ *FSRs*: Vol 24/2/ Vol 25/4,5,6. Vol 26/1. Vol 28/1,2. ■ *Sixth Quark Journal* No.3 1985.

2.7

UFO STATISTICS

by Claude Maugé

■ **CLAUDE MAUGÉ**: Born 1946. Studied physics and psychology. By profession a teacher. Outside ufology his interests include strip cartoons, classical music, science fiction, archaeological 'mysteries', ancient astronaut theory, psi phenomenon, psychology and neurosciences.

■ **UFO involvement**: Interested by virtually all aspects of the UFO phenomenon, but especially by: psychological, parapsychological and sociological aspects; epistemology of ufology; problems of the (non-)reliability of the milieu and the publications of prominent UFO authors; geophysical hypotheses; a possible socio-psychological explanation of the phenomenon. 'Put in a mixer and shake vigorously - (1) many 'sound and inexplicable' cases have later been found to be explicable or at least disputable: our files are saturated with countless cases totally unrelated to possible true UFOs. (2) at first sight UFOs and IFOs are indistinguishable. (3) the statistical proof of UFOs has no value. (4) the UFO milieu is generally not very reliable, and even the work of the most reputable ufologists is often open to serious criticism. (5) ufology is widely underlain by the 'ET myth' whatever the reality may be about ET visits to earth. (6) the UFO phenomenon has a fundamental socio-psychological component, whose impact is often underestimated. (7) we have the embryo of a socio-psychological model which we must study before entertaining more fantastic hypotheses.'

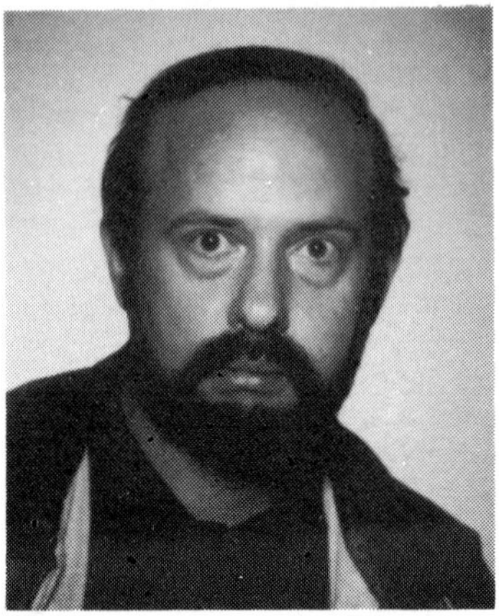

■ **Publications**: include papers in several UFO journals, notably *Inforespace*. Currently preparing a rather critical general review of ufology.

■ **Address**: 28 rue Lecuyer / 93300 Aubervilliers / France. Phone +33.1.48.33.80.81.

Ufology is constructed on foundations composed first and foremost of innumerable accounts of witness' sightings, but also of the numerous theoretical studies derived from these acccounts. Statistics play a fundamental role : some authors use them simply as a way of describing the phenomenon, some employ them in the construction of theory-models, others again consider them to be in themselves a proof of UFO reality.

My purpose here is not to review all the attempts to put ufology on a statistical basis. They are very diverse, ranging from attempts to estimate the total number of UFOs, to correlations with various phenomena, through descriptions of the main features of UFOs or ufonauts, or sociological findings about the witnesses. All of these would be of real interest, provided we were reasonably sure of their reliability.

However, several commentators have indicated, on the one hand, profound theoretical problems which underlie UFO statistics in general, and on the other, weaknesses in specific studies. I shall therefore start by considering statistics in general, and then examine some specific examples.

GENERAL THEORETICAL CONSIDERATIONS

While it is perfectly legitimate to calculate descriptive statistics on the basis of a specific data set, this is of only limited interest. Statistics become truly relevant only when they enable the crude features of one data set to be compared with those of another, or when they enable findings based on a limited set to be extrapolated to a more general set, or to assist in the construction of an explanatory model. But we are justified in making this kind of interpretation only when certain restricting rules have been observed.

As Julian has pointed out [**11**] UFO manifestations are of unknown nature, and occur outside our control; from this stem all the problems both of UFO research in general, and UFO statistics in particular. (Authors who have indicated the main difficulties include Fouéré [**5**], Hendry [**8**], and Rospars [**26**].)

The first requirement is that **statistical computations must be based on a random sample**. However, such a condition can never be fulfilled in ufology, not even if we take as our 'sample' all known cases or, more realistically, a very copious file such as UFOCAT. For the fact is that we do not know whether the cases we have on file are representative of all the actual sightings - less still, whether they represent the original objective events which caused those sightings (assuming that any such events occurred in the first place!).

The listing of a sighting in a data file depends on several factors. Vallee [**28**] has assumed that the crucial factor is **strangeness**: witnesses will not report cases which are too 'simple' but neither will they report cases which are too strange, which differ too much from what is expected. It is also possible that a **stereotype effect** exists: in that case, the UFOs most often reported would be those which best match up to the popularly accepted image. Westrum [**32, 33**], has shown that the reporting rate depends on the one hand on witness-related factors interacting with media influences, and on the other on the existence or absence of individuals or agencies to whom the sighting can be reported.

The second requirement is that **data must be homogeneous**: we may not mix unrelated data, but must use data that is all of a kind, derived from a defined group. But the unknown nature of UFOs prevents us from saying a priori if this requirement has been met. Even if we set on one side the fact that many sightings are potentially explainable by 'mundane' causes, it may or may not be true that the remainder form a single homogeneous class. The advocates of the essential unity of the UFO phenomenon believe this to be the case: other researchers, however, suspect that several different causes may be responsible, geophysical phenomena for example.

There is very little the ufologist can do about meeting these two requirements; but in principle he should be in a stronger position to meet the third requirement of viable statistics, that the **data should be reliable**. Yet in practice, ufology seldom rhymes with reliability. Virtually every catalogue contains a high proportion of cases which do not relate to one or more possible UFO core phenomena. What are we to make, for instance, of the figures presented in the Russian report by Gindilis, Menkov & Petrovskaya [**7**]? Hynek and Haines [**10**] consider them valid, but Besse [**1**] and Monnerie [**19**] have detected many weaknesses in the study, and Oberg [**20**] has pointed out that several sightings relate to space experiments from the (at that time secret) Plesetsk base.

It is possible to overcome this obstacle of data unreliability, but only by using very selected cases - I am thinking here of Smith's UNICAT. But statistics based only on selected cases serve no practical purpose because the process of selection has created its own bias: as Julian [**11**] rightly notes, any data set displays patterns, and it has to be determined whether they are significant or not. It will be interesting to compare results derived from UNICAT with those from an IFO set.

Data reliability does not solely consist in using sound cases. Both the creation of a file and the method of codification raise serious problems which have been well described by Rospars [**26**]. What kind of entries should we use? What variables should we code, and how? It is easy to ask these questions, not so easy to find answers. The variables must allow for a fair latitude in the witness' ability to describe what he saw, yet at the same time they must be reasonably discriminating. The coding must indicate precise modalities to the compiler of the statistics, yet somehow embody the various terms used by witnesses which can reasonably be regarded as equivalent. Hendry [**8**] has shown, for example, that such conditions are not met by the six parameters employed in the Battelle Institute study, and therefore questions its results: Willy Smith, on the other hand, disputes Hendry's criticisms. Without passing judgment on this particular case, we can see that there is considerable margin for doubt.

Though the existence of UFOs is open to question, that of human beings is well substantiated: and yet even sociological statistics are open to criticism. Consider, for example, two French opinion polls, the 1980 *IFRES - Le Parisien Libere* [**21**] and the 1981 *SOFRES - Bonne Soiree* [**6,**] both carried out by competent professional poll institutes. The latter found that 7% of the population of France have witnessed a UFO, a figure which roughly matches Gallup results in the USA: but the earlier poll gave only 0.3%! How could such a difference come about? Possibly due to the limitations of any opinion poll, such as the size of the sample: the IFRES poll questioned only 1033 people to find its three witnesses. Equally, the discrepancy may be due to the acceptance of the term 'UFO': the samples were selected according to standard statistical protocol, but no standard protocol exists for the variable 'meaning of the term UFO'.

THE POHER AND POHER / VALLÉE STATISTICS

I choose this example of 'general' statistics because it is based on a copious data set, which as presented in the Poher/Vallée paper [**25**] is frequently employed in the ufological literature. I have studied these statistics in detail elsewhere [**12, 14**], and present here only my main findings. Several of these are typical of UFO statistics in general, though few contain quite so many flaws.

Poher and his unnamed collaborators start with about 1000 UFO reports, collected for the most part from the UFO literature. The dubious cases are removed, leaving the '825 sightings' which form the basis of a complex statistical study in which many features are studied [**23**]. In a later paper [**24**] Poher uses them to demonstrate that the witnesses have really seen something which is inexplicable. The basic findings are finally used again and expanded in Poher and Vallée's paper [**25**]. However, each of these studies contains serious defects.

In the first place, Poher's 825 cases in fact number only 736. The discrepancy is due to the fact that certain classic cases are reported by more than one source: in Poher's list these are correctly put together as one item, but in the statistics they erroneously figure separately, thus constituting 825 alleged cases. Moreover, the elimination of multi-coded cases is not carefully done; if we eliminate cases thus duplicated, we reduce the figure still further to 710. These duplications may result from mistakes or imprecisions in the sources, but also from coding errors; these are numerous, amounting to some 10% of the cases, and in a quarter of those there is one or more serious error.

Furthermore, some of the sources which Poher uses, notably von Däniken, Misraki or Guieu, cannot be considered very reliable. There are few explained cases, but also few really sound ones: instead there are many - 22% - which seem easily explainable by mundane causes, and the great majority - 65% - are inconclusive cases whose reliability and non-reducibility are hard to estimate. Let us note here that, depending on the circumstances, Poher claims either that he deliberately compelled his collaborators not to exercise selectivity when listing the sightings, or that his study contains 'sound' cases (classed D according to GEPAN terminology). He can't have it both ways: either they are selected for soundness or they are not!

A further weakness is that 40% of his cases are too briefly (less than 1400 characters) reported by the original source: twelve are particularly short - less than 200 characters! Checking 449 cases, I found 236 which were either too short or dubious: extrapolating this ratio to Poher's complete set, we find that if we eliminate the unsatisfactory data we are left with only 418 - *barely half the original sample*!

Not only were the statistics based on this mix of good and less-than-good cases, but they unwittingly included 115 duplicate cases. Furthermore, charts in the original work [**23**] present results for French sightings and foreign sightings, though the latter *include* the French cases - a mistake repeated in subsequent papers [**24, 25**].

The famous comparison between durations of UFOs and IFOs [**25**] calls for special attention. The percentages in the 'non-French' chart correspond only partly to the raw results, and the value for observations lasting more than one day (about 8%) is manifestly absurd. The point abscissas of the curves are somewhat arbitrary, and the forms of the curves depend drastically on the width of the chosen classes. The 'identified objects' curve is totally arbitrary, and Hendry [**8**] is mistaken in thinking that it relates to 'pre-screened IFOs' as dealt with in his own study: Poher's 'IFO' curve is made up of mundane objects *immediately* identified as such by the witnesses, and consequently free of the emotional content that goes with a UFO experience or even that of a subsequently identified IFO.

Stranger still, we find that when Poher and Vallée use their UFO duration curve, which had been used in *l'Aeronautique et l'Astronautique* (*without* indicating the number of cases), in *Flying Saucer Review* (with mention of 508 cases), an additional point appears on the curve so that the total is close to the number 508. This value is evidently intended to denote the sum of 373 'non-French' and 135 French cases; but the 373 world cases in fact *include* the French cases, so they appear twice over! The curve itself is not wrong, but someone at some point has added to it a point so as to obtain the expected number.

In summary, then, what does our analysis reveal? Dubious sources, dubious cases; coding mistakes, methodological errors; confusion between data sets, and perhaps even data manipulation...

GEOGRAPHICAL DISTRIBUTION OF UFOS: THE EXAMPLE OF 'ORTHOTENY'

Some authors have rightly noted the existence of biases which taint studies of the geographical distribution of UFOs. (The same is true of temporal distribution.) Hendry [**8**] indicates reasons why CEs 'occur' in areas of low population, or why UFOs are sighted 'preferably' near natural features or human installations. Verga [**30**] goes so far as to deny that statistics related to population density have any value whatever. In this he is perhaps being too categorical; what is at issue is the competence of ufologists to handle the data. Epidemiologists, after all, manage to cope with such parameters competently enough.

Of all the studies of the spatial distribution of UFOs, orthoteny is no doubt the best-known example; it has been well reviewed by Scornaux [**27**]. Using the 1954 French wave, Michel [**17**] showed that sightings in a 24-hour period were arranged in alignments and geometrical structures in a way which chance would not account for. In particular, he emphasised networks centred on points where 'cloud-cigars' had been sighted. Moreover, on 24 September, six of the nine sightings known to Michel fell on a line connecting the cities of Bayonne and Vichy - the notorious BAVIC line. Such findings reinforced the hypothesis that the UFO constitutes an intelligent phenomenon existing in its own right: here at last was a quantifiable parameter. It was orthoteny which converted some scientists to ufology!

Michel's findings were hotly debated, particularly in the *FSR*, where contributors included not only Michel himself but also Saunders, Toulet, Vallée and Menzel. The latter in particular [**16**] noted some methodological errors on Michel's part: though arbitrary, it is legitimate to limit oneself to certain conditions (French territory; a 24-hour period; witness location as opposed to that of the UFO itself) but it is strictly incumbent on the researcher to respect those same limits in subsequent procedures - and this Michel had not done.

Eventually, there was general agreement that most of the findings could be attributed to chance; BAVIC remained the exception. But then this finding too turned out to be less solid than it had been made to appear. One sighting (Ussel) was shown to be 4.3 km from BAVIC, and two of the cases had not occurred on the specified date. Reduced in this way, even the BAVIC conincidence fell within the limits of chance.

If that were all, we could say there is no real fault in orthoteny, apart, that is, from Menzel's criticisms and the fact that Michel's sources were essentially derived from nothing more solid than press clippings. We could see it as an interesting attempt to discern a pattern in UFO sightings, and if it eventually proved to lack substance, well, the same is true of astrophysicists who themselves fell into the trap of a pseudo-'quasars orthoteny' [**34**].

Caudron however [**4**] has raised the possibility that Michel, perhaps unwittingly, might have 'horribly' manipulated his sources. He could have suppressed possible explanations offered by the sources themselves; he could have 'rearranged' dates (for instance, allocating a case described as occurring 'on the night of the 20th' to the 19th, 20th or 21st to suit his purposes); several sightings might be taken as relating to a single case, or alternatively several sightings supposed to be of the same object could be treated as separate cases.

To complicate matters still further, a veritable 'bavicomania' raged at one time: BAVIC was correlated to paleolithic drawings, geophysical phenomena, the birthplaces of prominent people or even the towns most frequently cited by Nostradamus! Michel himself [**18**] showed that BAVIC passes through two of the three main areas of France and Spain where paleolithic caves containing UFO drawings are to be found. Apart from the dubious nature of such identification, even here his statistical method was flawed, as I have demonstrated. [**13**]

Following in Michel's footsteps, many authors 'discovered' orthotenic systems in other parts of the world, though usually it is a question of 'permanent orthoteny' over an unlimited period rather than Michel's self-imposed 24-hour limit. Dohmen found orthoteny in Belgium, Druffel in North California, Fontes in Brazil, Ribera in the Iberian peninsula, Vallée in North Africa. In most of these cases chance seems able to account for the data, though the Belgian ones seem to fit the traffic lanes. Vézina & Leduc's study in Québec [**31**] however does seem more difficult to attribute to mundane causes. Their procedure is well conceived, bias and artifacts have been allowed for. Their conclusion is that the 'Beloeil network' with seven permanent orthotenic lines presents a genuine property of the UFO phenomenon.

Other researchers have 'discovered' geographical patterns even more sophisticated than orthoteny: more notable are Cathie's grid system, Fumoux' 'Isocelie', or Bernard's 'prophetic system' according to which the 1954 wave predicted de Gaulle's 1958 coming to power. However, as with most revelations of Sacred Geography or Earth Mysteries, when you place many points upon a relatively restricted area, you can find nearly all the figures you want.

PERSINGER'S TECTONIC STRAIN THEORY

Many attempts have been made to correlate UFOs with phenomena of natural or human origin, such as astronomical cycles - particularly solar activity; geomagnetic or geophysical features - particularly geological faults and seismic events; or mechanical events such as power failures. Of these, the most extensive is indisputably that of Persinger [**22**] who suggests that earth stresses generate electromagnetic luminous phenomena (ie UFOs) which can affect the environment and nearby witnesses. Persinger took various areas, and computed correlations between on the one hand the number of UFO reports and on the other the number of earthquakes of different intensities and other geophysical parameters and solar activity. Though there are certain problems with his findings, they are certainly interesting. Other authors in this book have commented on his theory as it relates to their field: I shall limit myself here to the statistical aspects.

First, it must be said that Persinger's data are not entirely reliable, because they come essentially from the books of Charles Fort, from *Fate* and from UFOCAT. Furthermore, seismic/geomagnetic variables are not always independent, and ufological data are (as we saw earlier in this paper) heterogeneous: both of these factors can bias statistical calculations. Selected functions and the correlations obtained vary according to the region being studied; in part this is traceable to geological variations, but in the absence of a model at least partly quantifiable, we may also suspect the presence of artifacts. Some of Persinger's results are not so well founded as the author claims: the theory is for instance unable to predict in retrospect the major European UFO waves of 1954 and 1973-74.

More fundamentally, the fact that a statistical function gives apparently accurate results is no guarantee of its validity to explain physical reality. Vallée & Vallée [**29**] had already reminded us of the fact that any periodic or pseudo-periodic phenomenon can always be correlated, with striking precision, with one or more astronomical cycles, simply because there are so many of them of various kinds. So such a correlation becomes meaningful only when we can show that cause-and-effect are operating. It is to be feared that Persinger's results may be demonstrating to us nothing more than artifacts of this kind. Moreover, the fact that Persinger obtains good results without taking into account sociological factors, though these could be expected to play an influential role, causes us to wonder whether his results are not *too* good to be accurate?

DISTINGUISHING UFOs FROM IFOs

It is evident that any detail in a UFO report can be found in one or another IFO report; and we know that some complex cases, formerly accepted as UFOs, were later recognised as sophisticated IFOs.

We must face the possibility that the residue of 'unknowns' in our files include numerous sophisticated misperceptions which could be explained only with great difficulty. We must recognise that the richness and precision of a report, and the confidence of the witness who makes it, are no guarantee of its reliability: witnesses who are correct and witnesses who are mistaken present just as many details and are just as positive about what they saw. So it would be a mistake to regard any low strangeness case as likely to be an IFO and every high strangeness case as a probable UFO.

One of the most promising attempts to resolve the UFO/IFO problem is that of Hynek [9] who studied some 400 cases and concluded that many individual features, still more those features in combination, were 'different from the properties of those events, phenomena and objects generally offered as explanations for the UFO phenomenon'. However, Hynek seems to have employed, as his basis for this comparison, sightings in which the phenomenon was identified at the time, so that there was no comparable emotional context. For this reason his findings should be treated with caution; hopefully they may be confirmed by whatever results are obtained when the more solidly compiled UNICAT file of Willy Smith is set against 'equivalent' IFO cases.

The problem of distinguishing UFOs from IFOs is fundamental to ufology, but even if we knew how to resolve it, our problems would not be at an end. For example, if UFOs are due to extraterrestrials manipulating us, true UFOs might be totally indistinguishable from IFOs.

Paradoxically, even when we know that a data set is heavily contaminated by IFOs, we can still detect patterns. No doubt these artifical coherences arise from the complexity of factors involved - the problems of perception and misinterpretation, including social and cultural influences; interaction with ufologists and/or the media; the fact that most sightings are misperceptions of a very few kinds of stimuli; not to mention the action of chance. But knowing that such sources of bias exist does not instruct us how to make allowance for them: all it does is remind us that we must be cautious before we accept any finding at face value.

CONCLUSION

In this paper I have briefly referred to some of the weaknesses displayed by certain UFO statistics, but one could easily have chosen other examples. The real problem is that ufology is a very complex field of research. To their credit, many ufologists have gone looking for data. But if their findings are to be of scientific value, they must conform to fundamental scientific rules of procedure; and this is especially true in the field of statistics.

REFERENCES

1 - **Besse,** Philippe, *Etude comparative des resultats statistiques elementaires relatifs aux observations de phenomenes aerospatiaux non identifies, Note technique no 2,* GEPAN, Toulouse, 1980: 61. ■ 2 - **Bougard,** Michel, Le leurre de l'indiscernabilite, in *Inforespace*, Brussels, dec 1984, No 8 hors-serie: 22-25. ■ 3 - **Breysse,** Denys, La duree des phenomenes OVNI: aide a la discernabilite in *OVNI-Presence*, Vevey, Switzerland/Aix-en- Provence, France, dec 1984/feb 1985, no 32, 22-34. ■ 4 - **Caudron,** Dominique, Talk at the *Journees Ufologiques Montlucon 82,* Montlucon, France, April 4, 1982. ■ 5 - **Fouéré,** René, Statistique et connaissance en matiere de recherche sur les soucoupes volantes, in *Phenomenes spatiaux*, Paris, sept 1975, no 45, 3-11. ■ 6 - **Gravelaine,** Joëlle de, Enquete BS-SOFRES: Soucoupes volantes et propheties, vrai ou faux? in *Bonne Soiree*, Paris, 12 nov 1981, no 3118: 12-13. ■ 7 - **Guindilis,** L.M., Menkov, D.A., and Petrovskaia, I.G., *Observations de phenomenes atmospheriques anormaux en URSS., Note d'information No 1,* GEPAN, Toulouse, 1980. **Guindilis,** L.M., **Menkov,** D.A., and **Petrovskaia,** I.G., *Observations - of anomalous atmospheric Phenomena in the USSR: A statistical Analysis,* CUFOS, Evanston, Illinois, 1980. ■ 8 - **Hendry,** Allan, *The UFO Handbook*, Doubleday, Garden City, NY, 1979: 241-269. ■ 9 - **Hynek,** J. Allen, Properties of the UFO phenomenon, in *MUFON 1984 UFO Symposium Proceedings*, MUFON, Seguin, Texas, 1984: 163-166. ■ 10 - **Hynek,** J. Allen, and **Haines,** Richard F., Implications of and comments on "Observations of anomalous atmospheric Phenomena in the USSR: A statistical Analysis", *Journal of UFO Studies*, Evanston, *vol.2*, 1980: 95-101. ■ 11 - **Julian,** Paul, Statistical Analysis, in D.S. Gillmor (ed), *Final Report of the Scientific Study of Unidentified Flying Objects* (Condon Report), Bantam, New York, 1969: 804-810. ■ 12 - **Maugé,** Claude, Regards critiques sur un fichier au-dessus de tout soupcon..., in *OVNI-Presence*, Vevey/Aix-en-Provence, sept 1983, no 27: 30-40. ■ 13 - **Maugé,** Claude, Lecture critique: "Palaeolithic UFO-shapes" d'Aime Michel, in *Annuaire du C.I.G.U.*, Paris, 1985, no 2: 201- 227. ■ 14 - **Maugé,** Claude, 'Ufology and statistics: the case of Poher's file', to be published in *Magonia*, London. ■ 15 - **Maugé,** Claude, 'Persinger's Tectonic Strain Theory: Greatness and weaknesses,' *Magonia*, London, nov 1986, no 24: 13-18 ■ 16 - **Menzel,** Donald H., UFOs - The modern myth, in C. **Sagan** and T. **Page** (eds), *UFOs - A scientific Debate*, Norton, New York (1972), 1974: 163-174. ■ 17 - **Michel,** Aimé, *Mysterieux Objets Celestes*, Arthaud, Paris, 1958 (several editions by various publishers, with the original title or entitled *A propos des Soucoupes Volantes*). Trans.: *Flying Saucers and the Straight-Line Mystery*, Criterion, New York, 1958; Neville Spearman, London, 1960. ■ 18 - **Michel,** Aimé, Palaeolithic UFO-Shapes, in *Flying Saucer Review*, Snodland, England, nov-dec 1969, *vol 15*, no 6: 3-11. ■ 19 - **Monnerie,** Michel, Quand les Russes s'emmelent..., in *Inforespace*, Brussels, aug 1981, no 57: 3-13. ■ 20 - **Oberg,** James E., The great Soviet UFO cover-up, *MUFON UFO Journal*, Seguin, oct 1982, no 176: 6-10, and nov 1982, no 177: 6-10. ■ 21 - *Le Parisien libere*, Paris, June 13, 1980: 13. ■ 22 - **Persinger,** Michael A., Possible infrequent geophysical sources of close UFO encounters: Expected physical and behavioral- biological effects, in R.F. **Haines** (ed), *UFO Phenomena and the behavioral Scientist*, Scarecrow Press, Metuchen, N.J./London, 1979: 396-433. ■ 23 - **Poher,** Claude, *Etude statistique des Rapports d'Observations du Phenomene O.V.N.I.*, private publication, 1971 and 1976 (There is an English version). ■ 24 - **Poher,** Claude, Etudes et reflexions a propos du phenomene "O.V.N.I.", in *L'Aeronautique et l'Astronautique*, Paris, 1975, no 52: 69-74. Reprinted in J.C. Bourret (ed), *Le nouveau Defi des OVNI*. France-Empire, Paris, 1977: 242-258. ■ 25 - **Poher,** Claude, and **Vallée,** Jacques, Basic patterns in UFO observations, in *Flying Saucer Review*, Snodland, England, nov 1975, *vol 21*, no 3/4: 8-13. I presume this paper repeats Poher and Vallee's contribution at the *AIAA 13th Aerospace Sciences Meeting*, Pasadena, January 20-22, 1975. ■ 26 - **Rospars,** Jean-Pierre, Etude des problemes lies a la creation d'un fichier informatique, in *Analyse du probleme du pre-traitement des donnees, Note Technique no 1*, GEPAN, Toulouse, 1979: 48-75. ■ 27 - **Scornaux,** Jacques, L'orthotenie: un grand espoir decu? in *Inforespace*, Brussels, from oct 1975, no 23, to may 1976, no 27. ■ 28 - **Vallée,** Jacques, *Le College invisible*, Albin Michel, Paris, 1975: 137-148. *The invisible College*, E.P. Dutton, New York, 1975. ■ 29 - **Vallee,** Jacques, and **Vallée,** Janine, *Les Phenomenes insolites de l'Espace*, La Table ronde, Paris, 1966. *Challenge to Science: The UFO Enigma*, Ballantine Books, New York, (1966) 1978. ■ 30 - **Verga,** Maurizio, 'Revising the geographical distribution of UFO events', in *Journal of transient aerial Phenomena*, Peterborough, England, apr 1984, *vol 3*, no 2, 111-116. ■ 31 - **Vézina,** Jean, and **Leduc,** Marc, *Application de l'Orthotenie aux Observations du Quebec*, UFO-Quebec,

Dollard-des-Ormeaux, Canada, 1983. ■ **32** - **Westrum,** Ron, 'Social intelligence about anomalies: the case of UFOs,' in *Social Studies of Science*, 1977, *vol 7*: 271-302. ■ **33** - **Westrum,** Ronald M., 'UFO reporting dynamics', in R.F. **Haines** (ed), *UFO Phenomena and the behavioral Scientist*, Scarecrow Press, Metuchen, N.J./London, 1979: 147-163. ■ **34** - **Zuiderwijk,** E.J., 'Alignment of randomly distributed objects', in *Nature*, 18 feb 1982, *vol 295*, no 5850: 577-578.

3
ASSESSING THE PHENOMENA

3.1

ASSESSING THE PHENOMENA

From time to time it is suggested that there should be - even that there already exists - a science of ufology.

As it stands, the suggestion is nonsense: there cannot be a science of something whose nature is unknown and whose existence *per se* is in doubt. Psychical researchers might as well talk of a science of poltergeistery, cryptozoologists of a science of lake monsters.

But though it would be premature to assign to any of these phenomena a science of its own, that assuredly does not exclude the possibility of studying them in a scientific way. Even the ill-fated Colorado University project, though it concluded that 'the scientific study of UFOs' *should* not be done, did not suggest that it *could* not be done.

Today's ufologists are proving that it *can* be done, as is demonstrated by the selection of papers in this section. One has only to look at the manuals and handbooks produced by various organisations [**eg. 1, 2**] as well as by individual researchers [**eg. 3, 4, 5**] to see that today's ufologists set themselves very high standards. So much so that it may be asked whether the ufologists themselves are capable of living up to their own counsels of perfection?

Be that as it may, there is ample testimony to the higher standards observed by today's ufologists compared with their predecessors of the early days. One obvious area is the cataloguing of cases. In most countries where any serious UFO research is conducted, a radical reassessment is currently in progress to weed out spurious or dubious cases from catalogues, and thus create a data base of practical value. Dr Willy Smith's international UNICAT project [**6**] is the most ambitious of these undertakings, while Michel Figuet's FRANCAT [**7**] - a re-evaluation of his own magnificent dossier [**8**], itself a landmark publication in its day - is an indication of how standards have risen in less than a decade. In Britain, Mike Wootten is carrying out a similar task in respect of the BUFORA files.

These efforts are practicable only because recent technological developments have put sophisticated data-processing tools in the hands of virtually every UFO research group, no matter how limited its budget. In other areas of UFO research, high equipment costs mean that investigators are caught in a vicious circle: they cannot command the technical resources which would enable them to produce the results which would generate the scientific interest which would make such resources available!

When, on rare occasions, researchers have broken out of this vicious circle, the results have been impressive - as witness the Scandinavian **Project Hessdalen** [9] and Rutledge's **Project Identification** [**10**]. In each of those projects, the use of scientific method produced evidence which if not conclusive is certainly strongly indicative of an unidentified phenomenon whose nature must be of interest to science. For a tiny fraction of the sum spent to such little effect on the Colorado project, they afford positive evidence which makes nonsense of that project's negative conclusions.

REFERENCES

1 - **MUFON**, *Field investigator's manual*, edited by Raymond E Fowler (3rd edition, 1983)› ■ 2 - **BUFORA**, *UFO investigation: a field investigator's handbook* (1st edition, 1976). ■ 3 - **Adell Sabates**, Alberto, *Manual del ufologo* (Editorial 7½, Barcelona, 1979). ■ 4 - **Hendry**, Allan, *The UFO handbook* (Doubleday, 1979). ■ 5 - **Randles**, Jenny, *UFO study* (Hale, 1981). ■ 6 - **UNICAT project** is co-ordinated by Dr Willy **Smith** [1200 Murcott Court, Longwood, FL 32779, USA] with some 60 collaborators and associates throughout the world. ■ 7 - **FRANCAT:** rencontres rapprochees en France (1983) is an ongoing project compiled by Michel **Figuet** [avenue de la Gare, Besayes, 26300 Bourg-de-Peage, France]. ■ 8 - **Figuet**, Michel, & **Ruchon**, Jean-Louis, *OVNI, le premier dossier complet des rencontres rapprochees en France* (Lefeuvre, 1979). ■ 9 - *Project Hessdalen 1984; final technical report*, compiled by Erling **Strand** [UFO-Norge, Postbox 14, 3133 Duken, Norway]. ■ 10 - **Rutledge**, Harley, *Project identification* [Prentice-Hall, 1981].

3.2
DEFINING THE UFO
by Richard Haines

■ **RICHARD F HAINES**: Obtained his PhD from Michigan State University in the field of experimental psychology / physiology. He has been a research scientist for NASA since 1967, and has officially investigated numerous aviation accidents and incidents. He is married, with two daughters.

■ **UFO involvement**: He has been an active investigator for a number of years, and has authored articles on many aspects of the phenomenon with the aim of persuading his scientific colleagues that the subject warrants serious examination.

■ **Publications** include: *Observing UFOs* (Nelson-Hall 1980); *Melbourne episode* (on the Valentich disappearance) LDA Press, 1987; and as editor, *UFOs and the behavioral scientist* (Scarecrow 1979).

■ **Address**: 325 Langton Avenue / Los Altos / CA 94022 / USA.

One might presume that in order to define something one must first know what that "thing" is, or at least have some idea in which category it may be fit. It is clear that anomalous phenomena, whose behavior seems to lie outside the current boundaries of knowledge of modern science, cannot be defined in this same way. Indeed, an anomaly remains anomalous until a sufficient body of evidence is compiled with which to relate it reliably to a larger body of knowledge and/or to an established scientific discipline. Thus, the unknown is only unknown for a particular period of time; it is not necessarily unknowable, given sufficient human endeavor.

A definition is a formal statement of the meaning or significance of a word, phrase, etc. Consequently, in order to define the unknown properly there must be an underlying foundation or basis of understanding which can lead to a formal statement involving meaning and/or its significance to mankind, to science, or to some other philosophy of thought or action. It is quite clear, after reviewing most prior definitions for the idea known as "unidentified flying objects" (UFO), that there is far too much effort expended on collecting the "evidence" and far too little effort spent building a firm foundation of terminology upon which we all can communicate with one another around the Earth and which will form the basis for a scientific definition.

Many descriptive terms and phrases have been used over the years to refer to UFO. Most have corresponded to the underlying beliefs of their authors as to what they thought the phenomenon was. Thus, the term "Flying Saucers" arose as a result of Kenneth Arnold's now famous daytime sighting of June 24 1947 when he said, "...they flew like a saucer would if you skipped it across the water." [**2**] An unknown American journalist subsequently coined the term "flying saucer." As Paris Flammonde [**3**] correctly pointed out, US Air Force Captain Edward Ruppelt coined the phrase "Unidentified Flying Objects" in order to "distinguish what appeared to be rational sighting reports from ones sounding like excerpts from fairy tales or nightmares." It was in 1967 that Ivan Sanderson referred to "Unexplained Aerial Object" (UAO) for those instances where the phenomenon was apparently solid, and "Unidentified Atmospheric Phenomenon" (UAP) when it appeared ethereal or amorphous. [**10**] Underwater Unidentified Objects (UUO) referred to exactly that by authors in the magazine *Flying Saucers*. Flammonde himself [**4**] used the term "Unidentified Sensory Experience" (USE), while John Keel used a simple term "Anomalies." Most of these terms are more conveniences than scientifically useful working definitions.

Many definitions have been offered for the term "UFO". Indeed, the basic phrase is still badly misunderstood by people around the world today. In order for us to discuss the subject with precision, it is particularly important to define what is and is not meant by the term. It should also be understood at the outset that the synonymous concepts "aerial disc", "alien flying object", "anomalous aerial phenomena" (UAP), "extraordinary flying object", "flying saucers" (FS), "unusual light phenomena", and other such terms are also defined imprecisely if at all in most of the literature. It is as if the general idea is already so socially ingrained, intuitive, and "natural" that many people do not even need a definition any more. For such individuals the UFO is a fully acceptable "given". And so let us begin this chapter with a brief review of previous definitions.

THE UFO DEFINED

■ **1966 - US Air Force definition:** "The Air Force defines an unidentified flying object as any aerial object which the observer is unable to identify." [**12**]

Comment: Whether this definition was deliberate or just naive, it failed to be precise and set the stage for the Air Force to show that a majority of reported aerial events by untrained witnesses were explainable in prosaic terms.

■ **1969 - University of Colorado UFO study definition:** "An unidentified flying object (UFO)...is here defined as the stimulus for a report made by one or more individuals of something seen in the sky (or an object thought to be capable of flight but seen when landed on the earth) which the observer could not identify as having an ordinary natural origin, and which seemed to him sufficiently puzzling that he undertook to make a report of it to police, to government officials, to the press, or perhaps to a representative of a private organization devoted to the study of such objects." [**5 p.9**]

Comment: This definition is based upon several key concepts: (1) The UFO is a stimulus for a report and, thereby, stops short of dealing with the possible core identity of the phenomenon itself, (2) The witness is the only judge of the identifiability of the stimulus and not other qualified persons, and (3) The eventual report was what became the focus of attention rather than the original stimulus for the report. This definition effectively precluded any direct confrontation with the UFO. It was typical of an academic, theoretical, non-confrontational approach to the matter.

■ **1972 - Carl Sagan's definition:** "A UFO is a moving aerial or celestial phenomenon, detected visually or by radar, but whose nature is not immediately understood."

Comment: This definition would appear to underscore a bias that all UFOs will be understood eventually.

■ **1972 - Aerial Phenomeno Research Organization (APRO) definition:** "any airborne object which cannot be identified by the witness." [**1**]

■ **1972 - Dr. William K. Hartmann's definition:** UFO "...is an unidentified object or apparition considered strange by the observer... If (the phenomenon cannot be identified by investigation) it may be considered an extraordinary flying object, that is, something beyond the bounds of recognized natural phenomena. Even more startling, it might be called an alien flying object meaning a vehicle constructed by alien intelligence."

Comment: Here Dr. Hartmann relies upon the witness for initial classification (as being UFO) with the additional confirmation by investigators, in which case the UFO becomes an EFO (extraordinary flying object).

■ **1972 - Dr. J. Allen Hynek's definition in** *The UFO Experience*: "We can define the UFO simply as the reported perception of an object or light seen in the sky or upon the land, the appearance, trajectory, and general dynamic and luminescent behaviour of which do not suggest a logical, conventional explanation and which is not only mystifying to the original percipients but remains unidentified after close scrutiny of all available evidence by persons who are technically capable of making a common sense identification, if one is possible."

Earlier, Hynek defined the UFO Phenomenon as "the total class of the UFO Report and the UFO Experience" and the UFO Experience as "the content of a UFO Report." [**8**]

Comment: My observations on this definition are given later.

■ **1979 - Allan Hendry's definition in** *The UFO Handbook*: "Any anomalous aerial phenomenon whose appearance and/or behavior cannot be ascribed to conventional objects or effects by the original witness(es) as well as by technical analysts who possess qualifications that the original observer(s) may lack." [**7 p.4**]

Comment: Here, for the first time, both the eye witness and technically qualified persons are involved in determining whether or not the phenomenon is unidentified.

■ **1980 - Ronald Story's definition in** *The Encyclopedia of UFOs*: "Although a perfect definition is probably impossible (since, after all, the subjects of our study are "unidentified"), it may be advisable to limit the field of UFOlogy to those cases of sightings and encounters that do not seem (after a thorough and proper study by qualified persons) to be explainable in terms of any known phenomenon of nature or man-made device." [**11 p.97**]

DEFINING THE UFO

In *Observing UFOs* [**6**], I began by commenting on the definition provided by Hynek [**8**]. This was done because I felt that some small modifications needed to be made in order to clarify it. The reader should refer to Hynek's definition given above before progressing.

■ "Reported Perception"

Not only must one have a perception of the UFO, but one must also report that perception to someone else. It is this report, rather than the personal experience of the event, that is usually subjected to analysis. Indeed, there are no known ways of studying the original perception. The form and content of the UFO report, therefore, are the most critical links in the study of eye-witness accounts of UFO phenomena and also provide the basis for evaluating the credibility of the witness himself. For instance, if the witness first calls the chief of the local police department and tries to give as objective a report as possible of his experience, and if the police (in due course) contact the Center for UFO Studies, the credibility of the witness is likely to be greater than if he first calls his local newspaper reporter or calls a news conference about his sighting. Thus, our motives and underlying needs to gratify our ego play an extremely important role in determining how and why we report an encounter with a UFO, or any other unexpected or bizarre event.

Also, the reported perception of a UFO may not represent what actually took place.

■ "Object or Light"

Although almost all UFOs might be placed into one of these two categories, it would seem reasonable to add a third category - the "presence of some*thing*." By restricting our definition only to an object or light source, we make the implicit assumption of the existence of a three-dimensional object that possesses mass and/or which radiates energy. The UFO may or may not emit luminous radiation at all times (which may explain how some UFOs can suddenly disappear). When we use the term "light", we typically mean that the UFO is visible to the eye, ie that it evokes a sufficiently strong sensation that it is perceived. Yet the use of the term "light" is somewhat misleading, because the term is used in the literature to indicate both stimulus and response. For example, it is not uncommon to hear the expression, "I saw the light..." (stimulus term) and also, "The UFO appeared very light against the dark background" (perceptual response term). In a continuing attempt to keep these two types of terms separate, I will always define the term "light" as the response term. Light is the experience that is produced by an adequate stimulation of the visual system; thus, we see light. We do not see *the* light. It should be mentioned that the sensation of light can be produced without the stimulation of the visual system by electromagnetic energy within the visible spectrum. One means of doing so is by a sharp blow (impact) to the head or by the gentle application of pressure directly to the eyeball. Both actions produce a sensation known as a "phosphene" which generally appears as one or more hazy patches of light. Other light sensations can be produced by placing the head between the poles of a strong magnet, alternating magnetic field or intense electrical field.

By including the third category (ie the "presence of some*thing*"), we are not presupposing anything in particular about the nature of the object with regard to its emitting or reflecting properties but only that the presence of something is (somehow) perceived.

It is well known that humans sense the presence of objects by means other than their eyes, ears, nose, skin, and tongue. By including this third category we have made allowance for the possible "extra-sensory awareness" which may accompany a UFO experience. Many cases can be found in the UFO literature where the witnesses simply "felt" that something unnatural was taking place, yet they were not sure what it was. In many such cases the UFO was perceived through "normal" sensory channels after these earlier so-called premonitions. We need not necessarily assume some form of psychic or paranormal capability within the witness nor must we automatically rule out such capabilities by the inclusion of this third category.

■ "Sky or upon the Land"

Certainly we must also make allowance for those UFO sightings where the object was seen beneath the surface of a body of water. The UFO literature contains many examples of such sightings. This aspect of the UFO phenomena has been relatively neglected to date and should receive far more study because of the (possibly) important differences in pressure, fluid dynamics (boundary layer flow effects, drag), visibility, and other underwater factors that make it quite a different operational environment from the atmosphere.

■ "Logical, Conventional Explanation"

This seems to be the crux of Hynek's definition.

After both logic and convention have been applied by everyone concerned and the mystery still remains, then a second criterion must be brought to bear, namely "*close scrutiny of all available evidence*" by technically trained persons who are capable of judging the identity of whatever caused the perception. Certainly the two criteria of logic and convention are the first that must be used in attempting to understand and explain the UFO phenomenon. This is precisely how the scientific method has shown itself to be such a powerful tool in unlocking the secrets of nature. Still, I would suggest that a reasonably large amount of UFO sighting "data" cannot be properly approached through logical or conventional avenues. Indeed, much of the UFO evidence is so bizarre in nature that it defies logic and our modern-day ways of viewing reality. To rely upon logic and prior convention alone is to shut the door upon other possible approaches to the full analysis of the evidence.

Consider, for instance, the possibility that a class of UFOs exists only in two, not three, dimensions. An infinitesimally thin piece of paper possesses both length and breadth and so may be seen as a reflecting surface, but theoretically it can also disappear if it is viewed 90o arc to the plane of the two dimensions. Such a possibility severely strains the concept of what is "conventional", since most of us have been educated to think that nothing that is "real" can exist in only two dimensions. In this regard, we could also consider the hologram, the basic concept of which made little sense even fifty years ago. The reconstructed wave fronts of electromagnetic energy combine to yield a realistic, three-dimensional representation of reality. However, the coherent source(s) of luminous radiation can be extinguished, causing the hologram scene to suddenly disappear. What appeared to be present is suddenly no longer there. In a situation such as this, the application of logic alone may or may not account for such a perceptual experience, depending upon the set of initial assumptions that are made about the nature of reality.

Certainly it is illogical for objects that appear to possess solidity (that is, mass) to accelerate almost instantaneously or to disappear instantaneously. And it is highly unconventional for an aerial "object" to emit a luminous ray only a fixed distance from itself as if the ray were a solid object (medium?). Yet these kinds of phenomena are being reported with regularity.

By definition, logic is the science which investigates principles governing correct or reliable inferences about something. Yet to apply human logic implies that the same principles govern UFOs as govern our world. Until we understand the true nature of the core UFO phenomenon, it seems entirely reasonable to assume that everything within the universe obeys the same physical laws. But it is not logical to also believe that humans know everything possible about all of these physical laws; it is possible that the "core" UFO phenomenon simply obeys natural laws about which we know next to nothing.

Consequently, what approach might be followed in addition to logic and convention? Perhaps a type of "reverse logic" where all possible combinations of events surrounding the UFO phenomenon are systematically analyzed as if they represented a purposeful deception strategy on the part of another race of beings. [**14**] Or perhaps a deliberate analysis of all available data where the differences and not the similarities are considered; perhaps, as Dr. Jacobs has suggested (1976), we should take a new look at what makes UFO sightings different from each other. There may well be hidden within such diversity (heterogeneity, disparity, noncomformity) a certain key which will unlock the code cipher which has previously prevented us from seeing the phenomenon for what it really is.

■ "Close Scrutiny of all Available Evidence"

Perhaps the most frustrating of all aspects of the UFO phenomenon is its ethereal nature. Most UFO sightings are of the "I saw it but it rapidly flew away" variety. Many sightings are very short-lived; the serious UFO investigator is often left on the defensive, facing a derisive world that rightfully demands some proof. Thus, it is essential that all of the available evidence be studied, not just those portions of the evidence that are convenient to obtain and analyze or those features of the sighting in which one is personally interested. Such approaches are bound to overlook correlative evidence which could turn out to be critically related to a full understanding of the core phenomenon. Perhaps the UFO phenomenon represents the product of factors:

$$a : b : c : d : e : f : g = \text{UFO}$$

If this is the case, nothing less than a systematic comparison, correlation, and/or cataloguing of factors "a" through "g" will be required to understand the UFO. Perhaps the UFO phenomenon is represented by the relatively simple expression:

$$a : b : (d - e) / f : -g = \text{UFO}$$

If our individual analyses continue to ignore the possible relationships between the data points, as has been the case in the majority of analyses to date, we will never solve even the most simple "expressions" of the UFO phenomenon.

■ "Common Sense Identification"

To the previously discussed requirement that logic and convention be applied to our understanding of the UFO phenomenon is added the concept of common sense identification of the evidence by persons who are technically capable of making such identification. If the intent of this part of the definition is to urge the use of one's common sense as a first step in the interpretation of UFO data, then this is a reasonable criterion. But if common sense is to be the last (available) criterion, then we may inadvertently ignore evidence that seems to violate our common sense understanding of the world about us. Indeed, our scientific understanding of the nature of reality is still limited. Some have suggested that our ability to conceptualize the nature of reality is bounded by physical constructs such as the quantum efficiency "barrier", the speed of light "barrier", the conversion of energy "barrier", and so on. And, although these limits have been verified in many instances as being reliable representations of certain specific physical characteristics of nature, there may be other, more general, laws which transcend them and which are totally unknown to man. Because these so-called barriers have not yet been exceeded does not necessarily prove that they never will be.

Therefore common sense is not sufficient in and of itself for developing an adequately broad perspective on the UFO phenomenon. The basic rationale for making changes in this part of Hynek's definition is presented below:

■ 1. The fact that someone reports his perception of a UFO does not, and indeed cannot, determine whether the object or phenomenon that produced the perception existed in reality. Certainly the converse is also true, for many things exist that are never reported.

■ 2. The presence of a UFO need not be restricted to some visual apparition but might be experienced either through some other sense mode or, perhaps, even through an indirect or unconscious awareness of its presence. Many experts consider the visual sense to be the only true space perception sense mode and the visual characteristics of a UFO are often its predominant ones. Nevertheless, man's other sensory capabilities can also play an important role in the initial detection of a UFO and, later, in identifying particular characteristics it possessed. For instance, one can recognize certain odors long after the original olfactory experience has occurred. One might also recognize the sound made by a UFO well after the encounter.

■ 3. What is commonly considered to be "close scrutiny" of the UFO evidence needs to be critically re-examined. What may constitute a complete analysis of a UFO sighting report to the investigator performing the field research is seldom complete enough for the specialist who may attempt to discover such things as the credibility of the witness, the reliability of the data recorded, the degree of accuracy (variability) of the field measurements obtained, and many other objective and subjective events that surrounded the sighting. Thus, the degree to which a UFO report can be scrutinized "closely" - and, by the way, usefully - depends not only upon the training and practical experience of the field investigator but also upon the training, creativity, and practical experience of the specialists who analyze the data. The witness, field investigator, and specialist form a single, highly interrelated team, each member of which plays a supportive role in developing a complete and useful sighting report.

■ 4. Since our common sense is largely bounded by the state of current knowledge concerning the nature of reality, it should also be supplemented by human intuition, ie immediate insight and instinctive perceptivity on the part of all three members of the "team" discussed above.

Before we attempt to modify the definition of what constitutes a UFO, taking into account the points raised above, let us return to the first part of Hynek's definition, in order to introduce a second definition which has been offered by Jacques Vallée. Hynek states that a UFO is "the reported perception of an object or light..." Since it is the report that is usually analyzed and not the original event, the definition should emphasize this fact while at the same time allowing scientific studies to be conducted on the various phenomena that are experienced.

This is Vallée's definition of the UFO phenomenon: "*Manifestations of the UFO phenomenon are to be found among reports of the perception* of a visual image, commonly interpreted by the witness as that of a material flying object, which possesses either or both of the following properties: a) an appearance which, to the witness, is unusual; b) a behavior which, to the witness, is unusual." [13]

This definition emphasizes a particular aspect of all available UFO reports rather than concentrating upon the perceptual event. In the definition offered below, the italicized portion of Vallée's definition is incorporated in order to emphasize the fact that it is the UFO report and not the original experience that is usually analyzed. Both Hynek and Vallée should be congratulated for their contribution to UFOlogy in providing these definitions.

THE UFO REDEFINED

This is the definition of a UFO that results:

Manifestations of the UFO phenomenon are found among reports of the perception or indirect awareness of an object, light source, or presence of something in the sky, upon the land, or beneath the surface of a body of water, the appearance, trajectory, and general dynamic, luminescent, or reflective qualities of which do not suggest an explanation that conforms with current conventional or logical explanations and which remains unidentified after all evidence surrounding the sighting has been studied by technically capable persons, including the field investigator (involved in the case), who have applied both common sense identification as well as intuition to their analyses.

This definition may be found wanting. Hopefully, it will be useful to those who seek to separate the subject of UFOs from the many other bizarre aspects of nature.

REFERENCES

1 - Aerial Phenomenon Research Organization (APRO), undated public relations brochure.. ■ 2 - **Arnold**, K., and R. **Palmer**, *The coming of the Saucers*, Amherst, Wisconsin (private Publication), pg. 11, 1952. ■ 3 - **Flammonde**, P., *The Age of Flying Saucers*, Hawthorne, New York, pg. 5, 1971. ■ 4 - **Flammonde**, P., *UFO Exist!* Ballantine Books, New York, 1976. ■ 5 - **Gillmor**, D.S., (Ed.), *Scientific Study of Unidentified Flying Objects*, Bantam Books, New York, 1968. ■ 6 - **Haines**, R.F., *Observing UFOs*, Nelson-Hall, Chicago, 1980. ■ 7 - **Hendry**, A., *The UFO Handbook*, Doubleday & Co., New York, 1979. ■ 8 - **Hynek** J.A., *The UFO Experience - A Scientific Inquiry*, Ballantine Books, New York, 1972. ■ 9 - **Jacobs**, David, 'UFO research, the ETH, and other murky problems', *CUFOS Conference Proceedings*, 1976. ■ 10 - **Sanderson**, I.T., *Unidentified Visitors*, Cowles Education Corp., New York, pp. 8, 10, 1967. ■ 11 - **Story**, Ronald, *The Encyclopedia of UFOs*, 1980. ■ 12 - **US** Air Force, *Project Blue Book*, February 1 1966. ■ 13 - **Vallée**, Jacques, *Anatomy of a phenomenon*, Regnery, Chicago, 1965. ■ 14 - **Westrum**, Ronald, 'Question of deception by UFOs a possibility', in *Skylook*, June 1975.

3.3

INVESTIGATING THE UFO

by V.J Ballester Olmos

■ VICENTE-JUAN BALLESTER OLMOS. Born in Valencia, 1948. University qualifications include physics, industrial engineering & computer programming. Professionally he has 11 years experience in the auto industry and is currently Insurance & Benefits Manager for Ford, Spain. He is married with two small daughters; he is fond of Western country music and Jack Daniels whisky.

■ **UFO involvement**: Specialises in landing reports, and his main research activities are centred on the gathering, investigation, cataloguing, computer processing and statistical analysis of close encounter reports. Other interests include methodological issues - the application of the scientific method to aspects of the UFO problem, and the development of accurate techniques for field investigation. In 1982 he received a grant from FUFOR for the study of close encounter reports in Spain and Portugal, and in 1983 he shared with John Schuessler (NASA) the Alvin Lawson Award, as editor-in-chief of *UPIAR Research in Progress*, for his work in 'advancing a scientific understanding of the UFO phenomena.'

■ **Publications** include: with Jacques Vallee, *Type-1 phe-nomena in Spain & Portugal (Flying Saucer Review Special* no 4, 1971): *Catalogue of 200 Type-1 UFO events in Spain & Portugal* (CUFOS 1975): *OVNIS, el fenomeno aterrizaje* [UFOs, the landing phenomenon] (Plaza y Janes 1978): with Miguel Guasp, *Los OVNIS y la ciencia* [UFOs & science] (Plaza y Janes 1981): *Investigacion OVNI* [UFO investigation] (Plaza y Janes 1984): with Juan A Fernandez, *Enciclopedia de los encuentros cercanos con OVNIS* [Encyclopedia of close encounters with UFOs] (Plaza y Janes 1987): with Juan A Fernandez, *New catalogue of UFO landing reports in the Iberian peninsula* (FUFOR 1987).

■ **Address**: Guardia Civil, 9 / 46020 Valencia / Spain. Phone (home) 96-3613108 / (work, 08.30-17.00) 96-1791627.

'It may only be mysterious because we do not understand it.'

Fred Hoyle,
October the First is too late.

INTRODUCTION

It is an empirically-demonstrated fact that most alleged UFO observations derive from conventional stimuli (natural or man-made), subjective perceptions, or simple hoaxes. Hendry [1] has disclosed that during the nearly two years he was the chief investigator of the *Center for UFO Studies*, 88.6% of incoming reports were explained.

A recent study of mine, partially financed by a grant from the *Fund for UFO Research*, has centered exclusively on UFO landing events; it reveals that 60.7% of the cases under consideration received a satisfactory explanation. As a by-product of this work [2,3] I compiled a catalogue of 355 such 'negative' reports. The breakdown of causes is as follows:

- 31.2% **fictitious** (hoaxes, frauds).
- 25.1% **meteorological** (ball lightning, whirlwinds, ionisation, lightning effects).
- 13.5% **miscellaneous** (vehicles, fires, lights).
- 10.7% **mental** (hallucinations, illusions, psychological, psychopathological, hypnopompic / hypnagogic visions)
- 8.2% **astronomical** (planets, moon, stars, meteoroids).
- 7.1% **aeronautical** (balloons, aircraft, rockets, re-entries).
- 4.2% **biological** (misinterpreted people).

Two significant findings emerge from these figures:

■ We are surrounded by innumerable error-facilitating phenomena.

■ At least so far as landing cases are concerned, it is a myth that hoaxes and mystifications are rare; in fact they are the largest single category of IFO explanation.

The present paper has been developed on the basis of these findings, and aims to establish guidelines which may contribute to unbiased and more accurate UFO investigation. [4,5]

How can investigation be defined in the context of the UFO phenomenon? *UFO investigation ought to be the collecting, checking, analysis and diagnosis of information provided by percipient-narrators in regard to their alleged UFO experiences.*

INFORMATION COLLECTION

Information concerning alleged anomalous phenomena should be considered valid only when it is obtained directly from the witness. Press and other indirect accounts have limited weight and become valueless in the context of a rigorous, methodical UFO study. A face-to-face in-depth interview with the witness who refers the case is strictly necessary to compile objective data about the incident for further evaluation. Observation of some basic rules can lead to the acquisition of better quality information in field investigation.

An elementary principle in any UFO interrogation is that it must start with a request to the witness to tell what happened; in depth, fully and without interruption by the investigator.

Only when the story has been told in full should the witness be subjected to a long battery of questions - some of them standard, others specific to the particular event. It is at this stage that manuals come into force. The best aids for the questioning of UFO witnesses are those compiled by Basterfield [**6**], Fowler [**7**], Stanway & Randles [**8**]: these provide a quantity of appropriate questions, including specialised questionnaires appropriate to distinct types of UFO sighting. Further theoretical and analytical support may be found in the books of Haines [**9**] and Hendry [**1**].

The entire inquiry should be recorded on tape, with a view to subsequent transcription and study. It is essential that the material be published in some form, however limited the availability, for unpublished data has no value at all.

It is important that questioning be conducted with a neutral attitude. The literature of the psychology of eye-witness testimony makes it clear that leading questions, embodying response elements, influence the witness and affect his reply: clearly this must be strongly avoided. [**10**]

Where there are multiple witnesses, questioning must be conducted independently, to prevent mutual influence, and to obtain fresh, original accounts from each observer for purposes of comparison.

The written report should faithfully reflect the witness' mode of expression, be it scholarly or down-to-earth. Where a dialect or foreign language is used, the relevant descriptive terms should be included along with the literal translation.

The witness should be persuaded to make a sketch of what he saw, even if he demurs on grounds of having no artistic ability. The inclusion in the dossier of any such graphic representation, however naive, will serve as an indication of how much the investigator has embellished the observation in an artist impression or reconstruction.

The personality of the witness, together with his degree of familiarity with the UFO phenomenon, should be assessed. With regard to the former, a variety of psychological tests may be used, which can be supplemented by interviews with neighbours and others concerning the witness' reliability; it should go without saying that any such inquiry about the witness' reputation should be conducted with the utmost discretion, for ethical reasons. It is advisable to conduct some of the inquiry in the witness' own home, with a view to obtaining the reactions and opinions of other members of the family; in addition, this provides an opportunity to note the witness' reading habits; if they should indicate a preoccupation with UFOs or any other anomalous/occult matters, this could be very relevant to the assessment.

The necessity for an interdisciplinary research team for field work is self-evident. No such thing as the perfect investigator exists, due to the varied and complex nature of the UFO/IFO problem; consequently an investigation by a single individual, no matter how qualified he may be, will not cover the spectrum exhaustively and may be liable to error. Ideally, the investigation group should include on the one hand those who will assess the case from a natural science perspective (engineers, physicists, technicians) and on the other those trained in social disciplines (psychologists, psychiatrists, doctors).

A serious UFO inquiry is radically different from a mere journalist interview. In general, the journalist is not there to question the witness' story, simply to report it; the serious investigator, by contrast, will see it as his function to call in question not only the interpretation but even the reality of the account he hears.

After the initial data-collection, very often during the preparation of the case report, gaps or contradictions in the evidence will be noted. Such defects can be remedied only by a return visit, no matter how time-consuming this may be. A good field investigation may require several visits to the location; it may be questioned how many high-strangeness reports published in UFO journals adhere to these standards!

A BASIC PROCEDURE

A basic procedure for serious investigation should take into account the following items:

■ The witness

Full name; address; phone number; profession; birth date. Age, civil status and occupation at the time of the sighting (which may be different from that at the time of the interview). If multiple witnesses are involved, independent data are required for each, together with details of interrelationship or other links between them.

Knowledge of aeronautics, astronautics, astronomy, meteorology, etc; interest in UFOs, the occult, parapsychology etc.

Previous UFO experiences or other anomalous incidents. The witness' activities at the time of the sighting.

■ Time and place

Date; time of day; duration of event.

Exact location with map co-ordinates. Local orographical and hydrographical data.

Facilities in the area - airfields, military installations, power lines and stations, water, nuclear &c; reservoirs; mines and industries; railways.

■ Meteorological & visual conditions

Data to be acquired from witness and/or checked with local meteorological centres: weather conditions, sky status (cloud, humidity, rain, fog, wind); temperature; position of sun/moon; visibility (eg - were stars visible?), moon phase, etc. Physical obstacles inhibiting observation or blocking part of trajectory.

Optical aids employed, if any - details of magnification and other features. How good is witness' eyesight?

■ The phenomenon

Full description, verbal and graphic, including:

Appearance: solid, metallic, igneous, luminous, gaseous, transparent; edges well- or ill-defined; structural details and surface elements.

Colour, luminosity, brightness (compared with sun, moon, planet, headlight, etc); colour changes, fluctuations in luminosity etc. Description of light radiated and objects illuminated.

If photographs, film or video exists, the document should be borrowed for analysis, along with all relevant technical data on the apparatus, settings used, as well as caption circumstances.[**11**] Any other recorded data such as audio or radar?

Behaviour of object: emission of sparks, smoke, vapour and other substances; morphological changes of shape or size; sounds or smells (these should where possible be compared with known sources).

■ Dimensions and distances

Estimating UFO dimensions is a complex operation, yet it is of vital importance. First, it should be determined whether the witness was able to give a precise estimate thanks to a known frame of reference or obvious proximity. As estimating dimension can seldom be precise, it is advisable to obtain the *angular diameter* or apparent diameter.

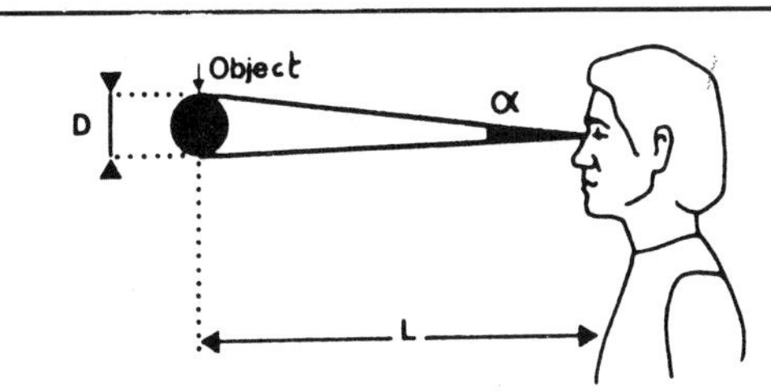

FIGURE 1.

Considering a spherical body [**Fig 1**] the angular diameter is the angle α subtended by that object to the witness' eye. In order to calculate its real diameter (D) we take the distance from the UFO to the observer (L) and apply the formula $D = L \times tg\alpha$. For small angles, where α is less than 20 degrees, we may use the formula $D \simeq L \times \alpha$. (D and L are measured in metres, α in radians (1 radian = approx 57 degrees).

The witness should be asked to extend his arm and say if in his estimation the object would be covered by the thumb (= approx 2 degrees) [**Fig 2**], closed fist (= approx 10 degrees) [**Fig 3**] or open hand (= approx 20 degrees) [**Fig 4**]. Alternatively, he may be asked to compare it with the moon (0.5 degrees angular diameter), a house, tree, car, star &c, which the investigator can use as a basis for comparison. Examples of indicative values are: a man of average height at 5 m = approx 20 degrees; an automobile at 25 m, or a football at 1.5 m = approx 10 degrees; a bus at 250 m = 2 degrees. [**12**]

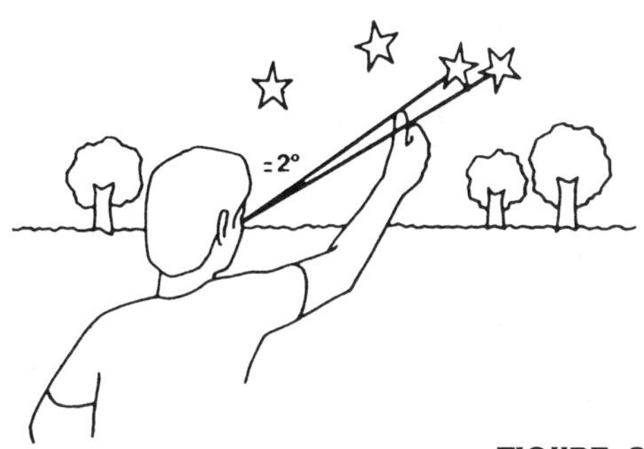

FIGURE 2.

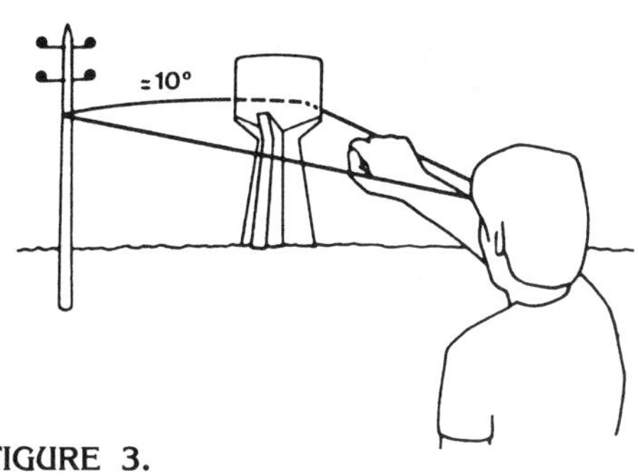

FIGURE 3.

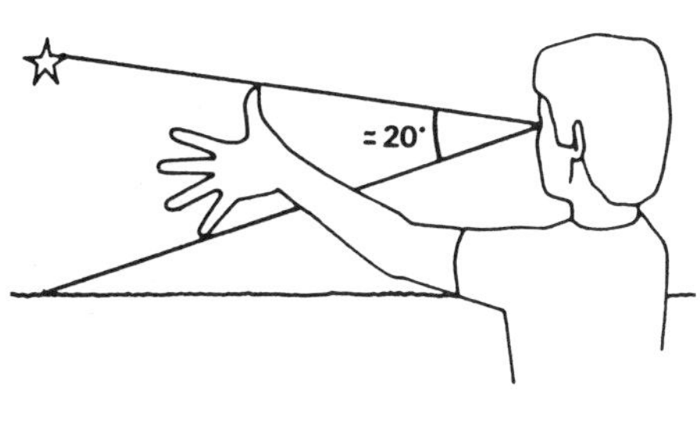

FIGURE 4.

The distance separating the object from the witness should also be ascertained if possible. Most probably this data can only serve in close encounter and landing cases: unaided estimate of this parameter for aerial phenomena is virtually useless due to its gross subjectivity. Elements in the landscape - hills, cottages, telephone poles, power lines etc - can be helpful, but accuracy of distance estimates deteriorate beyond 200 metres unless the witness is familiar with the area and the UFO is located unambiguously in relation to it.

In this context, the following elementary trigonometric formulae [see also **Fig 5**] may be relevant:

$$\text{sen}\ \alpha = \frac{h}{d}$$

$$\cos \alpha = \frac{L}{d}$$

$$\text{tg}\ \alpha = \frac{h}{L}$$

FIGURE 5.

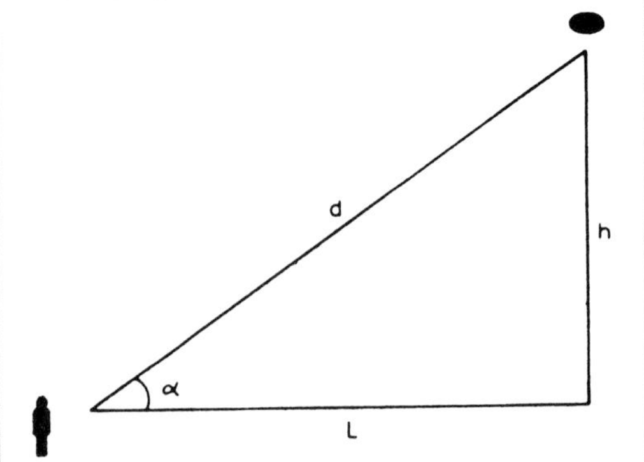

■ UFO dynamics

If several objects were seen, was there any flight configuration: was this formation comparable to the characteristics of military or commercial aircraft? If moving, a detailed account should be obtained - trajectory, changes in direction or altitude, cessation of movement. Estimates of speed should be compared with aircraft or meteors. Were dynamic data correlated with visual data - eg colour changes accompanying direction changes.

With the assistance of a simple scheme [**Fig 6**] the witness should indicate the dynamics of the UFO, supposing his position to be at 0; data regarding direction of appearance, movement and disappearance can be depicted in graphic form [**Fig 7**].

Data should include how the sighting commenced - was the object already there, did it manifest suddenly or slowly, was it ascending or descending; and how it terminated.

■ Effects & traces

Effects on people: if the witness experienced physiological or psychological effects during or following his experience, full details should be obtained and correlated with his general medical or mental background. Any *direct* connection between alleged body/mind effects and the UFO encounter should be explored and checked.

Effects on animals as response to the event should be noted. In the case of effects such as interference with electrical systems, radio or TV, engines, lights etc, full technical data on the equipment affected and the problems experienced should be compiled [**13**].

Ground traces should be accurately measured, including shape, dimensions and orientation. Photographs should be taken as early as possible,

FIGURE 6.

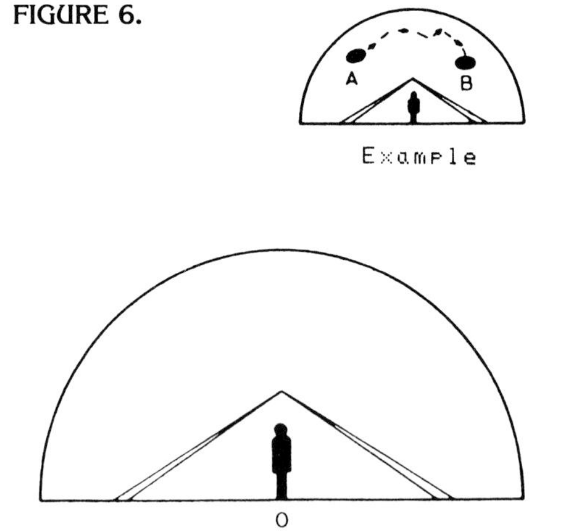

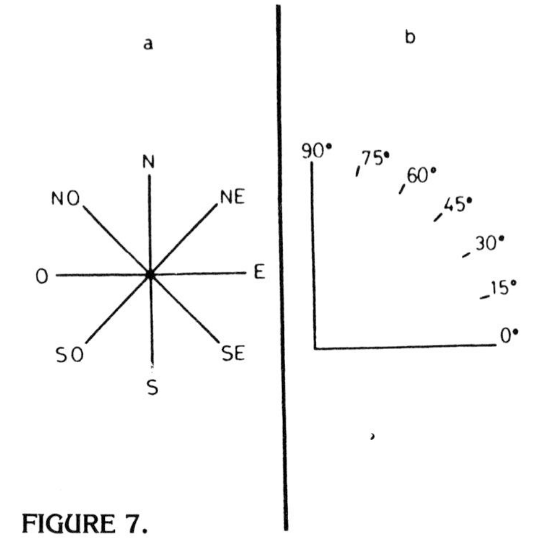

FIGURE 7.

including a ruler or some such reference item; a grid laid out on the terrain will facilitate accuracy. Radioactivity, temperature, pressure and other parameters should be measured. Where feasible, plaster casts should be taken of the imprints.

Soil samples from the traces should be collected for chemical analysis, together with control samples from nearby but unaffected areas. Vegetation which has been compressed, dehydrated, burned or otherwise affected should be photographed in situ, and samples obtained if feasible. Any deposit or material supposedly originating from the UFO should be collected if possible, at the least it must be thoroughly documented. Analysis of such samples will be a crucial item in the researcher's final report.

■ Occupants

Where apparently non-human entities are reported in the vicinity or in close association or actually emerging from/entering the UFO, a full description should comprise: number, appearance including anatomical features; clothing; equipment carried or used; distance from observer; actions and activities; nature of movement; duration of observation. Any associated smells, sounds - including of course communication. Alleged footprints; witness response.

Admittedly, these questions suggest science fiction. I do not wish to imply commitment to the ETH or any other hypothesis; but when witnesses claim to have observed entities in association with UFOs, it is our duty to collect all pertinent data, despite their improbable character.

INFORMATION CHECKING AND ANALYSIS

On-the-spot inquiry is essential for assessment and verification of the witness' narrative. Duplication of the event in real time will confirm or revise the time, duration and distance estimates provided by the witness; this in turn will provide a yardstick as to his overall reliability.

Search must be made for corroborative evidence, and particularly for additional witnesses. It can be very useful to talk to people living or working in the vicinity at the time of the incident.

If the field investigator's report has been well structured, this will facilitate critical analysis, leading to the detection of incongruities and incoherences in data, both internal or external to the report, such as a description of weather conditions which conflicts with the official weather report. Clearly, no witness report can be treated as factual; not that the narrator is necessarily lying, simply that there are so many factors helping to distort the sighting, so many processes and influences contributing to twist witness perception or memory, that to take a report at face value is intellectual suicide.

■ Evaluating witness subjectivity

In other publications [**4,14**] I have proposed a system for assessing the value of a UFO report in mathematical terms. Report co-ordinates are awarded objective measurements in order to establish a common standard. Three major dimensions of a report are defined and quantified - Information Quality; Strangeness; and Reliability. An algorithm linking these three parameters provides a *certitude index* for the case or group of cases under consideration.

I now propose a complementary system to quantify the *subjectivity* of a person reporting a UFO sighting. Based on a revised version of a proposal originating from GEPAN, it enables the degree of objectivity displayed in a given testimony to be evaluated. A subjectivity index (S) is defined for that purpose following four established criteria [**5**].

■ **CRITERIUM I** (CI): shows the level of consistency and coherence of the testimony. There must not appear any kind of internal or external incongruency or disagreement with data independent to the UFO information. There should not exist different versions of the incident narrated by the observer to distinct parties. The corresponding weights (W) are:

	Wi
Internal consistency of report	1
Lack of consistency	0
Unique version of event	1
Different versions	0

■ **CRITERIUM II** (CII): shows the personality and behaviour of the informant in relation to the event. Antecedent notoriety of the witness, interest in publicity or economical gain from the case, a significant inclination towards UFO or occult subjects, and prior sightings or anomalous experience:

	Wi
Antecedent notoriety	0
Lack of antecedents	1
Exploitation of UFO event	0
Lack of exploitation	1
Affection to the occult	0
Lack of affection	1
Other unusual experiences	0
No other experiences	1

■ **CRITERIUM III** (CIII): shows the impact of the UFO occurrence upon the percipient's belief system. Suspiciously, the experience may become a reinforcement mechanism to the observer's (positive or negative) personal beliefs about UFOs, or their nature and origin:

	Wi
Reinforcement of UFO beliefs	0
Absence, maintainance or change in beliefs	1

■ **CRITERIUM IV** (CIV): covers psychophysical and physiological aspects of the observer, including present or past neurological or mental illness, memory or perceptual disorders, etc; stressful family, emotional or labour relationships, including evidence of especially prolonged or unusual tensions or stress; and medical history, including drug usage or addiction with potential sensory counter-indications:

	Wi
Mental disorders	0
Lack of mental disorder	1
High stress	0
Lack of stress	1
Unusual medical history	0
Lack of unusual medical history	1

The maximum (M) and minimum (m) values that can be attained are:

	CI	**CII**	**CIII**	**CIV**	**Total**
M	2	4	1	3	10
m	0	0	0	0	0

The intrinsic valuation (v) of each set of criteria is not identical:

	Vi
CI	40%
CII	20%
CIII	10%
CIV	30%

These non-uniform percentages have been determined by the estimated specific weight of each criterium in the measurement of the human testimony.

■ The **Subjectevity Index** (S) formula is:

$$S = 1 - \left[\sum_{i=I}^{IV} \frac{P_i - m_i}{M_i - m_i} v_i \right]$$

where i = I, II, III, IV are the four described criteria; Wi is the weight or total value of each criterium; Mi and mi are the maximum and minimum possible values per criterioum; and vi is the valuation percentage or ratio of every criterium.

A more simple, developed version of the avobe formula is:

$$S = 1 - \left(0{,}2\,P_{I} + 0{,}05\,P_{II} + 0{,}1\,P_{III} + 0{,}1\,P_{IV}\right)$$

which indicates that the testimony subjectivity index is equal to the sum of the different relative weights of the involved criteria, properly adjusted by certain coefficients. The higher the value of S, the higher is the subjectivity of the information in question.

The index so obtained spans from 0 to 1 (0% – 100%). Only testimonies under 10% can be taken as *objective*, ie. testimonies which must be accepted by their scarce subjectivity. Over this figure, and up to 30%, cases seem normal but contain some elements casting *reasonable doubt* on the integrity of the testimony. Between 305 and 50% fall the testimonies which are uncertain and unreliable in both form and content, not conveying an external reality. Over 50% the testimony must be rejected, because there can be no confidence in its validity.

■ **The hypnosis tool**

Since the 1961 Hill case was publicised [**15**], and more heavily in recent years, hypnosis has been repeatedly used as a medium for witness memory recollection, particularly in alleged abduction cases.

Psychiatrist Martin Orne, an authority on hypnosis research, has stated that 'the technique may be helpful in the context of criminal investigation and under circumstances involving functional memory loss. Hypnosis has no utility to assure the truthfulness of statements since subjects may simulate hypnosis and are able to wilfully lie even in deep hypnosis; most troublesome, actual memories cannot be distinguished from confabulations either by the subject or by the hypnotist without full and independent corroboration.' [**16**]

It is evident that great caution must be exercised in the utilisation of hypnosis in the UFO context. Though considerable discussion has taken place on the matter, the only consensus is that the hypnosis itself should be carried out by a qualified and impartial professional. As regards the resulting information, it seems that it must always be regarded as doubtful. There is no longer any such thing as a virgin witness; everyone has been to some degree exposed to visual and verbal UFO documentation; at the same time, under hypnosis critical judgment diminishes, increasing the subject's suggestibility and rendering him more apt to respond to cues, conscious or unconscious, by the hypnotist. Pseudo-memories can be created in highly hypnotisable subjects, and enhanced recall under hypnosis is not free from errors [**17,18**]. It is not surprising, therefore, that in March 1982 the California Supreme Court concluded that 'hypnosis-induced testimony failed to meet a long-established legal standard requiring that scientific evidence be based on techniques generally accepted in the scientific community in which they were developed.' [**19**]

In the light of these shortcomings, the use of so uncertain a tool as hypnosis cannot be encouraged. If used, it should be under the most highly controlled conditions. Hendry [**1**] consulted three specialists in hypnosis, one psychologist and two doctors, and summarised their conclusions thus:

★ There is no total recall of the past under hypnosis, the subject may colour the output and the hypnotist can influence it.

★ It is possible to lie under hypnosis.

★ Abduction stories told under hypnosis may be subconscious fantasies.

★ If the subject 'lives' the experience displaying visible emotion - fear or anxiety - these signs probably confirm the reality of the narration.

Hypnosis by amateurs or by ufologists should be ruled out altogether, at the risk of jeopardising any potential the case might have possessed.

■ Instrumentation

The acquisition, verification and study of UFO-related data must progress from its present subjective state, where testing is rarely possible, towards more objective and consequently more reliable and systematic procedures. Ufologists should consider the scientific knowledge provided by such fields as meteorology, geophysics, atmospheric physics, microwaves, ultrasounds, ionisation phenomena &c, noting what instruments exist capable of application in UFO research, such as radiation monitoring [**20**], electric field detection [**21**] etc. UFO investigation will win scientific respect only when recorded data are available for laboratory testing.

The technology exists whereby investigators can benefit at every stage from field investigation to final analysis. Even on-site data gathering can benefit from elementary tools such as soil samplers, chemical reaction kits, sampling bags, water scoops etc. Also recommended are such instruments as a penetrometer, a portable survey meter and a goniometer.

INFORMATION DIAGNOSIS

We must proceed on the assumption that the human being is a fallible recorder, particularly when faced with unexpected and unknown events. No witness testimony can be taken at face value, because facts will inevitably, systematically be distorted or misrepresented. [**22**]

When all available information has been collected and organised methodically into a dossier, review can take place. The first step is to ask whether any natural phenomenon, manufactured object or mental process offers a configuration similar to the event as reported by the witness. If such a correlation exists, we may think it probable that the alleged UFO event is to be attributed to the same cause.

Even if no such similarity is evident at first sight, the investigator should still search for such an explanation before bestowing the UFO label on the case. A celestial planisphere and the astronomical ephemeris, for instance, have solved many aerial sightings... even alleged landings.

Ideally, an independent team should evaluate the inquiry and hunt for mundane explanations. The net end of any UFO investigation is to discover the truth, not to deceive oneself, though the effort may be laborious and often frustrating.

Only when the incident presents sufficient anomalistic aspects should it qualify for the UFO classification. Vague sightings cannot be classed as truly unidentified for no better reason than that the field investigator was unable to trace the stimulus that might have given rise to it. A UFO case must always have an *extraordinary* character to be classed as such: only high strangeness cases can seriously be considered as part of the UFO enigma, because they alone possess scientific potential.

A professional and scientific approach, such as that adopted by GEPAN [**23-27**], is the only route to follow if we are to establish the serious nature of our study and oppose those who abandon themselves to gullibility, blind beliefs and sensationalism.

REFERENCES

1 - **Hendry,** A., *The UFO Handbook. A Guide to Investigating, Evaluating and Reporting UFO Sightings*, Doubleday & Company, Inc., Garden City, New York, 1979. ■ **2** - **Ballester Olmos,** V.J. and **Fernández Peris,** J.A., *Enciclopedia de los encuentros cercanos con OVNIS* (Encyclopedia of the Close Encounters with UFOs), Plaza & Janes, S.A., Barcelona, 1987. ■ **3** - **Ballester Olmos,** V.J. and **Fernández Peris,** J.A., *New Catalogue of UFO Landing Reports in the Iberian Peninsula*, Fund for UFO Research, Maryland, 1987. ■ **4** - **Ballester Olmos,** V.J. and **Guasp,** M. *Los OVNIS y la Ciencia* (UFOs and Science), Plaza & Janes, S.A., Barcelona, 1981. ■ **5** - **Ballester Olmos** V.J., *Investigacion OVNI* (UFO Investigation), Plaza & Janes, S.A., Barcelona, 1984. ■ **6** - **Basterfield,** K., *Basic Investigator's Guide*, UFO Research, Australia, 1979. ■ **7** - **Fowler,** R.E. *MUFON Field Investigator's Manual*, MUFON, Seguin, Texas, 1975. ■ **8** - **Stanway,** R. and **Randles,** J., *UFO Investigation. A Field Investigator's Handbook*, BUFORA, Newchapel, 1979. ■ **9** - **Haines,** R.F., *Observing UFOs. An Investigative Handbook*, Nelson-Hall Inc. Publishers, Chicago, Illinois, 1980. ■ **10** - **Hilgard,** E.R. and **Loftus,** E.F., "Effective Interrogation of the Eyewitness", *The International Journal of Clinical and Experimental Hypnosis*, XXVII, 4, 1979, 342-357. ■ **11** - **Baker,** R.M.L., "Filming and Videotaping", *International UFO Reporter*, July-August 1984, 12. ■ **12** - *Le GEPAN et l'etude du phenomene OVNI*, CNES, Toulouse, 1979. ■ **13** - **Herr,** J.E., "Radio and Television Interference from UFOs", *The APRO Bulletin*, XXIX, 11, 3. ■ **14** - **Ballester Olmos,** V.J. and **Guasp,** M., "Standards in the Evaluation of UFO Reports", paper presented to the 1981 CUFOS Scientific Conference, Chicago, Illinois, September 25-27 1981. ■ **15** - **Fuller,** J.G., *The Interrupted Journey*, Dial Press, New York, 1966. ■ **16** - **Orne,** M.T., "The Use and Misuse of Hypnosis in Court", *The International Journal of Clinical and Experimental Hypnosis*, XXVII, 4, 1979, 311-341. ■ **17** - **Laurence,** J.-R. and **Perry,** C., "Hypnotically Created Memory Among Highly Hypnotizable Subjects", *Science*, 222, November 4 1983, 523-524. ■ **18** - **Dywan,** J. and **Bowers,** K., "The Use of Hypnosis to Enhance Recall", *Science*, 222, October 14 1983, 184-185. ■ **19** - **De Herrera,** J. "Resolving the Issue of Hypnosis", *The MUFON UFO Journal*, 175, September 1982, 15-17. ■ **20** - **Gupta,** J.P. and **Sachdev,** R.N., "A Microwave Radiation Monitor", *Journal of Applied Meteorology*, 15 September 1976, 1023-1025. ■ **21** - **Pontikis,** C., "Nouvel appareil de mesure du champ electrique de l'air", *La Meteorologie*, VI, 14, 1978, 37-41. ■ **22** - **Jimenez,** M., *Les phenomenes aerospatiaux non-identifies et la psychologie de la perception*, GEPAN Technical Note No 10, CNES, Toulouse, December 14 1981. ■ **23** - **Esterle,** A. *et al, Enquête 79/06*, GEPAN Technical Note No 8, CNES, Toulouse, October 26 1981. ■ **24** - **Besse,** Ph. *et al, Enquête 81/02*, GEPAN Technical Note No 11, CNES, Toulouse, March 8 1982. ■ **25** - **Audrerie,** D. and **Velasco,** J.J., *Enquêtes 81/07 et 81/09*, GEPAN Technical Note No 12, CNES, Toulouse, May 5 1982. ■ **26** - *Enquête 81/01. Analyse d'une trace*, GEPAN Technical note No 16, CNES, Toulouse, March 1 1983. ■ **27** - *Enquête 82/06, «L'Amarante»*, GEPAN Technical Note No 17, CNES, Toulouse, march 21 1983.

3.4.1

PHYSICAL TRACES

by Bill Chalker

■ **BILL CHALKER**. Graduated BSc with Honours from the University of New England, Armidale NSW, majoring in Physical and Inorganic Chemistry and Pure Mathematics. An industrial chemist by vocation, he currently works as a Quality Assurance Manager in the food industry. He lives in West Pennant Hills, Sydney, with his wife and their two sons.

■ **UFO involvement**: He was the first civilian researcher to gain access to the previously classified RAAF UFO files. He takes a special interest in physical trace cases, and co-ordinates the Australian Physical Evidence Study Group. He is a scientific consultant for the Australian Centre of UFO Studies, Australian representative for APRO, NSW state representative for MUFON, and Director of UFO Research for NSW.

'His aims are to isolate a large quantity of high quality information about "high strangeness" cases for the purpose of attracting scientists into supporting a sophisticated rapid intervention group programme.' He would also like to see the UFO phenomenon elevated to 'repeatable experiment' status in hope that this will bring the study of UFOs into the area of direct experimentation.

■ **Publications**: He has published extensively in UFO journals, including *FSR, MUFON UFO Journal, APRO Bulletin, International UFO Reporter* (for which he is contributing editor) and *UFO Research Australia Newsletter.*

■ **Address**: PO Box 6, Lane Cove / NSW 2066 / Australia.

Particularly since the sixties, we have seen increasing interest in a range of events that appear to substantiate the contention that UFOs possess a physical dimension. These events are collectively referred to as "physical trace" cases, defined by "those UFO cases in which definite physical changes in the immediate vicinity of a UFO sighting have been reported: marks and surface changes on the ground, damage to vegetation, residues and/or artifacts found and surface effects of some duration on buildings and vehicles." [**1**]

Although they can be extremely varied, the following "physical trace" types [**after Phillips 2,3,4**] have been reported:

■ PRIMARY EFFECTS

a) **Circular Sites**: with damage over the entire are - burned, depressed or dehydrated.
b) **Rings**: burned, depressed or dehydrated.
c) **Irregular Sites**: no particular pattern - burned, depressed or dehydrated.
d) "**Nests**": oval traces, generally depressed, with swirling effect.

■ SECONDARY EFFECTS

a) **Imprints**.
b) **Damage** to trees and other large flora.
c) **Craters**.
d) **Footprints**.
e) Plants or soil **removed**.

■ RESIDUES

Solids, powder, and liquid, including filaments and occasionally artifacts (ie alleged pieces of UFO itself).

The simple premise behind interest in this range of events is that we have something tangible to examine. Ted Phillips, a leading specialist in trace cases, writes "If UFOs are not available for study in the laboratory, physical traces certainly are". [**5**]

Witnesses reporting these sorts of events are certain that they have encountered a real phenomenon. The vexing issue for researchers is whether or not we can substantiate this consensus of UFO reality.

THE PHYSICAL TRACE EXPERIENCE TO DATE

The entire course of theoretical speculation since 1947 has pivoted about the critical question of UFO reality.

Artifact traces loomed large at the very beginning of the modern popularisation of the UFO mystery in the hoary guise of the Scully hoax. The book "Behind the Flying Saucers" [**6**] served to discredit the idea of retrieval of crashed UFOs until researchers like Stringfield [**7**] and Moore [**8**] led a resurrection of fascination with tales of the "ultimate" physical trace. The controversy about "crashed UFOs" continues unresolved. [**9**]

The notorious Maury Island fragments ushered in the flying saucer era, but fell far short as evidence.

Indeed the affair is widely regarded as a hoax - both a tragic and complex one. [**10**]

During the fifties and early sixties, landing reports, particularly those that involved "beings", did not get much of a hearing. Officially most were rejected without investigation. Such an approach may have been justified in the face of the contactee tales, but quite a few, somewhat more reasonable "landing" cases were caught up in this culling exercise. [**11**] Captain Edward Ruppelt, head of the USAF Project Blue Book from 1952 to 1953, stated "We had never picked up any 'hardware' - any whole saucers, pieces, or parts - that couldn't be readily identified as being something very earthly. The tar covered marble, aluminium broom handle, cow manure, slag, pieces of plastic balloon, and the what-have-you that we did receive and analyse only served to give the people in our Material Lab some practice and added nothing but laughs to the UFO project". [**12**]

One case - which Ruppelt tentatively labelled "The Best Hoax in UFO History" because it couldn't be explained - made official investigators ponder the "physical trace" question. The case of the Florida scout-master story was controversial. [**13**] "In the scout-master's favour were the two pieces of physical evidence we couldn't explain, the holes burned in the cap and the charred grass roots." [**14**] Recently, Jenny Randles argued "it is rather easier to believe that this was not a hoax than to believe that it was." [**15**]

Less than a month after the scout-master affair, perhaps the most frightening case of an encounter with a "UFO creature" allegedly occurred. [**16**] In the wake of the bizarre events near Flatwoods, West Virginia, on September 12 1952, physical traces were found, but, like so much tangible evidence, they were not documented to any satisfactory extent. [**17**] Investigations were undertaken but the reported physical traces were largely overlooked or superficially rationalised as having prosaic explanations. [**18,19**]

The 1954 wave, mainly centred in France during September and October, featured a number of interesting "physical trace" cases. Quarouble (Sept.10th), Chabeuil (Sept.26th), Premanon (Sept.27th) and Poncy-sur-L'Ignon (Oct.4th) are all "classics". [**20**] However, there has been considerable debate about the legitimacy of the 1954 wave. Barthel and Brucker argued that in many cases prosaic explanations, hoaxes, fraud and deliberate media manipulations were the causes. They argue that Premanon is identified and likewise, but less convincingly, Quarouble is dismissed. [**21**]

French UFO researchers of the "socio-psychological" school (ie *all* UFO reports are potentially reducible to either hoaxes or outright hallucinations, or misperception of prosaic things) [**22**] argue that the 29 reported trace cases in France during the period September-October 1954 are reducible in the following manner: "13 are well explained, 6 are doubtful, 10 cases remain, but only one (Chabeuil, 26 Sept.1954) or perhaps 2 (Chabeuil and Poncy-sur-L'Ignon, 4 Oct.) are sound. [**23**] At the time, though, the 1954 wave championed the reality of both the "physical" UFO landing phenomenon and the UFO entity enigma [**24,25,26**]. For example, Michel wrote of samples from the Poncy-sur-L'Ignon "trace" - "this morsel of earth knew the secret of the most mystifying event of the century or the most fantastic in all history." [**24**]

The extraordinary 1957 wave in the United States re-stated that perception of UFO "reality". The fascinating "electromagnetic" milieu of November 2-3 1957 centred around Levelland, Texas, has endured as an impressive argument for a "physical" phenomenon, [**27**] while the Olden Moore UFO landing event at Montville, Ohio, with holes, footprints and radioactivity cited as physical trace evidence, encouraged APRO to state that "a foreign object landed in that field." [**28**]

The Project Blue Book report of a USAF First Lieutenant, of November 23 1957, near Tonopah, Nevada, emphasises this position. That case involved 4 UFOs on the ground, an "EM" car stop and imprints on the ground consistent with "landing gear" ostensibly observed. It is a classic case, but one that the USAF put down to "psychological" causes (road hypnosis) despite an alleged duration of some 20 minutes. [**29**]

The classic artifact case (solid residue) also took place in 1957, the Ubatuba fragment affair, which APRO reported to be unusually high purity magnesium. [**30**] Subsequent analyses confirmed this finding, but the nature of the small amount of impurities has failed to eliminate totally the possibility of prosaic origins. [**31**] Recent investigations confirm that the isotope ratios are not inconsistent with terrestrial origin and possible prosaic sources have been suggested. [**32**] The Brazilian artifacts still command considerable attention and, at the very least, stand as one of the most thoroughly studied "UFO fragments" on record.

Less well known, but nevertheless interesting, is the Väddö case from Sweden in which two witnesses recovered an artifact from the site of a UFO landing near Väddö on November 9th 1958. The artifact turned out to be metallic, consisting of tungsten carbide, cobalt and a few traces of titanium. Although possibly of prosaic origin it was found immediately after the alleged UFO event at the site of the "landing" where a ground trace was also in evidence. The artifact was originally warm to touch; therefore leaving open a further zone of enquiry. [**33**]

During October 1959, at Mariannelund, Sinaland, Sweden, Gideon Johansson and his family witnessed an extraordinary CE3 event that also featured damage to a maple tree and a glassy deposit-type precipitate on power lines. The tree damage was caused when the UFO collided with it. EM and physiological effects were also reported. [**34**]

In 1961, the concept of a 'UFO" was still now known in Romania; however, this fact was irrelevant to Emanoil Manoliu, the son-in-law of the famous Rumanian writer, Mihail Sadoveanu. From the Neamt monastery, Manoliu observed a disc-shaped object above a hill by a nearby lake. It vanished with an extraordinary rush of air. The witness visited the presumed landing site with a priest, and found that "the grass had been singed and there was a light imprint in the soil, as if made by a hard object." [**35**]

On October 21st 1963, near Trancas in Argentina, effects were reported on carob trees and innumerable small white balls found forming a perfect cone 1 m high, inside a 10 m circle. The balls consisted largely of calcium carbonate. The traces were found on ground over which one of the UFOs had hovered. [**36**]

The Socorro case of April 24 1964, [described in section 2.3.5], has yet to be satisfactorily resolved as a bona fide UFO [**37**], a hoax [**38**], a secret experimental craft [**39**], or some other explanation. Four "leg" imprints and scorched foliage were found. Dr James E McDonald was advised of analyses of "fused sand", scorched flora and a few organic materials they couldn't identify." [**40**] Ray Stanford alleges that a NASA scientist advised him that the material was a zinc-iron alloy, previously unknown. The findings were subsequently denied, but Stanford disputes the official account. [**41**]

In August 1964, at Kallavesi Lake, Finland, Raimo Blomqvist claims he saw a UFO approach and hover near him. A small fragment was allegedly observed falling from the object into the shallow water on the lake's edge. The UFO then sped off. Blomqvist retrieved the fragment from the 20 cm-deep water. The 36 mm-long artifact was found to be mostly made up of iron oxide and a range of trace elements. X-ray analysis was undertaken at Abo Akademi University, where Prof. Edelman indicated it was "definitely not a geological entity", but "that material of this sort could be found close to active volcanoes, but only at a couple of locations in the world." Prof. Papunen at Turku University ruled out a meteor explanation, indicating that the amount and type of trace elements were not found in iron meteorites. UFO Research of Finland concluded, "the fragment is not a piece of ore, not of volcanic origin, not a meteoroid, and not a piece of any known machine." [**41a**]

Maurice Masse's paralysing experience at Valensole, France, on July 1st 1965, with lavender 'thieves' and a UFO, involved a cylindrical-shaped hole which formed the centre of a cross made up of 4 shallow grooves. [**42**] A French gendarmerie spokesman was quoted, "We've established the reality of the landing. There were landing gear impressions on the soil." [**43**]

Stephen Michalak claimed that at Falcon Lake, Manitoba, on May 20th 1967, he not only witnessed a UFO landing, but also touched it and sustained an array of injuries as a consequence. The site of the long-duration UFO landing also revealed a range of physical trace evidence, consisting of a ring of loose soil containing a bare patch of rock. [**44**] The affair was a controversial one, with the USAF Condon report indicating "many inconsistencies and incongruities" and finally concluding "This case does not offer probative information regarding unconventional craft." [**45**] Further investigations have failed to unambiguously resolve the case. [**46**]

In the same month, a French Foreign Legion reconnaissance group on Madagascar witnessed a UFO landing in daylight. The soldiers were paralysed until the UFO took off. However, 2¾ hours had passed without the witnesses perceiving it! The object left behind 3 marks on the ground set in a triangle. In the middle was a charred crater 3 m deep, with "some crystals of all colours, like bits of broken glass" at the base. [**46a**]

During the night of July 20th 1968, at a Soviet youth summer camp at Lake Kaarna, near Otepaa in Estonia, three students witnessed a UFO on the ground. After 5 minutes it disappeared. A student who went to investigate, saw a small human-shaped figure standing where the object had been. The figure "vanished suddenly into the air." At the site a 2 m "burnt" spot was found with 4 imprints around it. [**47**]

Within a period of 10 days during June 1969, two landings with physical traces allegedly occurred in the Ibiuna area of Brazil. On June 17, the lengthy observation of an unidentified "window" display led to the discovery of an 8 m anti-clockwise "nest" of swirled vegetation. A 6 m-wide anti-clockwise "nest" was confirmed at the site of a brief landing and take-off of a UFO witnessed by a local Justice of the Peace on June 26th. [**48**]

During the first half of 1971, Finland experienced a major UFO 'flap', including some interesting trace events. The Lake Saapunki UFO of January 3rd left behind green ice and other residues. Conflicting and inconclusive results failed to resolve the mystery, although it was concluded that the phenomenon "brought some particles to the spot, it created heat by some form of radiation, its brightness was tremendous." [**49**] Further, "the anaylsis suggests that something material made the depression and most definitely also left physical evidence of its visit." [**50**]

On February 5th 1971, 2 woodsmen working at Kinnula, Finland, observed a UFO land and witnessed a 'humanoid'. Petter Aliranta got close enough to touch the heel of the entity as it 'floated' back into the object. Aliranta had to let go, as it felt like he had touched a hot iron. He sustained an injury to his hand. After the UFO departed, 4 imprints were found consistent with where the 4 legs of the UFO had rested. [**51**]

During March 1971, a coastal artillery fort at Kuuskajaskari was brought to a full alert after a guard had observed a UFO landing. A subsequent patrol found a 5-7 m depression. [**52**]

The final trace event of interest in the 1971 Finnish 'flap' was at Lappi in May; after a UFO was observed landing, 3 holes were found in the snow and a black substance was found. No conclusive analyses were reported. [**53**]

During the same month, at least 2 independent witnesses saw a UFO sitting on 3 legs in a shallow hollow in a field at Stara Cerkew, near Kocevje, Yugoslavia. Alojz Krz claimed he observed the object from as close as 20 m. It frightened him considerably. At least half an hour later, 17-year-old Angela Rajhs came upon the object. She watched it for 4 to 5 minutes before beginning to cycle away. The UFO took off at this stage, turning in a wide spiral as it rose. The young woman and her parents returned to the spot the next day and found marks on the ground - "pointed" holes 15-20 cm in diameter. "The grass round about seemed to be burnt."

Among the best known and most controversial trace cases involved an illuminated, hovering UFO at Delphos, Kansas, on 2 November 1971 [narrated in shapter 2.3.10]. While many parties got involved, and some provided interesting results [**55 through 67**], in almost all cases the line of information was terminated. One of the few scientists to persist was Dr Erol Faruk, an organic chemist who carried out the analysis at a university in England. He found that 'the information obtained from the soil analysis can in fact be assembled together in a way that leads to a scenario fitting exceedingly well with the sighting report.' It accounts for the alleged temporary luminescence, the white 'blistered effect' on the ring surface, the soil hydrophobicity [**67a**], the ring elongation in the wind direction, the alleged initial moistness of the ring soil and the reported anaesthetic effects.

Some of Faruk's findings are consistent with a 'fairy ring' explanation, but he has clearly revitalised the debate on this controversial case by reducing the options to two: the Delphos ring has 'either got to be of biological origin, something like a fungal ring, or it's got to be an authentic case." [**68**]

The controversy over the case continues, fuelled by possible time anomalies and post-sighting experiences of witness Ronnie Johnson [**69**]. Legitimate UFO events or not, Delphos still serves as a catalyst for a maturing interest in physical trace cases.

A remarkable trace report, even including a shoot-out, occurred on 26 June 1972 when a UFO which appeared at Fort Beaufort in South Africa got a hot reception from the locals. A daylight sojourn of more than 4 hours, punctuated by some 15 rifle shots from farmer Bennie Smit and two policemen, ended when the small UFO disappeared into thick 'impenetrable' bush, where the seven witnesses could hear it crashing through the undergrowth. They followed; and though they could find no sign of the UFO or of its passage through the thicket, other traces were found. [**70**] Nine circular 'fist-like' imprints, 7 cm in diameter, were found arranged in sets of three. Analysis of samples indicated that 'if a foreign object had come into contact with the samples, it certainly did so without disturbing its composition in any way." Cynthia Hind concluded:

The wrecked tennis court at Rosemead - on baffling incident from the 1972 South African wave. [Cynthia Hind, *African encounters*]

"the Fort Beaufort UFO still remains unidentified and as puzzling an object as it was at the time of its first appearance." [**71**]

A number of other trace events featured in the 1972 South African wave, including an incident that involved damage to a tennis court at Rosmead. [**72**]

An array of physical traces were found in the wake of a spectacular UFO landing event at Columbia, Missouri, on June 28 1973. The incident involved a brightly-glowing circular object approaching a mobile home. Electrical power was affected, a large tree limb fell down, numerous imprints were found and leaves were found brown and wilted at the site. [**73**] Ted Phillips stated "analysis has given us no real indication of what caused the dehydration of the leaves, other than possibly heat. We were not able to do anything with the imprints because they were substantially deteriorated." [**74**]

Near Langenburg, Saskatchewan, Canada, on September 1st 1974, farmer Edwin Fuhr, while engaged in daytime wheatfield swathing, saw a metal dome apparently sitting in the grassy field. He approached on foot to within 5 m and saw that the grass around the base of the object was moving and the object was spinning at a high rate. Fuhr quickly returned to the swather. From that higher vantage point, he was able to make out four more identical domes in the field. After several minutes, the objects suddenly rose into the air in a step formation, hovered for 1 to 2 minutes, then suddenly ascended into low cloud and disappeared. Fuhr found 5 rings of grass each flattened clockwise. Four of the rings were 3 - 4 m in diameter and one 2 - 3 m. A week later a further ring was found, and yet another 3 nights later, completing a pattern in the traces found till then, namely a circle of rings. Analyses of samples did not indicate anything unusual. [**75**]

Two separate trace cases occurred in Spain during January 1975 - at Quintangortuno, involving army witnesses, and at Las Bardenas, possibly involving the Air Force. [**76**] The extraordinary Stonehenge apartment events of January 12th, in which a CE3 episode took place just across the Hudson river from Manhattan, also featured a number of imprints (12 - 15 small triangular spots). [**77**]

The physical trace found in the wake of a UFO landing at Medford, Minnesota, on November 2 1975, is an important one, particularly because of the nature of the analytical follow-up. Dr Edward Zeller, Professor of Geology, Physics and Astronomy at the University of Kansas, Radiation Physics Division, Space Technology Laboratory, undertook thermo-luminescence testing of samples for radiation. 'Some of the samples show almost ten times the amount of luminescence that other do and that's unusual. We wouldn't expect that level of variability in soil samples that under the microscope look very similar. The Medford site samples looked to be quite uniform initially, and therefore we would expect them to have similar luminescent properties. We find large-scale variation in the glow curves, but no large-scale variation in the microscopic appearance of the samples. The only thing we can say is that these high-variability conditions are unusual. Exactly what they mean, I can't tell you." [**78**] Dr Zeller concluded, "Like so much of the other data which has been obtained on the UFO phenomenon, the results of the thermo-luminescence studies on the Medford case are inconclusive. An anomaly seems to exist between the expected natural order of things and the observed relationships. Unfortunately, inadequate information is at hand and convincing proof of the cause of the anomaly cannot be obtained." [**79**]

"The most important spot on our planet may be a remote ranch deep in the Uruguayan outback. According to local ranchers, police and residents in nearby towns, more than 70 UFOs have landed at this ranch..." [**80**] So wrote Bob Van Der Velde in the APRO Bulletin, of his investigations into the extra-ordinary procession of physical trace evidence played out on the La Aurora estancia, south of Salto, Uruguay, where the disturbing death of the owner's dog, Topo, was linked to a UFO close encounter. [**81**] A startling array of physical and physiological effects have been reported over more than a 5-year period, of which the "Aurora Circles" are the most persistent evidence. They vary from 7-30 m in diameter, each generally being "a large circle on the ground where the grass had been burned away, then had grown back much greener than the surrounding grass. In each circle there were 3 impressions, forming a triangle, as if they had been formed by pod-shaped landing gear. In these impressions no grass had grown back..." [**82**] The Uruguayan army had taken an interest, installing "Danger - Radioactive Area" signs at various locations. Van Der Velde wrote, "For sheer numbers of UFO sightings, La Aurora certainly has any other location in the world beat hands down. And almost all are multiple-witness sightings by highly reputable people." Hoaxing, Van Der Velde states, "is possible, but unlikely. It is possible because we saw not one single piece of evidence that could not have been manufactured." [**83**] La Aurora could certainly benefit from an extensive scientific enquiry.

At Gaberke, Yugoslavia, on February 11th 1977, in the wake of the departure of an egg-shaped UFO, five imprints were found at the presumed landing site. "Glimmering dust" found at the location turned out to be a common mica. No conclusive evidence was found of any significant anomalies in the traces. [**84**]

At the Sturgell family property, near Jenkins, Missouri, on October 8th 1978, something was seen in a field near the house by various family members over a 2-hour period. That "something" became the centre of attention when it rose off the ground: six people observed it moving away. After 5 to 10 minutes, it seemed to converge on a second object and simultaneously disappeared. At the site of the "landing", a 1.3 m circle of "scorched" grass was found. Inside this area, there were three smaller circles. Dr Zeller found no evidence of radiation or heating in samples provided by Ted Phillips. Further testing by other laboratories also indicated no anomalies. [**85**] Phillips said of the case, "This report is listed in the high-strangeness trace reports, considering the credibility and numbers of witnesses, daylight observation, duration of sighting, distance between the UFO and witnesses, and the traces. This is one of the best." [**86**]

Scottish forestry worker Bob Taylor was the subject of an apparent 'physical assault' by UFOs near Livingston, Scotland on November 9th 1979. In the wake of his encounter with a strange domed object in a forest clearing, and an attack by 2 small spheres with protruding "spikes" that left him unconscious, physical traces were found at the site. The ground traces consisted of 2 parallel 'tracks' about 3 m long and 3 m apart, and many holes, each about 10 cm across. [**87**] X-ray fluorescence studies by Dr Colin Farrow, along with further tests by the Physical Data Section of BUFORA, all failed to reveal any differences between samples from the site and nearby control areas. No explanation has been determined for the case, but Scottish researcher Steuart Campbell has hypothesised an encounter with a rare and extraordinary form of 'black ball lightning'. [**88**] [He has since altered his opinion to an astronomical explanation.] Objective evaluation suggests that a real physical event may have taken place involving ostensibly extraordinary structured objects.

On January 9th 1981 occurred a case which in one sense marked the coming-of-age of the physical trace experience: an extensive scientific investigation was undertaken of a UFO landing case, and some intriguing anomalies were found by the official French UFO agency GEPAN. The witness, Renato Nicolai, saw a UFO land briefly in the grounds of his residence near Draguignan, Trans-en-Provence, in the south of France. The UFO left behind a 2.4-metre ring consisting of a 0.1-metre-wide annulus.

While the sighting itself was not all that remarkable, the quality of the investigative and analytical follow-up was impressive. GEPAN's parent organisation, CNES, the French equivalent of NASA, undertook analyses in its laboratories. Further testing was undertaken at the SNEAP lab, at laboratories of universities in Toulouse, Metz, Pau and Rangueill, and at the biochemical laboratory of the National Institute of Agronomy Research.

Here for the first time was a government UFO agency publishing extraordinary results about a UFO landing case. Dr Bounias' biochemical studies at d'Avignon-Montfavet indicated that young leaves from plants in the immediate vicinity of the landing site "withstood the most serious losses, evolving toward the content and composition more characteristic of old leaves." The chlorophyll pigment in the samples was weakened between 30 to 50 per cent. Attempts to duplicate the changes were unsuccessful; however, the GEPAN report on the case indicated "it could be tied to the action of some type of electric energy field." Further, the report stated, "It was possible to qualitatively show the occurrence of an important event which brought with it deformations of the terrain caused by mass, mechanics, a heating effect and perhaps certain transformations and deposits of trace minerals."

GEPAN concluded that the information gleaned from the study of the incident was "another confirmation of a very significant event which happened on this spot." "This GEPAN investigation is the most enriching of all those made up to the present." [**89**] [The case and its investigation have, however, come under serious criticism from other French organisations.-Ed.]

At Ross, Ohio, on April 10th 1983, 2 separate motorists experienced possible "EM" effects while observing a UFO. Ostensibly at the same time, the primary witness to the subsequent UFO landing first experienced household "EM" effects and disturbances with his dog. He observed a strange light display in an adjacent field. As the witness was about to call police, the light source began to rise, until at altitude it "suddenly took off like a jet aircraft." It left behind a 15 m-diameter circle, with a 1 m burned area in the middle. A range of laboratory tests failed to give any significant results. [**90**]

A thoroughly disconcerting case occurred at Varzi, Italy, on June 5 1983. At least 3 people saw a UFO take off from a nearby field of tall alfalfa. Two of the witnesses saw an unidentified man approach the UFO while it was on the ground! He was then seen fleeing, whereupon the UFO rose up slowly and then grazed along the field some 1 - 2 m above the alfalfa before rising vertically, hovering momentarily, and finally picking up speed and height and departing. Ostensibly, at the site the alfalfa appeared to be crushed in a circular area some 2 - 3 m in diameter, with whitish "mist" or "ashes" all around. Unfortunately, next day the alfalfa crop was cut, and by the time investigators arrived 5 days later there were no noteworthy features at the site. If we had the benefit of the "witness" who got within metres of the UFO on the ground, and had the trace survived for detailed analyses, the Varzi landing would have been all the more remarkable. [**91a**]

Also in Italy, farmer Guiseppe Cocozza encountered a hairy, helmeted entity in an alfalfa field at Lapazzita on October 8th 1984. As he retreated, the farmer saw the figure itself move away with "sparks" coming from either side of its body. The entity disappeared behind a hazel bush. About a minute later, a box-shaped UFO rose from the ground. At an altitude of about 600 m, it made an acute-angle turn and headed off towards the nearby mountain range. Signor Cocozza found numerous long hoof-like prints and a number of holes, all ostensibly made by the entity. In a clearing among hazel bushes, further imprints were located that were linked to the UFO landing. They included 2 elliptical marks 2.3 metres apart, and 6 roughly cylindrical holes all terminating in truncated cones. One of the investigating groups concluded from measurements at the site that the UFO may have weighed nearly one metric ton and that "a physical phenomenon of an unknown nature did indeed occur at Lapazzita." **[91b]**

This brief international survey shows that the physical trace phenomenon is an enduring aspect of the UFO mystery, having manifested for the entire duration of the modern era of the UFO controversy. And like the UFO phenomenon itself, it is global in its extent.

Fortunately there are a growing number of researchers specialising in the area of UFO physical trace cases. Ted Phillips, with the publication of his *Physical Traces associated with UFO sightings - A preliminary catalogue* in 1975, focused attention on this aspect of UFO research. **[92]** Now more than a decade later his original data-base of 561 reports has mushroomed into more than 3,000 reports. **[93]** Vincente-Ballester Olmos, one of Spain's leading UFO researchers, has addressed the question of trace cases on the Iberian peninsula. **[94]** Maurizio Verga has undertaken excellent work in his studies of Italian physical trace cases. **[95]** Jacques Bonabot **[96]** and Wim Van Utrecht **[97]** have published work on Belgian trace events.

It is time that this sort of excellent work is replicated in many more countries. This work has already begun in some, but there is a long way to go. Now is the time for co-ordinated international research aimed at refining and improving our physical trace data-base.

THE AUSTRALIAN PHYSICAL TRACE EXPERIENCE

For many years I have undertaken a specialised study of physical trace cases in Australia. **[98]**

In 1979 I presented a study of 237 accounts of Australian "physical traces." **[99]** These accounts were broken down into the following types in **Table 1** (below):

Type I: Physical trace with probative UFO correlation. (13.9%)
Type II: Physical trace with possible UFO correlation. (19.4%)
Type III: Physical trace of apparent/possible natural origin with possible UFO correlation. (1.7%)
Type IV: Physial trace with possible unusual phenomenological correlation. (11.4%)
Type V: Physical trace of probable or apparent natural origin. (16.5%)
Type VI: Physical trace of probable spurious, hoax or doubtful origin. (4.6%)
NEI: Physical trace with paucity of related information. (24.9%)
Other: Physical trace which by its apparent nature prevents any confident categorisation. (7.6%)

Table 1: Types of physical traces.

Clearly the high percentage of accounts for which there was not enough information (24.9%) is an indicator of the UFO controversy at large. Combined with Type V events, some 41.4% (or 98 out of 237 cases) are of limited merit. Only Types I, II, III and IV (44.7%) were considered to be of real merit. Types V and VI served to calibrate the data.

Apart from the flap of 1954, the year of 1966 saw the first real UFO wave of significance in Australia. The term "nest" entered popular parlance with the Tully area flap. George Pedley's experience and the "nests" discovered on Horseshoe Lagoon rightly became classics of the "nest" genre. **[100]** Victoria, however, took the centre stage with the incidents at Burkes Flat **[101]** and Clayton. The former, which may have involved a related fatality, is indicative of unidentified phenomena on a more probative level, with apparent perturbations of light and interaction with the soil at the site of the incident. The Clayton account, while being of a "nest", is perhaps equally as disturbing when it is known that the site was burnt out following "official" inspection. **[101a]**

The next major "physical trace" flap occurred during 1969, mainly centred in northern New South Wales and South Australia. The Bungalwalban trace is of particular interest at this time and indeed was the catalyst of considerable publicity. 1976 was a particularly good year for trace events in Australia, with the best of these being those at Penrith, Kettering **[102]**, Karrawina, and Nemingha **[103]**. An intriguing UFO milieu was centred in the Leitchville-Euchuca area of Victoria during late 1977 and early 1978. There were a large number of traces reported but very few had a probative UFO connection. **[104]**

The Australian data I have described in the following pages has been included on the basis of types of events. Trace details only of each event have been given. These have been further grouped under the features that characterise them.

This study of the cross-section of Australian physical trace data is a potent microcosm of the worldwide experience. It highlights the range of information that has become available to the UFO researcher in the area of possible physical evidence for UFOs.

We have a body of accounts, albeit small, that

clearly refer to physical traces with a strong probative UFO correlation. These documented events are complemented by similar accounts wherein the UFO correlations are not as strong. These combined accounts (Types I and II) give a picture of apparent interactions with the environment, ostensibly produced by UFOs, that is largely consistent with the world picture.

Type IV reports, although sometimes similar to those of Type I & II, cannot be entirely reconciled with these categories. Indeed, in some accounts we seem to have descriptions of apparent phenomena which may even fall outside the traditional framework of UFO experience, as defined by contemporary research. It is apparent that much further work is required to see whether we can reconcile these phenomena.

Type V reports stand as a tribute to the infinite variety of unusual natural phenomena which lie in wait for the careless, the uncritical or the gullible researchers. These events highlight the need for careful consideration by all investigators and researchers of the data we are accumulating. If we are uncritical of our own methods and data, then we will continue to wallow in the controversy that exists now.

Type VI reports (the hoaxes etc) caution us to approach remarkable events with due caution. Careful investigations and documentation techniques will aid in preventing these sorts of cases finding currency with the community at large. They only serve to muddy the water. [**105**]

For some, Type III cases may seem a contradiction. Natural phenomena produced by UFOs? There is a small body of data both in Australia and overseas that suggests UFOs may interact wit the environment and produce the characteristics that plague us in Type V accounts. Could the UFO phenomenon produce such things as "fairy rings" etc? The idea at first seems ridiculous. However, in some cases, either the UFO effect on the soil triggers an accelerated manifestation of natural phenomena (as Jacques Vallée speculated for the Delphos case), or the initial ground trace effects lay the ground-work for eventual take-over by natural phenomena, due to some sort of de-stabilisation effect in the natural environment of the site. [**106**]

SELECT CASES FROM AUSTRALIA [107]

■ PREHISTORY, WEST KIMBERLY, WA.

The aboriginal tribe, the Bad, revered "a supreme being" called Djamar, who according to tradition, manifested in a manner highly suggestive of "something" landing and leaving behind a physical record. The young initiates of the tribe are led to the stony bed of a creek and are shown the holes where Djamar had planted his "bull-roarer".

"Earnestly the old men impress on the youths the terrible force of the original *tjurunga,* by pointing out the baldness of the surrounding hills and the damaged bark of the trees struck by Djamar when he whirled the bull-roarer. It smashed the rocks of the foreshore." [**108**]

Year Type:	I	II	III	IV	V	VI	Total	
pre 1950	2	1	-	1	2	-	6	pre 1950
1950 - 1959	1	2	1	1	3	1	9	1950 - 1959
1960 - 1964	1	1	-	-	1	-	3	1960 - 1964
1965	2	-	-	-	-	-	2	1965
1966	4	2	-	-	3	1	10	1966
1967	1	-	-	-	1	-	2	1967
1968	1	2	-	2	-	1	6	1968
1969	5	7	-	3	9	1	25	1969
1970	2	3	-	3	-	-	8	1970
1971	1	4	-	2	2	2	11	1971
1972	3	1	1	-	3	1	9	1972
1973	-	6	-	5	6	2	19	1973
1974	1	4	1	3	1	-	10	1974
1975	1	4	1	3	2	-	11	1975
1976	4	3	-	1	2	2	12	1976
1977	2	5	-	1	2	-	10	1977
1978	2	1	-	1	1	-	5	1978
1979	-	-	-	-	1	-	1	1979
	33	46	4	26*	39	11	159	
(* One account in Type IV not dated)								

Table 2: Distribution of trace types by year.

■ 1925, NEAR MOORA, WA.

Two young men, one of them a 14- or 15-year-old English migrant named Thomas Green, came upon an object resting in a paddock. It was like 2 saucers placed edge on edge. Around the outside were oval-shaped windows. The object was resting on 4 legs, not of "any colour of the spectrum" and seemed to be shimmering as when something is seen through a heat haze. There was no sound and it appeared to be deserted. The young men fled the object; however, they returned several days later to find that it had gone. Where it had rested, the earth had been scuffed about. [**109**]

■ 1927, NEAR FERNVALE, NSW.

A complex milieu of strange phenomena featured the multiple-witnessed observation of a UFO landing. Two brothers returning from playing cards with neighbours observed an approaching large round dull light beneath a large disc-shaped object, that also appeared to have a dome on top. As it passed overhead, the object lit up the valley with a brilliant light, then seemed to turn and land nearby. The neighbours watching the progress of the brothers home, also saw the object land. The lights eventually went out and the area was then in darkness. Next day a complete circle of "scorched" grass about 10 m in diameter was found at the site.

■ 1970, JUNE, EMERALD BEACH, NSW.

At about 12.45 am, a truck-driver was nearing the Emerald Beach area, when he saw a bright light on the ocean side of the highway. He observed a circular object rise from behind timber, some 500 m from the road. It rose for a few seconds, then hovered for about half a minute at an estimated altitude of 20 m. Relative to the trees, the UFO appeared to be about 10 m in diameter, and what appeared to be flames were noticed along the bottom. The object then slowly returned to the ground: it was partly obscured by timber "while on (the) ground but still had light rays going up at an angle from top and sides." It was still on the ground when fear forced the driver to leave the area.

When I found out about this sighting in May 1973, it was with some reluctance that the percipient accompanied me back to the site with his student son.

"There was a 'circle' approximately 10 m wide, the long grass all about it making it well defined. Inside the circle, the long grass was almost completely absent, and what sparse grass was evident seemed to be much more yellow and 'dead'. Ferns outside the circle were green and growing well, but inside the circle most of the ferns were half-'dead' - with a strange greying on the plants. The sandy soft soil was quite grey.

"Overall the physical appearance of the plant life in the circle was radically different to that outside the circle...

"Very close by, a less well-defined 10 m circle was found. In the circle, dead tree limbs and logs were found. The plant life was in the same condition.."

A further 4 circles were found on the following day. These varied from 4 - 7 m in diameter. The smaller circles highlighted further finds, including "imprints" or impressions. The area had a number of burnt trees.

The traces matched very well with the reported observation, and afforded the opportunity of cautiously interpolating a reasonable scenario for what took place back in June 1970. The object may have come from the north, grazed trees (burning them), then tried to land, knocking over trees in the process. It then moved up again (now being seen by the witness for the first time), hovered and came down in a clearer area some 10-15 m to the north. When it settled, the waist-high grass which surrounded the object would have produced the observed effect of a V-shaped beam of light extending into the sky. This hypothesised mechanism of trace formation does not explain the 4 smaller circles.

Spectroscopy and other tests revealed no significant differences in the soil samples taken inside and outside the "main circle". [**111**]

■ 1975, MARCH 22ND, NR NEBO, QLD.

A party of 2 young men and 3 girls were returning from a droving trip on the night of March 22nd along the new Mount Flora to Dingo beach road in northern Queensland.

At about 10.30 pm, at a point some 90 km from Nebo, the group noticed a strange light amongst the timber ahead on the left-hand side of the road. Then, as they drew closer, they made out a rather curious object in a gravel storage area just off the road.

As they drew level with the strange object and were bringing the car to a stop, a tremendously loud bang seemed to emanate from the thing. The noise was likened to the sound heard when in close proximity to a shot-gun being fired. The vehicle seemed to shake in response for a moment. The suddenness of this loud report frightened the group.

The object appeared to consist of a row of flashing dull white-to-yellow lights, apparently attached to a large "box-like" mass about 1 m above ground level, with a circular mass situated directly above. This sphere, apparently some 3 m wide, consisted of several concentric rings of non-flashing bluey-green lights, with a central black disc. Some of the witnesses noticed what appeared to be a "pole" connecting these 2 masses and 4 legs faintly discernible at the base of the complex. The whole object seemed to be about 2.5 m high and some 3 m wide.

After the frightening bang, the group drove further down the road. Some of the witnesses saw that the upper circular mass of bluey-green lights "seemed to be watching us", as if "they were keeping us under observation."

The driver turned the vehicle around and then, once they were level with the object again, stopped. This time there was no loud noise. The two men wanted to get out, but all three girls in the back seat were terrified. They locked the car doors and pummelled the driver with their fists, imploring him to drive away.

The group drove 15 km and stopped at a roads camp. There they found road construction workers, and proceeded to describe the frightening spectacle.

The two men convinced one of the construction workers to accompany them back to the area. The girls were too frightened and waited at the camp. The trio found that the object was no longer at the storage area, but confirmed the presence of unusual indentations at the spot. The shaken party then made their way home.

Next day they reported the event to the Nebo police. One of the officers accompanied them back to the site. A quote from his report on "UFO sighted whilst landed on the Dingo-Mt.Flora Road", served to adequately define the impact of the experience on the witnesses:

"Whilst at the scene I mentioned to Caroline , aged 12 years, that if we waited for a bit, the UFO might return. The child became quite upset and was obviously frightened. She continued to be disturbed whilst at the location and constantly looked all around as if she expected something to return."

Caroline's written statement concludes with the following: "I *never* want to see one of them again."

On March 25th, an investigating officer from Townsville RAAF base, and an RAAF photographer, examined the site of the unusual incident. Quoting from the RAAF officer's report:

"The unusual marks on the ground consist of: three oval shaped areas; one roughly circular area; and a rectangular area... The impact(ed) (areas) appeared to be very recent with no weathering of the particular areas in question. Some gravel in the areas...was freshly fragmented... This was quite obvious to the eye as the bright colours of the unweathered exposed centres of the gravel, stood out among the surrounding weathered stones in the immediate vicinity..."

Samples were taken and a number of Townsville RAAF officers were asked to view the samples, "and

<u>Type I events: Physical trace with probative UFO correlation</u>

(i) <u>concentric rings</u>:

- 1965, Eton Range, Qld - 46'4" with ring width of 3'2"
- 1971, Tooligie Hill, SA - 45" circle, ringed by 2' wide trench 3 or 4" deep. 24" wide band of flattened wheat surrounding trace
- 1972, Tooraweenah, NSW - figure 8 formed by 4'widecircle with 8" annulus adjacent to 2'6" wide circle with 4" wide annulus

(ii) <u>elliptical "nests"</u>:

- 1966, Corndale, NSW - 20' x 15' flattened grass, deeper around perimeter
- 1969, Glenorchy, Tas - 18' x 12' burnt grass
- 1976, Penrith, NSW - 100' x 45' long grass swept in outward direction

(iii) <u>irregular shaped trace</u>:

- 1966, Tully - rectangular patch of couch grass ca. 5'x6' about 6' from main "nest"
- 1969, Windsor, SA - diamond shaped with smaller similar shaped on one end. associated imprints.

(iv) <u>depression</u> :

- 1966, Bourkes Flat, Vict - 3' wide impression 5" deep with sandy soil cleanly scooped out

(iv) <u>circular nests</u>:

- 1966, Tully, Qld - 30' clockwise trace of reeds, later 2x10', 12' & 8' "nests" found in close proximity
- 1966, Clayton, Vict - 25 to 30' nest of crushed grass
- 1969, Windsor, SA - 30' nest of grass
- 1970, Emerald Beach, NSW - 2x30', 2x15', 1x13½', 1x21'
- 1976, Kettering, Tas - ca.25' scorched grass circle
- 1976, Karrawina, Vict - 71' circle

(v) <u>agitated debri</u>:

- 1947, Maffra, Vict - roadside & maize debri blown about
- 1978, Echuca, Vict - traces in driveway, dirt & gravel blown about

(vi) <u>human physical effects</u>:

- ca.1932/33, Nambour, Qld - blisters & tightness in head
- 1963, nr. Moe, Vict - headache
- 1978, Euchuca, Vict - headache

(vii) <u>animal effects</u>:

- 1963, nr. Moe, Vict - animals reacted violently, cows avoided site over which UFO hovered
- 1965, nr. Vaucluse, NSW - dogs reacted
- 1969, Childers, Qld - dog reacted
- 1969, Windsor, SA - dogs reacted
- 1978, Euchuca, Vict - dogs, sheep reacted

(viii) <u>Imprints</u>:

- 1966, Tully, Qld - 3 imprints on floor of lagoon under nest
- 1967, St. George-Mitchell, Qld - 3 imprints 18" sq. in triangle
- 1970, Emerald Beach, NSW - 5 in 15' nest, 3 in 13½", 4 in 15'
- 1972, Murray Bridge, SA - 3 small pits
- 1975, nr. Nebo, Qld - 4 imprints in gravel storage area, 6'8", 7'6", 9', 5'6" apart; imprint sizes: 1'x7", 1'x 7-8" 10"x7-8"
- 1976, Penrith, NSW - 4 plate-sized "pod-marks" in a straight line.
- 1977, nr. Orange, NSW - 4 imprints in 5.3m, 10.1m, 4.3m & 5.8m arrangment

(ix) <u>precipitate</u>:

- 1976, Nemingha, NSW - white precipitate over car

(x) <u>other vegetation/terrain effects</u>:

- 1965, nr. Vaucluse, NSW - vegetation dying
- 1968, Heyfield, Vict - grass wilted
- 1972, nr. Katoomba, NSW - grass died at site and refused to grow again
- 1974, nr. Goulburn, NSW - area 200 yards wide all burnt
- 1977, Crows Peak, Oberon, NSW - grass browned off
- 1978, Cowra, NSW - ground burning at base of light beam

(xi) <u>Other</u>:

- 1954, Dandenong, Vict - magnetised fence, "drained" torch, etc
- 1965, Eton Range, Qld - scorching of trees
- 1966, Tully, Qld - "footprints", sulphur smell
- 1966, Bourkes Flat, Vict - "light bent", related fatality?
- 1969, Childers, Qld - hair on end, entities collected "samples" of cane, rocks, etc.
- 1969, Casino, NSW - luminous ring, light phenomenon
- 1970, Emerald Beach, NSW - burnt, dead trees, tree limbs, etc.
- 1971, Tooraweenah, NSW - small pile of sand found along with figure 8 trace
- 1972, Murray Bridge, SA - effect on car ("EM" case)
- 1976, Nemingha, NSW - apparent "EM" event, spontaneous combustion of rag which in contact with white precipitate
- 1976, Karrawina, Vict - missing cow
- 1970, Onslow, WA - fire
- 1977, Crows Peak, nr. Oberon, NSW - tree leaves browned off

<u>Type II events: Physical trace with possible UFO correlation</u>

(i) <u>concentric rings</u>:

- 1977, Leitchville, Vict - 8m. wide, 38 cm circular band (Church property)

(ii) <u>elliptical "nests"</u>:

- 1969, Bungawalban, NSW - 60'x15' flattened saccaline

(iii) <u>irregular shaped traces</u>:

- 1969, Renown Park, SA - 15' wide area with 4' x 5' rectangular area, scooped out area
- 1973, Bostobrick, NSW - white powder, charred limb, etc

(iv) <u>depressions</u>:

- 1973, Old Junee, NSW - 15' diameter indentation
- 1974, Strathalbyn, SA - 2' diameter depression 8-9" deep in centre of 12' diameter patch

(v) <u>circular nests</u>:

- 1966, Bankstown, NSW - 19'6" clockwise nest
- 1968, Hill River, SA - circular depression of tangled flatten weeds
- 1969, Tully, Qld - 29'6" clockwise rotation, 12' clockwise
- 1969, Bungawalban, NSW - saucer shaped ring
- 1971, Atkinson's Dam, Qld - 3 flattened areas 10', 25' & 8'
- 1971, Christmas Ck, Kempsey, NSW - 2x12' & 1x19' "burnt" nests
- 1971, Norwood, Tas - 10' flattened area of undergrowth
- 1974, Strathalbyn, SA - bare patch 12' diameter
- 1977, Bamawn Central, Vict - 2.4m.wide ring
- 1977, Slaty Ck. Creswick, Vict - 3m. wide ring
- 1978, Newstead, Vict - 4 circles, smallest 16 paces, largest 26 paces
- 1970, Thaduna Mine, WA - nest
- ca. 1970, Pine Ck, NT - 40' circle

(vi) <u>human physical effects</u>:

- 1959, nr. Cooktown, Qld - death, severe physical effects on percipient
- 1973, nr. Coffs Harbour, NSW - "blind eye", permenant eye damage
- 1974, nr. Grafton, NSW - fatal car smash, "healing"

(vii) <u>animal effects</u>:

- 1969, Bungawalban, NSW - cows avoided area
- 1977, Slaty Ck. Creswick, Vict - cattle avoided area

(viii) <u>imprints</u>:

- 1969, Renown Park, SA - 3 imprints 2" in depth, 5' from approx. centre of trace area
- 1969, Caltowie, SA - half inch holes around wheat stalks
- 1973, Old Junee, NSW - ca. 6 pod marks 4" diameter spaced at regular distances
- 1975, Highland Farm, Tas - ca. dozen small indentations in moss, ca. 2 cms deep and 3 cm wide

without exception all agreed that the stones appeared to be freshly broken when compared with the weathered sample from the surrounding areas.. No test for residual radiation was conducted at the site."

The investigating officer indicated that the impacting had been produced by a heavy weight or pressure. He could offer no satisfactory explanation to what caused the impressions in the gravel pit, nor could he account for the object seen. [112]

■ 1976, FEB. KETTERING, TASMANIA

After being woken at about 1 am by his young child crying, a 39-year-old man saw what at first appeared to be a plane coming down from the eastern sky on the shore of Little Oyster Cove. A widespread glow emanated from the area. Thinking it could have been a plane accident, the man hurried towards the light, still in a dressing gown. From a small rise he had an unobstructed view, some 25 m down the slope, of an extraordinary dome-shaped object. The source of bright white-to-yellow light was from windows around the object. The exterior looked like aluminium, with ribbing or ridging from the top. Below the windows, a small ledge led into a base, with a short vertical side. Through the 3 or 4 windows, the witness saw a tall cylindrical object (which he likened to a ship's compass mounting) and "motionless grey shapes" (like car seats with headrests seen from the rear - "entities" some people have suggested?)

A humming noise, like an electric motor turning over, could be heard as he drew closer. Then, as the object rose from the ground, the noise increased in volume. It gained elevation slowly, then increased speed, moving away at about a 60-degree angle into the eastern night sky. The object receded into a dot in the sky and was gone. The whole incident lasted 6 to 7 minutes.

The witness went back to the spot in the morning and found that the rough grass appeared to be scorched in a circular area, consistent with where the object had rested. This grass later died and was subsequently replaced by a "tougher cutting grass." By April 1977, the affected area stood out as much greener than the surrounding area. The area, about 6 m wide, was then a darker olive-green colour. Investigation revealed no significant differences in the thermo-luminescent content of soil and mineral particles taken from within the affected area and from

(ix) precipitates:

1962, Caroda, NSW - "angel hair"
1969, Grafton, NSW - "angel hair"
1970, Collins Cap, Tas - "angel hair"

(x) other vegetation/terrain effects:

1958, Lake Gardner, SA - fire, ground soft & hot
1966, Toorbul Point, Qld - shrivelled & scorched mangrove plant life
1969, Flinders Park, SA - dug up grape vines
1973, Tyringham, NSW - grass greyer in colour & thinner
1976, Baulkam Hills, NSW - ground trace, strips of dead grass and trees apparently affected

(xi) other:

1966, Bankstown, NSW - pungent smell
1968, Tully, Qld - nests, detector triggered, associated missing film
1969, Tully, Qld - detector triggered, trees deteriated
1969, Flinders Park, SA - strange afterglow
1969, Renown Park, SA - "footprints"
1969, Bungawalban, NSW - fernery collapsed
ca. 1970 - Pine Ck. NT - pathway of trees not growing, "hatchway" mark on perimeter of circular trace present
1971, Atkinson's Dam, Qld - magnetised rocks, white powder, broken & twisted tree branches, partly withered wattle tree & sticky white material
1971, nr. Gladstone, Qld - "oil residue" on car bonnet, "teleportation" burnt mark on bonnet
1972, Bents Basin, NSW - car caught fire
1973, nr. Armidale, NSW - browned leaves
1974, Tayene, Tas - bonnet "cleaned"
1974, Falconbridge, NSW - transformer relocated
1932, Guilford/southern NSW - "meteoric hole"
1975, Fingal, Tas - 2 damaged areas of wattle tree & saplings
1975, Lake Sorell, Tas - luminous mist
1975, Norah Head, NSW - several small trees & scrub knocked over
1976, nr. Wingen, NSW - car effects, torch failed etc
1976, Daw Park, SA - "footprints", entity
1977, St. George/Moonie, Qld - foreign material under car bonnet
1977, Leitchville, Vict - perfect circle (Fehring property)
1973, Garmain, NSW - traces

Type III events: physical traces of apparent/possible natural origin with possible UFO correlation

1950, Dorrigo-Bostobrick, NSW - "fairy ring" 20 to 25' in diameter
late 1972 - Camden, NSW - 6-8' patch of grass - fungal trace?
1974, Maitland, NSW - 2 circles ca.9 ms. in diameter
1975, Cygnet, Tas - black fungal type residue

Type IV events: Physical trace with possible unusual phenomenological correlation

(i) concentric rings:

1977, Port Neill, SA - 4.3m. doughnut ring

(ii) elliptical "nests":

1968, Cairns, Qld - 70'x30' cane flattened
1969, Afterlea, NSW - 30'x12' reeds flattened & entangled
1971, Lynchford, Tas - 30'x15' grass/blackberries with spiral pattern in centre

(iii) irregular shaped traces:

1971, South Plympton, SA - 2x9"x5" rectangular markings
1975, Narrogin, WA - rectangular oats impression 48'x25' with 28' radius arcs on 2 corners

(iv) depressions:

1970, nr. Boggabri, NSW - 6' depression 6" deep with 7 smaller holes and white powder
1974, Jandowae, Qld - 2m. depression 30 cm deep with 8 holes scattered around inside depression

(v) circular nests:

1968, Tully, Qld - 8' & 10' nests plus 3 more nests (size unspecified)
1973, Wentworth Falls, NSW - circular area (possibly smut)
1973, Bordertown, SA - 7 circular anticlockwise impressions in oats, largest nest was 14' wide
1973, Wokurna/Snowtown, SA - 8' anticlockwise impression in wheat
1973, South St. Roma, Qld - circular marks in sugar drip crop
1974, Nth Parramatta, NSW - circular impression with black silver substance, limb on tree snapped off
1974, Pullabooka, NSW - ca. 5.9m wide thistles flattened in anti-clockwise direction
1975, Tranmere, SA - 2x3' anticlockwise flattened areas of strawberry plants

(vi) imprints:

1971, Lynchford, Tas - 6 irregularly spaced indentations in elliptical trace

(vii) precipitate:

1973, Gawler, SA - "nylon" angel hair report

(viii) other:

ca.1946/47, Middle Ck. nr. Grafton, NSW - clothesline "torn" out of ground
ca.late 50s/early 60s, Bentleigh, Vict - oily line on washing
1969, Christies Beach, SA - 3x9" circles in equilateral triangle of sides 5'6"
1969, Eden Valley, SA - 3 circular scorch marks on car bonnet
1970, Toorooka, NSW - "slag" like residue
1975, Brisbane, Qld - tar-like material
1976, Eurobin, Vict - fused metal etc, 3 football size burn marks
1978, Huskisson, NSW - extensive damage from "fireball"
1970, Kedumba, NSW - circular burnt patch of timber, strange smell and missing cattle
no date, North Qld, fragment, unconventional alloy

Type V events: Physical trace of probable or apparent natural origin

(i) fireball damage (eg. Parramatta 1820)
(ii) migratory spiders web (eg. possibly 1953 Caufield & 1961 Meekatharra)
(iii) meteorites (eg. possibly 1958, Tarcutta)
(iv) "fairy rings" (eg. 1972, Navarre & 1973, Willow Tree)
(v) "smut" (eg. 1969, Grafton & 1966, Eyre Pennisula)
(vi) slime mould (eg. 1969, Parkholme)
(vii) sooty moulds (eg. 1969, Tumbulgum)
(ix) fire (eg. 1971, Punchbowl)
(x) lightning (eg. possibly 1975, nr. Murray Bridge)
(xi) exfoliation (eg. 1977, Leigh Creek)

Type VI events: Physical trace of probable spurious, hoax or doubtful origin

pre 1955,Oct., North Qld - W.C. Hall account - "miraculous transformation" of property after "flying saucer encounter", spurious photo
1966, Aug.11th, Rural Vict - the Marlene Travers rape story - trace burn marks and pregnancy alleged
1969, June 23rd, Sydney, NSW - triangular traces on golf course
1971, Aug. Lynchford, Tas - burnt circle in paddock probable hoax
1971, Aug.2nd, Queenstown, Tas - 30' burnt area probable hoax
1972, June 18th, Warragamba, NSW - concentric circles 33' & 26', 3" deep hole near circle of flattened grass
1973, South Coast, NSW - trace allegedly ¼ mile long, apparent spurious account
1968, Dec.28th, Goulburn area, NSW - arm wound, hoaxed photos, contactee tale
1973, Edmonton, Qld - "catwoman" saga, "Girlie" and her alleged "home" a UFO was subject of extensive contact/contactee enquiry
1976, Jan.6th, Adamstown, NSW - trace hoax - flour, etc.
1976, May 24th, Robertson, NSW - "UFO crash" story, "fungal" ground trace

outside.

The results indicated that no large doses of ionising radiation were associated with the object. The thermo-luminescence technique allowed the analyst, Dr G Stevens, to state:

(i) The death of the grasses was not caused by substantial heating of the soil. The soil on the surface had not been heated above about 170 degrees C and soil about 5 cm down had not been heated above about 155 degrees C.

(ii) The death of the grass and subsequent stimulated re-growth was not caused by large doses of ionising radiation. [**113**]

■ 1977, MAY 26, NR ORANGE, NSW

At about midnight, on a farming property about 11 km east of Orange, Mrs H was in bed reading a book, when she heard their dog barking and a corralled horse whinnying and stomping around its enclosure in a most agitated manner. Thinking some stray animal or dog had wandered into the area, she was about to get up to investigate, when her 16-year-old son rushed into her bedroom.

He too had heard the agitation of the animals and had looked directly out his bedroom door window. Some 90 metres away in an approximately north-west direction from the house, he saw a very bright light complex, either on or near the ground, but below the nearby hill line. It was ostensibly on the hillside. The whole thing seemed to slowly increase in brilliance, then upon reaching a brilliant intensity, began to wane in brightness, taking on an orange-red hue just before the illumination was extinguished. The light display originally consisted of about 4 bright white lights in a row. However, after the display went out, the hillside was in darkness.

She immediately went with him to his bedroom, but could not see anything. She then went through the house to the front door, from where she was surprised to see that a paddock across the road, running in front of their property, was brightly illuminated by an apparent monochromatic white light source. (The earlier action had taken place immediately behind the house.)

In about a NNW direction, she made out a bright elongated rectangular object which appeared to have about four "square windows" along its side. This whole complex appeared to move slowly over and around the crest of the hill (the same hillside as above, but now much further to the witness's right). Mrs H ran back inside the house and returned to the fence with her son. All that could then be seen was a bright glow in the same area, but this too eventually disappeared.

Collaborative incidences include the noise heard on the property by the mother, her son and her husband, the disturbance amongst animals on the property, noise over neighbouring properties, animal disturbances on other properties, and at least two independent sightings of UFOs at the same time by local shift workers.

When morning came, Mrs H's son went up to the area where he saw the light source on or near the ground. He found nothing, and school attendance required him to give up any further inspection. Later that same morning, his mother went up to the spot and found two unusual indentations, which consisted of circular areas denuded of grass with a covering of very finely granulated soil. Mrs H gave up looking any further because of the bitter cold, but she told a friend of the family, who in turn informed UFO Research (NSW) of the incident. The author (B.C.) contacted a local representative, Mr Terry Bishop, immediately.

Terry Bishop made a preliminary investigation and confirmed that there were in fact 4 indentations of the type pointed out to him by Mrs H. During the intervening period, it had rained and snowed. Because of this, the traces had deteriorated in condition but were still clearly visible. They were all about 5 cm in diameter and arranged in a trapezoid shape. There were no other apparent effects on the grass, except for apparent effects on a compass near one indentation, but these could not be confirmed with the subsequent more detailed investigation. This was conducted on Sunday, June 1st, by the author and colleagues.

The length of the "trapezoid's sides" (or distances between indentations) were 5.3 m, 10.1 m, 4.3 m, and 5.8 m. Both percipients reported after-image effects which reflected the brilliant nature of the light source involved. The boy described only an after-image effect which he felt was normal after exposure to a bright light, but his mother described seeing black squares before her eyes when she went indoors after her observation.

Apart from spectroscopic analyses (which revealed nothing untoward), the soil samples from the site (both imprint and control samples) were also subjected to inspection via the thermo-luminescence process by Dr Stevens. In the case of the Orange site, superphosphate had been spread about a week previous to the event in question, thereby supplying a natural reference for dosimetry. It was found that if any ionising radiation was involved, the ground would have received less than 100 rad and that any heating involved in forming the cleared patches would have been below 205 degrees centigrade. [**114**]

■ 1980, SEPT. 30TH, NR ROSEDALE, VIC.

A spectacular UFO-related physical trace event occurred during the early hours of September 30th 1980, on a 600-acre property some 8 km from Rosedale.

Mr B, 54, farm-hand and caretaker, was awoken at 0100 hours (daylight-saving time) by disturbance amongst the stock and a strange screeching whistling noise. Cattle were bellowing and a horse was running around in a state of panic. The witness went out to investigate. It was a clear, mild and still moonlight night.

He saw an aerial object appear between a cyprus hedge and shed, some 200 m from his position. It appeared to be a domed object with a white top, moving at about 2 m above the paddock.

The witness at first thought it was a plane going to crash, but soon realised that it had neither wing nor tail. He could now make out orange and blue lights on its surface, and estimated its diameter at about 8 m. Its height was about 5 m.

The object continued to move over the property, passing a hay-shed and then appearing to head towards an open concrete water tank about 400 m from the house. The object appeared to either hover immediately above or rest on top of the tank for about a minute.

The UFO then appeared to rise up several metres and seemed to drift off and land on the ground some 15 m north of the tank.

With the welfare of the stock in mind, the witness went inside to change, and within 5 minutes or so had ridden on his motorcycle up to the paddock where the object had landed.

A whistling noise continued to be heard and the object was in sight all the time as the witness rode up to it. As he neared it, an odd sensation overcame him, which he could only describe as feeling "like a plate of jelly."

Mr B stopped his bike between 10 - 15 m from the object. At no stage was there any effect on the bike. The witness could now see the object clearly.

It seemed to consist of two sections - a white dome on top and a larger orange section underneath. Around this bottom section there appeared to be circular windows or lights, estimated to be about 3 m apart and approximately 17 cm in diameter. These seem to give the impression that both parts were rotating in an anti-clockwise direction. It seemed to stay on the ground for about 2 to 3 minutes.

Suddenly, the noise level increased to "an awful scream", like a jet engine reversing for landing. The witness had to place his hands over his ears. Something like a black tube appeared around the base of the object, and this seemed to inflate to a tremendous size, just beyond the diameter of the object. There was a tremendous bang, and the object lifted up and gradually rolled out off the landing site, reaching a height of about 3 m.

The witness was almost knocked off his bike with a blast of hot air. The bike's headlight illuminated the base of the object as it moved away, enabling the percipient to observe that the black "tube" seemed to be deflating towards the centre of the base. Also around the rim of the base were 6 evenly-spaced "spokes" or V-shaped things.

At about 10 m out from the landing site, and at an altitude of 3 m, the object fell silent. The witness saw material falling away from the base of the object. This debris largely consisted of stones, cape-weed and cow paddies (dung).

The witness then rode straight onto the landing site and watched as the object travelled off in an easterly direction, never higher than about 30 m. It grew gradually smaller until it was lost to view.

Around him in the moonlight, the witness was able to make out a ring of "black" flattened grass, some 10 m across.

Stunned, he was eventually able to somehow ride back to the house. Inside he noticed on the clock that the time was 0150 hours. After a cup of coffee, the witness found that his wrist-watch had stopped at 0110. It re-started after a few minutes when he laid it down, but it stopped whenever he put it on. The problem persisted for about 3 days.

Unable to sleep properly, the witness was up early. He made his way down to the paddock where he had seen the object land during the night. With daylight, he found the ring standing out quite clearly in the paddock. The paddock was a blanket of yellow flowers, but at the landing site, the ring was near black or brown in colour - consisting of grass flattened in an anti-clockwise manner to a width of 0.5 m. Inside the ring was only green grass. The yellow flowers had been removed. The total diameter of the site was just under 10 m. Evenly spaced within the ring were 6 "spokes" of relatively undamaged grass. In a definite path leading out of the site to the east was debris, ostensibly seen falling from the object during its departure the night before.

In total, the event involves many extraordinary elements besides the single-witness close encounter, a UFO-correlated physical ground trace, effects on the witness (headaches, nausea, etc) and his watch, other trace effects, effects on stock, the disappearance of about 10,000 gallons of water from the tank, and possible secondary witnesses. [**115**]

CONCLUSIONS

Writing of physical trace cases in his 1979 handbook, Allan Hendry wrote: 'The physical evidence is only interesting if the testimonial allegations of their UFO origin are true. The most common notion of a truly valuable physical trace would be one in which a material of unearthly nature was present, like 'green kryptonite'. Yet the American Chemical Society recently announced the cataloguing of the four-millionth unique chemical substance! Asserting that virtually any material could not have an earthly counterpart, either man-made or in nature, would be almost foolhardy.' [**116**]

He suggests that isotope ratio analyses could be an important evaluation tool. [**117**] A good example of his argument is contained within the controversy surrounding the book *Alien honeycomb*, whose Australian authors claimed to have recovered extensive fragments of a UFO that exploded over a remote Queensland property. They insisted that these contained 'unknown elements' and 'configurations that will present science with some fundamental problems', but were curiously unforthcoming as to lab reports on the fragments or what connection they might have with a UFO. However, samples of the same substance were obtained from the same source by independent researchers and shown to be 'woven fabrics' of 'multifilament fibreglass'. [**117a**]

So long as the physical evidence continues to be ambiguous, Hendry concludes, we cannot disprove that they may be due to one of the following:

■ Startling natural agency (eg ball lightning) causing real traces

■ Naturally formed 'traces' artificially employed by the IFO witness to concretize his sighting to others - causality falsified, perhaps unintentionally

■ Hoaxed trace created by witness, perhaps unintentionally, in a dissociated fantasy state, to concretize his unrelated IFO (or fantasy) sighting to others

■ Consciously hoaxed trace and UFO story. [**118**]

The annual obsession in England with 'mystery circles' in recent years may involve examples of Hendry's options. [**118a**]

Jenny Randles has also focused critical attention on this area: 'The danger is always that the memory will unconsciously adapt itself so that the details of the sighting fit in with a quite irrelevant mark, uncovered by any intensive search of the "landing area". We have had camp-fires, wind-vortices, and even a lump cut up by a council lawn-mower, all appearing at first sight as "proof" that a UFO had landed nearby. It only requires a typically zealous investigator or witness. Indeed, I am somewhat doubtful whether it is ever worth *searching* for traces. Experience shows that it is only too easy to find something and then wrongly assume its relevance. It may be better only to examine traces found when the witness quite clearly spots the UFO causing them...' [**119**]

The evidence for what may be a bona fide UFO physical trace phenomenon is consistent with a rare physical explanation. Randles may have clarified part of the problem: 'I remain pretty certain that *some* cases do involve physical energy transfer (eg microwave radiation) and that a decidedly real material phenomenon (beyond which I will not specify) is responsible for some reports, and so must at times leave traces. There is an enormous gap between a phenomenon being *real* and it being *alien* (although too many uflogists see these words as synonymous). On the strength of the evidence of traces alone, I see no reason to bridge this gap. However, trace evidence should not stand alone. Its study is valuable. But I do not expect it to prove one way or another whether UFOs are in any sense alien.' [**120**]

Verga concluded from his study of Italian cases that 'practically all of the so-called UFO data are useless in terms of scientific evaluation' [**121**] and Hynek put the finger on the real problem when he wrote:

'Here we come face to face with the charge that after thirty years of dealing with UFO reports we still have no really convincing "hard data", ie parts of a UFO, unimpeachable residues from soil samples, unequivocal evidence that a UFO caused damage to animate or inanimate matter. Yet the fact is that we *do* have large amounts of such evidence... I grow livid when such charges of "no data" are made. After years of frustration without the funds to pay for adequate laboratory and other professional work, I bristle at the lack of understanding on the part of the scientific skeptics, who wouldn't get to first base without well-funded research projects with staff, travel and laboratory facilities...

'All we have are abortive, often amateurish attempts at data gathering, data analysis, and feeble attempts at laboratory studies (on a charity basis, of course), all of which dwindle into inconclusion and frustration... It is my contention that "hard" data may well have been present in many UFO cases but their discovery and definitive establishment has repeatedly gone by default for lack of professional (funded) treatment. It has always been a case of 'too little and too late', necessitated by the use of volunteers bolstered only by their unselfish devotion to the pursuit of an overwhelming mystery.' [**123**]

I am glad for Hynek's sake that before he died he was able to see at least the beginnings of some 'thorough, professional study' in the work of GEPAN, specifically the Trans-en-Provence case of January 1981. Indeed, given personal access to the GEPAN files, at the direct invitation of the French government, he found all of the GEPAN cases to be very well investigated. [**124**]

On the basis of the physical trace evidence and the collective evidence contained within the whole spectrum of UFO research, I believe a physical dimension to the UFO phenomenon has been substantiated. What has next to be determined is whether or not this physical evidence is consistent with a true 'alien' reality. The well-supported study of UFO-related physical trace events could make a crucial contribution to the resolution of this challenge.

REFERENCES

■ 1 - **Phillips**, *Physical traces associated with UFO sightings*, CUFOS (1975) foreword. ■ 2 - *Phillips*, 'Landing traces, physical evidence for the UFO', *Proceedings, MUFON Symposium 1973*. ■ 3 - **Phillips** CUFOS (1975) ■ 4 - **Phillips**, 'Physical traces of UFOs' in Story, *Encyclopedia*, (1980) ■ 5 - **Phillips**, 'Physical trace landing reports: the case for UFOs', in *Proceedings, MUFON Syposium 1975*. ■ 6 - **Scully**, *Behind the Flying Saucers*. ■ 7 - **Stringfield**, see refs in Section 2.7.1. ■ 8 - **Berlitz & Moore**, *The Roswell incident*; Moore, 'Crashed saucers: evidence in search of proof', in *Proceedings, MUFON Symposium 1985*. ■ 9 - **Jacobs & Hall** in *IUR* (Jul/Aug

1985). ■ **10** - See section 2.2.2. ■ **11** - **Ruppelt**, *The report on UFOs*, p 24. ■ **12** - Ibid, pp 278-9. ■ **13** - 'Florida scout-master's encounter' in Story (1980). ■ **14** - Ibid, p 243. ■ **15** - **Randles**, *UFO reality*, p 143. ■ **16** - **Story** 1980, p 127. ■ **17** - Ibid, p 128. ■ **18** - **Sanderson**, *Uninvited visitors*, pp 39 - 52. ■ **19** - **Barker**, 'Invading visit' in *UFO Report* (Dec 1976). ■ **20** - For example **Michel**, *Flying Saucers and the straight line mystery* (1958); Quarouble p 46-7, Chabeuil p 82-4, Premanon p 91-2, Poncy-sur-L'Ignon p 132-7. ■ **21** - **Barthel & Brucker**, *La grande peur Martienne*. ■ **22** - **Randles**, *The UFO world*, (BUFORA, 1986). ■ **23** - **Maugé** in *Magonia* 13 (1983). ■ **24** - **Michel** (1958). ■ **25** - **Carrouges**, *Apparitions de Martiens* (1964)› ■ **26** - **Vallée**, in **Bowen** [ed] *The humanoids*, (FSR 1966). ■ **27** - **Mebane**, 'Hallucinated machines at Levelland' in **Michel** (1958); **Vallée**, *Anatomy of a phenomenon*, p 136; **Hynek**, *UFO experience*, p 123; **Story**, *UFOs & limits of science*, (1981) p 136. ■ **28** - *APRO Bulletin*, (Jan 1958), also **Michel** (1958) p 253. ■ **29** - **Hynek**, *The Hynek UFO Report*, p 182. ■ **30** - **Lorenzen**, *Flying Saucers - the startling evidence*, p 104. ■ **31** - **Story** (1981) p 90 ■ **32** - *APRO Bulletin* (July 1985), citing **Sturrock**. ■ **33** - **Nordin**, 'The Väddö case' in *Nordic UFO Newsletter* (1981/1). ■ **34** - **Liljegren**, in *FSR* 16/6; *UFO-Sweden Newsletter* no 2 (Sep 1970). ■ **35** - **Hobana & Weverbergh**, *UFOs from behind the iron curtain*, p 161. ■ **36** - **Galindez**, 'Trancas after 7 years' in *FSR* 17/3. ■ **37** - **Powers** in **Bowen**, *The humanoids* p 130; **Hynek**, *UFO experience* p 144 & 223; **Steiger**, *Blue book* p 106; **Stanford**, *Socorro 'Saucer' in a Pentagon pantry*; **Hall** in **Story** (1980). ■ **38** - **Klass**, P, *UFOs exlained*, p 124; **Story** (1981). ■ **39** - **Firestone** et al in *UFORAN* 3/4 (1982). ■ **40** - **Hall** in **Story** (1980) p 343. ■ **41** - **Stanford** (1976). ■ **42** - **Bowen** et al in *FSR* 11/5, 11/6, 14/1; **Vallee**, *Passport to Magonia*, p 19; **Bourret**, *Crack in the universe*, p 98. ■ **43** - **Blum**, *Beyond Earth*, citing **Bowen**, FSR. ■ **44** - **Michalak**, *My encounter with the UFO*; **Bondarchuk**, *UFO sightings &c*. ■ **45** - *Condon Report* p 316 [Ballantyne ed]. ■ **46** - **Rutkowski**, 'Falcon Lake incident' in *FSR* 27/1' ■ **46a** - **Julien**, 'Landing in Madagascar' in *FSR* 23/1 [from *LDLN* 160]. ■ **47** - **Lina**, 'Landings in Estonia' in *FSR* 24/1. ■ **48** - **Bemelmans**, 'Reports from Ibluna' in *FSR* 16/1. ■ **49** - **Karavien**, 'The Saapunki UFO' in *FSR* 17/5, also 17/2 & 17/4. ■ **50** - **Makinen**, 'Flying Saucers invade Finland', *Saga*, Oct 1971. ■ **51/52/53** - **Kuningas**, 'The humanoid at Kinnula' in *FSR* 17/5. ■ **54** - **Krmelj**, 'Landing in Yugoslavia' in *FSR* 24/3. ■ **55** - **Phillips**, *FSR Case histories* 9. ■ **56** - **Phillips**, CUFOS 1975 p 79. ■ **57** - **Story** 1981 p 77. ■ **58** - Ibid p 81. ■ **59** - **Dickinson & Lucas**, *Dictionary of mushroom*, Putnam 1979. ■ **60** - **Vallee**, *Invisible college*, p 35. ■ **61/62** - **Phillips** in **Story** (1980). ■ **63** - **Klass**, *UFOs, the public deceived* p 125. ■ **64** - **Phillips**, in **Fuller** [Ed] *Proceedings of the First International UFO Congress* (1980). ■ **65** - **Hendry**, *UFO handbook* (1979). ■ **66** - **Sheaffer**, in **Story** (1980). ■ **67** - Author interview with **Phillips** (1986). ■ **67a** - In a letter to the author, dated 16 April 1987, Faruk writes: "I would like to emphasise that it was not the compound that was hydrophobic but the soil itself which was *coated* with the compound to render it hydrophobic. This aspect of the soil chemistry is explained more fully in my report." ■ **68** - Ibid, and with **J Clark**, and with **E Faruk**; also papers by **Faruk** in *IUR* (1987), and unpublished. ■ **68a** - See ref 59, also **Dick**, 'Some biological explanations for UFO trace cases and related phenomena' in **Moravec & Prytz** [ed[*UFOs over Australia* (1985); Bayliss **Elliott**, 'Concerning fairy rings in pastures', *Ann.App.Biol.* 13: 277-288 (1926); **Parker-Rhodes**, 'Fairy ring kinetics', *Trans.Brit.Mycol.Soc.* 38(1) 59-72; **Shatz** et al, 'Fungus fairy rings in Eastern Colorado &c', *Jnl Agricultural Research* XI/5 (1917). ■ **69** - Ibid 67. ■ **70** - **Bowen** in *FSR Case histories* 11. ■ **71** - **Hind**, *African encounters* p 44. ■ **72** - **Bowen**, *FSR* 19/1, and **Hind** p 126. ■ **73/74** - **Phillips**, *FSR* 19/6. ■ **75** - **Hynek & Vallee**, *Edge of reality* p 265; also ref 71 p 68; also **Phillips** MUFON (1975). ■ **76** - **Redon**, 'Landing near Burgos' in *FSR* 23/2; also *Skylook* 89 (1975). ■ **77** - **Bloecher** in *FSR* 22/3 & 4; also **Hopkins**, *Missing time*. ■ **78** - **Landsburg**, *In search of extraterrestrials*, p 14. ■ **79** - **Zeller**, 'The use of thermo-luminescence' in *Proceedings CUFOS* (1976). ■ **80/81/82/83** - **Van der Velde** in *APRO Bulletin* 30/4 & 5 and 26/2. *MUFON Jnl* 125. ■ **84** - **Krmelj** in *MUFON Jnl* 118. ■ **85** - **Seneker** et al in *MUFON Jnl* 135; **Phillips**, ibid 141; **Phillips** MUFON (1985)› ■ **86** - **Phillips** (1985). ■ **87/88** - **Keatman** et al in *FSR* 25/6. 26/1 & 3; **Campbell** in *JTAP* 1/2, and in *The unexplained* 2990 et seq. ■ **89** - GEPAN, *Note technique* 16; *MUFON Jnl* 193. ■ **90** - **Wilhelm** in *MUFON Jnl* 186. ■ **91** - **Chiumiento** in *FSR* 30/6, *IUR* 9/6. ■ **91b/92/93** - **Telarico** in *FSR* 32/1. ■ **94** - **Ballester Olmos**, *OVNIs - el fenomeno aterrizaje*, p 267. ■ **95** - **Verga**, personal communication; also *Notizario UFO* no 101. ■ **96** - **Bonabot**, *Bulletin de GESAG* 79. ■ **97** - **Van Utrecht**, in *SVL-Journal* 4/15. ■ **98** - **Chalker**, *ACUFOS Bulletin* 9; *Preliminary catalgoue of Australian UFO trace cases*. ■ **99** - **Chalker**, 'Physical evidence for UFOs in Australia - preliminary study' UFOCON (1979); abridged version in *MUFON Jnl* 157. ■ **100** - **Chalker** in **Story** (1980); **Seers**, *UFOs, the case for scientific myopia*; *UFO research, Queensland* (Sep 1977); **Magee** in *FSR* 12/2; **Seers** et al in *FSR* 15/3; *Australian FSR* no 5; *Australian FSR UFOIC Edition* no 9. ■ **101** - *Australian FSR VYFORG Edition* no 5; *Australian UFO Review UFOIC edition* no 10; **Chalker** in *UFORAN* 5/3 (*UFO Nyt* Jul-Okt 1985). ■ **101a** - *The Clayton Calendar* produced by Grade 6c-5c of Westall High School; see also *Australian FSR Victorian edition* no 5; also personal communication with **R Fischer**, formerly of VUFORs (1977). ■ **102** - **Roberts** et al in *FSR* 24/3. ■ **103** - **Chalker** in *FSR* 22/5, 23/3. ■ **104** - VUFORS & **Norman** in *Australian UFO Bulletin* (1978); **Chalker** in *Australian UFO Newsletter* (1978). ■ **105** - UFOIC newsletter. ■ **106** - Eg **Dick** in *UFOs over Australia* (1985); **Hendry** (1979); **Story** (1980). ■ **107** - Author's personal files and as specified. ■ **108** - **Worms**, 'Ojamar the creator' in *Anthropos* XLV (1950); also **Eliade**, *Australian religions*, Cornell (1973). ■ **109** - Personal communication from Bill **Barton** (PUFORG). ■ **110/111** - Personal investigation by the author. ■ **112** - RAAF investigation *HQTVL S/40 AirPt3(15)* (20.5.1975); see also **Chalker** in *MUFON Jnl* 143. ■ **113** - See ref 102. ■ **114** - **Chalker** in *UFO Newsletter (UFO Research NSW)* (Nov 1977). ■ **115** - **Basterfield & Chalker** in *UFORAN* 2/1 (1981); also *FSR* 26/6; also **Gildea**, in *Australian UFO Bulletin* (1980), repr.in *Australian Annual Flying Saucer Review* (1981). ■ **116** - **Hendry** (1979) p 129. ■ **117** - Ibid; also **Herbison-Evans**, 'Extraterrestrial isotope ratios' in *UFOs over Australia*. ■ **117** - **Pinkney** et al, *Alien honeycomb* (1980); **Chalker**, *UFORAN* 2/1; 'The great UFO debate' (re *Alien honeycomb*) in *People* magazine (Jan 21 & 28 (1981)). ■ **118** - **Hendry** (1979) p 148. ■ **118a** - **Fuller** et al, *Mystery of the circles*, BUFORA (1986); also **Randles** in *Northern UFO News* 120. ■ **119** - **Randles**, *UFO reality* p 139. ■ **120** - **Randles**, 'Comments regarding physical trace cases', European Working Team (1982). ■ **121** - **Verga** in *Magonia* 16, also in *MUFON Jnl* 198. ■ **122** - **Story** (1981). ■ **123** - **Hynek**, 'The 10 best cases' in *Frontiers of science*' (May-June 1981). ■ **124** - **Andrus**, *MUFON Jnl* 208 p 13.

3.4.2

PHYSICAL TRACES: REAL EVIDENCE?

by Maurizio Verga

■ **MAURIZIO VERGA**: Born 1963. Professionally, a textile technician.

■ **UFO involvement**: He has been involved in UFO research since 1977, taking a particular interest in close encounters and trace cases, about which he has written many articles. In 1985, together with other Italian researchers, he founded the Centro Italiano Studi Ufolgici and is currently one of its directors.

Over the past three years he has paid special attention to the role of the computer in ufology; in addition to developing some original software, he is editor of a specialist publication *The Computer UFO Newsletter* (available from the address below).

■ **Publications**: He is author of *ITACAT*, a 450-page manuscript about the 'commented casuistry' of Italian close encounters; and has compiled a catalogue of sightings with alleged physical traces.

■ **Address**: Via Matteotti 85 / 22072 Cermenate (Co) / Italy. Phone (031) 77.16.00.

One of the most intriguing aspects of UFO phenomena is the presence of traces related to UFO-sightings - or, in many cases, to *non*-sightings: for an anomalous ground mark will frequently be credited to alien spacecraft, even though no UFO has been reported - such is the power of the UFO myth.

If anything can provide physical proof of a tangible phenomenon interacting with our reality, these traces should do so. Offering objective evidence, independent of subjectively perceived reports derived from the senses of the witness, they may be - with the possible exception of photographs - the only counter-argument to set against the psychosocial interpretation. With the extraterrestrial hypothesis somewhat out of fashion, its faithful supporters rely heavily on traces to keep its tenets alive. But how reliable are they?

WHAT IS A TRACE CASE?

The 2500-3000 recorded trace events - one in five of all close encounters - offer a rich and varied catalogue of phenomena: burnt areas of ground and vegetation, flattened patches in cropfields or on the bare soil, dessicated plants, broken branches, holes in the ground, footprints attributed to humanoids, liquid or powdery residues, metallic fragments - and many more.

But how does such a finding come to be classified as a UFO event? My own definition of a trace case is as follows: 'An event where the discovery of a trace, either on the ground or on vegetation etc, or of a substance of any kind, is linked to a manifestation of what is conventionally known as the UFO phenomenon, whether such a manifestation has been reported or merely presumed. The link may be made by the witness, by the investigators, or by others not connected with the case'.

Note that we are speaking of a 'UFO phenomenon' as such, and not of some amorphous 'stimulus for a UFO report' such as is preferred by sophisticated definitions. [See Section 3.1 'Defining the UFO'] The reason is one of simple logic: a physical effect presupposes a physical cause, and those who are inclined to link a trace with the phenomenon are generally inclined to do so in terms of the popularly accepted myth.

For the researcher, however, physical traces are not so easily explained, and offer a complex conceptual problem. Thus we have had proposals for an 'interdimensional entity', able to assume physical characteristics; others have suggested kinship with other kinds of physical phenomena such as PK (psychokinesis) and RSPK (recurrent spontaneous PK or 'poltergeist').

Such far-out speculations are fuelled by the patent contradictions of trace phenomena. In some cases, traces are found on the ground where a UFO has been seen; in others, a supposed landed UFO leaves no trace. Even allowing for witness unreliability, we are faced with an inconsistency. What is the unkown factor behind this inconsistency; is it, as I personally think (for the moment at any rate!) linked with the individual characteristics of the witness?

Of course, if it should turn out that UFOs are entirely subjective in origin, we would have to account for the paradoxical association of subjective and objective phenomena. We would have to assume that the traces are caused either by subconscious action on the part of the witness, or by deliberate hoax. Easier to account for would be the *absence* of traces where we might have been expected to find them; this would simply be due to the witness' inability to manufacture them, either on the material level or because he is inhibited by a subconscious wish to draw attention to the subjective character of his experience.

NATURAL CAUSES

Even in cases where anomalous traces undoubtedly exist, we are by no means committed to accepting the proposed link with the UFO phenomenon. Nature offers an abundance of means whereby strange traces may be caused - fungi, plant sickness, lightning strikes, animal habits, whirlwinds and tornadoes, and much more, while man makes his own contribution with helicopters, defoliation, fires accidental or purposeful, chemical accident etc.

While these should be the *first* explanations to come to mind, specific circumstances may dictate otherwise:

■ **1** - The witness may have had a Type-1 sighting: in such a case, he will be predisposed to tie in that primary experience with anything else he may find that is at all strange. His cultural belief system, together with his own emotional state, will encourage him to make such a link in all sincerity.

■ **2** - Sometimes, such a link may be made less sincerely: in an effort to make his primary sighting more credible, the witness will link it with trace phenomena he *knows* to have no connection with it. (Even in conventional science there are instances of researchers deliberately producing evidence they know to be spurious, to support phenomena they believe to be genuine.)

■ **3** - The investigator, too, has his own beliefs, his own emotional state; so, though generally let us hope to a lesser degree, he too may either go along with dubious trace-UFO link proposed by the witness, or even propose one on his own initiative.

■ **4** - Nor must we forget the outright hoax - which can consist of either:

- ■ traces deliberately manufactured, or
- ■ pre-existing traces 'discovered' on the site and exploited to add credence or excitement to the story.

Most hoax traces are of the first kind, and we find all kinds of crude efforts to manufacture traces in accord with whatever variant of the UFO myth the hoaxer subscribes to.

Proving that such traces are spurious is both difficult and time-consuming, and it is understandable that with the limited means and time most investigators can afford, they are often unable to study the evidence with the requisite care to prove it decisively to be spurious. The consequence is that many cases remain in the catalogue which probably - given sufficient investigation - could have been shown to be hoaxes.

What virtually all hoaxes have in common is that they support the most literal popular image of the UFO as extraterrestrial craft. Circular traces reflect the disc-shaped stereotype: 'leg' marks reflect conventional notions of landing gear: burn marks reflect conventional ideas that UFO propulsion is effected by means of something not much more advanced than our own jets!

THE RESIDUE

In summary, it is possible to point out two fundamental aspects of the traces question, which should encourage investigators to rethink their attitudes towards the matter:

- ■ The explanation of most trace reports is to be found in terms of both natural and artificial causes. The range of these is so wide that their identification is often next to impossible.
- ■ It is impossible to accept some investigation reports as a basis for scientific data. Investigators are too often guilty of subjective responses and emotional involvement. This makes investigation of traces very difficult. Not being at the site oneself one can only assign 'possible' or 'probable' identifications, to the detriment of serious research.

The consequence is that practically all the so-called trace data are useless from the viewpoint of scientific evaluation. What are we left with? A residue, small but by no means negligible, which seems to point to the apparent physical reality of an apparently unknown phenomenon - though, of course, not necessarily one of alien or extraterrestrial origin.

But even so, we must recognise that the best of our investigation and research does not allow for strict scientific determinations to be made. Since the UFO phenomenon is itself undetermined, we can say only that it is just one of many conceivable explanations for the as-yet unexplained traces; other explanations may be more conventional, albeit extremely rare.

The conclusion is simple: If we wish to develop UFO research as a serious research field, we must be prepared to abandon deep-seated dogmas and widely-held illusions. One cannot reach out for understanding while clinging on to belief.

In particular, we should not cling to the belief that physical traces are evidence of a physical UFO phenomenon, unless we have stronger reasons for doing so than we possess at present. Despite what is widely believed - even by many ufologists - it is by no means certain that the UFO phenomenon has a basis in physical reality: in which case it follows we must look for an alternative explanation for physical traces. And even if UFOs exist as physical phenomena, the link between them and traces must be established more closely than it is at present.

Perhaps, when *UFOs 1947-1997* is published, the situation will be better?

3.4.3

EFFECTS OF UFOs UPON PEOPLE

by James McCampbell

■ **JAMES McCAMPBELL**: A University of California degree in engineering physics led to a wide-ranging career in research and design in the nuclear field and engineering management, including the Space Environment Simulator at NASA Huston, environmental protection for the Alaskan pipeline, and work for the Solar Energy Research Institute. Finally in 1980 he established his own marketing and consulting company.

■ **UFO involvement**: As might be expected from such a background, his approach to the UFO phenomenon has been consistently pragmatic: 'Civilisations presently unknown to mankind may exist in some extra-dimensional sense from which UFOs penetrate into our realm of existence, however they fully partake of our physical reality while they are under our observation. As they certainly interact with the physical environment, details of such interaction should be studied from a scientific point of view... Explanations should not be sought in the realms of religion, psychology, biology, paranormal or the occult, though these are valid lines of inquiry as corollaries to UFO sightings.' He has served as MUFON's Director of Research since 1975.

■ **Publications**: *Ufology, new insights from science and common sense* (1973) is not only an expression of the above position, but is widely respected as one of the most constructive contributions to the scientific UFO literature. This has been supplemented by numerous articles in *MUFON UFO Journal* and elsewhere.

■ **Address**: 12 Bryce Court / Belmont / CA 94002 / USA. Phone (415) 593 8848.

INTRODUCTION

A vast reservoir of technical data on UFOs lies in the published reports of witnesses. And it can be tapped by the careful study of details in single, well-documented events or in the composite from many similar cases. Validity of the data is assured when the reports contain technical information that could not possibly have been known to the witnesses. Ironically, testimony from simple, ordinary folk can therefore be the most valuable. It is essential to focus attention upon the phenomenon reported rather than the identity of the witness or other diversionary issues.

When a UFO produces some observable effect in our environment, it should be amenable to scientific analysis, that is, it should have a scientific explanation. Thus competent investigation of UFO cases will usually disclose the exact mechanism that produces the observed effect or, at least, identify one that might be responsible.

All observed effects of UFOs except purely mechanical processes and artifacts, carry implications of electromagnetic and gravitational fields in their vicinity. [1] Technical studies of individual effects can establish limits to the parameters of those fields. So detailed studies of the wide range of effects should lead to a significant understanding of the UFO field. Limitations deduced from one effect may well be different from those of another, and still another. By overlaying these various constraints, specific parameters of the UFO fields should become progressively more apparent.

Previous studies by the author and others have converged upon microwave radiation from UFOs as a candidate cause of many of their effects. So a general discussion here can lay a foundation for understanding what microwaves are, how they are described and, in succeeding sections, how they can interact with people to produce a variety of responses. Microwave radiation is that portion of the electromagnetic spectrum that lies in the frequency range of 300,000,000,000 to 1,000,000,000 cycles per second - abbreviated to 300,000 MHz (megacycles) to 1,000 MHz. Corresponding wavelengths are 10 to 0.1 cm. The specific frequency in a given event should be known. Next, the manner of delivery is important, whether continuous or pulsed, and if pulsed, at what repetition rate and what pulse width. It is easily seen that a strong but very short pulse followed by a relatively long interval before the next would deliver only a small amount of power. Thus one speaks of peak powers, average powers, and duty cycles. It need not be difficult to visualize a description of pulsed microwaves. Consider microwaves of 1,000 MHz being pulsed at 100 Hz having a peak power of 300 milliwatts per square centimetre (mW/cm1^{2}) etc. but an average power of only 2 mW/cm^2. A further concept to be encountered is that of *threshold* namely the lowest power level at which any given effect takes place.

Physical effects of UFOs upon people can hardly receive a comprehensive treatment in a brief section, still less those responses which appear to be psychological and even paraprychological. They have not been touched upon here but there is a mass of data that should be examined, particularly since the possibility exists that they may actually be only physical responses to radiation.

SIGHT

Almost everything known about UFOs is derived from direct, visual observation of unfamiliar things in the sky, or, occasionally, on the ground. In addition many witnesses have reported strange creatures associated with UFOs and involuntary visits aboard the craft, but as these aspects are covered elsewhere, they are ignored here.

HEARING

■ 1. BULLETS

Several witnesses have responded to an approaching UFO in the manner of the Old West, that is, by drawing a bead and firing with a rifle or pistol. The bullets have been heard to strike metallic surfaces and whine off in ricochets. [**2**] Also, the landing of nearby UFOs has been heard as a thud such as would be expected from a not-so-gentle setdown of a ponderous machine. [**3**] While these sounds offer no clues to the UFO fields, they suggest that the objects under study are not imaginary, vaporous, holograms, ball lightning, or earthquake lights.

A survey of close encounter cases by the author classified five distinct types of sounds emanating from UFOs. [**4**] They were:

VIOLENT	(roar, explosion)
LOW PITCH	(hum, buzz)
RUSH OF AIR	(whoosh, swish)
HIGH PITCH	(shrill, whistle)
SIGNALS	(beeps, pulses).

■ 2. VIOLENT

Very early in the morning of September 30, 1980 near Sale, Southern Australia, George Blackwell awoke to a whistling sound. It came from a wingless craft 8 m across that displayed colored lights as it spun. It flew slowly at low altitude finally settling to the ground near a large water tank. The witness approached to within 15 m when the whistling sound became very loud. Then he heard an awful *bang* accompanied by a blast of air and heat as the object took off vertically and flew away. [**5,8**]

A highway patrolman saw a strange object sitting on the ground in the San Joaquin valley of California. It was early morning on a wintry day. Suddenly, the object became surrounded by a mist. Then a brilliant glow appeared as the object rose off the ground. A few seconds later, he heard an explosion as the UFO departed. The sound was clearly a shock wave from the UFO as the time delay was appropriate for the distance and the speed of sound.

Explanation

Shock waves appear to be generated only at take-off. While sitting on the ground, the propulsion system is presumed to be turned off, that is, no external field surrounds the UFO. Power would then be required to initiate the field. The sudden appearance of mist in the San Joaquin case is a vital detail. That region in California is noted for very dense, ground fogs resulting from ground cooling due to radiant heat loss to the cosmos during long winter nights and high humidity near sloughs and swamps. Water vapor adjacent to the UFO could have been condensed by a reduction either in temperature or pressure. Because the phenomenon was accompanied by a shock wave, a change in temperature alone can be ruled out. The newly generated field must have exerted an outward force on the atmosphere thereby reducing the pressure close to the surface. A very small pressure change, indeed, would suffice to cross the dew point and condense water vapor from saturated air at 100% humidity. Such condensation can sometimes be observed in the low-pressure zone above airplane wings. Again microwaves emanating from UFOs are suspected because, at certain wavelengths, they are resonantly absorbed by water molecules with an accompanying transfer of momentum, that is, a force. Resonances are at wavelengths of 0.17 cm with four stronger ones below 0.1 cm. Continuation of the process of pushing the air out of the way is the likely reason that UFOs can fly faster than the speed of sound without creating sonic booms. [**6**]

■ 3. TONES

The most prevalent types of sounds are either low or high pitch. Words used by witnesses often succinctly and specifically denote the pitch. For example the former might be approximated by a humming bird, the latter likened to the squeal between stations on old-fashioned AM radios. Two revealing cases have recently come to light after being hidden for decades:

At 4.00 a.m. on July 25, 1957 several workers were taking a break at the Daye Steel Plant in Huangshi City, Peoples Republic of China. Upon hearing a humming sound, they noticed a bright spot in the clear sky that was increasing in apparent size. As it came closer it was seen as a circular plate giving off a dazzling white light and leaving a white trail. During a 2 to 3 minute observation, it flew over the frightened observers at 1000 m producing a whistling sound that was lounder than a jet. As the *object approached the witnesses* the low pitch changed to high pitch: no mention was made of any intermediate tones. [**7**]

The next example, collected by the CIA in southern Belgian Congo in 1952, remained secret until released in 1983 under a lawsuit pursuant to the Freedom of Information Act. Two fiery objects glided in sweeping curves over uranium mines. They were seen in several perspectives as disks, ovals, and thin lines. During 10 to 12 minutes of observation, they emitted hissing and buzzing sounds. Commander Pierre at a small airfield jumped into a fighter plane and took off in pursuit. He was able to get within 150 m of the objects that were disc-shaped, aluminum 12 to 15 m in diameter, with a rim of fire. They were emitting a whistling sound that could easily be heard over the airplane engine. Note that the sound changed from low pitch to high pitch as the *witness approached the objects* without mention of intermediate tones. [**8**] In both cases the range closed, with movement of the *object* in China and of the *witness* in the Congo.

Explanation

It has long been recognized that people can hear electromagnetic radiation in the microwave region such as radar and microwave radiation from UFOs was suspected as the cause of humming sounds. Relatively little was known about this phenomenon 15 years ago but it had been well established that the aural response was caused by short bursts of energy corresponding to pulsation of the microwave source. In some uncertain manner, the pulses stimulated the organ in the inner ear that sends signals to the brain. The tonal value perceived by experimental subjects corresponded to the pulse rate of the source. Also, the location of the source was usually thought to be behind the head as the direct response of microwave bypassed the time delay of ordinary, slow-moving, sound waves reaching the more remote ear. This process, known as binaural audition, is one of several clues to recognizing the direction from which sounds originate. Vigorous research during the 1970s brought this highly complex phenomenon into sharp focus. [**9**] But for the present purpose, many details must be omitted so some statements are subject to various technical restrictions that are not mentioned. Generally speaking, it has been shown experimentally that people are able to hear pulsed microwaves from 200 to 3,000 MHz with peak power densities of 300 mW/cm^2 and average power densities as low as 0.4 mW/cm^2 with pulse widths of 1 to 100 (usec) microseconds. As the shape of the response curve is a steep sided mesa, the range of pulse width is probably about 10 to 40 μsec. In terms of average power density the threshold is approximately 120 μW/cm^2. Therefore, very low-intensity, microwave radiation pulsed at 50 to 100 cycles per second would be 'heard' and aptly described as humming. Experiments with animals showed that cats were 20 to 30% more sensitive than people but one dog tested was 5 times more sensitive. That result may explain, why agitated dogs are the first indication of many UFO events.

An entirely different mechanism, known as the thermoplastic process, appears to be responsible for the high pitch sounds. Absorption of energy in biological tissue produces an extremely small increase in temperature. Due to thermal expansion of the tissue, a corresponding increase in pressure is produced that then propagates through the medium as a sound wave. A microwave pulse impinging upon the head thereby creates a pressure wave that propagates through the skin, muscle, bone, and brain tissue and reverberates inside the cranium. These vibrations are carried by bone conduction to register as sound in the auditory nerve. Microprobes have been surgically implanted in the auditory nerves of animals to measure the frequencies of pulses stimulated by this mechanism. It has been found that *the frequency depends only upon the size of the head and the acoustical properties of brain tissue*. An extremely intricate, theoretical analysis by Dr. James C. Lin accurately duplicates the experimental data for guinea pigs and cats. [**10**] For example, the calculated frequency for cats ranged from 30 to 40 kHz whereas the measured value was 38 kHz. The measured value for cats is within their normal hearing range, up to 60 kHz, but well beyond the limit of human hearing at 20 kHz. The calculated threshold for cats was 589 mW/cm^2 for a head radius of 3 cm. For a man with a head radius of 7 cm, the calculated frequency range from 10 to 15 kHz based upon theoretical models expected to yield upper and lower limits. The calculated threshold for man, 2183 mW/cm^2, is extremely high compared to safety limits in the U.S. for short-term exposure of only 10 mW/cm^2. Anyone hearing a shrill whistle from a UFO would be in serious danger.

Thus experiment and theory show that the pitch perceived from impinging microwave pulses result from two, distinctly different, mechanisms. At weak intensities and pulse rates in the low audio range, the pulses directly stimulate the inner ear and are interpreted as humming sounds. For very intensive radiation pulses, pressure waves reverberate inside the head creating the impression of high pitch whistles. No known mechanism produces tones of intermediate frequencies. Thus the sounds stimulated by microwave radiation from UFOs would be discontinuously dependent upon the distance to the UFO. [**11**]

SMELL

The idea that UFOs might produce some unique odours originally carried a touch of humour. But they really do! An early survey of the literature turned up 18 cases where witnesses noticed peculiar odours and attempted to describe them. Comparisons with sulphur dioxide, as in rotten eggs, were the most numerous. Other descriptions referred to benzine and its derivatives. Finally, a number of descriptions almost certainly identified ozone.

Explanation

Irradiation of various gases with microwaves produces a wide variety of gas atoms and free radicals, the required components for chemical reactions. In air, nitric oxide is produced. The efficiency of this reaction is greatly enhanced when the radiation is pulsed. Ethane and methane are decomposed but benzene is stable in the radiation. In other words, a pulsed source of microwaves in air can generate nitric oxide and, in subsequent reactions, the benzene family that has been detected near UFOs. As benzine is not decomposed by the field, any formed would tend to accumulate to detectable concentrations. These concentrations need not be great considering the extreme sensitivity of the olfactory sense. Oxidation of sulphur by microwaves has been accomplished in the laboratory, namely conversion of sulphur dioxide to sulphur trioxide. Similar oxidation of sulphur, contaminating the atmosphere from automobiles and other sources, into sulphur dioxide could well account for the most commonly reported sulphurous odours.

There is a curious relationship between this aspect of UFOs and the controversial subject of ball lightning. Many of the same odours have been reported in association with small balls of light at close range. Electrical discharges in the atmosphere change energy states of various atoms and numerous chemical compounds are formed. Nitrogen is elevated to a metastable state having several interesting properties. It produces a soft, white glow that continues for some time after the discharge terminates. Such excited nitrogen is called 'activated' because it readily combines with other atoms whereas ordinary nitrogen gas does not. It combines with hydrogen to form ammonia (NH_3) and with oxygen to form nitric oxide (NO). Below about 150°C it reacts with other atmospheric gases to form nitrobenzene ($C_6H_5NO_2$), an oily substance having a strong odour like bitter almonds. Also produced by electrical discharges in air is the highly reactive ozone (O_3) that can be detected around sparking electrical machinery.

As an aside, it is observed that the slow decay of activated nitrogen giving off a white glow is probably the cause of white, luminous trails so often seen behind UFOs as they traverse the sky. Activated nitrogen may also cause the slowly decaying clouds that are sometimes left at landing sites when UFOs take off.

It is clear that odours reported in UFO events are precisely those that would be expected from chemical reactions in the atmosphere triggered by electrical discharges or microwave radiation. Very few witnesses were cognizant of the technical details so their testimony can be taken at face value. The presence of microwaves seems assured but, unfortunately, the data do not allow any quantitative deductions. [**12**]

TASTE

Three hunters in the Ocala National Forest of Florida were looking for a lost deerhound at 9:00 pm on December 14, 1975. They spotted a hemispherical object 8m hign with 5 "legs" about 4.5m long. Emitting a bright blue-white light, it hovered over a powerline then moved away as the witness approached to within about 220m. During the half hour observation their CB radio failed, a humming sound was heard, a strange odour hung in the air, and "... they had a *funny metalic taste* in their mouths." (NB: the coincidence of the other phenomena.)

A Canadian case on October 23, 1967, involving 17 witnesses and 5 objects, seems to be significant although the details were poorly described. A real estate salesman approached to within 220m of objects that had landed in a vacant lot. "Everything he ate tasted the same and there was a *taste of copper or metal in his mouth*." The objects flew away over some power lines that lighted up and the salesman's car and the steel flagpole at the show house were later found to be magnetized.

Explanation

Recalling these and other such reports, the author's curiosity was raised by a casual remark of a friend. She had undergone a treatment of electrolysis for hair removal. When the electrode was placed on the cheek, she experienced a taste sensation "like eating tinfoil" that lasted about 15 minutes after the treatment. The implication was obvious. Some electrical or magnetic effect produced the same sensation in an electrolysis patient as in a UFO witness! A professional electrologist furnished some details. Low-voltage electicity is applied to a hair root at 13.56 MHz or with direct current. In her experience, the taste occured only when using DC. It is most prominent during an "after treatment" on the lower portion of the face using, as a cathode, a freely rotating, conducting cylinder covered with damp gauze. The author reluctantly submitted to such treatment and decisively experienced the phenomenon as the device rolled over the cheeks, lips, chin, and especially the jaws. The taste is hard to describe and the word "metallic" came to mind but seemed inadequate. There was a tingling component and a strange bitterness. The location on the tongue was the lower edge of the front half where the tongue contacts the teeth. [**13**]

Technical information on this subject is hard to find but a comprehensive, survey article may be available in some medical libraries. [**14**] The phenomenon has been known since the pioneering work in electricity. It was discovered when two dissimilar metals were applied to the tongue, creating a primitive battery. Test subjects over the years have always had difficulty in describing the taste. Much research has developed a wealth of detail about the phenomenon. While individual responses vary considerably, the threshold for detection is a current of about 100 microamperes. The taste increases with stronger currents. Its onset is immediate but it decays very slowly. The sensation is evoked by direct current pulses as slow as 0.5 per second that is perceived as continuous. Alternating current is also effective but not above 1,000 Hz. While the cause has not been unequivocally established, it appears to be a combination of direct action of electricity on the taste cells and normal, chemical effects of products of electrical breakdown of saliva.

A fundamental theorem of electromagnetism is that a magnetic field, while changing intensity, will induce an electric field that, in turn, drives a current in a conductor. So the current causing metallic taste could arise from a transient magnetic field alternating at less than 1,000 sec^{-1} or one being turned on-and-off in that range. But the human body is almost as effective an antenna as a copper wire of the same length. So short blasts of electromagnetic energy could also produce eddy currents of sufficient strength to stimulate the taste. In any event, the essential requirements are a current of at least 100 microamp that may be DC or pulsing up to 1,000 sec^{-1}. By examining other pertinent data from UFO sightings one might be able to establish which of these two mechanisms in involved.

REVIEW OF MAGNETIC EFFECTS

Magnetic fields associated with UFOs have produced a wide variety of effects strongly suggesting a static or slowly changing field. They have *induced permanent magnetism* in ferrous objects such as signs and flagpoles. Many *wristwatches have been stopped* during a UFO sighting then later found by a jeweller to be magnetized. Such residual magnetism could have been produced only by static fields or ones changing intensity very slowly: rapidly pulsing fields, on the other hand, would erase magnetism. That technique is used to erase magnetic tapes and to 'degauss' ships. The author has duplicated most types of *radio interference* from UFOs with static, magnetic fields. [**15**] The most sensitive components of transistor radios are coils in tuned radio-frequency and intermediate-frequency circuits. The magnetic field modifies the physical property of their ferrite cores. The circuits are thereby detuned from the selected station. Reception begins to fade at about 350 gauss and is entirely blocked at about 800 gauss. Such fields are moderately strong, being typical for bar magnets. Continued increases in field strength will shift the tuning to the next station of higher frequency. A radio can be tuned across the whole dial in that manner. Radios originally set at stations in the upper end of the dial will be driven completely beyond the AM band where they can receive navigational signals in Morse code.

Slowly pulsing magnetic fields around UFOs have been suspected to cause agitation or *spinning of compasses*. Intuition suggests that sustained rotation of a compass can be produced by a weak magnetic field only if it is pulsed at a rate approximating the natural, resonant frequency of the compass. That point was verified in experiments by the author in which spin rates of liquid-filled compasses were sustained from 6 to 20 rpm depending upon the strength of the applied magnetic impulses. Overly strong impulses threw the compass into wild agitation. On February 2, 1973, Captain Peter Telling was piloting a commercial flight in Australia. At first fearing a fire in his starboard engine, he spotted an intense bluish-white light 7-14m in diameter at a distance of 10m. It paced the airplane for 20 to 25 seconds. His automatic direction finder, gyrocompass, and *magnetic compass* all went haywire and spun at 12 rpm. [**16**] The pulse rate of the magnetic field was thus measured to be as slow as 12 rpm = 0.2 sec^{-1} or one pulse every 5 seconds.

Actually, the magnetic fields from UFOs have been precisely measured with scientific instruments in the field! [**17**] French aerospace scientist, Dr. Claude Poher, former head of GEPAN, studied the relationship between UFO sightings and major disturbances of the earth's magnetic field. France maintains a series of research stations monitoring atmospheric conditions, nuclear explosions, and the three components of the geomagnetic field. They are generally located in remote areas to minimize electomagnetic interference. During the fall of 1954 when UFO sightings were unusually frequent, fifteen events were found in which the exact location and time of the sighting corresponded with a major disturbance of the magnetic field at the research station. While moderately strong fields are measured in gauss, very weak fields are measured in gammas, the ratio being 1 gamma = 10^{-5} gauss. Maximum disturbances in the vertical component of the field ranged from about 5 gamma to about 80 gamma for distances of 24 to 100 km. The geomagnetic field in France is about 0.454 gauss with a declination of 10 degrees west and a dip of 60 degrees downward toward the north. Hence, the vertical component would normally be (0.454) sin 60 = 0.393 gauss = 39.300 gamma. The measurements are thus seen to be extremely sensitive, namely on the order of 1 part in 1,000. Five experimental data points clustering around 5 gamma at 85 km are taken as a baseline. As magnetic fields diminish from their source inversely as the third power of the distance, Poher's data allow the calculation of the source strength, or magnetic moment, of the UFO. It is found to be 7.7 x 10^{11} amp $metre^2$! That figure is phenomenally high compared to current research on super-fields and the hint of advanced technology from unearthly sources is inescapable. The magnetic field strength at any distance from UFOs can also be calculated from the scientific measurements. It would be 425 gauss at a distance of 130m from a UFO, a typical range at which electromagnetic effects are observed and consistent with the experimental data on radios.

From the foregoing review of magnetic effects, it appears that magnetic fields from UFOs are static or pulse very slowly. It is, therefore, unlikely that they could produce significant currents in the body because such induction is proportional to the rate of change of the field strength. The rate of change of a static field is, of course, nil.

In contrast, direct evidence indicates that pulsed microwaves are a strong candidate. In 1958, a four-year, comprehensive, medical survey of the physiological effects of radar was completed at Lockheed Corporation. Many employees were routinely exposed to low-intensity radiation during final tests of aircraft radar. Their medical histories were compared with those of employees who had not been exposed. Despite various minor symptoms, no pathological changes were observed for occasional exposures up to 13.1 mW/cm^2 in the S- and X-bands having frequencies of 1,550-5,200 and 5,200-11,00 sec^{-1} respectively. Almost 6% of 335 people exposed to the S-band field experienced a "buzzing or pulsing sensation," a phenomenon with which the reader is already familiar. "Less than 1%..." presumably meaning three individuals, experienced "sparking between dental fillings or a *peculiar* metallic taste." [**18**] (My emphasis.) There seems little doubt that pulsed microwaves are perfectly capable of stimulating the taste, particularly at power densities greater than 13.1 mW/cm^2.

FEELING

In almost every instance of short range observations of UFOs, witnesses have experienced a sensation of heat. The intensity may vary from a mild warmth to a frightening and painful burn. Frequently the witness retains a semi-permanent record of such encounters in the form of a sunburn or even blisters. The burns are generally limited to areas that are directly exposed to the UFO.

Explanation

If a UFO is encased in a brilliant plasma, it will radiate energy in a broad band of frequencies or wavelengths. Extending well beyond the visible spectrum, the flux of energy will include longer and shorter wavelengths in the infrared and ultraviolet regions. Infrared radiation is the mechanism by which heat is transmitted at a distance. If, on the other hand, the UFO is not covered with a plasma and a metallic surface is visible, it can still radiate substantial intensities of infrared due to elevated temperature, particularly if it is self-luminous, glowing in a soft orange color like the heating elements of an electric stove. The radiant energy transmitted per unit area and unit time may be expressed as millicalories per square cm per second (mcal/cm^2 sec) and compared to energy received from the sun. The solar irradiation constant, the energy striking an area perpendicular to the rays, amounts to 32.3 mcal/cm^2 sec. So the rate of heat input to a witness can be roughly estimated from the description of the experience or more accurately if the witness were asked for a direct comparison. Assuming isotropic emission from the UFO, one can calculate the total energy emitted by the UFO in that bandwidth. But that is not the whole story.

■ 1. 'SUNBURNED' SKIN

Manuel Amparano, a policeman in Kerman, California, observed a bright object in the sky during the night. It emitted a blue flash then departed straight upward in seconds. Upon returning to the station, he was found to be sunburned as red as a lobster. The effect faded in four hours. The burn was only on the portion of his body directly exposed to the UFO. His *long-sleeve uniform afforded no protection* but he was completely shielded by the door of the patrol car. [**19**]

In Baden, Pennsylvania, on August 13, 1965, a middle-aged man saw a disc in the night sky fly in front of the moon. It was estimated to be 100 m in diameter at a distance of 700 m. Its orange lights weakened as it became very intense blue for 3 seconds. Shortly afterward a shock wave was felt. Within 20 minutes his eyes became painful and he gradually lost his vision for a few days. Oddly his entire body was sunburned as if by "ultraviolet." [**20**]

Explanation

Obviously, ultraviolet could not have produced the sunburn because it could not have penetrated the clothing! The same applies to the California policeman. Microwaves, however, could penetrate clothing and burn the skin but be reflected by a car door. Early experiments by the U.S. Navy explored the heating sensation of microwaves. Energy from 10cm waves and longer penetrates deeply and is dispersed throughout the body. Hence only a small fraction is absorbed at the surface where biological heat sensors are located. But shorter wave lengths are preferentially absorbed in the skin and are thus more effective in stimulating the sensation of heat and causing burns. They are almost as effective as infrared! The experiments showed that the threshold for feeling warmth from microwaves of 1 cm in an exposure of a few seconds was about 2 mcal/cm^{2}sec. [**21**] In other words, people can feel the warmth from 1 cm microwaves at less than one-tenth the energy flux from the sun. Burns would naturally be caused by much higher intensities.

■ 2. HOT OBJECTS

David Winter experienced a typical automobile failure while driving home in British Columbia at 2:15 a.m. on December 13, 1967. It was a clear, cold night with the temperature about 20 to 25 oF. He pulled off the road to look under the hood for the source of trouble. Only then did he notice an object hovering about 15m above the ground about 100m away. It was shaped like a dome, flat on the bottom, displaying red and green lights with what appeared to be portholes emitting light. The surface looked like wire-brushed steel. He noted that his battery felt warm. Becoming apprehensive, he then got back into the car while watching the object drift closer in a gentle rocking motion. He became frightened upon discovering that his hair felt warm. Later he said ...and the copper ring on my left ring finger got rather warm and unpleasant to feel and I finally took it off. I have a sterling ring on my right little finger. And it wasn't as hot as the copper ring but it was still getting unpleasant so I decided to take that off too. And I notice my watch getting a little.... I have a metal watch band here and it got warm ..." Also, "A metal button and metal fly in my pants and they got hot." During a second inspection of the car, he retrieved a flashlight from a tool box and noticed that its metal frame became hot but the lens remained cold. Metallic parts of the car had become hot but the tires felt as cold as the air.

Explanation
Observe the contrasts between the items that were heated versus those that were not. Non-conducting materials (rubber and glass) remained at ambient temperature whereas electrical conductors (steel, copper, and silver) became hot. The watch band may have been gold but its material was not stated. Warmth of the battery was caused by heating of the battery acid, a conducting medium. **[22]** Undoubtedly, a high-frequency electromagnetic field was inducing eddy currents in the conductors that produced resistance heating. Differences in the temperatures of the rings would be expected due to the different electrical resistivities of copper and silver and their individual dimensions. **[23]**

■ 3. ELECTRICAL SHOCK
In the late 40s and early 50s, most UFO sightings were high-altitude flybys unless it was that witnesses were more reluctant to confess to close encounters and investigators to report them. It was not until the 1954 flap in France that witnesses in substantial numbers reported UFOs at very short ranges and an accompanying feeling of tingling or electrical shock. Then in 1958 near Lima, Peru, a UFO descended and hovered near a truck, bus, and car. Passengers in all three vehicles felt an electrical shock at the same time that their engines failed. NICAP was the first organization to take a particular interest in such electromagnetic effects and to publish an extensive record of the events. **[24]**

Explanation
Radar systems operating at microwave frequencies have become so powerful that the hazard of electrical shock to workmen has become serious. Special protective clothing has been developed that covers the entire body, head, face, hands, and feet. Made of metalized nylon, it reflects electromagnetic energy away from the wearer. A special feature assures electrical continuity across the seams. A surface layer of neoprene prevents closing a circuit between two objects at different electrical potentials that might be touched at the same time by a workman. **[25]**

Human-like creatures seen in association with UFOs are invariably described as wearing skin-tight, one-piece uniforms covering the whole body including the feet. They are notably without buttons, zippers, pockets, discontinuities, and seams. One witness peering into the goggles of a UFOnaut observed a fine, wire-mesh screen that would effectively shield the eyes against microwaves. UFOnauts are apparently taking the same precautions that we are in the presence of intense microwave fields. In such environments near UFOs, unprotected witnesses would be expected to feel the induced currents in the skin as a tingling sensation or an electrical shock.

BY-PASSING THE PHYSICAL SENSES
Some physical effects are visited upon the witness although they are not immediately registered by the ordinary senses.

■ A. PARALYSIS
At the time of an engine failure in the presence of a UFO, the witness may be surprised to discover that he is unable to move. A specially graphic example was the experience of a farmer in Saskatchewan. He climbed down from a swather to investigate a 3m, silver-colored, dome-shaped object that was hovering close to the ground and spinning in deep grass. Upon backing away and remounting the machine, he noticed four more similar objects spaced out along a nearby slough. The first object then rose up to about 60m followed by the second, then the third, and so on. During these manoeuvers he was paralyzed. In a taped interview he later said "I sat there like I was froze, I couldn't move nothing." Further elaboration was telling and clear:

"I didn't have the strength to move anything on it (the farm machine). See, its a hydrostatic drive, automatic like a car, steering also. I couldn't move anything, all I had to do was push the lever or turn the steering wheel, but I couldn't. I felt like I was hypnotized or paralyzed, I had no strength. I tried to move that lever but I couldn't. Just a touch of your finger - it will move. Nothing seemed to work right. I was scared, I've been scared before, but nothing like this. I wanted this hand on the gear shift and this one on the steering wheel and you think I could move it? I couldn't budge it." **[26]**

Explanation
Of primary concern here are the fundamental properties of motor control nerves. In some ways they resemble electrical wires but the similarity cannot be carried very far. A central core of protoplasmic material, a moderately good conductor, is surrounded by a sheath or membrane of a fatty substance that is a moderately good insulator. Orders to outlying muscles, sent by the central nervous system, travel along these fibers as a wave of electrical potential. The travelling pulse, known as

an action potential, always has the same intensity in a particular fiber. At any point along the fiber, it is either present or it is not. It never shows up only partially or at a potential different from the norm. Energy for transmission of this signal derives from the fiber itself, not from driving force at the input end. The sheath is interrupted at intervals of about 1 mm, called Ranvier nodes, and the transmission energy is supplied by the passage of certain ions through the membranes in these short segments. The width of the pulse is about 1 millisecond and it travels at various speeds, depending upon the size of the fiber, typically about 10 m/second. Measurements of electrical potentials inside the sheath show that a fiber at rest is about 0.07 volts negative compared to the external solution. An action potential travelling down the fiber has a positive amplitude of about 0.10 to 0.12 volts. Therefore, at the moment the action potential occupies a position in the fiber, its interior experiences a momentary swing that is about 0.04 volts positive compared to the outside.

Experimental electrodes implanted in the fiber at any location can trigger the standard pulse by impressing a potential difference across the membrane of about 0.02 volts or greater. Pulses then travel outward in both directions along the fiber, although they would normally travel in only one direction. After the pulse has passed through one segment of the fiber, a finite time is required for that segment to return to normal. During the recovery period, it is completely incapable of transmitting another pulse. For about one millisecond the fiber cannot be stimulated at all. For roughly another millisecond, it can but only by a stimulus stronger than usual. If a stimulus below the threshold of 0.02 volts followed by another within about 2 millisec, then the second one may evoke a response even though it too is weaker than the threshold. The first stimulus opens the gates so to speak, for the next one.

If microwave radiation were capable of providing the requisite stimulus, then action potentials would be induced. It has been found, in fact, that microwaves can create the necessary electrical tension across the membrane. By inserting miniature electrodes into nerve fibers, the potential difference between the inside and the outside can be measured. Irradiation by microwaves induces potentials that are typically in the milivolt range, but are sometimes as high as 0.10 volt, five times stronger than the threshold value of 0.02 volt. As action potentials triggered by this mechanism would be identical in every respect to those that are sent by the central nervous system, there would be no way that receptors could detect them to be fraudulent. Muscular responses would be absolutely dictated by such artificially produced signals. A muscle contraction persists for about 500 millisec before relaxing. So a series of pulses impacting a muscle at a faster rate would produce an indefinitely, sustained contraction. As all skeletal muscles occur in op-

	ELECTROMAGNETIC FIELD				
	Microwave ?	Threshold (mW/cm²)	Frequency (MHz)	Pulse Rate (sec⁻¹)	Pulse Width (microsec)
PHYSICAL SENSES					
Sight	No	-	-	-	-
Hearing: Bullets	No	-	-	-	-
Shockwaves	Yes	?	>60,000	?	?
Low Pitch	Yes	0.012	200-3000	50-100	1 - 100
High Pitch	Yes	2183	Any	Any	Any
Smell	Yes	?	Any	Enhances	Any
Taste 100 µAmp	Yes	<13.1	Any	<1,000	Any
Feel: Heat	Yes	8.37	30,000	Any	Any
Hot Objects	Yes	?	Any	Any	Any
Elec Shock	Yes	?	Any	Any	Any
BYPASSING PHYSICAL SENSES					
Paralysis	Yes	?	≃ 3,000	>500 Enhc	Any
Injuries: Burns	Yes	?	30,000	Any	Any
Internal	Yes	?	< 3,000	Any	Any
Hair Loss	No	-	-	-	-

Summary of infrared electromagnetic parameters.

posing pairs, their indescriminate and simultaneous contraction would freeze them in rigid opposition, that is, paralyze the body.

Any legitimate action potential from the central nervous system, representing some intended muscular behaviour, would be annihilated upon collision with the extraneous signal travelling in the wrong direction. Thus action potentials triggered by microwaves interfere with volitional control. Partial loss of motor control would be produced by slower pulses of microwaves, a reported UFO effect. [**27**] Because of health hazards, humans have not been intentionally exposed to high-intensity microwave fields so there is no experimental verification of the above analysis. However, motor disruption and partial paralysis by microwaves have been experimentally observed in chickens, pigeons, sea gulls, and small animals. [**28**]

■ 2. RADIATION INJURIES

An Ohio farmer and his wife were watching TV one night in November 1958 when the set acted up and went black. Then a strange light from the window caused them to look outside and discover a large object some 6m in diameter hovering over their backyard. The husband went outside to investigate. He remained still (paralyzed?) as the object moved directly over him. Immediately he felt ill and within 48 hours was dead, "...his insides fried as though by the heat of a microwave oven." [**29**]

A similar exposure of lesser severity may have been the cause of major health problems in the extremely well-documented Cash-Landrum case near Houston on December 29, 1980. It has probably been investigated more thoroughly than any other case and much has been written about it. [**30**] In the briefest possible summary, two principal witnesses were dazzled by a diamond-shaped object hovering low over a highway. Around it at some distance were a large number of helicopters of recognizable types. Exposure to the bright light, heat, and other radiation lasted 5 to 10 minutes. Both victims suffered severe burns, blisters, loss of hair, internal injuries, and at least 18 other symptoms.

Explanation

The investigators, including medical professionals and other physicians who cared for the patients over an extended period, fully recognized that the above injuries were caused by radiation of a broad spectrum including X-rays, microwaves, infrared, and ultraviolet. They also emphasize that the object described by the witnesses was simply not identifiable by them, nothing more. Also the presence of helicopters raised the question of whether the object might have been an experimental aircraft of the United States Air Force. The main points here are that 1) infrared and probably short microwaves produced the burns, 2) internal injuries were probably caused by the heating effect of the more penetrating, longer microwaves, and 3) loss of hair was due to the well-known effect of ionizing X-rays with probable contributions from microwaves. An atmospheric plasma produces a strong component of X-rays by the deceleration of electrons colliding with molecules and ions in the highly agitated, ionized gas. This process, known molecules and ions in the highly agitated, ionized gas. This process, known as Bremsstrahlung, also generates a broad spectrum of photons having lesser energies and correspondingly longer wavelengths in accord with the reported injuries in the Cash-Landrum case.

WEIGHING THE EVIDENCE

It has been shown from scientific sources that microwaves from UFOs could account for most physiological responses of witnesses, except for such mundane matters as visual observation and hearing bullets ricochet. For the senses of hearing, smell, taste, and feel, the formerly puzzling effects were traced to specific mechanisms that are capable of producing them. Some interactions between microwaves and the sensory organs appear to be mysterious, may be unknown to the general public or even experts in other fields, but are well established facts. In addition, much information was found to describe the interactions quantitatively. It should be helpful at this point to assemble that data in **Table 1** and analyse the various constraints imposed by the sensory physiology.

Scanning down the column of thresholds in Table 1 highlights the extreme sensitivity for hearing a humming sound at 0.012 mW/cm^2. It is little wonder that this response frequently causes the witness to look around for the source and discover an object in the sky if he were not previously alerted by the family pet. The humming sound is so consistently reported that the corresponding field parameters are considered to be typical. So a pulse rate of about 50 to 100 cycles per second is implied in accordance with the frequency of audio tones described as humming. That rate is well below the limit of 1,000 sec^{-1} required for inducing metallic taste. In order for microwaves to be heard, they must be between 200 and 3,000 MHz and have pulse widths between 1 and 100 microsec but probably between 10 to 40 microsec.

The feeling of heat begins in the upper frequency ranges at 2 mcal/cm^{2}sec. But direct comparison with the other thresholds requires a conversion into compatible units leading to the equivalent value of 8.37 mW/cm^{2}sec. [**31**] As this threshold for feeling heat is about 700 times higher than that for hearing, it is no surprise that the sensation of heating is restricted to short-range cases whereas a UFO at a considerable distance can be heard. As pointed out previously, the threshold for high-pitch sound, being some 22,000 times greater than for the hum, would endanger the observer. No further evidence allowing determination of thresholds could be found.

As to the frequency of the radiation, there is a pattern of consistency. Whereas hearing requires frequencies of 200 to 3,000 MHz, paralysis implied approximately 3,000 while internal injuries require less than 3,000. All frequencies are capable of producing high-pitch sounds, metallic taste, odours, heating of conductors, and electrical shock. These effects, therefore, could all be generated within the frequency limits imposed by the humming sound. On the other hand, something unique appears to be happening when shock waves are generated because they require frequencies greater than 60,000 MHz to couple with the molecules in the atmosphere. A clue may be afforded by the blue flash that was reported in two cases above, but this question is unresolved.

CONCLUSIONS

Careful study of UFO case histories can reveal considerable detail on the sensory responses of witnesses. Furthermore, a parallel survey of scientific literature in variety of subjects will sometimes disclose specific mechanisms that may be responsible for the reported effects. Finally, experimental data in the literature or obtained by the investigator can provide quantitative information about the physiological responses and the parameters of UFO fields. It has been found that most UFO effects on people can be attributed to a complex field consisting of two components, namely:

- **1)** An electromagnetic field in the microwave region having
  - **a)** frequency in the range of 200 to 3,000 MHz,
  - **b)** pulse repetition rate of 50 to 100 sec^{-1}, and
  - **c)** pulse width of 1 to 100, more likely 10 to 40 microsec.

  Theonset of physiological responses begins with a humming sensation at an average power density of 0.4 mW/cm^2 but field intensities many thousand times greater may be experienced.
- **2)** A magnetic field that varies intensity slightly about every two seconds. The intensity at the witness is on the order of 1,000 gauss for close encounters.

An extensive series of laboratory and field experiments could reduce the range of uncertainties in the field parameters, and eventually lead to a full understanding of UFO propulsion systems.

Reports of UFOs emphasize two major points: Firstly, they hover in the sky with no indication of a familiar propulsion system such as propellers, jets, or rockets. No momentum is transferred to the atmosphere and there is a notable absence of violent and noisy downwash. The objects appear to defy gravity. The other point is their strange manner of flitting about. Observers are frequently startled by a sudden acceleration far exceeding normal experience, also by instantaneous stops and right-angle turns at high speed. Not only do UFOs appear to be antigravitational, they behave as though they had no inertia.

In the General Theory of Relativity, Dr. Albert Einstein postulated the Principle of Equivalence. It states that the property of matter, called mass, is the same whether responding to gravitational forces or to accelerations. For the mathematically inclined reader, that means that the small 'm' in the universal gravitational equation ($F = GmM/r^2$) is identical to the small 'm' in the inertial equation ($F = ma$). That identity has been demonstrated in satellite experiments to a precision of 1 part in 10^{14}. So what does that mean? If a method should be developed to nullify the effect of gravity, it would automatically and necessarily nullify inertia! A hovering UFO that directly defeats gravity would have an inherent ability to fly without the familiar restrictions of inertia.

It is remarkable, indeed, that witnesses in all countries, languages, and educational levels from scholars to primitives have been describing the phenomenon correctly for 40 years although very few were acquainted with General Relativity. We have not listened well.

REFERENCES

■ 1 - **McCampbell,** James M., 'The Scientific Challenge of UFOs', *The MUFON UFO Journal*, No 194, April 1984. ■ 2 - **Fowler,** Raymond E., *Casebook of a UFO Investigator*, p 45, Prentice-Hall, 1981 and *Interplanetary Visitors*, p 112, Exposition Press, 1974. Also see **Salisbury,** Frank B. *The Utah UFO Display*, p 94, Devin-Adair, 1974. ■ 3 - **Pratt,** Bob, Editor, translated by James E. O'Brien, 'GEPAN's Most Significant Case', *The MUFON UFO Journal*, March 1984. ■ 4 - **McCampbell,** James M., *UFOlogy*, Chapter 4, Celestial Arts, 1973. ■ 5 - **Basterfield,** Keith and Bill **Chalker,** '*New Physical Evidence Cases in Australia*', MUFON UFO Journal, No 156, February 1981. ■ 6 - **McCampbell,** James M., 'An Hypothesis Concerning The Origin of UFOs - Horses Under The Hood', p 37, *Thesis-Antithesis*, Proceedings of a Symposium sponsored by the Los Angeles Chapter of the American Institute For Aeronautics and Astronautics, September 27, 1985; and 'UFO Technology And Technicians', p 109, *The Golden Gateway To Astronomy*, WAA/ALPO/AANC Joint Conference on Astronomy, San Francisco, August7-10, 1975. ■ 7 - **Stevens,** Wendelle C. and Paul **Dong,** *UFOs Over Modern China, A Survey of the Phenomenon*, UFO Photo Archives, 1983. ■ 8 - **Fawcett,** Lawrence and Barry J. **Greenwood,** *Clear Intent*, Prentice-Hall, 1984. ■ 9 - **Lin,** James C., *Microwave Auditory Effects and Applications*, Charles C. Thomas, 1978. ■ 10 - Ibid., p. 157. ■ 11 - **McCampbell,** James M., 'Hum And Whistle A UFO Tune', *The MUFON UFO Journal*, No 205, February 1985. ■ 12 - **McCampbell,** James M., *UFOlogy*, p. 38. ■ 13 - **McCampbell,** James M., 'A Taste For UFOs', *The MUFON UFO Journal*, No 205, May 1985. ■ 14 - **Bujas,** Zoran, 'Electrical Taste', Chapter 10, *Handbook of Sensory Physiology*, Volume IV, Part 2, *Chemical Senses*, Lloyd M. **Beidler,** Editor, Springer-Verlag, 1971. ■ 15 - **McCampbell,** James M., *UFO Interference With Radios*, In press. ■ 16 - **Hauck,** Dennis W., Editor, 'Pilot Experiences Electromagnetic Effects', *The MUFON UFO Journal*, No 107, p. 11, October 1976. ■ 17 - **Hynek,** J. Allen and Jacques **Vallée,** *The Edge of Reality*, p. 89, Regnery, 1975. ■ 18 - **Barron,** Charles I. and Albert A. **Baraff,** 'Medical Considerations of Exposure To Microwaves (RADAR)', *Journal of the American Medical Association*, Vol. 168, No. 9, pp. 1194-1199, November 1, 1958. ■ 19 -

Hynek, J. Allen, Editor-In-Chief, 'California Policeman Burned By UFO', *International UFO Reporter*, Vol. 3, No.9. p.10, September 1978. ■ **20** - **Vallée,** Jacques, *Passport To Magonia*, Case 677, p.313, Regnery, 1969. ■ **21** - **McCampbell,** James M. 'UFO Interference With Automobile Electrical Systems, Part I: Headlights', *Proceedings of the 1976 CUFOS Conference*, Lincolnwood, Illinois. ■ **22** - **McCampbell,** James M., 'Overheating of Car Batteries', *The MUFON UFO Journal*, No. 167, January 1982. ■ **23** - **McCampbell,** James M., 'UFOs And Hot Rings', *THE MUFON UFO Journal*, No. 189, November 1983. ■ **24** - **Hall,** Richard H., *The UFO Evidence*, P. 73, NICAP, 1964. ■ **25** - **McCampbell,** James M., *UFOlogy*, p.77. ■ **26** - **McCampbell,** James M., 'Interpreting Reports of UFOs', *Proceedings of 1975 MUFON*, Symposium, Des Moines. ■ **27** - **McCampbell,** James M., *UFOlogy*, P.75. ■ **28** - **Milroy,** William C. and **Sol** M. Michaelson, 'Biological Effects of Microwave Radiation', *Health Physics*, pp. 567- 575, Vol. 20, June 1971. ■ **29** - **Stringfield,** Leonard H., *Situation Red, The UFO Siege*!, Doubleday, 1977. ■ **30** - **Schuessler,** John F., 'Cash-Landrum Case: Speculation About The Medical Effects', p. 108, *MUFON 1984 UFO Symposium Proceedings*. ■ **31** - A convenient approach is to convert watts and cal/sec. 1 erg = 1 erg x 1 BTU/1055 joule x 1 joule/10^7 erg x 252 cal/BTU = 2.39 x 10^{-8} cal. Then 1 watt = 1 joule/sec = 10^7 erg/sec x 2.39 x 10^{-8} cal/erg = 0.239 cal/sec and dividing through by 1,000 gives 1 mW = 0.239 mcal/sec. Hence the threshold = 2 mcal/cm^2sec x 1 mW/0.239 (mcal/sec) = 8.37 mW/cm^2.

3.4.4
RADAR AND THE UFO
by Martin Lawrence Shough

■ **MARTIN SHOUGH**. Born 1953. Married, living in the village of Steyning, West Sussex, England. Enjoys painting, classical music (he plays a variety of instruments and has performed his own compositions on stage and on radio), and writing (he was a finalist in the 1986 Sussex Poet of the Year competition). He also enjoys the English countryside and English country pubs. A photolithographer by training, in 1985 he set up his own small publishing business.
■ **UFO involvement**: Since co-founding a Sussex UFO group affiliated to Contact UK which was active in the early 1970s, he has maintained an interest in anomalous phenomena. Specific interests are: the UFO problems and the philosophy of scientific method: statistical analysis: and radar/UFO events.

'UFOs are in the first place a problem not for physics but for psychology - the psychology of *our own attitudes*. We do not know what to believe; but more importantly we do not know *how* to believe or what we should accept as proof, as Ruppelt pointed out three decades ago. We certainly have a UFO problem, and what we need is not proof but therapy. The data *are* inconclusive, to be sure, but as Samuel Butler wrote, "Life is the art of drawing sufficient conclusions from insufficient premises."'
■ **Publications**: He has spent more than a year on a detailed study of one of the cases treated here, the Bentwaters/Lakenheath radar/visual case, to be presented in a forthcoming report at greater length .

Also in preparation is a uniform catalogue of reported radar/UFO events from 1947 to the present.
■ **Address**: 25 Mill Road / Steyning / West Sussex BN4 3LN / England. Phone 0903 81 3231.

The present article considers briefly the physical principles of radar; its capabilities and limitations; previous studies of the value of radar evidence in investigating anomalous aerial phenomena; selected radar and radar-visual events; some interpretations of the evidence; and conclusions and recommendations for further work.

THE NATURE OF RADAR

RADAR (**RA**dio **D**etection **A**nd **R**anging) is an echo location system which displays the positions of targets within a certain volume of space around a transmitting/receiving antenna. Fundamental to all types of radar is the visual display of information on target range and azimuth [direction]. How this is accomplished in analogue primary surveillance radars will be described here since most of the events discussed involve such systems.

Radio energy in the microwave band is fed to an antenna which radiates a shaped beam, the antenna revolving to sweep a volume of space. Energy returned from reflective targets is gathered by the same antenna and fed to a cathode ray tube display which indicates by a bright spot or 'blip' the position of each target. Azimuth indication is determined by the orientation of the antenna when an echo is received, the electronic sweep of the radar scope being directly controlled by varying voltages from a potentiometer coupled to the antenna drive shaft. Range information is given by the round-trip time of the reflected energy, measurement of which is made possible by emitting the energy in pulses: after each pulse the transmitter is switched off and the receiver 'listens' for echoes collected by the antenna. Since the velocity of propagation of electromagnetic energy is known, the delay of the echo can be used to determine range.

In primary surveillance radars of the type under discussion, the whole process is managed in practice roughly as follows. A self-oscillating output device such as a magnetron, which produces its own pulse waveform, is fed by waveguides to a feed horn located at the focus of the antenna, whose geometry (typically parabolic) creates a shaped beam which is narrow in azimuth to give acceptable positional accuracy and broad in elevation to cover altitudes up to several tens of thousands of feet. Reflected pulses from targets caught within the beam are amplified and fed to the plan position indicator (PPI), which displays what is in effect a plan view or map of the area swept by the revolving beam. A received signal causes an electron beam to paint a luminous spot on the PPI at a position corresponding to the azimuth of the antenna and the echo delay time. Each returned pulse creates a spot of excitation, and because the radar beam takes a certain time to pass the target a number of pulses will be reflected with each sweep. The 'blip' therefore appears as a short arc (in the case of, say, an aircraft or similar 'point target') composed of the integrated spots from a number of consecutive pulses. A short period of persistence is usually designed into the screen coating so that the blip decays slowly (over perhaps a second or so), aiding the operator in interpreting the relationship of one blip to the next which may not be painted for several seconds.

Pulse lengths are on the order of one microsecond, and the pulse repetition frequency (PRF) is typically hundreds of pulses per second. The half-pulse length is the value which determines the range resolution of the set: thus, the range resolution of a 1 microsec. pulse which is 984 feet long will be in the region of 500 feet, meaning that the set will not discriminate between targets with a range separation of less than this figure. (In practice, this is a minimum because of the poorer resolution of the display; furthermore, one target may shadow another if they are in the same line of sight from the antenna.) Resolution in azimuth is a function of the width of the beam.

The analogue PPI display models the actual radar environment to scale and with a fidelity which is both bothersome to the routine professional user and of value to the researcher. Much of what appears on-scope before sophisticated signal processing has nuisance value in air traffic control but might be of interest to, say, meteorologists or ufologists: one man's signal may be another man's clutter.

CAPABILITIES AND LIMITATIONS OF RADAR

Every radar's radiation pattern is unique, being partially determined by the siting of the antenna in relation to local topography, and is furthermore inconstant in time due to changing propagation conditions.

Surveillance radar coverage is roughly a toroidal volume centered on the antenna whose depth and height above ground vary with range. As range increases power density falls, cross-sectional beam area increases, and the height of the bottom edge of the beam above ground also (beyond a certain threshold) begins to increase. This last property is due to the curvature of the earth's surface, which is greater than the curvature of the radar ray paths caused by normal atmospheric refractivity. The result is the creation of an artificial horizon below which (under typical conditions) no targets can be detected.

A model of the radar horizon as a simple line of sight modified by atmospheric refractivity is an idealisation never achieved in practice. The ideal surveillance beam shape towards which designers work has a sharp and level bottom edge, consistent range at all altitudes, and a level top edge with no power wasted at high altitudes where no aircraft will fly. In reality, the best approximation to this pattern attainable by antenna design is disturbed yet further by factors such as the nature of the terrain (its changing elevations and the varied scattering and reflecting properties of the surface), the height of the antenna above ground and its siting in relation to surrounding structures, and the differential of atmospheric transparency to radar waves, which varies with elevation. Furthermore, due to the inverse-square attenuation of electromagnetic radiation, the beam does not have a definite shape at all.

The result is a complex pattern which can be defined only by operational criteria. Nowhere within the radiation pattern is detection certain: the practical probability of reliability (and thus maximum range) might be, say, 90%, depending not only on the target but on the power of the radar, the sensitivity of the receiver and the noise-level of the amplifier, variations in elevation and reflectivity of the terrain and ground structures, and atmospheric conditions.

A further problem is 'lobing'. Although most of the energy goes into the main beam, its shaping has many ragged edges and some energy spills over into lobes radiating sideways, or even backwards 180°, and the receiver has the dubious benefit of antenna gain in these directions as well. The principal cause of lobing is reflected ground-incident energy, which interferes with the waves of the main beam to create finger-like lobes in the beam's vertical profile, generating a pattern of vertical coverage resembling a spread hand rotating from the wrist. The result is gaps and peaks which can cause targets to appear and disappear confusingly. Sidelobes are also generated which radiate at a significant azimuth angle from the main beam, though much attenuated, and there may be several pairs of these, becoming weaker as the angle from the main beam increases. The main problem is that since the target azimuth displayed on the PPI is always that of the antenna orientation, any targets detected in sidelobes will be displayed at spurious azimuths.

ANOMALOUS PROPAGATION

Further, the beam can be modified in startling ways if the normal refractivity of the atmosphere is altered by abnormal temperature and humidity. Under these conditions radar energy may reflect echoes from targets on the ground within or even far beyond the normal range. Normally diffuse, such grounds returns could, in special conditions, appear as isolated echoes resembling those from point targets. Even without anomalous propagation (AP) conditions, the radar scope can show all manner of weather returns (eg rain, hail) plus the permanent ground clutter of the radar's immediate environment, although there are methods to reduce or eliminate such problems.

MULTIPLE-TRIP ECHOES

Due to a phenomenon known as multiple-trip returns it is possible, under AP conditions, for the radar to display echoes at spuriously close ranges from targets which are in reality beyond the unambiguous range of the set. For a target moving radially with respect to the antenna its displayed speed and course will match its real speed and course; only the range will be in error. For targets moving tangentially, displayed speed will be much slower than real speed (proportionally to real range) and courses may be very distorted.

GHOST REFLECTIONS

Multiple reflections of the transmitted pulse can occur between an aircraft and an efficient ground reflector (such as an empty lorry or metal building structure) or between two or more aircraft, generating spurious moving targets. Such ghosts appear beyond the aircraft range at a distance proportional to the added round-trip time to the reflector and on a radius passing through the aircraft; thus, as the aircraft flies past the reflector its ghost echo can attain high angular speeds and even appear to follow or intercept the aircraft.

RADIO FREQUENCY INTERFERENCE

Accidental RFI can be caused by other radars, voice communications, navigational aids and many other sources emitting in the crowded electromagnetic spectrum. Self-induced interference from a radar's own components can occur, and even out-of-band signals can, if strong enough, generate secondary intermodulation products which may be displayed. Typical interference effects are radial or spiral patterns appearing across the tube face, but sporadic interference pulses could produce brief, isolated false echoes, Since the spot will only appear on the PPI at the instant the interference occurs, a situation could conceivably arise whereby a cyclic source of interference emitting discrete pulses with a frequency slightly out of phase with the scan rate of the receiver would generate a series of 'echoes' slightly displaced on each scan, creating a false track.

INVERSION REFLECTIONS

A special case of anomalous propagation may arise when an elevated inversion layer partially reflects radar energy to the ground. The pulse may return by the same path and paint a spurious echo. Convincing moving targets may appear if, as is commonly the case, the inversion layer is rippled by waves moving across its surface under the influence of winds.

Less predictable effects may be caused by phenomena which are grouped under the heading clear air echoes or 'angels'. Many such echoes are now attributed to insects; however, relatively localised atmospheric structures are believed on occasion to produce direct returns on sensitive radars.

PREVIOUS STUDIES OF UFOS ON RADAR

Numerous authors have discussed radar and radar-visual events over the last four decades, but the status of this evidence has remained uncertain - indeed it has become less certain since the problems of interpreting radar images have become more widely understood in recent years. No single case has yet been accepted as unequivocal, although a handful of cases are sufficiently well documented and sufficiently intriguing to have been widely espoused as "probable" UFOs. Without exception the publicly available information on such events is inadequate to determine their cause, and in probably the majority of cases crucial data are either lost to us or were never recorded in the first place. To this extent radar evidence takes its place next to every other type of evidence available to the researcher, and one is reduced to estimating probabilities. This in itself is not an unusual situation at the frontiers of scientific research - fugitive and uncertain data are the very lifeblood of science - but it does demand a type of systematic analysis which has yet to be applied.

The number of radar events reported as UFOs is difficult to estimate. A NICAP compilation in 1964 listed about 60 [**1**], and a thorough search of the literature might be expected to yield about twice that number today. The proportion of events unreported is unknown but presumably large. Undoubtedly the watershed in radar-UFO studies was the Condon Report of 1969 [**2**] in which two previously unknown incidents appeared: Lakenheath, 1956, and South Central US RB-47, 1957. The Report was also the first study to attempt a collective analysis of radar events: 35 cases were examined for a variety of possible causes, the emphasis being on the question of whether anomalous propagation conditions could account for otherwise unexplained targets. Thayer's study [**3**] was based largely on USAF records from the Blue Book files and wherever possible utilised local radio refractivity index data to model propagation conditions at the time of the event. The result of this analysis was that 19 cases (or about 54% of the sample) were determined to be probable AP, 8 had explanations as man-made devices (about 23%), in one case there was no 'UFO' to explain, and in 7 cases (20%) Thayer's conclusion was 'unknown'. Of these seven cases Thayer regarded two as indicative of atmospheric propagation phenomena 'so rare that they may constitute unknown phenomena", whilst there was "a small but significant residue" of radar-visual cases which had "no plausible explanation" as man-made objects or propagation phenomena. Thayer recommended future investigation of both these categories of "unknowns", concluding with a list of desirable investigative procedures.

In the section of his summary 'Radar Sightings of UFOs' [**4**], Condon quotes Thayer's statement that "there was no case where the meteorological data tended to negate the anomalous propagation hypothesis". The scientific community ought to be shocked, not only because Condon failed to quote Thayer's relevant conclusions and recommendations, but because the remark he did quote is taken seriously out of context. Thayer was referring specifically tc the sub-category of probable AP cases, not to the entire sample, and it is hard to resist describing

Condon's error as one of prevarication.

Subsequent to the Condon Report a number of significant publications appeared treating radar-visual events, and the two cases cited above yielded a rich harvest of new analyses. In December 1969 the American Association for the Advancement of Science Symposium on UFOs heard contributions dealing with radar events from three of its sixteen participants; Kenneth Hardy, an Air Force weather radar specialist; James McDonald, atmospheric physicist at the University of Arizona; and Donald Menzel, Harvard astrophysicist. Hardy discussed anomalous propagation, echoes from birds and insects, and backscattering from layered atmospheric structures, concluding that painstaking analysis has always been necessary to understand these and other once-puzzling radar phenomenon. Bewildering propagation anomalies may occur which will only be explained by well-designed experiments. McDonald's published paper discussed in detail four radar-visual events, two of which (the Lakenheath and RB-47 cases) had been evaluated as "unknowns" by Thayer. In his analysis of the 1952 Haneda AFB, Tokyo, and 1957 Kirtland AFB, New Mexico, cases McDonald disputed Thayer's conclusions of, respectively, anomalous propagation and unidentified private aircraft. McDonald concluded that there remained "scientifically very important unsolved problems with respect to UFOs", that the Lakenheath event in particular presented "evidence of some phenomena defying ready explanation in terms of present-day science and technology", and that acceptance of the Condon Report's negative recommendations would be "scientifically inadvisable." Menzel's paper discussed anomalous propagation effects studied during his US Navy radar research in World War II, pointing out that these phenomena were very puzzling to scientists and military operators until the theory of refractive trapping had been worked out. Similar phenomenon could account for targets reported latterly as UFOs. Menzel discussed the 1952 Washington DC National Airport incident, concluding that the Blue Book analysis attributing the targets to AP, endorsed by Thayer though contested by McDonald [**5**], was valid.

In discussion, Carl Sagan, planetary scientist at Cornell University, and Robert Baker, an astronautical engineer with UCLA and Computer Sciences Corporation, considered the possibility of using US space-surveillance defence radars to acquire new data on possible anomalous phenomena. MIT physicist Philip Morrison suggested that the "interesting" radar-visual events cited by McDonald could arise from "spoofing", possibly involving classified technology, as a test of defence readiness by friendly intelligence or foreign powers. Astronomer Thornton Page of Wesleyan University observed that whilst the reality and solidity of radar targets is in general very difficult to establish without collateral evidence, the combination of several simultanenous observations makes the presence of a solid object very probable. In a short written contribution, David Atlas, University of Chicago radar propagation specialist, commented that although some radar observations require 'almost incredible atmospheric structures' to be explained as AP effects, nevertheless it is reasonable to expect that such structures will be understood in time. [**6**]

In July 1971, the journal of the American Institute of Astronautics and Aeronautics published an account by McDonald of the 1957 RB-47 incident [**7**] and in September 1971 an analysis by Thayer of the Lakenheath event. Both papers recommended further investigation and were widely regarded as signalling a new level of professional respectability for UFO studies.

1972 saw the publication of a book by J Allen Hynek, astronomer at Northwestern University and former scientific consultant to Blue Book, in which ten radar-visual events were outlined with the conclusion that 'good radar-visual cases, properly investigated, are rare. Those that do exist, however, cannot be easily dismissed.'[**8**] A different conclusion was reached by avionics journalist Philip Klass in 1974.[**9**] Klass presented lengthy analyses of the Lakenheath and RB-47 events in which he was highly critical of the conclusions of Thayer and McDonald and developed ingenious scenarios to explain both cases. In general, Klass felt that anomalous radar phenomena could all be explained by conventional objects, malfunctions and meteorological principles, compounded by the 'susceptibility of radar operators to being misled by spurious targets.' Klass's work is undoubtedly among the most influential in the radar-UFO literature.

There has been little movement towards consensus on the status of radar events in recent years, though a mood of cautious scepticism has spread through ufology since the mid-seventies which is reflected in a less sanguine attitude to the trustworthiness of radar evidence. The complexity of the radar environment aside, cases enjoying the benefit of preserved scope photographs, tapes or even contemporary written logs are very rare, and so the soft-data problem of interpreting human testimony to a large extent remains. In 1979 Randles and Warrington wrote:

"In our examination of cases involving radar observations we have found enough indication that almost all can be explained in terms of possible imperfections or misinterpretations of the displays, and see little substance in the alleged evidence provided by such cases." [**10**]

They make the interesting observation that the majority of cases on record belong to the 1950s, and argue that there are "no known recent radar observations", suggesting that this can be explained by the "troublesome adolescence" of radar development. Although it is a considerable overstatement to assert that radar events are an extinct ufological subspecies, it is true that the number of known incidents has fallen in recent years. This trend may have a different interpretation, however, as we will see later.

In summary, it has to be said that there has been very little in the way of systematic analysis of the radar-UFO data available. The data are only accessible through a search of scattered sources, and until a central file can be assembled few meaningful conclusions are possible about the class-properties (if any) of the total population of "unknowns". We will see that some tentative conclusions may be drawn from the study of small samples, but these are inevitably compromised by uncertainties about the reliability of much of the information. Forty years on, the radar evidence for unknown aerial phenomena still rests on the precarious credibility of a handful of individual cases.

SELECTED EXAMPLES OF RADAR-UFO EVENTS

■ SELFRIDGE AFB, MICHIGAN, 9 MARCH 1950

Two factors make this an intriguing case: from a scientific point of view, the detection of what was apparently the same unidentified target on two radars of different design; and from an historical point of view, that it led to high-level official recommendations through channels bypassing the low-priority Project Grudge system for fresh action on radar UFOs. A SECRET letter from the Air Adjutant General, Headquarters Continental Air Command, to the Director of Intelligence, Washington DC, concluded:

"The frequency of reports of this nature has recently increased; instructions have therefore been directed to all radar installations within this command to report scope sightings of unusual objects... It is recommended that reports of unidentified object sightings be reconsidered for submission from all Zone of Interior Air Force agencies." **[11]**

The event which prompted this letter occurred during radar monitoring of a night flying exercise by F-80s of the 56th Fighter Interceptor Group near Selfridge. A target was observed by an Air Force radar controller and three other operators on the PPI of the CPS-5 surveillance radar and simultaneously on the HRI (Height Range Indicator) scope of the CPS-4 height finder. The height finder emits a horizontal fan beam from a nodding antenna and operates at a very different frequency (S-band) from that of the CPS-5 (L-band). The "clarity, narrowness and definition of the presentation was definitely that of an aircraft" and comparable to the return from an F-80, according to the controller. The target moved with rapid alterations in height and speed, generally in the area of the fighters and "sometimes approximating their courses", but about 20,000 feet above their highest assigned altitude (checked by radio) of 24,000 feet. Over a period of 6 minutes the controller and another operator noted range, height, azimuth and time data in grease pencil on the scope heads. The target was observed for over an hour, during which time "several extreme instances of gaining and losing altitude" were observed, the target on the HRI scope rising and falling "up to 20,000 feet very rapidly" with "erratic" changes of speed observed on both scopes. On at least two occasions the target hovered motionless for a mean period of two minutes. Maximum stimated speed was 1500 mph, although the controller noted "the possibility of inaccuracy" in the timing at this point. Later, when the target was "giving indications on both scopes without fade", logged speeds were between about 330 and 480 mph, with climb rates up to 6000 ft/min. The highest logged climb rate coincided with the highest logged ground speed. The motion of the target during the six minutes before contact became intermittent on the CPS-5, and thereafter on the CPS-4, fading finally at 120 miles, are shown in **Figure 1.**

The controller's report on this incident, which is one of the most admirably careful documents of its type on record, states that positional checks performed with the F-80 pilots established that the CPS-5 was "very accurate on this particular night" and that no "known or prevalent weakness" of the CPS-4 could be found to explain the HRI indications. "All possible errors" were explored "exhaustively" with base technical personnel without result.

The Project Grudge evaluation of this case was "unidentified", but with the rider: "probable balloon". No specific balloon launch could be indicted, nor did Grudge offer any defence of this evaluation. Indeed it is hard to see any grounds for suspecting a balloon given the astonishing windspeed implied and the fact that the target evidently moved in many directions. Heading for the 1500 mph run was roughly NE, for example, whereas the target departed on a heading roughly SE. Furthermore, the faster run occurred earlier when a balloon would be lower, which is the opposite of the behaviour natural to a balloon climbing through winds which increase in velocity with altitude.

Birds, insects and ordinary weather returns cannot account for the target. Nor is it likely that instrument faults or remote RFI could affect two electronically independent radars with different receiver bandwidths - mutual interference being similarly improbable. No effect attributable to sidelobe returns could account for such a target. Anomalous propagation is a poor hypothesis in this case because the refractive effects due to atmospheric temperature/moisture gradients are very sensitive to frequency: as the analysis by USAF radar specialists noted, "the great difference in frequencies...and the evident correlation of observations almost rule out the possibility" of AP. No purpose is served by supposing multiple-trip effects: firstly the p.r.f. of each set must be the same; secondly, ground returns due to super-refractivity are very unlikely on the height finder since the mean antenna elevation (during the six-minute plot) is about 6° and the horizontal fan beam would radiate very little energy near 0° in comparison with the CPS-5 at ranges beyond the normal radar horizon - yet the target was painted with relative ease by the CPS-4, often only intermittently by the CPS-5; once again, *corresponding* distant ground returns on the two scopes are highly unlikely due to the different refractive curvature of their different frequencies; the presentation resembled an echo due to a point target such as an aircraft and showed a consistency not typical of ground returns due to super-refractivity; and multiple trip effects cannot of themselves create target movements of this nature.

Birds, insects and ordinary weather returns cannot account for the target. Nor is it likely that instrument faults or remote RFI could affect two electronically independent radars with different receiver bandwidths - mutual interference being similarly improbable. No effect attributable to sidelobe returns could account for such a target. Anomalous propagation is a poor hypothesis in this case because the

refractive effects due to atmospheric temperature/moisture gradients are very sensitive to frequency: as the analysis by USAF radar specialists noted, "the great difference in frequencies...and the evident correlation of observations almost rule out the possibility" of AP. No purpose is served by supposing multiple-trip effects: firstly the p.r.f. of each set must be the same; secondly, ground returns due to super-refractivity are very unlikely on the height finder since the mean antenna elevation (during the six-minute plot) is about 6° and the horizontal fan beam would radiate very little energy near 0° in comparison with the CPS-5 at ranges beyond the normal radar horizon - yet the target was painted with relative ease by the CPS-4, often only intermittently by the CPS-5; once again, *corresponding* distant ground returns on the two scopes are highly unlikely due to the different refractive curvature of their different frequencies; the presentation resembled an echo due to a point target such as an aircraft and showed a consistency not typical of ground returns due to super-refractivity; and multiple trip effects cannot of themselves create target movements of this nature.

Moving targets beyond the unambiguous range, say aircraft, could be displayed at spurious speeds and courses by multiple-trip returns (though the returns could not appear to hover for two minutes unless the aircraft did - that is, unless it was a helicopter), but displayed speeds will always be equal to or *less than* the true speed, not greater, and furthermore the echoes will be confined to the true

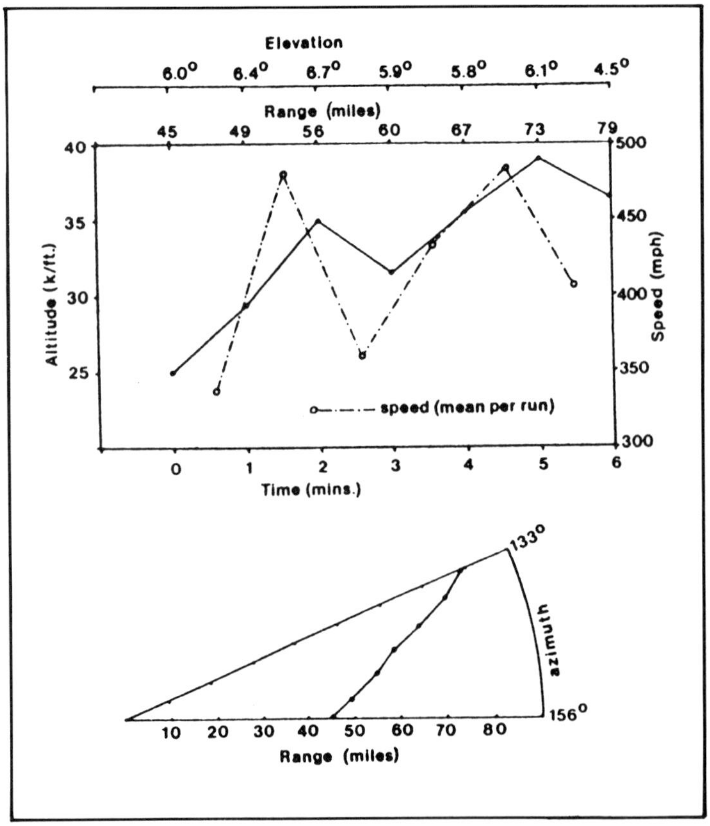

Figure 1 - Range, altitude, azimuth and speed data recorded for unidentified radar target at Selfridge AFB, Michigan, on 9 March 1950.

azimuth whereas in this case a fairly consistent pattern of behaviour was observed at azimuths differing by 180° (it strains credibility to imagine that multiple-trip returns from different targets at various azimuths could give the appearance of a series of connected movements by one target). Clear air echoes by direct returns from microscale atmospheric discontinuities are ruled out by the speeds observed. Forward scattering from moving waves on an inversion surface is ruled out also by speed, by the frequency sensitivity of this effect (which makes echoes on both 'scopes improbable), by the divergent headings of the target (thus independent of winds), by the rather high elevation of 6° shown by the HRI (too high for grazing incidence), by the repeated stationary episodes, and by the attenuation of the signal as it approached the extremes of its displayed range, becoming intermittent and finally fading (which is the opposite of the behaviour of echoes due to forward scattering, which decrease in intensity with *proximity* to the antenna as a result of the increasing incidence angle). No aircraft flying in 1950 could remotely approach the performance displayed by this target: even helicopters could not hover at such altitudes out of ground effect, and speeds of 480 mph would only be attained by a fighter using a considerable percentage of full power; even allowing wind speeds at 30,000 feet of perhaps 100 knots a helicopter would be too slow and could not achieve climb rates up to 6000 ft/min with a simultaneous ground speed of 480 mph.

The only half-plausible hypothesis in this case is that of a 'ghost' - a secondary echo from an aircraft due to either a ground reflector or another aircraft. Details hinting at this are the consistent high altitude of the target (roughly twice the altitude of the F-80s being monitored), the controller's statement that the "presentation was definitely that of an aircraft" but smaller than the F-80 returns, and the fact that the target "seemed to stay in the area in which our fighters were flying, sometimes approximating their courses." A ghost due to one of the F-80s would always appear on the azimuth of that aircraft but at a greater range and altitude. The F-80s were flying at 24,000 feet and *below*, so that the target altitude of (initially) about 45,000 feet *could* fit a ground reflection; but the relative ranges and azimuths are unknown. Arguments against a ghost reflection, however, are rather strong. Firstly, the repeated stationary episodes rule out a ground reflection. For a reflection between two aircraft to achieve this would require a reflection geometry that is possible, but highly improbable even once let alone twice, and certainly not for periods of two minutes. The consistent presentation of a single good return on both scopes for periods of several minutes, plus a consistent track heading during departure over a distance of about 50 miles or more, are not features suggestive of reflections between aircraft.

Of importance to show the interpretation of this event is the failure of the CPS-5 to at first show the target indicated by the CPS-4 at high altitudes. This is not easily understood in terms of a ghost reflection from an F-80, since the aircraft responsible (*ex hypothesi*) was simultaneously being painted by the CPS-5 and the reflection geometry would be the same for both radars, as it obviously must be (again, *ex hypothesi*) to account for the subsequent simultaneous paints. On the other hand, the relative performance of the two radars does make sense in terms of their practical capabilities with real targets at high altitude. As the report of technical personnel, Headquarters, Continental Air Command, pointed out:

"Further validity is lent to the contention of the reports by statements that first indications, which were at high altitudes, were observed on the CPS-4 height-finder before being observed on the CPS-5 surveillance radar set. This follows logic and field experience, inasmuch as the high-altitude coverage of the CPS-5 is known to be poor... It is to be noted that previous field experience with a CPS-5 surveillance radar set has indicated that targets picked up at ranges and altitudes indicated in subject report would probably have a reflection aspect ratio on the order of magnitude of a B-29 or greater." [**11**]

■ KANEDA AFB, TOKYO, AUGUST 5-6 1952

This case was carried as "unidentified" in Project Blue Book files, and has been subsequently analysed by Thayer [**3**] and McDonald [**12**]. Thayer suggested that this radar-visual event could be explained by anomalous propagation and a diffracted image of the star Capella, conclusions contested by McDonald.

At about 2330 local time on the night of August 5, two Haneda control tower operators observed a blue-white light of unusual brilliance in the NE and began studying it with binoculars. About ten minutes later, Haneda tower received a telephone call from Tachikawa AFB, 21 miles WNW of Haneda, independently calling attention to a "brilliant light over Tokyo Bay", a direction which, as McDonald pointed out, implies a bearing significantly south of east. These two lines of sight [**see Fig.2**] intersect in fact over the northern part of Tokyo Bay, where radar contact was subsequently made by ground radar and airborne intercept radar.

Haneda called the Ground Controlled Intercept (GCI) radar unit at Shiroi (N of Tokyo Bay) shortly after 2330 asking if radar had a target on a bearing NE from Haneda. The Shiroi CPS-1 surveillance scope showed three or four stationary targets "at a position 050° bearing from Haneda, as reported by the tower", over Tokyo Bay. The CPS-4 height finder could not pick up the targets, but it was noted that ground clutter was excessive at the low altitudes visually estimated by Haneda tower, and it is consistent that the targets could only be detected on the low beam of the CPS-1. For 15 minutes no change was reported from Shiroi and visual observation of the light continued from Haneda. According to the tower operators, the light rose slowly by a few degrees during the hour it was in sight.

At 2345 a target was detected on the Shiroi high beam and an F-94B was scrambled from Johnson AFB to the west. The F-94B got off at about 0003-4 after a delay due to fuel system trouble. At 0001 Shiroi had a target in a right orbit of 4 miles radius over Tokyo Bay, speed varying from about 100 - 150 knots and "stopping and hovering occasionally". When the target's orbit took it inland it was partially lost in the CPS-1 ground clutter pattern near Tokyo. At about 0012 the target emerged from the clutter and commenced a second orbit, fissioning now into three targets, one somewhat brighter than the other two. The three targets maintained about one-quarter mile separation through the second similar circle over the bay. As the targets reached the southernmost extent of their orbit and began to turn north of west back towards the coast, the interceptor, coming down over the NW of the Bay, was given a vector of 320° onto the largest target and instructed to search for the object at 1100 o'clock, range 4 miles. The time of this vector was 0015. At 0016 the 3 cm APG-33 air intercept radar on board the F-94B picked up a target at 10° port, range 6000 yards, coinciding very closely with position supplied by Shiroi. The interceptor followed the target in a starboard turn as it moved rapidly across the scope, both aircraft and unknown being painted by CGI radar. The unknown target had increased speed to between 250 and 300 knots as the interceptor approached, and now pulled away from the F-94B which was unable to close to within its radar lock-on range of 2500 yards. Pursuit continued for one and a half minutes until the APG-33 lost its target and both aircraft and unknown disappeared into the ground clutter pattern of the CPS-1. At 0017 30 Shiroi GCI recalled the interceptor to search the area of the Bay, without result, and at 0033 Shiroi released it from its mission, handing off to base control at Johnson.

In this case the extent of the correlation between radar and visual sightings has been subject to dispute. Both Thayer and McDonald argue that the object seen from Haneda was probably not related to the orbiting target intercepted by the F-94. McDonald's argument is that no lateral movement of the light was reported great enough to correspond to the arc of 30° subtended by the diameter of the radar orbit (8 miles) as seen from Haneda. Thayer remarks that in addition the light was still visible from Haneda at least 5 minutes after radar contact had been lost and the "UFO had left the area at a speed well in excess of 300 mph." That the object (if there was an object) had left the area is of course an assumption based on loss of the target from the AI radar and failure of Shiroi GCI to plot its emergence from the Tokyo ground clutter. It is possible that the "object", though lost to the radar, remained in the area to be seen visually for a few minutes.

The question of the movements of the light seen from Haneda is more interesting, and McDonald called this "the single most important ambiguity in the case file." He conceded that "the weight of evidence" does indicate that the object was seen to move, but concluded (a little inconsistently) that this movement had no relation to the orbit of the radar target. Yet the tower operators' statements describe

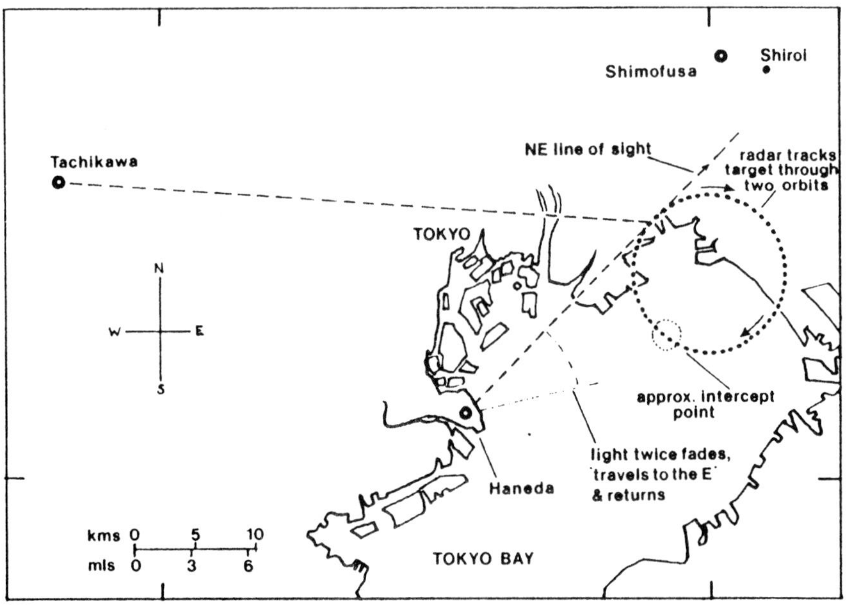

Figure 2 - Map of radar and visual sightings made in Tokyo Bay area, 5-6 August 1952.

the light initially stationary in the NE-NNE, then travelling to the E with an apparent gain in range so that it "became difficult to follow closely, except as a small light", returning to a stationary (or nearly stationary) position in the NE at its original brightness, then repeating the movement to the east and back before disappearing "when the jets (sic) were around... it seemed to know they were there." One controller stated: "I watched it disappear twice through the glasses. It seemed to travel to the East and gaining altitude at a very fast speed, much faster than any jet." Granted that these statements are not as clear as they might be, nevertheless phrases such as "travel to the East" from a position NE-NNE and "difficult to follow closely" at least arguably imply non-radial motion, and the fact that this motion was observed twice is rather easily related to the two wide orbits made by the radar target. Motion from NE "to the East" is not inconsistent with the 30° subtense of those orbits at Haneda, even if the times and exact bearings cannot be established.

Thayer attributed the light to a dramatically diffracted mirage image of the star Capella, which was at 8° elevation, 37° azimuth from Haneda at 2400. The light was described as "intense", "brilliant" and "blinding" enough to fatigue the eyes of the obsrervers and was of a blue-white colour. McDonald argues that since estimates of size and brightness were scaled directly against known light sources and a pilot balloon by tower personnel, these estimates should be taken seriously. Roughly consistent magnitude estimates emerge from comparisons made with Jupiter (appearing low in the east and looking relatively faint by contrast with the object, though with a magnitude itself of about -2.0) and with a 1.5 candle light carried by a meteorological balloon released from Haneda at 2400 with a known range from the tower of 2000 yards. McDonald estimated a magnitude substantially brighter than -3.0 for the object. The angular size of the light, which was large enough to be described as circular in shape, was scaled by comparison with the known diameter of the pilot balloon and comes out at about 3.0 minutes of arc, or about one-tenth the apparent size of the full moon. Further structure was visible around the central disc: a broad, dark annulus (described as a 'round dark shape' or 'darker object') about 12 arc minutes in diameter with three or four smaller lights around the curve of its lower edge. Only the lower edge of the dark shape was distinguishable from the sky background, and there was "a glare around the whole thing". This detail was observed through 7x50 binoculars.

An attempt by Thayer to account for this display by an admittedly conjectural propagation mechanism (which 'must be quite rare') involving a sharp temperature inversion overlaying collected patches of mist and through which the image of Capella would generate an annular diffraction pattern, was minutely criticised by McDonald on a quantitative basis. The possibility of illusion due to optical contrast effects, however, cannot be ruled out as an explanation for the reported structure.

The independent line of sight to the object from Tachikowa was, as McDonald emphasised, more than 45° away from Capella. However, it was only a few degrees from the position of Jupiter which was bright in the east, so the possibility should be considered that this sighting was of Jupiter. Set against this, it is impossible to estimate the likelihood of independent simultaneous misinterpretations of two different astronomical bodies, but the probability is presumably low, particularly when combined with subsequent multiple-radar contact with a target appearing to correlate with motions observed visually and detected in the area triangulated by these two independent lines of sight.

There remain many unanswered questions in this case. Why was the object not observed visually from Shiroi or from the interceptor? Why were three radar targets initially acquired when only one object was seen visually (unless, of course, one assumes that the three or four smaller lights seen close to the central light somehow correspond to these targets)? Why was only one object seen visually even after radar reported the target fissioning in three? Despite these and other anomalies, the radar events alone are very difficult to account for and AP involving orbital tracks and concurrent air/ground detection at very different frequencies and incidences seems out of the question. In summary, attempts to explain this event to date appear too contrived and require too many assumptions and coincidences to be probable.

■ LAKENHEATH, NEATISHEAD AND BENTWATERS, ENGLAND, AUGUST 13-14 1956

Since the publication of the Condon Report, this has been the most famous radar-visual case in UFO history. Analyses by Thayer [**3,13**], McDonald [**12,14**] and Klass [**9**] are the major published sources, with many other more or less accurate presentations scattered through the literature. Thayer and McDonald concluded that most or all of the radar indications observed had no adequate explanation, whilst Klass argued that typical AP effects compounded with equipment failure and observer error could explain all details of the case.

This sequence of events occurred over a six-hour period between 2130 GMT on August 13 and 0330 on August 14 1956, and involved multiple concurrent radar and visual observations of what appeared to be high-speed, self-luminous objects displaying unconventional manoeuvrability. The opinion of personnel involved and the conclusion of subsequent base-level investigation at Lakenheath was that the radarscope images represented airborne radar-reflective targets of unknown nature. At least five separate incidents were reported, involving at various times six ground radar sets and one airborne interception radar. Four incidents involved

Ground Controlled Approach (GCA) radar at Bentwaters USAF base; a fifth involved coastal air defence and Ground Controlled Interception (GCI) radars at Neatishead, Norfolk (RAF), Air Traffic Control (ATC) radar and GCA radar at RAF/USAF Lakenheath, in addition to AI radar aboard an RAF interceptor. Some twenty radar personnel were directly involved, with up to nine air-visual and ground-visual observers reporting related sightings. During the principal phase of the fifth event, correlating targets were simultaneously observed on at least five (possibly six) of the above radar scopes, concurrent with possible ground-visual and air-visual observations, and were interpreted as returns from a high-speed object exhibiting apparent control.

The following qualitative precis establishes the sequence of events and their general context as indicated by the contemporary Blue Book intelligence reports, the statements of the Lakenheath ATC Watch Supervisor, and the testimony of the RAF Chief Fighter Controller at Neatishead. There are inevitable gaps and contradictions after more than 30 years which will be addressed (briefly in the space available) in due course.

Late in the evening of August 13 a single high-speed (estimated 4000 mph) uncorrelated target was detected by Bentwaters GCA radar. At about the same time some 15 slow-moving targets crossed the scope in a different direction, appeared to merge on the display, then moved off-scope. Five minutes later another single high-speed target was observed to cross the scope on a heading different from either of the previous tracks. Less than an hour later a further single high-speed target crossed the scope on a heading the same as the previous target, and simultaneously visual observations were made by control tower personnel and the crew of a transport aircraft in a landing pattern over the field of a "bright light" which passed over the field and "under" the aircraft. At this time Bentwaters GCA alerted Lakenheath requesting confirmation of any uncorrelated targets.

At some time subsequent to this alert, ground observers at Lakenheath independently reported a luminous object approach the field at low altitude, stop, then move away on a different heading. Later two similar objects were observed which approached one another then moved away "in formation together." At this time Lakenheath GCA radar operators were observing targets in the vicinity of the base which exhibited "substantially the same" behaviour. One stationary target was observed 20-25 miles SW of the field and thus in a position to be detected by ATC radar (which had a 7-mile minimum range). ATC Center called GCA asking if they had a target at the above location: both scopes showed the target, which was puzzling to ATC personnel because the Moving Target Indicator (MTI) on their radar should have eliminated stationary targets. After a few minutes the target began to move at a speed of 400-600 mph and again stopped suddenly about 20 miles NNW of the field.

At this point the ATC Watch Supervisor called his superiors and reported the situation. As the target continued its high-speed straight-line movements around the area, a conference line was set up from the ATC radar room. The AF Communications Squadron Commander, the Base Commanding Officer and others, including an RAF liaison officer, were all patched in and at length a decision was taken to scramble two RAF interceptors. By this time Neatishead GCI had been alerted and could see the target on their scopes also as the first of two Venom NF2a nightfighters from RAF Waterbeach approached Lakenheath under their control.

Watched by radars at Lakenheath and Neatishead, about forty miles NE, the Venom was vectored onto the target, reporting radar contact and visual contact. As the interceptor closed range, AI radar lost the target and simultaneously ground radars showed the target circle rapidly behind the interceptor to begin a tail-chase. For some minutes the pilot attempted to shake the target from his tail unsuccessfully. About five minutes into this engagement the target was lost on Neatishead radars with a rapidity which was interpreted as a sudden descent out of the radiation pattern, and shortly the pilot was released from GCI control. Lakenheath continued to display the target as it followed him a short distance in the direction of Waterbeach. About 10 miles S of Lakenheath the target stopped and remained stationary, executed one or two short moves, then left Lakenheath radar coverage at a constant 600 mph to the north.

The complexity of this case is such that to do it justice would require a good-size book. [A detailed report is currently in preparation. MLS.] Here, a few of the apparent problems raised by ambiguities and contradictions in the source material will be mentioned and some interpretations of the evidence briefly reviewed.

Firstly, let us look at the four radar events at Bentwaters between 2130 and 2255. Of these only one involved simultaneous visual observations; nevertheless all four events are difficult to account for by conventional aerial objects or propagation/electronic anomalies. Three events involved single high-speed targets resembling aircraft returns which crossed the scope from one sector to the opposite; the remaining event involved a slow-moving cluster of targets which also crossed the scope center (approximately) between opposite sectors. The essentially radial motion of all these targets is interesting. Such motion on a radial-timebase PPI is at first sight suggestive of spurious signals generated somewhere in the amplifier or receiver circuitry. However, the motion of a target due to a spurious input between opposite sectors in this way would require an impossibly fortuitous relationship between two different and immediately consecutive input pulse patterns synchronised to the half-rotation period of the display. The notion of electronic artefacts has been advanced by Klass [9], but nothing short of a very sophisticated electronic-countermeasures simulation exercise could create a false target in this way, and the existence of such a capability with 1956 analogue technology is hardly credible.

No known propagation mechanism can account for targets with displayed speeds of thousands-of-mph. Some attention has been given, however, to the possibility that the cluster of slow targets at about 2130 might have been due to partial reflection from moving waves on an elevated inversion. This hypothesis was advanced, with reservations, by Thayer; rejected without reservations by McDonald; and adopted without reservations by Klass. Central to this hypothesis is the relationship between the reported target motion and the speed and heading of the winds over the Bentwaters area. Since the radar displays slant range to the target according to the total out-and-back path length of the reflected signal, and since the geometry of reflection from the layer to the ground and back doubles the path length, it is obvious that displayed range will always be twice the actual slant range to the moving wave. Thus, as the wave propagates across the inversion surface at wind speed, the reflected echo moves across the PPI in the same direction at twice wind speed. Klass points out that the cluster of echoes "faded considerably" during their recession NE, and the "winds aloft were to the *northeast* - the direction that the cluster of UFO-blips was moving." Furthermore, the reported speed of the echoes (between 80 and 125 mph) is "roughly twice the velocity of the winds aloft that night." [9]

On the face of it, this relationship is convincing. But there are several considerations which argue against inversion reflections, of which we shall mention three.

Firstly, the relationship with wind direction is not as unambiguous as Klass and (to a lesser extent) Thayer suggested. Surface winds were indeed within a few degrees of the reported heading, blowing from 230°. But these are not the winds whose speed Klass quotes. Surface winds were only 5-10 knots, so unrelated to target speeds of 80-125 mph. Winds in the correct range of speed occurred above 6000 feet, but these winds were steady from 260° and so *about 35° from the reported target heading.* Thus such an assumption ought not to be imported without discussion.

Klass's study emphasises the merging of this cluster of returns into a single stationary target, but makes no attempt to interpret this behaviour. Thayer, however, remarked that "the reported stationary episodes...would, taken at face value, rule out the moving-layer reflection hypothesis..." [13] These two stationary periods (in the face, *ex hypothesi*, of up to 60 mph winds) for a total duration of many minutes make no sense in terms of reflections from an elevated layered structure, and there is no internal reason to dismiss these rather specific details.

Probably the strongest argument against the inversion-reflection hypothesis concerns the reported fading of the returns beyond a range of about 14 miles, which feature Klass appears to regard as symptomatic of an unreal target. But the intensity of a signal returned from a distant ground target by a partially reflecting layer exhibits precisely the opposite of the reported behaviour. The targets were first observed at a range of 8 miles, overflew the radar appearing "as normal targets on the GCA scope", then "faded considerably" at about 14 miles in total contrast to the behaviour characteristic of inversion reflections.

The final event at Bentwaters, the 2255 radar-visual, raises the question of the Perseid meteor shower which has been regarded by some commentators (in particular Klass) as responsible for this and most other visual reports made that night. In fact, the original Lakenheath intelligence report contained the statement: "Observers report unusual amount of shooting stars in sky. Further state the objects seen were deinitely not shooting stars..." Hynek's 1956 evaluation as consultant to Blue Book noted this statement and rejected the Perseid hypothesis as "highly unlikely". Meteor wake returns would seem like a simplifying explanation, but the CPN-4 surveillance scope could not have picked up wake returns for reasons including the power and frequency of the set and the geometry of the track in relation to the antenna, in addition to which the reported speed is an order of magnitude too low. Furthermore, the position of the Perseid radiant is *50° away* from the reported heading.

Moving on to the subsequent incidents at Lakenheath, the centrepiece of the entire case is the interception, when so many ground and airborne radars painted the same target simultaneously. No serious attempt has been made to explain this extraordinary phenomenon, nor does it seem likely that any explanation will be forthcoming. The Neatishead GCI station (or "Happidrome", as such installations were quixotically known) consisted of no less than five electronically independent radar units from which height, range and azimuth data were fed to a range of consoles, the combination of inputs being selected by the operator for display according to the changing situation during intercept. The entire control and display system was duplicated in back-up and monitored by a second interception team. This system alone brought into play radars with different frequencies, different pulse lengths and possibly different PRFs. [19,22]

At Lakenheath, the L-band radar introduced a third frequency and a different PRF. It is implied that the S-band GCA CPN-4 continued to track the target during the interception, though attention is focused on the role of ATC at this time. The Venom's AI radar, a modified American SCR-720 with the very British designation of Mk.10, operated at a wavelength of 9 cm with a PRF variable from 375-1500 Hz depending on range-scale.

Lakenheath and Neatishead are separated by some forty miles, and the area of the interception in the southerly sectors from Lakenheath and southwest from Neatishead covered perhaps 200 square miles or so. Under these circumstances, the chance of a freak reflection echo (seriously proposed by Menzel [15]) creating a 'ghost' of the Venom is essentially nil, and no known propagation anomaly corresponds either to the behaviour observed or to the various separations, azimuth/elevation angles

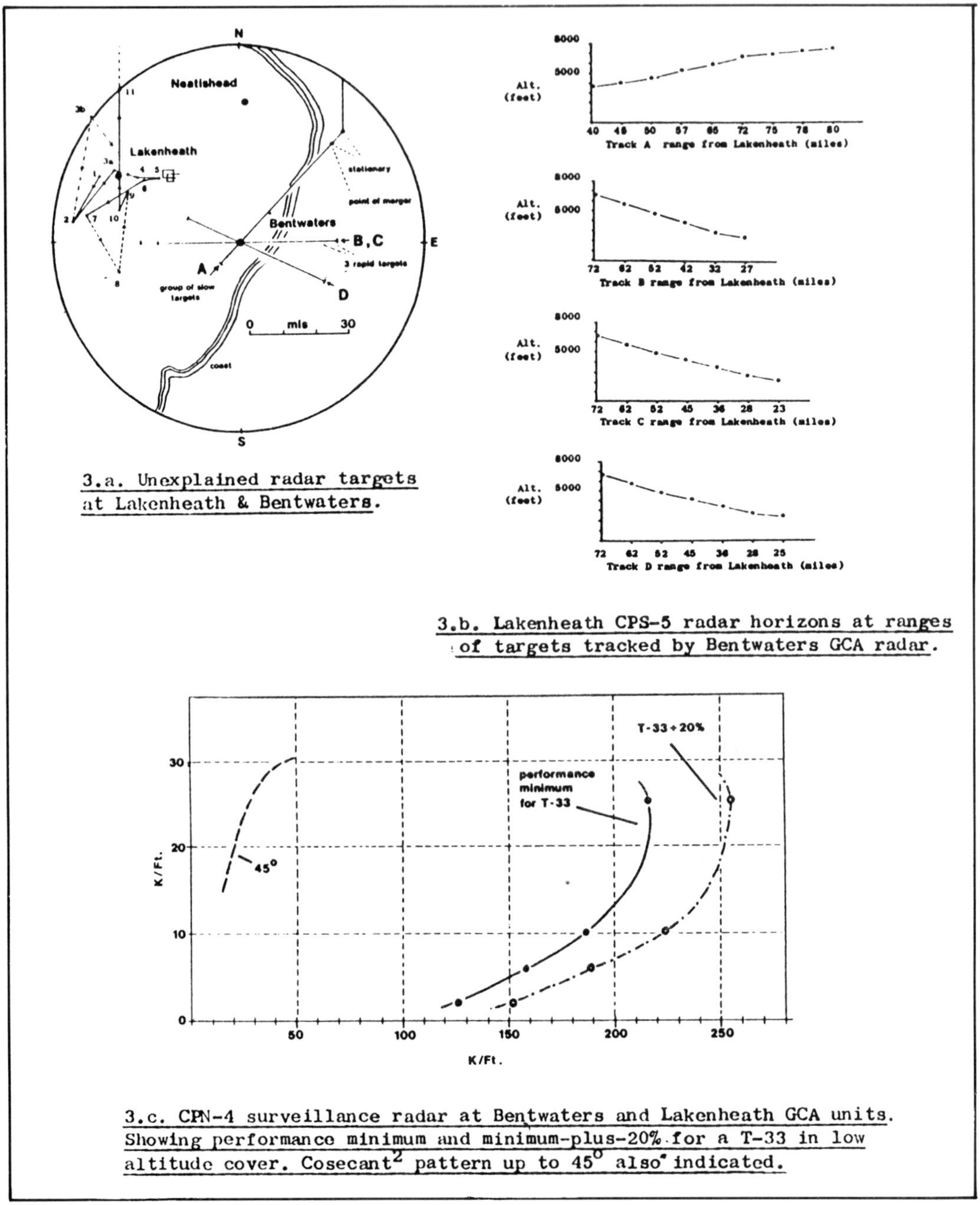

3.a. Unexplained radar targets at Lakenheath & Bentwaters.

3.b. Lakenheath CPS-5 radar horizons at ranges of targets tracked by Bentwaters GCA radar.

3.c. CPN-4 surveillance radar at Bentwaters and Lakenheath GCA units. Showing performance minimum and minimum-plus-20% for a T-33 in low altitude cover. Cosecant^2 pattern up to 45° also indicated.

Figure 3 - Radar observations at Bentwaters, Lakenheath and Neatishead, 13-14 August 1956. 3A) Map of radar tracks within circle representing Bentwaters' CPN-4 maximum range. 3B) Lakenheath CPS-5 radar horizons at ranges of targets tracked by Bentwaters. 3C) Range/altitude performance of CPN-4 for target cross-section equivalent to a Lockheed T-33 jet trainer.

and frequencies of these several fixed and mobile radar systems. Multiple-trip effects and electronic faults are also ruled out. It is very hard to conceive of any sort of atmospheric structure which could achieve the speeds and movements independently reported, or mimic in such fashion the appearance of rational behaviour. The target was not weak or intermittent but consistent and of a strength comparable to that of the Venom, according to the RAF Chief Fighter Controller, who adds that it appeared in every respect to be an aircraft target except for its extraordinary speed and manoeuvrability. [**17,19**]

Much controversy has surrounded certain attempts (especially by Klass) to de-mystify the events by means of highly ingenious interpretations of the testimony. Firstly, doubts have been expressed about the apparent absence of concurrent radar detection by Bentwaters and Lakenheath. The Bentwaters targets should, objected Klass [**9**], have been well within range of Lakenheath's CPS-5, and the Lakenheath events fell largely within Bentwaters' CPN-4 range. Thayer also found this "slightly disturbing". [**13**] Yet it does not by any means follow that targets within the ranges of two radars will be detected by both: it is necessary to consider the curve defining the lower limit of vertical coverage for a target of given cross-section at a given range; the scan rate of the antenna and the speed of the target; the role of the radar, probable levels of operator vigilance and the area of a controller's responsibility, and so on. Wherever approximate implied altitudes can be inferred from plotted target ranges and the probable radiation patterns of the radars concerned, the probability of concurrent detection is found to be low, in the sense that the high-speed Bentwaters tracks (for example) would yield only two or three widely separated paints on the CPS-5, and even noticing them in a relaxed ATC environment with "little or no traffic" would be a matter purely of luck. Furthermore, this result assumes a simple linear projection of the observed tracks beyond their points of final contact: over the actual observed track lengths none of the reported targets are well placed for concurrent detection by the CPS-5. Lakenheath's CPN-4 would have stood a better chance due to its high scan rate - but the GCA trailer was not even manned until the action began later at Lakenheath. Bentwaters' chances of observing the interception would be very slim except possibly at high altitudes, and if returns near the CPN-4's maximum range were intermittent or non-existent, it would not be surprising; whether or not the GCA unit was even manned at this time is unknown, as is the completeness of the subsequent report from that unit. Neatishead's role was different from either of the other two installations; charged with defence of the UK their concentration, as the Chief Fighter Controller points out, was on possible inbound targets to seaward, and until alerted by Lakenheath they would tend to ignore traffic inland. When this alert came, the target was immediately found. [**19**]

Klass's analysis made no attempt to interpret the nature of this target in detail, although it was suggested that some of the events observed at Lakenheath were the result of a faulty MTI which could under certain circumstances generate spurious signals. That the MTI was faulty was suggested by the fact that the target was still displayed whilst apparently stationary, although the MTI circuit should have filtered it out. In fact, the resolution of the PPI is not sufficiently fine to discriminate between stationary targets and targets moving in a small area: a target orbiting or moving back and forth at a speed of about 40 knots or more will be in principle indistinguishable from a stationary target. In practice, the limited persistence of the excitation of the tube phosphor (no more than a second or two) does not allow target positions to be compared with great accuracy from scan to scan, so that the practical limit of detectable motion is higher still. In addition to these arguments, it is also true that a rapidly-rotating body, although genuinely stationary, could return phase-shifted signals which would defeat the MTI filter. MTI faults could not explain concurrent observations by Lakenheath GCA radar, as Klass well knew, which is why his analysis all but suppressed the existence of this installation. Nor can they explain a correlating target detected by Neatishead GCI (which, to remove any possibility of independent coincidental faults, was not even fitted with MTI).

The centerpiece of Klass's study was his deduction that the interceptor pilot was alone in a fighter designed for two, trying to fly the plane whilst simultaneously grappling with unfamiliar radar equipment across the width of the cockpit. This hypothesis, which has been quite widely accepted, rests on a few phrases spoken by the pilot as recalled by the Lakenheath ATC Watch Supervisor: principally, "I've got my guns locked on him" and "clearest target I've ever seen on radar." Klass argues that because the pilot does not refer to a radar operator and uses the first person singular at all times, he could have been alone, a possibility also suggested by his apparent reference to a radar lock-on, since the APS-57 AI radar did not have a lock-on facility. If, then. the pilot were struggling to operate the radar (which would be difficult even to see very clearly) without a proper understanding of its capabilities and limitations, the value of his reported radar confirmation of the target is very doubtful.

However, pilots always use the first person singular (the "royal 'I'", as it has been rather well described) and, having a proprietorial attitude to their aircraft, will not say "we" just because somebody else happens to be in the next seat. Furthermore, the interpretation placed on the recollected words of an English pilot by American personnel may not be entirely reliable. In any event, it is virtually certain that the radar operator was on board: to fly at night on an operational intercept without him would be futile and suicidal, and that Operations would ever scramble a plane with half a crew (unless all seven other crews of 253 Squadron on standby night duty at Waterbeach that night were struck down) is inconceivable.

Many other aspects of this case could be discussed, but the final word must be reserved for the most serious apparent conflict of evidence, which concerns the control of the interception. Strangely, both the RAF Fighter Controller and the USAF ATCC Watch Supervisor (the latter supported by information in the 1956 intelligence report) are convinced that the interception was under their control. The Watch Supervisor recalls supplying vectors to the aircraft, recalls receiving some brief transmissions from the pilot and recalls hearing an air-to-air conversation between the two Venoms after Venom-number-one broke off the engagement. The AFR 200-2 report compiled by Lakenheath GCA and intelligence personnel soon after the event agrees that the Venom was "vectored to the target by RATCC." The RAF Controller, on the other hand, denies that any part of this was possible, and for what seem to be very good reasons: this was, after all, an RAF interceptor under RAF control; interceptions were Neatishead's job; the RAF GCI regime of the 'fifties was the very paragon of discipline with very tightly defined restrictions on radio traffic, highly confidential R/T frequencies and a private jargon of codewords; and lastly, the Controller remembers quite clearly what the pilot did and did not say. No air-to-air transmissions were monitored, according to this version, and the only transmissions from the pilot of Venom-number-one were the codes: "contact", "Judy" (meaning that the radar operator had the target dead to rights on his own scope and required no further assistance from GCI), followed by the words: "lost contact - more help" after the target was seen to circle behind the Venom. Is it possible to reconcile these contradictory accounts?

The answer is that by making the not-unreasonable assumption that the military authorities perceived a highly unusual situation to exist, all the pieces of the puzzle fall quite naturally into place. First of all, let us ask whether it is likely that Lakenheath RATCC was using the Neatishead GCI frequency. The RAF Fighter Controller's published statement in 1978 [**16**] argued stridently that this was "impossible" since only the interception team would know this frequency. Subsequently [**17**] he stated that he believed a request for this frequency was received, but the Lakenheath Watch Supervisor's statements [**3,18**] make no reference to such a request or betray any awareness of the existence of Neatishead GCI, which suggests the possibility that this request came from elsewhere. It does indeed seem unlikely that the RATCC team supervisor, a sergeant in the USAF Communications Squadron, would himself have the authority to initiate such liaison with a secure RAF facility even had he known who to call, and equally unlikely that the Chief Fighter Controller would pass this highly confidential GCI frequency to an unknown air traffic controller over the 'phone without instructions from higher authority. So wherever this request originated, another agency must have been involved, higher up the chain of USAF command and in liaison with RAF authorities. It seems that monitoring the GCI frequency was deemed desirable at some level, but Lakenheath may have had a rather different role to play for the reason that the GCI frequency could not operate effectively as an open communications channel. The GCI regime is not at all concerned with gathering intelligence; its function is simply to guide an aircraft efficiently onto the tail of its target with the bare minimum of talk for obvious security reasons, so conversation would not be desirable or even possible through the GCI system. Thus, although GCI communications would have priority during the interception, if higher authorities wished to query the pilot or passively receive real-time intelligence on the "UFO", another frequency could be assigned which would be available for use at the pilot's discretion as and when the changing situation permitted. The natural destination of any such transmissions would be Lakenheath, for there the controllers had been working with the target for some 50 minutes before Neatishead was even alerted and a conference line had been established, with USAF and RAF authorities hooked into the supervisor's switchboard. Thus, communications to Lakenheath would not be for the benefit of the curiosity of USAF radar personnel, but would feed through Lakenheath directly to this conference line. There is thus a rational motive for such an arrangement, and whether Neatishead would be informed would be entirely a question of their "need to know". In view of the necessarily circumscribed role of the GCI facility and the parsimony characteristic of British military intelligence, it seems unlikely that Neatishead would be deemed to have a need to know.

Having established a motive, the key to the means is the Venom NF2a's R/T system, which consisted of two VHF transmitter-receivers each with its own 10-channel controller providing a total of 20 pre-set frequencies between 100 and 156 MHz. Channels could be selected by a rotary knob, and the VHF unit in use could be selected by a simple spring-loaded switch near the pilot's left hand. To talk out, the pilot or radar operator must depress a press-to-transmit (P-to-T) switch which opens a circuit to the chosen VHF unit. Unless this P-to-T switch is closed, the aircraft is dumb. Similarly, if one VHF unit is switched in, the other is switched out, and on the latter's selected frequency the aircraft is again dumb, and if the control knob is rotated to a different channel the same applies. In other words, neither Neatishead nor Lakenheath can distinguish between the P-to-T switch being released and transmission being switched either to the other VHF unit or to a different frequency on the same unit. The aircraft can talk to either ground station without the knowledge of the other. Furthermore, and most important, Lakenheath cannot tell when the aircraft is listening to them, when the aircraft is listening to GCI, or even whether the radio on the aircraft is switched on at all. Thus having no need to know the details of RAF interception procedures, the personnel in the ATC radar room at Lakenheath would have no reason not to assume that, having once been in radio contact with the aircraft, they remained in contact during the intercept. The pilot, meanwhile, would now be following instructions from his controller at Neatishead, deaf to vectors that might from time to time be supplied by Lakenheath but appearing to respond by obligingly closing on the target.

By what means might such an arrangement be set up without radio contact through Lakenheath or Neatishead when the aircrew would be sitting in the aircraft at the Waterbeach operations readiness platform throughout the night "ready to push the starter button"? [**19**] The Venom had a confidential telebriefing facility, a port in the tail boom which connected the pilot to the operations briefing room by a secure landline which disconnected automatically as the aircraft taxied away. Mission instructions given in this way could not be accidentally compromised because the activation of the telebriefing line automatically disconnected the VFH units. Indeed, so secure are mission instructions considered that the Squadron Operations Records Books, which contain details of the briefing given to the pilot that night, will not be transferred to the public archive until the year 2031! [**20**]

If the motive and the means have been established, what about the opportunity? Does this scenario work in detail to make sense of the sequence of events as reported? The RATCC Watch Supervisor stated that on first radio contact with the Venom he relayed details of the target's behaviour, its possible altitudes and the report received from Bentwaters - "all the background information." This initial transmission appears definitely to have been acknowledged. After the interception, a brief conversation was monitored between Venom-number-one and Venom-number-two as the latter was approaching the area; number-two also spoke briefly to Lakenheath before returning to Waterbeach. Let us look first at these two phases of the incident, which the RAF Controller insists did not occur but which are at least partially substantiated by the contemporary intelligence report.

According to the Watch Supervisor, radio and radar contact with the Venom were established 30-35 miles SW of Lakenheath (although Waterbeach is only 20 miles SW - he explains this by pointing out that the aircraft would take off to the SW as usual into the prevailing winds, consuming 10 miles or more executing a climb and turn to the NE [**18**]). The range of the aircraft from Neatishead at this time is therefore 70-75 miles, and the fact that radio contact with Lakenheath was only established at this time raises the question of whether radio contact with Neatishead would have been possible. The main factor here is the aircraft altitude: at 10,000 feet the VHF radio would have a maximum range of about 100 miles air-to-ground [**21**], but at lower altitudes this range would drop, and the fact that radar contact was established at this time fixes the aircraft altitude (according to a best-estimate of the low-level coverage of the CPS-5 and the Watch Supervisor's altitude estimate based on experience) at between 2000 and 3000 feet. It is thus very probable that the aircraft would not be in contact with Neatishead GCI until it had gained further altitude or closed range, and at this time one would expect the pilot to take the opportunity of talking to Lakenheath.

At the time of the radio contact with Venom-number-two and the air-to-air conversation reported by Lakenheath, Neatishead had stopped painting the target and officially released the interceptor from its mission. Thus the explanation for the absence of such a conversation from the RAF Fighter Controller's account is simply a question of timing: at this time the interceptor was no longer under the control of GCI and was not talking on their frequency. For Neatishead, the incident was already over. Venom-number-two was in all probability not yet within range of GCI: note that the Watch Supervisor recalled - "he was not on radar at this time, probably had just taken off and was too low for us to pick him up, or too far away - we had most of the scopes on short range so we could watch the UFO closely..."[**3**]. "Short range" would be in the region of 30 miles, since the area of the action at this time was within 10-30 miles in the southerly sectors from Lakenheath.

Now we come to the main phase of the interception proper. The sequence of events reported by the Watch Supervisor (and the intelligence TWX to several USAF commands in addition to Blue Book) is that after a period with no reported acknowledgement from the Venom, during which it was closing on the target, the pilot called Lakenheath when the target was at about 12 o'clock, 2600 feet and reported: "I've got my guns locked on him". As the Watch Supervisor recalled this message it was prefaced with: "Roger, Lakenheath...", in apparent acknowledgement of RATCC instructions. The intelligence TWX simply states: "pilot advised target was on radar..." It does not seem unreasonable that, given the role RATCC personnel believed themselves to be playing, the Watch Supervisor could interpolate the word "Roger" in his recollection twelve years later. Now during this period the Venom was in contact with GCI twice: once reporting "contact", then shortly afterwards the code "Judy". "Judy" means that no further GCI assistance is required because the radar has a firm target, and so from this moment the pilot is not listening to his controller. He is thus free in principle to switch his frequency to that of

Lakenheath, and although the RAF Controller points out that at this time both pilot and navigator would be "concentrating hard" on target position data being read over the intercom, it perhaps overstates things to describe the words "I've got my guns [locked] on him" as "nattering to Lakenheath." [**17**]

We thus have the pilot reporting "Judy" then leaving the GCI frequency. Immediately on switching to Lakenheath's frequency the pilot reports the situation in a few words. This transmission does not interfere with last-minute range data from the radar operator since the operator can at any time interrupt - the intercom link is opened by depressing a press-to-mute footswitch which simultaneously disconnects the VHF receiver. Since the target is now dead ahead at 12 o'clock and within range of the Venom's four 20 mm Hispano cannon, the only radar information coming over the intercom will be range updates, but in fact it is doubtful whether the radar operator would have had time to begin counting down the remaining 2000 feet of range since the target was almost immediately lost.

According to the RAF Controller, after the pilot reported "Judy" only a "few seconds" or "one or two sweeps on our scopes" (10-20 seconds at 6 rpm) elapsed before the object had looped round and got behind the Venom [**16**] in a manoeuver which was interpreted as a positive-gee loop up and over the aircraft but which could equally have been a negative-gee loop below the aircraft (the Controller was watching a PPI monitor remoted from the interception cabin consoles and had no altitude information available). The SCR 720 AI radar had operator selectable elevation tilt limits between -20° and +40°, and a manoeuver with a downward velocity component of only 100 mph would take the target out of the radar coverage beginning from O° relative elevation in a little over two seconds at 1000 feet range. A target moving at the speeds reported by ground radar (600-800 mph) could disappear from dead-ahead in less than 0.4 sec at this range. (Under full power the Venom would close with the stationary target at a rate of about 750 feet/sec, so this range would be reached about 2 seconds after Lakenheath reported the target at 2600 feet, 12 o'clock from the aircraft). Again, if the target completed its loop in 10-20 seconds after the pilot reported "Judy", it would be lost from the AI radar's forward elevation coverage in a small fraction of this time. (A travel of 180° in 10-20 seconds implies an angular speed of 9-18°C/sec, corresponding to a vertical velocity of 100-200 mph at 1000 feet range neglecting accelerations). It seems consistent with the report from GCI, then, that the target was lost almost immediately after the pilot left the GCI frequency and therefore at about the very moment he was speaking to Lakenheath, which is also consistent with the Watch Supervisor's statement that the pilot had just reported that he had his guns on the target "then he paused [this would be the radarman interrupting the VHF link to report signal loss over the intercom] and he said, 'Where did he go? Do you still have him?'" Lakenheath answered that the target was now behind him.

It would be at this moment that the pilot would decide he needed more help from his controller and would switch back to the GCI frequency. This he did, calling "Lost contact - more help." He was told by GCI that the target was now behind him and given fresh instructions to evade his pursuer. [**16**] GCI would give him not only target range and bearing more accurately than Lakenheath but also altitude data which Lakenheath was not equipped to supply. This transmission is the answer to a question which has exercised the ingenuity of several commentators, notably Klass: that is, when the pilot next contacted Lakenheath and was able to "confirm that this [circling] had occurred" (according to the Watch Supervisor and corroborated by the intelligence TWX), how did the pilot *know*, when the Venom has no tail radar and restricted rearward visibility? The answer, of course, is simply that he knew because he had checked with Neatishead GCI.

During the subsequent chase, which lasted from 5-10 minutes, the pilot would be free of the need to concentrate on instructions from his radar operator since the target remained behind the Venom and the AI radar was redundant. At this time he would be at liberty to report the situation to Lakenheath, GCI communications permitting. It is doubtful that he would have much attention to spare, however, and under these circumstances it is consistent that his words to Lakenheath were reportedly "occasional" and "scared". After 5-10 minutes GCI had lost the target from their scopes due (it was believed) to a swift descent out of the radiation pattern, and the interceptor was released from GCI control. Two brief radio contacts with Lakenheath occurred as the CPS-5 continued to track the target in the vicinity (or apparent vicinity - relative altitudes being unknown) of the homeward-bound Venom for "a short distance." The second Venom then called Lakenheath on the same frequency, the target meanwhile having stopped and proceeded north at 600 mph to eventually leave the radar coverage at about 50-60 miles range.

The above construction of events is conjectural but it is entirely self-consistent and makes sense of what might otherwise appear to be serious anomalies. To this extent it is a good hypothesis, although at present security restrictions prevent it being tested against information in official records currently held by the Air Historical Branch of the Ministry of Defence in London and, presumably, US security agencies. Notwithstanding some uncertainties, however, the Bentwaters/Lakenheath/Neatishead events are today, three decades on, probably the most impressive of their kind on record.

CONCLUSIONS AND RECOMMENDATIONS

None of the cases here discussed is free of ambiguities, information of uncertain reliability, the frustrating absence of key details, and the same could be said of the many other events which one would like to discuss. In even the best documented cases there remain dark corners that future researchers will probably never fully illuminate. Nevertheless, events such as those we have dicussed are, *prima facie*, suggestive of the existence of tangible aerial phenomena escaping any current scientific classification insofar as the available data fail to convincingly support any other view.

In each of the cases discussed here, an explanation could be given if one were permitted to ignore or modify key items of testimony on the basis that nothing could be less likely than a "real UFO" (whatever that might be); after all, we know that errors occur - we do not know that UFOs do. Nevertheless, such an approach is at best *ad hoc* and open to the charge of being more sophistry than science. The most that can reasonably be done is to attempt to find collateral evidence, perhaps latent in the statistical population, that such a procedure would be justified; however, the reliability of statistical inferences is difficult to assess when the total available population is small.

In summary, the statistical properties of the limited sample considered are ambiguous, although there is some suggestion that the circadian distribution of the sample may correlate with the development and decay of atmospheric stratification responsible for anomalous propagation. It may be relevant to note here that *in general* visual sightings associated with radar-UFO events are of low to medium definition.

A number of events, however, are extremely difficult to interpret in terms of AP or other conventional phenomena. Some events involve targets whose duration, consistency of strength, continuity of behaviour and (in a few cases) apparent reaction to the environment suggest an unclassified airborne physical "object" as the most straightforward interpretation. That is to say, if such a phenomenon were consensually available, in the sense that phenomena such as AP, balloons and "ball lightning" are available, then it would reasonably be regarded as the most probable cause of these events.

The phenomenon's characteristics would include flight capabilities ranging from hovering to supersonic speeds, rapid accelerations and high rates of climb. It would be a reflector at radio (and possibly optical) wavelengths, and an emitter at optical wavelengths (though not always). Optical emission would typically be incoherent white light, though blue and orange are occasionally reported. Cases exist which would seem to require a phenomenon which is not always an optical reflector: ie Colorado Springs Airport, Colorado, May 13 1967, where surveillance *and* precision approach radars tracked an inbound target low over the field at 200 feet in daylight and fair visibility although neither a following flight nor control tower personnel with binoculars could see anything. [**3**] This case, described by Thayer as "one of the most puzzling on record", is unexplained.

Fusion of two or more targets below the limit of PPI resolution is sometimes reported, as is fission of larger targets into "elementary" targets. Radar cross-section would be variable, with an elementary target typically approximating that of a small jet fighter or smaller. Generally speaking, the targets observed in the most interesting cases behave in a remarkably versatile but not supernatural or irrational way. It seems likely that some of the capricious extremes of behaviour (occasional sudden disappearances, for example) could be explained by the normal imperfections inherent in radar systems and their propagation environment.

Visual sightings are typically of round white or blue-white lights with a small but sensible angular extension. Fission or fusion of two or more lights is sometimes reported, and angular rates range from zero (stationary) to many degrees of arc per second. An impression of non-inertial manoeuvrability is sometimes conveyed. In general, visually reported behaviour is at least qualitatively similar to that displayed by radar, and there do appear to be cases in which the radar-visual correlation can be considered good.

The fact that the radar-UFO file is dominated by cases from the 1950s (which is not to say that startling events have not been reported since) may be explained by a lower false alarm rate in modern radars and an increased understanding of the complexities of the radar environment. However, it could also reflect other factors such as the effective closure of the military record since the mid-sixties, the increased use of SSR radars and the development of clutter-rejection systems. Most of the older radar cases involve military radars operated by the USAF and owe their public visibility to the existence of the Blue Book record. Since declassification of the Blue Book files following the termination of the project in December 1969, and their subsequent transferral to the National Archive in Washington DC, a number of previously unknown cases have come to light adding to the number catalogued for the early years of UFO history. Since this date, the only significant information on new military radar events has been obtained with some effort through Freedom of Information suits. In the civil sector the widespread introduction of SSR (Secondary Surveillance Radar) and synthetic displays in recent years has already been mentioned. The very object of this technology is to narrow the field of attention of both operators and radar in air traffic control, increasing the efficiency of aircraft identification and routeing to the benefit of air safety but reducing the probability that anomalous targets will be attended to. Air traffic, especially in the civilian sector, is an enormously more demanding problem than was the case thirty years ago. The more sophisticated radar signal processing becomes in response to these demands, the narrower the filters - both electronic and perceptual - through which rare phenomena unanticipated by, or actively suppressed by, the system design must pass. One example of clutter rejection which has come into widespread use is non-linear polarisation, which is a rotation of the electric vector of a portion of the output wave causing signals reflected from bodies of a chosen sphericity or ellipticity to be rejected by the receiver. In normal use this technique suppresses returns from hail or rain droplets, but it can be seen that it will prejudice the detectability of other targets with a similar degree of overall symmetry.

Despite these difficulties, a number of intriguing incidents have occurred during the post-Condon era. In the autumn of 1975 a number of radar-visual events occurred in the vicinity of Air Force Bases and missile sites along the northern tier defences of the United States and Canadian Forces Stations across the border. Documentation of these incidents, in which penetrations of weapons storage and other secure areas by unidentified lighted objects were tracked by radar (sometimes multiple radars), was obtained with some difficulty by Citizens Against UFO Secrecy (CAUS) through FOI requests. A compilation of this fragmentary material by Fawcett and Greenwood [**24**] does not permit detailed analysis, but it is clear that the security reflexes of the USAF were jolted by these incidents, of which a number are clearly not AP-related, and it would appear that UFOs remain a problem - though now a private problem - for the military intelligence community.

On 19 September 1976 a multiple radar-visual event near Teheran, Iran - [see also Section 2.3, Case 12] - prompted a report within the US Defence Intelligence Agency (DIA) describing an interception by F-4 Phantoms of the Iranian Air Force of an "object" at 25,000 feet with a rectangular pattern of strobing coloured lights. Both F-4s reported weapons-control, INS and communications failure in its vicinity. Radar lock-on was achieved with a target comparable to a 707 tanker in cross-section. A smaller object was observed to detach itself from the larger body and force an F-4 into an evasive turn. This object appeared to outperform the F-4. Another object left and was seen to approach the ground at high speed, where it was reported by civilian observers. The UFO, noted the DIA report, was seen by "multiple witnesses in different locations... both airborne and from the ground" and their "credibility was high"; the sightings were "confirmed by radar", electromagnetic effects were reported "by three separate aircraft" (one civilian airliner and the two F-4s), and the brilliance of the object caused pilots to lose their night vision. The manoeuvrability of the object was "inordinate". The DIA evaluation of the case information characterised it as "unique, timely and of major significance." Only a fragment of the documentation believed to exist on this case has been obtained by FOI requests in response to initial newspaper reports. [**24**]

Observations of unidentified radar targets continue to occur in the decade of the 'eighties. Whilst we are not close to understanding the nature of some of the most puzzling events, a great deal more is known today about the value and limitations of this type of evidence than was the case in the innocent days when any uncorrelated return could become a "flying saucer". Attitudes to the evidence are more sophisticated and radar theory itself is more advanced. But a great deal remains to be done. Recommendations for future research would range from exploring the design of dedicated systems, instituting short- or long-term monitoring projects with existing instruments in areas of high report density, and saving data from routine civil or military radar operations, to consolidating the existing data-base for the purpose of effective statistical analysis.

Defence and space surveillance radars are highly dedicated systems in which huge numbers of uncorrelated (though not necessarily anomalous) targets are dumped irretrievably by the software. Suggestions have often been made [**eg.25**] to the effect that sub-routines could in principle save anomalous data from disposal, but the information content may be low [**26**] and there may be a conflict of scientific and defence interests. The development of UFO-dedicated radar systems with signal processing tailored to favour targets with certain parameters (presumably derived from analysis of the existing data-base) would be perhaps worthwhile, but the cost would obviously be prohibitive without funding of a kind it is unrealistic to anticipate at the present time. Monitoring projects using existing radars have actually been undertaken on various scales. In the autumn of 1967 investigators from Colorado University, Stanford Research Institute, Environmental Science Services Administration and other bodies visited an Air Force Base in California to study anomalous targets being reported intermittently on tracking and search radars. Targets were observed by the investigators, who were able to attribute them to anomalous propagation and birds detected due to the sensitive tracking radars being used in a search role for which they were not normally used. [**2**] A full-time UFO monitoring facility, Project Starlight International, was set up near Austin, Texas, in the mid-seventies. [**27,28,29**] A short-term monitoring project was undertaken in the Hessdalen Valley, Norway, in January and February of 1984 following a dramatic increase in the incidence of reports from this area. This enterprise received support from the Universities of Oslo and Bergen and attracted the co-operation of the Norwegian Defence Research Establishment. Thirty-six radar tracking incidents were recorded over a five-week period. One target, which was simultaneously observed visually and filmed as a continuous light source, reportedly gave paints on the radar only on alternate sweeps, an oddity for which no immediate explanation suggests itself. The data, however, have yet to be fully digested. [30]

Parallel with such activities, it is important to work with the data already available. Geographical, seasonal, circadian and other distributions should be studied in relation to propagation conditions conducive to false echoes. The existence of previously unsuspected atmospheric structures should not be ruled out, and the study of radar-UFO events may lead to new knowledge in this area. Phenomena related to ball lightning or other atmospheric electrical effects should also be considered as a possible explanation of some anomalous targets. The high *prima facie* strangeness of some events, however, argues that the search for still more exotic hypotheses could yet bear fruit.

REFERENCES

■ 1 - **Hall,** - R.H., *The UFO Evidence,* NICAP, Washington D.C., 1964. ■ 2 - **Gillmor,** D.S.(Ed.), *Scientific Study of Unidentified Flying Objects,* Bantam, New York, 1969; Vision Press, London, 1970. ■ 3 - **Thayer,** G.D., 'Optical and Radar analyses of Field Cases', in: **Gillmor,** op.cit. pp.115-176. ■ 5 - **Condon,** E.U., 'Summary of the Study', in: Gillmor, op.cit. pp.7-50. ■ 6 - **McDonald,** J.E., *Prepared Statement on Unidentified Flying Objects,* Hearings before the Committee on Science and Astronautics, US House of Representatives, July 29 1968, US Govt.Printing Office, Washington DC, 1968, pp.32-85. ■ 7 - **Sagan,** C., & T.**Page** (Eds.), *UFOs - A Scientific Debate,* Cornell University Press, Ithaca and London, 1972. ■ 8 - **McDonald,** J.E., 'UFO Encounter I', *Astronatics & Aeronautics* 9 (July 1971), AIAA, New York, pp.66-70. ■ 9 - **Hynek,** J.A., *The UFO Experience - A Scientific Inquiry,* Abelard-Schuman, London & New York, 1972. ■ 10 - **Klass,** P.J., *UFOs Explained,* Random House, New York, 1974, pp.175-233. ■ 11 - **Randles,** J., & **P.**Warrington, *UFOs - A British Viewpoint,* Robert Hale, London, 1979, p.103. ■ 12 - **Hynek,** J.A., *The Hynek UFO Report,* Sphere, London, 1978, p.123. ■ 13 - **McDonald,** J.E., 'Science in Default: Twenty-two Years of Inadequate UFO Investigations', in: **Sagan** & **Page,** op.cit. pp.52-122. ■ 14 - **Thayer,** G.D., 'UFO Encounter II', *Astronautics & Aeronautics* 9 (September 1971), AIAA, New York, pp.60-64. ■ 15 - **McDonald,** J.E., 'UFOs Over Lakenheath', *Flying Saucer Review,* Vol.16 No.2, March/April 1970, pp.9-17. ■ 16 - **Sachs,** M., *The UFO Encyclopedia,* Corgi/Transworld, 1981, p.33. ■ 17 - **Wimbledon,** F.H.C., letter to the Editor, *Flying Saucer Review,* Vol.24 No.1, June 1978. See also: *Sunday Times,* April 9 1978. ■ 18 - **Wimbledon,** F.H.C., personal communication, Sept 15 1986. ■ 19 - Copies of letters in author's possession: from T/Sgt. Forrest Perkins Feb.1968 to Colorado U. UFO Project, 6th & 12th August 1975 to Stanton Friedman. See also **Gillmor,** op.cit. pp.248-251. ■ 20 - **Wimbledon,** F.H.C., personal communication and interview, Sept.1986. ■ 21 - Communication from Public Record Office, Kew, Richmond, 17 November 1986. Station Record Books for Waterbeach up to Dec.1955 have been transferred to the PRO, but even these are closed to public inspection for 75 years. Squadron ORBs and Group records after 1946 and 1950 respectively are (if they survive) held by the MOD, and the PRO "cannot say for sure" when they will be transferred or what restrictions on public access may then be imposed. ■ 22 - This and other technical details of the Venom NF2a avionics are contained in recently de-restricted Ministry Air Publications held by the RAF Museum, Hendon. ■ 23 - **Hynek,** J.A., *The Hynek UFO Report,* op.cit. pp.122-144. ■ 24 - **Steiger,** B. (Ed.), *Project Blue Book,* Ballantine, New York, 1976, pp.348-370. ■ 25 - **Fawcett,** L., & B.J.**Greenwood,** *Clear Intent,* Prentice-Hall, Englewood Cliffs, New Jersey, 1984, pp.16-56. ■ 26 - **Baker,** R.M.L., Statement before US House of Representatives Committee on Science and Astronautics, 1968 (Ref.6), p.137. ■ 27 - **Hendry,** A., *The UFO Handbook,* Sphere, London, 1980, pp.230-234. ■ 28 - **Stanford,** R., 'Instrumented UFO Monitoring - A Status Report on Project Starlight International', in *Socorro Saucer* (appendix B, pp.184-191), Fontana (revised edition) 1978. ■ 29 - *Journal of Instrumented UFO Research,* PSI, PO Box 5310, Austin, Texas 78763. ■ 30 - **Sachs,** M., op.cit. pp.259-260. ■ 31 - *Final Technical Report,* Project Hessdalen, PO Box 14 N-3133, Duken, Norway.

Recommended sources for radar technical background

■ **Skolnik,** M.I., *Introduction to Radar Systems,* McGraw-Hill, New York, 1962. ■ **Blackmer,** R.H. et al, *Radar and the Observation of UFOs,* in: **Gillmor,** op.cit. pp.655-716. ■ **Cole,** H.W., *Understanding Radar,* Collins, London, 1985.

3.5

ASSESSING THE WITNESS: PSYCHOLOGY AND THE UFO REPORTER

by Alex Keul and Ken Phillips

■ **Dr ALEXANDER KEUL**. Born at Wien (Vienna), Austria, 1954. Obtained a PhD in meteorology and astronomy 1978 and completed a PhD study in psychology and journalism 1985. He is currently University Assistant for General Psychology at Salzburg University, where he is researching the hermeneutics of unconscious processes.

■ **UFO involvement**: Interest in the topic started with field investigations in 1972, and co-operation with APRO and MUFON. His psychological education changed his point of view radically. He is now an ETH-skeptic, best known for the work he has carried out in collaboration with Ken Phillips - the 'English witness project', intended to enrich our knowledge about UFO reporters, particularly their life histories and unconscious processes.

■ **Publications**: Following Austrian field investigation reports in UFO journals of the 1970s, he organised and contributed to the IUPIAR colloquium on 'Human Sciences and UFO Phenomena' at Zistelalm, nr Salzburg, 1982. The philosophy and first results of the 'English witness project' appeared in BUFORA's *JTAP*; the final results are presented here and at BUFORA's 1987 Congress.

■ **Address**: Plainstrasse 62/122 / A-5020 Salzburg / Austria. Phone 0622 53689.

■ **KEN PHILLIPS**: A mathematics teacher by profession, married and living in Hampstead, North London, Phillips names as his life's ambition to get out of teaching...an ambition doubtless stimulated by his discovery that research into the behaviour of witnesses seems to hold out more hope than the harder sciences of resolving the UFO enigma.

■ **UFO involvement**: In the mid-1960s he began to hear about flying saucers' over Warminster, and the sincerity of the accounts had a profound emotional effect. He joined BUFORA in 1968 and has been an active investigator since 1969, currently acting as National Investigations Co-ordinator for both BUFORA and ASSAP.

Having always been struck by the prevalence of psychic factors in the UFO experience, and the way in which witnesses suffered at the hands of the more exploitative elements of society, he welcomed the shift of emphasis from the nuts-and-bolts' to the psychosocial aspects of the phenomenon. Together with Dr Alexander Keul of Vienna University he has conducted revealing witness studies, as their contribution to this book illustrates.

■ **Address**: 16 Wedgewood Walk / Lymington Road / West Hampstead / London NW6. Phone (01) 435 0349.

Until ten years ago, the empirical human sciences had grossly neglected the UFO reporter. Thirteen studies on the sociology, psychology and psychiatry of UFO reporters, carried out up to 1986, are reviewed here, along with work conducted by the authors The overall findings are:

■ The content of UFO reports cannot be stastically distinguished from fantasy.

■ Recent studies tend to see the UFO reporter as psychologically different from the general population, particularly 'close encounter' (CE) / 'abduction' reporters.

■ Sociological data collected by the authors in Austria and Britain support Vallée's finding that UFO reporters are an average general population subgroup. Psychological findings will be presented at BUFORA's Congress 1987.

■ Close encounter reporters in both Austria and Britain claim high rates of ESP occurrence. Six of the ten British CE reporters claimed to have had ESP events *before* their alleged sighting, indicating a close ESP/UFO interdependence, as opposed to mere UFO-induced ESP: this opens up interesting possibilities for future research.

■ A simple experimental simulation of a UFO sighting, carried out in England, supports Haines' finding that extreme caution is called for when evaluating the reliability of witness drawings of UFOs they claim to have seen.

INTRODUCTION

Forty years after the first modern rush of UFO reports and publicity in the USA, the authors are aware of 13 empirical multiple case-studies (besides the routine opinion polls), 9 of them within the last ten years. The research interest of the scientific community cannot be called enthusiastic - UFOs and their reporters represent one of the top "taboo areas" in social and medical sciences.

In the 1969 Catoe bibliography on "UFOs and Related Subjects", Izzo counted only 11 references about human perception out of about 1600 entries. [**13**] Only two edited compilations and papers on UFOs and the social sciences have been published. [**6,11**]

Whereas competent case-studies on alleged "extrasensory perception" (ESP) do not omit a routine assessment of the witness/agent [**eg 2,22**], the initials UFO could as well stand for "*U*nidentified *F*eelings of the *O*bservers", who despite controvertible evidence and hostile social and scientific reactions, persist in claiming they saw something strange or alien.

STATE OF THE ART

Summing up briefly the results of multiple case-studies undertaken so far, it has been said that:

- "close encounter" reporters exhibit normal age, sex, occupation and activity characteristics. [**27,28**]
- US UFO reporters are status inconsistent persons. [**29**]
- eighty-three US UFO reporters showed no obvious psychological difficulties in paper-and-pencil tests. [**25**]
- US UFO reporters are normal, average citizens without psycho-pathological signs. [**23**]
- US UFO reporter sketches could not be distinguished statistically from non-sighters' fantasy drawings. Also, tests with people asked to copy a sketch of a UFO presented for a prolonged period of time, and with amateur UFO field investigators drawing UFO details stated in a written text description of a UFO, produced results that were not particularly accurate. [**11**]
- all Austrian UFO reporters out of a group of ten studied with a test battery showed psychopathological symptoms, three reporters a severe psychopathology. [**14**]
- five of six "close encounter" reporters studied suffered psychotic disorders. [**17**]
- psychological and medical paper-and-pencil tests done with four US "close encounter" reporters ended with the diagnoses: all normal. [**24**]
- both US "abduction" reporters and non-reporters experienced perinatal imagery under hypnotic regression. [**16**]
- seventy-seven US UFO reporters, in paper-and-pencil tests, indicated more belief in the occult and in government secrecy, but no differences in cultural alienation, malevolent world view and personal well-being, compared to 398 non-reporters. [**30**]
- ninety-three US UFO reporters (including "close encounters") studied with paper-and-pencil tests showed increased spiritual growth (positive values towards life, belief in spiritual truths, psychic sensitivities) after their experiences. [**3**]
- nine US UFO "abduction" reporters revealed high intelligence, weak identity (esp sexual identity), social vulnerability, and interpersonal caution (paranoia scale elevation), originality, high anxiety and a narcissistic disturbance (identity disturbance, lowered self-esteem, relative egocentricity) when studied with a psychological test battery by a psychologist not informed about their reports. [**1**]
- paper-and-pencil tests done with 225 US UFO reporters (incl alleged "contacts") showed a high level of psychic energy, a tendency to question authority and situational pressures/conflicts. "Contactees" were found to endorse unusual feelings, thoughts and attitudes, to be suspicious/distrustful and to be creative, imaginative or possibly schizoid. [**21**]

- Ten of these studies explicitly dealt with US UFO reporters, one with Austrian and one with French reporters.
- Eight dealt with general UFO reporters (including "close encounters"), five exclusively with "close encounter" / "abduction" reporters.
- Two used sociological techniques, five used paper-and-pencil psychological tests, two psychological test batteries including projective techniques, two psychiatric interview techniques, one hypnosis and one object sketches.
- Four found UFO reporters to be "all normal", one "status inconsistent", one that object sketches were "indistinguishable from mere fantasy", one that abductee reports were "indistinguishable from mere fantasy", two diagnosed "severe psychopathology", one "occult / government secrecy beliefs", one "increased spiritual growth", one "narcissistic disturbances" and one "high energy, suspicious, schizoid".

The spectrum of scientific views thus includes:

- "UFO events are psychopathological events." [**6,7**]
- "UFO events could be mere fantasies." [**5,9**]
- "UFO events are experienced by special people." [**2,12,13**]
- "UFO events are reported by ordinary, average people." [**1,3,4,8**]

As the labels "normal/abnormal" depend on which behavior/fantasies/values are found "normal" by the researcher and his/her surrounding society, a likely solution of the divergent results obtained so far is that researchers with a pro-ETH/pro-UFO belief system tend to see "no obvious psychopathology" whereas anti-ETH/anti-UFO belief holders notice the opposite. This constitutes a dialectic contradiction which, according to developmental psychologist

Jean Piaget, leads to development onto a higher level.

What we can safely say as a result of these past studies is that UFO reports cannot be distinguished from fantasies by means of their contents, that with the exception of papers by Sprinkle and Schwarz UFO reporters seem to show psychological differences from the general population, especially "close encounter"/"abduction" reporters. Does data from Europe support or contradict these conclusions?

RESEARCH PLAN

The speculative level of theorizing without empirical data [**9,10,19**] or posing the reductionist, value-dependent "normality" question [**14,17,23,25**] should be abandoned. A more fruitful approach would be to continue research on the question of differences between UFO reporters and the general population and on the psychological mechanisms at work in case of sudden perception of an ambiguous stimulus.

■ **AREA 1** - Sociological and medical (non-psychiatric) data on UFO reporters could support one of two possible hypotheses:

Hypothesis A: "UFO reporters are an average general population sub-group".

Hypothesis B: "UFO reporters differ in some respect from non-UFO-reporting members of the general population".

The features to be studied could be: age, sex, education, profession, employment, income, social status, marital status, children, state of health etc. Statistical comparisons with official census/survey data should be done. According to Vallée [**27,28**] "close encounter" reporter data should meet hypothesis A. A minor error would occur by the number of UFO sighters being part of the official census data.

■ **AREA 2** - Psychological studies of UFO reporters could focus - as non-UFO-reporter surveys [**8,18**] have done - on interests, attitudes and beliefs, especially strong belief systems, to support one of the two possible hypotheses:

Hypothesis A: "UFO reporters have average general population attitudes and beliefs/belief systems".

Hypothesis B: "UFO reporters have different attitudes and beliefs/belief systems than non-UFO-reporting members of the general population".

The features to be studied could be: religious beliefs, meaning in life, interest in UFO books, science fiction, parapsychology, astrology, spiritism, the 'Bermuda Triangle', 'ancient astronaut' hypotheses, political views, opinion on extraterrestrial life, life after death etc. Special attention should be paid to reactive effects of the UFO event (the investigation being ex-post-facto, ie post-phenomenal, major attitudes and beliefs could have developed/changed due to the event itself) and an appropriate control group.

■ **AREA 3** - A special study could try to shed light on the role of alleged ESP in UFO events, a point stressed by Schwarz [**11**]. A US study found UFO reporters (incl "close encounters") "showing sizeable increase in psi abilities" [**3**] and "sensitivities such as clairvoyance, telepathy, precognition, deja vu, out-of-body experiences..." [**4**] Unfortunately, alleged ESP events *before* the alleged UFO event as well as the time of the first alleged ESP experiences were not covered by the questionnaire. Questions on alleged ESP events before and after the alleged UFO event should be posed and the outcome compared with published survey data.

The academic question of whether ESP or "psi" "really" exists or not will be touched here as it possesses the same epistemological flavour as the "psychopathology debate" to some extent. Our pragmatic position is to treat ESP as equivalent to a strong belief system or the assertion that a UFO was seen, and to examine the joint appearance of assertions, ie whether there are people who claim a UFO sighting *plus* ESP events and hold an uncommon belief system.

■ **AREA 4** - On the assumption that even during observations of a physically real, instrument-detectable stimulus, unconscious material and socially transmitted UFO folklore tend to merge with the ambiguous visual perception data similar to what happens with a Rorschach ink blot test card, it would be fruitful:

a) to study report data on conventional visual stimuli (moon, planets, stars, fireballs), particularly if reported as UFOs, to ascertain the range of descriptional deviations; ie. "natural setting" - and

b) to do simple laboratory experiments with diaslides or films depicting a "UFO" stimulus to find out more about blurring effects, continuing the UFO drawing tests by Haines [**11**]; ie. "artificial setting".

MATERIAL AND METHOD

Due to an almost complete lack of UFO reports from Austria after 1980, new field investigations were done in Great Britain, where case reports kept flowing in to Ken Phillips (BUFORA / ASSAP).

Both screened and unscreened material has been used in social science UFO studies. By 'unscreened' is meant that the report lacks technical efforts by specialists to identify what has been seen. Such raw material, contining only a fraction of technically unidentifiable reports, was used for the extensive Warren [**29**] and Zimmer [**30**] studies ("I think I once saw a UFO").

For the present research effort, only screened case material has been taken into consideration.

Austrian case reports were screened together with a professional astronomer, weather service and Austrian air traffic controllers. British cases were screened by field investigator Ken Phillips with the help of local authorities and airport personnel.

The case selection modus in both countries was:

- only technically unidentified (screened) sightings
- preferably less than a year old
- male/female, age and occupation classes as general population
- both distant and "close encounters", ie alleged UFO(s) outside or within the reporter's perceptual frame of reference.

For the collection of sociological and psychological data, an interview scheme - the ANAMNESIS - was developed. The third version (Fischer, Keul & Phillips 1985 - see appendix) comprised 62 questions to be asked by the interviewer. Up to date, 30 filled-in ANAMNESIS sheets of the earlier versions 1 and 2 as well as seven of the long version 3 format (most of the field interviews done by Phillips) have been evaluated.

After most field interviews, a Rorschach projective personality test ("ink blot tables") was done with the UFO reporter. As modern general population standards for Austria and Great Britain are non-existent, phenomenological inter-group comparisons are the only way of evaluation which will be done in the near future. Amateur investigators are *not* encouraged to use this test because of the evaluation problems and because of the fact that in Great Britain Rorschach cards are not sold to people outside the psychological and medical profession and it is prohibited by law that they are passed on to be used outside diagnostic research projects and psychotherapy.

For the perception test of research AREA 4, a diaslide provided by Phillips was used.

RESULTS AREA 1

Twenty-one Austrian UFO reporters (13 distant events, 8 "close encounters") and 26 British UFO reporters (16 distant events, 10 "close encounters"), ie a total of 47 reporters, agreed to be field interviewed with the ANAMNESIS.

Of the Austrian reporters, 11 came from Vienna, 9 from Lower Austria and one from Salzburg City. All had contacted the Vienna authorities by their own accord after the alleged events. Of the British reporters, all but one came from the area of Southern England; most cases were from the Milton Keynes region where Phillips lived at that time. Contact modes were various - direct, via local press or other UFO group members.

Eleven of the Austrian reporters (52%) had less than a year's delay between alleged event and ANAMNESIS. In Britian, 10 reporters (38%) fall into that category.

ANAMNESIS data from Austria and Britain were statistically compared with:

- a list of 117 Austrian reporters of technically screened UFO events from 1972 to 1979 comprising age, sex, profession and report type,
- British 1980 unemployment figures (Employment Gazette July 1985),
- Austrian 1980 unemployment figures [**20**].

The list of 117 Austrian reporters of technically screened UFO events from 1972 to 1979 comprising age, sex, profession and report type was statistically compared with Austrian number of families and children [**5**], age distribution, male/female ratio, and livelihood categories (pupils/students, working population, pensioners)[**20**].

Inter-group differences (distant: "close" reports Austria: Britain), differences to total reports Austria 1972-79 and to general population figures of the two countries were tested with Chi-square or, for small expected frequencies (below five), Fisher-Yates was used instead [**7**].

The following results were obtained:

- Data on all Austrian reporters 1972-1979 concerning age group under/over 30 years, male/female sex and three main livelihood categories (pupils/students, working population, pensionists) *did not differ significantly* from the general population 1981.
- Inter-group analysis and comparison with general population values *did not yield significant differences* in the case of male/female sex, children, unemployment.
- *The only significant difference* between Austrian distant and "close encounter" reporters (Chi-square, 1%-level), between Austrian distant event reporters and the general population (Chi-square, 5%-level) and between the Austrian distant event reporters and all UFO reporters Austria 1972-79 (Chi-square, 5%-level) is an *old age artefact* caused by case selection procedures (more recent cases ready for the ANAMNESIS had a high percentage of old reporters).

Therefore, as far as we can see with the data sets used for this statistical study, *the Vallée findings that UFO reporters do not deviate from the average population of a country regarding sociological parameters as sex, age and occupation/livelihood, are correct for Austria and Great Britain.*

RESULTS AREA 2

Findings in this area of research will be presented in a paper for BUFORA's 1987 International UFO Conference at London.

RESULTS AREA 3

An ESP question had been part of the ANAMNESIS right from the beginning of our project in 1981. We recorded self-reported ESP experiences. Austrian data obtained in the earliest phase of the investigations were incomplete. However, in the "close encounter" category four of eight people definitely mentioned ESP. There was no public survey available with which to compare possible Austrian reporter data.

Coverage of the British scene was far better: 22 of the 26 interviewed reporters, when asked, said they had experienced ESP. Six of the 16 distant event reporters claimed ESP events, two of them before the alleged UFO sighting, five described repeated events. Self-reported phenomena included (definitions by the reporters): precognitive dreams / precognition (5), telepathy (3), apparitions (2), PK (1) and healing (1). Three reporters claimed alleged multiple phenomena (eg telepathy, healing and precognitive dreams).

The effect was stronger in the "*close encounter*" group: *of the ten people involved, nine reported ESP events, six of them before the alleged UFO sighting,*

Figure 1. 'UFO' stimulus drawings. (Reduction.)

eight repeated occurrences. Self-reported phenomena ranged from precognitive dreams / precognition (3), PK (3), apparitions/visions (3), healing (2), OBEs (2), automatic writing (2), telepathy (2), clairvoyance (1) to "astral travelling" (1). Four people reported multiple phenomena. The fact that the majority of these people started with alleged ESP episodes *before* the UFO record is a challenge to the popular assumption "UFOs cause ESP". It is far too early for causal speculations of any kind, but the strong affinity should be noticed. Schwarz [**11**] and Davis [**3**] have pointed into the right direction of research.

The Audience Selection survey of 1980 on self-reported ESP in Great Britain reviewed by Haraldsson [**12**] stated that 64% of their respondents said they had had "some psychic experience". Against the general population background of this figure it would not be surprising if two or three British UFO reporters claimed one ESP event in their lifetimes, but the concentration of "ESP-proneness" in the "close encounter" group still remains outstanding.

RESULTS AREA 4

To give the reader some idea about the following topic, **Figure 1** shows the result of a "UFO diaslide" drawing test done with 14 people, mostly academics, interested in UFOs, in 1982. Drawings were made immediately after a short projection time of the "UFO diaslide".

Following the idea put down above under AREA 4 b), we have experimented with a design similar to that of Haines [**11**].

A diaslide depicting the night-time view of a luminous, structured "UFO" with bottom and top portion details visible was displayed via slide projector to the auditorium for a fixed time span (under one minute). Exact descriptions of display material and duration are not published to enable us to repeat the experiment - even with readers of this report - in the future.

The experimenter (Phillips) asked the voltuntary participants to observe closely and, after switch-off, sketch what they had seen and give a duration estimate.

The test was conducted three times in England with a total of 61 experimental witnesses - first at a Crawley, Sussex, Astronomical Society meeting (April 19 1985), then at a Milton Keynes Astronomical Society meeting (October 4 1985) and finally during a BUFORA meeting at the London Business School, Regent's Park, London (October 5 1985). Thus, 32 participants were more amateur astronomy-related, whereas 29 were more UFO-interested.

Drawings were collected and sent to Keul in Austria for evaluation. The idea of showing a "UFO" diaslide and asking the viewers for sketches afterwards has its European premiere at Zistelalm, Salzburg, Austria, in July 1982 involving 14 participants of the International UPIAR Colloquium on Human Sciences and UFO Phenomena and Alexander G. Keul as experimenter [**15 - see Fig 1**].

Statistical evaluation of the sketches and duration estimates showed the following structures:

■ *Duration*: If a ±5 seconds interval around the true exposition time is defined as "*average fit*", then *one third to half of the viewer groups* gave estimates falling into this category. About one sixth to one third of the viewers reached a "good fit" (±2 seconds deviation from true time). About one third estimated a shorter than "average fit" duration, one seventh to one third over-estimated it. The roughly one third:one third:one third distribution of under-, average and over-estimations *is no safe base at all for assessing the quality of single "witness" estimates* "blindfold" (without knowledge of the true duration - the normal situation in the field).

■ *One third to half of the "witnesses" drew almost exact shape outlines* of the whole object seen, *about half drew distorted images*, one sixth and less depicted completely dissimilar shapes. The chance of obtaining a correct or distorted/worse "witness" shape sketch at random is about 50%.

■ *The main bottom structure* of the "UFO" *was drawn by one third to half of the witnesses and omitted by half to two thirds* in their sketches. Again, the chance of picking out at random a sketch with valid/invalid main secondary structures is 50%.

■ *Bottom secondary structures were correctly sketched by one sixth to one third of the participants*, one third to half of the audience gave wrong shapes and the same number of people drew none or fuzzy shapes there.

■ *Top main structures were correctly depicted by one third to half of the witnesses*, one fifth to one third drew wrong shapes and the same number of participants sketched none or fuzzy shapes. This is the same proportion of right drawing details as in (3) for the main bottom structure.

■ *Half to nine tenths of the sketchers gave the correct orientation of the "UFO" in space*, one tenth to one fourth sketched a rim perspective, about the same number gave the object a completely different spatial orientation and roughly the same number again drew an uncertain or no spatial orientation at all. Spatial orientation seems to be the best remembered visual parameter.

■ *Confabulations, ie non-existent details* entering perception or recall through the mind of the observer (eg from UFO or Science Fiction literature read before the experiment) *were found in about one fourth of the sketches produced by amateur astronomers' meeting participants, but in almost half of the drawings by ufologists' meeting participants.* The difference is marked, but not statistically significant (Chi-squared test). Most of the non-existent details could be identified by the evaluator as parts of a "classical UFO shape" similar to the experimental structure used, ie *an unconscious completion tendency* was shown by people who had read the respective literature - mostly ufologists, not amateur astronomers.

■ A general scoring attempt to look for *good and bad overall observers* - one point each for average duration fit, correct shape outline, main and secondary structures correctly drawn, right perspective and no confabulations - showed *no difference at all between the arithmetic mean of recalls by amateur astronomer meeting participants and UFO meeting members* - both x ('arithmetic mean') were 3,8, *but a somewhat greater variance* (ie more good *and* bad observers) *for the UFO meeting visitors* (standard deviations for amateur astronomers' meeting 1,58, for ufologists' meeting 1,97).

The overall results obtained with a sample of English "experimental UFO witnesses" indicate that:

■ observation duration (exposition time under a minute) is equally correctly estimated, over- or under-estimated, giving a 50:50 chance to get a good or bad duration estimate at random,

■ major structures of the "UFO" stimulus are correctly reproduced by a maximum of 50-60% of the "witnesses" and distorted or forgotten by the rest, ie structural details are badly reproduced in general,

■ spatial orientation of the stimulus is remembered best (by 50 to 90% of the viewers),

■ confabulated (non-existent) details enter nearly every second drawing, when UFO literature has been studied previous to the simulated observation,

■ UFO interested persons showed the same average structure recall (overall reliability) as those interested in amateur astronomy, but a somewhat greater variance.

Our experimental conditions (exposure time under a minute, color diaslide, no film used, emotional disposition different from a "real sighting" etc) are certainly limits to generalizations, but it is nevertheless remarkable that a finding of Haines - the not particularly accurate drawing results even if people are allowed to copy right from the original - has been independently reproduced in England. The first experiment in Austria, with 14 participants (mostly UFO-interested ones) and a color slide showing a more ambiguous shape than the slide provided by Phillips, resulted in an even greater divergence about shape and major structural details [**Figure 1**].

We think we have positively shown that an observer's eyes and mind are no video recorder or computer diskette that the field investigator only needs to "re-wind" to extract exact information, but that people who try to draw uncommon shapes they have seen - especially when the observation was short and details scarce - make great mistakes in time and structures, are better with spatial orientation, and that "ufological bias" or unconscious channels to UFO folklore material allow a lot of things that were not actually there to materialize in the drawings.

As our simple experiment was based on the assumption that some physical stimulus exists in some UFO events and the results are rather frustrating for the demands of natural scientists eager to analyze hard data, you can easily imagine what comes out of a computer program statistically mixing this sort of data like a washing machine - data of people from different cultures, UFO reports translated from one language into another and a salient proportion of case histories where the existence of a physical stimulus is at least doubtful.

CONCLUSION

After 30 years of speculation, disinterest or lonely single-handed research, several teams of critical people including trained psychologists have been active in the last five years. Compared to what we *should* know about the psychology of UFO reporters, we know nothing; nevertheless we definitely know more than five or ten years ago.

The main findings and their interpretations have been presented here - not in a popular jargon, but with technical terms whenever they occurred. The interested reader is referred to dictionaries of psychology/psychoanalysis [eg. *The Penguin dictionary of psychology*]. If we venture to put the overall findings down as three points, they may run:

■ UFO reporters do not seem to be a "sub-culture", but display more or less the same sociological characteristics as everyone else in a community.

■ UFO reporters, on the psychological plane, seem to be more critical and sensible, creative and powerful than their contemporaries. Reported psychological findings describe artistic people, more open to unconscious forces and less rigid in their roles, with all the benefits and draw-backs of such a position. A higher self-reported rate of ESP events also fits in here.

■ Experimentally simulated "UFO events" (assuming a physical stimulus as focus of attention) teach us to be critical and cautious about what people think they have seen, regardless of their profession and intelligence. The tendency of the human mind to re-structure, omit what has not been seen clearly or put in imaginary details is strong.

Consequently, we advocate *more psychological studies* about UFO witnesses under carefully controlled conditions and with open minds. We do not think that the ANAMNESIS is the *only* instrument to be used in the field, but it should not be the last one, reserved for "special occasions". And it should be used ethically correctly - not to put pressure on reporters, not to find out "secret sins" or with an attitude of sensational journalism. We do not hold any legal responsibilities for possible abuse of the system. But we would be happy to learn of new cases where researchers followed this track further on - beyond.

REFERENCES

1 - **Bloecher, Clamar & Hopkins,** 'Final report on the psychological testing of UFO 'abductees'' FUFOR 1985. ■ 2 - **Bononcini,** A., Martelli, A., 'Psychological investigation of subjects who are protagonists of alleged PK phenomena: a preliminary report' in *Journal of the Society for Psychical Research* 52.794, 1983. ■ 3 - **Davis,** L., 'How the UFO experience compares with the near-death experience as a vehicle for the evolution of human consciousness', unpublished MA paper for John F Kennedy University, 1985. ■ 4 - **Davis,** L., personal communication to K Phillips, 22.10.1985. ■ 5 - **Familienbericht,** 'Bericht uber die Situation der Familie in Osterreich", Wien, Bundeskanzleramt, 1985. ■ 6 - **Farabone,** R (ed) 'Proceedings of the International UPIAR colloquium on human sciences and UFO phenomena', UPIAR. Milano, 1983. ■ 7 - **Finney, Latscha, Bennett, Hsu,** 'Tables for testing significance in a 2x2 contingency table', Cambridge University press, 1963. ■ 8 - **Fox,** P., 'Social and cultural factors influencing beliefs about UFOs', in **[11]**. ■ 9 - **Gordon,** R.A., 'People who see flying saucers' in **Science**, 12.3.1971. ■ 10 - **Grinspoon,** L., **Persky,** A.D., 'Psychiatry and UFO reports', in Sagan & Page (eds) *UFOs, a scientific debate*, Cornell, 1972. ■ 11 - **Haines,** R.F., (ed) *UFO phenomena and the behavioral scientist*, Scarecrow, 1979. ■ 12 - **Haraldsson,** E., 'Representative national surveys of psychic phenomena' in *Journal of the Society for Psychical Research*, 53.801, 1985. ■ 13 - **Izzo,** F., 'The scandal is 0.7%', in **[6]**. ■ 14 - **Keul,** A.G., 'Personlichkeitsvariable and Realitatsprufung von ungewohnlichen Zeugenaussagen', private, Wien, 1980. ■ 15 - **Keul,** A.G., 'What could be this?' in **[6]**. ■ 16 - **Lawson,** A.H., 'Birth trauma imagery in CE-III narratives' in **[6]**. ■ 17 - **Mavrakis,** D., Bocquet, J.P., 'Psychoses et OVNIs' in *Canadian Journal of Psychiatry* 28.3, 1983. ■ 18 - **McIver,** S., 'What kind of people join a UFO group?' in *Journal of Transient Aerial Phenomena*, 2.5, BUFORA, 1983. ■ 19 - **Meerloo,** J.A.M., 'The flying saucer syndrome and the need for miracles' in *Journal of the American Medical Association* 203.12, 1968. ■ 20 - Osterreichisches Statistisches Zentralamt (OStZ) , *Statistisches Handbuch fur die Republik Osterreich,* Wien, Osterreichische Staatsdruckerei, 1981. ■ 21 - **Parnell,** J.O., 'Personality characteristics on the MMPI, 16PF and ACL, of persons who claim UFO experiences', unpublished dissertation, University of Wyoming, 1986. ■ 22 - **Roll,** W.G., *The poltergeist*, Signet, 1974. ■ 23 - **Schwarz,** B.E., 'Psychiatric and parapsychiatric dimensions of UFOs' in **[11]**. ■ 24 - **Schwarz,** B.E., *UFO dynamics*, Rainbow, Moore Haven, 1983. ■ 25 - **Sprinkle,** R.L., 'Hypnotic and psychic implications in the investigation of UFO reports' in Lorenzen, C.E. & J. (eds) *Encounters with UFO Occupants*, N.Y. Berkley. ■ 26 - **Sprinkle,** R.L., 'UFO research: problem or predicament?' in *Pursuit*, 10.4, 1977. ■ 27 - **Vallée,** J., 'The pattern behind the UFO landings' in 'The Humanoids' *Flying Saucer Review* special issue, 1966. ■ 28 - **Vallée,** J., 'Analysis of 8260 UFO sightings' in *Flying Saucer Review* 14.3, 1968. ■ 29 - **Warren,** D.I., 'Status inconsistency theory and flying saucer sightings' in *Science* 170, 1970. ■ 30 - **Zimmer,** T.A., 'Social psychological correlates of possible UFO sightings' in *Journal of social psychology* 123.2, 1984.

3.6

COMPUTERS IN UFOLOGY

by John Spencer, Jacques Vallée and Maurizio Verga

Computers have been with us for many decades; from what is recognised as their origins in Charles Babbage's invention, through the clumsy multi-valved computing engine called ENIAC used by the US Army for ballistic range finding, into the 1960s in which real computer power in the sense of data base storage and manipulation became available as valves were replaced by transistors and finally into the modern day where the transistors have been replaced by microchips producing the desk-top and personal computers.

The computers of the 1960s had phenomenal power in both what they could do and what they could store but this power was available to very few. The computers themselves were extremely expensive and limited in availability to the very large corporations. Computer programmers, technicians and operators were highly skilled specialists available at great cost, again, only to these organisations, and the computers themselves were extremely large and bulky. (One American leading computer manufacturer even in the early 1970s was proudly displaying in London's Oxford Street a computer which amongst its many talents could play progressively complex games of chess with an opponent - this computer weighed approximately 1 ton and required a further 21 tons of cooling equipment to keep it operating!) These computers were extremely delicate and required special dustfree environments and extremely complex handling procedures.

Ufology is, and has always been, the domain of the enthusiastic amateur and the vast majority of work in this field has been done by such enthusiasts working in their spare time, for no pay or reward, and using what facilities were available to them within their price range and convenient to their lifestyles. It is therefore only the invention of the personal computer (PC) that has put computing within the range of Ufologists and this revolution in computer technology is very recent; reaching back a mere handful of years in terms of any real power in storage or programming being available to the Ufologists.

Understandably then there is no real co-ordination across the globe in terms of what uses computers are being put to by Ufologists. Such is always the history of the early days of any invention and without exception every computer project that Ufology has undertaken, or is currently undertaking, is in the nature of experimentation, rather than application, of this new powerful tool.

Firstly, there are many different areas in which computers can be of service to Ufologists. **Maurizio Verga** in his paper 'Computer and ufology: the present scene' lists the following seven possible applications of the computer to the subject:

- Processing of parameters involved in a UFO sighting (apparent size and distance, angle of elevation, etc....) according to witness reports. This would enable comparison of data from well investigated reports to check differences due to perceptive and psychological error.
- Checking reports against data base of stars and planets to eliminate these misinterpretations.
- Storage of cases in computerised form by a common data base for each kind of machine, if possible. This would allow for easier and quicker exchange of data as well as better presentation.
- Development of statistical analysis on fundamental data of available reports.
- Establishment of a 'bulletin board system' able to connect members by electronic mail and to offer different kinds of information via modem links.
- Low cost production of a magazine or a newsletter through a powerful word processing program or other special software.
- Storing of bibliographies about selected matters with flexibility of display or retrieval.

There is one further usage to be listed here; to produce a data base of UFO group members able to display or retrieve information relating to their geographical spread, their spread of interests, the spread of available assistance they have offered to their association, lists of equipment available for use by the ssociation etc. **James Danby,** of BUFORA, has produced just such a data base for BUFORA members and although still in its early days is already proving a valuable tool to that organisation.

One further drawback in the use of computers in Ufology, due to the fact that the technology is still young and usage is still experimental, is that the work is being carried out across the globe on many, and incompatible, machines using data bases not common or transferable to other machines, making an exchange of information difficult. The following is a summary of computer usage in Ufology as prepared by Maurizio Verga.

THE GREAT CATALOGUES

Amongst the applications of computer in Ufology,

the establishment of large catalogues of cases is, without any doubt, the most well-known. The chief purpose was the development of statistical analyses (nearly all some simple frequency distributions) in search of constants inside the database. The problems associated with these colossal projects (time and financial constraints, personnel, access to computer, etc...) have always produced the closing of or, at best, a complete paralysis of the activities.

The great catalogues of sightings stored on big computers (mainframes) represent the past now: they were linked to the technologies and ideas of those times. However a brief look at these projects can be interesting.

■ UFOCAT (UFO CATalogue)

Practically, it was the first great UFO catalogue established on a computer: it has been presented several times as the evidence of the presence of an unknown phenomenon. It seems it succeeded in storage about 80,000 events (approximately). Unfortunately, most of them had a very scarce quality and a lot were not associated with the common idea of the 'UFO phenomenon'. The most recent statistics drawn from UFOCAT have been published around the end of the 1970's. [**1, 2, 3, 4**]. Since then there has been little more. It is probable that its activity has been 'frozen'. Some years ago CUFOS, put on sale some material drawn from this computerized catalogue, particularly the codebook employed for the coding of the events.

■ PROJECT URD

This is a project of storing world-wide data on a mainframe (IBM360/165) started in 1973 in Sweden. [**5, 6, 7**] This ambitious project, directed by **Bertil Kuhlemann,** seems currently inactive even though some statistics have been published in a Norwegian magazine. [**8**] It's chief aim was the establishment of a very large file of international sightings, as a basis from which to carry out some complex statistical analyses. The project has produced various material about it's work, including a preliminary 100 page report, which showed the results up to 1980.

■ UNICAT

This is another project of computerization of general UFO data, proposed by **Dr Willy Smith:** it seemed to be designed to co-operate with (or to replace?) UFOCAT. Each event would be entered in the computerized system under the form of a brief summary. UNICAT has essentially remained an idea: there has been no concrete development of the international co-operation which should be the starting point of such a project.

THE NATIONAL CATALOGUES

Some ufologists have acknowledged the practical difficulties in producing a catalogue of international UFO data, as well as its intrinsic uselessness (it is enough to think of the impossibility in checking all foreign cases). They thought it right to address their efforts towards a national database: and even then the work to do was always enormous, but results were more concrete, sometimes partially achieving the objective. These catalogues gather any kind of UFO event, they are structured in different ways and they have been developed on various kinds of computers.

■ UFODATA

This is a project of storing on a mainframe the whole Danish UFO and IFO database. It was started around the end of the 1970s, employing a software written for the study of the social sciences (SPSS). By such a sophisticated program some preliminary statistical studies were carried out by **Per Andersen,** UFODATA creator and director. [**9**] The project now has about 2,100 stored cases, but it goes on very slowly inside the activities of the Danish group SUFOI. Andersen is planning to transfer the whole work on a microcomputer, so that it could be available to a higher number of people. [**10**]

■ UFOCOMFILE (UFO COMputer FILE)

Australian researcher **Andrew Cole** started this project about the storage of Australian UFO cases on computer in 1976, using a big UNIVAC computer. Cases were entered by encoding the information of each report. The project - to which most Australian researchers contribute - is developing very slowly, due to limited collaboration. In July 1985 an internal one page *Bulletin* was published: it should produce a greater interest towards the project, but results don't seem to be encouraging. UFOCOMFILE has now been put on an Alpha Micro 100 personal computer owned by Andrew Cole, so that any dependence on an external computer (accessible only from time to time) is eliminated.

■ UFODOC

This is a database program, written by the Dutch researcher **Henry Kampherbeek,** devoted to the storage of Belgian and Dutch UFO data. [**11**] The software was developed for the Commodore 64 and a few hundred cases have already been entered. Using a similar program, Kampherbeek established a special database customized for bibliographic references regarding UFOs. Many applications of this have been developed by researchers for their own documents, but always employing different software. This produces many difficulties in exchanging files between colleagues. One of the aims of CUFON is to propose a standard program in this field.

■ TASCAT (TASmanian CATalogue of UFO events)

This catalogue has been established on a C-64 by **Paul Jackson**. It includes about 200 sightings that have taken place in Tasmania (Australia) and collected by TUFOIC. Each event has a certain amount of information, most of which is coded for entry to the database. Thanks to the options of the program, it is possible to process entries in any way. [12]

■ **BUFORA Computer Project**

Members of the British UFO Research Association are using micro-computers, especially the Sinclair Spectrum. One of the aims of the Association seems to be the establishment of some sort of computer network, in order to exploit all available resources (something very like to the Italian RUC: see below). Unfortunately, a not very enthusiastic participation is producing some difficulties for this interesting enterprise. **Mike Wootten** prepared on his Spectrum 48K a catalogue of British UFO sightings happening in the 1980s, employing a commercial database program. Preliminary statistical analyses and graphs have already been produced, but all this is only the first step towards a much more comprehensive work.

■ **UFOBANK**

This is a sophisticated database program for Apple IIc and IIe prepared by **Marco Battaini** (ICUFOS computer consultant). It is especially devoted to the storage and processing of a national database structured on a local (provincial) basis. The software can produce statistical analyses with tables and graphs of various kinds, both on a screen and printer. At the moment there are about 900 stored cases. A simpler version has been prepared for the C-64 and it is currently employed by many Italian ufologists to store our UFO data in the form of provincial files.

SPECIFIC CATALOGUES

Catalogues of relatively small databases on personal computers are currently the most successful applications. In fact, the 'restricted' quantity of data allows for work by a single person in quite expedient time. These are very specialist catalogues (relating, above all, to close encounters), employing database programs written for that purpose. During the last year there has been an increasing interest for such applications from more and more researchers and new work is likely to be carried out in the future.

■ **BECASSINE**

This is a particularly interesting project carried out by French researcher **Denys Breysse,** employing an Amstrad CPC 464. It is a series of programs (really remarkable from the point of view of the software) able to process wholly an international database of 'close encounters of the third kind'. Cases have been inserted as a series of information: a lot of them, especially regarding the description of the witness' experience, have been coded. The main aim of this work is the development of statistics on the whole database-sample entered in the system (estimated at about 1000 cases, 200 of which have already been stored). This, together with an attempted analysis of the "motifs included in the reports, should lead to an explanation of some characteristics of the CE 3 phenomenon and the myth linked to it. [**13** ,**14**].

■ **ARGENCAT (ARGENtinian CATalogue)**

Guillermo C. Roncoroni of the CIU. group of Buenos Aires established the Argentinian catalogue of Type-1 events (the so-called close encounters) on an IBM/36. It includes more than 300 cases stored in code relating to the several parameters of the typical UFO sighting. In parallel to the catalogue (which is continuously updated) there is a series of statistical analyses, most of which are presented as bar graphs and pie charts.

■ **COMPITACAT (COMPuterized ITACAT)**

This is a "package" of three different series of programs plus a common "demo" prepared by **Maurizio Verga**. [**15**] The series refers to:

ITACAT (catalogue of Italian close

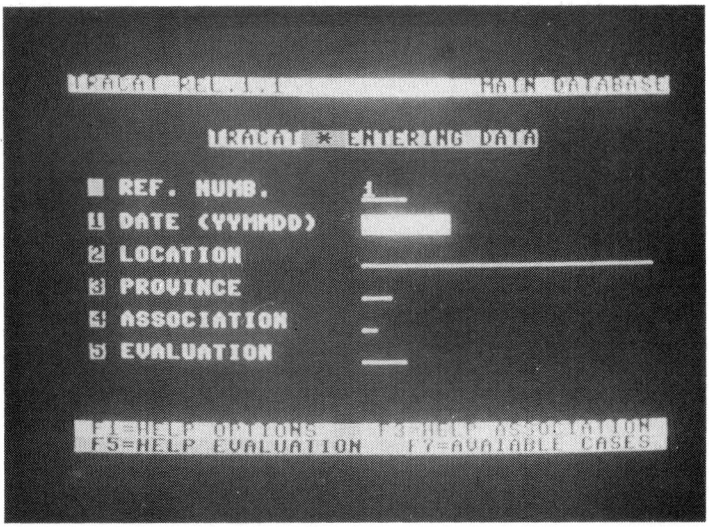

The initial TRACAT data entry screen.
[Photo: C. Guarisco.]

encounters, 450 cases).

ITACAT N (catalogue of explained Italian close encounters, 100 cases).

TRACAT (catalogue of Italian trace cases, 180 cases).

All software runs on Commodore 64/128 and it is available both on tape and floppy disc. Each series is made up of:

- a long program with many text screens presenting explanations and further information about the whole work.
- a graphic program with a presentation of the work, the powerful database and its file.

The database (written together with Italian ufologist **Marco Bottaini**) is able to manage all fundamental data of the stored cases. There is also a special 'demo' version of it, suitable to be shown during conferences and meetings open to the public. Moreover, it is a program with some simple statistical analyses about Italian landings: results and bar graphs are shown directly on the screen.

Beyond this particular version, the above mentioned catalogues have been stored on a very powerful database program for Commodore 128; the famous 'SUPERBASE': this allows for the addition of other information for each case (its sources, above all).

OTHER PROJECTS

Besides storing UFO catalogues, the computer is employed for the development of other kinds of programs or special applications. Among them, are the several bibliographic works carried out all over the work by many researchers on a personal basis. In Italy, for example, there are two particular projects inside ICUFOS: the first one, edited by **Marco Bottaini** on an Apple IIc, collects all bibliographical resources (books and magazines) owned by many Italian ufologists, while the second one, carried out by **Paolo Toselli,** is devoted to a bibliograpy of papers and books drawn from the scientific literature that could be useful in ufology.

But beyond the 'direct' applications of computers in our field, there are other special enterprises (COMPUFOMNET, RUC, etc...)

■ EDA (Elaborazione Dati Avvistamento)

The English translation of the name of this program is 'Sighting Data Processing'. The software, able to run on a Commodore 64, allows the processing of many different parameters coming from the witness' tale. Probable sizes, altitude, distance and speed are some of the parameters you can obtain supplied from the related information drawn from the investigator's report. Even though this program handles data related to human perception and evaluation, I think it could supply some interesting information, both to the on-field investigator and the researcher. EDA - which can process reliability/strangeness coefficients - has been written by **Sergio Bianchi** and **Luigi Di Ruzza** of GSE a valid Italian local group. [**16**]

■ COMPUFON (COMPuter UFO Network)

This is a network of personal computers owned by ufologists (nearly all from USA) and connected with a central data bank, and carrying out a Bulletin Board Service. The whole project has been directed by **Michael Hart**, essentially as a MUFON project. COMPUFON was born in 1985 making use of a small ATARI 800XL as it's central unit, then replaced by a IBM PC/XT with a 20Mbyte hard disc. At the end of 1985 the Network had about 100 members and among the services offered we can mention: the pages of a UFO magazine, *Aerial/Space Phenomena Review*; the public mail; the FOIA papers; the announcements.

M. Hart published a monthly *Bulletin* (also available directly through the Bulletin Board) devoted to COMPUFON activities and description of available material. Unfortunately, many problems produced the 'freezing' of the Network for a long period. In March 1986, Hart re-founded this important information service, changing it's name (now COMPUter UFO Management NETwork) structure. Members, who must directly ask for their own password and access, can connect to the system one or two evenings per week during it's experimental phase.

■ R.U.C. (Rate Ufologica Computerizzata)

This is an informal association established inside ICUFOS with the object of stimulating and coordinating the activities of about 40 Italian ufologists having personal computers (mainly Commodore 64 and Apple II, but the first one is certainly the most common). Aims of the Computer UFO Network - directed by **Maurizio Verga** - are several, but two of them have to be mentioned:

- 'the storing of the Italian UFO database on a local basis, using a common database program for Commodore 64.
- 'the composition of texts to be published on the new fine ICUFOS magazine, UFO - Rivista di Informazione Ufologica through a common word-processing program.

Among the RUC projects there is the establishment of a sort of UFO 'Bulletin Board Service' (like COMPUFOMNET), open to all researchers able to connect to the central unit via modem. Such a Service should offer information of various kinds, for example news about the most recent sightings, catalogues of cases, bibliographies, an 'electronic' bulletin, the possibility of exchanging messages among users and so on. Another important objective, even though a long-term one, is the development of new UFO software. RUC members receive a bulletin detailing it's activities and proposals of future work to be carried out.

■ **THE COMPUTER UFO Newsletter**
This is the only publication in the world exclusively devoted to the use and application of computers in ufology. A lot of international researchers contribute to the *Newsletter* edited by **Maurizio Verga**, wholly written in the English language, with articles on research projects, ready programs, proposals of common works and new software. There is a column, 'Offer of software', where there is an offer at cost price of all UFO programs available at the moment (about 30) for different kinds of computers. Furthermore, there is also an offer of the print-outs of many programs. The *Newsletter* is published from four to six time per year and it is available through a subscription. [**17**]

OTHER UFO PROGRAMS

There is other software related to ufology developed on various computers: essentially, these are catalogues of cases, some of which present a certain interest. Unfortunately, the information to hand at this time is not complete, so that only a few very brief comments can be made:

■ German researcher **Adolf Schneider** has prepared many different kinds of catalogues of UFO sightings: ANIMAL (cases with animal effects); LANIBE (Iberic landings collected by V.J. Ballester Olmos); NELIB (identified Iberic landings); ULIGHT (cases with extreme bright UFOs); EMGUFO (cases with electromagnetic effects); PHYSIO (cases with physiological effects on the witnesses); MINUFO (very small UFOs); UFODYNFO (UFOs with changes of shape).

■ **Richard Haines** (author of **Observing UFOs** and **UFOs and the behavioural scientist**) established a catalogue of sightings made by air-crews using an IBM PC.

■ Belgian researcher **Ronny Blomme** has just finished an interesting program for Apple IIe able to supply a skymap in any date and location. Printing the map produced by this program enables the checking of the position of most celestial bodies and, eventually, to find an astronomical explanation for some sightings.

■ In the USA **David Christensen** launched a project of storing the whole American UFO bibliography on a TRS 80 computer. In 1985, the available sources produced a 200 page print-out.

■ The well-known Swedish researcher **Anders Liljegren** carried out a preliminary catalogue of sightings of the "ghost rockets" which took place in Sweden in 1946. It was established on a IBM/36, the same machine used for SWECAT.

■ Another program dealing with the positions of stars and planets has been prepared by the French researcher *Daniel Mavrakis* on a SUPERBRAIN personal computer.

■ A Portuguese ufologist living in Canada, **Victor Lourenco**, prepared two catalogues available on Apple II and IBM PC: VAO (Portuguese general UFO sightings), and CATHUM (catalogue of close encounters of the third kind that have taken place in the Iberic peninsula). Both employ a sophisticated commercial software package (PFS).

■ Canadian researcher **Marc Leduc** stored the Quebec UFO database on an Apple IIe.

■ We have news about a US program (for Apple IIe) containing the whole listing and the statistical results of unidentified cases from Project blue Book.

The above summaries indicate the usages to which computers have been put, or are being put, but it is also of extreme interest to study in some detail the practical aspects of one or two of these projects in terms of handling the input, database etc. not least because this shows the problems the ufologist has in dealing with a wide range of ill defined data.

TOWARDS AN 'INTELLIGENT' UFO DATABASE

Jacques Vallee in his paper 'Towards the use of artificial intelligence techniques in the screening of reports of anomalous phenomena' presents the following detailed descriptions of his development of the OVNIBASE program: "Today we know enough about the behaviour of UFO phenomena and also of the various sources of misidentification to design a standardized, intelligent front-end to effect adequate screening. It can be implemented using a software expert system running on a personal computer. The author found the *NEXPERT* SYSTEM, developed by Neuron Data, Inc. to be a suitable vehicle for implementation of a screening system which can be operated by clerical personnel using

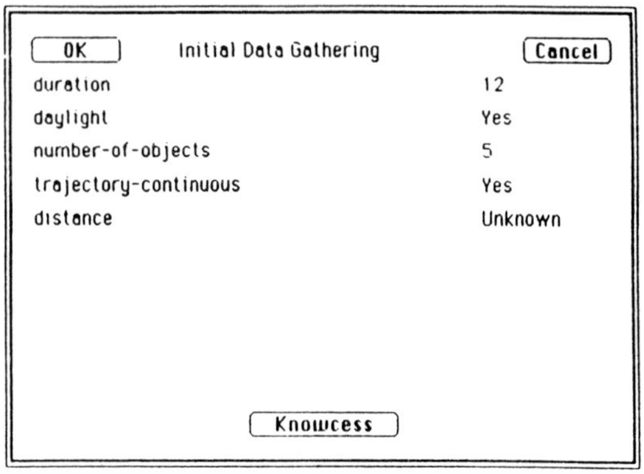

Figure 1 - Sighting report form in OVNIBASE.

a Macintosh computer. [18] The name of the system is OVNIBASE. [19] These next paragraphs discuss and illustrate its use in actual sighting analysis. **Figure 1** shows a simple form that the operator will be required to fill out at the beginning of case investigation. The form prompts the user for five parameters that can be elicited from the witness over the telephone.

At this point it is noteworthy that the questions to be asked to screen out the 'noise' are not necessarily the same questions one would ask during an actual field investigation. For example *duration* is a key factor in screening, as a discriminant among various hypotheses, while *shape* is often irrelevant.

The reader should also recognize that OVNIBASE does not attempt to make any judgment regarding psychological hypotheses such as hoaxes and hallucinations. In this first stage at least, the filter disregards witness-related information and even the actual number of witnesses.

Figure 2 shows another example of the OVNIBASE system in operation.

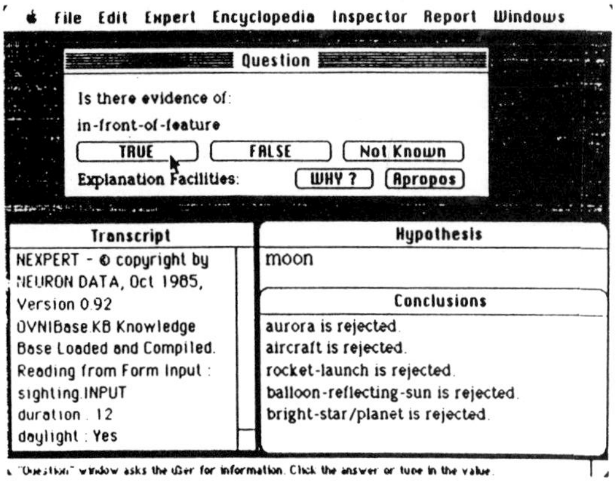

Figure 2 - The inference process in OVNIBASE.

The computer has rejected several possible conclusions (lower right window) and it is currently concentrating on the hypothesis that the object described could have been the moon. Now it is asking: "Is there evidence that the object was seen in front of a feature of the landscape?" The user can reply immediately to this question or he can ask for clarification by pointing to the WHY? box.

Through a succession of such questions and answers the system will gradually narrow its focus to reach a conclusion. This is a more desirable approach than the traditional questionnaire technique. In the standard questionnaire most questions are irrelevant, given the answers to previous questions. Hence they only serve to confuse the witness instead of eliciting useful information. For example, given the fact that an object was seen as a point of light, the next question should not be 'did it have a tail assembly?' but 'describe its motion in the sky', or 'what was the weather?' On the other hand, if the witness is trying to tell us that a two-ton chunk of metal has just fallen in his backyard any question about the weather is ludicrous.

Figure 3 illustrates another aspect of OVNIBASE, namely the ability to use the graphic display features of NEXPERT to form 'networks' of rules and hypotheses.

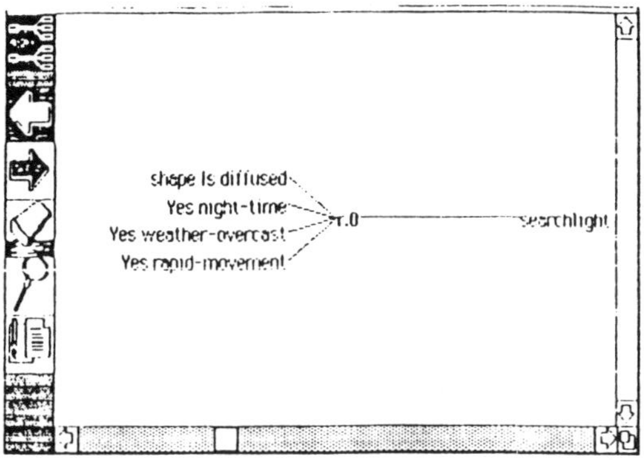

Figure 3 - Graphic illustration of a rule.

In this very simple illustration we see the structure of the rule leading to the 'searchlight' hypothesis.

For more detailed discussion of the features of the system, the reader is referred to the *User's Manual* for the first prototype of OVNIBASE. [19]

In this first version we have not made any attempt to include on-line identification of bright stars and planets [20] which could be added in future versions. Also, we have purposely limited the range of possible 'explanations' to the twenty most common hypotheses. It is the intent of the author [J. Vallée] to augment the system with additional features, rules and hypotheses once some basis of actual experience has been accumulated with the first version. Hence we welcome comments and suggestions. We also encourage others to build their own expert systems using NEXPERT or similar software.

A final word on the objective of the system as we have envisaged it, OVNIBASE seeks to eliminate at least 30% but no more than 70% of all incoming reports. The reason for this is that we know from previous studies that approximately 80% of all cases can be determined to have natural causes. If the filter eliminates less than 30% it does not significantly save human effort. But if it eliminates more than 70% it probably enters an area where human judgment should take over.

Those cases that are 'filtered out' are filed for re-examination by an investigator, but this examination is given lower priority. NEXPERT allows us to save the whole interaction transcript as an 'audit trail'. In this case, the system will provide the dominant conclusion and the reasoning that led to it. **Figure 4** shows an example of such reasoning.

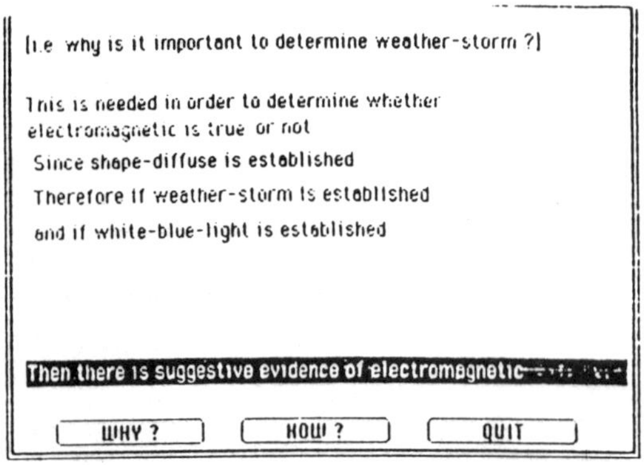

Figure 4 - Example of 'reasoning' in OVNIBASE.

Finally, those cases that pass the filter, and are brought to the user's attention as 'possible UFO', are listed with the sequence of inferences that led to eliminate every common natural hypothesis. The responsibility then falls back on the analyst to pursue the case in person, possibly through a field investigation.

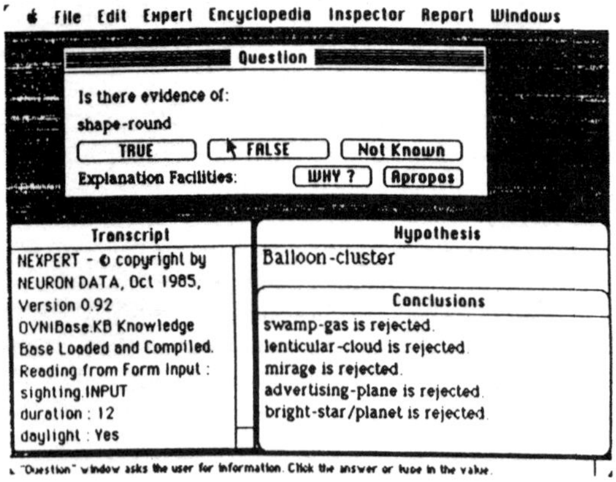

Typical screen for system interaction to OVNIBASE.

We envision OVNIBASE as a knowledge base gathering the rules for recognition of the most frequent natural causes of UFO reports. It can be viewed as an inexpensive screen for such reports, to be used by clerical personnel while on the phone to a witness reporting an anomalous phenomenon. Its objective is to eliminate most misidentifications, and to enable a skilled scientific analyst to spend his or her time on those few cases genuinely worthy of full investigation."

THE ABUSE OF COMPUTERS IN UFOLOGY

Maurizio Verga states that "the computer won't be the modern *deus ex machina* able to solve the UFO enigma" and this is clearly the case. Computers are much misunderstood by the general public, not least in their capacities. In science fiction a popular theme is the debate as to whether a complex computer is only able to mimic human activity indistinguishably from the real thing or whether there is genuine intuition or feeling. Whatever the fiction, the factual truth of today's most powerful computer is that there is no question of intelligence, or intuition. A computer can store massive amounts of information but retrieval of that information is dependent upon the proper programs and the proper input and the computer-users knowledge of both.

A computer cannot think; but it is capable of producing solutions to problems, mathematical, diagrammatical etc, with much greater accuracy and speed than the human brain, but again the production of accurate information is dependent upon an accurate database being put into the computer in the first place.

If, for example, we instruct the computer that two plus two equals three, then from then on it will, with great speed and accuracy, be able to add up two and two and produce the answer three. Computer users in all fields are aware of the problem of GIGO (Garbage In, Garbage Out). The problem faced by the ufologist is that we ourselves are not yet sure what information constitutes 'useful' and what information constitutes 'garbage'.

From the massive amount of witness reports there is a limited way in which the data can be input to the computer. It is difficult to 'weight' information from more reliable sources against that from less reliable sources without introducing human bias; it is difficult to instruct the computer that one particular sighting which may for example give technical descriptions of a vehicle should be taken more seriously than another with similar descriptions where the first has, perhaps, other witnesses and the second is almost certainly the product of psychological effects.

To take this example further let us suppose that both reports produce descriptions of a classic flying saucer shape with a particular pattern of lights. The first report may have been corroborated by other witnesses, by physical traces, etc, whereas there may be strong evidence that the second report is a psychological problem in the mind of the apparent witness (*perhaps even arising from an awareness of the first report.)* The danger is that a badly constructed database will report the physical descriptions of the craft and the lights in both cases. If the database was then accessed for, shall we say, classic saucer shapes and then further accessed to divide these into particular formations of lights, the database would then produce two virtually identical descriptions and the ufologist would delight in his computer having apparently corroborated the first report because there is also a second on file showing much the same data. Such a database might not be able to easily display the strength of opinion of the investigator in the first case or the doubts of the investigator in the second.

Ufology then should not fall into the trap that was the biggest problem for large corporations in the early days of computers. This trap is that the computer department is a complete separate section of the business, making up its own rules and deciding what output is available and producing it. It took a great deal of wasted time and money in these corporations to realise that the way to design a computer program is to involve all of the people who will use the program including those who prepare the data for input, those who input data and those who require the output and that the output of the computer should be designed according to the needs and requirements of the user-departments rather than the needs and requirements of the computer department itself. In our context therefore the data base for UFO analysis would be useless if the initial investigators report forms do not make the parameters for input clear to the investigator. However, the investigator should be involved in the preparation of the report forms as he or she is going to have to use them 'in the field'.

A further important matter to consider in the use of computers in ufology is that at some appropriate time *some conclusions must be drawn* in order to subdivide a database growing from widely different stimuli such as hoaxes, planets and stars, IFOs, etc in addition to the 'high strangeness' cases. There is no point in simply putting every UFO report into a massive database which will then only be able to produce statistics meaningless because of the variety of input.

To explain this by way of example, let us suppose that we created a database of all terrestrial vehicles. We would prepare thousands of 'case reports' of cars, planes, buses, coaches, helicopters, ships, submarines etc. In order to produce meaningful information we would then have to subdivide the database into, for example, those objects which travel on water, which fly in the air, which have certain configurations of wheels, etc. and then we could study in detail the objects which fall into each of those categories and examine the differences between them but without that subdivision the data base would be meaningless. It might report, for example, that of one million reported vehicles 85% had wheels, 30% had wings, 15% travelled beneath the surface of the sea, etc.

We should also not be fooled into thinking that the computer can in any way solve the UFO enigma. To take our above example one stage further, it we were to take all our one million vehicle reports and ask the computer to solve the 'vehicle enigma', presumably the best it could do would be to produce a hybrid vehicle made up of all the reports and which does not itself exist at all!

Computers are a powerful tool which properly used will give enormous assistance to ufologists the world over and will, hopefully, enable them to one day solve the UFO enigma but it should be recognised from the outset that they alone will not answer the questions. They may be likened to the advantage given to carpenters by powerful electric wood carving and drilling machinery. Properly used they can be time saving and labour saving. Delicate and beautiful woodwork is not created by powertools, but by the talents and ingenuity of woodworkers and so the UFO enigma will not be answered by computers but by the talented and intuitive thinking of human minds.

REFERENCES

■ 1 - **Merrit**, F. (1978) 'Notes additionelles sur UFOCAT' *Ufo info* 13: 52. ■ 2 - **Merrit**, F. (1978) 'Notes statistiques sur le phenomene OVNI' *Ufo info* 13: 53, p16 -18. ■ 3 - **Merrit**, F. (1978) 'Notes statistiques a propos d'UFOCAT - duree de l'observation selon le type de rapport', *Ufo info* 13: 54, p10 - 12. ■ 4 - **Merrit**, F. (1978) 'Appunti statistici sul fenomeno UFO,' *UFO and Fortean Phenomena* 12: p3 - 10. ■ 5 - **AA, VV**(1981) 'Project V R D', *UFO Research Australia Newsletter* 2.4.16 - 20'; and **Liljegren** A. 'Further notes on U.R.D.' 2:4,p20-21. ■ 6 - **Kuhlemann,** B. (1980) 'Some reflections on UFO research and international co-operation', *Journal UFO* 2: 1,p22 - 23. ■ 7 - **AA. VV.** (1980) *Project V.R.D. report 1 - Characteristics of a UFO report file, 100* page print-out. ■ 8 - **Strand,** E (1984) 'Statistik - fra U.R.D.' *UFO* 3: 1, p20 -22; 4:3, p28 - 29. ■ 9 - **Andersen,** P (1986) 'Project UFODATA, a status report', *CUFON* 1: 2, p5 - 8, ■ 10 - **Andersen,** P (1986 'Project UFODATA a status report' *CUFON* 1: 4, p17. ■ 11 - **Kampherbeek,** H (1985) 'UFODOC: a system for Dutch/Belgian cases' *CUFON* 1: 2,p5 -8 ■ 12 - **Jackson,** P (1985) 'Tasmanian UFO catalogue program notes', *CUFON* 1:2, p18-20. ■ 13 - **Breysse,** D (1986) 'A database for entity cases', *CUFON* 1: 4, p.3-5. ■ 14 - **Breysse,** D (1986) 'Checkpoint number two', *CUFON* 1: 4, p3-5. ■ 15 - **Verga,** M (1985) 'A Computerized catalogue of Italian close encounters', *CUFON* 1: 1, p10-13/bis. ■ 16 - **Bianchi,** S and **Di Ruzza,** L (1986) 'A program for the investigator', *CUFON* 1: 3, p16-18. ■ 17 - To subscribe to *The Computer UFO Newsletter* please send an International Postal Money Order (no cheque will be accepted) of 18,000 Italian lira (surface mail) to M. Verga, via Matteotti 85, 22072 Carmenate (Como) ITALY. ■ 18 - The author [JV] is grateful to the founders and staff of Neuron Data Inc for their guidance in the use of the NEXPERT system. Neuron Data is located at 444 High Street, Palo Alto, California. For more information about NEXPERT, see also *INFOWORLD* (Sept 2, 1985) 'A rule-based expert system introduced for the MacIntosh'. ■ 19 - *OVNIBASE User's manual*, (version 1.0). The system requires a Macintosh computer with 512K memory. 'MacIntosh' is the trademark of the Apple Corporation and 'NEXPERT' is the trademark of Neuron Data Inc. ■ 20 - Several computer programs are available to provide a determination of the visible planets and stars for a given place and time. See, for example, the article by Mavrakis D and Olivier, M.P. 'Determination Informatique de l'Aspect de la Voute Celeste', *INFORSPACE* No 68, June 1985 Vol 14. Reprints are availabel from the authors at G.E.R.S., 2 Avenue de Normandie F-060000 Nice, FRANCE. Complete program listings are also given in the book *Celestial Basic* by Eric Burgess (Berkeley Sybex 1984).

4
EXPLAINING THE PHENOMENA

4.1

EXPLAINING THE UFO

Using the UFO data to create a model of the phenomenon may seem premature when there is still considerable doubt as to what data is admissible. Some ufologists have argued that we should hold off theorising until we are sure of the facts.

But if, after 40 years of collecting data, we are still so uncertain how much of what we've collected is of any value, maybe there's something to be said for trying a different approach. That is, to use our 'best' data - the items which really do seem to be of value - to construct models. Any subsequent data can be tested against those models: if they confirm the model, that will encourage us to think we were on the right track. If they contradict it, we have to choose between rejecting the data, or re-structuring our model.

In practice, right from the very beginning, ufologists have been unable to resist the temptation to try their hand at model-making. The first explanatory model for the UFO was 'secret Russian device': as late as six years after the Arnold sighting, an article asked 'Are the flying saucers Russian-owned?' [**1**]

Renato Vesco's fascinating books, of which the first is translated as *Intercept but don't shoot* [**2**], start from the premise that UFOs began as secret devices designed in Britain and tested in Canada. Even though few of us would accept that theory - however much some of us might wish to! - Vesco's books are full of valuable research findings: a good example of how model-making can be a useful exercise even if the model itself has to be discarded.

A more recent example of model-making is Michael Persinger's work on geophysical causes and psychological effects [**3**]. Again, few ufologists think he has come up with the ultimate explanation; but there is no doubt that he has made a useful contribution to our thinking.

Sometimes UFO model-making can seem no more than what most model-making is, game-playing. But 'as if' speculation can be a serious pursuit. If the UFO data, accumulated over 40 years, displays consistent behaviour patterns, it is legitimate to seek for a meaning behind those patterns. What kind of technology *could* result in such behaviour? By asking that question, a number of researchers - Ken Behrendt in the US [**4**], Jean-Pierre Petit in France [**5**], and many more - have pushed their speculations in directions which could be of lasting value to science. Even if it should turn out that UFOs as physical objects don't exist, the very idea that they *might* exist may stimulate us to explore paths which lead to discoveries of real and practical value!

REFERENCES

1 - **Mallan**, Lloyd (ed.) *The mystery of other worlds revealed* (Fawcett, 1953). ■ 2 - **Vesco**, Renato, *Intercettateli senza sparare*, (1968): *I velivoli del mistero* (1969): *Operazione Plenilunio* (1972). The first is translated as *Intercept but don't shoot* (Grove Press, 1971). ■ 3 - **Persinger**, Michael, 'Possible infrequent geophysical sources of close UFO encounters' in Haines (ed) *UFOs and the behavioral scientist* (Scarecrow, 1979) and many papers in *Perceptual & motor skills* and elsewhere. ■ 4 - **Behrendt**, Ken, *UFO propulsion systems* (private, 1978), and subsequent issues of his journal *Aura*. ■ 5 - **Petit**, Jean-Pierre, *Le mur du silence* (Berlin, 1983); also various articles and interviews.

4.2.1

THE PARADOX OF UFO DESIGN

by Jenny Randles

■ **JENNY RANDLES**. Born 1951. After quitting a university physics course, she taught geology and geography in schools; later specialised in audio-visual teaching, obtaining a diploma in media communication. Since 1978 she has been a full-time professional writer and broadcaster.

■ **UFO involvement**: First became interested in UFOs in 1968, joining BUFORA a year later. In 1973 she was a founder member of NUFON (Northern UFO Network) and joined MUFORA, the Manchester association. She has served as BUFORA director of field investigations, and as an investigation co-ordinator for ASSAP.

This experience-based approach has led her to a conclusion which affirms at least some degree of UFO reality: she remains open to the possibility of alien intervention, but almost certainly not of the conventional 'space-ship' type, yet 'whatever doubts or reservations I may have about the nature of UFOs, I am positive that UAP (Unidentified Atmospheric Phenomena) exist. I believe we have excellent, consistent witness testimony describing appearance, behaviour and attendant physical effects of at least one type of unknown natural phenomenon... I think it is high time scientists began to take it seriously, for it is a scientific problem and not one for sensation-seeking authors or mystery movies.' (*UFO Reality*)

■ **Publications** include: (with Peter Warrington) *UFOs, a British viewpoint* (Hale 1979); *UFO study* (Hale 1981); (with Paul Whetnall) *Alien contact* (Spearman 1982); *The Pennine UFO mystery* (Granada 1983); *UFO reality* (Hale 1983); (with Brenda Butler and Dot Street) *Sky crash* (Spearman 1984); (with Peter Warrington) *Science and the UFOs* (Blackwell 1985); *The UFO conspiracy: the first forty years* (Blandford 1987) and numerous articles. She is also editor of *NUFON News*.

■ **Address**: 37 Heathbank Road / Cheadle Heath / Stockport SK3 OUP / England.

INTRODUCTION

There is really no such thing as the UFO phenomenon. Instead we have many different phenomena. This seems to be the inevitable conclusion one must reach, because of the variety in witness descriptions of what they have seen.

Let us take a look at some of the objects reported as UFOs to get an idea of the scope of this problem:

■ In 1947, when the first major wave of sightings occurred, Kenneth Arnold saw his famous 'crescents' skipping through the sky like 'flying saucers.' Crescent UFOs have been rather uncommon since then. Yet, oddly, many of these early reports involved squadrons of UFOs flying in formation - exactly as the American pilot had claimed. In the records of BUFORA for the 1980s, only two or three cases of such multiple UFOs can be found. What has happened to the 'craft' which Arnold saw? [1]

■ In 1957 another type of UFO was seen by dozens of people around the Texas manufacturing town of Levelland. These were orange 'balls of fire', which incidentally seem to have stalled many car engines. The 'ball of fire' is quite different from what was reported by Arnold over the Cascade Mountains. But it is a type which has endured and is one of the most frequently observed throughout the world. In Hessdalen, a Scandinavian valley, they are taking regular photographs of it. [2]

■ In 1967 police officer Herbert Schirmer from a Nebrasksa town became one of a growing number of people to claim that they have been taken aboard a UFO by its occupants. The object he saw - landing on the road in front of him - was of the sort that would be considered typical by someone unfamiliar with the complexities of this subject. It was the traditional 'saucer' shape with a rim across the middle. This is what many think of when the term UFO is mentioned. But it is not very widely seen, and even then comes in a baffling assortment of shapes and sizes. [3]

■ In 1977 Great Britain had a major wave of sightings. Another car engine was stalled, this time in Nelson, Lancashire. But the UFO, which seems to have had an electro-static field surrounding it, was unlike the one that interfered with trucks and cars in Texas twenty years before. This was shaped like a cigar with a mass of multi-coloured twinkling lights. As with several other forms the UFO takes, the cigar is another which crops up in our store of cases, this time on a fairly regular basis. [4]

Looking back on these forty years, I could recount stories that describe quite a few other shapes. Some of them (for instance the 'ball' and the 'cigar') are found in abundance. Others (eg one like a pawnbroker's sign - three balls of light in tripod formation) are common enough to be seen as a pattern, but relatively rare. The whole matter is extremely confusing and apt to drive one to despair when any effort is made to sort out the mess.

Yet we can approach the problem from a number of different points of view. Imagine making a collection of 'things in the sky' which *discounts* UFOs. What do we see?

Well - there are stars and planets. These are just twinkling (or non-twinkling) balls of light, usually no bigger than pin-pricks but sometimes visibly large (eg the moon). Colours are normally white, but can be yellow, blue, orange, red - in fact anything.

There might also be creatures in the sky - No, not aliens! I mean birds. These also tend to have fairly similar shapes, but come in different sizes and fly alone or in groups.

Then we have man-made craft - such as aeroplanes. The variety of these is growing all the time. Helicopters with rotors on top. Cigar-like airships. Sleek jets with swept-back wings that streak across the sky. Lumbering transport planes with heavy engines which seem so slow that they should fall from the air.

And we must not forget the natural phenomena - such as optical reflections and patches of light. Or clouds - they come in almost unlimited shapes and sizes, with no two ever being the same.

You might find this a curious exercise. What purpose does it serve? A very simple one in truth. For we tend to look at these things in isolation. We know a cloud *is* a cloud, or a bird *is* a bird. We know this because we have learnt by experience to group them into categories. But imagine a time when primitive man did *not* understand these things. Then - in a sense - all objects in the sky were UFOs. Only by a process of learning across many centuries did we distill out from the confusing and endless variations the categories which allow us to explain any particular phenonemnon.

What is to say that this process has ended? That we are not still involved in such a learning pattern? For there are yet many things in the sky that we do not understand, and which we call UFOs. We *assume* that they have one solution. But it was that mistake which once prevented us from distinguishing the cloud from the bird. Perhaps much of our problem of the multiple UFO shapes lies in our refusal to accept that we are dealing with several, totally unique, new phenomena - and not one thing which seems to defy standardisation.

SOME FACTS TO CONSIDER

Generally speaking, when somebody sees an object that he takes to be a UFO, it turns out *not* to be a UFO at all. It is, in fact, an IFO (Identified Flying Object). The precise percentage of IFOs in any sample does vary (according to the competence of investigators and the extent to which they filter out obvious misperceptions). But it is usually agreed to be about 90 out of every 100 sightings.

Of course, almost by definition, most of the things which produce IFOs are those known phenomena in the sky which have such a wide range of shapes and sizes. So we can see the primary reason why shapes in UFO reports vary such a lot. It is the IFO shapes which are varying. [**5**]

An area of study too often neglected by researchers is what I call the 'Puzzle IFO'. In these cases the identification is known, beyond any reasonable doubt, and yet the witness has described what they saw in utterly perplexing and puzzling terms. There are many cases, for example, where the moon has led to a strange close encounter, although there is no reason to doubt the basic credibility of the witness. [**6**]

What we need to do is to understand the common factors which might transform the ordinary object in the sky into an exotic form of UFO. Are they problems in the perception systems of the witness? Is there a *need* to believe in 'alien' UFOs. Could there be an external influence 'bending' the mind and creating the distortion of what is viewed? Such questions require urgent exploration and must form a more significant part of UFO research in the *next* forty years. We are far too inclined to throw away the IFO cases, proclaiming that once solved a report has no value. Indeed it *does* have value. It may be the key to the entire mystery.

Psychologists who have studied road traffic accidents have made discoveries that form interesting comparisons with these Puzzle IFOs. A number of things are now known to affect the account by an eye-witness. Every police officer or lawyer knows that when ten people see a car crash, there are ten separate versions of what took place. They are broadly similar, but also different. Some of the most influential things appear to be the interests of the observer, his preferences or beliefs and the effect of suggestion when he is giving his testimony. [7]

In an accident situation the onlooker might fail to notice any detail about one driver because he is attracted (sexually or otherwise!) to the other one. They may also subconsciously alter their memory of what took place because of something as seemingly irrelevant as racial prejudice. If one driver is black and the other white, the prejudiced witness has a tendency to redress the balance of blame in favour of his prejudice. And even more illuminating are experiments in the manner of extracting testimony. Ask witnesses whether they saw headlamps smash before or after a collision and you will get specific answers - even when no headlamps *ever* smashed. The wording of the question has planted the suggestion that they did and the witness changes his memory to assume he saw this non-existent event.

Putting these facts into a UFO context is interesting. The previous beliefs held by a witness will affect what they 'see'. Their prejudice (for or against) 'alien' UFOs will alter recollections without them being aware of it. And the form of questioning by the field investigator profoundly adapts the story reported.

Indeed, such problems are worse in a UFO situation because we are subjected to many social pressures (from sensational books and movies to TV adverts for things like coffee), all of which set our attitude towards UFOs along polarised and often far from rational pathways. These certainly have some bearing on the exact nature of what people report. [**8**]

Of course, in a car accident there may well be individual distortions. But nobody reports that the car was really a Boeing 747, or the SS Titanic. Applying this logic to UFO sightings we find the main problem with Puzzle IFOs. There is a missing factor which we need, to explain why the original stimulus has altered so much that it is literally unrecognisable.

One of the best ways to see this is to examine cases where a major IFO event was seen and reported (as a UFO) by hundreds of people at the same time. Space junk re-entries (particularly before these became regular occurrences) are useful for this. When on 31 December 1978, at 19.05 GMT, the booster from a Russian satellite, Cosmos 1068, burnt up over the North Sea, the conditions in Britain were perfect for many witnesses. Nobody knew the true explanation for the moving train of light which passed across the sky. Almost everyone assumed it was a UFO.

I collected a sample of 100 reports made by witnesses. The consistency between them was astonishing. Witness sketches showed cigar-like objects with plumes of flame coming from the rear and a line of windows (which were not there - this was an illusion caused by the trailing debris). None of the cases involved descriptions which defied comprehension - eg saucers or discs. There were no reports of serious effects, car stops or other things found in UFO close encounters. From the accounts that were given, it was possible to judge the cause. Estimates of height, size, even time of occurrence, did surprisingly vary. But the shape was one of the *most* consistent. [**9**]

All of this shows just what a problem these Puzzle IFOs are. It is far from easy to explain them as simple misidentifications by baffled witnesses.

IN SEARCH OF A SOLUTION

I think we can now define a new kind of classification for genuine cases, excluding all the obvious misperceptions. This would include three groups of reports:

■ ANOMALOUS UAPs

These Unidentified Atmospheric Phenomena (UAP) are the sightings of 'balls of fire', such as those being photographed at Hessdalen. They *seem* to be natural, atmospheric phenomena and some may be of novel origin. There may be one, or a number of different kinds of UAP. The Paul Devereux and Michael Persinger suggestion of 'earthlights' seems to be one excellent possibility. [**10**] There may well be others. The important thing that allows us to categorise the UAP as *separate* from other cases is that it can be seen by anyone who happens to be in the right place at the right time. The average number of witnesses per case works out in the region of 2.6 - *exactly* the same as with ordinary misperceptions. In those IFO cases the result is understandable, because the object to be misperceived is also visible to anyone who happens to be there. The UAP is, therefore, seen very similarly by all who witness it. Its 'ball-like' shape is rarely distorted. This kind of event is completely *OBJECTIVE*.

■ PUZZLE IFOs

As we have seen already, whilst these *are* misidentifications, they have more in common with UFOs than with ordinary IFOs. The case of a couple (one of whom was a scientist) driving north from Shropshire, England, into Cheshire late one night in October 1983, is useful in illustrating my point. They had a protracted encounter with an object that shone beams of light into their car and terrified them. They thought long and hard before reporting it to the Jodrell Bank Radio Telescope (who passed the story on to me). Despite the complete sincerity of the couple and their definite rationality and high intelligence, it is impossible to dispute that they must have misperceived the moon. Nobody else in Shropshire or Cheshire experienced the moon as a UFO that night. Something - and we do not know what - caused this couple to have a peculiar experience. The Puzzle IFO is then seen to be characterised as a *provable* IFO viewed (very often) by two or more people together, as in this case. [**11**] However, nobody else in the surrounding area, who might be expected to see a UFO if one was actually there, witnessed the event. It is essentially a mixture of *SUBJECTIVE* experience triggered by an *OBJECTIVE* thing.

■ EXOTIC UFOs

These may also be called close encounters, although distance (as this term implies) might not be the crucial factor, so I find it preferable to use another name. We might suggest that they are categorised as cases where no surrounding witness observes the phenomenon and even multiple witnesses together do not share it beyond a broad outline. There are certainly examples where a measure of agreement is reached later, but it is usually not possible to say how much this depends upon the level of communication between witnesses. In multi-witness close encounters the percipients are most always related in some way (or at least close friends), so this factor is bound to be strong. Cases are known where one witness, at a factory for example, did not see or hear anything whilst his fellow security guard had a bizarre encounter with an exotic UFO which the other man certainly *ought* to have observed. [12] It is also apparent that the *closer* the encounter, the more the witness per case ratio tends towards 1.0. 1.0 witnesses per case is, of course, perfect subjectivity. Nobody but the witness undergoes the experience. So the exotic UFO is primarily a *SUBJECTIVE* experience.

THE PROBLEM OF PHOTOGRAPHS

This system of classification leaves a difficulty. What do we do about photographs of apparently structured craft? If no true alien devices are creating the data, there should be none. Yet there are!

Of course, most photographs are *not* of Exotic UFOs. The genuine pictures tend to be of fuzzy blobs and lights, which might well be UAP. We know that many of the best-looking photographs of actual craft are hoaxes, and we cannot prove that the few which remain unexplained will not eventually have to be so consigned. There are no inexplicable photographs of structured craft on the ground, involved in close encounter cases, and no bona fide pictures of what might be UFO occupants. After forty years the absence of this sort of evidence strongly supports my argument and does not support those who contend that UFOs are physical machines from an alien source.

What of the few puzzling cases? At McMinnville, Oregon, in May 1950, a disc-like object flew past a farm and was photographed. [13] This is one of those cases that *does* appear to be genuine. Perhaps, in a very small number of instances, some truly alien device does fly past - at a distance. Or, it seems more likely, these real photographs depict earth technology - such as experimental aircraft that remain on the secrets list. If you wish to cling to an exciting idea then one could always fall back on the possibility of time-travel machines - in other words, still earth technology, from the far future.

There are certainly cases where what seems to have been the same (or near identical) object was observed by witnesses widely separated, who had no knowledge of the other sightings of this device. Only the real observation of some actual craft makes sense in those instances. A disc seen by a Luton, England, schoolboy in 1957 also appears to have passed over the Rogue River in Oregon in 1949. [14] More recently, many British cases involve a "stingray" or "manta-ray" type of UFO which has enough consistency to apparently be the same type of craft.

However, the object seen at Luton and in Oregon also appears to have been witnessed on the ground in 1964 - at a Kansas Air Base. This implies it was military hardware. And there are suspicious circumstances about the British "manta-ray" cases. They began at a time when the US Air Force developed a 'stealth' aircraft known as the F-19. It has supposedly been flown in the UK and bears a striking resemblance to what these UFO witnesses relate. It might well be considered useful for such secret technology to be reported as a UFO. This prevents international defence sources (who scoff at UFOs) from taking the often accurate witness statements seriously.

THE OZ FACTOR

When dealing with Puzzle IFOs and Exotic UFOs there is an invaluable clue. Witnesses tend to describe a set of symptoms which allow recognition of this type of case. I call them the Oz factor.

The most common features of this are;-loss of environmental sounds (as if the witness is suddenly surrounded by a bell-jar and cut off from the world), a strange sense of calm which descends upon them, a feeling of disassociation (often described as being 'half in this world and half out of it') and a distortion in the sense of time, where the duration of the close encounter becomes almost impossible for the witness to judge.

The Oz Factor appears to be an indication that the witness has altered his state of consciousness. The Exotic UFO experience is not taking place in the normal wide-awake state, where the misperception of an aircraft (for example) might follow. Nor, of course, is the witness asleep! In fact, I believe there are indications that he is in a distinct state - which I call 'Quasi-Conscious', because it has the semblance of full consciousness but it is not quite like it. In order for such a switch to have occurred (and the Oz Factor often seems to be an induced form of sensory deprivation - making the witness *tune out* external data and *tune up* attention to some subjective 'message') some part of his mind must have recognised an important necessity. The message, which without the Oz Factor might be ignored and merely whisper in his subconscious, must be allowed to over-ride the perceptions and get through to attention. [15]

POSSIBLE SOLUTIONS

Let us summarise where this study of the paradox of UFO design has brought us.

Most UFOs are ordinary misperceptions of mundane things - simple, straightforward IFOs.

Many of the remaining cases (which are proportionately few, but numerically a large number, collected globally across forty years) are what we have called UAP. They are natural phenomena that are *really* there, can be scientifically studied and anyone may potentially witness them.

A very few cases *might* be craft of a structured kind - possibly from some other source (eg time-travellers). However, more likely these are earth-based technology on the secrets list. If they are alien (ie extra-terrestrial) they are extremely rare and very covert in their behaviour and do *not* constitute more than a tiny proportion of UFO sightings.

This leaves a few per cent (perhaps just one or two) of cases that have yet to be accounted for. They are both what we have called Puzzle IFOs and Exotic UFOs. We might suggest three scenarios to explain them:

■ CUSTOMISED ALIEN UFOs

Perhaps some *very* alien UFO device, with properties that border on the fantastic, might be visiting earth. Quite unlike our aircraft, these would be individually customised and fluid in nature. The problem when discussing any form of alien theory is that we are constrained to think in human terms and it is most improbable that any alien intelligence would be a mirror of something humans *could* imagine. But if we cannot imagine it, then we might have difficulty perceiving it. Indeed - what might well occur is that we would each see the UFO according to our own personal concept of 'alien'. This would largely be based upon stereotyped science-fiction images and would vary around a common theme. It would also adapt with time as our cultural beliefs altered. This is remarkably similar to what we *do* have in the real UFO phenomenon. But the question of subjectivity in Exotic UFO cases still dogs us. Why is the UFO not seen by anyone in a position to do so?

■ PSYCHIC UFOS

Devereux has suggested that we are able to affect UAP with our mind, altering their shape through psycho-kinesis. In other words, the amorphous UFO alters according to our beliefs or desires into a structured shape. Whilst this may occur in isolated UAP encounters, it seems unlikely to explain Exotic UFOs. It stumbles over the same difficulty of subjectivity. For if one person 'moulds' the *real* UAP into a personalised shape, others ought to be able to see it.

■ SPACESHIPS OF THE MIND

There is one suggestion which I believe the facts most support for Puzzle IFOs and Exotic UFOs. A communication is being 'beamed' at us from an alien source. It comes in the form of a message to consciousness. Only people with a developed form of psychic awareness (ie they tend to have strange experiences throughout their lives) can detect this. Usually it is below the threshold of their detection. But occasionally (either when some mechanism focuses attention, or an unknown process allows it to happen) the message is pushed through into full awareness. This normally happens by the Oz Factor precipitating a change in state of consciousness. In the Quasi-Conscious state the message from this alien source is getting through and then becomes 'dressed up' in appropriate images. These images must have a similar theme (because they reflect the essence of the message). But they will vary from person to person, according to individual background. The term 'alien' will be expressed in a personally relevant science-fiction manner and if we look behind the detail of the encounter and pick out the theme we will be able to decipher the incoming message. In this sense UFO investigators would be rather like interpreters of dreams!

The importance of the Puzzle IFOs is that the mind can make use of a real stimulus in the environment to become the focus for the message. It is the stage upon which the drama is acted out.

This is certainly a bold theory which seems extravagant. However, it appears to overcome the paradox we began with. It also seems to be supported by research that is being carried out into witness-centred UFO experiences [see Section 3.5]. It is at least worthy of exploration.

REFERENCES

1 - **Arnold,** K & **Palmer,** R *The Coming of the Saucers* (Amherset Press, 1952). ■ 2 - **Wheeler,** D *The Lubbock Lights* (Award Press, 1977). ■ 3 - 'Close Encounters', in *The Unknown*, England, November 1985. ■ 4 - Frightening car-stop near Nelson, in *FSR*, England, 1977 Vol 23 No 2. ■ 5 - A good guide to some of the problems of IFO shapes can be found in **Hendry,** A *The UFO Handbook* (Sphere Books, 1980). ■ 6 - A classic Philip Taylor investigation for BUFORA is summarised (pages 82-88) **Randles,** J & **Warrington,** P *Science and the UFOs* (Basil Blackwell, 1985). ■ 7 - **Hunt,** M *The Universe Within* (Harvester Press, 1982). ■ 8 - One of the best aspects of the 'Condon Report' was its detailed study of human perception in a UFO context. You are advised to read this carefully (especially pages 559-567). **Condon,** E (Ed) *Scientific Study of UFOs* (Bantam, 1969). ■ 9 - A review of this research can be found on pages 44-49. **Randles,** J *UFO Reality* (Robert Hale, 1983). ■ 10 - **Devereux,** P *Earthlights* (Turnstone Books, 1982). ■ 11 - **Randles,** J & **Warrington,** P op cit, pages 132-133. ■ 12 - **Randles,** J & **Warrington,** P *UFOs: A British Viewpoint* (Robert Hale, 1979). ■ 13 - 'UFOs on Film', in *The Unknown*, England, September 1986. ■ 14 - 'In search of a stereotype', in *FSR*, England, 1983 Vol 28 No 4. ■ 15 - A more detailed discussion of all these problems can be found in **Randles,** J *Sixth Sense* (Robert Hale, 1987).

4.2.2

THE UFO PROPULSIONISTS

by Kenneth W. Behrendt

■ **KENNETH W. BEHRENDT**. Born 1951. BA (1973) & MS (1980) in chemistry from Rutgers University. He has held various technical positions as quality controller in the electronics field, pharma-ceutical chemist, and engineering consultant for a metal refinery. He is married with two children.

■ **UFO involvement**: Teenage interest in 'the unknown' led to a serious search for explanations, particularly as to 'just how the UFOs achieve their anomalous flight characteristics and produce the various propulsion system secondary effects.' The investigation of a friend's abduction encounter brought about a friendship with Tom Benson, and this in turn led to a deeper involvement in UFO research.

Since about 1980 articles in serious UFO journals have chronicled his efforts to rationalise the technical phenomena associated with UFOs, notably their propulsion and secondary effects, in the light of an expanded physics he refers to as 'anti-mass field physics.' This has provided him with a working hypothesis which offers a satisfactory explanation of how the various effects might be caused, and incidentally provides support for the ETH. 'I believe our technical understanding of the UFO phe-nomenon is now sufficiently advanced for us to duplicate it.'

■ **Publications**: *UFO propulsion systems, origins and purposes* (1978). In 1985 he commenced publication of *AURA (Annals of Ufological Research Advances)* which treats the anti-mass field theory in depth. His first book-length work *The physics of the paranormal*, 1987, applies anti-mass field theory to various paranormal / parapsychological phenomena. (from Arcturus, PO Box 2213 Scotia, NY 12302).

■ **Address**: 274 Second Street / Elizabeth / NJ 07206 / USA.

All materialistic ufologists hope for a satisfying solution to the so-called UFO mystery that will explain the origin of these craft, the purposes of their crews in visiting earth, and the technological means by which this is achieved. Unfortunately, in the absence of direct and reliable contact with extra-terrestrial beings, we may *never* know from what star systems our visitors originate or their purposes in earth's atmosphere and oceans. However, without direct contact we *can* still determine the technological means by which their vehicles operate. By carefully collecting accurate and detailed sighting data, organizing it and extracting the overall behavior and performance patterns it contains, the scientific method should allow us to determine, in time, the means of propulsion utilized in UFOs and how *all* of the various secondary effects are produced.

The final hypothesis that provides this partial solution must meet four criteria. First, it must *adequately account for all of the data* presently available on UFO structure and performance; secondly, it *should be internally consistent*, which simply means that one part of the hypothesis should not contradict another part of the same hypothesis; thirdly, this final hypothesis *must be predictive* so that it can explain UFO related phenomena not originally used in the formulation of the hypothesis; and, fourthly, the hypothesis must be detailed enough so that it will *be capable of experiental verification or denial*.

Unfortunately, in the last forty years ufology has concentrated mainly on the acquisition of UFO data and only a small percentage of the credible literature deals with attempts to rationalize the performance capabilities of UFOs and the secondary effects associated with their presence.

Practically all of the hypotheses advanced in an effort to provide the desired solution to the mystery have failed to meet the necessary criteria or conditions for a good, workable hypothesis. Most often they could not account for all of the available data and would become internally inconsistent when efforts were made to extend them. If the theorist lacked training in the contemporary physics of his day, his hypothesis might be so vague or qualitative that it could not be used to make predictions about the as yet not precisely known UFO phenomena, such as the structure and arrangement of a UFO's internal propulsion equipment. In almost every case, the hypotheses advanced lacked the mathematical rigor needed to experimentally test their validity.

As can be seen, the attainment of a final hypothesis that *does* meet these difficult criteria is highly desirable because it should allow us to readily *duplicate* what has been so frequently demonstrated for us by our extraterrestrial visitors. With the duplication of the UFO phenomena we can expect an immediate and profound change in the way we live our earthly lives. Transportation will be revolutionized as we manufacture our own UFO-like craft that can easily fly us from one side of our planet to the other *in minutes.* We can finally complete the exploration of our solar system, establish colonies on some of the other planets or moons of our system, and begin planning our race's first interstellar voyages. There should also be tremendous advancements brought about in the fields of energy generation, medical science, metallurgy, physics, etc.

With the above in mind, let us now explore some of the attempts made by ufologists in the last forty years to shed some light on this all-important aspect of the subject. Although the literature relating to propulsion and secondary effects is sparse, it is still not possible to give a full and detailed treatment of all of it within the confines of a single chapter. However, an attempt will be made to present some of the main themes in the evolution of our concepts on UFO propulsion and related matters.

Early ufologists were immediately impressed by the ability of UFOs to hover, rapidly accelerate, and perform violent aerobatic manoeuvers *without* any visible means of propulsion. They noted that craft whose landing marks indicated weights in the tens of tons seemed to also have secondary effects involving magnetism, and it appeared logical enough to them that powerful magnetic fields were the secret to UFO propulsion. For example, on June 24 1947 a camper in the Cascade Mountains, Oregon, USA noticed his compass needle spinning wildly about as a UFO overflew his position. These types of cases, coupled with the many in which a UFO witness's wristwatch was stopped due to exposure to a powerful magnetic field, seemed to indicate that magnetic forces were used to move UFOs.

The early UFO contactees were all obliged to strengthen their claims of personal encounters with

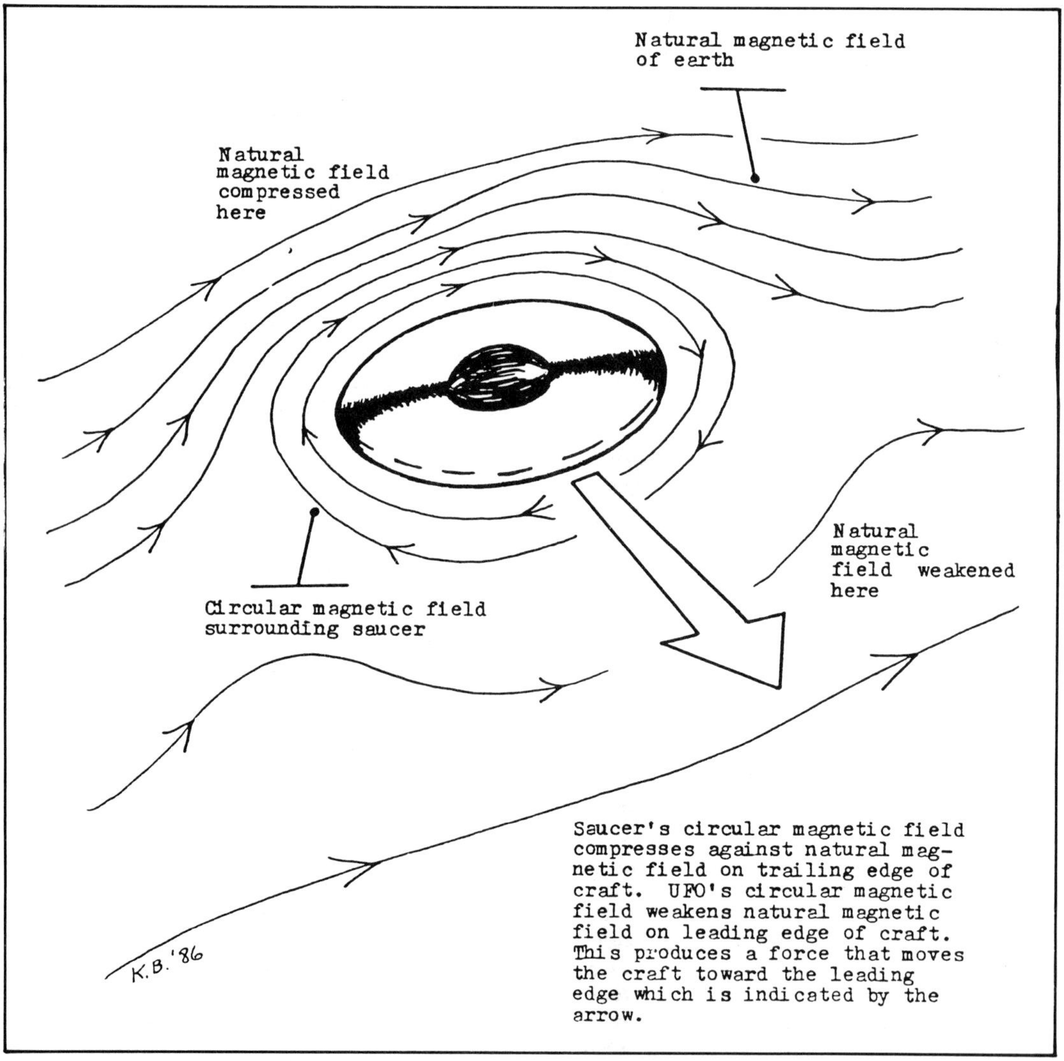

Figure 1 - Saucer using magnetic fields for propulsion.

extraterrestrials by describing the methods of propulsion that they used in their craft. The American contactee George Adamski (1891-1965) presented the idea that a flying saucer or "scout ship" could rapidly manoeuver about earth's atmosphere by creating a circular electromagnetic field about the ship that would move it by pushing against the earth's weak magnetic field (with an intensity of only about 3/4 of a gauss at the mid-northern and mid-southern latitudes). For travel between planets in our solar system, a mother-ship would employ the same principle except that it would utilize the magnetic fields emanating from our sun and other planets. [1]

Adamski's approach is illustrated in **Figure 1** and it is obvious that he envisioned the magnetic fields from UFOs interacting with external natural magnetic fields to produce translational motion in a manner similar to the way in which the magnetic fields of a motor's armature windings interact with the magnetic fields of the motor's field windings to produce rotational motion.

The problem with this approach is that it is impossible to produce the necessary magnetic field about the UFO using *any* kind of scheme in which electrical current flows about a complete circuit *within* the craft. However, even if a magnetic field of the appropriate configuration could be produced, it would have to be enormously powerful to account for the observed acceleration of the UFOs *if they are assumed to have their full expected masses*. Such intense magnetic fields would not only stall automobiles, but actually twist and deform their steel bodies and chassis as the magnetic fields induced in these structures forced them to align with the UFO's magnetic field. Two UFOs utilizing this form of propulsion would violently smash together if they tried to fly side by side in formation. Also, such a system of propulsion limits the UFO to flying at right angles to the external magnetic field lines the craft utilizes.

Such a propulsion scheme says nothing about the means for producing the craft's powerful magnetic field, nothing about the source of energy which will generate the craft's magnetic field, and nothing about how the craft and crew will be protected from lethal inertial forces while undergoing violent manoeuvers. For example, it is known that a right angle turn by a UFO travelling at only 100 miles per hour would kill most human pilots. The magnetic propulsion scheme says nothing about how a UFO crew could be protected from being pulverized while performing a right angle turn at *thousands* of miles per hour. Some early non-contactee ufologists attempted to get around these objections by assuming that all UFOs were automated or carried robot crews. One author, Gerald Heard, provided a unique solution to the problem of inertial forces applied to ufonauts' bodies by rapidly accelerating UFOs. [2] He simply concentrated on the sightings of smaller UFOs (sometimes referred to as "probes") and assumed that they carried intelligent bees from Mars with hard crystal-like bodies that would not be pulverized during violent aerial manoeuvring. Perhaps he thought the humming sounds associated with many UFOs were produced by their tiny insect crews!

If UFOs are assumed to have their full, normal masses in flight, then simple calculations show that they would have to have enormously powerful engines to operate as they do. For example, suppose that a witness reported spotting a saucer hovering near ground level that was 32 feet in diameter and which suddenly rose and disappeared into a cloudless sky in only ten seconds. Calculations show that the UFO would have to rise to an altitude of 20.83 miles in ten seconds to shrink to a point too small for the human eye to resolve. If the craft's acceleration was constant, then its crew would have felt the crushing inertial force produced by an acceleration of 68.38 g's and at the end of its ten-second climb the craft would be moving at 15,000 miles per hour. If the UFO weighed 10 tons (or 20,000 pounds), its engines would have to produce a force of 1.368 *million* pounds. Its engines would have to have had a power output of 27.36 *million* horsepower or 20,000 *mega*watts. Thus, its power output would be equivalent to about 2,500 of the 11,000 horsepower Pratt & Whitney jet engines that power the American B-52 Stratofortress bomber or to about twenty 1,000 megawatt nuclear power plants operating at peak output!

When we realize that such power would have to be safely generated within the limited confines of a small vehicle interior and would have to operate without any apparent means so that the UFO's hull can be a single, closed metal surface, we can appreciate the formidable challenge that a working UFO propulsion hypothesis presents to the theorist *if UFOs are considered to be massive in flight*. Most orthodox scientists who have reviewed these kinds of calculations, and assumed UFOs have their full, normal masses in flight, have tended to become skeptical about the existence of genuine extraterrestrial UFOs in general.

Early attempts to rescue the magnetic propulsion hypothesis and provide the enormous power levels required to move massive craft were made by such researchers as the Canadian engineer Wilbert B Smith (died 1962). He was the director of Canada's Project Magnet in 1949, which was one of the few open government efforts to seriously study UFOs. Concentrating on the small percentage of UFOs that display rotating hull surfaces, he proposed that their motion would cut the earth's geomagnetic field lines to produce large quantities of electrical power. Thus he likened rotating UFOs to giant electrical generators, whose power output would then be used to heat and expel air or another ejectable mass carried by the craft for thrust. He could not explain how a rapidly moving UFO could protect itself from being heated to incandescence by air friction, and assumed that the craft's rotating motion protected it. To overcome the problems inertial forces present to pilots aboard violently manoeuvring UFOs, Smith assumed that all UFOs were automated. Calculations of the amount of rotation of the craft's hull surfaces needed to generate the enormous power levels massive UFOs would need, indicate that a saucer using Smith's propulsion hypothesis would tear itself apart with centrifugal forces.

Toward the end of the 1950s and beginning of the 1960s, UFO propulsionists began to search for other than conventional ways to explain UFO performance and generate the huge power levels that *apparently* massive UFOs would need to achieve anomalous flight. They turned their attentions toward the use of such exotic energy sources as cosmic energy and nuclear power such as fusion.

As explained in a book by Aimé Michel [**3**], an engineer of the French Air Force, Lieutenant Jules Plantier, had been working on a novel hypothesis for UFO propulsion as early as 1953. Plantier's approach assumed that all space is permeated by a form of high-powered energy that was the source of cosmic rays. The ufonauts had simply developed equipment that could convert this sea of energy into motive force that would power a massive UFO in a planet's atmosphere or in the space between star systems.

In liberating this cosmic energy for motion, a UFO would be surrounded by a *local* electromagnetic field that could be varied and applied at will and which would account for all of the secondary effects associated with UFO propulsion.

Plantier's hypothesis was the first to attempt to explain the color changes associated with *changes* in UFO motion. Mathematically his hypothesis could indicate that rapid accelerations would envelop a UFO in a red glow, a high-speed turn would produce a green glow, and hovering would produce a white glow.

To explain how UFOs overcome aerodynamic heating during high-velocity flight, the Plantier hypothesis assumed that the UFO's local EM field would drag some of the air surrounding the craft along with it to act as an insulating cushion.

It is also significant to note that not only did Plantier's approach rationalize several of the secondary effects associated with UFO propulsion, but he also suggested that the universal energy tapped by UFOs would interact and selectively cancel out the earth's or the universe's pull on a massive UFO so as to allow it to move in any direction due to the gravitational pull of the earth or universe still allowed to affect the craft through its local EM field.

Plantier's hypothesis was ultimately unsatisfactory because it did not give the details of how the ufonauts would use cosmic energy to selectively "shield" their craft from the gravitational pulls exerted on it and is thereby incapable of experimental verification or denial. However, it is historically interesting as the first hypothesis that attempted to *mathematically* rationalize the secondary effects noted for UFOs. It also suggested a way to protect ufonauts from inertial forces since the accelerating forces are applied equally to the massive craft and its crew.

Discouraged by the vague nature of such concepts as "universal seas of energy", many propulsionists chose to give their hypothetical saucers more understandable power sources.

One propulsionist, R.H.B. Winder, in a series of articles for *Flying Saucer Review* [**4**] offered his design for a discoidal craft that would be able to hover and undergo a vertical acceleration of 30 g's.

As shown in **Figure 2**, the Winder vehicle was slightly over 30 metres (100 feet) in diameter and weighed 1000 tons. It had a raised dome that was really a low pressure fan that would draw in cool, electrically neutral air from above the vehicle and force it to flow over a fusion reactor in the center of the hull. Here the air would be ionized by powerful neutron and gamma radiations from a fusion reactor and would also serve to cool the reactor.

Once ionized, the positively and negatively charged air particles would be momentarily held in cylindrically symmetrical, cusped containment magnetic fields (created by two containment coils with opposite current flows that contain the D-He^3 plasma undergoing fusion) before leaking down into the region below the craft. At this point a large 30-metre-diameter lift coil would be activated so its magnetic field would slowly pulse from a central field strength of 100 kilogauss (about 200,000 times as strong as the earth's magnetic field) to one of 200 kilogauss. These high-power magnetic fields were achieved by using super-conducting niobium/tin electromagnets that could carry hundreds of thousands of amperes at low temperatures.

As the lift coil's magnetic field intensified in strength, it would compress the ionized air trapped in its magnetic field lines and this air was then pushed out below the craft to provide the enormous thrust needed to accelerate such a massive object. Winder calculated that if the lift coil pulsed 1.4 times per second, then each pulse would expel 135 *tons* of air at a velocity of 680 feet per second. A force of 30,000 tons would then be transmitted back to the craft through the lift coil's magnetic field to accelerate the craft at 30 g's. The craft could also be made to hover if there was one pulse every 7.5 seconds that expelled 1,800 tons of air at a velocity of 40 metres per second.

Winder's design suffered from many problems. Aside from the shielding that would be needed to protect the craft's occupants from the lethal radiations of a centrally-located reactor, there was the problem that the craft would pose for ground crews or observers who would be exposed to 130 km/h blasts of superheated air that would be hot enough to ignite the surface of a tarmacadam road!

Additionally, a craft using this method of propulsion would, when hovering, rise and fall about 60 metres with each pulse of the lift coil's field. Needless to say, this would make a controlled and safe landing of the craft virtually impossible, while the powerful magnetic fields involved could have catastrophic results for several craft flying in close formation.

Most importantly, Winder's propulsion hypothesis said nothing about protecting the crew from the effects of high g acceleration. Because he assumed that UFOs have their full mass in flight, he was forced to use a fusion reactor with a sufficiently high enough power output (10,200 megawatts for hovering and 12,200 megawatts for full acceleration at 30 g's) to drive his hypothetical 1000-ton ship. Also, his craft was incapable of space-flight unless it could be modified to carry an enormous amount of material to expel for thrust. No means was provided to protect against or eliminate aerodynamic heating of its surfaces in flight, even though other ufologists such as the American Coral Lorenzen were suggesting that UFOs eliminate aerodynamic drag by ionizing the air surrounding their hulls, deflecting it away from the craft with magnetic fields. [**5**]

In an effort to minimize the power needed to propel a UFO as it overcame the forces of gravity and to protect its crew from inertial forces, the propulsionists of the 1960s turned to a variety of anti-gravity hypotheses that would all eventually prove unsatisfactory.

The English engineer Leonard G. Cramp offered his famous "G-field" hypothesis in two books. [**6,7**] He claimed that the occupants of a rapidly-accelerating UFO felt no inertial forces acting on their bodies because all of the atoms in their bodies as well as in their craft accelerated *at the same rate* in an artificial local gravity field produced around the craft by a set of "G-field projectors" that it carried.

His hypothesis *does* allow a UFO to overcome gravity and inertial effects whilst still allowing the craft and crew to have their normal masses in flight. He unfortunately could provide no details on how such G-field projectors would operate. Also, such a system would probably be unusable for the same reasons that fixing a powerful magnet in front of a small steel car will not produce motion in the car as long as the

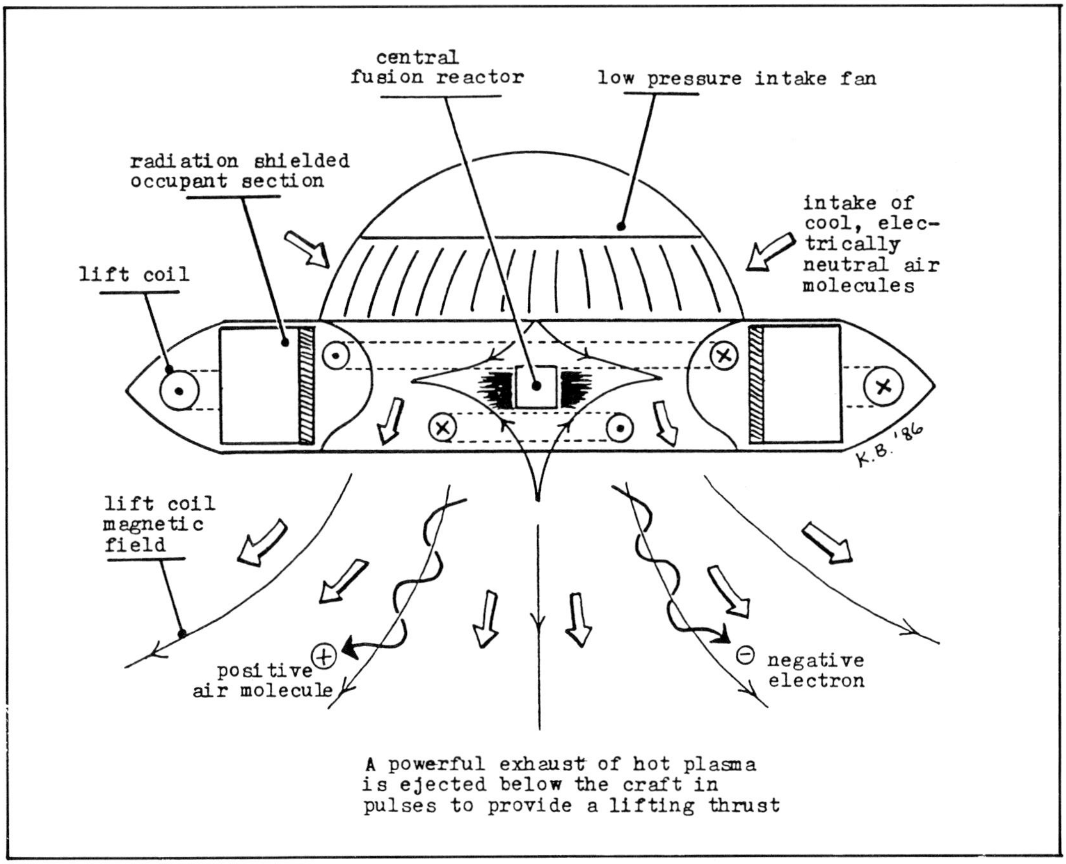

Figure 2 - Winder's concept of Flying Saucer design.

magnet is physically attached to the car.

Researchers such as the American physicist T. Townsend Brown [**8**] had developed electro-gravitic devices wherein it was claimed that certain high-capacitance dielectrics would exhibit a propulsive force toward their positively-charged plates when subjected to a high voltage of 50 to 300 kilovolts. Small suspended discs utilizing this effect were capable of motion, but orthodox physicists tended to dismiss the phenomenon as due to "electric wind" which was just a flow of ionized air around the highly-charged discs. Although they glowed like real UFOs and were capable of motion, no experiments have ever indicated that any electro-gravitic device had experienced a loss of mass in operation.

During the 1970s most of the UFO propulsionists had grown disenchanted with the anti-gravity approach and began to finally abandon the extraterrestrial hypothesis because of the failure of its adherents to develop a working hypothesis that would allow the craft's performance and secondary effects to be duplicated by earthly versions. It is at this point in the history of the subject that many embraced the extradimensional hypothesis which avoided the problems of vehicle propulsion by assuming that the craft were not really spacecraft as we understood the term, but rather devices for travelling through space/time or from a higher or lower set of dimensions into our four-dimensional universe.

Researchers such as the American Alan C. Holt [**9**] proposed a unified-field-theory model that attempted to describe all matter and energy in the universe as the manifestation of hyperspace energy currents. According to his hypothesis, a UFO could change its location by converting electromagnetic energy into gravitational energy. Using laser pulses, magnetic fields, and electron beams, his "resonance spacecraft" would generate oscillating energy patterns in a metal torus that would then interact with the postulated hyperspace energy patterns to negate the effects of local gravity fields. He envisioned a craft which, when only slightly out of resonance with its local hyperspace energy pattern, would perform the violent anomalistic motions sometimes noted for UFOs. When greatly out of resonance with its local hyperspace environment, his craft would then instantly travel through space/time to its resonant position in the universe, which could be very far from its starting point.

Another American researcher, Daniel Eden, has proposed a novel explanation for the "multiple image" UFO photographs that apparently show the UFO materializing in several different locations during the brief time that the camera's shutter is open. [**10**] He proposed that these photographs demonstrate that the craft is actually rapidly oscillating or "coining" from a dimensional space/time continuum higher than ours to one lower than ours. Thus, he solves the problem of overcoming gravity and inertia in our space/time continuum by having the UFO's pilots constantly adjusting the location in our universe that the craft passes through.

There are many problems with the extradimensional approach to UFO propulsion and dynamics. They all rely on the assumed existence of such things as parallel universes and an array of vague and as yet undiscovered effects that would allow access to these assumed realms. They say little definite about the many secondary effects such as automobile engine stalling, the extinguishing of incandescent electric lamps, interference with radio and television reception and power distribution, and the levitation of automobiles and drivers near large hovering UFOs. Neither does this approach explain the alarming phsyiological effects noted, such as the skin burns and paralysis sometimes received by human witnesses in close proximity to UFOs.

During the 1970s and 1980s, only a handful of ufologists had remained faithful to the extraterrestrial hypothesis and sought materialistic solutions for the phenomenon that would be capable of experimental verification.

The American ufologist James M. McCampbell proposed the idea that UFOs were material craft whose builders had developed a technology that allows them to greatly reduce the mass of objects. [**11**] He has attempted to rationalize the various colored glows surrounding the craft in terms of the irradiation of the air surrounding the vehicle by powerful microwave radiations it was emitting.

Although he has not provided a mechanism to explain how the craft would lower its mass so as to reduce its gravitational and inertial properties, his research into UFO microwave emissions has successfully explained the so-called "hot ring effect". This effect is sometimes noted by close encounter witnesses when they feel their finger rings getting hot. Apparently the rings can act as miniature loop antennas that can turn received microwave radiation into electrical currents that will heat up a metallic ring.

This writer has also remained faithful to the ETH and believes that we will only be able to eventually duplicate the propulsion systems utilized by the UFOs, and be able to reproduce the secondary effects associated with this technology, if we assume UFOs are physical craft that engage in travel between star systems by moving through *our* universe in a manner that uses a technology only *a little* more advanced than what we already possess!

During the last decade, this writer has managed to systematically develop a new hypothesis for UFO propulsion and secondary effects which successfully meets *all* of the criteria for a usable working hypothesis.

This new hypothesis is referred to as the "anti-mass field theory" or "AMF theory" although, technically, it is still closer to being a hypothesis than a full-fledged theory.

It begins with a new model to describe how objects produce the gravitational and inertial properties which we measure and use to define the "mass" of the object. The new model assumes that all of the sub-atomic particles in the atoms that compose an object emit or radiate a kind of *non*-electromagnetic radiation that expands away from the object at the speed of light. It is the refraction or bending of this radiation as it interacts with the radiation emitted from other objects which produces the force we call "gravity" that tends to pull all objects together. When an object moves, its motion forces the invisible radiation it emits to bend and this bending creates the force we call "inertia" which tends to retard or oppose the acceleration and deceleration of objects. Contemporary physicists may refer to this unseen radiation emitted from the sub-atomic particles of an object as the object's "gravity field". This writer, however, prefers to call it the object's "mass field".

From the above it should be obvious that if we could somehow partially reduce or partially neutralize the mass field emitted from an object, then that object would lose some of its gravitational and inertial properties and would *effectively* have a lower mass. If *all* of the mass field emitted from an object could be extinguished, then that object would become totally massless.

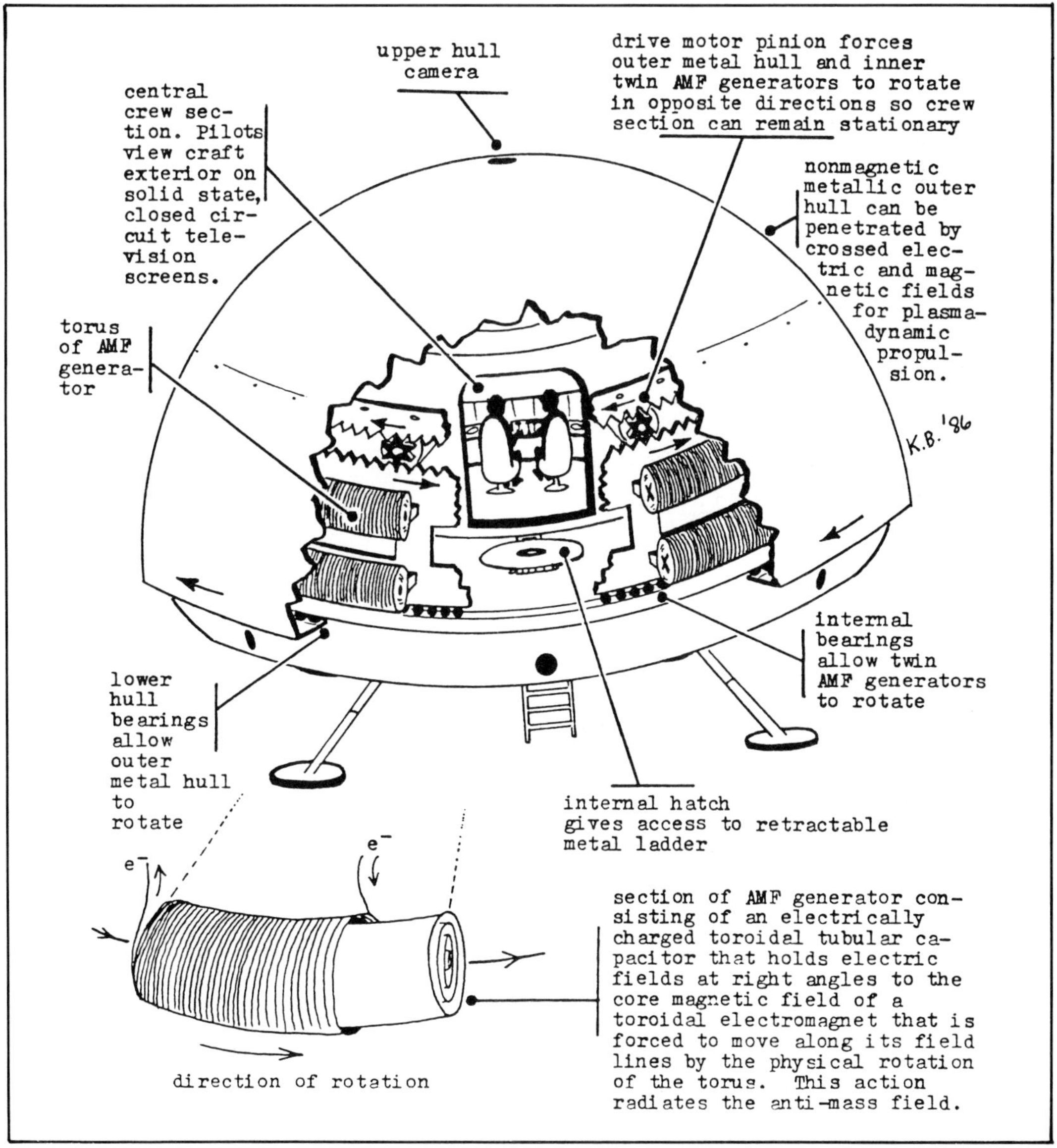

Figure 3 - Rotating hemispherical UFO equipped with twin AMF generators (sections removed to facilitate view of interior). This craft is designed for atmospheric operation only and is carried by a mothership.

The beings who designed and built the extraterrestrial craft that visit our world have learned how to neutralize the normal mass fields emitted from the atoms of their craft and crews' bodies. According to AMF theory, this is accomplished by equipping their craft with devices known as "anti-mass field generators". These devices emit or radiate a field whose "polarity" is opposed to that of the craft and crew's normal mass field and which cancels out or negates this mass field. With little or no mass, a UFO and its crew can buoyantly float in a planet's atmosphere without the enormous expenditures of energy that massive craft require. They can also travel through interstellar and intergalactic space at velocities exceeding that of light while massless without violating Einsteinian relativity. [**12,13**]

AMF theory goes on to provide a *detailed* mechanism for the means by which an anti-mass field is generated and a general description of the equipment needed to produce this new field effect. Basically, as shown in **Figure 3,** the AMF generator built into a UFO emits its anti-mass field when a magnetic field is force to move *along* its field lines at right angles to an electric field. AMF generators are usually toroidal or donut shaped and consist of a toroidal electromagnet that produces a powerful magnetic field at the core of the torus. The core also contains a toroidal tubular capacitor that consists of charged toroidal plates that hold electric fields at right angles to the core's magnetic field.

The magnetic and electric fields inside the toroidal AMF generator are not sufficient by themselves to generate an anti-mass field. It is still necessary to move the core's magnetic field along its field lines, and this is usually achieved by *physically* rotating the entire device. This requirement is obvious from the many UFOs that display rotating hull surfaces. In these cases the craft's AMF generators are attached mechanically to its rotating hull surfaces and rotate counter to them inside the hull. When such a craft has landed, it will slow and stop the rotation of its AMF generators and regain its full mass. Since it now has gravitational and inertial mass again, it may weigh tens of tons and press its landing gear into the soil of the landing site. Prior to lift-off, the craft will increase the rotation rate of its hull surfaces, and their internally moving AMF generators will emit its anti-mass field. The craft will then become almost massless and can rapidly leave the site when propulsive forces are applied to its hull. No matter how violent the take-off, the crew will feel little if any inertial forces applied to their nearly-massless bodies.

When operating in earth's atmosphere, some UFOs use simple rocket thrusters to apply motive force to their hulls. Because the craft is buoyant due to its AMF, its thrust can be used solely to provide horizontal motion. Such craft, however, are limited to velocities of only a few thousand km/h if excessive hull heating is to be avoided.

A more sophisticated means of thrust used by *most* UFOs is referred to as the "plasmadynamic mode of propulsion" in AMF theory. A plasmadynamically-propelled UFO uses its anti-mass field and various magnetic fields emanating from a *non-magnetic* metallic hull to convert the layer of air immediately surrounding its hull into a rich plasma or mixture of positively-charged atmospheric ions and negatively-charged electrons. This rich plasma is then exposed to crossed or perpendicular electric and magnetic fields that are projected into the plasma from propulsion equipment located inside the UFO's hull. These crossed electric and magnetic fields then apply what are known as "Lorentz forces" to the charged plasma particles and force them to flow *around* the craft's hull at enormous velocity. Since the plasma is forced to flow around the hull without touching it, aerodynamic drag is virtually eliminated and a massless UFO can achieve extremely rapid accelerations in our atmosphere without producing turbulence such as the "sonic boom".

AMF theory can further be used to explain how the boundary layer of plasma surrounding a moving UFO can be made to emit a visible glow. As the plasma's charged particles move through the crossed electric and magnetic fields near the craft's hull, the charged particles will move with an odd cycloidal motion. This motion forces them to emit a form of electromagnetic radiation known as "cyclotron radiation". Calculations show that if the magnetic fields near the hull have a strength of about 1000 gauss and the masses of the electrons in the plasma are reduced to about one ten-thousandth of their normal values by the UFO's anti-mass field, then these electrons can emit *visible* cyclotron radiation. The AMF theory explains how this process can generate cyclotron radiation in the infrared and ultraviolet regions of the spectrum. It is these radiations which cause the heating, skin burning, and eye injury secondary effects associated with UFO propulsion systems.

The AMF theory has, so far, successfully explained virtually all of the UFO-related secondary effects that it has been applied to. For example, it provides a mechanism to account for the way UFOs cause automotive failures and power blackouts. In these cases distant magnetic fields can interact with the UFO's anti-mass field reaching them to ionize air near the magnetic fields. This ionized air is electrically conductive and can short-circuit high-voltage circuits such as automobile ignition systems and high-tension power lines near their support towers.

AMF theory is still in a process of development and refinement, but it is *already* sufficiently detailed enough to allow us to begin the research needed to duplicate UFO propulsion. Those readers interested in a more in-depth treatment of this new propulsion hypothesis are invited to read *Annals of Ufological Research Advances*, or *AURA* for short, which can be obtained from: Arcturus Book Service, PO Box 2213, Scotia, New York, USA, 12302.

REFERENCES

1 - **Adamski,** George, *Inside the Spaceships* (Abelard-Schuman, London, 1955).. ■ 2 - **Heard,** Gerald, *Is Another World Watching? The Riddle of the Flying Saucers* (Bantam Books, New York, 1953).. ■ 3 - **Michel,** Aimé, *The Truth About Flying Saucers* (Criterion Books, New York, 1956).. ■ 4 - **Winder,** R.H.B., "Design for a Flying Saucer", *Flying Saucer Review*, 1966, Vol.12, No.6, p.21; 1967, Vol.13, No.1, p.13; 1967, Vol.13, No.2, p.20; and 1967, Vol.13, No.3, p.9.. ■ 5 - **Lorenzen,** Coral E., *The Great Flying Saucer Hoax* (William Fredericks Press, New York, 1962, p.139).. ■ 6 - **Cramp,** Leonard G., *Space, Gravity and the Flying Saucer* (The British Book Center, New York, 1955).. ■ 7 - **Cramp,** Leonard G., *Piece for a Jigsaw* (Somerton Publishing Company, Cowes, Isle of Wight, England, 1966).. ■ 8 - **Moore,** William, "The Wizard of Electrogravity Revisisted", *UFO Report*, Winter 1981, Vol.9, No.4, p.42, New York.. ■ 9 - **Holt,** Alan C., "Starcraft: The Anti-Gravity Fleet", *Science Digest*, May 1982, p.78, New York.. ■ 10 - **Eden,** Daniel, "Effective Mass and the UFO", *Pursuit*, Fourth Quarter 1984, Vol.17, No.4 (whole No.68), Little Silver, New Jersey, USA.. ■ 11 - **McCampbell,** James M., *Ufology: New Insights from Science and Common Sense* (Celestial Arts, Millbrae, California, USA, 1976).. ■ 12 - **Behrendt,** Kenneth W., "Introduction to Anti-Mass Field Physics", *AURA*, Aug.1985, Vol.1, No.3, p.1, Elizabeth, New Jersey, USA.. ■ 13 - **Behrendt,** Kenneth W., "Beyond Relativity Theory and the Light Barrier", *AURA*, Feb.1986, Vol.2, No.5, p.1, Elizabeth, NJ, USA.

4.2.3

AMBIGUITY IN UFO BEHAVIOR

by Robert C. Girard

■ **ROBERT C. GIRARD**. Traces his own fascination with UFOs and other unusual subjects back to 1950, when at the age of 8 he saw a flying disc one evening while he was playing with neighbourhood children. After decades of suffering that vague disorientation, that nagging feeling of not quite fitting into the rest of the human species which is common to many seekers, he founded, in 1980, the Arcturus Book Service.

■ **UFO involvement:** Operating out of small and hopelessly cluttered offices in Scotia, New York, USA, he offers books by mail on a variety of phenomena, including UFOs, ancient astronauts, parapsychology and hollow earth theory.

■ **Publications**: 'Ambiguity in UFO behaviour' represents a rare session at the typewriter for Bob Girard, who claims to feel uncomfortable with the notion that one's writing is obsolete even before it is set into type. However, in addition to purveying the writings of others he has also authored *The Cosmic Sheepdog*, a characteristic attempt to get beneath the surface of anomalous phenomena such as UFOs and seek an understanding of the underlying forces which are implicit in these baffling manifestations. There are times when he seems on the verge of understanding The Great Secret, and times when it seems to elude him skilfully.

■ **Address**:PO Box 2213 / Scotia / NY 12302 / USA. Phone (518) 374 2115.

This article does not draw from a wide and scintillating range of UFO literature. The subject of ambiguity in UFO behavior does not really require much in the way of direct quotations or paraphrased material culled from 1600 major and minor works about UFOs published in these 40 years of UFO history; with even a modest sampling of UFO study under one's belt, one should easily gather that the concepts treated in this section takes a fast quantum leap from the informational, or "real" level, to the metaphysical, or "subjective" level. This essay is largely an exercise in extrapolation - something that anyone of a questing spirit can indulge in. The very fact that you, the reader, have somehow come to hold this book in your hands, and have your eyes focused on this page, indicates that you are already quite prepared informationally for what comes next.

A BARRAGE OF CONFLICTING DATA

■ **November 10, 1952**. A Polish immigrant to the United States, George Adamski, who had had success in photographing flying saucers on an amateur basis since 1951, encounters a 2-metre-tall "Venusian" wearing a "jump-suit" in the desert near Desert Center, California. After some trial-and-error attempts at communication, the Venusian indicates that his people have come to earth in peace, and proceeds to answer Adamski's many questions - including one concerning the dangers involved in atmospheric testing of nuclear weapons, dangers which pose threats to civilizations beyond the earth itself. [**1**]

■ **September 12, 1952**. A total of 7 residents of Flatwood, West Virginia - a mother, her 5 sons and a national guardsman - investigate a report made by two of the sons that a flying saucer has landed on top of Flatwood Hill. While poking through the brush they encounter a 3-metre-tall "monster" with a red-orange face and glowing green eyes; in addition, they are overwhelmed by a terrible stench which makes them violently ill for hours afterward. The witnesses all have to be treated for shock, and traces made by a heavy object are found in the soil at the site. [**2**]

■ **August 26, 1952**. A Mr.R., friend of anthropologist George Hunt Williamson and an amateur radio operator, receives the following message from Zo, on Masar (Mars), on a frequency of 450 Khz:

II SWWAS Y CT ZO DE ZO DE ZO K K OK II ZO AFAAS Y II II MT WNWA II ZO ZO YANT NW YN WL WONT BE THERE UNTIL 1420 CMT KMC KTK RRB FLG INW IMH. FROM MASAR: YOU WILL SEE US IN THE SUN AT HIGH TIME TOMORROW VV THIS CAN BE THE SALVATION OF SARAS (Earth) IF ALL PLANS GO ACCORDING TO OUR WILL CAN YOU. II KA KARAS IS STILL IN THE AT. WE SHOULD BE IN YOUR AT. TOMORROW IF ALL GOES ACCORDING TO PLAN WITH COUNCIL. [**3**]

■ **November 28, 1954**. A Venezuelan truck-driver and his helper encounter a spherical object blocking the road near Petares, a suburb of Caracas. As one of the men gets out to investigate, a 1-metre-tall hairy being comes toward him. The helper tries to grab the creature, but it strikes him and knocks him 5 metres away. The helper then uses his knife, trying to stab the creature's shoulder, but it glances off as if hitting metal. A second creature emerges from a hatch in the sphere and blinds the helper with a light emanating from a metallic tube. While this is happening, the driver (who had remained in the cab) sees two other similar creatures carrying rocks and dirt leap into the sphere, along with the creature which had struck the helper. The craft then shoots off and is out of sight in seconds. [**4**]

■ **October 25, 1957**. In a house near Petropolis, Brazil, a girl lies dying of stomach cancer. Her family is gathered around, expecting her death before the night is out. Suddenly there is a bright light outside, and on running to the window, the girl's brother sees that a UFO has landed near the house. Then two beings about 1.20 m tall enter the house. They have red-blonde hair, small Oriental-style eyes, and wear "incandescent" uniforms. One of the beings gestures to the girl's father to come forward. The being places his hand on the father's forehead, and he describes for the being telepathically the girl's symptoms and condition. Then, by using a device which shines with a bluish light, all present are able to observe the interior of the girl's body in a kind of living X-ray. The beings perform an operation on the girl which lasts half an hour. Afterward, they give her father a container which appears to be made of stainless steel and which contains 30 white capsules. The girl has to take one each day for 30 days, but long before that time is up she is cured of her cancer, as is verified by her doctor. [**5**]

■ **May 20, 1967**. Near Falcon Lake, Manitoba, Canada, Steven Michalak is taking samples of rocks when he notices two strange flying devices. One of them lands, and Michalak sketches it. It is of a seamless construction. Suddenly a door opens, and he approaches the craft. He tries calling into it in several languages, to no avail, and the door closes again. As Michalak touches the craft, the rubber portion of his gloves melts, and the craft begins to revolve in a counter-clockwise direction. Michalak is blown to the left by a blast of hot air which sets fire to his clothing, and which causes a strange checkerboard pattern of second and third degree burns on his chest. Later, after suffering severe nausea and diarrhoea and losing 10 kg, he is thought to have received a dose of X-ray or gamma radiation of between 100 and 200 roentgens, which would have proved lethal if the duration of the exposure had been longer. [**6**]

TWO TYPES OF ALIENS

These few examples of the thousands of "true stories" one discovers in UFO literature are diverse enough to indicate some very ambiguous signals being sent to us, providing the stories are all "real". The ufologist's problem is to find the kind of "logical"

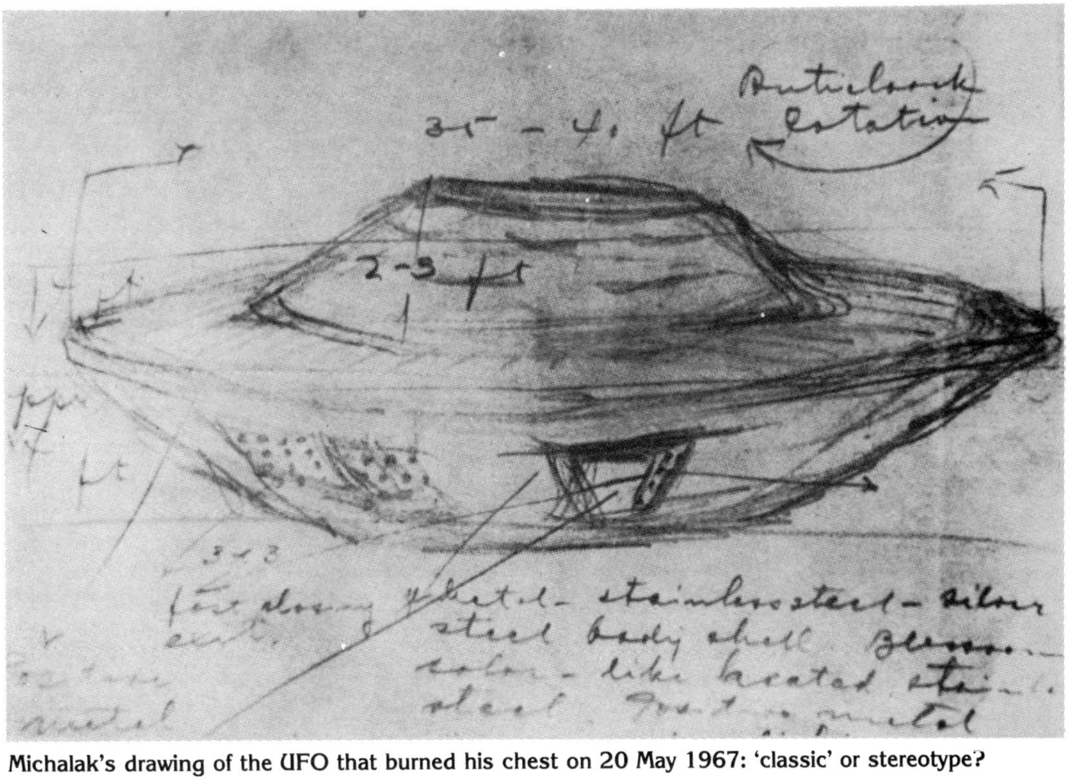

Michalak's drawing of the UFO that burned his chest on 20 May 1967: 'classic' or stereotype?

common denominator among them that will enable him or her to solve the riddle being posed by these strange craft, their occupants and their strange behavior. Forty years ago the solution seemed relatively simple; these ships (the occupants were not to be reported consistently until the 1954 French Wave) must have arrived from some nearby extraterrestrial location, with the moon, Mars and Venus being the most likely points of origin. In those days little was known of the conditions prevailing in our own solar system, and less was known about UFO crews. It would be years before the first introductory aliens would astonish Frenchmen with their odd little ships, their diving-gear uniforms, their paralyzing rays and their sometimes absurd attempts at communicating with humans. It would be still more years before humans began to be abducted by UFOnauts in significant numbers, more years still before hypnotic regression became a common approach toward retrieving abduction experiences - and even a few more years before the first suspicions that UFOs may *not* automatically come from outer space would appear in print, in the form of John Keel's and Jacques Vallée's articles and books. Such suspicions would be reinforced as our manned and unmanned space probes touched down one by one on the hostile surfaces of the moon, Mars and Venus, finding not so much as a single living bacterium.

As UFO experiences continue to accumulate in card files, dossiers and computer banks, and as more ufologists come to specialize in specific areas of UFO study (for example, UFO propulsion theory, landing trace analysis and study of UFO percipients), one common denominator begins to emerge; AMBIGUITY. It is as if, within a concept which in itself is incomprehensible to many humans, not only are the data often in violation of known physical "laws", but are themselves wildly inconsistent. The UFO Experience, in the end, appears self-contradictory.

The most striking source of ambiguity involves the observed behavior of the two distinct types of "extraterrestrials" most often reported in UFO encounters:

- The tall, often fair-haired, light-skinned being usually associated with the early, first-generation contactees (who were not abductees, it should be noted), and who still command a small but persistent following among that faction of seekers who "channel" messages from orbiting space brothers who are in earthly environs to save us from ourselves.
- The dwarfish, often gray-skinned, large-headed, slant-eyed beings who seem to have arrived on the UFO scene after the fair-skinned beings, and who are nearly always associated with the classic UFO abductions and their characteristic treatment of their human abductees as laboratory specimens, done without the least compassion for the individual subject or for the larger Human Condition on Earth.

A quick (and admittedly over-simplified) comparison of the observed behavior of these two types of aliens [**see the panel**] will bring into focus their ways of interacting with humanity.

BATTLEGROUND EARTH

If we were dealing with only two space-going civilizations here, there would be little problem accepting that their motivations are necessarily different, according to their different points of origin. But ambiguity arises - and even floods over us - when we search further and realize that members of both basic alien types claim to come from a very large number of extraterrestrial locations. The fair-skinned faction is often portrayed as representing a confederation of worlds or planets, and are, as such, a group of interstellar do-gooders. The dwarfish faction is often cryptic or even misleading about their home planets, but even they have revealed that they come from a wide variety of star systems. In addition, there is the enormous problem posed by the huge number of UFO configurations and sizes, and by the absolutely bewildering variety of reported UFOnauts, uniforms and equipment. This "snowflake effect", in which no two ships or crews appear exactly alike, fairly screams out to be interpreted as either A) a single civilization so space-capable that every citizen appears able to take a little spin over to the earth as easily as we humans head for a country picnic on a weekend afternoon, or B) members of *numerous* space-capable races are here, having found earth so fascinating as to make a journey measured in light years at the least somehow worthwhile. Both possibilities stretch one's credulity to its limits.

But now to add a final bit of ambiguous irony; there exists yet another story, which I heard first (and first-hand from the person to whom it happened) in March of 1986. Without betraying either the identity of my source or many of the details of this extremely complex tale, the most interesting element of all is a stunning role-reversal involving the two basic alien types! In this story (which was told to my source by a US military officer acting *on the record in the line of duty*), the dwarfish beings, who were the creators of homo sapiens some 30,000 years ago (as Cro-Magnon Man), appear as "good guys" in the sense that they are trying to assist humanity through direct contact (with US government officials, a program dating back to the mid-1940s) to prepare a defense (Star Wars) against an attack from none other than the tall, fair-skinned aliens who are the natural enemies of the dwarfish aliens. This assistance is not given out of any kind of compassion for humans as sovereign creatures with inherent rights of our own as a viable species, but simply because humanity is the experiment and the property of the creating race. As the story goes, both types of alien hail from the same solar system (that over-worked system known as Zeta-1 and Zeta-2 Reticulum). The races are enemies, and each possesses space-going abilities. The Nordic faction is out to destroy its enemy completely, and therefore humanity, as property of the dwarfish faction, finds itself in a no-win situation: 5 billion souls trapped on the battleground of an imminent interstellar war. Either we are destroyed, or we remain property.

An entire book could (and should) be written about this story, but that is beyond our purpose here. There is one bit of comforting news to add: the military official who briefed my source is a known specialist in DIS-information concerning UFOs. However, comforting though it may be, it also means that not only are we subject to conflicting data as seen and given to us by the aliens themselves, but now there are *humans* contributing to the ambiguity surrounding UFO behavior!

That essentially is as far as anyone can take this topic at this point. There is simply not enough *fact* available to continue - not at the "amateur Ufologist" level, at least. Each of us must, therefore, approach the UFO mystery (and relate it to other mysteries) in our own way. Ufology is, after all, an intensely personal Quest for understanding. Ufologists are essentially mystical seekers, and not merely objective scientists. Each reader of this article is at a different level of evolution, at a different point along the same path leading to greater personal understanding. Personally, I have been on the path since about 1950, when I happened to see as a young boy a UFO which remains as perfectly visible in my memory today as it did on that twilight evening 37 years ago. These 37 years on the Quest by no means qualify me as an expert on the subject. I often think that I know *less* about it as each new insight I gain is absorbed into the whole of my impressions, and dilutes still further the strength of earlier certainties.

Perhaps that is the point to all of this. Ambiguity seems to increase with one's knowledge of the UFO Experience. I have by no means solved the UFO Riddle in these pages, nor have I even come close to surrounding the problem of ambiguity in UFO behavior. However, I was given the chance to dwell a bit on this topic for this book, and this chance did give me the opportunity to discover what was on my mind today regarding UFO ambiguity. I discovered that this ambiguity is certainly *present* if one analyzes a large body of UFO reports - but that I don't know the final cause of it any more than you, the reader.

NORDIC-TYPE ALIENS	DWARFISH ALIENS
■ 1. Select their subject after screening him on earth for "worthiness".	■ 1. Subject selected at random, perhaps to thwart interception of their program by human authorities.
■ 2. Beings lure subject to the contact point via "hunches". Subject is often invited intothe UFO.	■ 2. Beings swoop down on subject on dark roads, often paralyze subject and prevent escape method, using light rays or gases. Subject then abducted onto UFO.
■ 3. Beings are tall, blonde, finely-featured, athletic in build; in short, "angelic" in aspect.	■ 3. Beings are often dwarfish and human*oid*. They are often ugly and terrifying to subject, especially since humans are nearly always unprepared to experience abduction.
■ 4. Beings claim to be from a "confederation" of civilizations, with many races serving on the same ship. Every attempt is made to help subject feel welcome among them.	■ 4. Beings are cold and methodical. No comforts or friendliness are offered to subject. Preparation for experiments begins.
■ 5. Patient explanation and instruction about ship, crew and mission. Subject may ask as many questions as he or she likes.	■ 5. Subject often restrained or tranquilized during experiments. No instruction or explanations; few if any questions permitted of subject.
■ 6. Messages of hope, encouragement and spiritual content are given to subject. Philosophical and New Age principles are emphasized, as well as warnings of impending catastrophe if humanity does not reform itself.	■ 6. Answers, often vague or cryptic, given to subject's questions. Widely differing answers are found when studying this type of experience on a case-by-case basis.
■ 7. Voyages to "known" places such as the moon or other places familiar to earthmen. Trips also to various parts of the earth, and guided tours through installations, cities etc.	■ 7. Occasional voyages to "unknown" places, often bizarre or frightening. Views only, no escorted tours given.
■ 8. Reaffirmation of friendly intent, and fond farewells from the aliens as the visit nears its end. Subject often encouraged to speak of the experience.	■ 8. Memory of abduction erased by aliens. Messages sometimes implanted deep into subconscious mind of subject (who is powerless to resist the implantation).
■ 9. Duration of experience often measured in hours, sometimes in days.	■ 9. Duration of experience often measured in minutes, less often in hours, rarely in days.
■ 10. Subject returned comfortably to pick-up point or home by aliens.	■ 10. Beings often dump subject in a place different from the pick-up point, sometimes far away.
■ 11. Subject suffers no ill after-effects. Possible beneficial effects such as increased psychic ability, etc.	■ 11. Subject often traumatized, and suffering physical or emotional distress. Symptoms of "radiation sickness" common, also nightmares, neurosis and compulsive behavior. Professional medical and/or psychological treatment often necessary.
■ 12. Follow-up contacts, with or without a UFO involved, are often promised and carried out.	■ 12. Follow-up contacts are often promised but not carried out. In other cases, however, follow-up contacts *are* made, without the knowledge or consent of subject.

KEEPING YOUR BALANCE

There are only a few scattered guide-posts marking the obscure path toward understanding what UFOs have to do with the larger Quest to discover the meaning and the truth behind our own existence. These are:

■ 1. It is nearly certain that the overwhelming majority of UFOs do not have an extraterrestrial origin.

■ 2. I can observe myself or other humans acting in such a manner that events are caused among lesser species of earthly life forms which are perceived by these life forms as phenomena when considered against their "ordinary" frames of reference.

■ 3. By extrapolation I may speculate that species sharing earth's biosphere with humanity and with the lesser forms of life exist *UP* the scale of life from humanity; and that these species, though unperceived by humans, may act in such a way that events regarded as phenomenal among humans may be accidentally or intentionally made to occur within the human community.

■ 4. Because I, as an investigator, do not know how many unperceived species may exist and may cause phenomena among humanity, I am subject to having to cope with conflicting data when studying such phenomena, and am subject to the resulting difficulty in determining what, if anything, is "intended" by such phenomenal events.

■ 5. There is evidence to suggest that there are malevolent as well as benign or benevolent aspects to phenomenal events, and that these in turn suggest the existence of different motivations behind them.

■ 6. There is information and insight which is beneficial to the individual seeker to be had from phenomena and from the study of phenomena. There is also very dangerous MIS-information. There is the suggestion that humanity may be no more than some other species' herd of cattle, or that another species manipulates the great bulk of humanity (unknown to it) in order to feed on the emotions generated by "being kept human" in a great stew of purely human dilemmas (the rise of AIDS being an interesting new ingredient in the stew, consuming the attention of millions of humans all of a sudden; this is how it works). A large number of such scenarios and possibilities - all involving the *non-freedom* of humanity - exists, and any or all may be true.

■ 7. While seeking greater understanding, and while trying to find the secret hidden in the swirls of ambiguity clouding your vision, you will serve yourself better by:

A. Observing everything around you, on every level, including yourself.

B. Keeping your intellectual and emotional balance.

C. Avoiding negative aspects which arise; bear in mind that malevolent opportunities exist alongside benevolent opportunities.

D. Relying ultimately on nothing but your own sense of judgment and direction, for that is the only frame of reference you can truly understand. Remember your own sovereignty, your own ability to act independently, your own power to over-ride external influences.

The most uncomfortable ambiguity is not that which is encountered when studying UFOs or other phenomena. Rather it is the ambiguity which is often found in one's own self. The more ambiguity one permits one's self to indulge in, the less able one will be to interpret ambiguities coming from outside. When a seeker suffers from self-ambiguity, the results can literally become nightmarish, and even fatal. Ufology never was for the curiosity-seeker, or the easily-frightened, or the insecure. It is for people who trust themselves and their ability to judge and to sense the correct way for themselves.

WORKS CONSULTED

1 - **Leslie,** Desmond, and George **Adamski**. *Flying Saucers have Landed.* British Book Centre, 1953. ■ 2 - **Wilkins,** Harold T. *Flying Saucers on the Attack.* New York, Citadel, 1954. ■ 3 - **Williamson,** George H., and Alfred C. **Bailey**. *The Saucers Speak.* Los Angeles, New Age, 1954. ■ 4 - **Lorenzen,** James L. and Coral H. *UFOs over the Americas.* New York, Signet, 1968. ■ 5 - *Flying Saucer Review,* Vol 13, No.5, 1967. ■ 6 - **Michalak,** Stephen. *My Encounter with the UFO.* Winnepeg, Osnova, 1967.

4.3.1

THE EXTRA- TERRESTRIAL HYPOTHESIS

by John Prytz

■ **JOHN PRYTZ**: Born Oyster Bay, NY, 1947. BS from State University of New York at Stony Brook, Graduate Diploma in Librarianship, Canberra College of Advanced Education. By profession Senior Reference Librarian at the Commonwealth Parliamentary Library, Canberra. Naturalised Australian. Interests outside ufology include cats; planetary astronomy & exobiology; science fiction; marine biology; cryptozoology and fortean phenomena &c. Collector of Australian beer cans and sci-fi movie soundtracks. Enjoys playing baseball, softball and ten-pin bowling.
■ **UFO involvement**: A member of ACUFOS (Australian Centre for UFO Studies) and ACT (Australia) representative for MUFON. In addition to articles and papers on a diversity of aspects, his activities have largely taken the form of putting his library expertise to work in the preparation of bibliographies and catalogues. He describes himself as 'a strong supporter of the ET hypothesis.'
■ **Publications**: include *Ufology and the UFO: an anthology* (Galaxy Press 1970); *In search of a subject: an Australian SETI programme* (ACUFOS 1981); *Information storage and retrieval for ufologists* (ACUFOS 1981); *Who's who in Australasian ufology* (ACUFOS 1982); ACUFOS bibliography series Volume One, *Ufology and exobiology* (1982) and Volume Two, *The Weird, the wild and the wonderful* (1985); co-editor with Mark Moravec of *UFOs over Australia* (ACUFOS 1985); and articles in numerous UFO and other journals in Australia and elsewhere.
■ **Address**: PO Box 87 / Deakin / ACT 2600 / Australia.

UFOs - by which I mean the bona fide, hardcore unidentifiable residue which remain UFOs despite intensive investigation and sufficient data - display behavioral characteristics which are the contrary of what is characteristic of natural phenomena - by which I mean not only familiar natural phenomena but also the rare, the exotic, and even the unknown.

Natural phenomena, even if not fully understood, will by definition show strong and fairly predictable patterns in time and place - sunspot cycles, cyclone activity, bird migrations &c. The introduction of intelligence into any equation makes for less predictability and rationality. Predicting economic trends, for example, is much less certain than predicting planetary orbits; sociology is a 'softer' science than botany; the evolution of art forms or educational theory exhibits less pattern than the devolution of a radioactive substance with a known decay rate.

UFOs differ from natural phenomena, not in not showing patterns, but because the patterns they show suggest 'free will' intelligence as opposed to blind obedience to natural laws. When we find UFOs interacting in real time with the UFO witness, as they did with Harley Rutledge and his team [**1**], it is clear that we are observing patterns of intelligence, in contrast to patterns of nature. But no less do such patterns differ from those of man-made hardware such as artificial satellites which, even though controlled by man, must obey the natural forces of motion, and unmanned balloons which follow the wind.

If we have trouble matching our wits against the UFO, that in itself suggests that whatever controls the UFOs has 'wits' of its own. But are we matching wits with a 'them' or an 'us'?

EXTERNAL OR INTERNAL?

Given a UFO witness, the big question is: on which side of his skin does the UFO intelligence manifest? Was the stimulus which led to his report external, reaching him via his five senses, or internal, originating from somewhere beneath his skin? Or to put it another way, do UFOs exist in their own right (perhaps as the traditional 'nuts and bolts') or are they reducible to processes which are properly the concern of the social, psychological and medical sciences?

The **external intelligence theory** (EIT) comprises a wide range of possibilities, including for example:

- terrestrial secret weapons
- time travellers from our future
- an atmospheric intelligence
- extraterrestrials.

The **internal intelligence theory** (IIT) comprises such possibilities as:

- hoaxes

- abnormal physiological and/or psychological causes; the 'pink elephant' syndrome, brain tumours &c
- normal physiological/psychological causes such as dreams and imagery.

Many other examples could be added to either list.

One of the reasons for doubting natural explanations is that no extensive alteration to the terrestrial environment occurred around the 1944-1947 period, other than the introduction of nuclear weapons testing and radioactive fall-out, which it hardly seems likely would have been enough to alter the chenical and physical properties of the atmosphere and thus produce natural UFOs. Yet some such cause would have been necessary to cause a massive influx of a new natural phenomenon.

The same argument applies to the IIT. If human beings are internally prone to visions of balls of light or metallic discs and cigars, for whatever reason, yet simultaneously interpret these visions as alien spaceships, then there is no rhyme or reason for UFOs to have made a sudden appearance in the mid-1940s, for the concept of extraterrestrial spaceships existed long before that. No internal cause-and-effect relationship is apparent between the social, political, scientific and psychological environment of that period and the genesis of the UFO phenomenon. [2] That the UFO phenomenon should be born then and there is inexplicable on the IIT and suggests that an *external* intelligence was at work...

The internal collective human society, human psyche, and/or human brain, do not undergo that sort of massive change - from pre-UFO innocence to post-UFO sophistication - in so brief a time period without a trigger of some kind. If that trigger was internal, how has it been maintained all this time? Forty years is a surprisingly long time for a fad to be stoked by its own power - but not so surprising if it was being fuelled by an *external* intelligence.

Had an internal trigger, however small, brought the UFO phenomenon from the subconscious to the conscious during the period 1944-1947, we would expect a flock of retrospective reports, sufficient to even out the number of UFO reports per year so that quantitatively there would be little to distinguish the pre-1944 from the post-1947 years. In practice, however, retrospective pre-1944 reports are relatively few and far between, suggesting *external* rather than internal stimulation.

If UFOs are internally generated, we should expect them to mirror human activity. But the fluctuations in UFO sightings - the American highs of 1952, 1957, 1966 and 1973, lows of 1951, 1959, 1963, 1969 and currently - are non-uniform, unpredictable, and seemingly without correlation: if they relate to any activity, it would seem likely to be of a kind *external* to humankind.

Correlation is lacking, too, between UFO reports and human population. If UFOs are generated by people, then Australia's 130% population growth since the commencement of the age of the UFO should be matched overall by a comparable rise in UFO reports. Needless to say, there has been no such rise. Nor, if the cause is *external*, should we expect one.

We find a similar absence of correlation in the matter of geographical distribution. UFO reports do not rise with population density, as we would expect with the IIT. On the other hand, an *external* intelligence behind the UFO phenomenon is just as likely to be repulsed by centres of human population as attracted to them.

FLAPS

The IIT is no less inadequate to account for small-scale concentrations of UFO activity. Why, all of a sudden, out of the blue (literally) should the inhabitants of a particular area, over a specific period of time, go 'round the twist'? Clearly the situation is considered abnormal for that time and place, otherwise the 'flap effect' could not have arisen and been noticed. This is true whether we are talking about some mysterious bug causing an epidemic of hallucinations, or a sudden ripening of social conditions so that reporting UFOs becomes acceptable, even respectable, for certain time periods only. Where did the mysterious bug come from, and where/why did it go? Why did the social conditions change, then change back again?

Flaps can be explained in the same way that we explain how it happens that the Sydney Cricket Ground receives a 'flap' of visiting strangers when an England-Australia test match is taking place. The Ground is a unique place for people to be at a unique time, not because of anything inherent in the ground itself, but due to an *external* cause. The English team is Sydney's equivalent of an ET visitation.

The same goes for other kinds of pattern. Aime Michel's orthoteny may be valid, or it may be due to statistical laws, probability theory, quirks of mathematics. But one thing is certain, no matter what is behind orthoteny, it absolutely cannot be any form of internal intelligence.

WITNESS BEHAVIOUR

The IIT has just as many problems, if not more, with the data we have gathered on how witnesses react. Its premise is that UFOs are caused by mental processes, yet are subsequently interpreted by those same mental processes as being something of an external nature, with a physical reality, often technological, frequently as ET spaceships.

Yet as a rule witnesses desperately seek first for a mundane explanation, looking to the press, the military, the police, friends, family, the medical profession, to say nothing of UFO groups, for reasonable and rational whys and wherefores. There is rarely in the first instance a leap to the exotic and the unnatural; that comes only after much personal self-examination and soul-searching. Here, as in other spheres of activity - nightmares, for instance - the average John Doe is perfectly capable of distinguishing internal from external stimuli. Survival depends on being able to recognise external reality; why should UFOs be an exception, thought to be external but in reality internal? The leap to EIT doesn't come automatically or through wishful thinking; the evidence must suggest it.

To establish the viability of the IIT, its supporters should be able to show that a significant number of UFO events were related by persons who were at the time under independent observation which refutes their account: for example, John Doe's claim that he was abducted by aliens from his office should be contradicted by the security camera which shows him sleeping on the job! A few such cases - if indeed they existed - would set the internal cat among the external pigeons!

What the witness tells us runs counter to the IIT. UFO shapes, as reported, are atypical of the popular paradigm of a spaceship - the most widely-held external concept. We have horizontal cigar-shapes and discs: we don't have vertical rocketships with fins so well known to the general public.

Nor does UFO behaviour match with how John Doe thinks of - and therefore imagines - external intelligence. Ask him to describe a hypothetical encounter with an alien spaceship and its crew - but make it in the early 1940s. The resulting description will in no way mirror post-1947 UFO behaviour, which clearly cannot have been inspired by the public's ingrained ideas. It seems far more likely that behind the phenomenon is an *external* process whose nature is unpredictable ('the universe is not only stranger than we imagine - it is stranger than we *can* imagine').

Not only do UFO reports *not* contain the elements we would expect - fins, wheels, sonic booms &c are hardly ever reported - but unexpected things *are* reported - neither 'angel hair' nor the 'falling leaf' motion are things you'd have picked in advance. We would also expect some cultural variation between different human societies: if internal processes are responsible, UFOs in Communist China should not mirror UFOs in Uganda, which should not mirror UFOs in Canada: yet we find that parallel UFO patterns cut across vastly different human societies.

Could that be because UFOs come from much deeper levels of our mental make-up, where cultural differences are irrelevant? Are we then to suppose we share those deeper levels with cats and dogs - for they also respond to UFOs! Isn't it easier to believe that animals and humans alike can all see UFOs because the UFOs are really out there in the environment?

To complicate the issue, we find that although accounts of UFOs and their occupants are generally consistent, patterns do vary from one part of the world to another. For example, the United States has many more reported UFO abduction cases in relation to population than Australia, which is hard-pressed to document even one single case. Yet Australians and Americans are *very* closely related in an historical, ethnic, social and cultural sense. To so differ in the matter of abductions therefore is suggestive of *external* factors.

But this brings us to the entire question of UFO occupants, and how humans expect them to be. Science fiction stories were full of 'bug-eyed monsters' - yet in UFO reports alien monsters are as rare as hens' teeth. If internal forces were at work, and human imagination could run wild, why not lots of creatures akin to the *Alien* or *The Thing*, *ET* or *War of the Worlds* octopods? Alas, it's *humanoids* - but *not* humans - by a wide margin.

And if it has to be humanoids, should not Australian aborigines see ebony humanoids, the Chinese yellow humanoids, and American Indians copper-red humanoids? Ufonaut descriptions, given the IIT, should mirror the ethnic spread, or parallel the personality and life-style of the witness. But there is no match, no parallel; and that is something easily accounted for if *external* intelligence is responsible, as is the fact that ufonauts are rarely reported as wearing personal adornment, or in association with art works or music - or even muzak. The fact that neither the UFO nor its occupants reflect before-the-fact conventional thinking or expectations is a strong reason for concluding that neither derive from human thought processes.

ABDUCTIONS

Abduction cases have been claimed as support for both the IIT and the EIT. Some insist that they must reflect external reality because of a number of multi-witness cases, along with physiological and/or psychological effects, testimony obtained under hypnosis, lie detector tests, and sometimes hard evidence such as ground traces, 'star maps' &c. IIT supporters use other cases - or sometimes the same ones - insisting that they are so weird, mystical and illogical that only mental illness, dreams/nightmares, or drug-induced hallucinations could be responsible.

It is of course a possibility that abduction cases are not, as a rule, 'either/or'; that some are internally generated while others reflect reality.

Internally-generated abductions should show no particular patterns, except those which mirror human data such as population distribution. No such patterns have been documented: if anything the reverse - ie abduction cases are inversely proportional to population density. We would also expect that each abduction should be a unique event, reflecting the individual personality, upbringing and life-style of the abductee. That would mean that the only common factor was the (imaginary) abduction.

In practice, however, common factors abound in the UFO abduction literature. There is a consistent pattern, as Budd Hopkins demonstrates elsewhere in this book and in his *Missing Time* ***3**. Such patterns, such data, run quite counter to any internal before-the-fact expectations. The paradigms of alien contact run along one of two lines: global invasion or diplomatic 'take-me-to-your-leader' exchange. In both, human beings are significant and important: whereas reports of UFO abductions suggest near indifference to human beings or, at most, a cold detached curiosity (eg 'medicals').

In retrospect, we see that this is what we should have expected from an alien race or time travellers. This is not contact between equals: the parallel is with a terrestrial biologist investigating a new species of ant. It is not a picture which is flattering to our egos: it is not the picture internal intelligence would have come up with.

PHYSICAL EVIDENCE AND FORTEAN PHENOMENA

And so we come to the physical, hardcore evidence. There is of course just no way that internal processes can account for physical traces, still photographs and motion pictures, radar returns, radioactivity readings, electro-magnetic effects &c. Furthermore, the IIT has degrees of difficulty with physiological evidence, psychological changes, all of which point clearly to an *external* explanation.

We could also mention related areas of 'evidence' lying outside the UFO experience as such, but potentially supportive of the EIT: transient lunar phenomena; the evidence which has given rise to ancient astronaut theories; vanishing ships, aircraft and satellites; long-delayed echoes; the Tunguska 1908 event; and a whole range of Fortean events. Whatever reality or relevance these may possess, they are certainly external rather than internal in nature.

WHICH EIT?

It is clear that the IIT comes a bad second to the EIT, whichever aspect of UFO reports we consider: but not all EITs are of equal value. Time travel, atmospheric intelligence and several other possibilities are no more than conjecture. Extraterrestrial intelligence and visitations, by contrast, have not only a theoretical under-pinning, but on analysis seem nearly inevitable.

■ Statistically, it is unlikely that mankind is unique as an intelligent life-form.
■ Most intelligent life-forms would have technological civilisations far older than ours: we are the new boys on the block.
■ Space travel is a known possibility. There is no violation of physical law.
■ That even if only one extra-terrestrial space-faring civilisation exists, the time it would take them to explore and colonise the galaxy, even at very low sub-light velocities, is but a tiny fraction of the age of the galaxy. Earth and Earthlings cannot hide!

So, where is everybody? The obvious conclusion is not that alien technological civilisations don't exist, but that the evidence for their existence isn't self-evident.

According to EIT, an EI visiting Earth would not of necessity have to correlate with human population density and distribution: which is what we observe. EI would be more restrictive than the range of human imagination allows for: observed. EI would exhibit interaction with the environment: observed. EI would not be random but display patterns in size, colour, behaviour &c: observed. EI would cut across ethnic, cultural, social, geographical and other boundaries: observed.

I can conclude only that some form of EI is behind the UFO reports. As to the nature of that EI, I have my own thoughts, as no doubt you have. But that's another ball game...

REFERENCES

■ 1 - **Rutledge,** Harley, *Project Identification* (Prentice Hall, 1981). ■ 2 - **Prytz,** John, 'UFO genesis' in *Mufon Journal* 175, Sept 1982. ■ 3 - **Hopkins,** Budd, *Missing time* (Marek, 1981).

4.3.2

UFOs AS NATURAL PHENOMENA

by Chris Rutkowski

■ **CHRIS RUTKOWSKI**: Has a degree in astronomy from the University of Manitoba, where he is currently in post-graduate research. He is a member of the Royal Astronomical Society of Canada and the Folklore Studies Association of Canada. He is also a member of the Experimental Creative Music Workshop.
■ **UFO involvement**: Has been actively investigating UFO reports since 1974, and is presently associated with UFOROM (Ufology Research of Manitoba) and CUFOS (Center for UFO Studies). He has written on a variety of UFO-related topics, including landing traces, belief systems and case studies. He has recently given particular attention to the Tectonic Strain and Earth Lights Hypotheses currently being proposed as a partial explanation for the UFO phenomenon. 'The topic of UFOs should be approached with common sense, as should any other topic. Believers should not necessarily be believed, but one should also be skeptical of skeptics.'
■ **Publications**: include articles for *Flying Saucer Review, Canadian UFO Report* and *Journal UFO*. He is editor of *The Swamp Gas Journal* and Contributing Editor of *The International UFO Reporter*.
■ **Address**: Box 1918 / Winnipeg / Manitoba / Canada R3C 3R2.

INTRODUCTION

When faced with the enigma of UFOs, many skeptics have offered their opinions on more "natural" and conventional explanations for the observed phenomena. Usually, these are given as alternatives to the popular extraterrestrial theory which has been put forward most often by proponents in discussions. Later, with suggestions of ultraterrestrial manifestations and parapsychological effects, it has seemed even more appropriate to advance conventional explanations. In recent years, with proponents becoming more critical and discerning, the skeptics' viewpoint, while not being wholly endorsed, has been given attention by serious ufologists. This is not to say that earlier proponents' works are being dismissed; what has happened is that as a developing science, ufology has become more refined, and internal constructive criticism and review is now the usual method of examining new ideas.

It is possibly for this reason that the concept of UFOs as natural phenomena has again received attention since about 1975. Originally introduced by skeptics and debunkers, the concept was usually rejected out of hand by devoted UFO buffs, and relegated to the dustbin. But with a definite explanation for UFOs still evading researchers, the "old ground" is being re-examined for useful information.

Actually, the problem is more complex than is generally realized. When considering "natural" phenomena, do we mean misidentification of common phenomena, or observations of poorly-understood phenomena, or observations of hitherto unrecognised phenomena? All three categories need examination, with reference to proposals by both opponents and proponents of the theories.

In the early years of the Flying Saucer Era, one puzzling phenomenon was called the "Mystery of the Green Fireballs". These nocturnal lights were exactly as their name implied, looking nothing more than large blobs of light with streaming tails. While considered unexplainable, skeptics quickly pointed out that the green fireballs could be just that - green fireballs, sometimes called bolides. Astronomers also failed to see the mystery in these lights, since they were a common sight in the night sky, being only pebble-sized chunks of comets or asteroids burning up in the atmosphere. In some cases, where the objects were observed to change direction or stop altogether, if these actions could not be traced to poor observational techniques or other confounding factors, then the bolide explanation could not apply. However, it is clear that most "green fireballs" were in reality natural phenomena [1]

This is an example of a natural explanation for a particular kind of UFO. Many other cases have been described in the literature, and it is easy to classify them as misidentifications. We can group these misidentifications into different categories, based on the kinds of phenomena observed. For example, a **Simple Misidentification** involves a common object observed but not identified, despite numerous clues to its identity. Calling Venus or Sirius a UFO falls into this category. A **Complex Misidentification** concerns less common natural objects seen under unusual conditions. This includes sightings of lone lenticular clouds along a horizon, large birds in flight illuminated from below at night, and will-o'-the-wisp.

Finally, an **Extraordinary Misidentification** would involve the observation of a unique natural event. In this category are "tectonic" and "piezoelectric" UFOs, which will be discussed later in this chapter.

Within the bounds of these categories, a wide array of natural explanations for UFOs can be found. Some are promising paths for understanding the UFO mystery, while others are spurious and add little to knowledge already gained. Together, however, they definitely show that all is not what meets the eye.

HISTORICAL OVERVIEW

In 1966, Philip Klass published a paper that has become an integral part of ufological literature. [**2**] He proposed that many low-altitude UFOs could be explained as luminous balls of plasma under certain conditions. He demonstrated that electric corona, discharged from transmission lines, could fit the description of some reported UFOs. He singled out the sightings at Exeter, New Hampshire, in 1965, as possible candidates for his alternative explanation. He also suggested that ball lightning could account for many observations, going into some detail in his explanation.

Klass' theory was rejected by most ufologists at the time; this theory was instrumental in labeling him a "debunker", as he sought conventional explanations for a well-known UFO flap. The biggest problem with his theory was that it invoked a poorly-understood natural phenomenon to explain a mysterious one. Even today, there is no consensus of how ball lightning is produced, although many theories have been put forth. Small plasmas have been created in the laboratory, but the mechanism of forming plasma balls in nature is certainly not clear. It is interesting to note that while discussions of UFOs often mention ball lightning, articles about ball lightning often mention UFOs, showing that atmospheric physicists are aware of the connection between the phenomena.

Corona discharge was advanced more recently by Callahan and Mankin in their paper on insect swarms as glowing UFOs. [**3**] They glued live insects to Tesla coils and subjected them to various voltages. They discovered that corona discharges could be produced around the bugs in this manner, and suggested that swarms of insects flying through strong electric fields could glow and be observed as UFOs. They chose the UFO reports in the Uintah Basin as comparisons, and found that the UFO cases agreed in general description to swarms of glowing insects. [**4**]

Again, however, their proposal centered around a phenomenon that was thought to be rare. Certainly few insect swarms can glow in the described manner because of the conditions required, yet there is no question that given the proper circumstances, insects could produce UFOs. The problem is that an alternative explanation for UFOs is only as good as its mechanism. In other words, how likely was it that insects were responsible for the Uintah reports? Because the insects could glow in the laboratory, was it logical to suggest they could perform similarly in nature? A further complication was that before the proposal by Callahan and Mankin, the skeptics already had explanations for the Uintah cases: Simple Misidentification of stars, aircraft and other conventional objects. It now seems likely that only a small percentage of Uintah UFOs could have been insects, since so many other explanations are available. But which cases?

In 1975, an interesting theory about another phenomenon appeared in print, unrelated to ufology. It concerned the observation that an analysis of cases of Spontaneous Human Combustion seemed to vary in number with the strength of the earth's magnetic field. It was suggested that somehow, geophysical events were related to Fortean events. Although others had speculated about the relation, it was about this time that the idea fought for more attention. [**5**] This eventually sparked a new controversy; it seemed possible that the ETH could be defeated by using only terrestrial physics to explain UFOs.

THE TECTONIC STRAIN HYPOTHESIS

The Tectonic Strain Hypothesis (hereafter called the TSH) was developed in slightly differing forms by several groups of researchers in the USA and Britain. Both groups attempted to address the problem of UFOs by examining natural phenomena for clues to the UFOs' identities. Their jumping-off point was the recognition that some UFOs bore a strong resemblance to ball lightning and other electrical discharges. If a widespread energy source were available, then UFOs could be explainable if the source could create them.

In North America, the most prolific writer on the TSH is Michael Persinger, a physiological psychologist at Laurentian University in Sudbury, Ontario, Canada. By the time you read this, as many as thirty articles on the theme of the TSH may have been published by Persinger. [**6**] His early version of the TSH was first made available in 1977 with a book he wrote with Gyslaine Lafreniere, titled *Space-Time Transients and Unusual Events*. [**7**] The book gave the results of their statistical calculations of Fortean events occurring over the USA. In addition, they gave the results of correlations between several kinds of Fortean phenomena as well as some phenomena and the population distribution in the USA. But the most startling statements were those that indicated a relationship between Fortean events and the changing geophysical parameters of the earth in its passage around the sun. All Fortean events, they believed, could be explainable as effects produced by geophysical factors. The problem remained of how to verify such a remarkable theory.

The answer seemed to come a few years later, when Persinger published a landmark paper in the scientific journal *Perceptual and Motor Skills*. His article, titled 'Earthquake Activity and Antecedent UFO Report Numbers', received relatively little attention at the time, but eventually shook the ufological community when its implications sank in over the next several years. [**8**] Persinger, meanwhile, continued to publish many more refinements of the TSH, often in collaboration with other researchers. [**9**]

His paper on earthquake activity was quite simple in concept; it showed a statistical correlation between the numbers of UFO reports and the level of seismic activity in a specific area. There was no question of the fact that the curves produced did match quite well, and the argument seemed sound enough. Earthquakes seemed to occur before, during or after UFO sightings in a certain area.

Persinger had come up with a fascinating intepretation of his statistical results, based upon geophysical effects on human behaviour. His explanation was this:

- within the earth, rock is under stress;
- under stress, rock gives off electromagnetic radiation;
- this radiation can travel to the earth's surface;
- the radiation can become visible as a glowing mass of light;
- the light is observed as a UFO.

the effects of the radiation depend also on the distance to the observer. Far away from the radiation, the observer only sees a UFO. Closer, he or she sees "structure" in the plasma, imagining portholes, separate lights and a dome.

But the most profound effects could occur in close proximity to the plasma. Persinger has suggested that because of the intense electromagnetic fields, the plasma could affect the physiological responses of the observer, causing him or her to "visualise" an extraterrestrial contact, hearing voices, feeling imaginary objects and experiencing a totally illusory event. And, if the hapless witness was to get too close to the plasma, he or she would be subject to epileptic fits, blackouts and even death by electrocution. [**10**]

The appeal of this theory is that it does not invoke extraterrestrials or ultraterrestrials at any point, being a purely "terrestrial" explanation. All the described effects are explained in a scientific context, without going beyond the boundaries of orthodox science.

In support of the suggestion that radiation can be produced from rocks under stress, Persinger has pointed to the work of Brian Brady, of the US Geological Survey. Brady has found that core samples subjected to extreme stress in his laboratory gave off minute spark-like lights just before fracture. [**11**] It was proposed that in nature, these lights would be of much larger proportions (because of the much larger volumes of rock involved), and could be the UFOs observed by witnesses. This view was endorsed by John Derr, also with the USGS, who compared the stress plasmas with earthquake lights, something he has been studying for many years. [**12**] Earthquake lights are usually described as luminous hemispheres near the ground, preceding or during an earthquake. Several theories have been proposed regarding their creation, among them the ionization of air and other gases near the fractures. [**13**] But the TSH provides another explanation, whereby the fracturing rock produces radiation that is observed as light, and the electromagnetic field produces the observed shape of the earthquake lights. We can then visualize smaller tremors being associated with smaller lights, of "UFO proportions".

Persinger was not the only one to speculate along these lines. Most notably, Paul Devereux in Britain was also working toward a TSH-like concept. His book *Earth Lights* described how UFO reports in Britain seemed to occur near geological faults. [**14**] He suggested that this was more than coincidence, and stated that Persinger's work might apply to Britain as well. Devereux also detailed his own experiments to crush rock samples, observing luminosities in the process. [**15**] It seemed that miniature UFOs could be produced in the laboratory in agreement with the TSH, but the question remained whether nature herself could be as accommodating.

Evidence in support of the TSH came from another kind of Fortean phenomena that had been documented for many years by researchers around the world. These were the "spook lights", mysterious balls of light that seem to "haunt" certain spots around the world. Many studies of the lights have been done, and they are included in most collections of Fortean data. [**16**] Often, the lights appear in swampy areas, and are sometimes attributed to "marsh gas". (Methane is produced from decaying material at the bottom of bogs, and rises to the surface where it may spontaneously ignite and appear as softly-glowing patches of light. These lights are given other names around the world, such as "*le feu follet*", "will-o'-the-wisp" and "*ignis fatuus*". Though methane can be implicated in some UFO cases, it is unlikely to be misidentified as a bright ball of light except under extraordinary circumstances.)

Other lights seem to favour certain hills or mountains. Some are seen along a particular path or roadway, such as those at "Spooksville" in Missouri, or in the case of the Woodridge lights of Manitoba. [**17**] One site has been studied in great detail by *Vestigia*, a research group working in New Jersey. Along a certain set of railroad tracks in Washington Township, Vestigia has set up numerous pieces of equipment to record the appearance of a recurring spook light. Over several years, Vestigia has produced many photographs and its members have made many visual observations of the light from various distances and angles. [**18**] Their results were even presented to a meeting of the American Geophysical Union, with mixed reaction. [**19**] Vestigia has described their theory of "Earth stress lights", whereby stresses within the earth create electrostatic charges that ionize air. Within electromagnetic fields, the ionized air would form a plasma that would be visible as a glowing ball of light. The implication that this was the proof of the TSH seemed to be plain.

The TSH is somewhat more complicated than a simple "cause and effect" relationship. It does not say, for example, that an earthquake "causes" a UFO (or vice versa). What it does say is that there exists an underground "strain field" that both earthquakes and UFOs have in common. Because a certain volume of rock is under pressure, the volume is an irregular three-dimensional field. As the stress shifts due to various influences including floods, tidal forces and other geophysical effects, the strain field moves and deforms. Also, because strain can take a long period of time to accumulate and relax, the effects are not immediately observable. It is for this reason that a particular seismic event might be statistically correlated with a UFO sighting that may have occurred several months previous to or after the event. As well, because it is the strain field itself which is being tracked, the seismic event might be separated from the correlated UFO sighting by a considerable distance, up to several hundred kilometres.

In terms of the geophysics involved, we can see how the TSH is apparently supported by current scientific thought. We know, for example, that the sun is ultimately our primary source of energy on earth. Our daily lives are governed by the sun; the course of our civilization has been influenced by the sun. We are being constantly bathed in a sea of particles strewn from the sun, not to mention being locked safely in a habitable orbit by its gravitational field. The solar wind is deflected by the earth's own magnetic field, which varies under the influence of the heliosphere. These changes are recorded daily by sensitive instruments around the world, so we have a fair idea of how the solar-terrestrial fields interact. [20]

It seems logical, then, to assume that this influence carries further to biological systems on the earth. Do these terrestrial fields affect us, or otherwise produce visible effects? This is the essence of the TSH argument. Are these lights in the sky (or on the ground) attributable to terrestrial electromagnetism? Or can our minds be somehow affected by these forces, causing us to have visual and audial illusions?

It has been reported in scientific literature that electromagnetic radiation is in fact produced when rock is subjected to stress. Unfortunately, the magnitude and frequency of the radiation seems to vary greatly from test to test. [21] Often, there are electromagnetic precursors to earthquakes, and this has led to some speculation on seismic forecasting using electromagnetism as a tool (it is immediately obvious how important this research could be to seismologists). However, these precursors are of varying intensity and do not paint a consistent picture of how they can be employed to the benefit of scientists.

It is thought that the electrical charges build up through systems of microcracks as rock expands and contracts due to strain. [22] Underground water may play some part in this process, though, again, the actual mechanism is not clear. All that can be said at this time is that electromagnetic radiation is produced by rock stress. This may also be related to two types of luminescence: piezoelectricity and triboluminescence. The former is the mechanism by which crystals glow when compressed; the latter occurs when large numbers of particles are brought into contact with each other, creating a kind of friction. [23]

Another problem is that electromagnetic radiation is greatly attenuated in many kinds of rock. [24] This means that any radiation thus produced underground would be generally stopped from penetrating to the surface. Some suggestions have been made that electrical "channelling" might allow the charge to travel long distances before dissipating, though again, this is speculation.

Of course, before we can consider variances in strain fields, we must look at a larger perspective. The TSH has also been linked to variations in geophysical indices, indicative of changes in the sun-earth interactive magnetic fields. We may suggest that the fields interact in some fashion, producing the desired effects. Yet, what about the effects of gravity? We can easily see the effects of the solar and lunar gravity upon the earth, as evidenced by the tides. But even these effects have not been shown conclusively to be related to earthquakes. Tides cannot yet be proved coherent with earthquake occurrence, though the TSH implies that changes in another kind of solar influence, the solar wind, may be part of its mechanism.

The strongest case for the TSH is its statistical argument. There is no question that in paper after paper, the presented data show positive correlations. Usually, this means that numbers of UFOs and seismic events are plotted against time, to show they occur concurrently. However, the relationship is not necessarily one-to-one, as allowances are made for "lag" or "lead" times in the case of the earthquakes. For some reason, the correlations are stronger if seismic events ranging from several months previous to several months after a UFO sighting are included. This has been explained as a result of the mutual strain field existing over long periods of time, building up and relaxing over a certain period. [25] A UFO report in June, for example, might be correlated with an earthquake in either January or December, or any time in between. But to further complicate the matter, the correlations are said to hold true throughout a large geographical area. This space variation might mean that a UFO report might be related to an earthquake (or tremor) several hundred kilometres away. Combining the two, it could be suggested that a UFO sighting taking place today in London could be related to a seismic event in Scotland, several months ago, according to the tenets of the TSH.

Such a variance in space and time has led to some criticisms on the grounds that allowing such liberal parameters might permit the inclusion of other factors. [**26**] The rebuttal to this is that in order to understand certain phenomena, such as atmospheric physics, one must recognize subtle changes over large areas and over long periods of time. [**27**] This is the proper "increment" that is mentioned in discussions of the TSH.

The data itself is a problem, since although the geomagnetic data is taken from relatively consistent sources, the UFO data for the TSH studies is taken from places such as Fate magazine and UFOCAT. Allan Hendry has pointed out that UFOCAT cannot be used for statistical studies because of the way in which it was produced. [**28**] While some entries are case reports, many entries are newspaper articles or other published notes and lists. As well, UFOCAT was not designed to discriminate between UFOs and IFOs, so many "explained" UFO reports are included. Therefore, TSH studies using UFOCAT data inevitably include IFOs.

The consequences of this situation are that "real" seismic events are being correlated with "unreal" IFOs. Observations of aircraft or stars are shown to be related to earthquakes (separated in time and space). A possible counter-argument is that the IFOs are just the statistical "noise" which confounds researchers, whereas the "real" UFOs are the "meat" of the matter, and the correlations hold true because the true unidentifieds are in fact correlated with the seismic events. [**29**] But we can wonder to what extent this may hold true; most ufologists recognize that the vast majority of UFO reports are explainable, and it is these that constitute the "noise". What is remarkable is that unsorted UFO/IFO mixtures and sorted UFO reports vary together over time, suggesting something more than a slight similarity. [**30**] It can be argued that our selection of "noise" does not differ from "meat" in certain respects.

Statistics are a very useful tool for analysing data. The meaning of the statistics, however, is open to intepretation to researchers. Since there generally is no fault with the statistics themselves, errors can be attributable only to the data used in the calculations. Sometimes, errors of interpretation can lead to bizarre results. One fine example of misintepretation of association is the observation that there is a positive correlation between the number of storks' nests and the number of births in Europe. We can conclude that more storks are bringing babies, or that as population increases, so does the number of buildings and the number of chimneys around which the birds can roost. Another example is the story of a man who wrote a letter to an airline requesting that their pilots refrain from turning on the "Fasten Seat Belts" sign, since each time it goes on, the turbulence increases. In both examples, though the statistics themselves were not flawed, the interpretation was erroneous. [**31**]

Similarly, even if UFOs and seismic events are positively correlated, the evidence that they are actually related is still forthcoming. In early statistical studies in support of the TSH, numbers of UFOs were correlated with seismic activity or earthquakes within about 150 kilometres of the sighting locations. However, in one recent study, because there were no seismic events within this range to correlate with a large concentration of UFO reports, the range was increased to 1000 kilometres in order to find correlatable events. [**32**] This was qualified by noting that different UFO sighting locations possess different geological characteristics, and that some areas would be able to support larger strain fields than others. Though this seems a rational deliberation, considering the large distance scale involved and the complex nature of sub-surface rock formations, this could also be construed as only a hand-waving argument.

The statement that UFOs may be miniature earthquake lights is also worth considering. John Derr has suggested that UFOs might be representative of very mild tremors, of magnitudes less than 2 on the Richter Scale, possibly even below magnitude 1. [**33**] However, such tremors are virtually lost in background noise, and cannot be detected by most seismic stations (with exception to the detailed networks in Southern California, for example). This begs the question of how such a relatively minor release of energy could create a plasma-like UFO in the air above the ground, allowing that a physical mechanism to produce the UFO exists. Also, since such tremors are always occurring, it is not obvious why UFOs are not constantly being observed, especially over seismically-active areas.

Another consequence of the TSH is that it suggests that natural radiation affects us in several ways, and that we can become temporarily "unbalanced" by this radiation, causing our brain to create false realities. To the ufologist, this means that UFO witnesses are hallucinating, but on a much grander scale, this means much more to the psychologist. Neatly, the TSH can explain psychotic behaviour by having this natural radiation affecting the minds of sane persons and rendering them insane. Indeed, it has already been said that the TSH offers a way to explain such things as religious fervour by the brain's reaction to outside radiation. [**34**] (We can wonder, though, whether we can expand the TSH to include man-made radiation. Certainly people living in close proximity to a radio transmitter would be affected by its output, if the premise of the TSH were to hold true.)

Finally, it should be noted that UFOs are not the only phenomena that are correlated with strain fields. Paranormal and Fortean events have also been postulated to be related to rock stress and geophysical factors such as solar flares. [35] In a very broad sense, then, the TSH may be used to explain all Fortean events, regardless of location, intensity and frequency of occurrence.

CONCLUSIONS

In summary, the Tectonic Strain Hypothesis poses an interesting problem for the scientist. As a hypothesis, the concept of explaining UFOs in terms of a natural geophysical mechanism is quite appealing, since it appears that it is a testable idea. In theory, it should be possible to verify whether UFOs are caused by underground strain fields.

However, while strained rock certainly exists, the strain field itself is a mystery at this time. Its behaviour cannot be predicted from the meagre evidence available, mostly because of the complex nature of rock formations. Before proceeding to use strain fields to explain a puzzling phenomenon, we must assume that such fields actually exist. Then, these fiels must generate energy in some poorly-understood fashion, releasing it into the environment and wreaking havoc with human sensory processes. Beyond explaining nocturnal lights, all degress of close encounter cases can be solved in terms of effects upon the human body, the ground (trace cases) or the air (angel hair).

In the wake of the TSH, psychologists are left to explain why witnesses would be so consistent in their descriptions of their UFO experiences. Because of the complex nature of our society, it is likely that many variables would have roles in making the UFO phenomenon what it is, and account for such elements as flaps and space-time distributions of cases over geographical areas.

But it is the mechanism that eludes us more than any other aspect of the TSH. While it might seem plausible that the constituent elements of the TSH follow each other to produce a rational argument in creating UFOs, the connections are not at all secure from a scientific standpoint. Even Persinger and Derr admit that: "There is still no direct evidence to support the existence of strain fields." [36] Since these fields are the foundation of the TSH, we can wonder why the TSH continues to support an undefined mechanism. It may in fact be easier to admit that UFOs are caused by extra- or ultra-terrestrials.

Some of the most damaging evidence against the TSH is its use of unsorted data to produce correlations. It is interesting how misidentifications of astronomical and aeronautical objects could be used in statistical correlations with geophysical phenomena to produce positive results. Certainly the use of long "lag" and "lead" periods to allow such correlations is questionable on the grounds that these periods can allow other factors to creep into the data. Given that a seismic event were to occur in a certain area, then to have a UFO be observed in that same area would seem to bear out the premise of the TSH (why should there be "lags" or "leads" at all, if the strain field is releasing energy?) But if the UFO is in reality an IFO, the data may not be valid at all. [37]

Paul Devereux has argued in favour of the TSH as an American counterpart to his earth lights theory. Yet, he has not wholly accepted his association with the TSH as an integral part of geophysical UFO theory. He admits that he has not employed statistical analysis to UFO and seismic data, but that he supports Persinger's analyses in principle. As well, his own experiments with fracturing rock have shown that anomalous lights can produce his speculated effects. These and other studies have been said to leave "no room for doubt" that the tectonic strain theory of UFOs reflects a real physical mechanism. [38] Yet there have been no indisputable, published experimental results that bear out this faith in the TSH.

This is not to say that the TSH has no merit. It employs scientific techniques and research in an earnest investigation into the UFO phenomenon, examining data for patterns and correlations, with a fresh approach. Persinger and Devereux should be commended for presenting their findings to the scientific community and to Fortean researchers for their consideration. There is no reason at all why some fraction of UFOs cannot be explained in terms of radiation released by rock stresses or fractures. In the short time that the TSH has been in existence it has gone through several improvements and changes to accommodate the few criticisms that have been leveled at it. [39] Until a physical mechanism can be clearly established and statistical arguments are relegated to a back-up position, the TSH must be regarded as what it was originally proposed to be - a hypothesis. Perhaps, in time, research by groups such as Vestigia will raise the status of the TSH, but until then, we are left with many unanswered questions, some asked by its own authors.

REFERENCES

■ 1 - There are several sources for descriptions of Green Fireballs. A good start is: **Ruppelt,** Edward J. *The Report on Unidentified Flying Objects* (Doubleday, NY, 1956) Chapter 4, pp.47-59. ■ 2 - **Klass,** Philip J. "Plasma Theory May Explain Many UFOs", *Aviation Week & Space Technology,* August 22 1966, pp.48-61. Also: "Many UFOs Are Identified as Plasmas", *Aviation Week & Space Technology,* Oct 3 1966, pp.54-73. ■ 3 - **Callahan,** Philip S. and **Mankin,** R.W. "Insects as Unidentified Flying Objects", *Applied Optics,* v.17, no.21, 1978, pp.3355-3360. However, the idea had been proposed over ten years earlier by Norton T. Novitt. His theory was presented in: **Soule,** Gardner. *UFOs and IFOs* (G.P. Putnam's Sons, NY, 1967). Chapter 19: "Could UFOs be Bugs?" pp.137-140. ■ 4 - Frank **Salisbury**'s fascinating studies of the Uintah Basin UFOs were detailed in: *The Utah UFO Display* (Devin-Adair, NY, 1974). He personally favoured the extraterrestrial hypothesis as an explanation for the major flap in that area. ■ 5 - **Gearhart,** Livingstone. "Geomagnetic Storms and Fortean Events", *Pursuit,* v.8, 1975, pp.38-40. However, F. LaGarde had earlier studied French UFO data and found that: "UFO sightings occur by preference on geologic faults." Quoted in **Devereux,** Paul (Reference 14), p.187. ■ 6 - The articles on the TSH by Michael **Persinger** are too numerous to include in a reference list such as this. His papers have appeared in each volume of the journal *Perceptual and Motor Skills* since v.53, 1981, although his first TSH-related paper in that journal was: "Transient geophysical bases for ostensible UFO-related phenomena and associated verbal behaviour?" v.43, 1976, pp.215-221. Other selected papers will be cited throughout this chapter. ■ **7** - **Persinger,** Michael A. and **Lafreniere,** Gyslaine F. *Space-Time Transients and Unusual Events* (Nelson-Hall, Chicago, 1977). ■ **8** - **Persinger,** Michael A. "Earthquake Activity and Antecedent UFO Report Numbers", *Perceptual and Motor Skills,* v.50, pp.791-797. ■ **9** - For example: **Persinger,** Michael A. and **Derr,** John S. "Geophysical Variables and Behavior: XXIII. Relations Between UFO Reports Within the Uintah Basin and Local Seismicity", *Perceptual and Motor Skills,* v.60, 1985, pp.143-152. This is an interesting paper because it uses an Appendix in Salisbury's book, not the actual case reports, to correlate with the seismic events. ■ **10** - **Persinger,** Michael A. "Geophysical Variables and Behavior: IX. Expected Clinical Consequences of Close Proximity to UFO-related Luminosities", *Perceptual and Motor Skills,* v.56, 1983, pp.259-265. ■ **11** - Although Brady's work is often cited, his results have not been published. His work was alluded to on several occasions, including the following statement by Persinger on the Canadian Broadcasting Corporation (CBC), on the national science program: *Quirks and Quarks,* Nov.8, 1980: "Dr. Brian Brady and his colleagues at the Department of the Interior in Denver, Colorado, have demonstrated in the laboratory the same kind of luminosities occurring before fractures in rock samples. Now mind you, because the rock sample is very small, the luminosities occur just a few milliseconds before. In very large areas the luminosities would be expected to be delayed by the appropriate amount of time - in this case months to even years before the tremor." Brady also appeared on the infamous NOVA episode on UFOs, giving a demonstration of his experiment for the cameras. He apparently also solved the remarkable New Zealand Kiakoura UFO incident when he discovered that the flight path of the planes involved followed a major geological fault, suggesting that the TSH was responsible. ■ **12** - **Derr,** John S. "Earthquake Lights", *Earthquake Information Bulletin,* v.9, no.3, pp.18-21. Derr was interviewed at a meeting of the American Geophysical Union, and his comments on earthquake lights as UFOs appeared in: **Simon,** C. "Looking Out for Luminous Phenomena", *Science News,* v.124, 1983, p.412. As an APRO consultant, he has prepared several reports regarding specific aspects of UFOs. ■ **13** - For example: **Lockner,** D.A., et al. "A Mechanism to Explain the Generation of Earthquake Lights", *Nature,* v.302, 1983, pp.28-33. ■ **14** - **Devereux,** Paul. *Earth Lights* (Turnstone Press, Wellingborough, England, 1982). ■ **15** - **Devereux,** Paul, et al. "Bringing UFOs Down to Earth", *New Scientist,* Sept.1 1983, pp.627-630. Devereux is also involved with a group called The Dragon Project which is investigating the telluric forces and fields associated with standing stones, ley lines and UFOs. ■ **16** - For example: **Coleman,** Loren. *Mysterious America* (Faber & Faber, Boston, 1983). ■ **17** - **Loftin,** Bob. *Spooksville's Ghost Lights* (private publication, undated). The Woodridge lights are described in: *Winnipeg Free Press,* Dec.5 1972, p.6, and are noted in several Fortean lists. ■ **18** - Vestigia's work has been noted in several sources, including: **Coleman,** Loren. *Curious Encounters* (Faber & Faber, Boston, 1985, pp.81-84). Also: **Bearden,** Thomas E. *Excalibur Briefing* (Strawberry Hill Press, San Francisco, 1980, pp.9-16). Definitive information is given in its *Vestigia Newsletter,* published over the last decade. ■ **19** - **Wagner,** W.S. and **Visvanathan,** T.R. "'Earthquake Lights': A Potential Aid in Earthquake Forecasting", *EOS,* v.59, 1978, p.329. ■ **20** - This is a gross over-simplification of the effects. How these effects can be analysed is detailed in: **Mayaud,** P.N. *Derivation, meaning, and Use of Geomagnetic Indices (Geophysical Monograph 22),* American Geophysical Union, Wahington DC, 1980. ■ **21** - Some relevant articles are: **Gokhberg,** M.B. et al. "Radiofrequency Radiation During Earthquakes", *Doklady Akademiia Nauk SSSR,* v.248, 1981, pp.32-35. **Demin,** V.M. et al. "Nature of Mechanoelectric Radiation From Ore Bodies". *Doklady Akademiia Nauk SSSR,* v.260, 1983, pp.306-309. ■ **22** - **Mizutani,** H. et al. "Electrokinetic Phenomena Associated with Earthquakes", *Geophysical Research Letters,* v.3, no.7, 1976, pp.365-368. ■ **23,** -These mechanisms are noted in Devereux et al, already cited in Reference 15. ■ **24** - **Hill,** D.A. "Radio Propagation in a Coal Seam and the Inverse Problem", *Journal of Research of the National Bureau of Standards,* v.89, no.5, 1984, pp.385-394. ■ **25** - **Persinger,** Michael A. "Geophysical Variables and Behavior: IV. UFO Reports and Fortean Phenomena: Temporal Correlations in the Central USA", *Perceptual and Motor Skills,* v.54, 1982, pp.299-302. ■ **26** - **Rutkowski,** Chris A. "Geophysical Variables and Human Behavior: Some Criticisms", *Perceptual and Motor Skills,* v.58, 1984, pp.840-842. However, even Devereux has pointed out problems with Persinger's analyses, in *Earth Lights* (Reference 14), p.73. ■ **27** - A rebuttal appeared as: **Persinger,** Michael A. "Geophysical Variables and Behavior: XXVI. A Response to Rutkowski's Critique of the Tectonic Strain Hypothesis for UFO Phenomena", *Perceptual and Motor Skills,* v.60, 1985, pp.575-582. ■ **28** - **Hendry,** Allan. *The UFO Handbook* (Doubleday & Co., NY, 1979, p.247). ■ **29** - This argument has been employed by Persinger in his defense of the TSH. ■ **30** - **Rutkowski,** Chris A. *The UFOROM Datafile - MANUFOCAT* (private publication, Winnipeg, Canada, 1983). ■ **31** - Many other examples are clearly presented in: **Campbell,** Stephen K. *Flaws and Fallacies in Statistical Thinking* (Prentice-Hall, NJ, 1974). The given examples are noted on pp.172-173. Campbell shows how easy it is to misinterpret statistics and receive erroneous results, even using "correct" equations. ■ **32** - **Persinger,** Michael A. and **Derr,** John S. "Geophysical Variables and Behavior: XXXII. Evaluations of UFO Reports in an Area of Infrequent Seismicity: The Carman, Manitoba Episode", *Perceptual and Motor Skills,* v.61, 1985, pp.807-813. ■ **33** - **Simon,** C. "Looking Out for Luminous Phenomena", *Science News,* v.124, p.412. ■ **34** - **Persinger,** Michael A. "Religious and Mystical Experiences as Artifacts of Temporal Lobe Function: A General Hypothesis", *Perceptual and Motor Skills,* v.57, 1983, pp.1255-1262.

■ **35** - **Schaut,** G.B. and **Persinger,** Michael A. "Geophysical Variables and Behavior: XXI. Global Geomagnetic Activity During Spontaneous Paranormal Experiences: A Replication", *Perceptual and Motor Skills,* v.61, 1985, pp.412-414. ■ **36** - See reference 32, p.813. ■ **37** - **Rutkowski,** Chris A. "Geophysical Variables and Behavior: XXXIV. Further Comments", *Perceptual and Motor Skills,* v.63, 1986, p.18. ■ **38** - **Devereux,** Paul. [letter] *CUFOS Associate Newsletter,* v.6, no.2, 1985, pp.2-3. ■ **39** - Other published criticisms include: **Bullard,** Thomas. *Mysteries in the Eye of the Beholder* (PhD Thesis, Indiana University, 1982), p.564. As well, Steuart **Campbell** has published several critical comments about Devereux's Earth Lights theory, resulting in a lively debate. For example, a letter in New Scientist, Dec.15 1983, p.799, started some interesting discussion.

4.3.3

BRITISH SPOOKLIGHTS

by David Clarke & Granville Oldroyd

■ **DAVID CLARKE**. Born Sheffield, England, 19 years ago. Currently studying Archaeology & Prehistory at the University of Sheffield. An active member of the Sheffield Society for Research in the Paranormal, South Yorks & North Derbyshire Earth Mysteries Group, and ASSAP. His interests are fell-walking, rock-climbing, folklore, ecology, and 'the preservation & restoration of our ancient heritage.
■ **UFO involvement**: He is South Yorkshire area investigator for BUFORA. Particular interests: all aspects of historical research, especially airship scares and other rumour-generated events; the geophysical aspects of UFO sightings. A contributor to Bolide, and more regularly to WYUFOG's *UFO Brigantia*, and is involved in its 'Project Pennine.'
■ **Publications**: With G Oldroyd, *Spooklights: a British Survey* (1985). In preparation: *1913 Airship Scare catalogue*, (co-author) for FUFOR; a publication on legends and earth mysteries of S. Yorks and N. Derbyshire; and *Strange Sheffield*, for ASSAP's Project Albion. Joint editor of *Northern Earth mysteries*.
■ **Address**: 6 Old Retford Road / Handsworth / Sheffield S13 9QZ / England.

■ **H GRANVILLE OLDROYD**: Born Grange-over-Sands, 1942. Outside his occupation as a self-employed gardener, researches railway history and is active in steam engine preservation, possessing a 10-ton steam road roller of his own.
■ **UFO involvement**: Research into historical aspects of the UFO phenomenon, notably pre-1914 airship scares considered in their political and social aspects; and World War One rumours for possible similarities with the UFO belief system. Has himself witnessed several UFO events.
■ **Publications**: With David Clarke, *Spooklights, a British Survey* (1985); collaborator (with Nigel Watson) in the forthcoming *1913 airship scare catalogue* (FUFOR).
■ **Address**: 16 Longlands Lane / Heysham / Morecambe LA3 2NS / England.

"I am told, though, that so many people have seen objects that looked like spaceships that 'there must be something in it'... Maybe there is, but think of all the people in the history of the world who have seen ghosts and spirits and angels. It's not what you see that is suspect, but how you interpret what you see."
Dr. Isaac Asimov, 1966.

Since the beginning of recorded history man has been puzzled and fascinated by strange lights in the night sky. They come and go, and their appearances have become woven into the legends and folklore of cultures throughout the world. Only in recent years - since 1947 - has the modern myth of extraterrestrial visitations been attached to these lights which, to earlier generations, were attributed to spirits of the dead, mischievous elements or omens of disaster. Although scientists have consistently failed to face up to the challenge of studying and analysing this abstract and paradoxical problem, there is obviously much of interest to be discovered from such a venture. For behind the mass of eyewitness testimony there undoubtedly lurks solid evidence for an unknown natural phenomenon with inherent potential to revolutionise our current conception of space and time.

Throughout the ages these manifestations have always been interpreted in the light of the contemporary cultural frame of reference. Primitive societies view the strange lights as evil spirits and signs from the Gods, and regard spots haunted by the lights as sacred places where burials were made and temples were erected. Prior to the 19th century countrydwellers in Europe, especially in the Celtic countries, saw the lights as fairies, boggarts and other supernatural creatures, and regarded their haunts with awe and respect. Scientists of the day dismissed these lights as superstitious nonsense and explained eyewitness accounts as caused by marsh gas or "Will o' the Wisp" although no one has yet explained, captured or recreated a will o' the wisp in the laboratory or convincingly explained how one can be produced from any amount of decaying matter present in marshes. Nowadays that will o' the wisp has disappeared from the countryside it has become fashionable to explain the sightings as ball lightning (which, like will o' the wisp, raises more questions than it answers), or as visitors from outer space.

SPOOKLIGHTS IN FOLKLORE

There can be little doubt that many present-day UFO sightings accounts would have, in past ages, been attributed to Will o' the Wisp or Jack o' Lantern. Indeed, a recent encyclopaedia description of the phenomenon has noted that "it has given rise to many superstitions and figures in the folklore of many countries and probably has accounted for some of the reported sightings of 'flying saucers'". The scientific term for these lights was "*ignis fatuus*", meaning 'foolish fire', so-called according to Blount's *Popular Superstitions* "because it only feareth fools... Hence it is, when men are led away with some idle fancy or conceit, we used to say an ignis fatuus hath done it..

Dancing in murky night o'er fen and lake,
He glows to draw you downward to your death,
In his bewitch'd low, marshy, willow brake... "

This alludes to the most durable part of the legend - i.e. that the lights deliberately lead people to their deaths by enticing them to follow across bogs and fens. In Brand's *Popular Antiquities* is given the story of "a respectable person in Herefordshire"..(who) "presuming upon (his) knowledge of the grounds about his house, was tempted one dark night to follow one of these lights, which he saw flying over a piece of fallow ground. It led him over a ploughed field, flying and twisting about from place to place - sometimes it would suddenly disappear, and as suddenly appear again. It once made directly to a hedge and when it came near it mounted over, and he lost sight of it after a full hour's chase. On his return home he saw it again, but was already too much fatigued to think of renewing the pursuit."

Although the marsh lights have been "explained" conclusively through the ages as mere pockets of ignited methane no one has yet shown, according to a recent investigation [1], "how to achieve natural ignition of intermittent, disconnected bubbles of gas rising through the marsh." Furthermore, countryfolk have always regarded these phenomena as manipulations of some intelligence - fairy, boggart or some other malicious elemental, who took delight in enticing lost souls to their deaths. Even today, children place candles inside hollow turnips on All Hallow's Eve, to represent the evil spirit or Jack o' Lanthorn. These beliefs explain the curious vernacular names given to lights seen in particular regions of the British Isles - Hob o' Lantern, Jenny Burntail, Friar's Lantern, Joan-in-the-Wad, Kitty with his Candlestick, etc. These names all refer to the elementals said to control the lights.

In *Nature's Secrets*, a 17th century document, *ignis fatuus* is described as "the lowest meteor in the air (which) is the burning candle, or as some call it, Ignis Fattus. These pallid fires appear but at some times of the year, and that in certain places: and in those parts where they are most usual they are not commonly seen, but as forerunners of sultry heat in summer, and wet in winter, they are usually observed to appear in open weather."

Many obscure locations throughout the world have peculiar legends attached to them describing the appearances of strange lights, often spanning several centuries, around particular spots - more often than not ancient churches, old burial grounds, quarries and prominent local landmarks.

SPOOKLIGHTS ANCIENT SITES

Folklore clearly indicates that prehistoric sites - tumuli, standing stones and stone circles especially - were regarded as the haunts of elves, ghosts and the little folk by country dwellers. There is mounting evidence that at least some ancient sites were deliberately constructed upon spots that were traditionally known to generate or attract unusual phenomena by the ancient people. T. Sington, writing in *English Mechanic* (1919) speculated that "owing to some local conditions at present unknown... such lights would have attracted the attention of the inhabitants, who would have attached great significance to them, and might then have selected the site as a place of worship or sacrifice." He gives as evidence his own sighting of mysterious white lights in the vicinity of the ancient and spectacular Castlerigg Stone Circle, high in the Cumbrian fells over Keswick. Walking with a companion back to a hotel after an ascent of Helvellyn one pitch black night before the First World War they had seen a "rapidly moving light as bright as the acetylene lamp of a bicycle" cross the road above their heads near the stone circle. Afterwards they saw a number of similar lights moving around directly in the direction of the circle. At one point one of these lights came straight to the spot where the observers were standing - as it approached them "it slowed down, stopped, quivered, and slowly went out, as if the matter producing the light had become exhausted." [2]

Our own research into a particular spot on the western outskirts of Sheffield, South Yorkshire (a road connecting the villages of Worrall and Loxley), where unusual low-level lights have been observed over a long period of time have revealed to our surprise that the same spot, a sandstone outcrop called Loxley Edge on Wadsley Common, used to be the location of a megalithic standing stone called "the Landin Stone", destroyed in the 18th century when the site was turned into a quarry but marked for many years by a gibbet where notorious murderers were executed - adding to the eeriness of an already much-haunted spot. This connection with graveyards and burial grounds perhaps gave rise to the "Corpse Candle" tradition commonly heard of in Celtic countries. The Gaelic-speaking peoples traditionally regarded all spooklights as forewarnings of death, and in India a religious caste known as the Shanars believe old burial grounds are haunted by 'devil fires', known in Tamil as 'pey-neruppu' who are often seen gliding over marshy land as flickering lights. Around Darjeeling these lights are known as 'chota-admis', which the natives believe are borne by little underground people who walk or fly around at night carrying lanterns. To come upon such a creature unexpectedly was regarded as a sure sign of impending death.

HAUNTED SPOTS

Reservoirs, lakes and other stretches of water also appear to have a peculiar attraction for mystery lights and in more recent years for UFOs, particularly in the Pennine hills of Yorkshire. In 1912 the Earl of Erne, of Crom Castle, Co. Fermanagh, Ireland, wrote to the London *Daily Mail* to describe the appearances of a strange light over Lough Erne, nearby. "This light has been seen at intervals several times within the last six or seven years by 'all sorts and conditions of men' and women too. It is of a yellow colour, and in size and shape very much the same as a motor-car lamp. It travels at a considerable pace along the top of the water - sometimes against the wind, at other times with it. It lights up all objects within a certain radius and disappears as quickly as it appears." [**3**]

A similar light is said to have appeared over the lonely hillsides surrounding the small hamlets of Burton Dasset and Fenny Compton in South Warwickshire during the years 1923 and 1924. Although local folk had been whispering stories about the strange wandering lights since the middle of the 19th century, it was not until 1923 when the frequent appearance of "the light" around the old Saxon churchyard on the hillside reached the columns of the local and national press that the mystery came to the attention of outsiders. One local resident described the spectral light as "a strong and dazzling light like a motor-car headlight... a perfectly lovely sight, it flitted about and passed through bushes and over fences at a great speed; then with a final flash it disappeared."

The sightings at Burton Dassett (Saxon meaning: "abode of wild beasts") are worthy of particular attention as following newspaper publicity early in 1923 intense interest in the mystery was aroused and hordes of curious ghost-hunters descended upon the hills to catch a glimpse of the light. At least three visiting journalists actually saw the phenomenon, which one described as "well defined and spherical, it moved across our field of vision with its peculiar switchback motion from left to right disappearing as quick as it had come... like a dull yellow eye, it was glowering at us apparently from beneath a nearby tree... " The Burton Dassett "ghost" appeared to centre its attentions around the pre-Norman All Saints Church, and the ancient Beacon Tower on the highest point of the hills nearby. It was from this tower that another visiting journalist saw the light "fully a mile away, but its radiance was such that the sky was faintly illuminated for several miles... the light itself was steady and vivid, but the wide beams that were thrown upwards flickered like a failing lamp... " Between these two above named points are outcrops of iron-bearing rocks which have been extensively quarried, and the Burton Dassett faultline, with a downthrow of 65 feet, lies to the northeast. These are important clues which may help to explain the phenomenon, for on the same night in January, 1924, when the ghostly light made its most spectacular appearance an earthtremor was shaking the nearby counties of Herefordshire and Worcestershire. [**4**]

EARTHLIGHTS

The appearances of strange lights at places such as Burton Dassett may perhaps be explained by reference to the theory proposed by Paul Devereux in his landmark work *Earthlights* (Turnstone Press, 1982). Basically, this suggested that unusual lights, including those under the modern interpretation of UFOs, are plasma-like blobs of energy 'created' by frictional discharges from rocks in zones of geological faulting. In this way spooklights are "created" by electromagnetic leakage from the strain generated in faultlines during the period leading up to an earth tremor. Dr. Michael Persinger, a Canadian scientist, has specified certain features around which these electrical fields could produce visible luminosities - including hills, point sources and towers, reservoirs and powerlines (we would add quarries, railway lines and moving automobiles). Persinger also identifies several 'trigger' events which may spark off this effect, including changes in air pressure, the passage of frontal systems and gravitational influences such as sunspots and near approaches of the moon [**5**] which may cause strain to be generated in faultlines.

These lights appear to be surrounded by strong electromagnetic fields which seem to cause interference with radio reception and car engines; specific concentrations of this energy could well have many untold effects upon humans and animals who happen to be in the right place at the right time or who get too close to one of these dazzling lights. Persinger & Devereux have suggested that if these lights are capable of effecting electrical apparatus then they may be able to stimulate the production of hallucinatory imagery within the electric circuits of the human brain - perhaps resulting in something akin to an epileptic fit in some cases, and some kind of "inner illumination" in others. Many witnesses do experience physical symptoms following sightings - including conjunctivitis, nausea, drowsiness, dehydration and exhaustion. In each case individual witnesses will superimpose, or manipulate what they see to produce alien spaceships, images of the Virgin Mary, German airships or denizens of fairyland depending upon the predominant cultural perception of the unknown. This may explain why Catholic cultures see religious visions while technological cultures interpret the same stimulus - a flashing light - as the marvellous spacemen from Andromeda.

Further intensive research is continuing throughout the world into this fascinating and all-inclusive theory which so far has been the only convincing explanation put forward linking the objective part of the phenomenon with the subjective. Moreover, it is a developing idea that is changing with time - the famous "piezo-electric effect" has now been replaced by triboluminescence or TLS as the phsyical process whereby the 'earthlights' are produced. TLS is a "cold light" emission of visible radiation due to frictional forces causing electrons to jump from higher to lower energy levels. Experiments in which granite cores have been crushed in laboratories have produced luminous phenomena which could be explained as TLS, and which perhaps could be replicated on a larger scale in nature.

Although sightings of strange aerial lights since the year 1947 have been distorted by the current cultural myth surrounding (imaginary?) visitors from outer space, the underlying objective phenomenon remains the same. By 1967 American UFO investigator John Keel had realised that behind the illusory spacecraft there lurked "the real phenomenon", what he called "soft objects". ie. "sightings of transparent or translucent objects seemingly capable of altering their size and shape dramatically... most of these objects (are) temporary manipulations of matter and energy." [**6**] One of the most famous UFO sightings of recent years - the procession of brilliant lights that buzzed a freight plane flying between Wellington & Christchurch on the east coast of New Zealand on New Year's Eve, 1978 - can probably be explained by the geophysical hypothesis. Dr. Brian Brady of the US Bureau of Mines realised that the aircraft was flying parallel to the Alpine Fault - one of the major geological faults surrounding the Pacific - when the strange lights were observed. Similar correlations have been noticed between UFO sightings on the West Coast of the USA and the nearby active San Andreas Faultline.

THE PENNINE CONNECTION

In recent years UFOlogists in the north of England have been working to isolate and analyse a recurring phenomenon - known in local folkore as "the phantom helicopter", but in reality a brilliant ball of orange light - which has been seen by thousands of witnesses throughout the Pennine area. This particular phenomenon has been described consistently by so many people that there can be little doubt that it is a form of natural energy indigenous to the Pennine hills. It seems to have a partiality for reservoirs, lonely moorlands and hilltops, quarries, point sources and powerlines. These sightings appear to come in measurable waves, not always accompanied by waves of media attention. Concentrations of reports emanate each year from the moorland districts between Lancashire and Yorkshire - stretching from the Rossendale Valley across the moors and hills to the northeast to the Craven District around Skipton and Grassington (both areas riddled with faultlines & quartz-bearing rock), as far east as Ilkley Moor and Bradford. Although the more recent sightings have been clouded and distorted by the climate of 30 years' belief in space travel, waves of these sightings can be traced back centuries in the same areas always in different contexts - fairy lore, witchcraft scares, German signallers, phantom airships, etc. Intrepid UFO investigators who have been searching for evidence of "nuts and bolts" spaceships around Grassington and Carleton Moor have talked to local farmers who have been watching funny lights bobbing and weaving over the contours of the local hills for generations. Obviously these lights are not extraterrestrial vehicles, but terrestrial energy forms.

Similar lights appeared all over the country upon the outbreak of the First World War, and in 1915 military intelligence officers on Dartmoor were being led astray by Will o' the Wisps thought at the time to have been lights sent up by German spies. At 9.30 p.m. on September 4th, 1915, Lieutenant Colonel W.P. Drury, sent to track down to spies to their lair, saw "a bright white light considerably larger than a planet, steadily ascend from [a] meadow to an approximate height of 50 or 60 feet," whilst observing Dartmoor from a spot near Dartington Point. "Its course was clearly visible against the dark background of wood and hill," said Drury in his official report to the War Office,"... we were within a mile of the light and saw its ascension and transit distinctly... " [**7**]

During the 1914-1918 war any strange light in the night sky was interpreted as German signallers at work, as nowadays it would be put down to a UFO. In both instances the reports come in waves. The process has now gone one step further in that we are producing our own imagery (as in the close encounters), with or without the help of a non-human intelligence. The commencement of the Great War provided a stimulus for the belief in German signallers at work in Britain, but where was the stimulus in 1947, for space travel was not firmly rooted in the human consciousness until the mid-1950s. Perhaps we are capable of producing a belief system similar to the UFO one by ourselves. Was this capability utilized by a non-human (but not necessarily extra-terrestrial) intelligence for its own ends in 1947?

CONCLUSIONS

"We stopped and watched it for a while, then tried to walk around it, but it would move over and head us off. When we walked forward it backed up, and when we backed up it came towards us. Then we stood there with that thing about a dozen feet in front of us as silent as death itself. It was transparent. We could see a bunch of sagebrush through its body... we could see no body resembling bird or animal, nor could we see anything resembling legs to hold it up. It was just a ball of light, yet apparently this strange object could see us and it checked our every move."
- eyewitness account. [**8**]

Abundant evidence has now been collected to enable us to prove the existence of these luminous objects, or beings - which Jenny Randles has labelled "UAPs" (unidentified atmospheric phenomena). They have many notable characteristics - they are predominantly ball-shaped, with diameters varying from 10cm to more than 5 metres, though are more probably amorphous or gaseous in composition (i.e. many reports describe them passing through fences and hedgerows, which may have given rise to apparition reports such as the famous "White Lady" of ghostlore). Sometimes they appear to resemble giant human eyes, or brilliant motor-car headlights and pulsate internally. Close observers often see two lights above one another, one a kind of reflection of the brighter light "bobbing up and down as if on elastic". Others are composed of numerous small lights, which may split up into smaller combinations and then rejoin the main mass. They always display inquisitive or elusive behaviour and seemingly have an awareness of observers' movements and thoughts - reacting especially to intense enthusiasm and emotional excitement (e.g. the phenomena accompanying the Welsh Revival in 1905), in a way similar to poltergeist manifestations.

Primitive folk legends worldwide indicate that the lights "live" normally underground and only emerge on certain occasions - usually thunderstorms and earthquakes. Those legends also indicate that the lights are capable of metamorphosis, i.e. are shape-shifters and have the ability to materialise and dematerialise at will. It is hard to avoid the suggestion that the lights are living beings possessed of some kind of rudimentary intelligence. Various forms of "Sky Animal" theory were proposed by John P. Bessor, the Countess Wassilo-Serecki, and Trevor James Constable in the 1950s, and may even have been considered by the US Air Force as an explanation for certain UFO sightings, for a 1949 USAF report reads: "The possible existence of some sort of strange, extraterrestrial animals has also been... considered. Many of these objects acted more like animals than anything else." [**8**]

It could be that the lights are simply reacting to changes in the environment which merely give the impression of intelligent control. They may be responding to changes in the earth's magnetic field, temperature variations, and air density. Plants react to changes in temperature, light and the length of days without the need of intelligent action on their part. Some flowers, for instance, open only during sunshine. Perhaps, however, we should not be too hasty to dismiss the idea of intelligence, for they may have intelligence of a totally different kind to anything else we have hitherto encountered.

Whatever these phenomena may represent, there is no doubt that they exist and that they deserve a full-scale scientific investigation to determine their true nature. This has not been forthcoming due to the discouraging outer-space connotations given to all UFO reports, whatever their explanation. These strange lights are still appearing to this day throughout the world, and there is little doubt that future generations will continue to gaze with wonder at their mystical illumination of the night skies. Maybe one day, long after visitors from outer-space have been forgotten, and when the human race has come to a fuller understanding of the mysterious processes operating upon our mother planet will we be able to comprehend their *true* nature and significance.

NOTES AND REFERENCES

■ **1** - "Will o' the Wisp", by A.A. **Mills**, *Chemistry in Britain* 16:69, February, 1980. ■ **2** - "A Mystery", by T. **Sington**, *English Mechanic*, October 17, 1919, pg 152-153. ■ **3** - "The Yellow Light", London *Daily Mail* December 25, 1912. ■ **4** - For a full account of the Warwickshire sightings, see the David Clarke's *Spooklights: A British Survey* (Privately published, 1985), pgs 19-36. ■ **5** - The "Waimea Lights" which appear on the north central part of Hawaii, "are said to appear on the first two or three nights of the full moon close to midnight". See *Mysterious Fires & Lights*, by Vincent **Gaddis** (Dell, 1967), pg 77. ■ **6** - "The Principle of Transmogrification", by John **Keel**, *Flying Saucer Review*, Vol 15, No 4 (June-July, 1968), pgs 27-31. ■ **7** - PRO Admiralty 131/119 pp 343-346, December 6, 1915. ■ **8** - *Mysterious Fires & Lights*, by Vincent **Gaddis**, pg 91.

4.3.4

ALTERNATIVE THEORIES: THE SEARCH FOR THE GRAIL

by Dennis Stacy

■ **DENNIS STACY:** Born in 1946. Graduate in English from the University of Texas, Austin. Currently , he is a busy full-time writer, whose articles, interviews and pictures on a wide variety of subjects, from UFOs to science, travel and commentary, have appeared in newspapers and magazines round the world. Leisure-time pursuits include motorcycling, the game of Go, and exploring the back-roads of Mexico.

■ **UFO involvement**: Both from a personal standpoint and as editor of the monthly *MUFON UFO Journal,* he takes an interest in all aspects of the UFO phenomenon.

■ **Publications**: A regular contributor to *OMNI*'s 'UFO Update' column, and author of many articles in both specialist and popular journals.

■ **Address**: Box 12434 / San Antonio / TX 78212 / USA. Phone (512) 828 4507.

A 1986 *New York Times* headline lamented that 'Physics May Be Up Against the Wall This Time.' It referred to a *Scientific American* article by Yale physicist Alan Chodos, in which he warned of the present 'faddish' flocking of particle physicists to the newfangled "superstring theory."

Chodos called the latter idea, which seeks to unify gravity and the fundamental forces of nature with known and suspected subatomic particles, "the Holy Grail of the Ultimate Theory," a kind of "theory of everything." The problem, he complained, was that one of the key fundamentals of superstring theory could only be investigated at distance scales 100 quintillion quintillion times smaller than atomic nuclei particles. Such capabilities, of course, far outstrip our present (and imagined future) abilities to conduct or measure such experiments. The consequence, Chodos argued, was that, deprived of verifiable experiments, physicists might "wander off into unchartered regions of philosophy and pure mathematics."

As far as ufology is concerned, the parallels are obvious. Despite four decades of research and data collation, our examination of the UFO source itself continues to be conducted at remote range. At best we have a handful of statistics and computer printouts, a few photographic phantoms and some inconclusive "landing" traces, along with reams of intelligence agency documentation retrieved (in the U.S.) under the Freedom of Information Act, papers that hint as much of government confusion as conspiracy. The "embarrassment of riches" of which the late Dr. **Hynek** once spoke is as theoretical as it is anecdotal, as much bluff and dross as gleam of gold. Still, we search for the Holy Grail, for the one all-inclusive hypothesis that will neatly knot the separate strings of reported UFO phenomena. What we need is a single specimen. What we have, in its absence, is a sieve of speculative theories, few of which are testable in a laboratory sense.

Nor can we say we were not forewarned. The French Wave of 1954 was notorious for the number of supposed "humanoids" reported in association with landed UFOs. Unfortunately, the sometimes inane behaviour of said humanoids was even more notorious. Such absurdities led the French astrophysicist Dr. **Pierre Guerin** to formulate what has since become known, though not widely enough, as 'Guerin's Law': "In Ufology, any law is immediately falsified by subsequent sightings just as soon as it is formulated." (Another Frenchman, **Aimé Michel,** could not help but add his own corollary: "...including Guerin's Law.")

To guard against purely semantic games, however, we might look briefly at what Sir Karl Popper had to say about theories that ideally lead to laws. "Every good theory is a prohibition: it forbids certain things to happen. The more a theory forbids, the better it is." The father of falsifiability, the measure whereby a hypothesis is tested, also warned that "it is easy to obtain confirmations, or verifications, for nearly every new theory, if we look for confirmations."

With that philosophical pill out of the way we can begin to look at the various hypotheses that have been proposed over the last four decades to account for the UFO phenomenon in particluar and UFO phenomena in general. Story's *Encyclopedia of UFOs* [1] lists a mere eight potential candidates. They are:

- 1) Secret Weapon;
- 2) Hollow Earth;
- 3) Underwater Civilization;
- 4) Space Animal;
- 5) Extraterrestrial;
- 6) Time-Travel;
- 7) Ultraterrestrial, and
- 8) Psychic Projection.

By contrast, the index of **John Keel's** massive *Operation Trojan Horse* [2] suggests a total of 19 theories. As a further addendum, consider the work of Texas folklorist **Elton Miles,** who collected local legends explaining the so-called Marfa Lights, globules of luminosity that have been reported hovering and dancing over Mitchell Flat, near Marfa, in far west Texas, for more than a century. Miles was able to compose a list of no less than 21 "explanations" that ranged from secret military experiments to glowing mineral deposits to jackrabbits that had brushed up against phosphorescent vegetation, and then went bounding across the desert. If so many theories can be propounded for mysterious lights that remain in one place, one can only sympthise with the problems of considering all the hypotheses that purport to explain *moving* lights.

Foremost of the problems, of course, is where to begin? Do we start with Ezekiel's "wheel-within-a-wheel" or the early Anno Domini reports of flying Roman "shields," the Great Airship of 1897, the "Foo Fighters" of WW II, or the subsequent onslaught of "mystery rockets" reported from the Scandinavian peninsula in 1946, anyone of which, or all, might represent a missing evolutionary link? The easiest way out of the dilemma is to adopt **Charles Fort's** oft-repeated dictum - "One measures a circle beginning anywhere," - and begin with **Kenneth Arnold**'s landmark 1947 sighting. Whether we'll be able to circumnavigate our circle and return to our initial point of origin is debatable, but for all practical purposes it represents the point from which ufology itself may be said to be *continuous*, having been in business in one form or another from that time down to the present day.

Historically, Arnold's sighting released a pent-up flood of similar reports. For the first time scientific and/or military officials were compelled to make both private and public pronouncements about the phenomenon. The results were the first wave of many UFO theories to come.

On 10 December, 1948, the Directorate of Intelligence, Headquarters United States Air Force, and the Office of Naval Intelligence, Navy Department, jointly issued a "Top Secret" document entitled *Air Intelligence Report No. 100-203-79*, an "Analysis of Flying Object Incidents in the U.S." [3]

An interesting observation of this curious 26-page report was that "the conclusion that some type of flying object has been observed over the U.S. seems to be substantiated. It is not known at this time whether these observations are misidentifications of domestically launched devices, natural phenomena, or foreign unconventional aircraft...Descriptions of the flying objects fall into three categories: 1) disk-shaped 2) rough cigar-shaped 3) balls of fire. Varying conditions of visibility and differences in angles at which the objects may have been viewed introduces a possibility that a single type object may have been observed rather than three different types. This possibility is further substantiated by the fact that in the areas where such objects have been observed the ratio of the three general configurations is approximately the same."

Indications are that the Air Intelligence Report was an in-house revision of an earlier "Estimate of the Situation" prepared by the Air Technical Intelligence Center (ATIC) at Wright Field, later Wright-Patterson Air Force Base, Dayton, Ohio, in response to the growing number of UFO reports. The likewise Top Secret Estimate rose through the ranks until it reached the desk of then Air Force Chief of Staff General Hoyt S. Vandenberg, who kicked it back downstairs because it had concluded, without ample proof, according to the General, that UFOs were of an extraterrestrial origin. Subsequently, the estimate was declassified and the available copies destroyed. A similar fate was ordered for the "son of the Estimate," but for reasons unknown these orders were never carried out. Through the Freedom of Information Act (FOIA), American researcher Robert Todd was able to obtain the release of a copy of the Air Intelligence Report on 5 March 1985, almost 40 years after its initial appearance. Thus the Extraterrestrial Hypothesis (ETH), presuming the existence of real, nuts and bolts spacecraft piloted by intelligent beings from another planet, is one of the earliest on record. Military assumptions of Nazi or Soviet secret weaponry were relatively short-lived, though the notion continues to pop up in various places today.

Events were already conspiring, however, to give the ETH its first of many variations, and from the unlikeliest angle, too. During the first half of the 20th century, **Wilhelm Reich,** a former communist and Freudian psychoanalyst, had already cut a controversial swath through society. Over a 20-year period from 1920 until 1940, Reich conducted a number of individual experiments that led him to propose the existence of an all pervading "life-force." Since this seemed to be the same energy bound up then released in the sexual orgasm, Reich dubbed it "orgone energy," and set about developing accumulators, or organic "greenhouses," designed to collect and concentrate this universal energy.

By the time Arnold was seeing "saucers" in the

Pacific Northwest, Reich had established his own community, Orgonon, in Maine, at the opposite corner of the country. As early as 1952, visitors to Orgonon had reported seeing shiny objects overhead similar to Arnold's, but Reich himself paid little attention until a follower sent him a couple of UFO books, including **Keyhoe**'s *Flying Saucers Are Real.* Reich wondered how stationary UFOs could be distinguished from stars, and was soon conducting time-lapse photography experiments which convinced him some "stars" *were* UFOs and his work at Orgonon was under alien surveillance.

Among the orgone machinery Reich had assimilated was a tube-like device called a "cloudbuster." Certain clouds, Reich thought, had become contaminated with DOR ("deadly orgone"), or orgone energy altered by nuclear radiation. Tubes were aimed, the DOR drawn off, and the dark clouds subsequently dissipated. Reich tried the same experiment on blue lights hovering over Organon and the success seemed to be repeated; the blue lights faded and blinked out.

Reich concluded that the UFOs operated on orgone energy and called their occupants CORE men, for Cosmic Orgone Engineering. Unfortunately, the use of orgone as an energy source gave off a lethal exhaust, DOR, which Reich felt contributed to the formation of deserts. Besides drawing off DOR, the cloudbuster could also concentrate orgone and cause rain. Reich became convinced that deserts and UFOs were intertwined following a series of rainmaking experiments he conducted outside Tuscon, Arizona, in 1954. His first night in the desert he saw several UFOs, and as was his wont, gave them a name of his own, Ea, standing for 'Energy alpha'. The Ea's apparently were trying to thwart his efforts at making rain, helped in his own mind, by the "emotional desert" of mankind. In the posthumously published *Contact with Space*, Reich concluded, "There was no escape from the fact that we were at war with a power unknown to man on earth."

Reich's UFO phase (he died in an American jail in November of 1957, incarcerated for interstate sale and shipment of orgone accumulators used in the treatment of cancer) tends to get overlooked by his biographers, sympathetic and critical alike. The short shrift seems due to a combination of embarrassment and the fact that most biographers (of Reich or anyone else) are not well schooled in ufology. For those fortunate enough to be reading this book, however, a few parallels can be drawn between Reich's UFO philosophizing and subsequent developments in the field. Perhaps the most obvious of these if Reich's ready acceptance of the Extraterrestrial Hypothesis. Secondly, and no less importantly in light of alternative theories, is Reich's linking of UFOs with arid climates, primarily, and the terrestrial landscape itself in general. The former assumes a significant connection when we come to consider the work of Trevor James Constable, the latter when we look at the work of geocentric theorists like **Michael Persinger** and **Paul Devereux**.

But first we need to briefly review the thought of another remarkable man who, like Reich, was a pioneer figure in the development of western psychology. This, of course, is **Carl Gustav Jung,** also a psychoanalyst of stature who apparently felt compelled to address the UFO phenomenon during the twilight of his career. The work that concerns us here is his *Flying Saucers: A Modern Myth of Things Seen in the Skies*. [**4**]

Two characteristics caught Jung's eye in particular; the *circularity* of the reported UFO image, and its apparent *weightlessness*. The first Jung associated with the idea of the Sanskrit *mandala*, a word meaning "magic circle." The second observation carried connotations of non-materiality, and suggested that whatever UFOs might be, they were *not* made of titanium or any other metal alloy, but consisted instead of psychic "stuff."

Jung's undying contribution (or confusion!) shifted the focus from the hardware of the phenomenon to its psychic, or software, component. Reich himself had come perilously close to a similar viewpoint, but seems, finally, to have fixated on the exterior reality of the phenomenon. For Jung, the interior aspects of the UFO problem, its archetypical propensities, were equally, if not more, intriguing than its external aspects. There might well be other intelligent life forms out there, which astronomers increasingly questioned, but there was terra incognita *inside* humankind, too. In the words of Hermes Trismegistus: "As above, so below."

Jung regarded UFOs as a sort of "visionary rumor," a psychological projection of hopes and fears in an anxiety-ridden age fraught with the threat of nuclear annihilation. The circumference of psychological unity, of wholesomeness, could be rendered complete by mentally invoking the magic circle of the UFO. Like Reich, Jung postulated an emotional desert watered by life-giving rain. Unlike Reich, however, who appears to have projected his own paranoia onto the phenomenon, Jung seems to have seen UFOs in more benign terms, somehow intertwined with the human psyche, and perhaps even playing a significant role in its expression or development.

Under one guise or another, this perceived duality of the UFO continues to plague its students, cropping up most obviously in religious oriented theories that tend to ascribe either a "good" or "bad," angelic or devilish, nature to the phenomenon. Thus, a Christian fundamentalist like **John Weldon** (co-author with Clifford Wilson of *Close Encounters* [**5**]) can claim: "You have to conclude that we are dealing with something that is really indigenous to this planet - something that is more or less one and the same with occult phenomena, basically spiritualistic and, from the Christian viewpoint, demonic. It is something that is quite hazardous to get involved with."

Other Christian-based commentary, of course, may take exactly the opposite approach and include UFOs within the divine pantheon along with assorted heavenly messengers. Yet a third synthesis, typified by **Joseph Blumrich**'s *The Spaceships of Ezekiel* [**6**], seeks to interpret religious texts in contemporary, scientific terms, concluding that the "Wheels within wheels" reported by the Biblical prophet really *was* an alien spaceship. **Von Däniken,** a profit figure of another sort altogether, has made a career of claiming *all* early religious mythology relates to visitations (and interference) by extraterrestrial beings. Despite dubious claims of evidence, the Ancient Astronaut theory remains essentially unfalsifiable. It has a certain symmetrical gravity to it, but is basically a Chinese puzzle-box, explaining life on this planet by life on another. At some point we run out of planetary boxes and find ourselves back on square one, having circled the square, but achieving little else.

Reich's theory, however, had a fallout of its own in the work on one **Trevor James Constable,** a former follower and British chronicler of WW II aviation history. Constable not only experimented with the cloudbuster, but also turned to infrared photography, in a desert scenario, to demonstrate his own conviction that UFOs represent a prevalent, *invisible* phenomenon. Parts of Constable's own writings (he offers specific tips as to how similar photgraphy can be conducted, for example) are clear, but he also confuses the issue as to whether UFOs are real space ships or organic organisms omnipresent in the earth's atmosphere.

Ultimately, he opts for both interpretations. Some are spaceships, other "critters," as he calls them, though they remain intimately linked. "The critters fly faster than and easily outmanoeuvre contemporary aircraft, and they do this on biological power. The key to spaceship propulsion seemed to lie in the same realm," he wrote.

Of critters specifically, Constable says: "These creatures are amoeba-like life forms existing in the plasma state. They are not solid, liquid or gas. Rather, they exist in the fourth state of matter - plasma - as living heat-substance at the upper border of physical nature. They consist of calcium and fluids, the metal *and the fluids* both being in the plasmatic state. My pictures show that these aerial fauna are like unicellular life forms."

Constable's work deserves more than a footnote in the history of UFO theories, if for no other reason than he builds on a previous theory (Reich's) and provides clear instructions for repeated testing of his own. The history and results of his own experiments can be found in *Sky Creatures: Living UFOs*, a paperback condensation of his larger *The Cosmic Pulse of Life*. [**7**] For all that, Constable's research is not widely replicated by the UFO community, which could seemingly duplicate or disprove his findings relatively easily. At least one serious study followed, however, which resulted in a string of striking color and black & white photographs (Constable also claimed to have taken moving film of his critters). These remarkable pictures can be found in *UFO La Realta Nascosta* [**8**], by **Luciano Boccone**. Unfortunately, as far as I know, no English translation or edition exists at this time, a handicap which seriously hampers commentary on the Italian group's work as a whole, at least by this author. (It's an unfortunate fact of life that many fine works in French, Italian, Spanish and the Scandinavian languages, as well as others, go untranslated and largely unnoticed by English-speaking ufologists because there is no widespread "market demand" for them. This proscription does not apply to popularisations like those of Erich von Däniken, whose original German writings have had no trouble worming their way into worldwide print.)

Simply because a theory is popluar, however, is not necessarily cause for its dismissal, as we have seen in the case of the extraterrestrial hypothesis itself, of which there are two general categories dependent on interpretations of UFO "behaviour." In terrestrial terms these may be referred to as interventionist and non-interventionist. The first category posits a sort of objective, almost quantum conundrum-like observer who steadfastly refuses to intervene in the politics, history and evolution of the planetary culture under observation. It's the basic philisophical premise, for instance, behind the adventures of our own mass-media UFO, the Starship *Enterprise*. How such a purity of purpose is possibly to be maintained, though, is a problem quantum mechanics has not yet solved on a small scale, and one that seems evens unlikelier of solution on any larger scale. That is, the very act of observation is itself observed, which leads to inevitable changes and reactions in the civilization under study.

The alternative is to impart alien motives to UFOs which, of course, presume alien occupants. Said purposes may then coincide with earthly spiritual and environmental ones, or they may stand in opposition to what we perceive to be human progress. Among those who claims to have been contacted by alien beings there is no shortage of dire warnings of "heavenly" intervention if mankind as a whole continues upon its present course, dabbling in a nuclear arms race capable of exterminating life in a matter of seconds, or slowly strangling the planet we inhabit with various pollutants. In such a scenario the aliens only intervene because we have forced their hand.

Charles Fort was perhaps the first to warn otherwise. After noting the disappearance of Ambrose Bierce in Texas, he came across an Ambrose Small who had vanished from Canada. "Was somebody collecting Ambroses?" Fort wondered, having earlier speculated, "I think we're property." The implication was that we're farmed, in the same way that the McDonald's hamburger market demands now account for a significant slice of beef and potato production.

In its darkest manifestation the UFO phenomenon has frequently been associated with reported mutilations of cattle and other live stock, though the connections are tenuous at best usually depend on medical experiments or needs invovling plasma, or ways ot monitoring terrestrial pollution. Abductionists like New York artist and author **Budd Hopkins** [**9**] have postulated a more human focus, based primarily on anecdotal accounts of being taken aboard a UFO and subjected to (sometimes surreal) physical examination.

Hopkins has detected a wide range of alleged symptoms that include repeated abductions within a single family over a period of years, even decades, scars of supposed unknown origin indicative of tissue sampling, tales of artificial insemination, sperm collection and acts of intercourse, and in at least one instance a follow-up abduction in which the fetus was removed (!). The tabloid imagery continues with Hopkin's assertion that abductions may number in the thousands and are the products of extraterrestrial intellegence engaged most likely in genetic experimentation. Whereas Hynek, speaking of the sheer number of UFO reports alone, referred to "an embarrassment of riches," Hopkins barely blushes, even though much of his evidence is circumstantial and comes from hypnotised witnesses. The debunkers, who demand extraordinary proof of the existence of even *one* UFO, let alone thousands of logistically-staggering abductions, are understandably skeptical.

At least one of the questions endemic to abductions (why had no one of "note" ever been abducted?", will be answered by press time with the publication of **Whitley Strieber's** *Communion*, [**10**] a first-person account of the emotional trauma suffered by Strieber and family, and apparently inspired by a UFO kidnapping. Strieber is a prolific American writer who has authored or co-authored a string of both supernatural and factually-based stories. His success is such that *Communion* is sure to generate large amounts of publicity and counter-speculation among the public at large.

Strieber's experience is startling, to say the least, though hardly unique in the annals of abduction. In early January of 1986, he began having uneasy memories of a series of events that occurred the day after Christmas the previous year. These events involved bluish lights, missing periods of time, and humanoid creatures. Strieber, a disinterested skeptic at the time, thought he might be losing his mental faculties. The terror which almost overwhelmed him was later replaced by fascination and curiosity. Eventually, he came to the conclusion that these half-remembered incidents "might involve contact of some sort with nonhuman beings."

Whatever they represent, Stieber's visitations have continued. He claims to have seen "the visitors" seven more times between April and November of 1986. "In a few cases they have appeared while I was awake, most notably on August 27. On the other occasions they waked me up." The August event began at 11.35 at night, in a remote cabin in the woods, when the outside suddenly lit up like daylight. High up under a steep eave then came nine, evenly-spaced knocks. Strieber's cats reacted with abject terror; he himself went outdoors to investigate, noting "I feel that, as soon as I rose from the chair, I entered some sort of an altered state."

Opening the screen door, Strieber saw by his knee, less than a foot away, three tiny, gray beings, about half a metre tall, dressed in blue jumpsuits, with large heads and black, slanted eyes. Their gazes met, and Strieber felt a pleasant sensation course through his body, followed by the illusion of a field of yellow flowers where his swimming pool was. "I was aware that the three beings were quite real, but that the 'field' was a hallucination," says Strieber. His memory deteriorated after that, and he could only recall a vague impression of something awesomely huge overhead. The subsequent missing time amounted to a period of two and half hours.

Strieber has submitted himself to a battery of psychological and physical testing, including the polygraph, and seems destined to become the most thoroughly studied "abductee" ever. Interestingly enough, during the August encounter, though his mind was not afraid, Strieber's body apparently reacted with shock and he endured a near-death experience in which he fainted. He has since eschewed hypnosis, preferring "to struggle with the memories, to try to learn how to overcome the biological fear that seems to be impeding this experience." He has taken to long walks in the woods to overcome fearful tendencies.

Certain aspects of the Strieber encounters strike chords of recognition with other paranormal phenomena, including the ghostly knockings associated with poltergeists, visions of "little people" (Magonians?), and the NDE itself, as well as altered states of consciousness in general.

The similarities of the UFO experience have not gone unnoticed by students of parapsychology. **Lorraine Davis,** a student of JFK University in California, recently completed a Master's Thesis [**11**] in studies of consciousness in which UFO percipients are compared with those who reported NDEs, since both groups spoke frequently of bright lights, tunnel-like passages, and visions of humanoids. Like their NDE counterparts, some UFO percipients subsequently underwent psychological changes. These included increased psychic ability, adoption of less egocentric attitudes toward self and others, and a more universal, as opposed, to narrow sectarian, religious viewpoint.

Still, there remains a significant dichotomy to what might be called the ufological versus the parapsychological approach to the problem. Whereas the parapsychologist tends to see these phenomena as products, or possibly by-products, of as yet unrevealed powers or domains of consciousness, the tendency among ufologists is to seek answers in the realm of imagined future technology. Strieber, for example, reports he is presently engaged in experiments in which ultrasound is introduced via the ears to the brain. By employing slight differences in frequencies, the missing-time experience has reportedly been recaptured. If this finding holds up, obviously a known mechanism will have been discovered whereby current earth technology can effectively replicate one of the more perplexing aspects of the alleged abduction scenario. Demonstrating that this effect can be carried out at a distance (on unwilling percipients?!) would constitute a significant step in the "right direction."

Jacques Vallée and rocket ballistics expert **Thomas E. Bearden** have also proposed theoretical technologies that would duplicate reported UFO effects. Vallée's emphasis has been in the area of psychological and social manipulation of individual and group belief systems using "psychotronic" technology, machines that supposedly interact with human consciousness and vice versa.

Bearden's thrust [12] has been toward demonstrating the engineering reality of such technology and is based largely on his own interpretation of the work of Nikolai Tesla. Both systems exhibit the sort of conjurative characteristic implied by Arthur C. Clarke, who warned that future technology will appear to us as magic. This would be particularly true, of course, if either time or interdimensional travel on the part of the alienauts were permissible.

Vallée's recent writings on the subject sometimes seem too glib and general. By contrast, Bearden is almost *too* specific; from his way with words and idiosyncratic terms, one comes away feeling the theory is almost too obtuse even for its author. He claims, modestly enough, to have

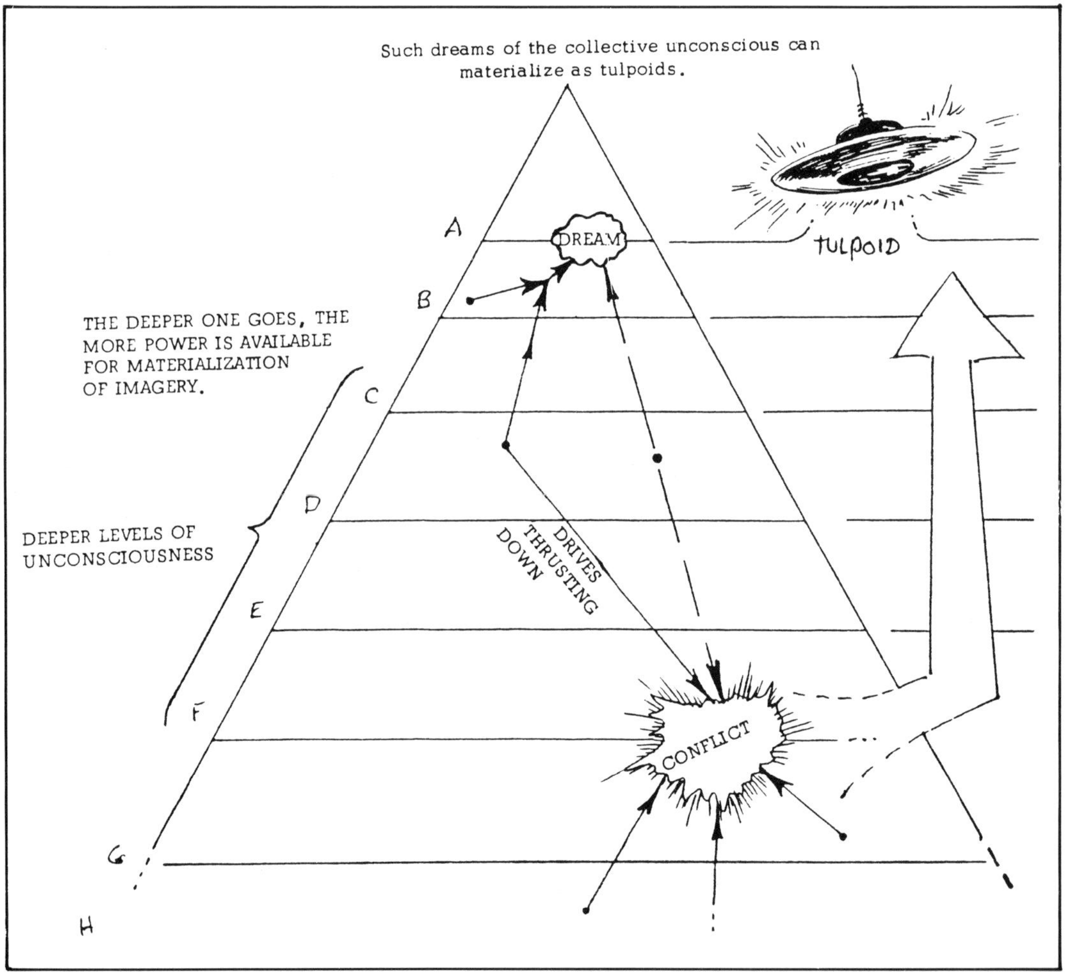

Dreams are unresolved conflicts, which can manifest as UFOs, according to Thomas A. Bearden. [From T.A. Bearden, *Excalibur briefing*]

"formulated a hyperdimensional theory of UFO's which, in a strange way, includes every other present theory of UFO's in a nonexclusive manner. Ther theory is...consistent with the present experimental basis of physics, although extending it."

According to classic quantum mechanics, the act of observation collapses the wave function of subatomic particles, rendering them detectable as either waves *or* particles, though in reality they are both simultaneously. Much is presently being made in the world of theoretical physics, not to mention parapsychology and ufology, as to whether this microintervention of consciousness, in the form of an observer, extrapolates into macroeffects, i.e., the "real" world. Hugh Everett III, working under the renowned John Wheeler, then at Princeton, worked his way around this apparent impasse by suggesting multiple observers. As a consequence of each "choice," or observation, the wave function still collapsed in this "universe" into either a wave or particle; but a new universe was also created in which the critical determining choice was not made. Thus a wave "here" becomes (or remains) a particle "there," in effect creating hyperspace. Unfortunatley for the interests of clarity, Everett and Wheeler's theory called for an infinite number of universes in which all the choices or observations since the beginning of time (or at least of observers) could be accommodated. An infinity of universes implies, for us, a real world in which each and every imaginable possibility exists, thus the bizarre variety of reported UFO shapes and occupants. *Somewhere* in hyperspace each of these alien ships and alienauts exists in physical reality, as real as our own apparently "singular" universe.

According to Bearden, crosstalk betwen these many "worlds" is not only feasible, but subject to engineering principles. Some of this seems to take place anyway, unconsciously, as a result of the remarkable nature of the human brain, both hemispheres of which act as scalar wave generators carrying mental information, or thought patterns. Ordinarily these are not manifested in our world because the informational content, or side-effect, is at right angles to our own 3-dimensional space. These waves can cross, or interfere with one another in space, however, and under certain conditions (tectonic strain and other geomagnetic and resonant energisers) their mental content may temporarily materialise. This answers, at least, the question of where UFOs come from and where they go when they are not transiently "visible" here. The mental information on the carrier waves is literally Jung's "collective unconscious."

Bearden's elaborate hypothesis of course, may strike one as either intuitively brilliant or inherently implausible. For this particular layman there is a feeling of being "headed in the right direction." Certainly it's as worthy of consideration as some of the more "mundane" explanation of UFO phenomena offered up by orthodox science. Consider only the following, found in *UFO's - A Scientific Debate*, under the august editorial imprint of Mssrs. Carl Sagan and Thornton Page. [**13**] In the chapter, 'Psychiatry and UFO Reports,' authors **Lester Grinspoon** (no Freudian analysis, please!) and **Alan D. Persky** refer to the Isakower phenomenon, "an unusual variant of the hypnagogic state."

Otto Isakower, writing in 1938, notices that "the visual impression is that of something shadowy and indefinite, generally felt to be 'round' which comes nearer and nearer, swells to gigantic size and threatens to crush the subject. It gradually becomes smaller and shrinks up to nothing. Sometimes there is fire somewhere."

Continuing, Isakower notes that "yes, these imprints seem very easy to detect; they are the mental images of sucking at the mother's breast and of falling asleep there when satisfied. The large object which approaches probably represents the breast, with its promise of food. When satisfied, the infant loses interest in the breast, which appears smaller and small and finally vanishes away."

In such a scenario presumably the UFO withdraws into the mother's blouse from whence it came. Aside from lending new meaning to the phrase "mother ship," however, ther excerpts quoted by Grinspoon and Persky leave one wondering about psychological origin(s) of the "fire" that is "sometimes...somewhere." Predictably in a reductionist treatment like this one, the other popular image of UFOs as "cigar-shaped" comes in for an equally popular Freudian interpretation. Hynek questioned why pink flying elephants weren't reported in a similar context. We wonder why, since sex is allegedly on everyone's mind, flying saucers aren't shaped like doughnuts, to better accommodate cigars, and why the two aren't constantly mating in the skies overhead?

By ranging from physics to psychology, we've now circumscribed a circle of our own, the sphere containing the UFO phenomenon. The rim where we stand, looking in, is crowded shoulder-to-shoulder with ufologists. Undoubtedly, we've leapt over many a theory and theorist in our circumnavigation, but that's the nature of the beast. The question is, How many theories of UFOs are there? The answer is: How many drops does it take to fill to Grail?

Circumspection shows us there are as many theories for the UFO as there are ufologists.

REFERENCES

■ 1 - **Story,** Ronald D, *The encyclopedia of UFOs* (Doubleday, 1980). ■ 2 - **Keel,** John A, *Operation Trojan Horse* (Putnam, 1970). ■ 3 - *Air Intelligence Report no 100-203-79* (10.12.1948), declassified & reprinted in *MUFON Journal*, 207, July 1985. ■ 4 - **Jung,** C.G., *Flying saucers: a modern myth of things seen in the skies*, (Orig. German 1958; Routledge/Harcourt Brace, 1959). ■ 5

- **Wilson,** Clifford, & **Weldon,** John, *Close encounters, a better explanation* (Creation Life, 1978). ■ **6** - **Blumrich,** Josef F, *The spaceships of Ezekiel* (Orig. German 1974; Bantam/Corgi, 1974). ■ **7** - **Constable,** Trevor James, *The cosmic pulse of life* (Merlin, 1976). ■ **8** - **Boccone,** Luciano, *UFO, la realta nascosta* (Ivaldi, 1980). ■ **9** - **Hopkins,** Budd, *Missing time* (Marek, 1981). ■ **10** - **Strieber,** Whitley, *Commuinion* (1987). ■ **11** - **Davis,** Lorraine, *How the UFO experience compares with the Near-death Experience as a vehicle for the evolution of human consciousness* (MA thesis, John F Kennedy University, 1985). ■ **12** - **Bearden,** T.E., 'Star wars now! The Bohm-Aharonov effect, scalar interferometry and Soviet weaponization' in *Pursuit*, Nos 65 & 67, 1984. ■ **13** - **Sagan,** Carl, & **Page,** Thornton (eds) *UFOs, a scientific debate* (Cornell, 1972).

4.4.1

UFOs AS PSYCHOLOGICAL AND PARAPSYCHOLOGICAL PHENOMENA

by Mark Moravec

■ **MARK MORAVEC** lives in Sydney, Australia. He completed a degree in psychology at Macquarie University in 1979, at which time he had already developed an interest in UFO phenomena and conducted field investigations. Combining these interests has led him to specialise in the psychological and sociological aspects of UFO experiences.

■ **UFO involvement**: He is currently the Co-ordinator of ACUFOS (Australian Centre for UFO Studies) which was established in 1974 at the request of Dr Hynek, to act in co-operation with CUFOS. Since then, ACUFOS has evolved into an independent national co-ordinating centre which promotes scientific research and investigation, national conferences and other activities. Mark also co-ordinates the Percipient Studies Project, which aims to research the human factors involved in UFO-related experiences by the in-depth psychological, sociological and medical study of UFO percipients.

Mark views his interest in UFO phenomena as part of his curiosity and appreciation for the world's wonders: whether the natural wonders of auroras and wilderness areas, the complexities of mind and behaviour, or the multi-faceted mysteries of anomalous experiences.

■ **Publications**: He has published articles in *ACUFOS Journal, MUFON Journal, The Skeptic* and *Australian Folklore* and elsewhere. He has authored or co-edited several publications for ACUFOS, including *PSIUFO Phenomena: a study of UFOs and the paranormal* (1981) and *UFOs over Australia: a selection of ACUFOS research findings and debate* (1985).

■ **Address**: PO Box 728 / Lane Cove NSW 2066 / Australia. Phone 02 498 3463.

UFOs may or may not have a physical existence. But they certainly do exist as psychological and sociological phenomena.

Why? Firstly, the human witness is our primary source of information. Secondly, since the UFO experience is the reported perception of an unidentified aerial phenomenon, it requires an examination of the process of human perception. And thirdly, as this brief survey will show, other psychological processes may also play a part in shaping the final reported experience.

In this chapter, we will explore the psychological and the alleged parapsychological dimensions of the UFO experience. UFO reports will be examined in the light of psychological reactions, perception, psychopathology, altered states of consciousness, beliefs and paranormal claims. We will also ask the question: can psychology explain the UFO phenomenon?

PSYCHOLOGICAL REACTIONS

■ **CASE 1 - Cowley, Queensland, Australia, 9th February 1979.**

A lone motorist encountered a dark, beehive-shaped object, from which a dull white light emanated, sitting on the edge of the road. As the object rose slightly, Mr H was blinded by a flash of light from the object. After blinking his eyes a couple of times, the percipent regained his sight but realised his car's headlights, dashlights and engine had ceased to function. He coasted to a truck pullover area, and after about 30 seconds, the lights came back on of their own accord and the engine could be restarted. Mr H said he did not know what the object was; it was totally strange to his experience. After the car had stopped, he had felt very unsettled, like the feeling one gets after being woken up by a nightmare. **UFO Research (Far North Queensland) Case QB79-013.**

How do people react when they observe an unidentified flying object? Two studies were carried out by the author to answer this question. The first study examined a sample of 56 unidentified, close encounter cases from the files of UFO Research (New South Wales). 46 cases specified a psychological reaction [**see Moravec, 1981a and Table 1**]. The second study used data from the Australian UFO Computer File (UFOCOMFIL). Out of 1,006 coded unidentified cases of all types, 90 (9%) specified a psychological reaction [**see Moravec, 1986 and Table 2**].

Both studies indicate that "fear" is the most common reaction to UFO experiences. "Curiosity" is the next most common reaction. In a number of cases in *Study 1,* both fear and curiosity were experienced simultaneously - indicating an approach-avoidance conflict where the witness wants to find out more about what he or she is observing but is afraid of the unknown consequences.

If we attempt to classify the psychological reactions in terms of positive, pleasant feelings versus negative, unpleasant feelings, we find that "negative" feelings predominate. However, this result is mainly determined by the large proportion of cases where "fear" is experienced. Reactions *subsequent* to a sighting tend to be continuations of reactions *during* the sighting. Even the dreams or nightmares subsequently experienced by some witnesses could well be a continuation of the initial fear reaction.

In a number of cases, physiological reactions also accompanied or followed the UFO experience [**see Tables 3 and 4**] as, for example, the impaired eyesight in Case 1.

The Studies indicate that insomnia and impairment of eyesight are the most common physiological reaction to UFO experiences.

Could physiological reactions be psychologically induced? For instance, "hair standing on end" is a classic physiological effects described in the UFO literature are psychosomatic in origin, rather than direct physical effects by the UFO.

Are psychological reactions to *unidentified* flying objects different from reactions to *identified* flying objects? There are case examples which show

TABLE 1: PSYCHOLOGICAL REACTIONS TO UFO EVENTS

(Study 1 - Moravec, 1981a - 46 cases)

Reaction	No. of Cases*	Percentage of Cases
Fear of Anxiety	32	69.6
Curiosity	7	15.2
Amazement	4	8.7
Amnesia	4	8.7
Puzzlement	3	6.5
Dreams or Nightmares	3	6.5
Disbelief	2	4.3
Excitement	2	4.3
Calmness	2	4.3
Mesmerisation	2	4.3
Lack of Control	2	4.3
Other (torment, disorientation, depression, annoyance, guilt, impending doom)	6	13.2

*Note: some cases involved more than one psychological reaction

TABLE 2: PSYCHOLOGICAL REACTIONS TO UFO EVENTS

(Study 2 - Moravec, 1986 - 90 cases)

Reaction	No. of Cases*	Percentage of Cases
Fear	35	38.9
Uneasiness or Agitation	19	21.1
Curiosity	21	23.3
Loss of Memory	4	4.4
Elation	4	4.4
Attention Drawn by a Feeling	6	6.7
Other (drawn to object, psychic phenomena, contactee)	3	3.3

*Note: some cases involved more than one psychological reaction

that it is possible for people to become quite alarmed and upset while watching the apparent motions of the planet Venus distorted by the atmosphere. After a study of 1,307 cases, Hendry [**1979, 104**] concluded that: "The fear elicited by the UFO and IFO sightings is not in direct response to what is being experienced, but rather to what is being anticipated in advance." People have been socially conditioned to believe in, and fear, "extraterrestrial spaceships." Thus, a percipient's dramatic emotional reaction may not necessarily indicate the presence of an "authentic" UFO, but rather that the percipient believes the event is a genuine unknown.

Hynek [**1974**] has referred to the "escalation of hypotheses" where a UFO witness may attempt to explain the phenomenon he is observing by a series of increasingly more complex and exotic explanations. For example, a person may observe the approach of an airborne light and interpret it, in turn, as an airplane, helicopter, a man with a torch and, finally, a UFO. In Hynek's view, this reaction adds credibility to the person reporting the UFO and shows that he or she is not automatically jumping to exotic interpretations until forced to by the strangeness of the experience. A number of cases in *Study 1* illustrated this process. However, it it possible that sometimes the witness may make an ultimately erroneous conclusion that he or she is observing a UFO.

In summary, the two studies show that the most common psychological reactions to UFO events are fear, followed by curiosity. There is also a wide range of other reactions, possibly dependent on each individual's personality or situation. The most common physiological reactions are insomnia and impairment of vision. Some physiological reactions may be psychosomatic, i.e. psychologically induced. Witnesses many react similarly to both UFOs and IFOs, hence a dramatic emotional reaction does not necessarily increase the credibility of a UFO report. Finally, the fact that fear is generated in many individual UFO experiences makes a powerful reason, in itself, for the continued study of UFO experiences.

PERCEPTION

■ **CASE 2 - Baulkham Hills, New South Wales, Australia, 24th February 1979.**

In the early morning hours, a student observed a bright, white light gradually ascend in the north-east sky over a 20-minute period. When viewed through binoculars, multi-coloured lights appeared to flash from the centre of the object. Investigation determined that the light's position and motion correlated with the rising of the star, **Arcturus. UFO Research (New South Wales), Case NA79-055.**

Ufologists will recognise this case as typical of what turns out to be the most common stimulus for UFO reports, namely astronomical objects. In this instance, it took me quite some time to convince the

TABLE 3: PHYSIOLOGICAL REACTIONS TO UFO EVENTS
(Study 1 - Moravec, 1981a - 11 cases)

Reaction	No. of Cases	Percentage of Cases
Insomnia	4	36.3
Sensitive or Sore Eyes	3	27.3
Headache	1	9.1
Hair "Standing on End"	1	9.1
Fainting Spells	1	9.1
Tingling Sensations in Arms and legs	1	9.1

TABLE 4: PHYSIOLOGICAL REACTIONS TO UFO EVENTS
(Study 2 - Moravec, 1986 - 9 cases)

Reaction	No. of Cases	Percentage of Cases
Impairment of Eyesight	3	33.3
Temperature Change	2	22.2
Headache	1	11.1
Ear Pain	1	11.1
Muscular Pain	1	11.1
Rashes	1	11.1

witness that he had seen a star distorted by atmospheric refraction and internal binocular reflections, rather than some alien object.

Why is it that a common celestial object can so often be transformed into something strange, mysterious and alien? Partly it is because of a lack of knowledge of the night sky; partly it is the expectation or belief of some to see spaceships in the night; and partly it involves the process of perception.

Perception is the process of sensing and interpreting the world around us. A number of physiological and psychological factors can help create illusions or introduced inaccuracies in eyewitness testimony.

For example, highly illuminated objects can appear larger than they really are, especially when they are much brighter than their background. Very bright square and triangular-shaped objects can appear almost completely round against a dark background. Continuous viewing of bright light sources can sometimes lead to the spurious perception of colour changes even though the emitted wavelength is constant. A suggested explanation for these "irradiation phenomena" is that the light radiation entering the eye scatters within the eye's transparent media and covers a larger area on the retina [**Haines, 1980**].

The "autokinetic illusion" occurs when a light source appears to move about erratically, sometimes oscillating or performing loops, even though it is actually fixed or stationary. This movement is most commonly reported when a single light source, such as a star or planet, is viewed continuously against a dark background without any easily visible reference points. The extent and direction of perceived motion is highly amenable to suggestion. An explanation for this illusion is that the eye engages in small involuntary retinal movements which are interpreted as an "objective" movement of the light source in the absence of a stable visual frame of reference [**Haines, 1980; Robinson, 1972**].

The single fact that most UFO sightings occur during the night-time hours has important perceptual implications. At night, very few landmards such as hills and trees can be effectively used to determine accurate object distance or size. Darkness may obscure the finer details of the observed object. The switchover of rod and cone cells in the eye at night causes "night vision," whereby a faint illuminated object may be detected but with limited clarity. A fearful reaction, such as a scream, on the part of one observer may cause a chain reaction of fear or hysteria to develop amongst other observers, thereby emotionally flavouring their observations. This reaction, easy to observe at night in an isolated area, may stem from a basic human fear of the dark and the unknown. Tiredness, or prolonged concentration on an unchanging environment, as might occur to a motorist travelling along a deserted, straight road, can make the individual more susceptible to misinterpretations of common phenomena [**Horne, 1985**].

A number of factors associated with an event can influence a witness's ability to report accurately. Accuracy improves with longer duration and if the event has features that attract attention and hold interest. There can be marked inaccuracies in the estimate of time, speed and distance. A number of studies have shown that people consistently overestimate the amount of time an event took. There are also witness factors. Mild stress produces alertness whilst intense emotion impairs performance. Expectations based on cultural beliefs, past experience, personal prejudices or temporary biases can distort perception. There are individual differences in eyewitness ability. Those people who are generally anxious, neurotic or self-preoccupied tend to make slightly worse eyewitnesses, perhaps because they do not adequately attend to important cues in their environment. Men and women pay more attention to particular items that attract their interest. Recall and recognition ability, and lack of susceptibility to misleading information, improves with age up to about age 15 to 20. Recall and recognition can decline after about age 60, but this varies according to the task and the individual [**Loftus, 1979**].

Once the information is stored in memory, further changes can take place. The longer the time lapse between the experience and its recollection, the less accurate and complete is the eyewitness acount. Post-event information can modify memory or cause the incorporation of non-existent details. It can also influence people's subjective feelings about an event. When a witness is uncertain, guessing can fill in the gaps, but be mistaken for a real memory on later recall.

Biases can be introduced when retrieving information from memory. An open-ended question generally elicits less complete but more error-free information, whilst a closed question elicits more complete but less accurate information. The best style of interrogation is to let the witness tell the story in his or her own words, then ask a series of specific questions to increase the range or coverage of the witness's report. Question wording can be critical. In one experiment, subjects were questioned after viewing a film of a traffic accident. Those subjects who were asked how fast the cars were going when they "smashed" into each other gave a much higher estimate of speed than those asked the same question but with the word "hit" substituted. When asked, a week later, whether they had seen any broken glass, the first group of subjects more often said yes, even though there actually was no broken glass in the accident. These subjects had incorporated into memory both elements of the original incident, and external post-event information supplied by the question, the word "smashed" having implied both a higher speed and the presence of broken glass. Thus leading questions can impart information and affect witness memory. Non-verbal communication, conveyed by tone of voice, movement of head and eyes, gaze and posture, can sway testimony in a certain direction [**Loftus, 1979**].

To summarise these findings, as applied to the UFO experience: Physiological and psychological factors associated with the process of perception can introduce inaccuracies in eyewitness testimony. It may involve characteristics of the event, such as very bright luminosity, movement illusions and sighting duration.

Or it may involve individual witness characteristics. As Haines [**1980**] has ably summarised, a short period of observation may limit the amount of detail which can be absorbed by the percipient, and may lead to a greater chance of misidentification. Different vantage points between witnesses can lead to different emphases in testimony. The emotional shock of seeing something novel and strange may distort or limit the reported details of a UFO experience. Perceptual capabilities can vary between individuals according to differences in cultural background and upbringing, intelligence, memory capabilities, vocabulary and verbal expression, and tolerance of stress. The contents of memory tend to fade with the passage of time. They may also become distorted or reorganised according to the individual's exposure to other information about UFO phenomena - in the form of other UFO sightings, literature and visual media portrayals of UFO phenomena, and discussions of the subject with other people.

Whilst human perception has its biases and limitations, it is not totally inept and untrustworthy. Were it so, we would be killed every time we tried to cross the street. Rather, human perception has its strengths and weaknesses. And as long as the investigator takes this into account, eyewitness testimony can still be a valuable source of information. By using such methods as reconstruction and replaying the UFO sighting at the site of its occurrence, the investigator can maximise the amount of useful and reliable information that he or she can obtain from the UFO percipient.

PSYCHOPATHOLOGY

■ **CASE 3 - Sydney NSW, Australia, 1979.**

Mr A had a strong impulse to go to the local airport. The impulse was so strong that he got a headache. He went onto the observation deck and saw a bright, round light in the sky which "took off past the moon". Amongst other experiences, Mr A sometimes feels that "they" are controlling his mind against his will and directing him to do things which he doesn't want to do. Some nights Mr A has sensed "invisible beings" near his bed. In one particular instance, he was awakened by the presence of an invisible being pointing to a burn mark (accidentally done when welding) on his forehead. He believes that the west coast of the USA will be destroyed by earthquakes or other natural disasters as punishment for the wickedness of man. [**Moravec, 1980**].

Are people who report UFO sightings psychologically disturbed? This impolite allegation has been made by various armchair commentators throughout the history of the UFO controversy. But it is only recently that some researchers have scientifically investigated this question.

Grinspoon and Persky [**1972**] are proponents of the traditional psychoanalytic beliefs in all-powerful unconscious processes, their expression in the form of symbols, and the regression of thought to a more primal, magical mode when under stress or conflict. They speculated that this regression of thought towards fantasy could occur in UFO reports by chronically disturbed individuals (such as cases of hallucinatory schizophrenia, the shared delusions of folie a deux, or psychopathic personalities wishing for personal gain) or transiently disturbed healthy individuals experiencing altered or trance states of consciousness (with breast or penis symbolism often evident in the hallucinated images). The authors did not, however, offer specific UFO case examples as support for their ideas. Also, Freudian concepts are themselves controversial within psychology.

Warren [**1970**] attempted to show that UFO sighters suffer from "status inconsistency". This refers to individuals who have different, contradictory rankings on different measures of social class, e.g. high education but low income. According to Warren, the psychological stress and social alienation of unmet expectations, particularly perceived status deprivations relative to one's peers, can lead to a rejection of authority and an involvement in escapist fringe activities. An analysis of 1966 Gallup Poll data showed the total sample of UFO sighters were more likely to be status consistent (contradicting the hypothesis), but the subset of UFO sightings by white males were more likely to be status inconsistent with a high education but a relatively low income or occupational ranking (supporting the hypothesis). These results were contradictory but suggestive. However, subsequent studies by Warren and by Swift [**1980**] have failed to support the status inconsistency hypothesis.

Keul [**1982**] and associates administered the Rorschach projective personality test and memory, intelligence and suggestibility tests to 10 UFO percipients. A clinical psychologist independently interpreted the test data. The percipients were divided into three categories. There were nil in the X category ("reality-orientated, psychic stable witness"); seven in the Y category ("moderate psychic disorders" such as hysterical reactions, neurotic fears and confabulation tendency); and three in the Z category ("severe psychopathological disorders"). From this study, the author concluded that "it seemed a valid hypothesis that psychopathology plays a considerable role in Austrian UFO cases." A further study by Keul and Phillips [**1985**] with a larger sample size failed to confirm a link between UFO experience and psychopathology.

Other studies have supported the view that UFO percipients are of average or above-average character. In two surveys conducted by Sprinkle [**1976**], a total of 82 subjects completed personality and vocational interest inventories. The majority of the participants claimed to have had a UFO experience. Sprinkle concluded that the subjects, as a whole, were "persons of average or above average education, with professional and academic interests, with an interest in human behaviour, and with no obvious psychoneurotic or psychotic reactions."

One psychological study has focused on UFO abductees - individuals who claim to have been taken aboard a UFO and been subjected to a medical-style examination by UFO entities. Psychologist Dr Elizabeth Slater administered the Rorschach, TAT and MMPI personality tests, and the adult WAIS intelligence test, to nine UFO abductees, without being informed beforehand of the background of her subjects. Evaluating the subjects, Dr Slater described them as unusual and interesting, with a variety of personality styles. They shared a "brighter than average intelligence and a certain richness of inner life that can operate favorably in terms of creativity or disadvantageously to the extent that it can be overwhelming. Shared underlying emotional factors include a degree of identity disturbance, some deficits in the interpersonal sphere, and generally mild paranoia phenomena (hypersensitivity, wariness, etc.)". Further, "there is no evidence in the tests administered (that) any of the nine subjects possess the various forms of psychopathology by which they might have invented their reported experiences of UFO abduction". [**Bloecher et al, 1985, 30, 35**]. The psychological traits of inner turmoil and wariness were interpreted as possible consequences of the trauma and social stigmatisation associated with the UFO abduction experience.

Summarising the results of the above studies, there is no firm evidence to support the hypothesis that UFO witnesses tend to be psychologically disturbed or socially maladjusted as a group. In the case of two studies that initially suggested otherwise, later replications with larger sample sizes failed to support the hypothesis of psychological disturbance. The Sprinkle and Slater studies also had an advantage in the use of well-regarded self-report inventory tests such as the MMPI. Some psychologists have criticised the Rorschach and other projective personality tests on the basis of limited standardisation and reliability. Indeed, "the final interpretation of projective test responses may reveal more about the theoretical orientation, favorite hypotheses, and personal idiosyncrasies of the examiner than it does about the examinee's personality dynamics" [**Anastasi, 1976, 578**].

Whilst UFO witnesses as a group are not psychologically disturbed, there is evidence to suggest that a very small proportion of witnesses are. The individual involved in Case 3 is an example. Mr A described a number of experiences typical of those reported by "paranoid schizophrenics". According to traditional psychological definitions, paranoid schizophrenia primarily involves disturbances in cognitive functioning, and may feature delusions (substantial misinterpretations of real events which significantly influence thought and behaviour), hallucinations (the "perception" of people, objects or events which do not physically exist), distorted self image (such as body "contaminated" or falling apart), bizarre or illogical associations in thought and speech, and autism (pronounced isolation and withdrawal from others and a retreat into a fantasy world). The most common delusion is a paranoid fear of being influenced and controlled by outside forces. Paranoia functions as a psychological defence mechanism which projects the individual's responsibility for personal failures and wrongdoings onto external "enemies" [**Moravec, 1980a; Buss, 1966**].

In the case of Mr A. the subjective experience of his mind being controlled by outside forces is typical of the paranoid individual. The "invisible beings" are hallucinations which help provide companionship and meaning to an isolated, alienated man. The predicted natural disasters are part of a pseudo-religious belief which functions to deemphasise the individual's own weaknesses by emphasising the failings of other people. Investigation of Mr A's background shows him to be a 56-year-old migrant who lives alone in a small room with only the barest of essentials. He has trouble staying at jobs; sometimes fights the people there ("they're all against me, and I don't know why"), and has sometimes wanted to kill himself. All these details show that Mr A has trouble coping with everyday life. His isolation, old age and the social dislocation of trying to settle in a new country have all probably contributed to his stress. His UFO sighting is only a low weight nocturnal light with no supporting evidence. The fact that he has read much UFO literature, with a preference for the "way-out" type of articles, indicates Mr A has merely incorporated UFO lore into his delusions.

The proportion of UFO experiences which can be attributed to psychological disturbance is very small. In Hendry's [**1979**] study of 1,307 cases, only 0.5% of sightings were attributed to this cause. My own experience from first-hand UFO investigations suggests that of every 100 cases reported, an average of only one to two cases are due to psychopathology. Often it is the same one or two disturbed individuals who re-surface every few years to expound their claims to someone new. In these handful of cases, personal difficulties have contributed to a psychological disturbance and the individual has incorporated UFO and psychic lore in his or her delusions.

ALTERED STATES OF CONSCIOUSNESS

Is there such a thing as a "UFO state of mind"? An "altered state of consciousness" is a mental state, induced physiologically, psychologically or pharmacologically, which is recognised as a significant deviation in subjective experience or psychological functioning from the individual's normal, alert, waking consciousness. It may involve a greater preoccupation than usual with internal sensations or mental processes, changes in the formal characteristics of thought, and some impairment of reality testing [**Ludwig, 1972**].

Elsewhere, I have suggested the hypothesis that: "Predisposed individuals, in certain situations, undergo an altered state of consciousness during which vivid, subjective sensations are experienced and interpreted in a personally meaningful (UFO) context". "Predisposed individuals" include those with a history of experiencing dissociated states of consciousness and those with a ready belief in personal psychic experiences (the "psychic personality"). The "situations" include those where there is a reduction or overload in sensory stimuli and/or where the individual is exposed to psychological, physiological or psychic stress. The "altered state of consciousness" could be a fugue, possession, multiple personality, or allied states. The "vavid, subjective sensations" range from flashes of light and simple geometric patterns to complex "abduction by UFO entities" scenarios. The interpretation "in a personally meaningful UFO context" involves the incorporation of the individual's unconscious beliefs and fantasies, and his or her knowledge of UFOlore [**Moravec, 1981b**].

A number of features are common to most altered states, including changes in thinking, time sense (e.g. "timelessness"), emotional expression (ecstasy), body image ("oneness"), perception (Hallucinations), meaning or significance (illumination), sense of the ineffable (indescribable experience), feelings of rejuvenation ("rebirth") and hypersuggestibility (fantasies accepted as objectively true) [**Ludwig, 1972**].

The following pages present a brief survey of UFO case examples and the altered state of consciousness (ASC) which appears to be implicated in each. Further discussion and case examples are summarised in Moravec [**1981b and 1982/83**].

HYPNOPOMIC AND HYPNAGOGIC IMAGERY

■ **CASE 4 - Watrane, Tasmania, Australia, February 1976.**

A man was in bed, just about to go to sleep, when he noticed the doorway appeared to get "darker." He saw three figures walk through the closed door and come to his bed. The figures were two to two-and-a-half metres tall, a dull black colour and had vague facial features. One figure placed a hand on the percipient's leg, making him go numb to the waist, while another figure tried to enclose the percipient's leg in a silver, glowing "sugar bag." When the man called out, a figure made his mouth and right arm also go numb. The percipient managed to throw his cigarettes, lighter and ash tray towards his wife who stirred and started to put on the room light. Meanwhile the entities let go of the man, pulled off the bag, and one by one stepped over his wife's bed and out the window which had burst open in an orange glow. The woman had not seen anything and the window was found to be still closed [**Moravec, 1981c**].

The intermediate state between wakefulness and sleep is referred to as "hypnagogic;" the state preceding full wakefulness after sleep is termed "hypnopomic." Psychologists have found that during these states, many people have experienced sudden, involuntary sounds and images such as hearing one's name called and seeing "faces in the dark." Very often the images are vivid and realistic, although their content may be bizarre [**Reed, 1972**].

In one study of hypnagogic imagery, the researchers found "that loss of volitional control over mentation [thinking] tended to occur first; then loss of awareness of surroundings; and finally, loss of reality testing (hallucination) occurred" [**Vogel et al, 1972, 78**]. There were several instances of bizarre, inappropriate or distorted images (e.g. the image of tiny, hairy people sitting inside the chest cavity) and magical, omnipotent thinking (one subject reported that he was a giant waving his hand over an entire town, and with each wave of his hand the lights of the town became dimmer). Note the resemblances between these examples and reports of UFO entities and "electromagnetic effects."

The Watrane case has a number of features characteristic of imagery, including the vivid luminescence of the glowing bag and the glow outside the window, the bizarre scene of the entities walking through a solid object, and the context of the experience occurring on the awake/asleep interface. Also note the lack of physical changes to the environment and single witness status of the experience.

A number of close encounter UFO reports could be instances of imagery. This includes both UFO experiences where the subject is in bed and is "awakened" only to observe a vivid light or exotic entity; and UFO experiences reported by solitary motorists who are tired, lose concentration and enter a hypnagogic state. The content of the imagery - spaceships and entities - are a result of a cultural belief in extraterrestrial life and its possible visitation of Earth. [**Basterfield, 1981**]

AMNESIAS

■ **CASE 5 - Springwood, NSW, Australia, 1973.**

A man was awakened by a blue light coming through the caravan roof hatch. He determined that the light was part of a blue beam, apparently projected from an aerial disc above the caravan. The percipient tried to wake his friend without success. The next thing he clearly remembered was finding himself about half a kilometre away from the caravan, on a track leading into the nearby valley. Although he could not clearly recall anything of this "lost time" of some two hours, he felt some "beings - caucasian types" were involved, and that he was "aware of their purpose." [**Moravec, 1981c**].

A number of altered states can be considered as examples of the psychological defence strategy of "dissociation." Dissociative amnesia is not a mere forgetting, but an active process whereby unpleasant features are blotted out of awareness following a traumatic experience. Case 5 is an example of an amnesiac reaction in the UFO context.

FUGUES

■ **CASE 6 - Lawitta, Tasmania, 5th February, 1979.**

A young man's car was lit up by an intense white light from overhead. The car radio went dead, the lights went out and the engine stopped. Later that night the percipient was found by police in a Hobart city street. They went to speak to him because he had no lights on his car. The man did not know who he was, where he had come from, or where he lived. The police searched him, found his address on personal papers and took him to a hospital, where he was said to be suffering from shock. He had a high pulse rate. When doctors shone a light into his eyes, the percipient started to recall what had happened. He said that after the car stalled he had spent 10 to 15 minutes trying to get it started. He could not recall driving to Hobart. [**Moravec, 1981c**].

A fugue state consists of "transitory abnormal behaviour characterized by aimless wandering and more or less alteration of consciousness, usually, but not necessarily followed by amnesia. A desire for escape from some intolerable situation is usually the immediatley precipitating factor in the production of the fugue....In fugues of short duration, the patient wanders aimlessly, is highly emotional and when found is agitated and confused. In long fugues, he travels far, appears self-possessed, and lives in every way like a normal person except that he is not where he should be" [**Kolb, 1968, 75**].

A fugue differs from simple amnesia in that there is an actual physical flight from the individual's current environment. Also, in a fugue the amnesia may extend to the individual blocking out memory of his or her own identity in addition to his her behaviour during the fugue state.

The percipient in Case 6 appears to have suffered a fugue of short duration. Note the percipient's lost memory of his personal identity and that he drove to a new location without awareness of doing so. He was clearly traumatised when discovered by the police and during the hospital examination. However, a purely psychological interpretation of the incident is complicated by the apparent physical effects on the vehicle. The car had a flat battery, an unexpectedly low oil level, and damage to the alternator switch and headlight wiring.

POSSESSIONS

■ **CASE 7 - "Uniontown," Pennsylvania, USA, 25th October 1973.**

"Stephen" and two other witnesses approached a red ball of light above a field. The light descended, changed to a white colour and rested on or close to the ground. The dome-shaped object made "a sound like a lawn mower." Nearby, two large apelike creatures moved along a fence. When Stephen fired his rifle directly into the larger creature, it emitted a whine. Suddenly the UFO vanished and the creatures slowly returned to the woods. The UFO landing area now glowed a brilliant white colour. Five UFO investigators later examined the site with Stephen and his father. Whilst being questioned, Stephen suddenly rubbed his hands and face and shook back and forth. When two people attempted to assist him, Stephen flailed his arms and threw the two to ground. The percipient continued his wild behaviour until he collapsed. Whilst being helped down the hill, Stephen had a vision of a man dressed in black who told him: "If man doesn't straighten up, the end will come soon." When handed his glasses which had fallen off, Stephen responded by asking whose glasses they were and conveyed that he could see okay. According to his parents, neighbours and physicians, Stephen had never acted like this before. [**Schwarz, 1974**].

"A trance is usually defined as a temporary change in the person when he seems to be a very different person from his usual self, familiar before the episode and found again when the trance is ended....In possession trance, as different from non-possession trance, the person is believed to be invaded by a spirit or a new sense of power for good or ill" [**Hilgard, 1977, 20, 21**]. Thus possession is an ASC with a specific, superimposed, supernatural belief.

In Case 7, the percipient had no memory of what happened during his wild and bizarre behaviour. The investigating psychiatrist concluded that there was no evidence for dishonesty, sociopathic behaviour or druguse; rather that Stephen had undergone a fugue state triggered by a traumatic UFO encounter and explicable in terms of the psychodynamics of his past life. As well as being a dramatic example of a fugue, the Uniontown case can also be interpreted as a possession state where the percipient behaved as if "taken over" by the UFO entity.

MULTIPLE PERSONALITIES

■ **CASE 8 - Stocking Island, Bahamas, June 1974.**

Dr Andrija Puharich, former mentor of Uri Geller, has associated with a number of "psychic mediums." One medium, Phyllis, channelled communications whilst in a self-induced trance state from alleged extraterrestrial entities named "Ryr" and "Tom." The entities gave information on cosmic philosophy, the nature of their civilisation and the role of the Puharich group in bettering the world. When Tom replaced Ryr as the main communicator, the medium's trance voice changed appropriately. During these communications, Phyllis was not consciously aware of what she was saying. The content of the communications was retold to her after she came out of trance. [**Holroyd, 1979**].

Multiple personality is a "condition in which the integrated personality fragments into two or more personalities each of which manifests a relatively complete integration of its own and which is relatively independent of the other personalities" [**Chaplin, 1975, 329**]. Where there are only two personalities, the state is usually referred to as dual or alternating personalities.

One view of the origin of multiple personality is that where there is an active incompatibility between repressed elements and the rest of the personality, the former may separate from the usual consciousness and organise a personality of their own. This new secondary personality has its own consciousness which often has no recollection of the usual primary personality and carries out acts independent of it. The disposition and character of the secondary personality usually differs from that of the primary personality since it is made up of thoughts and feelings rejected by the primary personality [**Kolb, 1968**].

The main difference between possession states and multiple personality is that the former may involve the simple transmission of messages without fully-developed identities, whilst the latter consist of fully developed personalities with their own individual identities.

Whilst multiple personality has commonly been considered a rare occurrence in the psychiatric context, a case can be made for its existence in the non-psychopathological, transient context of the UFO and psychic mediums. In the 1920s to 1940s, an American psychiatrist, Dr William Sadler, investigated many people claiming to be psychics or mediums. He wrote: "It is safe to conclude that many honest mediums are afflicted by some phase of double or multiple personality. In multiple dissociation there may exist in the mind a systematized, orderly group of complexes, among which 'reside' the controls and guides under whose direction the medium appears to operate....several distinct consciousnesses take turns, but with no regularity, in putting an appearance. To those not versed in these matters they seem to be strange and extreme changes of mood and behaviour, accompanied by the ability to change the voice, facial expression, and behaviour to suit the personality in evidence" [**Sadler, 1947, 282, 285**].

The same circumstances appear to operate in the UFO context. In Case 8, the content of the communications appears to originate from both the medium's subconscious (via transient multiple personalities) and the minds of the other group members, particularly Puharich who has acted as the common central thread in a number of contact groups.

AUTOMATIC WRITING

■ **CASE 9 - Sydney, NSW, Australia, June 1980.**

A group of women claimed to receive communications from "spirits of the dead" and "space entities" by means of visions and automatic writing. The main space entity told them that he was here to learn more about human beings and wanted to help the group. The woman who received messages via automatic writing explained that during these experiences her mind is blank and in a "meditative state." "I know that somebody or something makes my hand move. I can't write anything with my left hand yet it's only that which is written with...My mind is a blank but I'm aware that my hand is moving. And when they [the group members] ask questions I can hear the questions they ask. But it is not my mind that's giving the answeres, because the answers suddenly come out and my hand starts writing. So it's like being separate from the body...Somebody else is taking over my mind, and it's their thought going in here and making me write." The percipient does not know what she has written until it is read back to her after the session has ended. [**Moravec, 1981b and 1981c**].

Automatic writing is "writing carried out without conscious control" [**Chaplin, 1975, 49**]. Like fugues and multiple personalities, automatic writing is an example of an automatism or dissociation of personality "in which unconscious factors temporarily gain control, act independently and dictate behaviour" [**Kolb, 1968, 75**]. Amnesia may or may not be associated with experience.

Automatic writing has been with us for a long time. Many messages have been attributed to spirits of the dead. As UFO experiences have become more common, a proportion of messages have been attributed to UFO entities. In Case 9, the communications were initially attributed to spirits of the dead, and then to UFO entities. Thus belief and sociological factors appear to play a role in the interpretation of automatic writing experiences. The evidence points to the medium's own subconscious mind as the source of the messages.

AUTOHYPNOSIS

■ **CASE 10 - Bouahmama, Algeria, March1958.**

During the Algerian War, a French Foreign Legionnaire on sentry duty heard a whistling noise. He looked up and saw an enormous, elliptical-shaped object descend and hover silently 35-40 metres above the ground and 50 metres distant. "The object was surrounded by pale green light, and an intense conical beam of emerald-green light was coming from the centre of the underpart towards the ground. Legionnaire N.G. did not fire his rifle, nor did he pick up the telephone. He just remembers staring at the object for 45 to 50 minutes. The pale green and emerald colours were the most beautiful, relaxing and fascinating colours he had ever seen. Legionnaire N.G. had forgotten all about the war. All nervous and psychological tension had gone from his mind. He was just feeling happy." Then the noise came again, the object rose gently, and flew off at temendous speed. Neurological and psychiatric examinations found the percipient in good physical and mental health. [**Mesnard, 1973, 17-18**].

In contrast with artificially-induced hypnotic states, autohypnosis is a hypnosis which is self-induced. The Algerian case contains many features suggestive of a hypnotic state having been experienced by the witness: the entrancement by the fascinating colours of the phenomenon; the effect of relaxation and elimination of tension; the feeling of happiness; and the complete distraction from everyday worries. The percipient described his peaceful state thusly: "It was like time running very slowly...it was like being in another world."

HYPNOSIS

■ **CASE 11 - White Mountains, New Hampshire, USA, 19th September 1961.**

Betty and Barney Hill were travelling from Canada to home in Portsmouth when they observed a star-like light which appeared to get larger and brighter. After several kilometres of driving, the couple stopped to take a closer look at the object through binoculars. It was a pancake-like disc, glowing with brilliant white light, with two fin-like projections on either side and a double row of windows. Behind the windows, Barney could see six or more uniformed beings staring down at him. Terrified of possible capture, he ran back to the car and quickly drove off. The couple then heard a beeping sound and suffered a period of drowsiness. Disturbed by the fact that they could not recall what had happened to them over a period of two hours following their sighting, and because Barney had developed an anxiety and a series of warts, the Hills eventually visited a psychiatrist, Dr Benjamin Simon, who hypnotically regressed them to the time of the UFO incident. In separate sessions, the Hills recounted a story of abduction and physical examination by UFO entities. [**Fuller, 1974**].

The classic "interrupted journey" of Betty and Barney Hill paved the way for a new type of UFO report - the "abduction" experience - and the use of hypnosis in UFO investigations. Hypnosis has been used to both relax the subject after a traumatic experience and as a technique for retrieving information from subjects who have experienced a period of amnesia.

Hypnosis, as traditionally conceptualised, is an artificially induced ASC brought about through certain "induction" techniques. The basic characteristics attributed to hypnosis include passivity, redistribution of attention, increased fantasy and role behaviour, reduction in reality testing with increased tolerance for reality distortion, and hypersuggestibility [**Hilgard, cited by Honorton, 1974**].

The exact nature of hypnosis has been a matter of debate. Some researchers have suggested that it is a specific altered state of consciousness whilst others have suggested it is merely a conscious roleplay featuring a heightened suggestibility. Similarly, there has been extensive debate as to the reliability of information gained during hypnotic age regression. The popular belief that hypnosis is a technique which delivers absolute truth is negated by research which suggests that hypnotic regressions are not age accurate but rather situations where the subject creates a hallucinated environment appropriate to the suggestion, combines random memories from both the period and from years before and after, and contributes a certain amount of confabulation.

Hilgard [**1977**] cites a case where a subject was hypnotically regressed beyond birth and down the evolutionary ladder. The subject moved around the flooor, apelike, and could not talk. But according to a prearranged suggestion, she communicated by sneezing involuntarily when an appropriate letter of the alphabet was presented. When asked, "Where are you?", she selected the letters, C-H-I-M-P-A-N-Z-E-E. This case dramatically illustrates the extent to which a hypnotic subject will roleplay a regression on demand.

Could it be that the technique of hypnosis actually promotes abduction fantasies, given the right social context and the now readily available abduction lore? Lawson [**1977**] compared the narratives of "real" UFO abductees and "imaginary" abductees who were hypnotised and directed to imagine that they had had such an experience. The narratives of both groups revealed many parallels, including many presumed obscure patterns from the UFO literature. Lawson suggested several sources for the data: the imagination; general UFO information within the culture at large; extrasensory perception of UFO information from ufologists present or from other sources; and the incorporation of memories, such as past real-life surgery incorporated in a fantasised medical examination by UFO entities. One criticism of Lawson's work is that he has thus far made only selective, subjective comparisons of a few "real" and "imaginary" transcripts. What is needed is a controlled comparison utilising a large sample of cases and independent judges kept "blind" as to the identity of each transcript. One suggested explanation for the Betty and Barney Hill abduction case is that Barney Hill became entranced by staring at the star-like object he initially observed and, consistent with the increased fantasy and reduced reality-testing typical of hypnotic states, then fantasised an entity contact experience. Ten days after the UFO sighting, Betty Hill had nightmares of being abducted by UFO entities. The Hills were regressed independently but not before Betty had communicated details of her abduction dreams to Barney. These dreams contained details similar to what the couple were later to relate when hypnotised, and could therefore be the ultimate source of the abduction story. This psychological hypothesis may be complicated by certain physical evidence claims such as the discovery of a dozen bright, shiny spots on the trunk of the car following the UFO incident.

To summarise, the recall of observations and experiences during hypnotic age regression is not always truthful or accurate. The distortions produced during the memory process can also occur in hypnotic states. The validity of data obtained can be limited by a number of factors including the subject's ready compliance to the hypnotist's direct and indirect suggestions, and the incorporation of nonrelevant memories and fantasies.

A number of UFO experiences appear to have involved subjective perceptions during altered states of consciousness. There is scope for much future research into methods of induction and the personality and situational characteristics necessary to produce an ASC-mediated UFO experience. One important point requiring clarification is whether the ASC is responsible for the entire reported experience or whether a physical phenomenon is also involved. A number of cases exist where alleged physical damage has been done to the vehicles involved in the UFO incidents. Thus a purely psychological hypothesis may be insufficient to cover all the aspects of some UFO reports.

A critical research question is whether close encounter UFO percipients are more likely to be prone to experience dissociated states of consciousness. The Bloecher *et al* [**1985**] study of UFO abductees found no evidence of psycho pathology or personalities prone to fugue states or multiple personality shifts. Yet it also found, that under stressful conditions, six of the nine subjects showed a potential for transient psychotic experiences involving a loss of reality testing along with confused and disordered thinking that can be bizarre, peculiar or very primitive and emotionally charged.

Other anomalous experiences may also occur during altered states of consciousness. The images of an intense white light; a feeling of paralysis; movement through a tunnel; and an encounter with strange, non-human entities; have been reported in experiences as diverse as UFO abductions, lucid dreams, out-of-body experiences, near-death experiences, drug-induced hallucinations and mystical experiences. Thus similar imagery may emerge in UFO as well as other anomalous experiences occurring during an ASC. The difference depends not so much on the content of the experience as on the differing interpretations placed upon it. And the the interpretation varies according to the situational context in which the experience occurs, and according to the sociall-conditioned beliefs held by the individual percipient. [**Moravec, 1982/83**]

Three hypotheses might account for these constant images: **social conditioning** (where people incorporate generally circulated knowledge of "mysterious phenomena" into their hallucinatory experiences); **archetypes** (Jung's [**1969**] notion of unconscious images originating from a hypothesised "collective unconscious" common to all mankind); and **neurophysiology** (Siegel's [**1977**] conception that because of the common neurophysiological makeup of human beings, there is a finite number of images which the brain consistently hallucinates).

BELIEF

Examine the history of UFO phenomena and you will discover a panorama of conflicting and emotionally defended beliefs. It is almost as if the UFO functions as a Rorschach inkblot that reflects the individual's beliefs.

Consider the chain of people involved. There is the percipient who reports his or her experience; the investigator who documents and interprets the report; the outside "expert" who makes a pronouncement on the case; the mass media that circulates the story; and the general public that adopts certain attitudes towards the reported phenomena. All have made judgements and statements, often contradictory, which fuel the UFO controversy. What are these beliefs and how do they affect the UFO data?

BELIEFS OF PERCIPIENTS

■ **CASE 12 - Hollington, East Sussex, England, 4th October 1981.**

Mrs A was watching television when she felt "compelled" to go to the window, from where she saw a large, bright yellow object in the sky. Joined by her daughter-in-law, Janette, the two women watched enthralled for half an hour as the object wobbled and pulsated and repeatedly changed shape. Several times, as an aircraft came nearby, the object emitted smoke and hid itself behind the smoke. Janette reported seeing lights and structured sides to the object. Both women claimed to experience severe, recurrent headaches over the following three weeks, and Mrs A suffered a 14-hour blackout four days after the sighting. The witnesses were firmly convinced they has observed a spacecraft piloted by aliens. Upon investigation, the object was identified as the moon. [**Randles, 1982**]

This example of a misidentification of a common, natural object, with a strong belief superimposed, is extreme but not unique. The moon, the planets and the stars have sometimes been imbued with the most remarkable of properties.

According to sociologist Robert Hall [**1974, 215**]: "What people believe is usually organised into elaborate systems of belief... It appears that people perceive more readily and accurately those things that are consistent with their pre-existing knowledge and beliefs than things that are not.. It appears that ambiguous situations tend to be interpreted so as to fit in with and support pre-existing beliefs and knowledge, and gaps in knowledge tend to be filled with consistent improvisations."

Do people have preconceived ideas of what a UFO should look like? Haines [**1977; 1978/79**] compared UFO drawings made by alleged eyewitnesses with drawings made by non-witnesses. Comparisons of several hundred drawings showed no discernable difference in the UFO outline shape or its dome. One study found that UFO witnesses drew less miscellaneous details (such as apertures and markings). Overall, the studies imply that people do have at least some preconceptions of what a UFO should look like, perhaps from a commonly held social stereotype of media portrayals.

Many people believe that UFOs are alien spaceships visiting the Earth. The belief in extraterrestrial UFOs reaches its most extreme form in the case of the "contactees" - individuals who claim to have communicated with UFO entities and/or been temporarily taken on board the "spaceships". The strength of this will to believe is demonstrated by the 'Bay City' UFO cult documented by Festinger *et al* [**1964**]. Several of the cult members quit their jobs and cut their ties several weeks before a predicted natural disaster and their predicted pickup by flying saucers, neither of which eventuated.

In contrast to those UFO percipients who readily adopt an exotic belief, there are some who react in a more cautious manner by adopting Hynek's [**1974**] "escalation of hypotheses". These witnesses try to explain their observations in familiar terms where possible, only concluding they are unidentified when all other explanations are ruled out. Thus some UFO percipients *do* test out their observations and avoid leaping to hasty and exotic conclusions.

BELIEFS OF INVESTIGATORS

Several surveys have been conducted which give some insight into the beliefs or opinions of UFO investigators. The Moravec [**1981d**] survey polled 20 scientifically-oriientated UFO researchers associated with the Australian Centre for UFO Studies (ACUFOS). Greenawald [**1978**] polled 43 members of the USA-based Mutual UFO Network, being probably a mixture of scientifically-orientated investigators and less critically-minded enthusiasts.

The extra-terrestrial hypothesis (ETH) was favoured as the most likely explanation of UFOs by both Australian and American researchers. The ETH was nominated by 40 percent of Australian researchers - though sometimes in conjunction with other hypotheses - and by 88 percent of the American MUFON members, but this was on a forced choice basis (extraterrestrial / inter-dimensional / paraphysical / no opinion) which may have effectively restricted the variation in responses.

Whilst the ETH predominated, the Australian survey also showed support for a wide range of other hypotheses, particularly the inter-dimensional, misperceptions/psychological, psychic/paranormal and "many different origins" hypotheses. Significantly, 25 percent of the Australian researchers did not give a preferred explanation, stating that they didn't know or preferred to keep an open mind.

Ufologists may go through a sequence of beliefs as they continue their UFO investigations. Hendry [**1979**] suggests that many ufologists initially consider all UFO reports, concentrating on the physical evidence and favouring the ETH. Then, assuming a higher yield of information, the ufologist concentrates on the high strangeness Close Encounters of the Third Kind and psychic aspects. This leads him or her to believe that the witnesses' minds are being manipulated in some fashion and that most cases are paranormal. Some ufologists anchor on the first "nuts and bolts" stage. The motivating force in following the sequence is the struggle between the outcome the ufologist desires and frustration over what the evidence permits.

Hendry has viewed ufologists from an American perspective. In Australia and Europe another trend followed by some ufologists has been to consider all reports, concentrating on physical evidence, flirt with stranger paranormal cases, and then due to a perceived lack of solid evidence, favour the psychological/misperception hypothesis, perhaps accompanied by natural phenomena (such as ball lightning or hypothesised "earth lights").

We all have a tendency to believe in certain things; to become infatuated with certain ideas. There is nothing wrong in favouring a particular hypothesis; after all, hypothesis formulation is an accepted part of the scientific method. But one of the many important tasks of a ufologist is to recognise one's beliefs or biases, and to ensure they do not unduly influence one's investigations and reports.

BELIEFS OF SCEPTICS

After the UFO event has been interpreted by the percipient and the investigator, other commentators may contribute their interpretations. One of these commentators, the UFO sceptic, can be as much a prisoner of his own beliefs as some UFO proponents. In practice, there are two kinds of sceptics. The 'true sceptic' avoids taking up a belief. Instead, he or she critically evaluates both pro and con arguments and their associated sets of supportive evidence with equal scepticism. In contrast, the debunker has a preset attitude against the existence of UFO phenomena. Just as the 'true believer' readily accepts any outrageous claim, the 'true disbeliever' fervently denies anu UFO claim, ignoring any data or evidence contrary to his or her own view.

There are many examples, historically and contemporary, of sceptics who have been misled by their own beliefs: the eighteenth century French physicists who refused to accept hundreds of reports of stones falling from the sky, now known meteorites [**Westrum, 1982**]; the British astronomer royal who stated that "space travel is utter bilge"; and in the 1980s, the Committee for Scientific Investigation of Claims of the Paranormal (CSICOP) attack on pro-astrology research findings by using false statistical reasoning, the insinuation of hoaxing and an attempted cover-up of their mistakes [**Kamman, 1982**]. In the UFO field, some sceptics have attempted have attempted to explain away UFOs by using hypotheses that ignore vast chunks of UFO data and which have been seriously questioned by other scientists (eg. Klass' [**1968**] plasmas, and Callahan and Mankin's [**1978**] electrified luminescent insects).

What factors motivate sceptics to behave in the way that they do? There are some legitimate reasons why sceptics adopt an attitude of disbelief towards UFO claims. The most readily available information about UFOs is in the form of sensationalist and inaccurate tabloid newspaper stories. Scientists are limited by finite time and funds in the subjects that they can research. The phenomena appear to be elusive and thus difficult to study.

But less noble, non-scientific considerations also arise. There is a resistance to not only accepting, but also examining, data that conflicts with the current, dominant scientific ideology. "Indeed we might describe the body of scientific knowledge accepted at any time and the people who bear that knowledge as constituting an unusually strong belief system which resists inconsistent claims of knowledge... To the extent that observation challenges established beliefs, scientists resist accepting the observation," [**Hall, 1974, 220-221**]. This resistance can take several forms: avoidance or denial of evidence; illogical arguments ("some cases are false, therefore all are"); and buck-passing between scientific specialties. It is as if the researcher has experienced "anomaly anxiety" when faced with new evidence that doesn't fit the accepted parameters of knowledge.

The traditional aura of ridicule which has surrounded the UFO subject can lead to pressure and ridicule by peers which may influence research choices or even jeopardise a career. Astronomer J. Allen Hynek explained why he initially maintained a negative or neutral public posture to UFO research in the mid-1950s: "... at that time I was either an assistant or an associate professor at Ohio State, and Ohio State is not Harvard, nor the University of Chicago; frankly, I was much more concerned with my own career at the time. I knew if I really came on waving my arms I would have been declared a nut and my services would no longer have been required." [**Hynek and Vallée, 1975, 193**]

As well as individual ridicule, another disturbing tactic of some sceptics is the attempt to stifle debate and research on some topics. In 1983, the University of Nebraska-Lincoln sponsored a conference on "Exploring Unexplained Phenomena" with a major focus on UFOs. A prominent member of CSICOP contacted the University organisers and chancellor to vehemently complain about the sponsoring of the conference, questioning the credibility of the presenters and indicating that those organisations which publicly questioned the government lent support to the communist movement. [**Andrus, 1983**]

A sceptical attitude can be a useful approach to studying anomalous phenomena when it involves a critical, but objective, evaluation of data and hypotheses. But when objectivity is replaced by dogmatic belief in the non-existence of a phenomenon, and the tools of ridicule and character assassination are freely applied to stifle research, then it is clear that sceptical belief can have damaging consequences.

BELIEFS OF SOCIETY

The public circulation of a UFO report is usually the final link in a chain which started with the actual UFO event. The mass media, which often appear to place priority on how sensational an event is, rather than on accuracy (particularly with controversial subjects such as UFOs), may completely distort an already distorted account of a UFO event. Some UFO reports may be destined to be quoted again and again in many UFO books, attaining a kind of folklore status. These accounts, be they accurate or otherwise, form a major source of information which influences public beliefs about UFOs.

What beliefs does Western society hold about UFOs? If we take the American Gallup polls as a guide, a majority of the population believes that UFOs are real. Polls conducted over a 12-year period asked national samples of adult Americans whether UFOs are "something real or just people's imaginations". Of the 93 to 96 percent who had heard or read about UFOs, an increasing proportion thought that they were real: 46 percent in 1966; 54 percent in 1973; and 57 percent in 1978 [**Swift, 1980**].

Although there are dozens of hypotheses about the nature of UFOs, the majority of people automatically equate UFOs with alien spaceships. There has been established a cultural myth that we are being visited by spacecraft from another planet. Why do people so readily believe in UFOs as extraterrestrial visitors? Jung [**1969**] interpreted UFOs as a living myth which expressed unconscious collective concerns about such issues as nuclear war and overpopulation by positing the existence of extraterrestrial saviours clothed in the technological garb of modern times. The round, disc or spherical shapes of UFOs act as unconscious *mandala* (Sanskrit for circle) symbols respresenting wholeness, order, deliverance and salvation.

If there is a predominant belief in society that UFOs exist and that they are extraterrestrial spacecraft, how does such a belief influence the behaviour of UFO percipients, investigators and sceptics? The percipient may intentionally or unintentionally alter the characteristics of his or her testimony to fit in with the expectation that he or she is observing a spaceship. Persinger [**1979**] has suggested that even the media-generated assumptions associated with the terms "UFO" and "flying saucer" can modify memory and behaviour in the direction of the assumptions. The UFO investigator who is not aware of the need to uphold the utmost objectivity in his or her investigations, may emphasise or favourably modify those characteristics of the UFO report that fit in with his or her own beliefs. Even the sceptic may adopt the cultural myth of UFO equals extraterrestrial spacecraft, and thereby base his or her arguments for the non-existence of UFOs on mistaken assumptions.

We have examined the beliefs of percipients, investigators, sceptics and society. As we follow the chain beginning with the UFO event, we find that the percipient, the investigator and the sceptic can all input their sometimes biased views and thereby change the UFO event as reported. The sensationalised distortions by the mass media and the overall social beliefs about UFOs can further transform the data [**see Figure 1**]. The end result is that the published UFO report may be very different from what actually happened. The investigator must ensure objectivity is maintained in his or her investigation, and the researcher must remain aware of the potential biasing influences of people's beliefs.

PARAPSYCHOLOGY

Parapsychology is the study of events which allegedly involve a human awareness of or influence on the environment without normal sensory contact or action. Some UFO researchers have claimed that there is a parapsychological component to the UFO phenomenon - either because there are certain UFO reports which appear to include the occurrence of paranormal events; or because there are aspects of UFO appearance and behaviour which suggest a paranormal process or origin. Whilst the claims of parapsychology are in themselves controversial, this should not stop us from examining the alleged parapsychological aspects of UFO phenomena. For no data should be censored. Rather, all the data should be considered as long it is reliable and effectively documented.

'PSIUFO phenomena' are those cases where UFO and paranormal events apparently overlap [**Moravec, 1981c**]. There are a number of different types of cases, as the following examples illustrate.

MENTAL COMMUNICATIONS

■ **CASE 13 - Frankston, Victoria, Australia, 25th July 1972.**

On the 3rd of July, Mrs Maureen Puddy stopped her car to observe a blue, disc-shaped object above the road. On the 25th, she again observed the same object, but this time lost control of her car which slowed to a halt by itself. An inaudible "voice" spoke to her: "All your tests will be negative. Tell the media we mean no harm. You now have control." The car engine restarted itself and the object was gone. On the 22nd of February 1973, the percipient heard a voice say: "Return to the meeting place." Returning to the encounter location, she experienced a sequence of visions of UFO entities [**Basterfield, 1977; Magee, 1972**].

In mental communication cases, a person claims to have received communications from a source that is usually identified as a UFO entity. The communication may be received through a variety of modes including "telepathy", automatic writing, trance states or visions. The content of the communications can include an espousal of philosophical and spiritual concepts, and predictions of future events. Sometimes a group of people gather round one or more "psychically-gifted" individuals who channel incoming communications from the "higher intelligences".

POLTERGEISTS

■ **CASE 14 - Wooler, Ontario, Canada, 2nd July 1968.**

Fred and Wayne Coulthard observed an object with rotating red lights which agitated the family's horses and cats. Less then two hours later, poltergeist disturbances began in the house and continued for several days. A window shattered; cards, spoons and a glass were thrown around; and a strong odour of roses was detected in the kitchen [**Greystone, 1969**].

Poltergeists (literally "noisy spirits") feature the unexplained movement of objects, and have traditionally been associated with the "haunting" of people or places. In the UFO context, there are UFO cases which feature poltergeist-like effects such as "levitation", or which are preceded or followed by a classic, object-throwing poltergeist.

APPARITIONS

■ **CASE 15 - "Highland Farm", Tasmania, Australia, March 1975.**

A man observed two soundless flashing lights, beneath which was a yellow glow dimly

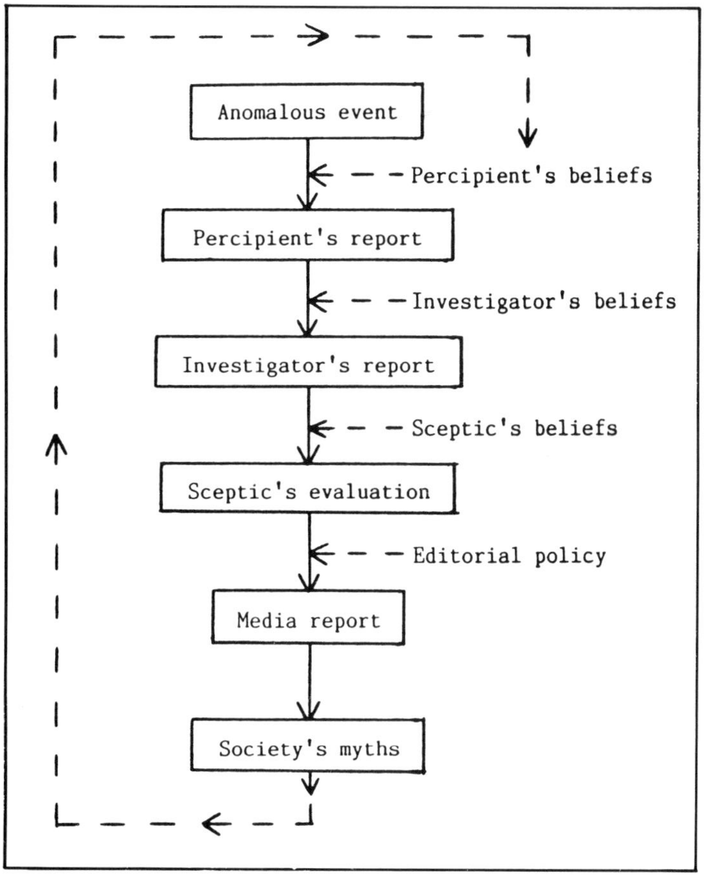

Figure 1 - The anomalous event, as transformed by beliefs. (Note: the ordering and relevance of each factor may vary from case to case, and also does not preclude the influence of other factors.)

illuminating the ground. The lights sped upwards at a steep angle. In the same month, two shooters observed an apparition on the same farm. One described it as a woman in period dress who glided up steps; the other as an oval area of light which pulsed until it faded away. There were other sightings of apparitions and nocturnal lights at the same locale [**Moravec, 1981c**].

Apparitions are hallucinatory experiences of the visual kind, usually involving a human figure. Some parapsychologists believe that apparitions are extrasensory communications which become conscious through a hallucinated experience.

HEALINGS

■ **CASE 16 - South-eastern France, 2nd November 1968.**

Dr X, a biologist, observed the approach of two red and silver, luminescent, disc-shaped objects. The two objects merged into one, and shone a white spotlight on the percipient. The object then "dematerialised" with a bang. Afterwards, the percipient realised that both a painful, three-day-old axe wound from chopping wood, and a ten-year-old Algerian War wound had completely healed [**Michel, 1969**].

Paranormal healings are rapid or instantaneous healings of physiological wounds, where such healings are not achievable by present medical techniques under the circumstances described. In some cases, paranormal healings appear to be directly associated with UFOs. Many UFO-healing cases appear to involve the direction of a powerful light onto the percipient prior to the alleged healing taking place.

GHOSTLIGHTS

■ **CASE 17 - Boulia, Queensland, Australia, June-July 1912.**

The channel country of western Queensland is the reputed haunt of the Min Min Light. Whilst on horseback in the early morning hours, Henry Lamond observed a glary, green ball of light. It moved at about 16 km/h at an estimated height of one and a half to three metres above the ground. The horse momentarily stopped trotting, lifted her head and pricked her ears. The light and rider passed each other, going in opposite directions. When the light was about 180 metres off, it suddenly faded away [**Lamond, 1937**].

Ghostlights are small lights which usually occur close to ground level and tend to reappear in the same location. The light may perform evasive-like manoeuvres when pursued, and may become associated with a local folklore of tragic death. Ghostlights appear to fit both the classifications of a UFO (unidentified, airborne light) and a haunting (recurrent, localised manifestation of possibly paranormal origin).

TIME LAPSES AND ABDUCTIONS

■ **CASE 18 - Jindabyne, NSW, Australia, September 1974.**

Whilst spot-lighting animals, an 11-year-old boy and a friend saw a bright white spherical light on the ground about 800 metres away. Several years later, the percipient began to have vivid "memories" of that evening and realised there had been an unaccounted for time lapse of two hours. According to what he recalled, the two had become surrounded by a blue light as they approached the object. They floated through a hatch into a grey rectangular room. They were placed on two benches and examined by several tall, hairless beings who attached many "wires" to the witnesses, parting and closing their clothes without tearing them. The percipients were eventually returned to the spot from where they had been taken [**Moravec, 1984**].

Some UFO experiences involve a "time lapse" where the percipient is unable to consciously recall the events which occurred during a certain period of time. When later hypnotised, or sometimes spontaneously, the percipient may recall an "abduction" experience involving involuntary seizure and examination by UFO entities. In many abduction cases, there are reports of paranormal events, such as the passage of a solid object through a seemingly solid wall; the temporary extraction and examination of bodily organs; "disintegrations" and "materialisations" of objects; and discrepancies in perceived time.

There are a number of possible explanations for PSIUFO cases. Some reports involve a *misinterpretation of common natural phenomena*. For example, object movements in poltergeist cases can sometimes be attributed to diverse causes from improperly hung doors to vibrations from motor vehicles and earth movements. Apparitions may sometimes be caused by reflections or misidentifications of petrol pumps, letter boxes and washing line clothes seen under poor observational conditions. Some ghostlights turn out be marsh gas lights, clusters of luminescent insects, light refraction effects and ball lightning.

A large proportion of cases can be attributed to *psychological causes*. In some cases, especially those featuring mental communications and apparitions, there is evidence of a psychological disturbance (psychosis) triggered by personal stresses unrelated to the UFO experience. In these particular cases, the individual has merely incorporated UFO and psychic lore in his or her delusions. Where there is a group centred around a "psychic" who receives communications from alleged UFO entities, there is usually an evolving belief system maintained and reinforced by individual group members to satisfy their own psychological needs. The "alien beings" can offer hope and security in a hostile, chaotic world, and can fulful a spiritual need not satisfied by the sometimes restrictive dogma of conventional organised religions. The experiences provide excitement in an otherwise mundane, everyday life, and the "psychic circle" serves the need to identify with and belong to a trusting group. The "mental communications" originate not from "alien intelligences", but from the human mind which has subconsciously projected some of the individual's own, disowned thoughts and feelings onto imaginary, external entities.

A proportion of apparition cases appears to be due to hypnopompic and hypnagogic imagery - the often vivid and bizarre hallucinations which can be experienced during the intermediate sleep/awake state of consciousness. Some UFO healings may involve psychosomatic complaints which are "cured" by suggestion following the UFO event. Where there is a time lapse without a conscious recall of events, the most likely explanation is an amnesia or fugue state. Whether this psychological state was triggered by personal stresses unrelated to the UFO event, or by a physically anomalous UFO event, remains to be determined. Cases involving a recalled abduction may include some element of hallucination or fantasy. In the case of abduction memories recalled during hypnosis, there is the additional problem of heightened suggestibility. This may lead the subject to try and please the hypnotist, and to pick up hints from the questioners and the environment, thereby creating biased testimony. Further psychological studies of abduction claimants are required to determine to what extent such claims can be explained by psychological processes.

A more controversial hypothesis is that the cases we have been examining have *paranormal causes*. It might be the case that UFO phenomena have a paranormal origin. If true, perhaps individuals with a history of psychic experiences such as apparitions and poltergeists are psychic and are more likely to see a UFO existing beyond the normal sensory range. Alternatively, UFO phenomena may be more akin to hallucinatory apparitions or the transient, unconsciously-produced physical manifestations of poltergeists rather than being normal physical objects.

Possible support for the paranormal hypothesis of UFO origin comes from cases where there is a tradition of tragic death and subsequent haunting; where there is a selective perception of events; where there is an association with other paranormal events such as apparitions and poltergeists; where the UFO has unusual physical aspects such as changing shape, materialising/dematerialising or casting no shadow; and where the phenomena appear to be dependent on the presence of a particular individual. There are also other features of UFO phenomena which are more readily explainable by a paranormal or psychological hypothesis rather than a physical hypothesis such as the extraterrestrial hypothesis. For example: the vast number of different UFO shapes and entity descriptions; the lack of any apparent purpose in "their" behaviour; and the relative lack of physical evidence. There are suggestive precedents for apparitions that uncannily imitate physical objects [**Tyrell, 1963**]; the experimental creation of poltergeists, such as the group of Canadian parapsychologists who created an imaginary character called Philip, and after regularly meeting for a year, claimed to produce raps and table movements [**Owen and Sparrow, 1976**]; lights of apparent paranormal origin, as in the flashing lights which centred around a 19-year-old girl in Clayton, North Carolina in 1962 [**Roll, 1976**]; and even accounts which describe visual sightings of out-of-body projections as balls of light [**Rogo, 1978**].

If UFOs are physical objects, they may still have the capacity to sometimes produce paranormal effects. The UFO experience might trigger or amplify psychic abililties such as extrasensory perception psychokinesis. Or mental communications and apparitions might be extrasensory communications from the UFO intelligence to the percipient. The main drawback to the paranormal hypothesis is that regardless of any UFO connection, paranormal experiences are controversial, being either in doubt or unexplained. Therefore, attempting to explain one unknown phenomenon, UFOs, with another alleged unknown phenomenon, psi, may not end up explaining anything at all.

Some PSIUFO cases may have *physical causes*. In the case of healings, research suggests that a pulsed, high frequency electromagnetic field source can be used to enhance the regeneration rate of peripheral nerve fibres, i.e. to speed up wound healing. The EM field is pulsed so that the heating effect on the tissue is much less than would occur if the energy were continuous. The biological effect of the EM field may operate at the cellular and/or nervous system (bloodflow and oxygenation) level [**Bentall, 1976**]. The possibility of UFO-promoted healing by electromagnetic radiation is appealing, given the other documented EM effects of UFOs in stopping or interfering with vehicle engines, headlights and radios. Many UFO-healing cases appear to involve the direction of a powerful light onto the percipient prior to the alleged healing taking place - indicating either a significant physical energy process or psychological effect. If there are non-psychosomatic UFO healings - by deliberate intent or as a side-effect

- then the medical implications are both startling and worthy of immediate attention.

Ghostlights may also have physical causes. The Vestigia group conducted an instrumented field study of the Long Valley Mystery Light in Washington, New Jersey in November, 1976. Observers sighted a small, yellowish-white light, took seven infrared photographs and recorded an electrical disturbance and geiger counter readings [**Wagner, Hulse and McGrath, 1978**]. This study indicates the presence of a physical phenomenon which might be geophysically-based given that the light has made frequent appearances in the same area over a 20 to 40-year period. The occasional observation of mysterious lights before, during or after earthquakes, has led to the suggestion that ghostlights have a geophysical cause. Persinger [**1976**] has hypothesised that in areas prone to tectonic stress and strain release, highly localised, transient "electic field columns" could form, ionise the surrounding air and produce luminosities which could move erratically along the lines of force, and interfere with both electrical equipment and the human brain, causing tingling sensations, paralysis and hallucinations. Whilst intriguing, the hypothesis has limitations in the use of supportive data of questionable reliability, the questionable assumption that such a phenomenon as a "localised electric field column" actually exists

TABLE 5 - THE ROLE OF PSYCHOLOGICAL PROCESSES IN UFO EXPERIENCES

Process	Context*	Experience
Misperception	Insufficient knowledge of natural / man-made phenomena	Spurious UFO sighting reports
Hoax	Attention-seeking	Fabricated sightings and physical traces
Psychosis	Stress / personal crisis / predisposition	Reports involving mental com munications / apparitions / paranoia
Folie a Deux	Psychosis plus dominance / subordinance relationship	Reports with false consensus by two or more percipients
Conversion Hysteria	Fear / intense emotions / bodily predisposition	Physiological symptoms of psychosomatic nature
Altered State of Consciousness	Reduction or overload of stimuli / history of ASCs etc	Reports involving time-distortion / dream-like elements etc
Hypnopompic / Hypnagogic Imagery	Sleep / awake interface	Reports involving mental com-munications / apparitions / entities
Amnesia / Fugue	Stress / trauma	Reports featuring time-lapse / disorientation / physical wandering
Possession / Multiple Personalities	Stress / trauma predisposition	Reporst featuring "invading entities" / "messages" from same
Automatic Writing	Personal crisis / spiritualistic beliefs / predisposition	Reports featuring written messages
Autohypnosis / Hypnotic Regression	Concentration for long periods / leading questions / desire to please hypnotist	Trance-like states / fantasised abduction by UFO entities

* Includes beliefs derived from socially-communicated knowledge of UFO lore.

in nature, and the fact that UFO and ghostlight sightings also occur at locations lacking an earthquake history, faultline or known quartz deposit.

If a more exotic hypothesis, such as the extraterrestrial hypothesis, is applied to the data, then ghostlights could be considered to be small, physical UFOs in the guise of "remote-control probes". Abduction experiences would be interpreted as actual physical abductions by UFO entities. Consistent multiple witness accounts and unambiguous physical evidence would be required to support such a hypothesis and to rule out psychological and other alternatives.

A proportion of close encounter UFO cases involve associated parapsychological experiences. These experiences include mental communications, poltergeists, apparitions, healings, ghostlights and time lapses/abductions. This finding is supported by the experiences of UFO investigators who have found that many close encounter percipients also report a background of paranormal experiences. Also, a study by Keul and Phillips [**1985**] found that British UFO witnesses reported significantly more ESP occurrences than the general population, with most ESP events having occurred before UFO sighting, and close encounter percipients having reported double the amount of psychic phenomena.

The critical question is what these reported paranormal experiences represent. A large proportion of PSIUFO cases can be attributed to psychological causes. Mental communications originate from the percipient's own subconscious mind rather than from any external entity. Apparitions are hallucinations experienced during an altered state of consciousness such as hypnopompic or hypnagogic imagery, or as a consequence of psycholgical disturbance. Some healings are psychosomatic. Time lapse and abduction experiences may involve fugue states and some element of hallucination or fantasy, although further research into the background of these percipients is required before a definitive conclusion can be made.

Some PSIUFO reports are due to natural physical phenomena. For example, many ghostlights involve refraction effects and ball lightning, often coloured by local legend. The feasibility of possible geo-electrical and paranormal mechanisms of causation for some reports remains to be determined.

The most challenging PSIUFO reports are those that involve objective physical events, such as the UFO poltergeists (assuming hoaxes can be ruled out) and the non-psychosomatic UFO healings. I have personally investigated a number of PSIUFO cases and have found them to be generally complex, sometimes puzzling, and almost always a fascinating part of the rich tableau of human experience.

CONCLUSION

Can psychology explain the UFO experience? Partly, it can. As we have seen, a large proportion of UFO experiences involves the psychological processes of perception, psychopathology, altered states of consciousness and beliefs [**see Table 5**]. A large proportion of PSIUFO cases also involves psychological processes.

However, the UFO phenomenon is not limited to psychological processes. For example, a number of the case examples in this chapter have involved physical effects on vehicle systems. Whilst there exist such provocative cases as the 1957 Levelland, Texas multiple car stops case [**Hynek, 1974**]; the claimed UFO landings with physical traces at Socorro, New Mexico in 1964 [**Stanford, 1978**] and Tully, Queensland, Australia in 1966 [**Seers, 1983**]; and the severe physiological effects Cash-Landrum case which occurred in 1980 near Huffman, Texas [**Schuessler, 1982**], then it is clear that there also exist as yet unexplained physical dimensions to the UFO enigma.

UFO reports and UFO percipients need to be examined in their psychological and sociological contexts, for these psychosocial forces can play an important role in shaping the UFO experience. There is much scope for future research. The foremost task is to give greater attention to a comprehensive study of the UFO percipient or witness. *Percipient studies* can be defined as the in-depth study of the human aspects of anomalous experiences, utilising the methods and knowledge of psychology, sociology and medicine [**Moravec, 1983**]. Two particularly relevant methodologies are a detailed profile of the UFO witness, through biographical interviews and psychological and neurological testing; and a two groups (experimental and control) comparison of UFO percipients and non-percipients.

Some of the many topics which could be addressed by the "percipient studies" methodology include whether the UFO experience can be artificially induced by altering the normal state of consciousness; whether "psychic" people are more likely to have UFO experiences; whether there are cross-cultural differences in abduction experiences; and which simple perceptual tests could be applied to measure eyewitness reliability.

The UFO experience offers a goldmine of data on human experience and behaviour. Social and behavioral scientists will find much that will interest them. The fact that the UFO experience is still a contemporary phenomenon means that the people it has impacted on can be studied at first hand. I predict that a greater involvement of social and behavioral scientists in studying UFO phenomena will lead to an increase in our understanding of both UFO reports, and human experience and behaviour in general.

REFERENCES

■ **Anastasi,** Anne, *Psychological Testing,* 4th Edition, Collier Macmillan, New York, 1976. ■ **Andrus,** Walter, 'Director's Message', in *MUFON UFO Journal,* 188, Oct 1983, 20. ■ **Basterfield,** Keith, *UFOs: the Image Hypothesis - Close Encounters of an Australian Kind,* Reed, Sydney, 1981. ■ **Bentall,** R., 'Healing by Electromagnetism - Fact or Fiction?', in *New Scientist,* 70: 997, 22 Apr 1976, 166-167. ■ **Bloecher,** T., **Clamar,** A., **Hopkins,** B., **Slater,** E., and **Westrum,** R., *Final Report on the Psychological Testing of UFO 'Abductees',* Fund for UFO Research, Mt Rainier MD, 1985. ■ **Buss,** Arnold *Psychopathology,* John Wiley and Sons, New York, 1966. ■ **Callahan,** Philip, and **Mankin,** R., 'Insects as Unidentified Flying Objects', in *Applied Optics,* 17: 21, 1 Nov 1978, 3355-3360. ■ **Chaplin,** James, *Dictionary of Psychology,* Revised Edition, Dell, New York, 1975. ■ **Festinger,** L., **Riecken,** H., and **Schacter,** S., *When Prophecy Fails,* Harper and Row, New York, (1956), 1964. ■ **Fuller,** John, *The Interrupted Journey,* Berkley, New York, (1966), 1974. ■ **Greenawald,** Walt, 'The Nominal UFO Researcher', in *The MUFON UFO Journal,* 125, Apr 1978, 13-15. ■ **Greystone,** W., 'Canada's UFO Poltergeist', *Beyond Condon,* FSR Special Issue 2, Jun 1969, 66-70. ■ **Grinspoon,** Lester, and **Persky,** Alan, 'Psychiatry and UFO Reports', in **Sagan,** Carl, and **Page,** Thornton, (Editors), *UFO's - A Scientific Debate,* Norton, New York, 1972. ■ **Haines,** Richard, 'UFO Drawings by Witnesses and Non Witnesses: Is There Something in Common', in *UFO Phenomena,* 2:1, 1977, 123-151. ■ **Haines,** Richard, 'UFO Drawings by witnesses and Non Witnesses: Is There Something in Common? Part II', in *UFO Phenomena,* 3:1, 1978/79, 259-271. ■ **Haines,** Richard, *Observing UFO's,* Nelson-Hall, Chicago, 1980 . ■ **Hall,** Robert, 'Sociological Perspectives on UFO Reports', in **Sagan,** Carl, and **Page,** Thornton, (Editors), *UFO's - A Scientific Debate,* Norton, New York, (1972), 1974. ■ **Hendry,** Allan, *The UFO Handbook,* Doubleday, New York, 1979. ■ **Hilgard,** Ernest, *Divided Consciousness,* John Wiley and Sons, New York, 1977. ■ **Holroyd,** Stuart, *Briefing for the Landing on Planet Earth,* Corgi, London, (1977), 1979. ■ **Honorton,** Charles, 'ESP and Altered States of Consciousness', in **Beloff,** John, (Editor), *New Directions in Parapsychology,* Paul Elek, London, 1974. ■ **Horne,** Peter 'UFO's and the Human Factor', in **Moravec,** Mark, and **Prytz,** John, (Editors), *UFOs Over Australia: A Selection of ACUFOS Research Findings and Debate,* Australian Centre for UFO Studies, Sydney, 1985. ■ **Hynek,** J. Allen, *The UFO Experience: A Scientific Inquiry,* Corgi, London, (1972), 1974. ■ **Hynek,** J. Allen, and **Vallée,** Jacques, *The Edge of Reality,* Henry Regnery, Chicago, 1975. ■ **Jung,** Carl G., *Flying Saucers: A Modern Myth of Things Seen in the Skies,* Mentor, New York, (1959), 1969. ■ **Kammann,** Richard, 'The True Disbelievers: Mars Effect Drives Skeptics to Irrationality', in *Zetetic Scholar,* 10, 1982, 50-65. ■ **Keul,** Alexander, 'The Austrian UFO Witness Project', in *UPIAR Research in Progress,* 1: 1, 1982, 41-43. ■ **Keul,** Alexander, and **Phillips,** Ken, '"The Unidentified Witness" - UFO Witness Psychology Results', in *ASSAP News,* in press, 1985. ■ **Klass,** Philip, *UFOs - Indentified,* Random House, New York, 1968. ■ **Kolb,** L., *Noyes' Modern Clinical Psychiatry,* 7th Edition, W.B. Saunders, Philadelphia, 1968. ■ **Lamond,** Henry, 'The Min-Min Light', in *Walkabout,* 1 Apr 1937. ■ **Lawson,** Alvin, 'What can We Learn from Hypnosis of Imaginary "Abductees"?', in *The MUFON UFO Journal,* 120, Nov 1977, 7-9; 121, Dec 1977, 7-9. ■ **Loftus,** Elizabeth, *Eyewitness Testimony,* Harvard University Press, Cambridge MA, 1979. ■ **Ludwig,** Arnold, 'Altered States of Consciousness', in **Tart,** Charles, (Editor), *Altered States of Consciousness,* Anchor, New York, (1969), 1972. ■ **Mesnard,** Joel, 'Tranquillizing Visitation at Bouahamama', in *Flying Saucer Review,* 19: 3, May-Jun 1973, 17-18. ■ **Michel,** Aimé, 'The Strange Case of Dr "X"', in *UFO Percipients,* FSR Special Issue 3, Sep 1969, 3-16. ■ **Moravec,** Mark, 'Mental Communications and Psychological Disturbance', in *Journal of the Australian Centre for UFO Studies,* 1: 3, June 1980, 2-6; 1: 4, Aug 1980, 2-6. ■ **Moravec,** Mark, 'Psychological Reactions to UFO Events', in *The MUFON UFO Journal,* 158, Apr 1981a, 12-14. ■ **Moravec,** Mark, 'A UFO State of Mind', in *Proceedings of the Sixth Annual UFO Conference,* Australian Centre for UFO Studies, Adelaide, 1981b. ■ **Moravec,** Mark, *PSIUFO Phenomena: A Study of UFOs and the Paranromal,* Australian Centre for UFO Studies, Gosford, 1981c. ■ **Moravec,** Mark, 'Survey of UFO Researchers', in *Journal of the Australian Centre for UFO Studies,* 2: 3, May-June 1981d, 2-5. ■ **Moravec,** Mark, 'The Psychology of Close Encounters', in *Journal of the Australian Centre for UFO Studies,* 3: 6, Nov-Dec 1982, 10-13; 4: 1, Jan-Feb 1983, 2-5; 4: 2, Mar-Apr 1983, 2-6. ■ **Moravec,** Mark, Percipient Sutdies, in *Journal of UFO Studies,* 3, 1983, 53-60. ■ **Moravec,** Mark, 'The Jindabyne UFO abduction case', in *UFO Research Australia Newsletter,* 5:5, Sep-Oct 1984, 6-10. ■ **Moravec,** Mark, *Human Reactions Study: A Preliminary Report,* presentation at UFOCON 9, Melbourne, Jan 1986. ■ **Owen,** Iris, and **Sparrow,** Margaret, *Conjuring Up Philip,* Harper and Row, New York, 1976. ■ **Persinger,** Michael, 'Transient Geophysical Bases for Ostensible UFO-Related Phenomena and Associated Verbal Behaviour?', in *Perceptual and Motor Skills,* 43, 1976, 215-221. ■ **Randles,** Jenny, 'A Close Encounter with the Moon', in *The Probe Report,* 3: 1, Jul 1982, 2-4. ■ **Reed,** Graham, *The Psychology of Anomalous Experience,* Hutchinson and Co., London, 1972. ■ **Robinson,** J., *The Psychology of Visual Illusion,* Hutchinson and Co., London, 1972. ■ **Rogo,** D. Scott, *Mind Beyond the Body,* Penguin, New York, 1978. ■ **Roll,** William, The *Poltergeist, Star,* London, (1972), 1976. ■ **Sadler,** William, *Mental Mischief and Emotional Conflicts,* C.V. Moseby, St Louis, 1947. ■ **Scheussler,** John, 'Radiation Sickness Caused by UFO's', in 1982 *MUFON Symposium Proceedings,* Mutual UFO Network, Seguin TX, 1982. ■ **Schwarz,** Berthold, 'Berserk: A UFO-Creature Encounter', in *Flying Saucer Review,* 20: 1, 1974, 3-11. ■ **Seers,** Stan, UFOs: the Case for Scientific Myopia, Vantage, New York, 1983. ■ **Siegel,** Ronald, 'Hallucinations', in *Scientific American,* 237: 10, Oct 1977, 132-140. ■ **Sprinkle,** R. Leo, 'Hypnotic and Psychic implications in the investigation of UFO reports', in **Lorenzen,** Coral & Jim, *Encounters with UFO Occupants,* Berkley, NY, 1976, 256-329. ■ **Stanford,** Ray, *Socorro Saucer,* Fontana, Glasgow, (1976), 1978. ■ **Swift,** David, 'Who Believes in UFOs?', in *Journal of UFO Studies,* 2, 1980, 7-12. ■ **Tyrell,** George, *Apparitions,* Collier, New York, (1953), 1963. ■ **Vogel,** G., **Foulkes,** D., and **Trosman,** H., 'Ego Functions and Dreaming During Sleep Onset', in **Tart,** Charles, (Editor), *Altered States of Consciousness,* Anchor, New York, (1969), 1972. ■ **Wagner,** W., **Hulse,** R., and **McGrath,** J., '"Spook Lights": the Vestigia Update', in *Vestigia Newsletter,* 2: 3, Fall 1978, 1, 3-7. ■ **Warren,** Donald, 'Status Inconsistency Theory and Flying Saucer Sightings', in *Science,* 170, 6 Nov 1970, 559-603. ■ **Westrum,** Ronald, 'Crypto-Science and Social Intelligence About Anomalies', in *Zetetic Scholar,* 10, Dec 1982, 89-102.

4.4.2

UFOs AND CONCEPTS OF REALITY

by Jenny Randles

While World War Two raged round about, the English country town of Cheltenham was almost untouched. One sunny afternoon in 1942, probably in March, 27-year old Eileen Arnold was walking home from her pre-natal appointment. She was approaching 8 months pregnant, and filled by the glow of motherhood: but she was also aware of another, stranger feeling.

'I was in a particularly sensitive state,' she comments. Walking the busy High Street she had a sudden 'implulse' to look skyward, and there she saw a weird oval object like nothing she had ever seen before. It seemed to eject 'quills' as a porcupine might do. But, even odder, as she observed this strange phenomenon, the world about her seemed to change. 'Traffic and people had completely vanished... I didn't even see the road and pavement'. All she saw was a rooftop and this peculiar object.

Today we would call that object a UFO: but in 1942 the concept of a UFO did not exist. [1]

The case of Eileen Arnold is rich with mysteries for us to ponder. The strange symptoms which she describes fit a common pattern found in many close encounters:

- loss of environmental sound
- time distortion
- apparent isolation of the witness

I use the term 'Oz factor' to categorise these characteristic symptoms: but that is simply a label, not an explanation. We are unable to understand how, if a *real* UFO was flying over Cheltenham High Street that afternoon, it was seen by only this one person. We do not know why it affected her consciousness in the way it did. Nor do we know whether it is important or irrelevant that Eileen subsequently had many experiences which we might call psychic - including messages in her mind from some unknown, or at least unidentified, source.

BEYOND THE 'EITHER/OR' RESPONSE

UFO encounters such as this - and it shares features with probably a majority of close encounter reports - require us to re-evaluate the entire subject. We are trained to view the world in simple 'black and white' fashion - either things are unreal, either they are absolute or they are real or they are unreal, either they are absolute or they are imaginary. But which is Eileen's experience? 'Real and absolute' is what she herself says: yet its personal nature makes us wonder if in truth it was unreal and imaginary?

Some aspects of the experience seem to support one view, some the other, and we feel a need to choose between them because that is how we have taught that the world operates. But could this be a fundamental error? Could this be why the problem of the UFO is so fraught with irreconcilable difficulties?

There is a principle in science which may be helpful at this point. It says that when a question throws up two apparently contradictory answers, both of which appear to have evidential support, then it is not a case of one *answer* being incorrect, but of the *question* being incorrectly phrased. So perhaps our question, 'Is Eileen Arnold's experience real or unreal?', is not the right question. If, between reality and unreality, there exists a pseudo- or a quasi-reality, the 'either/or' dilemma disappears.

Though we are trained to think in 'either/or' terms, both philosophy and physics provide demonstration that the universe is not so cut-and-dried as we think.

Philosophers ponder the nature of perception: how do we 'see' something - a rose, let's say. We think of our eyes and other senses as operating like a camera, processing information from light rays, sound waves, scents &c to create an image of the rose onto the screen of our mind in a purely mechanical way. But any attempt to reduce the brain to the status of a computer, however advanced, fail: in practice, what happens is that we process the sensory information to create reality *inside* our heads, makining deductive choices about their interpretation, and then selecting images from experience - what we might call our 'mind store'. This offers plenty of scope for error and subjective judgment, and the end product is far from being a straightforward photographic projection; as a film director adds his own input to what the camera sees, to produce an artistic creation. [2]

Bertrand Russell said 'The world may be called physical or mental or both or neither, as we please' - a view endorsed by researchers in all fields of science, particularly psychologists. We can appreciate this process in action with the help of Fig 1. What do you see? Plainly, there is a triangle standing out from the centre of the dark surrounding mass. But look more closely; there is no triangle. We have

FIGURE 1.

created it in our mind by inference. Yet even when we know it is in illusion, we continue to see the triangle. It is a product of our mechanical perception system, which we cannot over-ride. We have, in a sense, created the reality of the triangle where there was no triangle; and once created, it remains perpetually visible.

'NOTHING IS REAL' (John Lennon)

During the past 100 years physics has undergone a revolution as profound as when in the Middle Ages we finally accepted that our Earth is not the centre of the universe. Having discovered, through Isaac Newton and his successors, that there are simple laws which govern the behaviour of all objects - be they a rose, a rock, or a human body - we anticipated that from here on, science would add only refinements to this view. Instead, our probing of the atom revealed a ghost world where reality continually eludes our grasp.

The first indication came when scientists could not make up their minds about light. Some of the evidence suggested it was made up of tiny bullet-like particles, called *photons*. Such experiments as projecting a light-beam through a single hole in a stream of particles (electrons).

However, other experiments produced evidence that light is *not* a stream of particles but a field of energy. Project the light-beam through two slits in the card, and the two waves will create a pattern where they overlap on the screen. When a peak of Wave 1 meets a peak from Wave 2, the one reinforces the other; when it meets a trough, they cancel out. The resulting banded appearance makes sense only when light is conceived as an energy field composed of waves? Particles or energy waves? Seemingly contradictory answers, suggesting that the question had been incorrectly put.

Recognition of this fact led to a whole new branch of physics, quantum mechanics, whose consequences are still being explored. Aside from demonstrating the inadequacy of the 'either/or' approach, it also leads to the proposition that our minds play a key role in the shaping of physical reality.

Over-simplified though this brief exposition has been - see [**3**] for a fuller account of how bizarre it can get! - it shows that there are both psychological and physical arguments for questioning our conventional view of reality. Unfortunately, this has tempted some people to carry the analogy further than can be justified, resulting in a spate of popular books seeking to link ancient mysticism, systems of occultism and eastern philosophy to quantum physics, proclaiming that all reflect differing versions of the same story. Though some intriguing ideas have emerged, the effect has been to turn others off with a suspicion that such approaches offer nothing of any real value.

UFOs AND THE NEW VIEW OF REALITY

If we do not allow ourselves to be dissuaded by such doubts, it is fascinating to find that these findings of modern science are mirrored in what we know about the UFO phenomenon. It is almost as though we UFO researchers are privileged to be given a preview of what these findings entail: for we are faced with exactly the same dilemma when deciding the reality status of the UFO.

Not all UFO cases raise this dilemma, of course. There are natural, physical phenomena on the fringes of our understanding in atmospheric physics, geophysics or meteorology, which are not infrequently reported as UFOs: these I prefer to term UAPs (Unidentified Atmospheric Phenomena). Additionally, for many UFOs there are even more conventional explanations; though some of these IFO cases are so extraordinary - for instance, when the full moon is misperceived by a group of people - that they may share more with close encounters than we realise. [**4**]

The category of UFO report which chiefly challenges us with this dilemma is the *close encounter*: where a witness believes he has seen an alien craft, or its occupants, and may even claim contact with such. The account is likely to involve effects of some kind, either on the witness, or the environment, or both. While UAPs are visible to anyone present in a given place at a given time, provide photographic and other 'hard' evidence, and have a witness/event ratio close to that of any other real aerial object, close encounters are characterised by their subjectivity.

We can draw up a balance sheet of the 'real' and 'unreal' features of the close encounter:

REAL

- Some group and multi witness sightings.
- Identical in theme and essence.
- Profess alien origin.
- Convey messages that do not seem personal to the witness.
- Appear to interact with radar and generate photographs.

UNREAL

- Overall figures tend to appear to single witness; suggests subjectivity.
- Individual vatiations in themes and UFOs.
- Pre space-age 'UFOs' profess not to be alien (eg. fairies).
- Messages are trite; content never exceeds present state of knowledge.
- Hard evidence far less than it 'should' be; cases where UFOs do not show up on film.

There may well be other differences that could be added to this preliminary list; but these suffice to indicate the paradoxical character of the close encounter which can appear to operate in two modes which seem on the surface to be contradictory.

Are UFOs solid machines that fly around the sky to be seen by anybody, and manufactured by a visiting alien technology - simply advanced versions of our own space shuttle? Or are they illusionary things, real only in the mind of the percipient, considered to be alien at this point in time only because it is culturally appropriate to do so?

The problem is that both answers seem to be true according to the circumstances.

To explore the implications of quantum physics discoveries, theoretical models have been constructed which are testable experimentally. Such work carried out by a French team led by Dr Alain Aspect led them to report in 1982 that only two viable theories are left us.

The first is the 'Copenhagen' theory, so named because it was devised by a group of workers based in this city; it has stood for half a century and is still considered the front runner. It argues that whenever an event occurs with two possible outcomes, both exist in a kind of phantom state, until an observer crystallises one possibility into reality. The other one, we assume, never appears in our real world. It is this theory which leads to the suggestion that our mind is the architect of what we see as real.

The second, more recent theory, developed by three physicists, Everett, Wheeler and DeWitt, is named the 'many worlds' hypothesis because it proposes that *both* possibilities actually crystallise out, but we only happen to live in the work of one of them. In another 'ghost world' there is a 'ghost you and me' living with the consequences of the other possibility. However, as in practice we seldom have only two possiblities, but millions on millions, there is no limit to the number of you and me's nor to the number of possible universes, each slightly different one from the other, which they inhabit.

Whether we opt for the theory that it is we who determine what is real, or the theory that everything is real but we choose which we live with, these models can be successfully integrated with the UFO phenomenon.

UFOs AS CULTURAL DREAM

UFOs seem to be a cultural dream that has a quasi-reality. Some of the time, or in certain circumstances, they behave like real objects. The rest of the time, or in other circumstances, they behave like subjective experiences. Psychologist Carl Jung probed his way towards a concept based on these ideas just a decade into the modern UFO era. [**5**] He was aided in this because he had worked with quantum physicist Wolfgang Pauli on earlier theories of reality. Jung saw that UFOs were neither real nor unreal (or possibly both at the same time) and suggested that they represent an objectification of an inner belief which was so strong that it possessed global significance.

While most UFO researchers have shied away from these propositions, some have tried to see the subject as a living dream. Lyall Watson made a brave attempt to update Jung with his concept of the 'lifetide' - a kind of species consciousness which contains common elements of all human thought. [**6**] Watson proposed that the UFO is a distillation of our need for a superior intelligence - a need so prevalent among mankind that it has taken on a semblance of reality.

By a synchronicity which would have appealed to Jung, another expression of the same idea was simultaneously put forward in fiction form by (unrelated) sci-fi author Ian Watson. [**7**] In his view gifted people (channels for the inner myth) are able to turn the subjective experience into objective phenomena and so act as catalysts for the cultural belief. Once that belief has been strengthened by these 'real' phenomena, other gifted people can act as channels and reinforse the effect; thus UFOs become a self-generating reality, created because enough people **want** them to be a reality.

Lyall Watson credited Jacques Vallée with the first flowerings of his theory in ufological terms: Ian Watson dedicated his book to Bertrand Méheust for similar reasons. While both Vallée and Méheust came close to devising a UFO theory based upon a pseudo-reality, neither actually achieved it because ufology retains too much of the 'either/or' tendency.

Ever since the two Watsons published their ideas in 1979, scientific advances have only added to their insights. Psychiatrist Morton Schatzman's account of his work with 'Ruth' is particularly enlightening. [**6**] Ruth was having hallucinations of living people so powerful that the only convincing indication that they were hallucinations wa the knowledge that the real person was thousands of miles away at the time. Schatzman's experiments led to the disturbing conclusion that while in some ways Ruth's hallucinations were 'unreal' - e.g. they couldn't be photgraphed - in other ways they were 'real' - for instance, her perceptions systems behaved as though a real object was standing before her blocking out the background. The implication is that the hallucination possessed a certain degree of reality, at least so far as her perceptive system was concerned.

THE 'SPECTRUM' CONCEPT

In my own theoretical work, the 'either/or' concept is rejected in favour of what I call a 'spectrum', in which reality ranges from *normal* reality (i.e. objective, wide-awake, 'solid') at one end, to *synchronistic* reality (subjective, image-based, 'insubstantial') at the other. Between are various shades. [**9**]

UFO close encounters occur in one of these in-between states, a quasi-real state that is closer to the 'normal' end of the spectrum. This must be so, for events at this end of the spectrum are experienced in the context of the objective world - which is, we know, how they are experienced by UFO witnesses such as Eileen Arnold.

Eileen is what Ian Watson would term a 'channel' - and what others might call a medium, because her abilities often manifest in non-UFO ways. Whatever term we use, all we are really saying is that she has a good capacity for manipulating images in her mind; she can take a theme and build a good visual image out of it, just as Schatzman's Ruth was able to do. (I suspect Ruth would have made an excellent UFO contactee.)

How then do I 'explain' Eileen's experience?

As Eileen Arnold was walking down that Cheltenham street she began to slip out of normal reality. This manifested as a feeling of being sensitive. She was tuning in more to her consciousness and paying less attention to the world outside, as happens in other circumstances, for instance when we are driving alone on a quiet road, or lying in bed in the dark.

What made Eileen tune in? One the Jung/Watson theory we have a somewhat artificial concept of inner contact with a cultural myth, although how or why this should occur is by no means clear. Personally I see no reason why a real messages should not be responsible. After all, physics, psychology and the paranormal all demonstrate how it is possible - at this level of consciousness or mind - to detect messages across time and space. They come from the past or the future, or from other people - in a distress situation, for example; it is plausible that in the same way a real message might be beamed at us to warn of the need for earth to change direction (the theme of most alien contact messages). It would take little extension of what we know to imagine an alien civilisation broadcasting - perhaps by 'super-telepathy' - some kind of general galactic warning.

Perhaps Eileen simply heard, as it were, the phone bell ringing below the surface of her mind, and decided to find out who was calling. Next came the fading out of 'real life' sights and sounds, alterations to her perception which I call the Oz Factor; 'tuning out' sensory information is part of the process of tuning in to the message. As she turned the message into visual imagery, this was projected onto outwide world, resulting in her impression that the rest of the environment had vanished and only the UFO and the rooftop were visible; in other words, her superimposed hallucination was not quite perfect.

The precise form the UFO took would be constructed from Eileen's mind-store of images. In 1942 there had been no UFOs in the mesia, so her choice of images was (to our present eyes) anomalous: since then the objects seen have become more standardised. (Note, for instance, how many of the early 1947 sightings were of UFO formations - something very rare today: was this because the first widely publicised sighting was Arnold's report of a formation of UFOs which functioned as a stereotype until superseded by more acceptable forms?)

The UFO that is forged from the mind-store of a witness, even today, is at one and the same time unique to the individual yet falling within a generally acknowledged outline which owes its form to the cultural view of what UFO looks like, as formulated by the media &c. We each produce our own precise image to represent the concept 'alien'. So it is at the same time both personalised and shared. It is a visual dramatisation of the message detected by the mind of the witness who has temporarily left the normal reality mode and tuned in to the contact 'beamed' from somewhere.

Tentative as it is, something like this theory seems to be necessary to account for the paradox of the UFO close encounter. The implications are exciting. For example, it helps explain something that has deeply puzzled me: how qualified and experienced observers can make serious errors of perception and view the full moon and other commonplace phenomena as exotic UFOs. Having detected the message, and being in a position to dramatise it, the witness naturally seizes upon a real visiual stimulus on which to construct the illusion. Perhaps it is easier to distort the moon into a spaceship than to create one out of nothing.

If nothing else, I hope this brief discussion of what is both a complex and (I suspect) crucially important question has demonstrated that UFO mystery could have a great deal to say about the nature of reality. It may be timely for scientists who study reality perception to look at the UFO evidence and consider whether it may be a large-scale demonstration of the very phenomenon they are struggling to comprehend. Equally, it may be timely for UFO researchers to consider the fundamental issues of the subject of their research.

REFERENCES

■ 1 - **Randles,** J., *Sixth Sense* (Robert Hale, 1987; Salem House, 1987, pp 203-5) ■ 2 - My book *Sixth Sense* discusses the whole field of perception, sense detection and their relevance to the nature of reality. ■ 3 - **Gribbin,** J., *The search for Schroedingers Cat* (Corgi, 1985). ■ 4 - **Randles,** J. & **Warrington,** P., *Science and the UFOs* (Blackwell, 1985, pp82-8, 132-3). ■ 5 - **Jung,** C., *Flying saucers: A modern myth of things seen in the skies* (Routledge and Kegan Paul, 1959) ■ 6 - **Watson,** L., *Lifetide* (Hodder and Staughton, 1979). ■ 7 - **Watson,** I. *Miracle Visitors* (Gollancz, 1979; Grafton, 1980). ■ 8 - **Schazman,** M., *The story of Ruth* (Duckworth, 1980; Penguin, 1981). ■ 9 - **Randles,** J., *Beyond Explanation*? (Robert Hale, 1985; Ravette, 1986; Bantam, 1987).

4.4.3

THE PSYCHO-PHYSICAL NATURE OF UFO REALITY: A SPECULATIVE FRAMEWORK

by Jacques Vallée

■ **JACQUES VALLÉE**: Probably the most cited name in this book is that of French-born Jacques Vallée, who shares with John Keel the distinction of broadening the concepts of UFO research to the extent of requiring us to contemplate profound changes in our notions of reality.

A computer scientist working in the San Francisco Bay area, Vallee has French educational qualifications in mathematics and astrophysics, American qualifications in computer science.

■ **UFO involvement**: Vallée's interest in UFOs dates from 1961, when he was working with the French Satellite Tracking Programme, reporting to the Smithsonian Astronomical Observatory. Elusive objects whose behaviour was uncharacteristic of satellites would appear from time to time, but when one evening eleven data points were obtained on one such object, the tape was confiscated and erased.

This reluctance of science to face up to the UFO challenge has been a constant preoccupation throughout his subsequent involvement with the subject - an involvement distinguished on the one hand by a passion for logic which can be seen as his French inheritance, and on the other by a pragmatism which perhaps his residence in the United States has fostered. The combination has made him among the most respected and most influential of all ufologists.

■ **Publications**: *Anatomy of a phenomenon* (1965); *Challenge to science* (with Janine Vallée, 1966); *Passport to Magonia* (1969); *The edge of reality* (with J Allen Hynek, 1975); *The invisible college* (1975); *Messengers of deception* (1979). He is also the author of several science fiction works.

■ **Address**: 1550 California Street, Suite 6L-169 / San Francisco / CA 94109 / USA.

THE NEED FOR A UNIFIED APPROACH

What I will present here is more a speculative framework than a true hypothesis; we should only regard as a scientific hypothesis; we should only regard as a scientific hypothesis a statement presented in such a way that it is testable in repeatable fashion by anyone with the proper knowledge and instruments. It must also be possible to ascertain to what extent an hypothesis, when tested and proven to be true, actually "explains" the observed facts.

This audience does not have to be reminded that theoretical development does not stop with the testing of hypothesis. In the case of UFO's, however, it is especially important to keep in mind that an hypothesis may well be proven true while an apparently contradictory hypothesis is also proven true. (The hypothesis that the phenomenon of light is caused by particles is true, but so is the hypothesis that it is caused by waves). We must be prepared for the time when we will be in a position to formulate scientific hypotheses for the UFO phenomen, and then we may face a similar situation.

The framework I will present here is based on such an apparent contradiction, because I will argue that the UFO phenomenon can be thought of either as a physical one or a physic one. I do not consider this framework a scientific hypothesis because the testing of some of the ideas proposed here will require a better quality of data than we currently have. I do hope, however, that it will prove stimulating as a unified approach to a very puzzling phenomen that presents both undeniable physical effects suggesting a technological device or craft *and* psychic effects reminiscent of the literature on poltergeists and psycho-kinetic phenomen.

The feeling of absurdity and contradictory in these two aspects is not worse than scientific puzzlement during the particle/wave controversy. It has to do mainly with the inadequacy of our language to come to grasps with a phenomenon that defies our attempts at classification.

DIMENSIONS OF THE PROBLEM

Let us consider the characteristics of the sightings that are not explained by trivial natural causes; we can recognize six major "dimensions" in terms of our perceptions of these characteristics.

First of all is the **physical** dimension. Most witnesses

describe an object that occupies a position in space; moves as time passes; inter-acts with its environment through thermal effects as well as light absorption and emission; produces turbulence; and, when landed, leaves indentations and burns from which approximate mass and energy figures can be derived. Furthermore, it gives rise to photographic images and magnetic disturbances. Claude Poher and I have revived some of these characteristics in a previous paper before the AIAA and I will not repeat our observations here. The UFO phenomenon, in a physical sense, is consistent with a technology centred on a craft using a very revolutionary propulsion system. But there is more.

For lack of an adequate term I will call the second dimension **anti-physical**. The variables are the same as those in the previous category but they form patterns that conflict with those predicted by physics - an object that is described as physical and material is also described as:

- sinking into the ground.
- becoming fuzzy and transparent on the spot.
- merging with an identical object at slow speed.
- disappearing at one point while appearing elsewhere instantaneously.
- remaining observable visually while not detected on radar.

The third dimension has to do with the **psychology** of the witnesses and the **social** conditions that surround them. Human observers tend to see UFO's while in their normal environment and in normal social groupings. They perceive the objects as non-conventional but they try to explain them away as common occurences, until faced with the inescapable conclusion that the object is truly unknown.

Physiological reactions are another significant dimension. The phenomenon is reported to cause burns, "beeping" sounds, vibrations, partial paralysis, heat sensation, pricklings. Some witnesses have become temporarily blind when exposed to the objects' light. Others have described nausea, difficulty in breathing, loss of volition. The most frequently symptom in the days following a close-range encounter is drowsiness.

The fifth category of effects is labeled **'psychic'** because it involves a class of phenomena commonly found in the literature of parapsychology, such as:

- impressions of communication without direct sensory channel.
- levitation of the witness or of objects and animals in the vicinity.
- poltergeist phenomena: motions and sounds without a specific cause, outside of the observed presence of a UFO.
- manoeuvers of a UFO appearing to anticipate the witness' thoughts.
- premonitory dreams or "visions".
- personality changes promoting unusual abilities in the witness (as in the case of Uri Geller and others).
- healing.

These observations have been developed in my book *The Invisible College* (E.P. Dutton) and a detailed description would be beyond the scope of this paper. The fact that such data exist, however, is central to the framework I want to build here.

The sixth category could be called "cultural". It is concerned with society's reactions to the reports, the way in which secondary effects (hoaxes, fiction and science-fiction imagery, scientific theories, cover-up or exposure, censorship or publicity, sensationalism, etc.) become generated, and the attitude of members of a given culture towards the concepts that UFO observations appear to challenge. The greatest impact of the phenomenon has been on general acceptance of the idea of life in space and a more limited, but potentially very significant, change in the popular concept of non-human intelligence.

POSSIBLE NATURE AND PURPOSE OF UFO TECHNOLOGY

A framework for scientific speculation on the UFO phenomenon can be built on the identification (admittedly very coarse) of the sic major dimensions of UFO effects. If I must formulate a view of the problem in a single statement at this point that statement will be:

The UFO phenomenon is the product of a technology that integrates physical and psychic phenomena and primarily affects cultural variables in our society through manipulation of pysiological and psychological parameters in the witnesses.

This single statement can be developed as follows:

- The phenomenon is the product of a technology. During the observation, the UFO is a real, physical, material object. However, it uses either very clever deception or very advanced physical principles, resulting in the effects I have called "anti-physical", which must eventually be reconciled with the laws of physics.
- The technology triggers psychic effects either purposely or as a side effect of the presence of a UFO. These psychic phenomena are now too common to be ignored or relegated to the category of exaggerated or ill-observed facts. All of us who have investigated close range sightings have become familiar with these effects.
- The purpose of the technology is cultural manipulation - possibly but not necessarily under control of a form of non-human intelligence, and

the physiological and psychological effects are a means to that end.

CONCLUSION

We are now becoming familiar with display technologies that produce three-dimensional images with color, motion and perspective through physical devices. I am suggesting that UFO's are analogous to these display technologies but utilize a far wider range of variables to operate on the witnesses and through them on human culture. The long time scale and the global nature of these effects make it extremely difficult to test hypotheses involving such cultural effects.

Science-fiction has familiarized us with the concept of machines (or beings) projecting an image of themselves that systematically confuses observers. One could imagine that the UFO is a physical craft equipped with the means to interact both with the surrounding atmosphere and with the senses of its observers in such a way as to convey a false image of its real nature. One could also argue (as Jim McCampbell has done) that such an object could use microwave devices to create perceptual hallucinations in the witnesses (including messages that are heard by a single individual in a group).

Even such a complex scheme, however, fails to explain all the reported effects and the subsequent behaviour changes in close-range witnesses. We must assume something more, the triggering of deep-seated processes within their personality. The question then becomes: to what extent are these effects evidence of a purposeful action of the operators?

To answer this question, and to test more fully the hypothesis that UFO phenomena are *both* physical and psychic in nature, we need much better investigations, a great upgrading of data quality, and a more informed analysis not only of the object being described, but of the impact of the observation on the witness and his social environment.

5
UFOs
AND SOCIETY

5.1 UFOs AND SOCIETY

We know that UFOs exist because tens of thousands of people, at many different times and in all parts of the world, have reported seeing flying objects they cannot identify. We are not yet able to say whether a single phenomenon is responsible for all their experiences, or whether they have all had the same kind of experience. But the fact that everyone recognises a flying saucer when it appears in a TV commercial, or that any schoolchild can draw one, shows that a **shared concept**, at least, exists. A concept, moreover, which evidently has an extraordinarily strong appeal.

George Eberhart's recently published bibliography of ufology [**1**] is a 1298-page testimony to the hold the UFO concept has on society. It is a hold that takes many forms. The number of books about UFOs and periodicals devoted to them, the number of press articles and media reports, the number of UFO investigation groups and private researchers - these are all measures of the widespread interest the subject provokes in society as a whole.

But there is more to it than that, there is the particularly and peculiarly *strong* interest - strongly negative or strongly positive - that the idea of UFOs provokes in certain sections of society:

■ **Governments** - The Freedom of Information Act has revealed that for decades the US Government has concealed from the public its interest in UFOs, in a way it does not seem to have done about any other matter [**3, 7**]; why should it be so uniquely secretive in this respect?

■ **Skeptics** - Those who don't believe UFOs exist don't simply ignore them, they write book after full-length book to prove that they don't exist [**6, eg.**]: why do they feel so strongly?

■ **Hoaxers and pranksters** - A remarkable number of people apparently feel an irresistible urge to hurl hub-caps into the air or suspend lampshades on nylon thread and pass off the resulting photographs as UFOs; or they send fire-balloons over populous suburbs, or indulge in other such complex and often expensive deceptions [**5**]: what inspires such an expenditure of time and trouble?

■ **True believers of the pie-in-the-sky kind** - UFOs are the focus for great numbers of quasi-religious belief systems whose one common feature is the idea that UFOs originate from superior civilisations with a mission to save our world from our mistakes [**2, 4**]; how have UFOs come to acquire this reputation, which others see as 20th century folklore?

■ **True believers of the fire-and-brimstone kind** - UFOs are no less vehemently attacked as creations of the Evil One [**eg., 8**]; how have they come to be seen in this light?

The answers to these questions may take us to the heart of the UFO mystery. For it is clear that, no matter what the UFOs may be, they have achieved a permanent impact on society; they have entered into our mythology. Even if UFOs should prove to have no basis in physical reality, they will survive as an idea, just as the popular idea of witchcraft survives despite the fact that witches, as popularly conceived, never existed.

Of God, Voltaire said that had he not existed, it would have been necessary to invent him. Of flying saucers it might be said that our society *needed* something of their sort. It remains an open question whether they already existed and manifested in response to that need, or whether we invented them because we needed them.

REFERENCES

1 - **Eberhart**, George M, *UFOs and the Extraterrestrial contact movement: a bibliography* (Scarecrow, 1986). ■ 2 - **Evans**, Hilary, *Gods, spirits, cosmic guardians* (Aquarian, 1987). ■ 3 - **Fawcett**, Lawrence, & Greenwood, Barry J *Clear intent*, (Prentice Hall, 1984)› ■ 4 - **Festinger** et al, *When prophecy fails* (University of Minnesota, 1956). ■ 5 - **Keel**, John A, *Operation Trojan Horse* (Putnam, 1970) ■ 6 - **Menzel**, Donald H, & others, *Flying saucers* (Harvard, 1953); *The world of flying saucers* (Doubleday 1963); *The UFO enigma* (Doubleday, 1977). ■ 7 - **Moore**, William L, *Crashed saucers: evidence in the search for proof* (private, 1985); and many other research papers. ■ 8 - **Wilson**, Clifford, *UFOs and their mission impossible* (Word of truth, 1974).

5.2

UFOs AND SCIENTISTS

by Ron Westrum

■ **RON WESTRUM**: Born Chicago, 1945. Educated at Harvard and University of Chicago. Currently Professor of Sociology and Interdisciplinary Technology at Eastern Michigan University. He specialises in the sociology of science and technology, in which he has published numerous articles besides editing the newsletter *Social Psychology of Science* and co-authoring *Complex organizations* (1984).

■ **UFO involvement**: For many years he has been a sociological consultant for MUFON. This has led him to doubt the likelihood that UFOs are merely a creation of the human imagination. 'While most UFO reports are the result of mistakes, the evidence in favour of *some* UFOs representing extra-terrestrial spacecraft is strong. It is essential that these reports be investigated by properly trained technical personnel and not simply swept under the rug, as is currently the case.' His writings and presentations have consistently urged a greater involvement by scientists, and a more scientific approach by ufologists.

■ **Publications**: include frequent contributions to leading publications in both ufology and other fields of anomaly research. His paper 'Knowledge about sea-serpents' in Wallis (ed) *On the margins of science* (Keele University 1979) is an excellent example of how methodology can be most effectively deployed in anomaly research.

■ **Address**: Department of Sociology / Eastern Michigan University / Ypsilanti / MI 48197 / USA.

The response of the scientific community to the UFO phenomenon over the last forty years has been inadequate. Very little properly organized and funded scientific investigation has been carried out. What investigations scientists have conducted has taken place for the most part in their spare time or with bootlegged funds. Well-funded investigation has been rare and the findings from such investigation have done little to advance knowledge. Since the scientific community constitutes our major environmental monitoring system, this failure is important. Scientists have had an impact; UFO research has benefitted from their participation in terms of both theory and investigation. Yet, considering the importance of the question, the failure of the scientific community to investigate the UFO situation thoroughly is a serious breach of responsibility. For if *any* part of the UFO phenomenon represents extraterrestrial intelligence, the failure to investigate has lost us valuable time to cope and to respond.

In this chapter I will concentrate largely on events in the United States. This represents, I admit, a somewhat limited viewpoint. Yet a large proportion of UFO research has taken place in the United States, and it is in the United States that the scientific community has entered most fully into the debate over UFOs. [**1**] Furthermore, other countries have looked to the United States, with its respected scientific community, its huge military establishment, and its powerful electronic scanning systems, as a guide to their own conduct toward UFOs. Thus the United States has had an influence much greater than perhaps it deserved to have in the investigation of the UFO phenomenon. Finally, the response of the scientific community in the United States is typical of scientists' response to cryptoscientific anomalies, and thus to some extent can be used as a general model for the response elsewhere. [**2**]

INITIAL REACTIONS

The initial response of the scientific community to UFOs in the late 1940's and early 1950's was that UFOs were a fad that would soon pass away. One sociologist at Ohio Wesleyan University, whose gift for prophecy was not great, stated that "the flying saucer is an excellent subject [for sociology] in that it is almost wholly a manufactured concept, lasting for a short period of time, and so, easy to study." [**3**] Others in the physical sciences shared this view, and UFOs were commonly referred to in the press as a "fad," "craze," or "delusion." This attitude was strengthened by reports whose explanation turned out to be mundane. It was easy to assume that all reports, if scrupulously investigated, would prove to have everyday explanations.

In the United States, the exception to this attitude was constituted by scientists who were engaged with the military in classified research. From time to time some of these men would become convinced that some UFO phenomena were genuinely anomalous. In particular the "green fireballs" of Mexico seemed very anomalous for a time. [**4**] There was also a considerable interest in military circles about UFOs generally, and private views did not always coincide with opinions given to the press. This private set of opinions was a partial basis for a series of books by Donald Keyhoe, a retired Marine Corps officer, who kept public interest alive and eventually founded the National Investigations Committee on Aerial Phenomena. [**5**] But these opinions, either because or in spite of being reported by Keyhoe, had little influence on scientific opinion generally.

The context of early UFO reports included postwar jitters, the beginnings of serious science-fiction literature, and considerable doubt that space travel was possible. It is difficult to look back forty years and grasp how rudimentary were the intellectual tools of the time and how inadequate they were to cope with a possible extraterrestrial visitation. Computers had just been invented, along with atomic weapons and jet planes. Our sophistication about evolutionary biology was small, compared to the present day. Thus our understanding of biological intelligence was rudimentary; artificial intelligence was barely on the horizon. [**6**] Yet it was this relatively unsophisticated scientific culture which was being asked to consider the possibility of hyper-intelligences interacting with our planet and ourselves from another star. Since humans tend to use their own technologies as a basis for judgement, the rudimentary state of the appropriate scientific and technical apparatus was a serious limit on the imagination. It is not surprising, then, that the dominant response of the scientific community was that "flying saucers" were a social rather than a physical phenomenon.

This attitude received strong reinforcement in the first book written by a scientist on UFOs. Donald Menzel was an already eminent astrophysicist at Harvard University when he wrote *Flying Saucers* in 1953. [**7**] In this book Menzel ascribed most UFO sightings to optical illusions, using a theory that has since been largely discredited. Bruce Maccabee has shown how little of the reasoning used by Menzel and other scientific critics of the time could stand serious examination. But in matters such as UFOs the scientific community is not disposed to profound examination. Rather, it was easier to contrast the "scientific" intelligence of writers like Keyhoe. The latter seemed to deserve little attention from "the scientific reader" and little was accorded him.

"WAR OF THE WORLDS"

UFOs sightings continued, however, during the 1950's with notable sightings by pilots and military personnel. The Air Force UFO project, which had originated as Project Sign, turned in to Project Grudge, and finally to Project Blue Book. In 1953, a panel of eminent scientists, loaded with talent, was asked to review the evidence gathered by Blue Book. Even though the evidence was by no means unequivocal, the Robertson panel suggested that there was little to support the idea of "space travellers." Project Blue Book was to be continued, but largely to assuage public fears. Blue Book had also brought about a development that was to have an important impact later on: the involvement of Dr. J. Allen Hynek in UFO research. Hynek was an Air Force consultant, very little in the public eye, but meanwhile was receiving an informal education in UFO investigation. As Hynek rose in the astronomical community to Department Chairman at Northwestern, he was to prove very valuable to the UFO investigation community.

In 1955 Project Blue Book also issue a "Special Report #14" which reported on UFO cases investigated by the Air Force up to 1952. [**8**] The report, prepared by scientists at the Battelle Memorial Institute, was the most extensive scientific investigation of UFOs ever undertaken. The report is notable both for the very interesting cases reported and for the obvious attempts to reach reassuring conclusions from them.

The 1950's also brought the growth of religious interest in UFOs, and with it a rash of "contractees" who claimed they had spoken with people from Mars or Venus. These individuals, although eliciting a sympathetic public interest, did little to encourage scientists to investigate UFOs. In an era dominated by McCarthyism and fears of atom bomb fallout, UFO reports seemed little more than just another curiosity. But public interest was growing. The "collective unconscious" was churning out films like *War of the Worlds* and *It came from Outer Space.* Private UFO organizations also grew and developed during this time: such groups as the Aerial Phenomena Research Organization (1952) and National Investigations Committee on Aerial Phenomena (1956) were to play a major role in UFO research and its advocacy.

UFOLOGY GROWS

In the 1960's scientists took an increased interest in the UFO phenomenon. Most of this interest was caused by the growth of UFO organizations and their investigations. The data base of cases investigated by UFO organizations was larger, as shown by *The UFO Evidence*, published by NICAP in 1964. [**9**] The increasing quality of UFO writing, shown in books and journals, provoked interest by a number of scientists. Jacques Vallée, an astrophysicist and computer scientist, published *Anatomy of a Phenomenon* (1965) and *Challenge to Science* (1966), two books much more sensitive than Menzel's to the limitations of science, although both were flawed by lack of personal investigation. J. Allen Hynek, meanwhile, following his famous "swamp gas" remark, was becoming disturbed by his public posture as a government skeptic, when his own investigations actually make him think that UFOs ought to be more carefully studied. His change of heart became public through a series of papers and interviews leading up to his publication of *The UFO*

Experience: A Scientific Inquiry, probably still the best single introduction to UFOs. [**10**] Many scientists, pro and con, appeared and gave papers at congressional hearings and at a special panel at the American Association for the Advancement of Science. [**11**]

Increasing numbers of sightings and strong lobbying by UFO organizations also led to an Air Force-funded study, chaired by Edward U. Condon and based at the University of Colorado. The Condon commission was finally to decide that nothing of scientific value came from UFO investigation. Its report, released in 1969, although massive and superficially impressive, is marked by flawed design, intellectual evasions, and considerable padding. [**12**] It is characteristic that the Condon Report makes virtually no reference to the earlier (and far superior) Battelle study. Although some of the chapters of the Report contain useful information, overall the study was a waste of money. It is obvious that its major purpose was to whitewash the controversy.

MATURE UFOLOGY

During the 1970's and 1980's so many scientific contributions to the UFO phenomenon appeared that one can only survey them briefly. An important exception is *The UFO Handbook* by Allan Hendry, which synthesizes the work of Hynek's Center for UFO Studies. [**13**] Anyone beginning investigation of UFO reports must start with this outstanding study. In the 1970's the earlier complaint that scientists wrote very little on UFOs no longer had relevance. A large number of able researchers carried out investigations, wrote reports, published books and met at conferences arranged by the Mutual UFO Network (a spin-off from APRO) and the Center for UFO Studies. An "Invisible college" of scientifically trained UFOlogists came into being, and infused the work of organizations and UFO journals with some external legitimacy.

For the first time there was also an articulate group of skeptics associated with the aviation and space community: Philip Klass, James Oberg, and Robert Shaeffer. Although Donald Menzel published two more books on UFOs, these had little impact on public or scientific opinion. Very different was the impact of the new group, since at least two were journalists who enjoyed public controversy, and who were notably aggressive in attacking scientists interested in the UFO phenomenon. For the first time bitter personal attacks became common between proponents and opponents of UFO research.

Another feature of interest in this period is the lack of communication between researchers interested in UFOs and those involved in SETI, the 'Search for Extraterrestrial Intelligence'. The SETI community, largely made up of "visible scientists," is engaged in radio telescope searches for intelligent life elsewhere in the universe. Unlike interest in UFOs, SETI research became respectable, with a SETI section of the International Astronomical Union.

SETI researchers almost never cite UFO research, or associate themselves with UFOs. Funding and legitimacy for SETI would be jeopardized for doing so. [**14**] UFO researchers, on the other hand, have failed to link their investigations with the theoretical perspectives of SETI scientists.

This failure to link and articulate the two communitines has impoverished both. The two communities share a common problem: how to investigate and evaluate ostensible ETI activity. It may seem more "scientific" to do this with radio telescopes than with field investigations, but such a view displays a naïveté about the nature of science; what makes science good is not high-tech apparatus but the dialect counterpoint of theory and research. SETI has useful theories but no results. UFO investigation has generated a lot of data, but largely without theory. Obviously, these two activities should be coordinated.

QUO VADIS?

UFO research needs more science and more involvement from scientists. That this has not already occurred and is not likely to occur sometime soon reveals a deep weakness in the social organization of science. The question involved here is too serious, and frankly, the evidence is too strong, to leave UFO investigation in its current unsatisfactory state. Amateur and spare-time UFO research has done well, but it has not done well enough. Mankind simply cannot let this issue remain half-explored; it is too important to our welfare. If there is extraterrestrial intelligence, we cannot predict in advance what form its manifestations may take. Any possible manifestations should be promptly and exhaustively explored. We as a fragile species must *know*.

REFERENCES

■ **1** - David Michael **Jacobs,** *The UFO Controversy in America* (New York: New American Library, 1976). ■ **2** - See Ron **Westrum,** 'Social Intelligence About Anomalies: The Case of UFOs,' *Social Studies of Science*, Vol. 7 (1977); **Westrum,** 'Science and Social Intelligence About Anomalies: the Case of Meteorites,' *Social Studies of Science* Vol. 8 (1978). ■ **3** - Herbert **Hackett,** 'The Flying Saucer: A Manufactured Concept,' *Sociology and Social Research* Vol. 32 (May-June 1948), pp.867-873. ■ **4** - See Loren E. **Gross,** *UFOs: A History,* Vol. II (Scotia, New York: Arcturus, 1983) pp.17-53. ■ **5** - See for instance, Donald **Keyhoe,** *The Flying Saucers are Real* (New York: Fawcett Publications, 1950). ■ **6** - Norbert **Wiener** published *Cybernetics: Communication and Control in Man and Machine* (New York: John Wiley) in 1948. ■ **7** - Donald **Menzel,** *Flying Saucers* (Cambridge: Harvard University Press, 1953). ■ **8** - I have never seen a copy of the whole report. Commentaries have since been written, however, which quote it extensively. E.g. Leon **Davidson,** editor, *Flying Saucers: An Analysis of Air Force Project Blue Book Special Report #14* (White Plains, New York: 4the Edition 1971); Bruce **Maccabee,** *Scientific Investigation of Unidentified Flying Objects* (Silver Spring, Maryland: no date, circa 1981). ■ **9** - National Investigations Committee on Aerial Phenomena, *The UFO Evidence* (Washington, DC: 1964). ■ **10** - J. Allen **Hynek,** *The UFO Experience: A Scientific Inquiry* (Chicago: -Henry Regnery, 1972). ■ **11** - John **Fuller,** *Aliens in the Skies* (New York: Putnam, 1969); Carl **Sagan** and Thornton **Page,** editors, *UFO's: A Scientific Debate* (Ithaca: Cornell University Press, 1972). ■ **12** - Edward U. **Condon,** et. al., *Scientific Study* *of Unidentified Flying Objects* (New York: Bantam Books, 1969). ■ **13** - Allan **Hendry,** *The UFO Handbook: A Guide to Investigating, Evaluating and Reporting UFO Sightings* (Garden City: Doubleday, 1979). ■ **14** - See Ron **Westrum,** David **Swift,** and David **Stupple,** 'Extraterrestrial Intelligence: the Sociology of an Idea,' in James **Katz,** editor, *People in Space* (San Francisco: Transaction Books, 1986.

5.3

UFOs AND THE PUBLIC

by John Spencer
with additional material from John Barrett.

■ **JOHN SPENCER:** educated in north-west London. First became interested in UFO research in the mid-1960s. This led to sky-watching with two friends from his school days - Bob Digby and Stephen Gamble (both long-serving members of BUFORA's Council of Management) in the early 1970s. He has been a member of BUFORA for many years, and was its Treasurer until 1982 when he resigned to set up his own firm of Chartered Accountants. He remains Financial Director and Honorary Secretary.

■ **UFO involvement**: In 1984 BUFORA set up, within its research department, sections designed to investigate particular hypotheses, broadly distinguishing the extra-terrestrial, artifical terrestrial, natural terrestrial, psychological and less specific hypotheses - and to apply directional research to cases. John was involved in setting up the division investigating 'natural terrestrial'.

His interest in UFOs is particularly in the interaction of the phenomenon with the human mind.

■ **Publications**: He worked closely with the former editor of The BUFORA Bulletin on many projects including reviews of publications. He has authored for that publication an article on the dangers of misinterpreting the results of hypnotic regression. Apart from being joint editor of this book, he is joint editor of a forthcoming publication likewise produced under the auspices of BUFORA, due for publication in February 1988, in which UFO research will be reviewed for a wider and less specialised readership.

■ **Address**: 15 Bosworth Road / Barnet EN5 5LZ / England. Phone 01-449 3751.

Forty years ago, on the 24th June 1947, the modern UFO phenomenon was born. This statement is as incorrect as it is meaningless. What happened on that date, as readers of even rudimentary books on the subject will know, is that a civilian pilot, Kenneth Arnold, sighted from his aircraft nine objects in close formation in the vicinity of Mount Rainier, Washington, USA and described them to the Press at the time as moving in an unconventional manner "like a saucer would if you skipped it across water." In those words were born the expression "flying saucer" and the media from then on had a phrase which had caught the public imagination, the description the phrase implied was inadequate even as it was invented, as numerous reports were to be received of cigar shapes, egg shapes, etc. and very soon the expression unidentified flying object (UFO) soon came in to use. However, even today the expression flying saucer is perhaps the commonest general phrase to be found in the tabloid press. The opening sentence of this paragraph was inaccurate in yet another way; Kenneth Arnold's sighting merely gave a name to, not birth to, a phenomenon which had existed long before. Studies and theories have reached back through the centuries to biblical times and earlier, to perhaps the earliest paintings our ancestors scratched on cave walls.

The formation of nine flying saucers sighted by Kenneth Arnold were estimated to be travelling at speeds of approximately 2000-2750 km/h (350 to 1700 mph) [**1**]. No terrestrial aircraft at that time had flown so fast but even though man had not achieved these speeds they were not beyond the reach of credibility. Just five days before the sighting Colonel Albert M Boyd USAF in a Lockhead P 80 R Shooting Star achieved a record speed of 1010 km/h (623.61 mph) and within under six months Captain Charles E Yeager USAF in a Bell XS1 (later redesignated X1) made the first supersonic flight in history breaking what was believed to be a sound barrier by travelling at 1135 km/h (700.66 mph, 1.06 mach). Shortly afterwards, 26th March 1948, Captain Yeager in the X1 achieved a speed of 1555 km/h (959.8 mph, Mach 1.45). By the summer of 1951 the US Navy Douglas D 558-11 Sky Rocket research aircraft had achieved 2013 km/h (1242.68 mph), virtually the estimated speed of the Arnold saucers.

This above paragraph represents an important part of UFO research. The apparent development of the UFO has tended to very closely mirror the development of our own technology, and the possible reasons for this, at least from the view point of human logic, can be realistically broken down into five main areas; one or more of which may contain at least part of the answer to the question of the origin of the phenomenon. These areas are:

■ **FACTUAL** i.e. that our atmosphere is being invaded by flying vehicles of, presumably extra-terrestrial origins whose technological development happens to be only just ahead, and constantly just keeping ahead, of our own.

■ **FACTUAL,** but in the sense that our scientists, having observed the activities of presumably extraterrestrial craft in our atmosphere are inspired to research into areas that lead to advancement they would perhaps not have otherwise achieved. In short, we are copying them.

■ **SUBTERFUGE** i.e. our atmosphere is being invaded by presumably extraterrestrial spaceships from a civilisation considerably more technologically advanced than our own which does not wish us to know that fact. This may be because of 'like minds' or perhaps more simply that they hope that we will pass them off as vehicles of our own, giving them less fear of interruption as they go about their business, whatever that may be.

■ **CREDIBILITY**. i.e. that the witness to one of these UFO occurrences wishes to be believed. (In this sense we are not restricted to technological aircraft from Earth or beyond but can include any stimulus producing a UFO report) In order to be so believed then the report of the sighting must fit within certain credible parameters. This hypothesis, along with the others, will be examined in more detail later but it must be stressed at this point that while the above would be true of an outright lie, i.e. a prefabricated report, we are here considering something more basic to the human psychological framework, something that applies as much to witnesses who genuinely believe the report they make.

■ **'HOLLYWOOD'** (for want of a better term) i.e. that in as much as films are inspired by the reports of UFO, so the possibility must be considered that at least some UFO reports are inspired by films. Apart from actual hoaxes on this basis, we are here discussing the same psychological make-up as above; that of the desire for credibility of the sighting.

Firstly we must consider examples of the development of UFO's and of our own technology through a few of the many thousands of UFO reports over the ages. The first UFO "flap" since we ourselves have become aeronautical would be the airship flap of 1896/97 where a considerable number of cigar-shaped air ships were reported across the USA. At this time the first aircraft was six years away and nothing remotely resembling a flying saucer had yet been considered and the only air travel progress the human race was making at that time was in airships. 1852 saw the first aerial vehicle: Giffard's airship although this was incapable of being directed even in the lightest of breezes [**2**]. Of course, we always use the terminology of our time to describe what we see and no Kansas farmer in 1896 would use the expression 'airplane', which he would not then have heard of, but would use the expression 'air ship' which would at that time have been referred to in the broadsheets of the day. But it is not merely the terminology that matches, it is the description. We were dealing with airships that were "cigar shaped," precisely the shape of the airship then under development. The Adamski-style saucer was yet to make its apearance both in fact and in terminology.

Coming forward in time then to our Arnold sighting earlier mentioned what else was being reported around that time? There were, for one thing, the "ghost rockets" of 1946 with speeds ranging up to 800 km/h [**3**]. Also in 1946, on August 1st, Captain Jack E. Puckett flying a twin engine C47 from Langley Field to Mackdill Air Force Base, Florida reported a horizontal flying object moving at approximately 3,000 km/h [**3**] and described it as the size of a B-29 bomber.

In the 1950's we have of course the Adamski saucer although the main significance of this report is that of the contact with the "UFOnauts" rather than the technological capabilities of their ship. In 1953, however, Sgt. William Kelly in front of a radar screen in Yaak, Montana, USA reported 6 unidentified targets moving at speeds between 2,200 and 2,500 km/h [**4**]. On December 12th 1953 Major Charles E. Yeager achieved Mach 2.44, 2673 km/h, in a Bell X 1A.

On 29th June 1954 a BOAC Strato Cruiser travelling from New York to London reported a group of UFO's travelling at the same speed as the aircraft, approximately 600 km/h [**4**]. This may of course not be representative of their capabilities, however, as the witnesses believed the UFO was deliberatley pacing the aircraft.

1957, November 11th, and a passenger aboard Western Airlines flight 61, Mr. Robert P Hahn, sighted a UFO travelling at an estimated 8000 km/h [**5**]. This was ahead of our own technology of the time but only 2 1/2 years away were the flights of the X15 Rocket plane which achieved 3420 km/h, mach 3.19, in May 1960 and by June 1961 had achieved Mach 5.27, 5837 km/h. This plane, by November 1961 had broken the 6480 km/h record.

We have of course been considering experimental test aircraft in most of the above, but this is not to say that commercial passenger aircraft are that far behind. In the 1960's was laid down the foundations of Concorde which can now regularly fly at Mach 2.2, 2349 km/h and is now so familiar a sight that it is virtually ignored as it flies through the sky of South West London on its way to New York where it can put down its passengers just three supersonic hours after leaving their luggage in Heathrow!

Into the 1970's and a sighting in August 1974 at Lake Sarratoga, New York State, which recorded an immense blimp-shaped object at a speed in excess of 8,000 km/h, and much faster if the radar scope was recording some degree of upward movement. [**5**].

With regard to the descriptions of UFO's these tend virtually invariably to be aerodynamic. Discs, saucers, cigar shapes, egg shapes etc. are the most common; almost without exception reports are never of un-aerodynamic objects. The one main example of an exception to this is Carl Higdon's encounter on October 25th, 1974, where the object into which he was abducted was described as "Cube-like in appearance, shaped like a box flat on all sides without evidence of landing gear or doorways." [**6**] However, his description of the abduction suggests, if it is to be accepted at face value, matter transference rather than physical travel and perhaps for that reason does not contradict the point made. Perhaps it seems logical that such vehicles would be aerodynamic but this is a current, state-of-the-art piece of human logic. In fact, there is no reason to think this should apply in the case of our alleged extra-terrestrial visitors. Our own vehicles are aerodynamic for two main reasons:

■ Firstly, because our vehicles push through the air expending energy as they do so. The energy they have is that which is stored aboard in the form of fuel and therefore the more aerodynamic the craft either the faster or the farther it can travel.

■ Secondly, an aerodynamic shape reduces friction and subsequent over heating of the outer skin.

However, the most likely form of propulsion used by alien space craft, if one accepts that it is what they are, would appear to be some form of harnessing of the earth's magnetic field, which suggest that the craft's range and speed are not in any way limited by any onboard supplies of fuel. Furthermore, a technology capable of crossing the gulfs of space is not likely to have any great difficulty creating frictionless or friction-reducing material since this is almost certainly a problem of pure physics which would have to be a subject they had taken to considerably further extremes than our own.

Perhaps the answer therefore lies in the possibility that the craft are perceived to be aerodynamic to suit the limited, human thinking of the witness rather than anything extra-terrestrial.

Let us now go back to our five possible reasons why UFO reports appear to mirror the current state of technology. We suggested firstly that this may be the product of a simple fact; that the crafts were extra-terrestrial in origin and were visiting the earth for one purpose or another and happened to be not only reasonably similar in colour and capability to our own craft but not only reasonably similar in colour and capability to our own craft but developed at a rate similar to our own technological development. There are certainly some persuasive arguments in favour of this; given the state of our own technology the supposedly alien vehicles would never have had to perform much more spectacularly if all they wish to do was to avoid us. However, on the assumption that at least some of the sightings were not planned by the crafts' occupants we would expect to see them performing at their own best capabilities when they were sighted unintentionally. When we fly an aeroplane we do so to the limits of our own requirements or of the aeroplane's capabilities and we are not limited by the fact that a car, say, happens to travel much slower except in the rare event when the aeroplane is trying to shadow the car. On the other hand, given that their technology must be very much more advanced than our own, not least because they are capable of visiting an alien planet whereas we are not, then it seems fair to assume that advances they would regard as being significant in their technology would probably be unnoticeable by ourselves since we could not comprehend them. In short, the crafts that we see nowadays would not seem very different from those that we have seen over the past 50 or 100 years, possibly even over the past 2,000 years from our standard and view point. Modern man may be very proud of this year's new Fiat, Ford, etc, but a jungle-dwelling native is not likely to comprehend significant differences in cars today against cars of twenty years ago.

Our second hypothesis, that our own advances in technology are inspired by what we see of the extra terrestrial crafts' capabilities at least has certain human precedents. The breaking of the sound barrier itself was difficult to achieve and many experienced pilots believed it would be impossible. When Chuck Yeager did break the sound barrier, then suddenly it became a "norm." There was once much talk, in sporting circles, that a four minute mile barrier was impossible for a human being to break but following Dr. Roger Bannister's achievement a whole host of people have broken through this non-existent wall. The conquest of Mount Everest was considered impossible until Hillary placed the Union Jack on its summit in 1953 and those who have subsequently followed him have included a Japanese grandmother and a host of people who descend from the heights on skis. And so on and so on; the only common barrier that we have been looking at is the psychological barrier which, when the way is shown, can be easily surmounted. However, even if the inspiration of watching UFO's has contributed to our development it cannot be said to have played a major part as the development itself has been reasonably smooth and reasonably logical and not shown any of the massive leaps and bounds that would be expected from some form of external interference.

We thirdly considered subterfuge. The likelihood that alien space craft wish to be indistinguishable from our own is the least likely possibility of all as presumably it would not be anything but simple for them to produce an accurate copy of, say, a strato cruiser which could travel about virtually unchallenged. In any case, the pattern of reported events particularly with regard to UFO contactees does not suggest that concealment is important and some sightings have been very blatant in nature.

Our fourth hypothesis, that the descriptions given of the craft and its movement are dictated by the beliefs of the witness reflect a current trend in UFO research in that it is believed a full analysis of a sighting cannot be made until the witness himself is brought under scrutiny. We can illustrate this best by way of an example. Let us place ourselves in time in 1950 and we will suppose that our witness, a lone witness with no corroborative evidence to support his sighting, sees a fast-moving, apparently solid object traverse the sky at a fast speed. Firstly, it is likely that he will not have been able to do any scientific analysis on the speed, the timing of the sighting, and any photograph taken if any is likely to be unclear since he will not have been prepared for the contact. Let us suppose that he can report this sighting to a UFO researcher within a fairly short space of time, say two days. Our witness's first problem is that he must be believed. Bear in mind he is not prefabricating a lie here but setting up his own forms of reinforcement of his sighting. This question of the desire to be believed is crucial to this analysis and therefore we must digress for a short time and consider experiments conducted at Harvard many years ago and which have been repeated since with similar results.

In this experiment some thirty people were put in to a room where they were told they were going to be given certain rudimentary tests but they were not told the nature or aims of these tests. The test took the form of two lines of unequal length drawn on a blackboard, line A being longer than line B, but not so much as to be blatant. Each of the thirty people was in turn asked which line was the longest. The test was in fact this; 29 of the 30 people were Harvard University 'plants' and they would reply that they believed line B to be longer and in a significant percentage of cases the 30th person - the only true experimental subject - also claimed line B to be the longest. In subsequent analysis it was revealed that in many cases the person had deliberately lied because he did not want to be 'different from the norm' and in other cases where analysis went further still; under a lie detector test many of the experimental subjects actually believed line B to be the longer. In other words they had denied the evidence of their own eyes because of a self-conditioning exercise which had failed, quite reasonably, to take into account the possibility that they were being duped by 29 confederates.

To come back to our UFO scenario our witness has two days to think through the event before giving his report to the UFO researcher and in those two days this conditioning will take effect. Firstly, even though he may not have had a clear sighting of the shape of the vehicle he will create some sort of reasonable aerodynamic shape because logic will dictate to him that that is what it must have been. Even if he saw a perfect cube in flight the least he could do after two days consideration would be to round off the corners. With regard to the speed he probably has no idea whatsoever about the speed that the object was travelling and if he makes a guess based on the speeds of contemporary aircraft he may be tempted to double or treble this but not much more because he wishes to remain credible. On the other hand he may admit to the researcher that he has no real idea and he may try to work out a speed by, say, comparing it to the movement of a conventional aircraft. This is very flawed reasoning because firstly he has no idea of the size and therefore the height of this unknown sighting and obviously if sightings were taking place at a very low level it would require a very much lesser velocity to cover the same arc of sky than if it were flying say 20 times higher. Indeed, an inexperienced researcher may even collaborate unintentionally in this perpetration by asking say, 'how fast was the object travelling? in the sense that how long did it take to pass between two points, (say a tree and church spire)' and the witness might say 'five seconds' whereas in reality the witness probably has no real idea, and if the truth were seven seconds or ten seconds then the estimate is out by up to twice as much. Furthermore if the calculation on this basis concludes that the speed was, say, 50 times faster than a conventional aircraft either the inexperienced researcher or the witness may say "well this must be wrong it is not reasonable, perhaps I had the estimate of the duration wrong etc." This process not only explains the similarity between supposedly alien and terrestrial technology but may go some considerable way to "standardising" the UFO reports themselves, particularly in cases where the witness has read some article or the other on UFO's either prior to the sighting or between the time of the sighting and the time he gives a report to a researcher or newspaper; his reading possibly inspired by his own sighting but his report coloured by his own reading.

But let us now bring our scenario into 1980 where our witness sees exactly the same event. For the aerodynamic shape nothing much has changed in that current human technology requires an aerodynamic shape for expedient flight but perhaps the barriers are slightly down to those which existed in 1950, because since that time we have seen newsreel footage of spacecraft operating in an airless environment and perhaps the most unaerodynamic of all objects, the lunar landing module. Obviously these vehicles are not aerodynamic because they are not designed to operate in an atmosphere but the point is that the prejudices acting on a rational mind are slightly less and one might expect a modern day report to be perhaps more liberal in this respect, and this does tend to be what we find. Saucers, or whatever, tend to have more protruberances, windows and generally more exterior working parts although admittedly to date they seem to basically retain their overall aerodynamic structure. With regard to speed, however, there can be significant changes because since the 1950's we are obviously more accustomed to higher speeds. In the realms of fact, we are quite used to speeds of around 40,000 km/h being achieved by Apollo spacecrafts on their journeys to and from the moon and speeds of 30,000 km/h regularly achieved by the space shuttle in its earth orbital missions. It is not that we can particularly conceive of what these speeds mean, nor would they be easily achievable in any atmosphere, but if our rationalising witness comes up with a speed of approximately 30,000 km/h he will feel less inhibited about reporting that speed because in 1980 it would seem less ridiculous than in 1950 and the report would be no less credible for it. In the same way if a witness today reported seeing a UFO and reported it's speed as 'a million km/h' the witness would be accused of exaggeration at the least because such speeds are beyond reason, from our current state-of-the-art, but if that speed became a norm and we could all watch an aircraft fly at a km/h at, say, Biggin Hill then the witness would feel less inhibited about the report. This does not change the fact that either way the craft may well have been moving at that speed, it only makes the witness more likely to report it. So, as our technology advances so does the apparent technology of our alien visitors.

Additionally, between 1950 and 1980 there have been considerably more reported sightings of UFO's and considerably more press and other media coverage and it is a simple matter of fact that more people are aware of the UFO-phenomenon than perhaps ever before with almost everybody having read at least one report or another reinforced by statements that the phenomenon has existed for decades; whereas in the 1950's one could only claim that it had existed for years; at least in terms of media interest. Reports therefore can become more liberal as people begin to accept the subject generally.

Our fifth hypothesis is not really a separate area but is mostly supplementary to the previous hypothesis. The idea that Hollywood (and I use the term to embrace films, television programmes and other fictionalisations) has influenced us is very important. To give an example, continuing from our previous example, if our hypothetical witness believed that the vehicle he had seen was 5 km wide he would have been very reluctant to believe that himself in 1950 and would certainly have been reluctant to report it as such (our creditability problem again) because no air travelling vehicle had ever come remotely close to that size. Our same witness in 1980 might be considerably less reluctant to make that claim because he would be aware, possibly, that millions of people have indeed seen a three mile wide space craft with their own eyes. Not in reality of course, but in Steven Spielberg's film *Close Encounters of the Third Kind.* Spielberg actually puts such an image on the screen and thereby sensitizes us all to the image which then seems less alien (no pun intended) when someone reports the reality of that image.

Throughout the past forty years, and perhaps particulary in the 50's and early 60's, science fiction films and television serials have concentrated very much on the UFO problem and in many cases derived plots directly from it. Prior to the Arnold sighting, science fiction did not generally involve invasions from other worlds but tended, where extra-terrestrials were involved, to be more of an updated form of 'cowboys and indians' and perhaps the best known of these would be the 'Flash Gordon' serials of the 1930s and 1940s. It is also notable that prior to the Arnold sighting flying saucers were generally unheard of and space travel took place in 'advanced' airplanes; witness again the bullet-shaped vehicle in which Flash Gordon travelled. However, after the Arnold sighting there was a rash of 'invasions' and almost always by flying saucer, typically: *Man from Planet X* (1951), *The day the Earth stood still* (1951), *The thing from another world* (1951), *War of the worlds* (1953), *It came from outer space* (1953) [actually an egg-shape, not a saucer here], *Invaders from mars* (1953), *This island Earth* (1955), *Forbidden Planet* (1956) [we invaded them in this case, but we did it in a classic flying saucer], and *Earth versus the Flying Saucers* (1956). Consequently, the public is now sensitized to the subject as a whole, and to 'flying saucers' and extra-terrestrial intelligences in particular.

In conclusion, the past forty years of UFO's have allowed us to progress some considerable way towards finding the answers to the questions the phenomenon raises. This is not to suggest that we have yet solved the enigma or even that the above chapter answers more than a small number of the questions that need to be answered, but it begins to outline why we have learned to study the influences on the mind of the witness at least as much as the report offered in order to seek out those answers and modern UFO research is increasingly aware of this need.

REFERENCES

■ 1 - Paris **Flammonde**, *UFO exist.* ■ 2 - *The Guinness Book of Speed Facts and Feats.* ■ 3 - Ralph **Blum** and Judy **Blum**, *Beyond Earth.* ■ 4 - Hilary **Evans**, *The Evidence for UFOs.* ■ 5 - Margaret **Sachs** with Ernest **Jahn**, *Celestial Passengers, UFOs and Space Travel.* *6 Warren Smith, *UFO Trek.*

5.4

THE DAY FLYING SAUCERS INVADED THE CINEMA

by Nigel Watson

The easiest way to see a flying saucer is to visit your local cinema rather than some wind-swept hill-top. Invaders from outer space, and our own invasion of outer space, came to the cinema screens as soon as you could say "box office." The writings of Jules Verne and H.G. Wells inspired Georges Méliès' productions, an early and good example being *A Trip to the Moon* (Georges Méliès; 1903) [1] His films tended to feature wonderful inventions and journeys to exotic locations. They relied heavily on trick photography and staging that became Méliès' trademark. The first screen alian to visit Earth came to London. The lonely moonman has fun with his anti-gravity gas at the expense of Earth people, and this occurs, the title explains, *When the Man in the Moon Seeks a Wife* (Percy Stow; 1908).

However, between 1910 and 1945 visions of the future, mad inventors, time travel, death rays, radio beams, invisibility rays, and futuristic weapons tend to be of as much interest to filmmakers as interplanetary exploits. The aliens from outer space did not start plaguing us until we had settled the Second World War. In the 15-part serial *The Purple Monster Strikes* (Spencer Gordon Bennet and Fred Brannon; 1945) a Martian organises an invasion by killing a scientist and taking over his body. But it was not until the "flying saucers" hit the newspaper headlines, that the cinema worked over-time to bring them into view. A villainous scientist in the film serial *Bruce Gentry - Daredevil of the Skies* (Spencer Gordon Bennet and Thomas Carr; 1948) uses flying discs in an attempt to smash the Panama Canal.

The most obvious use of the contemporary interest in strange flying objects is given away by the title of *The Flying Saucer* (Mikel Conrad; 1950). Whereas in later science fiction films the aliens may be seen as a metaphor for the communists, *The Flying Saucer* has no need for such subtleties. It clearly shows the Russians stealing a saucer from a scientist in Alaska. Fortunately for the free-world and the continued production of Ma's applie pie the plans of the Russians are thwarted when the craft explodes in mid-air and the scientist gives his secrets to the U.S. Government.

1951 was a good year for flying saucer films. A serial called the *Flying Disc Man from Mars* (Fred C. Brannon; 1951) cashed-in on their popularity by re-making *The Purple Monster Strikes*. This time a Martian forces a scientist to help him re-build his flying saucer spaceship so that he can bomb Earth and take-over. In the final reel this unfriendly Martian (ironically called Mota - atom spelt backwards) is killed by an atomic bomb delivered by a young scientist.

In *The Thing from Another World* (Christian Nyby and Howard Hawks; 1951) a 20,000 ton unidentified aircraft crashes into the Arctic. When men from a nearby US military base investigate they find a fin of perfectly smooth, unknown metal, sticking out of the ice. Geiger counter readings in the area are high and when the men spread out to mark-out the edges of the craft, which they can see beneath the ice, they discover it is circular. A character exclaims, "We've found a flying saucer." The standard procedure for dealing with such craft is to release it with thermite bombs. One of the team thinks that, "We may have the key to the stars. A million years of history of waiting for us in that ice." What effect this would have on us is never considered because the bombs blow up the flying saucer and all that is left is a 8 foot tall alien. This time they decide to chop out the ice surrounding the occupant and take it back to base. Accidently the alien is thawed out and goes on the rampage. They discover it is a highly intelligent vegetable that is not handicapped by emotion or sex. It lives off blood and regards humans as a tasty treat to stick in its larder. Dr Carrington nurtures more of the creatures and grows to admire its intelligence and power, whilst Captain Hendry does everything in his power to kill it.

The film articulates several aspects of the human dilemma. In the bleak wilderness of the universe our society and civilisation is easily destroyed by impersonal nature if we do not work together. In particular, soldiers and scientists (the creators and users of atomic power) must work together for the good of mankind. At first the Americans believe the UFO is Russian, and so the external impersonal force of communism can be seen as an underlying threat. Furthermore, the alien can be seen as the unrestrained forces of id or superego that lurks within all of us. This led one critic to note that: "In *The Thing,* this means that although the blood- sucking carrot from another world is a head-over-heart veggie robot Red monster from the superego one minute, it is an extremist heart-over-head monster from the id the next. [2]

In *The Day the Earth Stood Still* (Robert Wise;

1951) Earth is not presented as a friendly sanctuary from the vast and deadly universe surrounding us. Instead, it is humanity who is the threat to the rest of the universe. Our tinkering with atom bombs cause Klaatu, and Gort, a huge robot, to land their flying saucer in Washington D.C. Their mission is to try to stop our aggressive political bickering, but in the end they have to demonstrate their superior power by bringing Earth's machines to a halt temporarily. Their solution is to leave a robot police force to look after us, since in the eyes of the rest of the galaxy, we are still irresponsible children who have too many dangerous toys to play with. The fears about nuclear power and East/West relations mirror the concerns that became increasingly expressed by contactees and ufologists in the subsequent years. The depiction of the flying saucer, and Gort, are probably the best re-constructions (or creations?) of how people at that time imagined the technology of UFO beings.

Humanity was also shown as heartless and cruel in *The Man from Planet X* (Edgar G. Ulmer; 1951). An alien visits us to obtain help for his dying planet, but all we do in return is blast his ship with bazookas. The same fate nearly occurs to the aliens who fall to Earth in *It Came From Outer Space* (Jack Arnold; 1953), but one man does have faith in them and helps them to repair their meteor-like craft.

By now filmmakers featured interplanetary attacks at every opportunity. Such films as Invaders from Mars (William Cameron Menzies; 1953), *Earth Versus the Flying Saucers* (Fred F. Sears; 1956), *Invasion of the Body Snatchers* (Don Siegel; 1956), *Plan 9 From Outer Space* (Edward D. Wood; 1956), *Invasion of the Saucermen* (Edward L. Cahn; 1957), *Teenagers from Outer Space* (Tom Graeff; 1959), all showed Them wanting possession of our minds, bodies and/or property. Earth attracts flying saucers and aliens like bees to honey if we are to believe these filmic fantasies.

In *This Island Earth* (Joseph Newman; 1956) the Metalunians even kidnap some of our scientists to help them fight the Zahgons. The battle is unsuccessful but we are treated to see colourful flying saucers and monsters. The image of the flying saucer is also used in *Forbidden Planet* (Fred M. Wilcox; 1956). This time the craft is operated by ourselves in the future. *United Planets Cruiser C-57D* is an early screen version of the *U.S.S. Enterprise*, and its mission to look after the spaceways leads to a battle with a crazy scientist's id. The opening and closing sequences of the saucer spinning through space are very effective. Its wobbly landing on a red desert strikingly shows a cone of light project from the spinning underside of the vehicle. As the red lights spin slowly to a halt a pedestal descends to act as a landing leg, whilst two landing ramps are lowered. Such details have featured in close encounter reports, and the interior of the vehicle which contains a television monitor, and a replica of the ship inside a glass bubble that acts as a navigation device, seems reminiscent of reports made by people who say they have actually been inside flying saucers.

Certainly the filmmakers sucked dry anything remotely connected with UFOs. Their popularity was one reason why producer George Pal decided to make the *War of the Worlds* (Byron Haskins; 1953). He said, "With all the talk about flying saucers, *War of the Worlds* had become especially timely. And that was one of the reasons we updated the story." [**3**] There was also an eye to achieving the interest that had tragically got out of hand when Orson Welles' Mercury Theatre on the Air broadcast an updated version of H.G. Wells' story on the evening of 30 October 1938. This radio broadcast, that caused thousands of Americans to believe that the Martians had invaded, was itself the subject of a television movie titled *The Night That Panicked America* (J. Sargent; 1975). Fortunately, Pal's Martian war machines that looked like flying saucers with vacuum cleaner attachments were not enough to scare anything but dirty carpets.

The 1960s, by contrast, offered little fare for science fiction films, for the real-life space race to the moon was more attractive and immediate than pictures of little green men swarming out of round metal tins. However, some notable films were made during this period. The *Village of the Damned* (Wolf Rilla; 1960) and a remake, *Children of the Damned* (Anton M. Leader; 1963), were based on John Wyndham's novel *The Midwich Cuckoos*. In both a new breed of children with supernatural powers are born to normal Earth women, and at the end the children are killed because of our own fears and ignorance. This same type of theme is dealt with in *It's Alive* and *It Lives Again* (Larry Cohen; 1973 and 1978). UFOs and virgin births are featured even more explicitly in *God Told Me To* (Larry Cohen; 1976) in order to provide a 'brilliantly repercussive investigation of individual and social repression, sexual repression, sexuality, guilt and faith.' [**4**]

In 1967 a Martian spaceship is found underneath the streets of London. On investigation it is found that the machine can still radiate energy even though its insect-like occupants are dead. Apparently we did not evolve naturally but were programmed thousands of years ago by the dying Martians to cover their genes. Disturbed by the excavations the spaceship sends out signals that bring alive our dormant Martian genes. As the machine absorbs and sends out power an image of a Martian, which looks like the devil, appears above ground. These events in *Quatermass and the Pit* Roy Ward Baker; 1967) suggest that we are nothing more than the property of aliens who have cultivated us for their own mysterious purposes. Just as in Arthur C. Clarke's novel *Childhood's End*, our racial memories, even our religions, are based on false recollections caused by alien interference.

The most important film of the decade was undoubtedly *2001; A Space Odyssey* (Stanley Kubrick; 1968), and it also deals with the evolution of mankind. This is not altogether surprising since Arthur C. Clarke co-wrote the script with Stanley Kubrick. In their story a black monolith stimulates apes to use weapons and this eventually leads to human civilisation and space exploration. Our technology raises us head and shoulders above our natural surroundings but it also turns us into emotionless robots. The monoliths in the film act as tools for the unseen aliens. Their role is very much like Gort the robot; they become aware of our increasing movement out from our cradle and they warn the rest of the universe of our presence. Finally one of the seamless slabs sends an astronaut on the next step of evolution, and he is transformed into a star-child. What happens next is best left to our imaginations, since the sequel *2010* Peter Hyams; 1984) is only a display of special effects with no greater message than that a new sun in the solar system will help cement East/West relationships.

Arthur C. Clarke has always laughed at reports of UFOs [**5**], but Kubrick was more open-minded about this subject. He said: "I'm really fascinated by UFOs and I only regret that this field of investigation has to a considerable extent been pre-empted by a crackpot fringe that claims to have soared to Mars on flying saucers piloted by three-foot-tall green humanoids with pointy heads. That kind of kook approach makes it very easy to dismiss the whole phenomenon which we do at our own risk." [**6**]

The hunt for a flying saucer by the Russians and Americans took place in China in the oddly titled *The Bamboo Saucer* (Frank Telford; 1967). They do find the saucer, and rocket into space with it, but they never find out who owns it. This low-budget film was based on the alleged crash of a UFO on Spitzbergen, Norway, in the early part of 1952, so perhaps the filmmakers knew more than we do. [**7**] Certainly Erich von Däniken [**8**] was certain that what we regard as our Gods were extraterrestrials and this theory is propounded in *Chariots of the Gods* (Harald Reinl; 1969). His ideas, plus a liberal loan of ideas from 1930s adventure serials and *Kiss Me Deadly* (Robert Aldrich; 1955), were knowingly and joyfully linked in *Raiders of the Lost Ark* (Steven Spielberg; 1981).

The 1970s seemed to have little interest in aliens from outer space. Gruesome and detailed horror films featuring all manner of disasters and possession by the devil were all the rage. Even when aliens did visit us they were corrupted by our society and reduced to disillusioned robots. This occurred in *The Man Who Fell to Earth* (Nicholas Roeg; 1976) which sometimes seems as if it was directed by an alien.

Suddenly aliens and flying saucers became cinematically respectable again when *Close Encounters of the Third Kind* (Steven Spielberg; 1977) hit the screens. Who would ever have guessed that Hynek's *The UFO Experience: A Scientific Inquiry* would provide the title and background information for a 19 million dollar epic? No one could ever have guessed that Francois Truffaut would play a part based on Jacques, Vallée, though it is possible that Vallée's book *The Invisible College* supplied the idea, used in the film, that the aliens could communicate with us telepathically and that if we are sensitive to such messages we can all become contactees.

The search for something beyond the insipid materialistic American Dream that is fired by the UFO encounters experienced by Roy Neary, Jillian Guiler and her son Barry, must have struck a chord with its record-breaking audiences. Like *Star Wars* (George Lucas; 1977) it has been dismissed as nothing more than adolescent escapism, that requires "only that their audiences react: they demand no commitment... " [**9**] What such a view ignores is that people want entertainment and a restoration of 'the sense of wonder, not intellectual discourse pushed down their throats at every opportunity. Indeed, the use of instinct, emotion and non-verbal means of communication (for example, lights, music, the now famous 'sky tones', radio signals, television and cartoon images) help express what is inexpressible by rational, cold, objective means. For some this is a return to faith in magic or religion as opposed to science. However, *Close Encounters* implicitly questions our arrogant belief that any of us - scientists, priests or other holders of knowledge - have the answers to life's mysteries. I suspect that some reviewers have been more uneasy about the magic of *Close Encounters* because it is made available to representatives of Everyman on our own doorstep in the present day, whereas the magical monoliths in *2001* which provide the dream of the millennium are available only to an elite who are able to travel millions of miles into space in the future. Perhaps *Close Encounters* temporarily gave a boost to the UFO subject by making it the centre of nation-wide if not world-wide discussion, but it is doubtful that just one film can change deep-seated opinions and attitudes.

As a consequence of the popularity and interest generated by *Close Encounters* several poor cash-in films were made. A ufologist is shown tracking down a flying saucer in *Foes* (John Coats; 1977). The same kind of idea is used in *Starship Invaders* (Ed Hunt; 1977) in which Robert Vaughn plays the part of a ufologist who has to fight off a nasty bunch of aliens headed by Christopher Lee. In *The End of the World* (John Hayes; 1977) Christopher Lee is taken over by an alien, who, with other aliens, wants to destroy Earth because our planet is polluted beyond redemption. A better effort is *The Glitterball* (Harley Cockliss; 1977) which features two boys who help an alien to return home to its mothership. In contrast to Spielberg's benevolent aliens, a remake of the *Invasion of the Body Snatchers* (Philip Kaufman; 1978) and *The Dark* (John 'Bud' Cardos; 1979) contain rather more frightening alien entities.

Thoughts that the United States Government is hiding a crashed UFO have been prevalent in the UFO literature since the 1950s, and such sentiments are articulated in *Hangar 18* (James L. Conway; 1980). Manipulation by Government agencies is revealed, this time deliberately for comic effect, in *Simon* (Marshall Brickman; 1980). The film centres on Simon, a psychology professor, who is brainwashed into thinking that he is an extraterrestrial by the Institute of Advanced Concepts. More manipulation by the authorities and media are revealed in *The War of The Worlds - The Next Century* (Piotr Szulkin; 1981). A reporter tries to tell the public that the Martians have landed but nobody will believe him; this is a veiled reference to the wider public concerns in Poland at that time (e.g. the threat of Russian invasion).

1982 was a good year for aliens in the cinema. In *Big Meat Eater* (Chris Windsor; 1982) the aliens fight for the radioactive waste emanating from a butcher's septic tank, but through sheer ingenuity the aliens are gunned down by the end of the picture. Another oddity is *Liquid Sky* (Slava Tsukerman; 1982) that includes a German ufologist and a fair mixture of sex, drugs and rock and roll which puts sky watching into the shades. Not much better is *Xtro* (Harry Bromley Davenport; 1982) that includes abduction by a UFO, rape by aliens, the birth of aliens that, not surprisingly, disrupt family life, etc. A remake of *The Thing* (John Carpenter; 1982) starts with a 1950s image of a flying saucer entering the Earth's atmosphere. Later - at least 100,000 years later - our present-day heroes find the ship buried under the Antartic ice. One credulous character says, with regard to the reality of flying saucers, "*Chariots of the Gods*, man, they practically own South America. They may have taught the Incas everything they know." Despite such touches of humour the film relies more on showing hideous alien shape changing and plenty of gore. Exploiting the horror film genre and the ideas of Erich von Däniken, *Time Walker* (Tom Kennedy; 1982) shows us that an alien with a deadly touch took over Tutankhamen's mummy. So when it is disturbed it quite predictably starts killing people.

Amongst all these deadly aliens it is quite a relief to see *E.T. The Extra-Terrestrial* (Steven Spielberg; 1982) who perpetuates the 1960s notion, as voiced by The Beatles, that *All You Need is Love*. Rather than the grandiose and noisy mothership that overwhelms humanity in *Close Encounters* by its sheer size and power the tiny creature who climbs out of his modest flying saucer in *E.T.* is capable of working miracles in our cynical world by showing that we should trust

in love and our own dreams (in the same way Speilberg can be seen as the miracle worker of the cinema). The message of *E.T.* seems to be that the threat to humanity is our own adult arrogance, not marauding invaders outside out own world . That message does not seem too remote from that delivered by Gort and Klaatu in *The Day the Earth Stood Still*, or by countless contactees.

The films mentioned portray Earth either as a utopia or dystopia. Sometimes the flying saucers bring us salvation, other times they bring us punishment for our sins. They either shock and frighten us or they reassure us that we are worthy of our existence now or at least in the future. At times the saucers act as a metaphor for personal and/or social, psychological and/or physical alienation. Other times the flying saucer acts as a symbol for optimism, beauty, and a means of going beyond our Earth to find new wonders to marvel at. Or the saucer can be seen as a warning against dabbling with things we do not understand and that we should remain on Earth until we resolve our problems before contaminating the rest of the universe with them.

I am sceptical about the existence of aliens who meet or communicate with people on Earth. The reports of encounters and the stories of contactees contain messages that the percipients wish to hear. They are a vocalisation of their innermost fears and fancies. To bring them to a conscious level they are framed within the UFO mythology. This mythology began simply with sightings of flying saucers that became elaborated by our society and culture. The visions of filmmakers and UFO witnesses alike have - consciously or unconsciously - articulated with varying degrees of success the concerns of mankind. There is a two-way interaction between film art and UFO observations. Unfortunately ufologists have tended to ignore the influence of the cinema on our perception of UFO phenomena whilst filmmakers have largely ignored the wealth of material within the UFO literature that could bring new insights into the human condition onto the screens.

In future we should keep one eye on the skies and the other on the cinema screen, and if you have any eyes to spare watch where your flying saucer is going.

REFERENCES

■ 1 - Bracketed information refers to the name of the film's director followed by the film's release date. ■ 2 - **Biskind,** Peter, *Seeing is Believing: How Hollywood Taught Us To Stop Worrying and Love The Fifties* (Pluto Press, London, 1984, pp134-5). ■ 3 - quoted in; **Brosnam,** John, *Future Tense: The Cinema of Science Fiction* (Macdonald and Jane's, London, 1978, p90.) ■ 4 - **Hardy,** Phil (ed.), *The Aurum Film Encyclopedia: Science Fiction* (Aurum Press, London, 1984, p329.) ■ 5 - See for instance his scathing criticism of the subject in his novel *A Fall of Moondust* (Pan Books, London, 1964 - orig. pub. 1961 - pp175-181. ■ 6 - **Agel.** Jerome (ed.), *The Making of Kubrick's 2001* (Signet, New York, 1970, p.339). ■ 7 - More details of this incident are contained in **Edwards,** Frank, *Flying Saucers - Serious Business* (Lyle Stuart Inc., New York, 1966, pp81-82.) In addition, John Keel notes that Mr V. Itkonen, a Finnish movie producer, was interested in this case. All investigations seem to show that it was a journalistic hoax. See: **Keel,** John, 'Mystery Aeroplanes of The 1930s: Part 2' in *Flying Saucer Review*, Vol 16 No 4, July/August, 1970, pp9-10. **Trench,** Brinsley Le Poer, *The Flying Saucer Story* (Neville Spearman, London, 1966, pp152-55) reports the story and quotes Second Lieutenants Brobs and Tyllensen who believe that flying saucers are using the Arctic regions. Such ideas whether factual or fictional were no doubt fuelled by *The Thing*. ■ 8 - Spelt 'Daeniken' throughout Phil Hardy's *The Aurum Film Encyclopedia: Science Fiction*, ibid. ■ 9 - **Pym,** John, 'The Middle American Sky' in *Sight and Sound*, Vol. 47 No 2 (Spring 1978) p128.

FURTHER READING

■ **Baxter,** John, *Science Fiction in the Cinema* (Tantivy Press, London, 1970). ■ **Cantril,** Hadley, *The Invasion From Mars* (Harper and Row, New York, 1966 - orig. pub. 1940). ■ **Siegel,** Richard and **Suares,** Jean-Claude, *Alien Creatures* (Reed Books, Los Angeles, 1978.) ■ **Sobchack,** Vivian Carol, *The Limits of Infinity, The American Science Fiction Film. 1950-75* (Thomas Yoseloff Ltd., London, 1980.) ■ **Strick,** Philip, *Science Fiction Movies* (Octopus, 1976.)

5.5
CONSPIRACY AND COVER-UP
by Hilary Evans

From the very outset of the Flying Saucer era, the question was raised: Is the truth about the phenomenon being concealed by interested parties, either as a deliberate conspiracy of silence or as a sustained policy of covering up the facts?

The question is of fundamental importance. For if anything of the sort is taking place, we who are seeking to resolve the UFO problem are facing a double challenge: first from the phenomenon itself, and second from those who are seeking to prevent us learning what that phenomenon is.

In such a situation it is easy to become paranoid, and many ufologists have become so. Others have become bogged down in the mass of detail and documentation which such a study necessarily entails, and in so doing have tended to lose perspective.

An in-depth examination of the evidence for conspiracy and cover-up would require us to present and analyse detailed information beyond the scope of this book. But what **can** do is ask the more general questions:

- What is the **probability** that such a conspiracy or cover-up is taking place?
- If they **are** taking place, what is their probable extent?

SHIFTING THE BLAME

It is a universal human trait to seek scapegoats whom we can blame for the accidents which befall us or even for our own mistakes. God and the Devil, Anarchists and Jewish International Bankers, Fascists and Communists, Witches and Freemasons, Secret Societies of every shape and colour - these have at different times and in different cultures been made to carry a share of false blame. And because there is generally a shred of substance in the allegations, the accusations have often festered, and sometimes erupted into appalling counter-persecutions in which one portion of mankind has turned on another, and having first stigmatised the innocent with spurious slander, proceeded to punish them for their supposed guilt.

Social psychologists have shown what sort of process may be underlying such events. Faced with the unknown or the seemingly unfair, people are reluctant to accept that blind chance or accident are at work; instead they look for a more tangible someone/something behind it. Anthropologist Evans-Pritchard, for instance, has shown how such a process underlies some manifestations of African witchcraft [**10**].

Sometimes people attack others to externalise tendencies they subconsciously feel in themselves. American social psychologist Cantril has shown this to be the case with the lynching of coloured people by whites which periodically occurred in his country until very recent times [**5**].

So, when faced with suggestions that 'someone' is concealing the truth about UFOs, we must consider the possibility that such unconscious psychological processes may be at work. At the most superficial level, we must consider whether researchers, frustrated by their inability to resolve the UFO problem, may come to think they are being deliberately hampered by some sinisterly-motivated 'them'. Most frequently the 'them' will be 'the government', but Satan has also been invoked [**25**], as have some obscure entities of indeterminate origin known as 'Men in Black' [**8**], and even the extra-terrestrial entities themselves. [**14**]

GROUNDS FOR SUSPICION

But of course that is certainly not the whole of the matter. Even if psychological forces are playing a part in determining the shape the suspicion takes, the grounds for that suspicion are physical enough. Just as there was in fact some basis for the accusations of witchcraft, just as anarchist bombs, Masonic secrets and the crimes of the Mafia are matters of fact, so there are undoubtedly real actions by governments which provide grounds for accusing them of being less than open about their UFO involvement.

In particular, thanks to the Freedom of Information Act in the United States, documents have been released which indicate that at a time when security forces were denying that they were concerned with UFOs, they were in fact taking a substantial interest. [**12,17**]

There is no question, then, that such activities took place: they are a matter of fact. The question we have to ask, therefore, is: To what extent were these activities part of an organised policy?

We know from other manifestations of government activity, not only in the United States, that the implementation of any policy is liable to be hampered either by conscious disagreement or by mere old-fashioned muddled thinking as to how that policy should be carried out. Other factors are also at work:

- On the macro level, changes in administration, which in the United States tend to permeate all levels of government, would make consistent implementation of any policy improbable.

■ On a lower level, individual motivation, such as drives individuals to reveal military secrets to foreign powers or to leak Watergate-type details to the media, is a further obstacle to the methodical execution of a policy of concealment.

To suppose that, despite such factors, a clear unswerving line could be pursued over a 40-year period, is to make the premise that UFOs are somehow the exception to normal experience.

Could that be the case? Could it be that, because UFOs are an exceptional phenomenon, they could indeed lead to exceptional behaviour? Even if this were so, even if we hypothesise that, contrary to all previous experience, somehow a consistent policy *could* be implemented and maintained, we must still demand evidence that this has in fact happened.

COVER-UP OF WHAT?

If concealment by government is taking place, it may be of:

- ■ Its own activities
- ■ Its efforts to find out the activities of others
- ■ Its possession of knowledge about the activities of others
- ■ Its ignorance.

■ ITS OWN ACTIVITIES

It is possible that governments are spreading disinformation about UFOs as a disguise for their own activities. On 20 September1977 a 'jellyfish-like' UFO was reported over Petrozavodsk; it was subsequently established that the Soviet government could identify it only too well - it was a Kosmos-955 spy satellite from their secret base at Plesetsk. But it suited them to let the general public think otherwise. [**19**]

On this occasion the concealment was discovered; but it may reasonably be asked, how often have similar concealments *not* been discovered? As we shall see, there are many cases in which governments are *known* to have been involved; in how many of them were they not only aware what was going on, but **responsible for it happening** in the first place?

In 1968 Italian author Renato Vesco published the first of three deeply researched volumes [**24**] proposing the thesis that UFOs are, in fact, disc-shaped aircraft secretly produced in Canada by the British government. His case is buttressed by a wealth of circumstantial evidence which makes his books some of the most fascinating in the UFO literature; but even in 1968 it wasn't easy to believe Britain could conceal such a secret from the rest of the world. After two further decades it is simply not credible.

Using UFOs to conceal secret activities might be an attractive solution to a short-term embarrassment, but any long-term conspiracy along such lines simply could not be sustained.

■ ITS EFFORTS TO FIND OUT THE ACTIVITIES OF OTHERS

Documents obtained through the United States Freedom of Information Act [**17**] reveal that clandestine investigation of UFO-related matters has undoubtedly taken place. But we must remember that clandestine investigation is taking place all the time in virtually every sphere of government activity. Study the history of security organisations, and you find that cloak-and-dagger game-playing forms a large part of their activities, and often becomes an end in itself. [**15**]

We don't need a psychologist to tell us what kind of motivations we would expect to find in the kind of person who enlists as a secret agent. Just as some people are motivated to leak information to the media or to foreign powers, so others are motivated to play spy games a la John Le Carre. So documentary evidence that clandestine investigations have taken place in the matter of UFOs is nothing surprising: rather, it is just what we would expect.

■ ITS POSSESSION OF KNOWLEDGE ABOUT THE ACTIVITIES OF OTHERS

If one keeps quiet about something one has learnt, it is so that one may exploit it to one's own advantage. If a government knows about UFOs but is keeping its knowledge to itself, this could be:

■ So that it can make a secret deal with those responsible for the UFOs. Apart from the improbability that any government would be so stupid as to seek a unilateral agreement of this sort, or that any extra-terrestrial force would be willing to go along with it, again we must ask: Could such an agreemment be maintained for years without the rest of the world realising that something was going on?

■ So that it can benefit from technological know-how or other guidance. Benefit implies use: but in these days when every country is spying on every other, even on its allies, any such use would rapidly be observed by others, whether it took the form of a sudden breakthrough in technology or of less tangible forms of progress. In practice, it is evident that the governments of the world are all at very much the same level, whether technological, economical or moral.

It has been suggested that more than one government is involved. But this simply escalates the difficulty of keeping anything secret: apart from anything else, it implies that governments, which are continually squabbling amongst themselves on a hundred other issues, are, on this one matter, in tranquil agreement!

Yet another possibility is that government(s) do in fact possess such knowledge, but aren't able to make any use of it. So they are keeping it under wraps until such time as someone comes up with the necessary additional information. But if that's the case, a total blanket will defeat their ends; instead, we should expect to see some indication that solutions are being sought to help them take advantage of their knowledge.

Such evidence exists, after a fashion. For what most baffles the researcher is the refusal of governments to make any kind of pronouncement about events **in which official forces or agencies were undoubtedly involved**. Even a handful of such events is impressive:

14.10.1943: discs reported during Schweinfurt raid [**4**]
7.7.1947: material found at Roswell, USA [**1**]
13.8.1956: radar-visual event at Lakenheath, GB [**21**]
6.11.1967: vehicle interference near Fordingbridge, GB [**11**]
9.8.1980: apparent landing at Kirtland AFB, USA [**16**]
27.12.1980: ambiguous event at Rendlesham, GB [**3**]
8.1.1981: alleged landing at Trans-en-Provence, France [**13**].

In each of these cases, official interest was displayed, often to a very considerable degree - for example, Col Halt's notorious memo and tape in the bizarre Rendlesham affair. Unquestionably, the officials involved were playing at **something**; was that 'something' part of a concerted plan, or simply an ad hoc response to a one-off situation?

Others would also point to the seemingly perverse handling of many official inquiries, for example:

■ In the United States, the so-called Condon Report [**7**]

■ In France, the blow-hot-blow-cold attitude of the government in regard to GEPAN [**2**]

■ In Britain, the undoubted 'caginess' of the Ministry of Defence [**3**]

■ In the Soviet Union, the unpredictable shifts in media attitudes to the subject.

Yet others would add the crash/retrieval syndrome, which has brought forth a tantalising quantity of intriguing testimony. [**23**] Unfortunately, every bit of it is either ambiguous or of uncertain provenance, and the possibility remains that it has all been fabricated by the alleged informants.

We should also take into account allegations that the CIA (for instance) may have been conducting a policy of deliberate disinformation.[**22**] Recent disclosures of CIA activities [**18**], and similar carryings-on in other countries, suggest that we cannot ascribe limits to what such forces may feel themselves justified in doing, given the incentive. But is the UFO phenomenon considered important enough to warrant going to such lengths?

Extreme proponents of the conspiracy theory go further still, extending it to cover the media, the scientific establishment and so on. Only such a thesis, they suggest, explains why virtually every television documentary about UFOs adopts a debunking approach, rather than an impartial assessment of what we ufologists believe to be a subject of world importance.

That skepticism or ridicule are the rule can hardly be denied. But such attitudes are not confined to UFOs: they are encountered in respect of all fields of anomaly research, from 'earth mysteries' to parapsychology.[**20**] This suggests that the explanation is to be found in social psychology rather than in any deliberate conspiracy.[**9**] If a deliberate cover-up exists in regard to UFOs, we would have to argue that there is a similar conspiracy against parapsychology.

■ ITS IGNORANCE

The stance adopted by the media and the scientific establishment makes better sense if we attribute it to psychosocial response to something they *don't* understand, rather than to any directive from above or in-house agreement to keep silent about something they *do* understand.

As for officialdom, it seems most likely that their responses - for instance, to the cases listed earlier - spring from their ignorance rather than their knowledge. As career public servants, they are unwilling to admit their ignorance to the general public; so they take refuge in the cloak-and-dagger game-playing of their security forces.

When Australian researcher Bill Chalker was given access to the UFO files of the Royal Australian Air Force, not only did he find no evidence of a cover-up, but on the contrary found that some individuals, at least, were aware that a cover-up would be counter-productive:

'Any attempt by us to suppress public interest (however misguided we may think that interest to be) only helps to support the general impression that we are sitting on fat files of information...we will never be able to dodge press innuendos and statements verging on public accusations, as long as we continue to play our unclassified UFO cards too close to our chests.' [**6**]

Chalker's conclusion was that the RAAF was as puzzled as the rest of us by the reports it received. We must consider the possibility that the same may be true of all those official bodies whom we suspect of conspiracy and cover-up.

REFERENCES

■ 1 - **Berlitz**, Charles, & **Moore**, William L, *The Roswell incident*, Grosset & Dunlap, 1980. ■ 2 - **Bougard**, Michel, 'Le point sur le GEPAN' in *Inforespace*, 44, 1979; **Gouiran**, Charles, 'Ballon-sonde et gaz des marais' in *LDLN* 219-220, 1982. ■ 3 - **Butler**, **Street** & **Randles**, *Sky crash*, Spearman, 1984; also **Randles**, J. 'Rendlesham Forest update' in *MUFON Journal* 204, April 1985. ■ 4 - **Caidin**, Martin, *Black Thursday*, Dutton, 1960. ■ 5 - **Cantril**, Hadley, *The psychology of social movements*, Wiley, 1941. ■ 6 - **Chalker**, Bill, 'UFOs and the RAAF' in *MUFON Journal* 175, Sep 1982. ■ 7 - **Condon**, E (dir) *The scientific study of UFOs*, Univ of Colorado, 1969: **Saunders**, D, *UFOs, yes!*, World, 1968. ■ 8 - **Evans**, Hilary, 'The men in black', in *The unexplained*, p.510, 1983. ■ 9 - **Evans**, Hilary, *Intrusions*, Routledge, 1982 . ■ 10 - **Evans-Pritchard**, E E, *Witchcraft among the Azande*, Oxford, 1937. ■ 11 - **Falla**, Geoffrey, *Vehicle interference project*, BUFORA 1979. ■ 12 - **Fawcett**, Lawrence, & **Greenwood**, Barry J, *Clear intent*, Prentice Hall, 1984. ■ 13 - GEPAN, Note technique 16, *Analyse d'une trace*, CNES, 1983. ■ 14 - **Guérin**, Pierre, 'Le probleme de la preuve en ufologie', in **Bourret**, J C, *Le nouveau defi des OVNIs*, France-Empire, 1976. ■ 15 - **Knightley**, Phillip, *The second oldest profession*, Deutsch, 1986. ■ 16 - **Maccabee**, Bruce, with **Moore**, Bill, *UFO landings near Kirtland AFB*, private 1985. ■ 17 - **Maccabee**, Bruce, *The government UFO connection*, and approx 600 pages of associated documents, Fund for UFO Research. ■ 18 - **Marks**, John, *The search for the 'Manchurian candidate': the CIA and mind control*, Times Books, 1979. ■ 19 - **Oberg**, James E, *UFOs & outer space mysteries*, Donning, 1982. ■ 20 - **Prince**, Walter F, *The enchanted boundary*, Boston S.P.R., 1930. ■ 21 - **Shough**, Martin, section 3.3.4 of this book. ■ 22 - **Spaulding**, William H, 'UFOs, the case for a cover-up' in *The Unexplained* p.1041, 1982. ■ 23 - **Stringfield**, L, *Retrievals of the third kind*, 1979; *The UFO crash retrieval syndrome, status report II*, 1980; *UFO crash/retrievals, status report III*, 1982. ■ 24 - **Vesco**, Renato, *Intercettateli senza sparare*, 1968 (trans: *Intercept but don't shoot*); *I velivoli del mistero*, 1969; *Operazione Pleniluno*, 1972. ■ 25 - **Weldon**, John, with **Levitt**, Zola, *UFOs, what on Earth is happening?*, Harvest House, 1975.

5.6

LEVELS OF MYSTIFICATION

by John Rimmer

■ **JOHN RIMMER**: A librarian by profession, in charge of a large public library at Purley in South London, part of which is the specialised collection of over 8000 books and periodicals on UFOs, Forteana, psychical research and the occult, which is the ASSAP Reference Library, probably the largest public collection inrope. Besides his ufological and paranormal preoccupations, he is interested in printing and graphics, politics, real ale and collecting playing-cards and tarots. He lives with his wife at Mortlake, on the site of the estate of Dr John Dee, the Elizabethan sage and alchemist.

■ **UFO involvement**: He has been interested in UFOs and related phenomena since the 1960s, when he helped establish *MUFOB (Merseyside UFO Bulletin)* which became one of the first magazines to introduce psychological & sociological analysis into UFO research. Since 1975 he has edited its successor, *Magonia*.

■ **Publications**: Twenty years of not only editing but also contributing to MUFORG / *Magonia* have occupied most of his writing time, but *The evidence for alien abductions* (Aquarian, 1984) is an impartial survey of this controversial subject.

■ **Address**: John Dee Cottage / 5 James Terrace / Mortlake Churchyard / London SW14 8HB / England. Phone 01 876 7246.

UFO researchers have their own idea of what would make the 'perfect' UFO report. I suppose, ideally, it would be something like this:

> The Reverend John Smith, a Church of England vicar who also happens to hold a current flying licence and is a part-time aircraft recognition specialist and RAF reservist, was walking to St Aloysious's Church for Evensong one day. He had his camera with him to take photographs of the Harvest Festival flower arrangements. He was accompanied by the Bishop of Bootle, a former Concorde test pilot. Just as they approached the church a structured metallic craft, circular, with arrays of interest-looking lights, flew low over them. The Reverend Smith managed to take several photographs of the manifestation, one showing it clearly outlined in front of the church spire, allowing its maximum distance to be accurately determined. The Bishop, an accomplished artist, who always carries a sketchpad with him, also managed to make several drawings of the object.
>
> Unbeknown to them, Mr and Mrs Henry Jones, respectively Secretary and Treasurer of the local branch of the United Kingdom Temperance Association, and keen amateur astronomers, also saw the object. Mrs Jones, a member of CSICOP, had a movie camera with her (she had just filmed the ceremony at which her husband had been awarded a Fellowship of the Royal Optical Society for his pioneering work in the understanding of the workings of the human eye) with which she was able to record the object's extraordinary trajectory which included several right-angled turns executed at high speed. Local buildings and landmarks were visible in the background to the films at all times.

Well, this is what the ufologist hopes for, but more likely they get something like this:

> Señora Dora Nakamura, a restaurant proprietress in the La Victoria district of Lima, Peru, reported that one day a remarkable little gentleman marched into her eaterie. He was a "little green man" (her very words) with one eye in the centre on his forehead. Allowing for his somewhat bizarre appearance, her exotic customer had down-to-earth tastes, ordering a portion of her chicken "with plenty of saffron and red pepper".
>
> Despite her understandable surprise at this turn of events, Senora Nakamura retained sufficient sang-froid to be able to accede to this request, serving the chicken hot'n'spicy as they presumably like it on Ganymede or wherever. The satisfied customer paid for his meal in strange coins marked with indecipherable hieroglyphics, and strolled out. Local UFO investigations trying to follow up the story were informed that Dora was "in delicate health" (no comment, one trusts, on the spicy chicken) and did not wish to say anything more about this matter, admitting that it was a hoax.

Well, that's that then. Just another barmy UFO story from South America. We know what those hot-blooded Latins are like - it's all that red pepper probably.

There seems to be a clear distinction between a 'genuine' case and a hoax. The 'genuine' witness may have innocently misinterpreted a mundane object or phenomenon which is easily identified by the investigator, but their initial report was not the result of a deliberate attempt to deceive. The hoaxer, on the other hand, sets out with the sole intention of... well, what exactly? If we look at the case of Dora Nakamura (and it's worth pointing out that this is a *genuine* UFO report. It can be found in *Flying Saucer Review,* volume 13, number 6) it does take quite a lot of working out just what the lady's motivation was in perpetrating such a hoax. Could it have been a rather odd publicity stunt: "They'll Travel Light-Years for a Nakamura Chicken Dinner" - not quite Saatchi and Saatchi material, but displaying that naive enthusiasm that is sometimes more effective than professional gloss!

Well hardly. Her sudden retreat from the consequences of her hoax - whether her ill health was physical, psychosomatic or just 'diplomatic' suggests something other than a light-hearted prank. Could it have been intended to provide a brief moment of fame (Andy Warhol's famous fifteen minutes), or plotted for financial ends, for sale to the Peruvian version of *The Sun*? She must have realised that such a totally absurd claim would provoke scorn and hostility - as indeed it did. A genuine hoaxer (pardon the oxymoron) would surely concoct a much more believable story?

Perhaps the borderline between 'genuine' and 'hoax' is not quite as clearcut as we might like to think. It is easy to see how a straightforward report of a low-key UFO event might be embroidered a little, almost unconsciously, by the witness, to make it seem a little more exciting, to impress friends and to give investigators with a satisfying story. The witness might be 'economical with the truth' to remove a few loose ends that get in the way of a smooth-flowing narrative to retail in the saloon bar of the Goose and Ferret. But even this is surely quite different from making up a complete experience from nothing at all.

There are of course people who make up complete, and very elaborate, experiences from pure imagination. We call them novelists, and if their name is Harold Robbins they get paid enormous amounts of money for doing it. Most get paid rather less, in some cases so much less that it's difficult to see why they bother doing it at all. Indeed, reading some biographies of writers, they begin to sound rather like Señor Nakamura, suffering ridicule, obscurity and breakdowns as a result of their effort. If asked why they bother, they'll say something like "I have something I need to say, and I say it in the form of a novel. If no-one else wants to read it, tough".

The inner motivation towards creativity is very strong, and we all know stories of writers and artists who have starved in attics rather than deny this creative urge. But isn't it possible that other people also feel the need to express their creativity in some way? People who perhaps don't even realise the nature of what is prompting their actions. Let us look, very briefly at a famous British abduction case - the so called 'Aveley Abduction'.

A young married couple, John and Elaine Avis, and their three children were 'abducted' during a late-night car journey home in 1974, as they returned to their home in Essex. Their story is similar to others described elsewhere in this book. Both the adults were subjected to medical examinations conducted by two types of creatures: tall, faceless 'controllers', and smaller ape-like creatures wearing white lab-coats. They were also conducted around the 'space-craft' they found themselves in, where they were shown, amongst other things, a type of TV screen which revealed a remarkable image. From a general view of the heavens, showing stars and planets, the view 'zoomed in' in one planet, which turned out to be our Earth. The view closed in more and more, revealing details of oceans and continents, closer and closer to north-west Europe. It began to reveal the details of the outline of the British Isles, then closer and closer, until as they watched in amazement the image finally revealed their own house in a small village in Essex.

The thing that strikes me most about this account is just what a beautiful artistic concept it is. In just one remarkable image we are shown not only man's place in one small corner of the universe, but also his unity and continuity with all of creation. It relates humankind to our planet and to our universe. It is the message of the mystic, and it is the message of the scientist.

It is interesting that after their experiences, both John and Elaine took radical new steps in their life-style. John began to take an interest in art, attending college (he had previously had no form of further education) and becoming quite an accomplished sculptor. Elaine also rekindled an interest in learning, which she had dropped since her marriage. It seems as if there was a lot of creative energy hidden in these two people, which because of their backgrounds and life-style they had not been able to exploit to the full. Perhaps the 'abduction' was an unconscious act of artistic creation, through which these half-submerged energies were finally released so that they could be channelled into more 'acceptable' artistic outlets.

There is no doubt that the Avis's underwent a very special and personal experience which they saw as being very, very real. No-one has ever suggested that their abduction was a deliberate hoax. But there have been some UFO cases, abductions and otherwise, where there is considerable doubt as to the genuineness of the witnesses' reports. Some are just out and out spoofs - the infamous 'Allingham hoax, for instance. But there are others which seem to end up in a welter of confusion and recrimination. Some of the famous American cases look like this: the Travis Walton case for example, in which an Arizonan forestry worker disappeared for several days, returning with stories of an abduction. This soon degenerated into a bitter war of words, with accusations and counter accusations rapidly burying any chance of an objective assessment.

There have been other cases, which it might be best not to mention by name here, where the chances are that the 'percipients' were hoaxers. Unlike the carefully stage-managed Allingham hoax, which resulted in nothing but an amusing puzzle for a generation of ufologists, some of these hoaxes have resulted in real unhappiness and anguish for the people concerned. Señora Nakamura suffered a breakdown of health, other hoaxers have found their world overturned by the consequences of their acts.

Most ufologists now accept that the Adamski photographs, and most of his testimony about 'Venusians' in the desert, are hoaxes. Most of his subsequent reports and writings are based on events which did not objectively happen, not even on events which he genuinely perceived as happening. Yet this does not make the Adamski 'case' any the less important. His ideas and images found a sympathetic echo in the phyches of thousands of other people who formed his cult following. Other people - sincere people - subsequently had Adamski-type experiences. It is almost as if Adamski created his own reality, which other people came to share. Something of the same process appears to be happening in France with one of the perpetrators of a famous hoax abduction at Cergy-Pantoise near Paris. Here it seems almost irrelevant that the growing cult is based on a hoax.

A hoax like the Allingham case, or the 'experimental hoax' conducted in Warminster in the 1960's, is quite self-contained. it is conducted in a controlled and rational manner, and at some time in the future the hoaxer is exposed or reveals himself. Hoaxers like Adamski or the young men at Cergy-Pantoise, or Dora Nakamura, on the other hand, do not act in a rational manner. They carry the hoax on, into ever more bizarre twists and turns: a living proof of Scott's comment: "O what a tangled web we

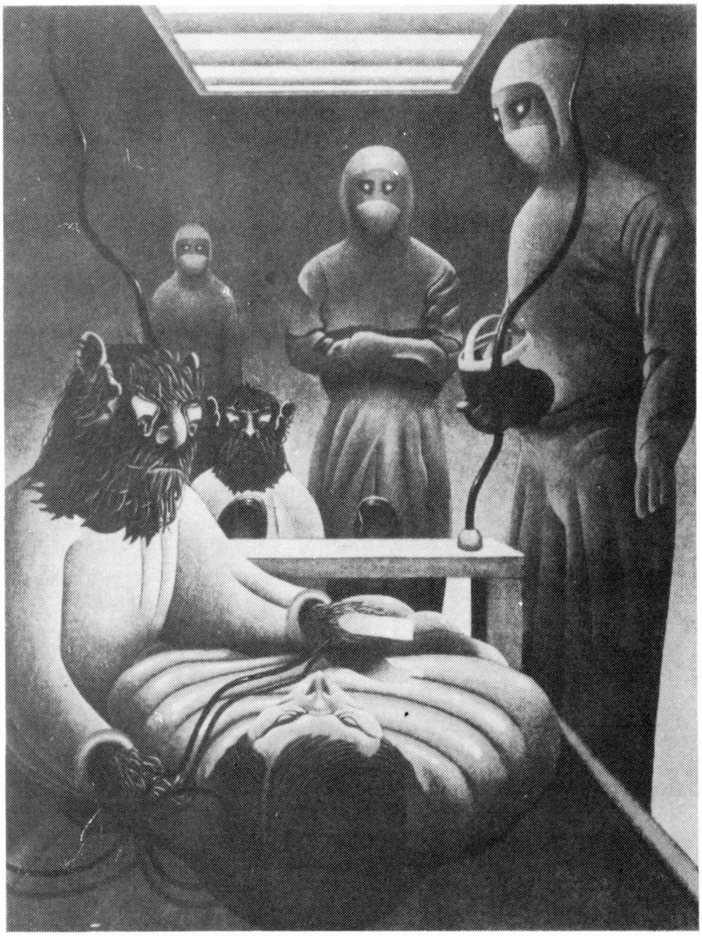

Artist's impression based on John & Elaine Avis' account. [From Hilary Evans, *UFOs: the greatest mystery*]

weave, when first we practise to deceive" Eventually, these hoaxers become so tangled in their own web that they become completely confused between reality and hoax. In fact the distinction becomes unimportant to them. The hoax has now taken on a life of its own - *their* life! They *become* the hoax.

It's an irony of ufology that one of the ways in which investigators dismiss the charge of hoax is by saying that the alleged perpetrator 'had nothing to gain by it', as though all hoaxes were only carried out after sober and careful analysis. This is far from the case. Most hoaxes seem to be carried out for strange, hidden motives, perhaps as a form of expression - artistic expression, even - of half-understood, half-concealed feelings and urges. The people undertaking hoaxes seldom consider the consequences - a broken life, or even, in the case of the hoaxers of Cergy who were fooling the Gendarmerie of the Paris region, a broken head!

One thing seems clear, the hoaxer is as much a part of the UFO problem as the 'genuine' witness. Perhaps more so: maybe in the anguished mind of Dora Nakamura and her fellow 'hoaxers' we are closer to the processes which produce the 'real' abduction and contact reports than we are in with a hundred 'honest' misinterpretations of natural phenomena or photographs of odd blobs in the sky, even if taken by an ordained minister!

5.7

UFO CULTS

by Kevin McClure

■ **KEVIN McCLURE:** After reading theology at Oxford, he works for the social services and lives with his wife and children in Leicester.

■ **Publications:** In addition to many articles in other people's journals, he founded and edited his own journal for a while; called *Common Ground,* it was devoted to the serious study of anomaly issues. *Stars and rumours of stars*, written with his wife Su, is a study of the anomalous events associated with the Welsh Revival of 1905. *The evidence for visions of the Virgin Mary* (Aquarian 1983), is not only the first overall study of this subject in English, but has been widely translated into other languages.

■ **Address:** 11 Asquith Boulevard / Leicester LE2 6FD / England. Phone: 0533 882800.

We are not interested in the UFO phenomenon because it is one that can be explained in terms of known science. With rare, and generally very dull exceptions, our interest is based on the element of the unknown. And the UFO phenomenon brings the unknown more closely and vividly to ordinary people than any others.

It is not only a visual unknown, not a matter of mere observation: as has become abundantly clear in the past forty years, there is far more than one sense involved in the UFO experience. And more than the five senses, too - the experience has changed personalities, changed the direction of percipients' lives. It has rearranged priorities and beliefs, ruined many reputations, and enhanced a few. The changes seem to occur with little intention on the part of the percipient - it seems that the drive to present oneself as a percipient, with a consequently unique and important point of view, is irresistible to certain people.

There is no older or more intrinsic expression of human personality than the religious urge, the need and desire to both explain the mysteries of human life, and to link them with an external, extra-human cosmology. In this there is one or more intelligence beyond our own, relating to our own, and giving it greater order and meaning. The UFO experience is one that on occasion appears to bring those external intelligences in direct contact with humanity. As such, it is hardly surprising that the percipients response to a complex close encounter, in particular, can often be interpreted in terms similar to those of traditional, established religion.

However, the impact of UFO experiences - or claimed experiences - can extend beyond the percipient or percipients and often has. Erich von Däniken, of course, suggests that the world's history is actually one of UFO visitation and misinterpretion. Whether he believes it or not is another matter entirely. Arthur Shuttlewood believed that UFO's are "the giants of past ages in modern guise". And Lord Clancarty - as Brinsley Le Poer Trench, an influential figure in British ufology - believes in the 'Sky People' who left Earth when Atlantis sank, and have been returning to assist in mankind's development. But this sort of 'continuous involvement' view of UFO appearances and involvement is an unusual one, and though there is certainly a strong element of belief in the following of all these three - perhaps substituting for evidence and reason - they are not typical of the contactee cults of the past 40 years. Let us look briefly at a few of those . . .

Most UFO cults have appeared in the United States, long the home of countless eccentric religious and near religious groups. The story of one of these cults is told in full by a trio of sociologists, Leon Festinger, Henry Riecken and Stanley Schachter. They 'planted' observers in a developing group centred on a UFO 'communicator' in Utah. The communicator was 'Marian Keech', who believed she had received the original message from her late father. She sat quietly and regularly thereafter, waiting to produce automatic writing. She was soon contacted by 'higher forces': first by 'the Elder Brother', and then by entities from the planets Clarion and Cerus (neither of which is known to astronomers). She received communications especially from one

Sananda of Clarion, who claimed to have been Jesus in an earlier time.

Mrs Keech did not publicise her messages enthusiastically, but others from existing UFO groups and mystical or occult groups soon showed an interest, and in August 1954 a press release was issued. This summarised not only the more philosophical parts of the communications, in which the media showed little interest, but also predictions regarding a coming physical disaster of vast proportions. The nature of the event, as reported by Mrs Keech varied at times, but as interest in the group grew its details became clearer. At the end of September the *Lake City Herald* published this typical report:

> "Lake City will be destroyed by a flood from Great Lake just before dawn, December 21st, according to a suburban housewife. Mrs Marian Keech of 847 West School Street says the prophecy is not her own. It is the purport of many messages she has received by automatic writing, she says... The messages, according to Mrs Keech, are sent to her by superior beings from a planet called 'Clarion'. These beings have been visiting the Earth, she says, in what we call 'Flying Saucers'. During their visits, she says, they have observed fault lines in the Earth's crust that foretoken the deluge. Mrs Keech reports she was told the flood will spread to form an inland sea stretching from the Arctic Circle to the Gulf of Mexico."

By now Marian Keech was referring to a group of communicators whom she called the 'Guardians', though Sananda remained the most important. Once the media had started to publicise the group Mrs Keech and her associates began to be afflicted by the problems that always beset UFO contactees. Increasing numbers of visitors called at her house, often when group members were present. She had explained to the group that if they did the right thing and were gathered together, ready, at the appointed time, they would not be drowned in the forthcoming flood, but would be carried away in one or more flying saucers. The extra-terrestrials could come to make contact at any time and in any way: so Mrs Keech and her group had to decide whether or not visitors were extra-terrestrials, and also whether they were good or evil extra-terrestrials.

The cult had now fallen into a classical pattern. It had a communicator, an explanation for the whole UFO mystery, a message of great importance, and a task for its members - not so much to publicise the disaster, as to prepare themselves to survive it. As the chosen date approached, the visitors became more frequent and more outlandish. Members of the group gave up jobs, possessions and relationships, and some took up unusual diets. All who could come together to await the fulfilment of their expectations. One condition of escape required by the Guardians was that all metal should be removed from the participants' persons. This led to some interesting arrangements for trousers and brassieres, and a lively discussion about dental fillings.

The last few days before 21 December were traumatic for the group members, as their hopes were first raised and then dashed by increasingly strange messages and predictions, all proving to be inaccurate. The greatest shock came on the day itself, when no flood arrived, nor any spacecraft to save them from it. The group fell prey to disillusion, and in due course dispersed.

The **One World Family,** founded by Allen-Michael Noonan, is a California based cult that has attracted some following, and many of its characteristics are typical of other groups. In Noonan's case it is said that he was working on a billboard when he was suddenly transported to another planet. He found himself surrounded by angelic creatures, seated around a fluorescent throne. A voice boomed, "Will you agree to be the saviour of the world?". Noonan agreed to do so. He has since remained in contact with an extra-terrestrial known as Ashtar, has made trips to an inhabited Venus, and regards himself as the Messiah. He is writing a massive reinterpretation of the Bible, the 'Everlasting Gospel', which his followers help him produce. He believes that he is the only mouthpiece for communications from Ashtar. Hallucinogenic drugs and the exercise of psychic abilities feature in the cult.

Noonan also claims that, with the practical help of the aliens, the One World Family will eventually take over the government of the U.S.A. and the running of the United Nations; but only after all professing Christians have been, as they ambiguously phrase it, "eliminated". Allen-Michael Noonan is one of the less wholesome characters to have founded a UFO cult.

A less sinister, but none the less remarkable cult group was the **Institute for Cosmic Research,** founded in Michigan in 1967 by a young man known as 'Gordon'. This group developed around the supposed construction of a flying saucer that would actually fly - the *Bluebird* - and the group lasted as long as its members had faith in the unique achievement that would climax its slow and painstaking creation. Gordon claimed that his birth was supernatural: he arrived in his mother's arms, clad in white muslin, while a UFO hovered over the house. He was, he said, one of the seven Great White Brothers (a common title in occult/contactee accounts). He also affirmed that he, and he alone, was in contact with extra-terrestrial entities from Io, one of the moons of Jupiter. There, he said, he had represented Earth at meetings of the 'Intergalactic Council'.

He told his followers that the Space Brothers had warned him that "Earth vortex is about to break because of an excess amount of hatred on this planet".

However, the Space Brothers had a plan: in order to change the ways of mankind, they had chosen "to provide Gordon with the technology to build a small flying saucer". Potential members of the Institute were told that only highly developed souls could be involved in work on it. They were to build the saucer and fly it into the skies. They would be joined by saucers from other planets and together would circle Earth for three days, darkening the skies. People would look up and wonder why - and then would fall on their knees and start practising 'Universal Law'.

In Gordon's cosmology the Sun was cold, and the stars, all of them, wre inhabited planets. Despite all this, which must surely have been hard to believe, it is clear that Gordon possessed considerable charisma. The group lasted seven years before the basic untruth of the claims dawned on his adherents. Even then, many of the group members were unwilling to accept the fact. It is desparately hard to admit that you have been *so* wrong for *so* long. The group had expended time, money, energy and faith: in some ways it was easier to go on believing than to have to cope with reality.

Another group that purveyed warnings of catastrophe transmitted from space beings called itself the **Light Affiliates**. They were active in the late 1960's in Burnaby, British Columbia. Their launching statement read:

> "We wish to notify all those interested that a phenomenon has occurred here in Vancouver. A young girl, age 22, suddenly began channelling on 23.10.69. Her source is a being identifying himself as 'Ox - Ho', who is relaying transmissions from a galaxy close to our own ... Her material is phenomenal in that she has been informed of the coming disasters, when to expect them, and what to do pertaining to the necessary evacuation of the danger areas and food supplies, etc, that will be needed".

The real name of the 'channel' was Robin McPherson, but she was renamed 'Estelle' by the 'being'. Her mother Aileen became 'Magdalene', her friend Sally became 'Celeste'. A young man involved in the early communications was given the evocative name 'Truman Merit'.

Ox - Ho explained that the day of judgement would begin on 22 November 1969. In these final

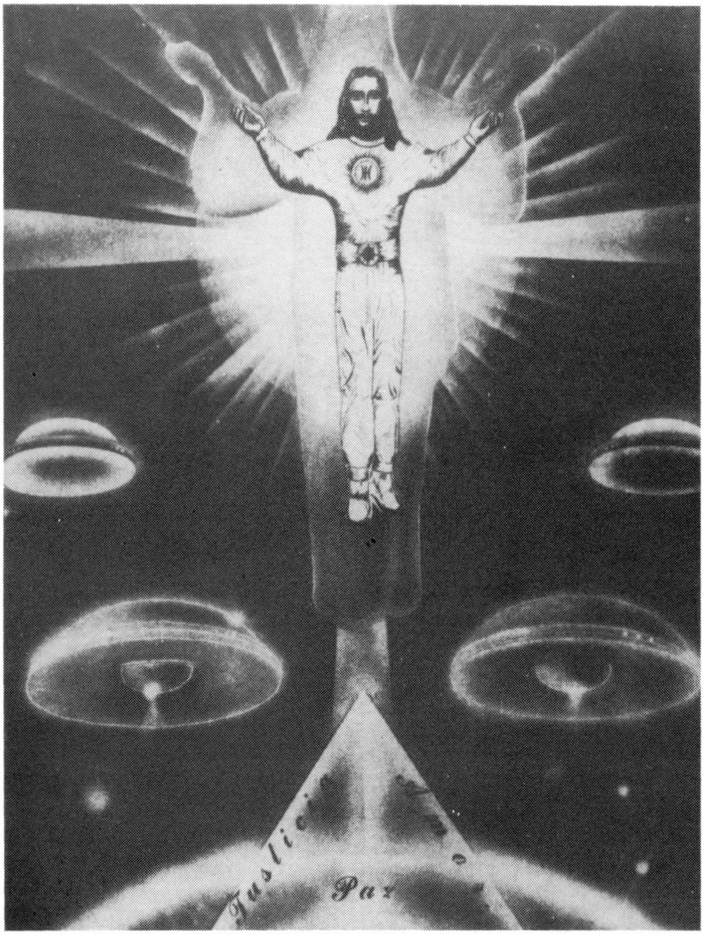

Flying saucers as religious artefacts. [From *Angeles ayer, extraterrestres hoy* **('Angels yesterday, ETs today'), Spain, 1985.**]

hours Man would be "given a last opportunity to repair his decadent house before the terminal series of disasters". If mankind did not take the opportunity to change, "the Space Brothers would remove the Chosen and return them to Earth after the planet had once again 'crystallised', and been spiritually, as well as physically, restructed". The 'restructuring' would involve the tilting of Earth on its axis, and the disappearance beneath the sea of large land areas. The members of the Light Affiliates were exhorted to evangelise wherever possible.

Nothing seems to have happened on the predicted date to fulfil the expectations of the Light Affiliates. Robin McPherson ceased to communicate, but her mother continued the task. In an interview with the writer Brad Steiger on the mid-1970's, she explained where the predictions had gone wrong.

> "We misinterpreted them, Brad, because it all happened so suddenly. The first visions I was given of destruction were very upsetting. I can see things now in a much broader perspective ...the thing is that it is the first ascension. The Brothers are trying to get as many people as possible into the Kingdom ... You know, I,ve been told by the Brotherhood that Earth is like an encounter therapy centre for the psychotics of the Universe ... I have been shown that the Earth is also wobbling very drastically on its axis".

It is sometimes less painful to find ways of demonstrating that your beliefs are fundamentally correct by means of some elaborate reinterpretation, than to concede that you have simply made a mistake.

The group that made the greatest impact during the 1970's was HIM - **Human Individual Metamorphosis**. This group appeared in California in 1975, and appealed to some of those who had dabbled in the drug culture, personal spiritual development, and 'New Age' mysticism. The movement was run by a middle-aged man and woman. They adopted names that were modest enough: Bo and Peep. Their teachings offered the advantages of life after death without the inconvenience of dying. Instead, the adherents were to ascend physically. One of the cult's publicity posters read:

"UFO's - why they are here. Who they have come for. When they will land. Two individuals say they were sent from the level above human and will return to that level in a spaceship (UFO) within the next three months. This man and woman will discuss how the transition from the human level to the next level is accomplished, and when this may be done ... If you have ever entertained the idea that there might be a real PHYSICAL level in space beyond the Earth's confines, you will want to attend this meeting".

Bo and Beep - formerly known as M.H.Applewhite and Bonnie Nettles - had convinced themselves that they were more than human, and had the strength of will and personality to maintain that impression; converts were quite clearly overwhelmed by them. At first they claimed that they would one day be assassinated and then would be resurrected - after three days. Later these claims were set aside. As in other such groups, members were expected to make sacrifices: to give up their names and possessions, abandon the use of drugs and alcohol, radio and television, and not to indulge in sex or even to read books. A perfect situation for psychological conditioning. The members generally lived in semi-permanent camps. The words of Bo and Beep in an interview, recounted by Brad Steiger, make clear their attitude to personal and family relationships.

"Husband and wife can take the trip at the same time - but not together. It would be impossible to become an individual if you went together on the trip... In order to leave this Earth's atmosphere, you must go alone and overcome whatever needs you have for any other individual or thing of this Earth. Anything for which you depend on another human being or any thing on this Earth must be overcome."

Being a member of HIM was more like being a Moonie than participating in a traditional religion, or even a traditional UFO cult. But the structure of the group was like that of other groups already described: there was a communicator, a message, a task.

No one has yet ascended to another physical realm above the atmosphere. Not many people seem to have got their money back, either. It turned out that Bo and Peep had met each other in a psychiatric hospital, where he was a patient, and she a nurse. Yet plenty of people remained willing to believe them and accept their discipline. Like so many fringe religions, it seems to have met spiritual needs shared by many people in uncertain times.

The most famous and long-lived UFO cult started in Britain in about 1955, when George King, alone in his flat in West London, heard a voice say 'Prepare yourself, you are to become the voice of Interplanetary Parliament'. Eight days later an Indian swami passed through a locked door and explained to King facts that led to the founding of the **Aetherius Society,** which now has active memberships in over 40 countries around the world, and certainly conveys an unusual image of Ufology to many uninformed observers - one that many of us may at times regret.

King had previously been involved in healing work, and in his book *You Are Responsible* hbe explained that he had to forsake his metaphysical studies, even though 'We believed that we were on the verge of discovering a new method of cancer treatment which could cure certain forms of this malignant scourge...'

It is unfortunate that King's informants did not permit the completion of this work, as instead he became involved in reporting communications and experiences that have since been rendered absurd by space exploration. King wrote of his travels to Venus and Mars - he stated that Mercury was the only uninhabited planet. He detailed a battle he fought on a massive flying saucer of an interplanetary space fleet, 40 million miles from Earth. In public meetings he gave trance messages from entities such as 'Mars Sector 6', the 'Master Aetherius', and even the 'Master Jesus', who was apparently living on or near Venus. Without this last claim, the society might have been taken a little more seriously.

Though the messages have at times been less than clear - Mars Sector 6, for example, speaking through an entranced George King: "Take those M - ions inside of yourself, then your brain cells will release an opposite female magnetic energy. This will counteract the hurricane-force." - the Aetherius Society clearly works on the simple basis of communicator, messages, and task. And the society's members seem to be both selfless and determined in their efforts to perform that task. They have made pilgrimages, often in difficult and dangerous conditions, to a number of the world's mountains, carryings out plans bearing names such as Operation Sunbeam, Operation Bluewater, and Operation Starlight. They have charged the 'spiritual energy batteries' in such places as Ben Macdhui in Scotland, Mount Kilimanjaro in Tanzania, and the Madrigerfluh in Switzerland. On the night of June 27, 1981, for instance, batteries E - 1 and E - 3 were charged at Holdstone Down in South-West England. The 160 members of the society who were present stored a total of 219 hours and 28 minutes of prayer energy in battery E - 1. Meanwhile, the extra-terrestrials put 1100 hours into battery E - 3. On the same weekend, as part of Operation Sunbeam, 6000 prayer hours of energy were sent from Jupiter to the psychic centre in Scotland.

And what becomes of all this prayer energy? At the time of the threatened invasion of Poland by the Soviet Union, in 1981, Operation Prayer Power was launched. The operation was made more complex because the Los Angeles battery had to be substituted for the inadequate Detroit one - "the Prayer Energies were not being picked up by Adepts 002 and 003 in position in their (invisible) Space Craft above the central base of operations in Los Angeles." George King reported during the operation that "the Great White Brotherhood Retreat in Kilimanjaro, East Africa, had now joined in the release pattern." At the end of the operation, Mars Sector 6 informed King that "there was a heavy resonance of Spiritual Energies over the whole of Poland." Perhaps there is something to be said for not trying to explain the function of prayer.

Few UFO cults last as long as the Aetherius Society - and few are so well-meaning, or so concerned about wider issues and concerns in the world outside their group. Like any other small groups held together by belief, both the UFO cults I have mentioned, and the great majority of the others I know of, are subject to the human needs and failings found in any religion. Often, it seems that the original experience - or the publicity resulting from it - has fulfilled a need in the principal figure that the development of the cult has continued, and that the content of the messages and the nature of the tasks has often interrelated with the nature and needs of the followers. Attention-seeking is probably the correct psychological term for it, but the attention only lasts so long as the promise of the cult remains viable. Few remain so for very long.

So much for the past - what of now, of 1987? Religious cults there are a-plenty, for these are interesting and stressful times, and nothing produces cults like worried and uncertain people. But the nature of UFO cults and belief-groups continues to change with the twists and turns in the public perception of the phenomenon itself. Time was when both sightings and contactee experiences were simply explained in terms of spacemen from nearby planets, with space programmes just a bit advanced from our own, and wisdoms and philosophies to match. Then, as our own space programmes progressed, visitors from the Solar System became less plausible - and much less frequent. So the experiences, the messages and their sources became gradually more exotic and more distant, till the 'new ufology' of the 1970's finally made the matter more complex than most reasonable, intelligent people could deal with, arguing in effect for varieties of abnormal psychology that endowed humans with powers previously ascribed only to deities and devils.

Since that time there has, of course, been a hiatus in sightings, in contactee experiences and, not surprisingly, in new cult groups; though there has been no real reduction in overall quantities of alleged communications with the 'Space Brothers' or whatever any particular group may name them. Spirit voices are always with us. But this is the age of swift and effective communication, and increasingly the age of the electronic church. To the West, Europe is assailed by the Evangelicals, and the unreason of Fundamentalism. To the East, the rise of Islam proceeds unchecked. Both of these religious forms have the characteristics of cult behaviour that we have observed in the behaviour of a few simple UFO groups, and it is not surprising that at the time of writing, in early 1987, I can detect the influences of both in the style and content of current UFO belief.

This falls into two fairly clear areas. Firstly, there is a clear return to the ETH - the Extra-Terrestrial Hypothesis - among influential groups on both sides of the Atlantic. To a belief in solid, tactile UFO's such as sit and glint on the sides of hills, or present themselves in magnificent photo-opportunities, ideal for the publication of coffee-table books by enterprising publishers. There is no more evidence for the

ETH than there ever was, but it is clearly an idea whose time has come - again. And secondly, and altogether more oddly, there is an interpretation based in Eastern religious experience to match the Fundamentalism of the ETH. This is publicised - indeed, it is shouted from the rooftops in every issue - by the Editor of the world's most respected UFO magazine, and apparently supported by its readership. In simple terms, it regards the UFO phenomenon as Satanically - or Ahrimanically (it amounts to the same thing) - controlled and inspired, with UFO-based entities as real beings, but ones sponsored and supported in the cause of the downfall of humanity. Which oddly enough, in its turn, is the view of the UFO phenomenon propagated by the American Fundamentalist movement.

Personally, I regard the collected evidence of the UFO phenomenon as tenuous and frail, but also as important and interesting. The cults and belief groups that have developed from it are themselves fascinating, but if I were to summarise their significance in the subject as a whole, and their bearing on its interpretation and understanding. I would have to conclude that they warrant our interest, and maybe our sympathy. But not a great deal of our time.

5.8

UFO ABDUCTIONS AS RELIGIOUS FOLKLORE

by Bertrand Méheust

■ **BERTRAND MÉHEUST:** educated at Dijon University and now works as a teacher. He has taught in Algiers and Gabon as well as in his native France.

■ **UFO involvement:** Though he has done a considerable amount of field investigation, his personal approach to UFOs is indirect, via the fields of science fiction and folklore, which he believes can teach us much about the UFO phenomenon as a social artifact. In 1980 he took the opportunity presented by residence in a remote district of Gabon to carry out 'Project Nabokok' which tested the response to depictions of UFO stereotypes of primitive peoples who had not been exposed to the 'flying saucer' myth (see *Inforespace* #55).

■ **Publications:** Besides many articles in journals such as *Inforespace* and *OVNI-presence*, he has written two very influential studies of unique importance: *Science fiction et soucoupes volantes* (Mercure de France, 1978); and *Soucoupes volantes et folklore* (Mercure de France, 1985).

■ **Address:** 89130 Mezilles / France.

A BRIEF ACCOUNT OF WHAT WE KNOW ABOUT 'LES 'RAVIS' [1A]

During the last 20 years, several hundred people - maybe more [**1B**] - in Europe, and above all in North and South America, have asserted that they have been taken on board 'flying saucers'. There they have been subjected to terrifying medical examinations accompanied by the taking of specimens and surgical operations, before being returned - deeply traumatised - to everyday reality.

Anthropologists, preoccupied with affirming the value of 'life as it is lived' and affirming their solidarity in principle with outcasts of every sort, have failed to notice the abduction phenomenon. So, with the professionals opting out, it has been left to the amateurs, with whatever means they had at their disposal, to gather witness reports. One inquiry after another, these private researchers have accumulated an impressive quantity of material, uneven in quality no doubt, but already sufficient to enable us to answer certain fundamental questions.

We know, for example, that abductions are not legends - not, that is, fictitious events depicted as real ones in order to make them appear more dramatic: in most cases, the time, the place and the identity of the witness are known precisely. Moreover, the majority of abductees seem of good faith, and display no psychiatric symptoms. Clearly this faces us with a logical difficulty: how can a person be healthy and sincere - to all appearances at least - yet persist in such nonsensical claims?

The first step towards resolving the paradox, we suspect more and more, must be to take a closer look at the insufficiently explored complexities of human subjectivity, and most especially in the psychology of altered states of consciousness. However, we must not expect to find the entire solution in this direction, for we know too that **objective** events seem to occur which flout our image of the world, despite all the efforts of skeptical inquirers to explain them in terms of everyday experience.

Meanwhile, other researchers have sought solutions within the witness' cultural background. The characteristic display of scientific marvels was the first feature to be noticed [**2**]. Then came attempts to compare encounters of the third kind and abductions with marvellous historical accounts drawn from folklore and ethnology [**3**], and this confrontation has revealed astonishing parallels between, on the one hand, experiences reported in these two traditional domains, and on the other, these new forms of human experience.

Here are some examples of these repeated patterns:

ABDUCTIONS AND PRIMITIVE LEGEND

■ Carl Higdon, 40 years of age, is a mechanic for a petrol company, the AM Well Service of Riverton, WY. He is a practical man, fond of sport and open-air pursuits, a passionate big game hunter. On 25 October 1974, he leaves at 4 pm to go hunting elk in Medicine Bow National Park, and decides to explore for the first time a section not easily accessible and little frequented by hunters. After parking his pick-up, he sets off into the undergrowth and walks for some time in a strangely silent forest. Encountering five elk, he puts his gun to his shoulder and fires.

At this precise moment Wonder invades the Wyoming forest. The sound of the shot is muffled, the bullet travels so slowly that he can see it in flight, and it falls to earth some 15-20 metres before him, completely crushed. Surprising, to say the least! The hunter goes to pick up his shot, puts it wonderingly in his pocket, then turns at the crack of a branch. A being of human appearance, very tall, yellow-skinned, with bristling straw-coloured hair, stands in the shade of a birch, some 20 metres away. He is wearing a black costume.

The being approaches and speaks, asking an unexpectedly, paradoxically banal question, 'How you doin'?' Taken by surprise, Higdon replies 'Pretty good.' 'Are you hungry?' the stranger asks. 'Yeah, a little.' The being throws him a package containing four pills, telling him to take one and that it will last him four days. He takes one, then the stranger asks Higdon if he wants to go with him. 'I guess,' he replied, and for the first time sees a transparent illuminated 'cubicle'. Next thing he knows, he is seated in the cubicle, with two other men in black seated alongside him and five elk behind in a cage. Hunted now rather than hunter, he sits in a sort of armchair, held in it by a vertical acceleration which at once occurs. The journey has begun.

After some time has elapsed, they seem to reach the beings' 'planet'. Higdon is not permitted to leave the 'cubicle', but through its walls he sees a sort of tower, surmounted by rotating lights, so unbearably bright that he complains. So his captors, with astonishing cynicism, say 'Well, we'll take you back; you're not any good for what we need.' And indeed, after a short return journey, Higdon is returned to the forest, dropped out of the 'cubicle' onto the rocky ground, which bruises his shoulder as he slips.

These "diabolical" events are recalled by him only the following day; right now, he finds himself simply walking at random, gun in hand, on a cow trail in an area unknown to him. By chance he comes across a vehicle stuck in the mud, equipped with a CB radio. One hunter, aching all over, gives a call for help and waits. In fact, due to his loss of memory, he has failed to recognise his own pick-up which is bogged down in a place unreachable by 2-wheel-drive vehicles, and which he had left 8 km away!

His mayday call is received, a police team comes to his rescue. The amnesiac is discovered about 23.15, beside his stranded vehicle, distraught in manner, his eyes red and tearful. He fails to recognise his wife who is with his rescuers, and he repeats over and over again the story of the pills and the men in black. His body is covered with scratches. The magnum bullet is found in his pocket, crushed and folded like a glove. At the County Memorial Hospital, to which he is taken straight away, the doctors find nothing abnormal, and his amnesia disappears after a day. He leaves, completely back to normal, on 26 October. [**4**]

■ On 6 January 1976, about 23.25, three American women, Mona Stafford, Louise Smith, and Elaine Thomas, are travelling by car towards Liberty KY. Suddenly they see an enormous object, lit with multiple lights, descending from the sky. At first they take it for an aircraft in trouble, but reject this idea when their car, caught in a beam of bluish light, becomes uncontrollable and starts to float. Panicking, the ladies are overtaken by an excruciating headache and lose consciousness.

When they recover their senses, their vehicle is 12 km further on, one-and-a-half hours have elapsed, and they have no memory of what has happened in the meantime. At Louise's home they discover on their necks red marks 10 cm long and 3 cm wide. All three are suffering from inflamed, tearful eyes. The worst afflicted, Mona, has to consult an eye specialist for acute conjunctivitis. Louise loses 14 kg and Mona 8 kg during the following weeks.

As fragments of strange memories come back to them, they decide to consult a psychologist, who has recourse to hypnosis: so it comes about that an abduction story surfaces. The stories thus obtained confirm one another partially.

Their abductors were the size of 10-year-old children, with alarming slanted eyes, elongated fingers, grey skin. A sort of vizor partially hid their faces, revealing an **unnerving** gaze. They separated the three women, and conducted them into a sort of cave whose interior was suffocatingly hot.

The abductees were then subjected to a terrifying medical examination. Their arms were pinned to tables, and a hot sticky liquid was poured over their entire bodies. Then the beings tried to twist their arms and legs, 'as though they were seeking to test how much stress human muscle and bone could withstand before breaking.' They took Mona's eyes out of their sockets, and examined them before replacing them.

The three women never knew how they got back to their vehicle. [**5**]

■ On 21 August 1980, a young American known as 'Megan Elliott' is on a visit with her parents in East Texas, together with her 18-month-old daughter Renee. The little girl develops an ear infection and a skin rash which deteriorate despite all efforts, and she screams to 'go bye-bye car.' Megan decides towards midnight to take her home, which means a 100 km journey along deserted roads.

After travelling some 50 km, the car radio malfunctions and the headlights dim; Megan feels as though her car has left the ground. She sees at her own level the tops of pine trees, agitated 'as if in a windstorm', and looks up to see the flat metal bottom of an object only a few feet away 'with a double row of bright lights in a circle." The car enters the object, and comes to rest in a brightly-lit room. Megan hears a voice inside her head say 'Get Renee and get out of the car.' Some little humanoids with big heads then probe her body and take samples. She has the impression of being aboard for several days.

She regains consciousness in her car, parked only 8 km from home. After somehow reaching her house, she stumbles indoors carrying her daughter in her arms. She feels dizzy and her head hurts. At 5 am next day, she already recalls the main details of her experience: her daughter's ear-ache and skin rash have cleared up and never return. Megan subsequently loses 7 kg and her family remark on changes in her personality. [**6**]

■ In the early hours of 26 August 1975, during a 300 km journey to Bismarck ND, Sandra Larson is abducted along with her 15-year-old daughter Jackie and a friend, 20-year-old Larry, who is driving. The three see 8 to 10 glowing globes descend towards their vehicle. The scene lasts only a few seconds, but a service station clock reveals that an hour has elapsed though they have no memory of it. Disturbed by the memory, Sandra decides to undergo hypnosis.

Under hypnosis she tells a classic abduction story, from which two notable features emerge: first, her abductors scrape the inside of her nose with some instrument, and second, they open her skull, take out the brain, then replace it. [**7**]

Now let's switch to a different cultural context. Here are some fragments from primitive legend - tales of dreams, visions, abductions by the spirits or initiation rituals.

Like Carl Higdon, a young Krahó was hunting deer when he encountered a deity whose role was to protect animals: 'One day he went to hunt deer. He was in the forest when a Xupé appeared to him. After asking what he was doing there, the spirit advised him to go hunt elsewhere. He returned to his village and was taken sick with a fever. During the night, the Xupé came to him, disguised as a black man, and inserted a substance into his head, his heart and his arms, which cured him. This substance also gave him the power to heal. [**8**]

Beings from space - or from our inner fantasies? [René Olsen / *UFO-Nyt*]

Wherever Voodoo is practised, we hear of abductions, particularly involving children. The young victim is taken to another place and generally remembers nothing: 'The procedure is always the same; the child suddenly disappears, often while he is walking with his parents. He is rediscovered in a convent, no longer able to recognise his family. Here is one story among many, told me by the cousin of a child who had been abducted in this way: "One day I was looking for an uncle (a fetish-worker, that is to say an initiate) who had gone to work in a distant field. Not knowing how to find the field, I took with me his 7-year-old daughter. We were walking and talking, when suddenly I was overtaken by a kind of fever and could see nothing. When I could see clearly again, the little girl had disappeared. I arrived in tears at the field where my uncle was working. He was not alarmed at the disappearance of his daughter and reassured me: she had assuredly been abducted by the fetish. And indeed we found her at the convent, stretched on a mat, unable to recognise anybody." [**9**]

Certain rites of initiation, in Africa for example, display a number of characteristic features in association: enclosure in a confined space, ritual killing, amnesia, rebirth. The young initiates are told they will be swallowed by a monster. Michel Hulin comments 'For the participants the ordeal has nothing metaphorical about it. Terrified, they believe their last hour has come, and more or less lose consciousness... and wake up at the far end of the initiatory enclosure, convinced that they have traversed the valley of death, but that those who killed them - the ancients, the ancestors, the deity - have mercifully brought them back to life.' [**10**]

In traditional cultures, ecstasies - whether deliberately sought or occurring spontaneously - are often characterised by this scenario: the subject is abducted by demons, who torture him. Among the Aranda, for example, a candidate witch-doctor quits the village and lies down at the entrance to the cave of initiation. At dawn, an Iruntarinia demon manifests. 'Seeing the man sleeping, he throws an invisible lance which enters his neck, pierces his tongue leaving a large hole, and re-emerges by the mouth... The spirits then carry him into the depths of the cave... The Iruntarinia remove from his body all the internal organs and replace them with new ones. The man returns to his senses, but for several days is in a state of stupor. The spirits have at the same time implanted magic stones in his body which protect him from all malevolent influence. [**11**]

A would-be practitioner among the Aranda is subjected to a comparable test by the Eruncha demons and the medicine men. They drag him underground, rub his body with rock crystals to break the skin, then insert fragments of crystal under his scalp, pierce the nail of his right hand and make an incision in his togue. [**12**]

Among the Tungus of Siberia a candidate is wholly dismembered by the spirits, who re-forge his body on an anvil and make him a new one. He returns to life with a new soul and body capable of resisting the dangers of his profession. [**13**]

In Australia, the Arunta demons drag the apprentice, as he wanders in the desert, into a terrifying phantasmagoria. 'The malevolent entity takes away his sense and hearing, so that he wanders all night like a madman... and throws *ngankara* stones which pierce his body... Then the spirit takes him to the entry of his subterranean dwelling, and hurls him time after time to the earth until he is lying unconscious... Then, using a sling, he pierces his occiput with the fibula of a kangaroo... At dawn he is taken by the spirits and left with mocking laughter on the outskirts of a nearby camp... The two oldest magicians take him back to the camp, where he recognises nobody, not even his closest relatives... the novice feels so sick and tired that he sleeps all day, growing thinner in the sight of all.' [**14A**]

THE UNDERLYING STRUCTURE: THE CONTEMPORARY 'RESEMANTISATION' [14B]

Let us try to perceive the structure which underlies these experiences. We see that, around the theme of death and rebirth, a certain number of recurrent motifs are expressed. The subject is isolated in the forest, realm of death and 'otherness'. There, he is overcome by a monster, dragged by spirits into a luminous cavern or imprisoned by elders in an initiatory enclosure which symbolises the mother's womb. Then he is tortured, mutilated, burned, flayed, crushed, scarred. The demons or the masters scratch or cut his skin, implant crystals in his body, tear out his entrails in order to replace them. On his return, he has lost all memory of his former existence... [**15**]

One would need to be singularly blind to the world of symbols not to perceive a timeless structure behind the variations which are described in contemporary abductions. The sequence of motifs is the same in both sets of experiences, ruling out any projection on my part. But - and this is the essential point - most of these motifs have been 'resemantised'. The ball of light which sometimes descends on the chosen one, becomes a glowing spaceship. The amnesia is attributed to a deliberate action on the part of the abductors, anxious to efface all traces of their mysterious activity. [**16**] The crystals implanted beneath the skin have been replaced by electronic gadgets intended for mental monitoring. [**17**] Ritual surgery becomes a medical examination; the initiatory cavern, a laboratory or operating theatre; even the tortures which formerly prepared the transfiguration of the subject are now inflicted by sadistic or superhuman experimenters. The stigmata and other physical marks are interpreted as the result of surgery or radiation. [18] The celestial journey of the shamans becomes the interplanetary excursion on board a spaceship. [19] Even the selection by the spirits of an individual by virtue of some hereditary characteristic - for example, the presence in his body of a particular bone [20] - is matched by such contemporary cases as that of Lydia Stalnaker, abducted near Jacksonville in August 1974, whose abductors told her she had been chosen precisely on account of her peculiar 'internal chemistry.' [21]

And finally there are the powers themselves. Whether they are real or imaginary - and it's a question which must be faced! - they crown both the abduction experience and its parallel with primitive fantasy, showing that this expression of human experience, however absurd it may seem in our technological world, possesses a logic of its own.

With regard to the 'tone' of these 'ethnodramas', three facts seem to merit our attention:

- the glacial indifference of the superhuman experimenters.
- the fusion of initiatory cave with spaceship and hospital.
- the *sacral promotion of medical fantasy.*

This last trait is particularly significant. Peter Brown has written somewhere that the frontier which separates the sacred from the profane is constantly being re-drawn, and that the supernatural world is the screen on which man projects, at any given moment, his relations with his own self and with the world. The cold austerity of the spaceship-hospitals deserves to be seen as a revelation of the collective subconscious.

PROBLEMS AND HYPOTHESES

As soon as we try to integrate contemporary abductions into the overall pattern of the collective imagination, we run into countless difficulties. Unquestionably these events involve both modern and traditional elements - but in what proportion? Are they primarily folklore, or are they primarily space-opera? Have we the right to juxtapose elements from cultures as different as the Aranda from that of present-day Texas?

At this stage, we can only note the parallels and propose hypotheses. The fact that the experiences share so many elements, and have in common their underlying structure, must be more than coincidence; at the very least, it points towards a permanence of certain elements in the universal language of the imagination, emerging in a certain state of consciousness, sometimes sought - as when the primitive shaman deliberately seeks the enlightening experience - sometimes spontaneous, as seems on the surface to be the case with today's abduction events.

Things become clearer if we admit that the abductions are in fact "nothing other" than types of religious experiences disguised in a technical imagery acceptable to the western man of today. Given this hypothesis, adbuctees may be considered as people who, in "primitive" civilisations, would possibly have become professional manipulators of the sacred, ie shamans or medicine men. But, as western culture no longer provides them with a socially acceptable outlet for their strange powers, their experiences are ridiculed, rejected, under-exploited, and their gifts become useless and parasitic.

This hypothesis does not imply necessarily that all the abduction stories have to be reduced to mere psychological factors, to the dramatic expression of inner conflicts; it implies at least that any theory about the abductees has to take into account the human, cultural environment in which these events occur, for they are, whatever the ultimate explanation may be, deeply rooted in the human mind.

This model enables us to explain why, while the experiences of the abductees share so many traits with the abductions of religious folklore, they show, on the other hand, striking dissimilarities which make them typical of our agnostic and technical civilisation. These differences are no less striking and must be taken into account in our understanding of the UFO lore.

Let us try to survey some of these dissimilarities. In traditional civilisations, one may become a shaman after an enlightening experience that is deliberately sought, or after a vision which occurs spontaneously. [22] But in any case, the subject learns how to repeat his visions, how to control them and to integrate them in his conscious life. [23] My first assumption is that in our culture visions occur only spontaneously, as nobody would think of using techniques to produce them. My second assumption is that the European or American abductee, as any average western man of today, no longer possesses the mental tools to cope with that type of experience.

As a result, he will not interact consciously with the strange world that has just opened to him. His involvement in the other world will not improve, even if his captors, as is supposed to occur regularly, come to visit him several times. [24] In other words, to continue my hypothesis, the abduction experience remains unexploited; it is a crude material given by the "producer", to quote Hilary Evans [25], and which, as it is not re-worked through appropriate techniques, is not likely to lead very far. Briefly speaking, the abductee knows only the first step of the stairs leading to the enlightening experience.

This does not mean at all that the abduction is not a deep experience. Undeniably changes seem to occur in the abductee's personality after his traumatic encounter; he generally no longer sees the world the same way; he opens his mind to a broader vision and becomes, to quote Leo Sprinkle, a "cosmic citizen." [26] But the facts tend to prove that these types of spontaneous experiences are not sufficient to induce a complete and durable change in the subject's personality if they are not authorized and reinforced by the group. Here is the point: today, the UFO abduction is not understood as a religious experience (if I am right, of course) and authorized as such; it is only tolerated as a technical, space-age myth. [27 Only the lunatic fringe takes it seriously. It is almost an illegitimate experience.

As a result, the abductee has to face:

■ *His own skepticism*: very often he does not believe, at the beginning of course, in his own abduction for he had never heard of any such experience! [28]

■ *His own subjectivity*: since the only tolerated myth is a space-age, technical one, he fails to recognise the events he has experienced as productions of his inner World, and projects them outwards into science-fiction speculations.

■ *His own agnosticism*: he fails similarly to understand his experience as a potentially religious one, for it is disguised in a technical myth which he takes at face value. [29]

■ *The rejection by his family*, by his friends, by his professional milieu. And very often this rejection tends to be more dangerous to his mental balance than the abduction itself. For, instead of being highly regarded by the group, the abduction of course is rejected as a form of psychological imbalance, or as a hoax.

We no longer believe that gods appear and speak to us in our dreams, but nevertheless we continue to dream. Officially we no longer believe in gods but actually we continue to dream of superior forces, and eventually some of us see them. The "producer" continues to produce; but his creations are no longer channelled by cults, rituals, and unversally accepted beliefs. This is quite a new situation. We are the first civilisation to construct a social life without any reference to the sacred. And, if my hypothesis is correct, we are observing for the first time the emergence of a sacred experience *utterly disconnected from its usual cultural channels*. So, even if the so-called abductions were "nothing else but" strange mental experiences, they would deserve more scrutiny from social sciences than they have received up to now.

REFERENCES

■ **1A** - The French term *'ravi'* means both 'abducted' and 'ravished' in the sense of 'being in a state of deep happiness'. ■ **1B** - These figures are given by Budd **Hopkins** in 'UFO abductions, the invisible epidemic' in *MUFON UFO Symposium Proceedings*, (1981) pp.44-47. Clearly they cover only a fraction of these experiences; the true figure is unknown. ■ **2** - **Méheust**, B. *Science fiction et soucoupes volantes* (Mercure de France, 1978). ■ **3** - **Méheust**, B, *Soucoupes volantes et folklore* (Mercure de France, 1985). ■ **4** - **Sprinkle**, Leo, 'Investigation of the alleged UFO experience of Carl Higdon', in **Haines**, R (ed) *UFOs and the behavioral scientist* (Scarecrow, 1979) pp.225-257. ■ **5** - **Gansberg**, J & A, *Direct encounters* (Walker, 1980) pp.24-31. ■ **6 Willis**, L, 'Mother and child Texas abduction case' in *MUFON UFO Journal* 167, Jan.1982. ■ **7** - **Clark**, Jerome, 'UFO abduction in North Dakota' in **Rogo**, Scott (ed) *UFO abductions* (Signet, 1980) pp.138-159. ■ **8** - Here is a variation on this theme, which it is interesting to compare with Higdon's account. A Cuna Indian was hunting in a forest without having much luck. While he was resting beneath a tree, a spirit appeared and asked him what he was doing there. The man said he was hunting, but without success. The spirit put a pastille on his tongue, telling him that it would instruct him, and he undertook to teach the man the art of catching game. [Barbara **Chesser**, 'The anthropomorphic personal guardian spirit in aboriginal South America' in *Journal of Latin American Lore*, 1(2), 1975, pp.107-126. The same ethnologist tells the story of a young Indian lost in the forest with a raging fever, who called on Vai-Mahse, the protecting spirit of animals. A being suddenly appeared beside him, who gave him grain and fragments of quartz before vanishing. In other South American variants, the spirit even asks the hunter if he is hungry, or stops his arrow in mid-flight [**Barroso**, Gustavo, *Mythes, contes et legendes indiens* (Paris, 1930). Higdon's story shows us how traditional mythological material re-emerges in living experience. A sort of 'quotation' takes place, without the hunter even being aware of it, and the ritual question 'Are you hungry?' is tinged, for the American who loves hunting, with a guilty ecological conscience. ■ **9** - **Schott-Billman**, F., *Corps et possession* (Gauthier-Villars, 1977) p.67. ■ **10** - **Hulin**, Michel, *La face cachee du temps* (Fayard, 1985) pp.147-8. ■ **11** - **Roheim**, Geza, *Les portes du reve* (Payot, 1973) p.247, citing **Spencer & Gillen**, *The Arunta* (London, 1927) II, pp.391-3. ■ **12** - **Eliade**, Mircea, *Religions australiennes* (Payot, 1972) p.148. ■ **13** - **Delaby**, Laurence, *Chamans Toungouses*, Etudes mongoles et siberiennes, Cahier 7, 1976, Laboratoire d'ethnologie at de sociologie comparative, Universite de Paris X, pp.44-5. ■ **14A** - **Martino**, Ernesto de, *Le monde magique* (Marabout Universite, Verviers, 1971) pp.116-7. ■ **14B** - 'Resemantisation' is the process whereby an image or symbol acquires a new meaning without losing its original meaning. ■ **15** - **Eliade**, Mircea, *Mythes, reves et mysteres* (Gallimard, 1957) pp.242-4. ■ **16** - British policeman Alan Godfrey was on patrol when he saw a luminous object hovering above the road. Suddenly he found himself back in his vehicle, but parked 100 metres distant, and 30 minutes of his time were unaccounted for. One of the first things he recalled was a voice saying 'You shouldn't have seen this thing. It wasn't meant for your eyes.' The voice, monotonous and impersonal, continued to repeat this prohibition. [**Randles**, J, *The Pennine UFO mystery* (Granada, 1983) p.127]. During his medical session, the abductee was told to forget certain details, and indeed hypnosis failed to fill every hole in his memory. [ibid p.167] This injunction to forget is a frequent theme in CE3s/CE4s; it is the modern form of the religious taboo, disguised as a post-hypnotic suggestion emanating from the ufonauts. ■ **17** - Charles Hickson, one of the Pascagoula abductees, was similarly persuaded that the entities had implanted a device in his body with which they could permanently monitor his thoughts. [Ted **Peters**, in *Cross currents*, 1977, 27, no.3, p.133]. ■ **18** - It is thus that we could interpret, among others, the psychological troubles experienced by Villas Boas after his 1957 abduction. [**Bowen**, C. (ed) *The humanoids*. FSR, 1966]. ■ **19** - Some abductees, in the course of their experience, are treated to a tour of space: eg the Spanish hunter Julio [**Ribera**, A, 'The Soria abduction' in *FSR* 30, 1985]. There is a manifest similarity to the celestial journeys of shamans. ■ **20** - Among certain races, such as the Tungus, the spirits surgically bestow an extra bone on the initiate, proving the legitimacy of his claim to shamanship. [**Delaby**, op cit, p.45]. ■ **21** - **Gansberg**, op cit, p.35. ■ **22** - **Eliade**, Mircea, *Le Chamanisme* (Payot) pp.21-43; *Mythes, reves et mysteres* (Gallimard, 1957) p.97. ■ **23** - This ritual and cultural regulation is evidently of decisive importance. It is practised in all traditional societies. The aim is to seize and control the ambivalent sacred forces to secure benefits for the community. Because they are well known, I will cite only one example; among the Tamangs of Siberia, initiation comprises four levels. 1) The neophyte has a vision of the call, still little structured; a terrifying experience which resembles those of our abductees. 2) He learns to induce this vision, but cannot yet control it. During this phase, the spirit speaks through the disciple and identifies itself. 3) The neophyte increases his control over the gods; he can use their powers for certain purposes. The tutelary spirit begins to utter, through the mouth of the shaman, a coherent discourse. 4) The shaman ascends to the heavens where he meets the spirits. In this final phase, the subject has complete control over his visions. The entire initiation process takes place under the control of an experienced guide. [Larry

G **Peters**, 'Tamang shamanism', in *American Ethnologist*, 1982]. ■ **24** - It is widely believed by ufologists that abductions and CE3s are one-off experiences, which tends to support the idea that they have had a real experience involving a flying machine. But this is no more than a pious legend. Many abductions are preceded or followed by other events. Betty Andreasson had altogether seven encounters from the age of seven. [**Fowler** R., *The Andreasson affair, phase two*, p.266]. Bob Luca, Jose da Silva, Mona Stafford and Maurice Masse are just four of many further examples that could be cited. ■ **25** - **Evans**, Hilary, *Visions, apparitions, alien visitors* (Aquarian, 1984). In his study of apparitions, Evans designates as 'The Producer' the spontaneous myth-creating function of the human subconscious. ■ **26** - **Sprinkle**, Leo, 'UFO activity and cosmic consciousness', at *APRO UFO Conference*, 1981. ■ **27** - **Méheust** 1985 op cit, especially the chapter 'Les lecons d'un periple dans l'imaginaire.' ■ **28** - **Gansberg**, op cit, p.50. This book contains a mine of information on the human repercussions of abductions. ■ **29** - Clearly I am here drawing on the ideas of Jung and his French disciple Gilbert Durand, regarding the 'camouflages' of the sacred in the modern world. [**Jung**, *A modern myth*: **Durand**, *Les structures anthropologiques de l'imaginaire*.]

5.9

UFOs AS SOCIAL AND CULTURAL PHENOMENA

by Hilary Evans

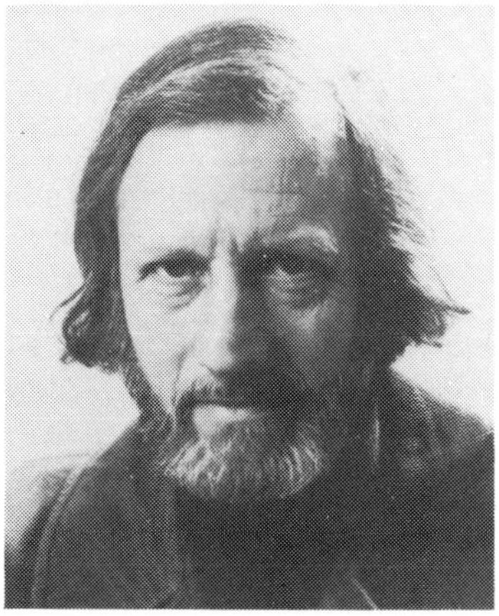

■ **HILARY EVANS**. Born Shrewsbury, England, 1929. Studied literature at Cambridge; wrote advertising copy before becoming a picture librarian. He has written several books on visual documentation and popular sociology. He is married, & has a daughter.

■ **UFO involvement**: A lifelong interest in the paranormal (he was at one time a council member of the Society for Psychical Research) led to his recognition that UFOs represent the richest field of accessible contemporary anomalous phenomena; he believes their cultural and sociological aspects should be studied along with their ostensible inherent characteristics, and that psychological study of witnesses should accompany analysis of what they report. He sees scientific study of the UFO phenomenon as our best opportunity to break through the 'reality barrier' which prevents our understanding the wide range of anomalous phenomena of which UFOs are only one category.

He is a council member of BUFORA, a co-founder of ASSAP (Association for the Scientific Study of Anomalous Phenomena) and compiler of BOLIDE (Ball Of Light International Data Exchange).

■ **Publications** include: *Intrusions: society and the paranormal* (RKP 1982): *The evidence for UFOs* (Aquarian 1983): *Visions, apparitions, alien visitors* (Aquarian 1984): *Gods, spirits, cosmic guardians* (Aquarian 1987).

■ **Address**: 1 Tranquil Vale / London SE3 OBU / England. Phone (home) 01 852 5040 / (work) 01 318 0034.

When Jung titled his landmark 1958 study *A modern myth of things seen in the skies* [1] he perceptively saw that, irrespective of whether or not there was any physical substance to the UFO phenomenon, it was in the process of generating its own mythology, its own sterotypes, its own cultural patterns.

Over the ensuing quarter century we have watched that mythology expand and enrich itself to the point where methodical study of the UFO reports has become immeasurably difficult because, before all else, the researcher has first to separate the primary phenomenon from these secondary accretions. Before the question of the nature of the phenomenon can be tackled, he has first to ask such questions as:

- When a witness reports seeing a UFO, is he honestly reporting a physical sighting, or is he involved in a purely psychological process in which his subconscious mind is using the UFO as trigger for a private psychodrama?

- If a truly physical event is occuring, to what extent is his account of it modified by what he has been conditioned to expect to see or by what he knows his neighbours will approve/disapprove?

- If the experience is fundamentally subjective, to what extent is his experience modified by his cultural environment, by prevailing and accepted stereotypes?

- When an investigator inquires into an alleged UFO event, is he doing so with complete impartiality, or is his ivestigation biased by the same factors as affect the witness?

- When friends, neighbours or the media disbelieve, even mock a UFO witness, do they do so out of honest conviction, or to hide their own subconscious terrors, or out of social conformity?

The same questions were asked, four or five centuries ago, about witchcraft: many commentators have noted the parallel between the UFO phenomenon and the witchcraft/demonolatry mania which raged from the 14th to the 17th centuries. Study of that mania throws valuable light on the current vogue; at the same time, it would be a mistake to regard the parallel as analagous in all respects.

Though scholars are still far from unanimous about what happened in the witchcraft mania, the general consensus is that for all the wealth of confessions, many of them voluntarily made, there was never any universal witchcraft cult as such: what was happening was that a great many misguided people, accused and accusers alike, were subconsciously *using* the witch and demon stereotypes as expressions of their private preoccupations. That is to say, the *idea* of witchcraft served a psychological and cultural purpose.

It is evident that Flying Saucers/UFOs are performing a similar role for many people today. French ufologist Michel Monnerie has perceptively labelled them an 'accepted myth' [2]: but they are not just a single myth. Without perhaps being all things to all men, they are certainly different things to different people, and this is reflected in some of the social reponses UFOs have provoked:

UFOs AND THE FUNDAMENTALIST CHRISTIAN

For many Christians, UFOs personify the forces of evil. Thus, in a 1961 booklet, Steuart Campbell writes: 'The appearance of UFO [sic] in our skies means the devil is intensifying his satanic campaign against good and against God.' [3] The literature of fundamentalist religion, in which UFOs are identified with forces of evil, is very extensive, and often backed by considerable study of the subject.

Though those outside this belief-system may feel this scenario to be improbable, there is no way at present that it can be disproved.

UFOs AS A SUBSTITUTE FOR RELIGION

For those who are dissatisfied with traditional religions, but feel the need of some external authority to whom they can look for ultimate salvation, UFOs offer a timely viable substitute as the vehicles in which cosmic guardians and space brothers visit our planet, bringing greater wisdom than we ourselves possess and offering a solution to the problems which our civilisation has not yet been able to resolve, such as war and aggression, not to mention a cure for cancer. Thus Laura Mundo tells us 'the space people love us as part of the universal family'. [4]

Those who are unwilling to discard existing religion have found ways of reconciling UFOs with Christianity. Thus in *Visitors from other planets* [5] we are told: 'Records of a manuscript will be found showing that Jesus had been transported into a spacecraft from the ages of twelve through thirty to receive specialized training for his role.'

Such claims are generally unspecific, and consequently hard to disprove; where they are specific, they can sometimes be shown to be erroneous. Thus, in 1954 Dorothy Martin, of Chicago IL, was warned by her space contacts of an imminent catastrophe which would overwhelm the United States, but reassured that she and her companions would be rescued by spacecraft. Those who believed her, including a college professor, sold their homes, quit their jobs, severed their family ties; but neither the catastrophe nor the rescue took place. [6]

UFOs AS PRIVATE PROJECTIONS

There is good reason to believe that UFOs have provided many individuals with a convenient means of externalising their private problems - casting them as scapegoats, spokesmen or saviours in critical situations. This hypothesis has been developed in two books [7], in which I show that UFO-related entities are one of several archetypal forms (others include the Virgin Mary and The Devil) which lend themselves to this kind of psychological process.

For example, it seems likely that the witnesses in two well-investigated cases, *The Andreasson affair* [8] and *The Tujunga Canyon contacts* [9], were projecting their internal crises as external UFO contact scenarios, evading responsibility for the way in which they resolved those crises by attributing it to some agency outside themselves. Where a Christian might have claimed that God or the Virgin Mary had ordered him to act in a certain way, the UFO contactee finds the UFO-entity more suitable.

UFOs AS FOLKLORE

For many, UFOs appear to operate on a deeper level; without having any specific religious function, they answer a sense of longing, provide an assurance of something beyond the here and now. Nor is this 'something' necessarily benevolent. In a recent address [10], Venetia Newall, president of the Folklore Society, reminded us that folklore is not always jolly romps and picturesque customs: much of it relates to deep-seated fears, and is sinister and cruel. Thus UFOs from the beyond may be the expression of mankind's sense of unspecified powers, yearned for by some, dreaded by others.

This is illustrated by the sense of awe which is frequently reported by observers; awe which is felt, moreover, even when it is subsequently established that the UFO in question was clearly the planet Venus or an advertising aircraft. When responses to UFOs, subsequently proved to be IFOs, take the form of being 'petrified, scared they'd zap a light at me...screamed for husband to get back in car...had a camera but too scared to use it...hope I never see it again...felt like the loneliest people on the block' [11], it is manifest that the banal sighting has released a deep-seated emotion, a tension which expresses itself in social attitudes which are in turn embodied in folklore.

UFOs AS SUPERTECHNOLOGY

For a minority, UFOs represent science-fiction come true. Here, too, they are an assurance that there is more to the universe than the humdrum life of Earth, but now any hint of threat is negligible by comparison with the promise that sci-fi fiction is not never-never fantasy but fact which may materialise at any moment. Many a UFO witness has described his reaction as one of delighted relief at finding that UFOs truly exist - 'My God! they're real!'

This has clearly been the incentive for many members of UFO research organisations: thus in 1950 Wilbert Smith persuaded a department of the

Canadian Government to sponsor 'Project Magnet' as a UFO detection system, though Smith's published writings do not hide his belief that 'a large number of the space brothers, whose special mission it is to safeguard the spiritual welfare and evolutionary progress of Earthlings, had banded themselves together to form a 'cosmic police force'. [**12**]

In 1967 the town of St Paul, Alberta, constructed a 'Landing Pad' for UFOs 'as a symbol of our faith that mankind will maintain the outer universe free from national wars and strife', and a similar Landing Port was built in 1976 by the citizens of Lake City, PA. [**13**]

UFOs AND THE SKEPTICS

No less notable than the attitude of the 'believers' is that of the skeptics, who have assailed UFOs and their champions with extraordinary virulence. The *Committee for Scientific Investigation of Claims for the Paranormal*, nominally dedicated to impartial investigation, has never attempted any balanced assessment of the UFO evidence. Astronomer Donald Menzel wrote, in the space of more than two decades, three full-length books offering alternative explanations - often ludicrously inadequate - for UFO sightings [**14**]: aviation author Philip Klass has also written three substantial books [**15**] which, while often doing an excellent debunking job on some of the wilder claims of UFO proponents, suggest some kind of negative obsession with a phenomenon in whose existence he does not believe.

Half a century ago Walter Franklin Prince, a Research Officer of the Boston Society for Psychical Research, made a survey [**16**] of negative reactions to claims of psychic phenomena. 'It seems,' he wrote, 'as though some enchantment seizes upon men of ability in their respective fields the moment they pass the boundary line of psychical research'. The same could be said of ufology: one has only to study the way the University of Colorado UFO Project (of 1966-1968 [**17**]) was handled by its eminent director, Dr Edward Condon, who would unquestionably have qualified as one of Prince's 'men of ability in their fields', to see how even persons of scientific training will abandon their habitual standards when confronted with an anomaly which - whatever its popular image - has acquired an aura of scientific unrespectability. The contents of this present study would surely suffice to show that UFOs constitute a scientific enigma of the greatest interest; yet throughout the 40 years the phenomenon has been around, serious interest by scientists has been minimal compared with their uninformed derision.

A VARIETY OF CULTURAL RESPONSES

In addition to these responses variously related to personal need, there are also notable differences in the way different cultural groups respond to UFOs. While the French tend to be characteristically 'philosophical' in their approach, often evolving complex hypotheses usually along psychosocial grounds, their German neighbours have for the most part adopted a more 'mystical' attitude, naively uncritical. The Spanish, too, are disinclined to be critical, but display a unique liveliness and ingenuity in their interpretation of the data. Britain and Australia have in general adopted a down-to-earth, matter-of-fact approach, while the United States is notable at one extreme for the most consistently serious research and at the other for having a near-monopoly of abductees and contactees.

For some researchers, the conclusion to be drawn from this variety of response is that there is no need for any primary or core phenomenon to exist at all. Instead, all that is needed to provide the stimulus is the *idea* of UFOs. Given the idea, anyone and everyone feels free to make use of it in whatever way suits them best.

This may well be true, but it cannot legitimately be used as an argument against the physical reality of the phenomenon. The fact that *some* people are exploiting the idea does not necessarily mean that there is no genuine phenomenon behind that idea.

At the same time, it would be equally illegitimate to argue that the existence of pseudo-UFOs implies the existence of true-UFOs. Folklore beliefs such as werewolves and vampires demonstrate that archetypes can be generated from misidentifed or misinterpreted phenomena.

Does this mean that the true nature of the UFO is irrelevant to the social and cultural response? Not exactly. There has to be a stimulus of some sort, and it may be said of the UFO that it was an idea whose time had come. David Hufford, in his study of the 'bedroom invader' phenomenon [**18**] showed how, once the phenomenon had been given a label, a great many people came forward and identified the 'bedroom invasion' experience as their own. Was this what happened in 1947 when in the wake of Kenneth Arnold's report, UFO reports flooded in from witnesses who had had strange experiences which they had previously been unable to relate to reality? [**19**]

It has been argued that the age of the flying saucer was a media event; but the media, with rare exceptions, is no more than a feedback device reflecting the preoccupations of the public. UFO historian Loren Gross has conclusively demonstrated the occurrence of UFO sightings before the 1947 sighting [**20**]: all that happened in 1947 was that UFO witnesses came out of the closet.

Another interesting social feature of ufology has been the search to establish the UFO as a timeless phenomenon [**21**]: the idea of 'UFOs throughout history' is often linked to the notion that we are under surveillance by superior beings, and has led to the proliferation of 'ancient astronaut' hypotheses of many quaint and curious kinds. [**22**] These have often been seized upon by the UFO cultists and structured into their belief-systems.

The evidence for these hypotheses has been shown to be fallacious [23] so that once again we find people latching on to an idea which, no matter whether it is true or not, happens to meet their needs.

THE IRRELEVANCE OF FACT

The overall conclusion, then, is that society has responded to the UFO in whichever way it has seen fit, without inquiring too closely how firm were the grounds for belief.

Does this mean that people don't care whether UFOs exist or not, so long as they have their beliefs? Not at all. Virtually everyone who claims UFO contact insists on the reality behind his claim, and it is psychologically certain that he needs this reassurance as much for himself as to convince the rest of us. True, witnesses are generally sadly uncritical in the evidence they offer or accept; phenomena that anyone with his wits about him could see to be a natural phenomenon or human artifact, even hoaxes manifest to the least suspicious mind, are in all sincerity offered as proof by people who seem to have abandoned whatever critical standards they use in their daily lives.

Not long ago, a researcher from New Zealand showed me a photograph of a flying saucer which he claimed to have taken in his own country, giving me a detailed account of the circumstances. I was subsequently able to identify his photo as having been taken in the United States some years previously. That man had nothing to gain by deceiving me; yet some inner compulsion had driven him to invent this totally untrue account.

That inner compulsion, whatever it ws, was his personal version of the response which the UFO arouses in so many people. Whatever the UFOs are, whatever degree of reality they possess, beyond question they embody a unique power to generate a remarkable range of responses, to release a remarkable depth of feeling.

UFOs AS A BELIEF SYSTEM

It is evident that among those who are involved with UFOs there exists a category of people for whom, though they pay lip-service to scientific research, this is not the real impetus. For them, belief comes first, and scientific research is of value only as it provides a basis for belief.

Clearly, they are not necessarily aware of this themselves, and for this reason it is not always easy to distinguish them. None of us is altogether free from subjective motivation, in whatever field of activity; even the most unprejudiced searcher after truth is to some extent affected by his cultural environment and his personal circumstances. This is no less true of quantum physics or cancer research than it is of ufology; it is one of the occupational hazards of being a member of the human race.

But UFOs, with their unique combination of more-or-less religious overtones (cosmic guardians and all that) with seemingly physical aspects measurable by science, have a special power to skew our judgements. In this respect, it is interesting and significant that while a fair number of UFO-people have some interest in science-fiction, it is very rare indeed for science-fiction buffs to be interested in UFOs. Why should this one-way interest be? The explanation is revealing:

Science-fiction expresses the dream of our time. Consequently, it is not surprising that those who delight in dreams are not so delighted by the proposition that their dreams are about to be realised in cold reality.

On the other hand, those who are involved with the actuality of UFOs are apt to be somewhat disenchanted by its down-to-earth aspects, and yearn after its wider aspects as represented by sci-fi.

'WHAT KIND OF PEOPLE JOIN A UFO GROUP?'

Shirley McIver's findings, presented under this title [24], are a useful indication of what UFOs mean to society, so long as we don't try to read more into them than they contain. Without wishing to offend my fellow-researchers, it seems to me that to study UFOs is like studying pathological patients to discover how

the human mind works. You do indeed learn a lot - but you must always bear in mind that what you are studying is not the norm but an extreme.

Thus McIver found that 80+% of UFO group members are male, which clearly conflicts not only with the population as a whole but with the sex ratio of UFO witnesses. Certainly, the inference is that males are more interested than females in finding out what UFOs are; but it does not follow that they are any the more interested in the phenomenon itself. Women may, for instance, feel that joining a UFO group is not the appropriate response.

Clearly there are limits to what information can practicable be obtained by questionnaires: even if we knew what questions to ask, it would be a matter of some delicacy to persuade people to reveal the motivations which underlie their involvement with UFOs, whether as witnesses, researchers or simply as readers of books on the subject. That 49% of McIver's respondents were also interested in physical research is surely meaningful; but would the skeptics be justified in saying that this simply bears out the finding that anyone who's a sucker for one pseudo-science is liable to be a sucker for them all?

Whether UFOs are for us objects of belief or scientific anomalies, there will be some of us who will abide by the evidence and others who will be reluctant to accept indications that out personal interpretation is unfounded. Equally, some of us who are skeptical that UFOs are anything more than unidentified UFOs are open to persuasion, while others are not to be shifted from their negative position.

Probably none of us likes the idea of being fooled; but that too works both ways, unbelievers can be as mistaken as believers. Ultimately, it is a question of what we are willing to accept as evidence, that in turn is dependent on how wedded we are to a particular belief, and that in turn again is dependent on how much we *need* that belief.

What is so remarkable about the UFO phenomenon is that it had divided us so profoundly; that some of us see it as a thing to take seriously while to others it is an amusing frivolity; that those who refuse to take it seriously range from simple indifference to virulent anger against those who think otherwise, even to the extent of physical attacks on witnesses; and that even among those of us who are convinced that UFOs should be taken seriously, there are some who do so on religious ground, some on moral grounds, some on scientific grounds.

None of which tells us very much about UFOs - but it tells us a great deal about ourselves.

REFERENCES

■ 1 - **Jung,** C. G. *Flying Saucers: a modern myth of things seen in skies* Routledge, 1959 (Orig. 1958). ■ 2 - **Monnerie,** M, *Et si les OVNI n'existaient pas?*, Humanoids Associes, 1977. ■ 3 - **Campbell,** Steuart *The Strong delusion* private, 1961. ■ 4 - **Mundo,** Laura, *The Mundo UFO report,* Vantage, 1982. ■ 5 - **Yolanda,** Nada, *Visitors from other planets* Mark-Age, 1974 ■ 6 - **Festinger, Riecken & Schachter**, *When Prophecy Fails,* University of Minnesota, 1956. ■ 7 - **Evans,** Hilary, *Visions, apparitions, alien visitors,* Aquarian, 1984; *Gods, spirits, cosmic guardians,* Aquarian, 1987. ■ 8 - **Fowler,** Raymond, *The Andreasson affair* Prentice-Hall, 1979, and *The Andreasson affair*: Phase Two, 1982. ■ 9 - **Druffel,** Ann & **Rogo**, Scott, *The Tujunga Canyon contacts,* Prentice-Hall, 1980. ■ 10 - **Newall,** Venetia, 'Folklore and male homosexuality', in *Folklore,* 1986-ii. ■ 11 - **Hendry,** Allen, *The UFO Handbook,* Doubleday, 1979. ■ 12 - **Smith,** Wilbert T., *The boys from Topside,* Saucerian, 1969. ■ 13 - **Curran,** Douglas, *In Advance of the Landing,* Abbeville, 1985. ■ 14 - **Menzel,** Donald H. *Flying Saucers,* Harvard, 1953; *The world of Flying Saucers,* Doubleday, 1963; *The UFO enigma,* Doubleday, 1977. ■ 15 - **Klass,** Philip J, *UFOs identified,* Random House, 1968; *UFOs explained,* Random House, 1974; *UFOs, the public deceived,* Prometheus, 1983. ■ 16 - **Prince,** Walter Franklin, *The enchanted boundary,* Boston S.P.R., 1930. ■ 17 - **Condon,** Edward U, (director), *The Scientific study of Unidentified Flying Objects,* University of Colorado, 1969; **Saunders,** David R, with **Harkins,** R. Roger, *UFOs? Yes! Where the Condon Committee went wrong,* World, 1968. ■ 18 - **Hufford,** David J, *The terror that comes in the night,* University of Pennsylvania, 1982. ■ 19 - **Bloecher,** Ted, *Report on the UFO wave of 1947,* private, 1967. ■ 20 - **Gross,** Loren E, *Charles Fort, the Fortean Society, and UFOs* private, 1976. ■ 21 - **Drake,** W Raymond, *Gods and spacemen throughout history,* Spearman, 1975, and six other volumes in the series. ■ 22 - **Misraki,** Paul (as 'Paul Thomas') *Les extraterrestres,* Plon, 1962 (English: *Flying Saucers through the ages,* Spearman, 1965,) is the most sensible of the genre. ■ 23 - **Castle,** E W and **Thiering,** B B, *Some trust in chariots*! Bailey Bros & Swinfen, 1973, is one of several books debunking the ancient astronaut hypothesis. ■ 24 - **McIver,** Shirley 'What kind of people join a UFO group?' in *Journal of Transient Aerial Phenomena* 3.1, 1983.

6
UFOs
AND SKEPTICISM

6.1

THE CASE FOR SCEPTICISM

by Michel Monnerie

■ MICHEL MONNERIE: He lives in Paris, where he works for the Archive Nationales, specialising in official seals.
■ UFO involvement: After many years as an active investigator, he became discouraged by the readiness with which witnesses misinterpret natural phenomena and conventional causes of UFO reports, and the similar readiness of investigators to accept those misinterpretations. This disenchantment lead him to discontinue active investigation, and instead to question the entire basis of UFO research, resulting in the publication of two books which had a profound effect upon UFO research in French-speaking countries.
■ **Publications:** *Et si les OVNIs n'existaient pas?* (1977); *Le naufrage des extraterrestres* (1979).
■ **Address:** 8 Passage des Entrepreneurs / 75015 Paris / France.

If we are willing to stop for a minute and think about UFOs without getting excited, we must admit that in 40 years of ufological studies there has been not one single observation of a UFO. Rather, ufologists have simply collected various stories, whose theme has always a common origin - generally an extra-terrestrial or at least an extra-human one.

During those 40 years there have been no investigations, no measurements, of *UFOs*: what has happened has been that some people, wishing to go beyond a simple anecdote, have measured... the witness's *memories*.

Like any other researchers on the margins of science, ufologists desperately want to be taken seriously. They supposed that scientific studies, using the most up-to-date discoveries, would prove how serious ufology is. Orthoteny, statistics, had a scientific look. Alas, the catalogues they used were a strange cocktail of magazine articles written by merry reporters, unchecked anecdotes and vague investigations conducted by naive amateurs. The failure of the resulting studies was hardly surprising.

Those who sought to prove that all UFOs were of extra-terrestrial origin had either to cheat, or to set aside many cases, in order to construct their theory. Those who sought to establish other supernatural explanations had to do the same. More and more ufologists came to admit that some cases had an ET explanation, others a parapsychological one, yet others were hoaxes, and so on.

For the past ten years ufologists have had to admit they were unable to explain witness' stories by one cause alone. The increasing complexity of the explanations, together with a higher standard of investigation making it obvious how many were due to error and misinterpretation, mean that ufologists must start again from the very beginning.

THE SINGLE COMMON ELEMENT

One common element is found at every step in ufology: Man. The witness is human - and so are the reporter, the investigator, the scientist, the ufologist, the philosopher: human, one and all. Instead of seeking an explanation in terms of ETs, ghosts, angels or devils, why not study the one certain element, man?

Instead of asking 'What are UFOs?' - a question which remains unanswered - let us ask:

- WHY do people believe they see UFOs?, and
- HOW do people believe they see UFOs?

To the best of my knowledge, I am the first ufologist to suggest that we should consider man as the centre of the problem. In two books [**1,2**] I proposed that UFOs should be studied from a psychosocial orientation. Those two books fundamentally changed ufology not only in French-speaking countries but elswhere in Europe. Many ufologists - they might be termed 'newfologists' - started studying socio-psychology, which yielded better results than ufological theories. Due to the language problem, this revolution has made its way more slowly in English-speaking countries: I am grateful to Bufora for giving me this opportunity to put forward my ideas.

WHY DO PEOPLE BELIEVE THEY SEE UFOs?

This is the easier of our two questions. Curiosity, hope, but also fear of the unknown are deeply ingrained in our natures. For centuries our minds have been focused on the supernatural world. People imagined devils, ghosts, leprechauns; believed in them, thought they were constantly around them, questioned their existence so little that it seemed quite natural to meet them physically once in a while. Folklore is rich in meetings with these fantastic beings, whose appearance may be vary according to the period or the cultural setting, but which always retain a family resemblance.

With the 19th century, though belief in the supernatural by no means ceased, it was now opposed and was no longer so omnipresent in people's minds, no longer acceptable as a universal explanation for the world about us. From now on, it was *science* which undertook the responsibility of explaining nature and its phenomena. The sky was no longer regarded as something fundamentally different from the Earth: stars were similar to the sun, planets were similar to the earth. (Not that these ideas were new, but now they reached a world-wide audience.)

When planets were seen to be just like Earth, ours became just a simple planet without any special privileges: when man lost his unique status, it became quite normal to imagine neighbouring planets as possibly inhabited. All at once, this new dimension fired the imagination of astronomers, and after them the philosophers and the novelists - indeed, they were often the same people.

By the end of the 19th century, the possiblilty that other worlds might be inhabited was accepted. As there seemed no limit to technical progress, so space travel began to seem feasible. A whole literature sprang up to exploit that theme. This was the great age of colonialism, and that literature depicted man as explorer and conqueror. Only a few writers - such as Wells in his *War of the worlds* - took a contrary theme, describing the invasion of Earth by ETs more advanced than ourselves.

The astronomers' belief that Mars must be rather similar to Earth inspired a real Martian romanticism: in no time Martians were widely known and consequently widely believed in, a myth which continued to grow during the 20th century.

At the same time 'anticipation literature' flourished, science fiction, books of popular science. Astronautics moved from dream to reality: the first rockets were built with the purpose of reaching outer space. By 1938 to leave Earth by rocket had come to seem a practical possibility. Sci-fi literature was widespread in the USA, and innumerable people believed firmly in the possible existence of the Martians - as witness their reaction to Orson Welles' broadcast of an updated *War of the worlds* in October that year. Americans - and many Europeans also - were actually living the space dream. For them it was all true, and its realisation only a matter of months, at most a few years.

World War Two momentarily interrupted those dreams, but it accelerated the technical progress which would make them real. By the end of the war, space conquest had come to look like a realistic enterprise: rockets now existed, a huge energy source was available in nuclear power, radar and long-distance radio relays would keep space travellers in touch.

It was precisely now, when everyone excited by space, that Arnold's observation occurred.

This one incident might have passed was unnoticed: instead it became extremely significant, provoking a series of similar observations. Americans, still in a state of shock from the war, feared the Russians and a possible invasion of their territory. The first rumours concerning mysterious flying objects express this fear of secret weapons, invasion... Lacking any basis in reality, this belief soon veered in another direction: with the Flying Saucers, the Martians and ETs became fact.

Prepared by years of sci-fi, by the enthusiastic optimism of astronomical and astronautical ideas, man now thought of himself as a citizen of the cosmos. Earth was no longer isolated: there was nothing far-fetched in the idea of traffic from one world to another. In this context, rumours about Flying Saucers seemed normal, *logical*. At one level they were technological rumours, such as had in the past been inspired successively by hot air balloons, zeppelins and airplanes: but these rumours were emotionally much richer, for now was added the fear or the hope of a meeting with other civilisations, with all their customary fantastic overtones.

For thirty years, these magnificent popular rumours ran wild, abundantly rich in material for the psychologist, the folklorist, the sociologist. What put an end to them was reality, the disenchanting results of real-life space exploration.

Parallel to the popluar rumours, however, saucers had become for some a myth, even a religion, thanks to the enthusiasm of the ufologists. Accustomed to thinking of planets as inhabited, of space travel as feasible, it was only natural they should believe they saw strange vessels.

Such is the answer to the question 'Why?'

HOW DO PEOPLE BELIEVE THEY SEE UFOs?

A rumour is like an epidemic. From the moment people started speaking about Flying Saucers, there were many who were shocked by any slightly unusual object they saw in the sky - shooting stars, meteors, even such everyday items as bright stars and planets. And by day, aircraft, balloons, birds, clouds, reflections...

This added up to a good many sightings. Ufologists, nowadays, no longer file cases which are only slightly strange. But let us not forget that it was precisely these cases which provided the foundations for the UFO myth.

Those witnesses who were more imaginative or more suggestible described more elaborate sightings, rich in details about the 'saucers' and their flights. Journalists reported many such stories. Soon, books were published, recording all these cases, whether honest, invented or fantastic, with no selectivity. They introduced fresh rumours - UFO crashes, the discovery of tiny pilots - which led, *ipso facto*, to stranger and increasingly stranger observations.

It is these sightings which provide the main data base for ufological studies. On the one hand too complex to be simply rejected as nothing more than a mistaken observation, and on the other hand not so strange that the witness can be dismissed as a madman or a liar, they might, taken as a whole, persuade the skeptic that UFOs are a reality. Practical ufologists exploited them as much as possible in their publications, lectures and interviews, until UFOs were taken seriously. In France, due to pressure from the most serious ufologists, an official organisation was created, GEPAN, which included several scientists among its personnel.

This isolating of the least unlikely cases, to give a serious look to the UFO phenomenon, has created the *illusion* of a scientific problem. But the attempt is self-defeating. There can be no justification for setting aside those cases which are either too simple or too complicated. Ufology is an integral whole, and must be studied and understood as a whole. And this can be done only by working from the one constant element: man.

FROM THE SIMPLE TO THE SOPHISTICATED

Those observations which contain little strangeness, in which there has been an obvious confusion with stars, aircraft &c, are an effect of the vocabulary of the rumour. Any light which the witness cannot precisely identify, he labels a UFO. Usually such a witness, despite what he says, has no knowledge or experience of what goes on in the sky, is not really interested in the heavens and has never really observed them. He sees a light, and calls it a UFO: 150 years ago, he'd have called it a balloon; later, a zeppelin, an aircraft, whatever was in fashion.

Stranger sightings follow the same pattern, but in a more sophisticated way. If a witness is surprised by an object which is outside his personal experience, or which seems out of place, he will start by trying to identify it with what he knows - aircraft, balloon, tractor etc: or, to be more accurate, with the *idea* he has of such objects. If this doesn't work, he will start to be afraid, asking himself: Could this be one of those UFOs they talk about? From then on he will be dominated by this idea, and will project what he knows - or thinks he knows - about UFOs. His imagination will translate the object's movements and metamorphoses according to the guidelines of the UFO myth, and he will give birth to a case which is logically acceptable - by the logic of ufology.

For instance: clouds passing in front of the moon, changing shape and appearance from one moment to the next. The witness - if he has not recognised the moon - will speak of a wheel which changes shape and size, which comes closer then moves further off, which swoops hither and thither then comes to a complete stop. Maybe he will see beams, portholes...

The moon is by no means the only object responsible for such confusions: a diversity of things seen, which not being understood were accepted as UFOs, have provided the raw materials for many cases collected over the past forty years. Each witness is a human being different from every other: unique. His own experience, his education, but first and foremost his suggestibility, determine how he interprets his sighting. The most suggestible may even experience an out-and-out day-dream, in which the movements of the original object will only vaguely approximate to the story presented. Those even more deeply affected will quit the real world to enter a self-hypnotic state, and will experience, in a sort of trance, the strangest kinds of case - contact, abduction - though to an outward observer they would be simply in a cataleptic state, facing an ordinary light whose nature they cannot grasp.

I could give innumerable examples of such cases which have subsequently been explained, but space prevents; besides, they can be found either in my own publications or those of the 'newfologists'.

If we start with the only element of which we are positively sure, the witness, it becomes possible to understand the way he reacts, and the unusual levels of consciousness in which he is led to see UFO where there is only an ordinary object looking extraordinary.

The classical ufologist will then raise another objection: the physical evidence. Alas, that too depends on man, and stands up no better to a critical examination:

■ **PHOTOGRAPHS**: the most spectacular are fakes, employing special effects, often very elaborate. Others show misinterpretation of the original source, ignorance of camera techniques, errors of all kinds which emerge as one studies the picture.

■ **TRACES**: some are made by the witness himself after the event, while in other cases the converse is true - people who come across mysterious trace invent a sighting to explain it. When the witness is honest, it is often a mere coincidence: following a sighting, study of the site reveals an anomalous mark which has in fact no connection with the sighting except that supplied by the ufologist's faith. In other cases, the trace has been left by the same object which created the sighting - helicopter landing, tractor etc.

■ **RADAR CASES and POWER FAILURES** have also to be filed as coincidences. An over-enthusiastic investigator will always find a relationship between the primary event and secondary incidents.

■ Finally, **TRAUMAS or PHYSIOLOGICAL EFFECTS** experienced by the witness may reasonably be supposed to be psychosomatic in origin.

CONCLUSION

In so short a space, I cannot expect that these arguments can convert believers. They must realise that the sociopsychological pattern is not automatic. Everyone who touches an electric pulg with his finger will feel the same shock; when faced with a stange light, no doubt 99 people in 100 will not so much as notice it, or if they do, not give it a second thought. Only the odd one will react otherwise; and the way he reacts will depend on his make-up, his cultural background, not to mention the state of his digestion. The process whereby strange or unusual scenes are tranformed into UFOs is not a systematic one. I can only urge scientists to test the socio-psychological explanation on really objective inquiries, and see for themselves.

When confronted with a witness, or reading his report, instead of getting excited at the thought that he may have seen a UFO, ask, 'What did he see that he thought was a UFO?'

First, look to astronomy for an answer. In 40% to 60% of nocturnal cases you will find that a bright star or planet was directly in line with the reported object; and you'll be astonished by what the witness describes when it is clear that he was looking at the Moon or Venus.

Next, look for other sources - aircraft, lighthouses, balloons, birds &c. Little by little the psychology of the witness will emerge in all its complexity.

The major failure in ufology comes from the fact that investigators, believing that UFOs exist, have lost their critical sense. A good investigator must be a skeptic. When confronted by the unusual, he must study the only real element he has - the witness. Is he lying? Was he mistaken? Why?

Even when being extremely suspicious, the investigator will once in a while encounter a case which utterly resists explanation. Does that mean the strange apparition is proved a real UFO? Alas, the investigator is just as much of a human being as the witness, and may lack the requisite knowledge and experience which would resolve this case.

Cases which defy explanation may well be of genuine importance, but that would not justify their being used as evidence that UFOs exist. In my first book, I proposed a 'principle of doubtful observation'. Because observation must always be considered doubtful, not one single typical UFO case introduction of the ET element.

Ufology is not the result of ET visitation or any other kind of interference from outer space; but that does not mean that it is without interest. Ufology is a modern folklore, whereby for forty years man has been preparing himself for the greatest transformation in his history: his entry into the Space Age.

A child prepares for adult life by reproducing in his games the events, feelings, jobs he will later encounter. In just the same way, men dream, imagine or play the Space Age. This is the best form of preparation for it.

Forty years of ufology have yielded a rich store of information for folklorists, sociologists and psychologists. It is now time to use it.

REFERENCES

■ 1 - **Monnerie,** Michel, *Et si les OVNIs n'existaient pas?* (Les Humanoides Associes, Paris, 1977). ■ 2 - **Monnerie.** Michel, *Le naufrage des extraterrestres* (Nouvelles Editions Rationalistes, Paris, 1979).

6.2

THE CASE AGAINST SKEPTICISM

by Willy Smith

"When you can measure what you are speaking about, and express it in numbers, you know something about it. But when you cannot - your knowledege is of a meagre and unsatisfactory kind."
Lord Kelvin.

INTRODUCTION

The problem I want to discuss here is not the reality of the UFO phenomenon, which after 40 years of UFO experiences is accepted by a large percentage of the population, but the more subtle point of the existence of an objective reality behind those anomalous manifestations documented by the UFO reports.

Although anyone who has looked into the information available with more than a superficial interest can hardly doubt that UFOs exist, two groups of people insist on denying their existence on different philosophical grounds.

First, we have the self-appointed debunkers, the perennial skeptics, such as Phil Klass, Ian Ridpath and a few other misguided souls. They are not particularly distinguished by their intellectual integrity and do not hesitate to depart from the truth by omitting facts that do not fit their pet theories. Their approach to the UFO problem is simple enough: if they succeed in "unmasking" all of the prominent UFO sightings, it follows that whatever cases are left could be equally well explained, and thus the non-existence of UFOs would have been proven. Leaving aside the small point that it is not possible to prove a negative, they carefully avoid even mentioning those cases that they know quite well could not be explained, and continuously attempt to engage the serious researchers in endless futile arguments.

I am not interested here in the professional debunkers, and I dismiss them without further ado with the following words from Dr. Hynek:

"One could spend all his enery confronting the skeptics. That same energy is much better spent investigating the subject. Why waste time on people who have not bothered to learn the basic facts? It's their problem!" [**1**]

The second group, the one I am concerned with, is formed of ufologists who, after finding in their work hundreds, nay, thousands of cases without scientific value, find their viewpoint shifted toward skepticism. This is healthy for the discipline and should be so. What is disturbing is that often that change of attitude seems to blind their critical faculties, and they are ready to accept as feasible farfetched hypotheses that pretend to explain the UFO phenomenon. Many of those so-called "hypotheses" are not even such, as for instance, the birth trauma hypothesis (BTH) or the socio-psychological theories (SPT) that have lately become so fashionable. Those explanations fail to satisfy the requirements that all scientific hypothesis must fulfill to be viable. They have no solid foundations and are usually presented not on the strength of experimental facts, but by the "hand waving" type of arguments.

Nonetheless, those ufologists, as they really know better, try to justify their negativism with more solid arguments and have thus fallen into another trap: the myth of the principle of indistinguishability, that is, that given a set of UFOs and a set of IFOs, they cannot be separated. If this is so, the argument continues, very likely all those manifestations that we take as UFOs are sophisticated IFOs, and in reality UFOs do not exist. And, they add, this is supported by the numerous examples of "classical" cases that in the fullness of time have been found to have mundane explanations.

My intention is not to argue the many fallacies of this reasoning, including the frequent setting aside of the wisdom of Occam's razor. There are so far two methods for determining whether UFOs can be distinguished: a comparison procedure, used numerous times in the past; and a unique statistical analysis of the information available, which has become possible only after the development of UNICAT. Although I will discuss both approaches, the object of the paper is basically to disseminate the second method.

TRADITIONAL COMPARISON METHODS

It is obvious that if one could establish on a statistical basis that differences exist between UFOs and IFOs, the problem of the existence of UFOs would be resolved.

This approach has two difficulties. First, we must have representative sets of the populations (IFOs and UFOs) that we intend to compare, that is to say, our UFO set is to contain only UFOs, while the IFOs set must be formed by only IFOs. Otherwise, the conclusions of any comparison would be baseless. The fact that no high-quality UFO data base existed until recently, and moreover, that a catalog of true IFOs is hard to come by, certainly did not deter a generation of investigators, perhaps with more enthusiasm than knowledge, from pursuing this effort.

The alleged pioneer of the indistinguishability myth is almost certainly Allan Hendry [2], and he has been quoted over and over by people who have not read his book with the critical spirit and depth that it deserves. I don't believe Hendry's intent was to prove that IFOs could not be distinguished from UFOs, but only that they could be easily confused if one was not careful. In addition, Hendry was not himself particularly attentive to detail, and his investigation of many cases was done by phone [2 p.88]. The astute reader will see that the Battelle Memorial Institute study [3] in fact proved that IFOs and UFOs could be distinguished [4] although Hendry, for reasons that are not clear to me, proceeded to dismiss their results by specious arguments [2 p.266].

The second difficulty is that one must then compare characteristics appearing in both sets that have been determined with reasonable accuracy. The six characteristics selected by the Battelle Institute study were shape, duration, speed, brightness, color and number. These characteristics were perhaps not the best possible ones, but they sufficed, and the analysis of the Battelle Institute shows that statistically UFOs and IFOs are different. As already indicated, Hendry wants us to believe the contrary, qualifying the information available as "loose." Anyone taking the time to study references [3] and [4] can verify that this statement is incorrect, as in order to properly appreciate *Special Report #14* one must read it with care.

The development of the UNICAT data base has created a set of high-quality UFO cases which could be used for the comparison. To obtain a reasonable IFO set is not easy, and perhaps the "knows" mentioned in reference [3] could be utilized. A second possibility would be to use catalogs of "negative" cases, such as NELIB of Ballester Olmos et al [5]. I have found, however, that the contents of NELIB are not by far 100% IFOs, but in some instances controversial cases that have been thrown there when it was clear that they did not contain sufficient information to make them acceptable. Another reason why I feel skeptical about NELIB is that ball lighting -a rather rare phenomenon- is offered as an explanation for a large percentage of the listed IFOs (18%). In spite of these shortcomings, I intend to use NELIB for comparison with UNICAT.

The above considerations led me to the conclusion that in order to have a catalog of 100% IFOs the only guaranteed procedure was to create it artificially. Thus, I asked the UNICAT associates and collaborators, as well as many other persons having limited knowledge of the UFO phenomenon, to list totally imaginary cases providing a few basic items of information that could be used later for statistical analyses. Those contributing the imaginary cases were not told the aims of the study, and I must confess that to prevent biases I advanced misleading information about my purposes. The result of this

PERCENT FREQUENCIES

	Parameters	Year: 1984 Cases: 400	1986 606
HV	hovering	46.00%	48.68%
US	UFO silent, no noise	45.75%	44.06%
AA	anomalous acceleration	22.00%	26.73%
TS	tremendous speed(faster than jet)	19.50%	22.11%
VA	vertical ascent	21.50%	20.30%
FT	fast takeoff	19.50%	19.31%

TABLE 1

collective effort is FALSECAT, and the few comparisons I have done so far have shown totally unexpected results.

The analysis of the information collected in FALSECAT has not been completed yet, and likewise, the statistical comparison of the UNICAT data base with other more or less mixed catalogs of UFO and IFO cases is still under way. The results will be presented in a separate paper, in the not very distant future.

This brings me to the second approach, which requires no comparisons and is based only on the information collected on the phenomenon.

THE DYNAMIC PARAMETERS

When Dr. Hynek and I started the development of UNICAT, one of the objectives was to prove in a manner acceptable to the scientific establishment that the UFO phenomenon was not only real, but also different from the subjects treated by other disciplines, and consequently deserving of serious consideration.

To satisfy this goal, for UFOs or any other topic, one must start by collecting a satisfactory and representative sample of the items to be studied. To emphasize the point, if one wants to study bananas, one does not collect fruits; or if one desires to study birds, one does not collect mammals. Consequently, the first piece of business was to assemble a database of UFO cases, from which IFO and doubtful cases would have been screened. This database, to be satisfactory, was not to be a mere catalog or listing of cases with coded sequential entries, like UFOCAT and many others. It was designed specifically for this application, with random access to any of the 250+ fields included in its format.

The question then was to identify those repeatable characteristics appearing in the UFO reports, and formulate the database on their terms. This is not an easy proposition, as we do not really know which properties are significant and which are not, a dilemma similar to that faced by Pliny when collecting all the information he could in his monumental treatise [**6**].

This first selection of the parameters applicable to the UFO phenomenon was done by Dr. Hynek on the basis of his experience, and was developed in papers presented by him at several scientific and ufological meetings in the USA and abroad [**7, 8, 9**].

As we acquired more experience and the development of the database advanced, new parameters were added until at present we have 225 parameters describing the properties of the UFO phenomenon. It also became clear that the parameters could be grouped by categories, and one of them was composed of "dynamic" parameters, which refer to the reported UFO motions.

For the purposes of this paper, I am interested only in the frequencies obtained for the dynamic parameters. We soon found out that six of those parameters appeared with very large frequencies. Those characteristic parameters, some of which perhaps could be better labeled kinematic rather than dynamic, are listed in **Table 1**.

The initial frequency study done in 1984, when the database had 400 cases, was repeated in 1986 with 600 cases. As shown in **Table 1,** the percentages have not changed much, which is very significant, as the added cases were furnished rather arbitrarily by UNICAT associates. Yet, a chi-square test shows that both sets are samples of the same population. This unexpected statistical consistency of UNICAT has also been verified while doing other studies in the database.

We notice that the first two parameters in the list appear with very large frequencies; in fact, almost one half of the cases in the database seem to be silent UFOs or hovering UFOs. The rest of the parameters exhibit frequencies of about 20% or more.

Now, the selection of the parameters was somewhat arbitrary, and *a priori* there is no reason to suspect that the cases with hovering UFOs, say, are related in any way to the cases showing tremendous speeds (TS). To verify this, we ran a parameter correlation. ie, we queried the database for those cases having any two or any three of the above parameters simultaneously.

2-PARAMETER CORRELATIONS

HV	TS	65
HV	AA	83
HV	VA	66
HV	FT	72
HV	US	148
AA	US	65
US	FT	45
FT	VA	39
VA	TS	44
TS	AA	93
AA	FT	62
FT	TS	44
TS	US	53
US	VA	44
VA	AA	57

TABLE 2

4-PARAMETER CORRELATIONS

AA	62	FT
93	17	72
TS	65	HV

#1

AA	62	FT
65	14	72
US	148	HV

#2

AA	62	FT
57	12	72
VA	66	HV

#3

AA	62	FT
65	17	44
US	53	TS

#4

AA	62	FT
57	11	44
VA	44	TS

#5

AA	62	FT
57	8	45
VA	44	US

#6

AA	83	HV
65	22	65
US	53	TS

#7

AA	83	HV
57	15	65
VA	44	TS

#8

AA	83	HV
57	14	148
VA	44	US

#9

AA	93	TS
57	12	53
VA	44	US

#10

FT	72	HV
45	14	65
US	53	TS

#11

FT	72	HV
39	7	65
VA	44	TS

#12

FT	72	HV
39	7	148
VA	44	US

#13

FT	44	TS
39	5	53
VA	44	US

#14

HV	65	TS
66	10	53
VA	44	US

#15

TABLE 3

If we take for example the parameters hovering (HV) and UFO silent (US), we find that the database contains 295 cases of hovering and 267 cases of silent UFOs, and that of those cases, 148 have both parameters simultaneously. Expressed in another form, almost 25% of the cases in the data base exhibit overlapping parameters HV and US.

This perhaps was to be expected, as we know that UFOs that hover are often silent. But what is terribly important is that if we consider all combinations of the parameters taken two at a time -- of which there are 15 possibilities-- we find that the numerical correlation extends to all of them, and that the order of magnitude of the numbers obtained is very much the same, as shown in **Table 2**. (A very visible three-dimensional display of the 2- and 3-parameter correlations has been obtained using the faces, edges and vertices of a regular dodecahedron.)

Similarly, there are 15 different possibilities if the 6 dynamic parameters are taken 4 at a time, which we have represented in **Table 3**. Each square is one of the possible cases, and the numbers listed on the sides are the values previously obtained from 2-parameter correlations. The numbers in the center of the squares indicate the number of cases having simultaneously the 4 parameters in the corners, and again we notice that the results are strikingly similar, although the characteristics represented by the parameters are intrinsically different.

It is evident from the above that the correlations between any two --or among any four-- of the most frequent dynamic parameters is very strong. Although not shown here, the study has been extended to 5-parameter correlations.

CONCLUSION

The conclusion is then that the most frequent dynamic parameters are not independent as initially assumed, but strongly correlated. And what is the meaning of the correlation? How can this be, when the reports providing the basic information collected in the database come from hundreds of individuals and from all parts of the world? Since the possibility of a gigantic collusion is unthinkable under the circumstances, the only alternative is that the common thread linking all this mass of information is the UFO phenomenon itself; and in fact, that the parameters are associated by the phenomenon which they describe.

To belabor the point, consider for a moment some well identified natural phenomena or man-made artifacts, and determine which of our six parameters apply to each one of them. We have added an additional parameter, TT (treetops) which describe the height of the observations and may be significant for the instances of misinterpretation.

As can be seen in **Table 4,** the known phenomena display three or four of the parameters, but none of them have simultaneously the parameters AA

	AA	FT	HV	TS	US	VA	TT
AIRPLANE		**	**			**	**
BALLOON			**		**	**	**
HELICOPTER			**			**	**
METEOR	**			**	**		
ROCKET	**	**		**		**	
PLANET			**		**		**
UFO	**	**	**	**	**	**	**

TABLE 4

(anomalous acceleration), HV (hovering) and US (UFO silent). Thus, we queried the database for those incidents exhibiting simultaneously those three parameters, as we know by exclusion that they CANNOT by any of the knowns listed in **Table 4**. We found, in fact, 37 such cases. In addition, 14 of those 37 cases also have the parameter FT (fast takeoff), and 22 of them display the parameter TS (tremendous speed). To obtain an idea of the "quality" of the cases, we add supplementary conditions, such as daytime, independent witnesses and close encounters. Of our 37 cases, 13 have independent witnesses (IW), 19 are close encounters and 6 of them took place in daytime.

The analysis, of course, doens't stop here, and it will take a long time before the information already contained in UNICAT is properly analysed. All we have done is to study 6 of the 225 characteristic parameters!

Based on the above, we can enunciate an **operational definition** of the UFO phenomenon as follows:

An observation resulting in a combination of the parameters that cannot be matched by any object manufactured by our present technology, or by a known natural phenomenon.

This is the first important result of the UNICAT project. As the addition of further information could not eliminate the anomaly, we have a corollary:

The UFO phenomenon is a new phenomenon.

REFERENCES

■ 1 - **Hynek,** J. Allen and **Vallee,** J.; *The Edge Of Reality*, 1975, p. 26. ■ 2 - **Hendry,** Allan; *The UFO Handbook*, 1979. ■ 3 - USAF *Project Bluebook Special Report #14*, dated May 5, 1955. Analysis prepared by Dr. L. Davidson, 4th edition, 1971. ■ 4 - **Maccabee,** Bruce: 'Scientific Investigation of Unidentified Flying Objects,' in *The Journal of UFO Studies*, Vol. 1 and Vol. III, undated, CUFOS. ■ 5 - **Ballester Olmos,** V.J. and **Fernandez,** J.A.; *Catalog of Negative UFO Landings in the Iberian Peninsula (NELIB)*: in preparation, to be published by the Fund for UFO Studies, Washington, D.C. ■ 6 - **Pliny** the Elder, *Naturalis Historia*. ■ 7 - **Hynek,** J. Allen; *The Properties of the* **UFO** *Phenomenon*, paper presented at the annual meeting of the AAAS in New York City on May 29, 1984. A more extensive version of this paper was presented at Princeton University later that same year. ■ 8 - **Hynek,** J.Allen; 'The Properties of the UFO Phenomenon,' in MUFON *1984 UFO Symposium Proceedings*, p.162. ■ 9 - **Hynek,** J. Allen; *Parameters of the* UFO *Phenomenon*, paper presented at the GEPAN meeting in Toulouse, France, June 24-25, 1985.

7
APPENDICES

7.1

CURRENT UFO RESEARCH ORGANISATIONS

These organisations, so far as we know, are:
- ■ currently active
- ■ doing either serious research or competant investigation
- ■ either publish their findings or are ready to share them and/or collaborate with other *bona fide* researchers.

We supply: ■ names of organisation; ★ names of contacts; and ▼ an address -- but we cannot guarantee that our information is accurate or up to date.

ARGENTINA

■ **CADIU** (Circulo Argentino de Investigaciones Ufologicas)
★ Oscar Galindez
▼ Casilla de Correo 218 / Cordoba.

■ **CEFAI** (Centro de Estudios de Fenómenos Aéreos Inusuales)
★ Roberto Banchs
▼ Casilla de Correo #9, Suc. 26 / CP 1426 / Buenos Aires.

AUSTRALIA

■ **ACUFOS** (Australian Centre for UFO Studies)
★ Mark Moravec
▼ PO Box 728 / Lane Grove / NSW 2066.
(Many other Australasian organisations are affiliated with, and can be contacted via ACUFOS.)

■ **Victorian** UFO Research Society
/ Judith Magee / Paul Norman
▼ PO Box 43 / Moorabbin / VIC 3189.

BELGIUM

■ **SOBEPS** (Société Belge d'Etude des Phénomènes Spatiaux)
★ Michel Bougard / Lucien Clerebaut
▼ 74 Avenue Paul Janson / B -1070 Bruxelles.

■ **SVL** (Studiegroep voor Vreemde Luchtverschijnselen)
★ Wim Van Utrecht
▼ Oever 28 / B 2000 Antwerpen.

■ **UFO** 21
★ Marc Broux
▼ 40 Konig Albertstraat / B -3500 Hasselt.

BRITAIN

■ **ASSAP** (Association for the Scientific Study of Anomalous Phenomena)
★ Ken Phillips (UFO investigation)
▼ 16 Wedgwood Walk / Lymington Road / London NW6
★ Hilary Evans (UFO & general inquiries)
▼ 1 Tranquil Vale / London SE3 0BU.

■ **BUFORA** (British UFO Research Association)
★ Arnold West
▼ 16 Southway / Burgess Hill / RH15 9ST.

■ **CONTACT** UK
★ Bernard Delair / Derek Mansell (Senior Research Officer)
▼ 48 Crown Road / Wheatley / Oxford OX9 1UL.

■ **LUFOIC** (Leicester UFO Investigation Committee)
★ Clive Potter
▼ 31 Grove Road / Leicester LE5 3HJ.

■ **MUFORA** (Manchester UFO Research Association)
★ Peter Hough
▼ 6 Silsden Avenue / Lowton / Warrington WA3 1EN.

■ **NLUFOIG** (North Lancashire UFO Investigation Group)
★ Gordon Barraclough
▼ 89 Bare Lane / Morecambe LA4 6RN.

■ **WYUFORG** (West Yorkshire UFO Research Group)
★ Andy Roberts / Martin Dagless
▼ 84 Elland Road / Brighouse HD6 2QR.

CANADA

■ **CCUQ** (Centrale de Compilation Ufologique de Québec)
▼ CP 103 / Drummondville / Québec / J2B 2V6.

■ **CCOI** (Corporation pour la Collection des Observations Inexpliquées)
▼ BP 161 / Saint -Brunot / Québec / J3V 4P9.

CHINA

- ■ **UFO** Research Centre of Yunnan
- ★ Shi Bo
- ▼ 24 Xiao -Wei -Yung / Zhu -Shi -Kou / Peking.

DENMARK

- ■ **SUFOI** (Skandinavisk UFO Information)
- ★ Per Andersen
- ▼ PO Box 6 / DK -2820 Gentofte.

FRANCE

- ■ **ADRUP** (Association Dijonaise de Recherches Ufologiques & Parapsychologiques)
- ★ Patrice Vachon
- ▼ 6 reu des Gémeaux / 21220 Gevrey Chambertin.

- ■ **AESV** - FRANCE (Association d'Etude sur les Soucoupes Volantes)
- ★ Yves Bresson / Perry Petrakis
- ▼ BP 324 / 13611 Aix -en -Provence Cedex.

- ■ **CIGU** (Comité Ile -de -France des Groupements Ufologiques)
- ★ Michel Coste / Thierry Rocher
- ▼ 10 rue de l'Ingénieur Robert Keller, 262/17 / 75015 Paris.

- ■ **GEPAN** (Groupment d'Etude des Phénomènes Aérospatiaux Non -identifiés)
- ★ M. Velasco
- ▼ 18 avenue Edouard Belin / 31055 Toulouse Cedex.

- ■ **GEPSI** (Groupe d'Etude des Phénomènes Spatiaux Inexpligués)
- ▼ 89 rue de Siam, 29200 Brest.

GERMANY

- ■ **CENAP** (Centrales Erforschungsnetz Aussergewöhnlicher Phänomene)
- ★ Walter Werner
- ▼ Eisenacherweg 16 / D -6800 Mannheim 31.

- ■ **GEP**
- ★ Gerald Mosbleck
- ▼ Postfach 2361 / D -5880 Lüdenscheid.

ITALY

- ■ **CISU**
- ★ Edoardo Russo
- ▼ Corso Vittorio Emanuele 108 / 10121 Torino.

NORWAY

- ■ **UFO** -NORGE
- ★ Odd -Gunnar Roed
- ▼ Boks 14 / N -3133 Duken.

POLAND

- ■ **Krakow** UFO Research Group
- ★ Bronislaw Rzepecki
- ▼ ul. Jozefa 22/14 / 31 056 Krakow.

PORTUGAL

- ■ **CNIFO** (Comissao Nacional de Investigacao do Fenómeno OVNI)
- ★ J. Fernandes / F. Fernandes
- ▼ rua Sà da Bandeira, 331 -3#, sala 31 / 4000 Porto.

SPAIN

- ★ Vicente -Juan Ballester Olmos
- ▼ Guardia Civil, 9, D -16 / 46020 Valencia.

- ■ **Cuadernos** de Ufologia
- ★ Julio Arcas Gilardi
- ▼ Rualasal 22 / 39001 Santander.

SWEDEN

- ■ **AFU** (Archives for Ufo Research)
- ★ Anders Liljegren
- ▼ PO Box 11027 / S -60011 Norrkoping.

- ■ **UFO** -SVERIGE
- ★ Hakan Ekstrand
- ▼ Box 175 / S -73300 Sala.

SWITZERLAND

- ■ **AESV -SUISSE** (Association d'Etude sur les Soucoupes Volantes)
- ★ Yves Bresson / Perry Petrakis
- ▼ CP 342 / CH -1800 Vevey 1.

UNITED STATES

- ■ **APRO** (Aerial Phenomena Research Organisation)
- ★ Coral Lorenzen
- ▼ 3597 W. Grape Drive / Tucson / AZ 85741.

- ■ **CUFOS** (J Allen Hynek Center for UFO Studies)
- ★ George M. Eberhart
- ▼ 2457 W. Peterson / Chicago / IL 60659.

- ■ **FUFOR** (Fund for UFO Research)
- ★ Bruce Maccabee
- ▼ PO Box 277 / Mount Rainier / MD 20712.

- ■ **MUFON** (Mutual UFO Network)
- ★ Walter Andrus
- ▼ 103 Oldtowne Road / Seguin / TX 78155.

7.2

BOOKS ABOUT UFOs

This list contains selected books considered by BUFORA Council Members to be the most important contributions to our knowledge and understanding of the subject during the last 40 years. This list does not include contactee narratives and other literature which, while both significant and illuminating, is probably not central to an understanding of the phenomenon as such. As a guide for further reading the following symbols apply: ● = recommended; ●● = essential; and ■ =an important regional study.

ARMAND. John, & HOLM- HANSEN. Bjorn
-- *UFO'er over Norge* (Gyldendal, 1971). ■

BALLESTER OLMOS. V.J.
-- *OVNIs: el fenomeno aterrizaje* (Plaza y Janes, 1978). ●
-- *Catalogue of 200 type 1 UFO events in Spain and Portugal* (CUFOS, 1976). ■
-- *Investigacion OVNI* (Plaza y Janes, 1981). ●
& FERNANDEZ PERIS. Juan A.
-- *Enciclopedia de los encuentros cercanos con OVNIs* (Plaza y Janes, 1987). ●
& GUASP. Michel
-- *Los OVNIs y la ciencia* (Plaza y Janes, 1981). ●

BANCHS. Roberto Enrique
-- *Las evidencias del fenomeno OVNI* (Alonso, 1976).

BARTHEL. Gerard, & BRUCKER. Jacques
-- *La Grande peur martienne* (Nouvelles editions rationnalistes, 1979).

BASTERFIELD. Keith
-- *Close encounters of an Australian kind* (Reed, 1981). ■

BERLITZ. Charles, & MOORE. William
-- *The Roswell incident* (Grosset & Dunlap, 1980). ●

BLOECHER. Ted
-- *Report on the UFO wave of 1947* (Private, 1967). ●

BONDARCHUCK. Yurko
-- *UFO sightings, landings and abductions* (Methuen, Toronto, 1979). ■

BOUGARD, Michel
-- *Des soucoupes volantes aux OVNI* (SOBEPS, 1976). ●
-- *La chronique des OVNI* (Delarge, 1977). ●

BOWEN. Charles (Ed)
-- *The humanoids* (Spearman, 1969). ●
-- *Encounter cases from Flying Saucer Review* (Signet, 1977) ●

CARROUGES. Michel
-- *Les apparitions de Martiens* (Fayard, 1963). ●

CHAPMAN. Robert
-- *Unidentified flying objects* (Barker, 1969).

CLARK. Jerome, & COLEMAN. Loren
-- *The unidentified* (Warner, 1975). ●

COHEN. Daniel
-- *The great airship mystery* (Dodd Mead, 1981). ●

CONDON. Edward U. (Dir)
-- *The scientific study of unidentified flying objects* (University of Colorado, 1969). ●●

DAVIS. Isabel, &BLOECHER. Ted
-- *Close encounter at Kelly, and others of 1955* (CUFOS, 1978). ●

De TURRIS. Gianfranco, & FUSCO. Sebastiano
-- *Obiettivo sugli UFO: fotostoria dei dischi volanti* (Mediterranee, 1975). ●

DEVEREUX, Paul
-- *Earthlights* (Turnstone, 1982).

DRUFFEL. Ann, & ROGO. D. Scott
-- *The Tujunga Canyon contacts* (Prentice Hall, 1980). ●

EBERHART. George M.
-- *UFOs and the extraterrestrial contact movement* (Scarecrow, 1987).

EVANS. Hilary
-- *The evidence for UFOs* (Aquarian, 1983). ●
-- *Visions, apparitions, alien visitors* (Aquarian, 1984). ●
-- *Gods, spirits, cosmic guardians* (Aquarian, 1987).

FAWCETT. Lawrence, & GREENWOOD. Barry J.
-- *Clear intent* (Prentice Hall, 1984). ●●

FERNANDES. Joaquim
-- *OVNIs em Portugal* (Nova Critics, 1978). ■

FESTINGER. L., RIECKEN. H.W., & SCHACHTER. S.
-- *When prophecy fails* (University of Minnesota, 1956). ●●

FIGUET. Michel, & RUCHON. Jean-Louis
-- *OVNI: le premier dossier complet des rencontres rapprochees en France* (Lefeuvre, 1979). ■

FLAMMONDE. Paris
-- *Tha age of flying saucers* (Hawthorn, 1971) ●
-- *UFO exist* (Putnam, 1976). ●

FOWLER. Raymond
-- *The Andreasson affair* (Prentice Hall, 1979). ●
-- *The Andreasson affair, phase two* (Prentice Hall, 1982). ●

FREIXEDO. Salvador
-- *Visionarios, misticos ys contactos extraterrestres* (Daimon, 1981).

FULLER. Curtis G. (Ed)
-- *Proceedings of the First International UFO Congress, 1977* (Warner, 1980). ●

FULLER. John G.
-- *Incident at Exeter* (Putnam, 1966).
-- *The interrupted journey* (Dial, 1966). ●●

GANSBERG. Judith M, & Alan L.
-- *Direct encounters: personal histories of UFO abductees* (Walker, 1980).

GAUTHIER. Jean-Pierre
-- *OVNI, le tour du phenomene en 80 photos* (Solar, 1979).

GIRAUD. Jean (Ed)
-- *Les soucoupes volantes: le grand refus?* (Moutet, for the GABRIEL group, 1979).

GOOD. Timothy
-- *Above top secret* (Sidgwick & Jackson, 1987).

GRECO. Massimo, & MUSCIO. Arrigo
-- *UFO: illusione o realta?* (CUN, 1985). ■

GROSS. Loren
-- *The mystery of the ghost rockets* (Private, 1974). ●
-- *The UFO wave of 1896* (Private, 1974). ●
-- *Charles Fort, the Fortean Society and UFOs* (Private, 1976). ●
-- *UFOs, a history. Vol. 1: July 1947 to December 1948* (Arcturus, 1982). ●
-- *UFOs, a history. Vol. 2: January to June 1949* (Arcturus, 1982). ●

HAINES. Richard
-- (Ed) *UFO phenomena and the behavioural scientist* (Scarecrow, 1979). ●●
-- *Observing UFOs* (Nelson Hall, 1980). ●●

HALL. Richard H. (Ed)
-- *The UFO evidence* (NICAP, 1964; reissued with an index by Sherman Larsen, private). ●●

HENDRY. Allan
-- *The UFO handbook* (Doubleday, 1979). ●●

HICKSON. Charles, & MENDEZ. William
-- *UFO contact at Pascagoula* (UFO Photo Archives, 1983).

HIND. Cynthia
-- *UFOs - African encounters* (Gemini, 1982) ■

HOPKINS. Bud
-- *Missing time* (Marek, 1981). ●●
-- *Intruders* (Random House, 1987). ●

HYNEK. J. Allen
-- *The UFO experience* (Regnery, 1972). ●●
-- *The Hynek UFO report* (Dell, 1977). ●●
& VALLEE. Jacques
-- *The edge of reality* (Regnery, 1975). ●●

JACOBS. David Michael
-- *The UFO controversy in America* (Indiana University Press, 1973). ●●

JUNG. Carl Gustav
-- *Ein moderner Mythus von Dingen, die an Himmel gesehen werden* (Rascher, 1958). Translated as *Flying saucers: a modern myth of things seen in the skies* (Routledge, 1959). ●●

KEEL. John A.
-- *Operation Trojan Horse* (Putnam, 1970). ●●
-- *Strange creatures from time and space* (Fawcett, 1970). ●
-- *Our haunted planet* (Fawcett, 1971). ●
-- *The Mothman prophecies* (Saturday Review / Dutton, 1975). ●
-- *The eigth tower* (Saturday Review / Dutton, 1976). Paperback was retitled *The cosmic question.* ●

KLASS. Philip J.
-- *UFOs identified* (Random House, 1968). ●●
-- *UFOs explained* (Random House, 1974). ●●
-- *UFOs: the public deceived* (Prometheus, 1983). ●●

Las HERAS. Antonio
-- *Informe sobre los visitantes extraterrestres y sus naves voladores* (Alonso, 1976). ■

LESLIE. Desmond, & ADAMSKI. George
-- *Flying saucers have landed* (Werner Laurie, 1953).

LITTLE. Greg L.
-- *The archetype experience* (Rainbow, 1984).

LOB. Jacques, & GIGI. Robert
-- *Les apparitions OVNI* (Dargaud, 1979).

LORE. Gordon I.R., & KEYHOE. Donald
-- *Strange effects from UFOs* (NICAP, 1969).

LORENZEN. Coral & Jim
-- *Flying saucer occupants* (Signet, 1967).
-- *Abducted* (Berkley, 1977).

McCAMPBELL. James M.
-- *Ufology* (Jaymac, 1973). ●●

McDONALD. James E.
-- *UFOs: greatest scientific problem of our times* (NICAP, 1967). ●●

MAGOR. John
-- *Our UFO visitors* (Hancock House, 1977). ■

MANEY. Charles A., & HALL. Richard
-- *The challenge of unidentified flying objects* (NICAP, 1961).

MATTERN. W.
-- *UFOs - unbekanntes flugobjekt?* [English version (not identical): *UFOs - Nazi secret weapon?]* (Samisdat, 1974).

MAVRAKIS. Daniel, & OLIVIER. Marie-Pierre ●
-- *Les objets volants non identifiables* (Laffont, 1986).

MEHEUST. Bertrand
-- *Science fiction et soucoupes volantes* (Mercure de France, 1978). ●
-- *Soucoupes volantes et folklore* (Mercure de France, 1985). ●

MENZEL. Donald H.
-- *Flying saucers* (Harvard, 1953). ●
& BOYD. Lyle G.
-- *The world of flying saucers* (Doubleday, 1963). ●
& TAVES. Ernest H.
-- *The UFO enigma* (Doubleday, 1977). ●

MICHEL. Aime
-- *Lueurs sur les soucoupes volantes* (Mame, 1963). Translated as *The truth about flying saucers* (Criterion, 1956). ●
-- *Mysterieux objets celestes* (Arthaud, 1958). Translated as *Flying saucers and the straight line mystery* (Criterion, 1958). ●

MICHEL. John
-- *The flying saucer vision (Sidgwick & Jackson, 1967).*

MONNERIE. Michel
-- *Et si les OVNIs n'existaient pas?* (Les Humanoides Associes, 1977). ●●
-- *Le naufrage des extra-terrestres* (Nouvelles Editions Rationalistes, 1979). ●●

MORAVEC. Mark, & PRYTZ. John (Eds)
-- *UFOs over Australia* (ACUFUS, 1985). ■

MURCIANO. Carlos
-- *Algo flota sobre el mundo* (Prensa Espanola, 1969).

MUSGRAVE. John Brent
-- *UFO occupants and critters: the patterns in Canada* (Global Communications, 1979).

OBERG. James E.
-- *UFOs and outer space mysteries* (Donning, 1982).

OLSEN. Thomas
-- *The reference for outstanding UFO reports* (UFO Information Retrieval Center, 1966).

OROFINO. Juan Carlos
-- *Los senderos del cielo* (Halbrane, 1983).

PACAUT. Rene
-- *Ils ont rencontre des extra-terrestres* (Lefeuvre, 1978).

PEREIRA. Jader U.
-- *Les extra-terrestres* (GEPA, 1974).

PIENS. Christiane
-- *Les OVNIs du passe* (Marabout, 1977).

PINOTTI. Roberto
-- *Visitatori dallo spazio* (Armenia, 1973).
-- *UFO: la congiura del silenzio* (Armenia, 1974).
-- *UFO: missione uomo* (Armenia, 1976).

RANDLES. Jenny
-- *UFO study* (Hale, 1981). ●
-- *The Pennine UFO mystery* (Granada, 1983). ■
-- *UFO reality* (Hale, 1983). ●
-- *The UFO conspiracy* (Blandford, 1987).
& WARRINGTON. Peter
-- *UFOs: a British viewpoint* (Hale, 1979). ●
-- *Science and the UFOs* (Blackwell, 1985). ●
& WHETNALL. Paul
-- *Alien contact* (Spearman, 1982).

REHN. K. Gösta
-- *Tefaten ar har* (Zindermans, 1972). Tralslated as *UFOs are here and now* (Abelard Schuman, 1974). ■
-- *UFO - utmaningen* (Zindermans, 1976). ■

RIBERA. Antonio
-- *Platillos volantes en Iberoamerica y España* (Pomaire, 1968). ■
-- *Sequestrados por extraterrestres* (Planeta, 1981).
-- *Encuentros con humanoides* (Planeta, 1982).
-- *Las máquinas del cosmos* (Planeta, 1983).**RIMME**

RIMMER. John
-- *The evidence for UFO abductions* (Aquarian, 1984). ●●

ROBIOU-LAMARCHE. Sebastián
-- *Manifesto OVNI du Puerto Rico, Santo Domingo y Cuba* (Punto y Coma, 1979). ■

ROCHA. Hugo
-- *Oenigma does 'Discos Voadores'* (ADV, 1951).
-- *Outros mundos, outros humanidades* (Educaçao Nacional, 1958).

ROGO. D. Scott
-- (Ed) *UFO abductions* (Signet, 1980). ●●
& CLARK. Jerome
-- *Earth's secret inhabitants* (Tempo, 1979). ●

RUPPELT. Edward J.
-- *The report on UFOs* (Doubleday, 1955). ●●

RUTLEDGE. Harley D.
-- *Project identification* (Prentice Hall, 1981). ●●

SACHS. Margaret
-- *The UFO encyclopedia* (Putnam, 1980). ●●

SAGAN. Carl, &PAGE. Thornton (Eds)
-- *UFOs: a scientific debate* (Cornell, 1972). ●●

SALISBURY. Frank B.
-- *The Utah UFO display* (Devin-Adair, 1974). ●●

SANCHEZ BUENO. Bernardino
-- *Os OVNI no passado remoto* (Bertrand, 1985).

SANDERSON. Ivan T.
-- *Uninvited visitors* (Cowles, 1967).
-- *Invisible residents* (Crowell, 1970).

SCHWARZ. Berthold E.
-- *UFO dynamics: psychiatric and psychic aspects of the UFO syndrome.* 2 vols. (Rainbow, 1983). ●●

SCORNAUX. Jacques, & PIENS. Christiane
-- *A la recherche des OVNI* (Marabout, 1976).

SCULLY. Frank
-- *Behind the flying saucers (Holt, 1950).* ●

SEAGBENT. D.A.J.
-- *UFOs: a scientific enigma* (Sphere, 1978). ●

STANWAY. Roger, & PACE. Anthony R.
-- *UFOs, unidentified - undeniable* (Newchapel Observatory, 1968).

STARTUP. Bill, & ILLINGWORT. Neil
-- *The Kaikoura UFOs* (Hodder & Stoughton 1980)■

STENDEK (Editorial)
-- *Si: estan aproximacion cientifica a los OVNIs* (Editorial 7½, 1978). ●

STEVENS. Wendelle, & DONG. Paul (Eds)
-- *UFOs over modern China* (UFO Photo Archives, 1983).

STORY. Ronald D.
-- *UFOs and the limits of science* (Morrow, 1981). ●
-- (Ed) *The encyclopedia of UFOs* (Doubleday, 1977). ●●

STRINGFIELD. Leonard
-- *Situation Red: the UFO seige* (Doubleday, 1977).

VALLÉE. Jacques
-- *Anatomy of a phenomenon* (Regnery, 1965). ●●
-- *Passport to Magonia: from folklore to flying saucers* (Regnery, 1969). ●●
-- *The invisible college* (Dutton, 1975). ●●
-- *Messengers of deception* (And/Or, 1979). ●●
& VALLÉE. Janine
-- *Challenge to science* (Regnery, 1966). ●●

VESCO. Renato
-- *Intercettateli senza sparare* (Mursia, 1968). Translated as *Intercept, but don't shoot!* (Grove, 1971). ●
-- *I velivoli del mistero* (Mursia, 1969).
-- *Operazione Plenilunio* (Mursia, 1972).

VIEROUDY. Pierre
-- *Ces OVNIs qui annoncent le surhomme* (Tchou, 1977). ●

WEBB. David
-- *1973 - year of the humanoids* (CUFOS, 1976). ●

WEGNER. Willy
-- *UFO-landinger i Danmark* (FUFOS, 1975,1978). ■

WEVERBERGH. Julien, & HOBANA. Ion
-- *UFOs in Oost en West; deel 2; UFOs boven het Oostblok* (Ankh-Hermes, 1972). Translated as *UFOs from behind the Iron Curtain* (Souvenir, 1974). ■

ZALBIDEA. V., & LIZAR. J.
-- *OVNI: analisis de un contacto* (Tropos, 1975).

ZEIDMAN. Jennie
-- *The Lumberton Report* (CUFOS, 1976). ●
-- *A helicopter- UFO encounter over OHIO* (CUFOS, 1979). ●

ZERPA. Fabio
-- *O OVNI e seus misterios* (APUL, 1977).

ZURCHER. Eric
-- *Les apparitions d'humanoides* (Lefeuvre, 1979). ●